CompTIA

SECURITY+
Get Certified Get Ahead
SY0-301 Study Guide

Darril Gibson
CompTIA A+, Network+, Security+, CASP,
SSCP, CISSP, MCT, MCSE, MCITP

ISBN: 1463762364
ISBN-13: 9781463762360
Library of Congress Control Number: 2011913176

CreateSpace, North Charleston, SC

Dedication

To my wife, who even after nineteen years of marriage continues to remind me how wonderful life can be if you're in a loving relationship. Thanks for sharing your life with me.

Acknowledgments

Books of this size and depth can't be done by a single person, and I'm grateful for the many people who helped me put this book together. First, thanks to my wife. She has provided me immeasurable support throughout this project.

The two technical editors, Duane Gibson and Bill Talbott, provided outstanding feedback and superb technical insight. Bill is an old friend from my Navy days, and he's currently doing great things as a consultant working for Microsoft. Duane (my brother) is an old friend from my childhood days, and he's widely recognized as a Cisco expert. They both have taught many Security+ classes and provided me with some great perspectives. I'm grateful they were involved in this project. I certainly appreciate all the feedback they gave me, but I want to stress that any technical errors that may have snuck into this book are entirely my fault and no reflection on them.

The entire team at CreateSpace was easy to work with and provided excellent services from the first contact through the entire editing and layout process. I'm thankful for all the work and support they provided.

About the Author

Darril Gibson is an accomplished author and professional trainer. He has authored or coauthored more than a dozen books and contributed as a technical editor for many more books. He holds many current IT certifications, including: CompTIA A+, Network+, Security+, CASP, (ISC)2 SSCP, CISSP, Microsoft's MCDST (XP), MCSA, MCSA Messaging (2000, 2003), MCSE (NT 4.0, 2000, 2003), MCDBA (SQL 7.0, 2000), MCITP (Vista, Server 2008, SQL 2005, SQL 2008), MCTS (Server 2008, SQL Server 2008), MCSD (6.0, .NET), and ITIL Foundations v 3.0.

He is the CEO of Security Consulting and Training, LLC, and actively teaches, writes, and consults on a wide variety of IT topics, including CompTIA Security+. He also teaches as an adjunct professor at ECPI University.

Darril lives in Virginia Beach with his wife and two dogs. Whenever possible, they escape to a small cabin in the country on over twenty acres of land that continue to provide peace, tranquility, and balance. You can send him an email at Darril@GetCertifiedGetAhead.com.

About the Technical Editors

Duane Gibson's certs are A+, Network+, Security+, MCSE, CCNA, CEH, and FCC-GROL. He has over 10 years' experience as a technical trainer.

Bill Talbott is the founder and CEO of Talbott Consulting and Training, Inc. and has been in the IT industry for over 23 years. He has been a technical trainer for the past 11 years specializing in the delivery of Microsoft, CompTIA and tailored curriculum for Universities, Fortune 500 and local companies.

Table of Contents

Introduction 1
    Who This Book is For 1
    About This Book 2
    How to Use This Book 2
    Remember This 3
    Vendor Neutral 3
    Web Resources 4
    Assumptions 4
    Set a Goal 4
About the Exam 5
    Number of Questions and Duration 5
    Passing Score 5
    Beta Questions 5
    Question Types 6
    Exam Format 7
    Exam Prerequisites 7
    Exam Test Providers 7
    Exam Domains 8
    Objective to Chapter Map 8
    Recertification Requirements 20
CompTIA Security+ Assessment Exam 21
Assessment Exam Answers 38
Chapter 1 Mastering the Basics of Security 53
Exploring Core Security Principles 54
    Confidentiality 54
    Integrity 55
    Availability 57
    Balancing CIA 58
    Non-repudiation 58
    Defense in Depth 59
    Implicit Deny 60
Introducing Basic Risk Concepts 60
Exploring Authentication Concepts 61
    Comparing Identification, Authentication, and Authorization 61

Identity Proofing 62

    Identity Proofing for Verification 62

    Self-service Password Reset Systems 63

Three Factors of Authentication 63

    Something You Know 63

    Something You Have 68

    Something You Are 70

    Multifactor Authentication 72

Exploring Authentication Services 73

    Kerberos 73

    LDAP 74

    Mutual Authentication 74

    Single Sign-on 75

    IEEE 802.1X 76

Remote Access Authentication 76

    PAP 77

    CHAP 77

    MS-CHAP and MS-CHAPv2 78

    RADIUS 78

    TACACS/XTACACS 79

    TACACS+ 79

    AAA Protocols 80

Chapter 1 Exam Topic Review 80

Chapter 1 Practice Questions 83

Chapter 1 Practice Question Answers 87

Chapter 2 Exploring Control Types and Methods 91

Understanding Basic Control Types 92

    Technical Controls 93

    Management Controls 94

    Operational Controls 94

    Controls Based on Functions 95

    Preventative Controls 95

    Detective Controls 96

    Corrective Controls 96

Exploring Access Control Models 97

    Role- and Rule-Based Access Control 97

    Using Roles Based on Jobs and Functions 98

    Establishing Access with Groups as Roles 98

    Using User Templates to Enforce Least Privilege 100

    Discretionary Access Control 101

    SIDs and DACLs 101

    The Owner Establishes Access 103

    Beware of Trojans 103

Mandatory Access Control 103
    Labels and Lattice 104
    Establishing Access 104
Understanding Physical Security Controls 105
  Access Controls 105
    Door Access Systems 105
    Physical Access Control—ID Badges 107
    Physical Access Lists and Logs 108
    Tailgating 108
    Mantraps 109
    Security Guards 109
    Video Surveillance (CCTV) 109
    Physical Tokens 111
  Hardware Locks 111
Understanding Logical Access Controls 112
  Least Privilege 112
  Access Control Lists 113
  Group Policy 113
    Using a Password Policy 114
    Domain Password Policy 116
    Device Policy 116
  Account Management 117
    Centralized and Decentralized Account Management 117
    Disabling and Deleting Accounts 118
    Time-of-day Restrictions 118
    Account Expiration 119
    Account Access Review 119
  Chapter 2 Exam Topic Review 120
Chapter 2 Practice Questions 123
Chapter 2 Practice Question Answers 128
Chapter 3 Understanding Basic Network Security 133
Reviewing Basic Networking Concepts 135
  Protocols 136
    Common TCP/IP Protocols 136
    IPv4 vs IPv6 142
    Subnetting 143
    Subnetting and Availability 143
    Calculating Subnet IP Addresses with a Calculator 144
  Understanding and Identifying Ports 146
  Well-Known Ports 147
    Combining the IP Address and the Port 148
    IP Address Used to Locate Hosts 149
    Server Ports 149

Client Ports..149

Putting It All Together 150

The Importance of Ports in Security.. 151

Port Scanners.. 152

Understanding Basic Network Devices 153

Hub 153

Switch 153

Security Benefit of a Switch.. 155

Port Security 155

Physical Security of a Switch... 156

Loop Protection 156

VLAN.. 156

Prevent Network Bridging 157

Router 157

Routers and ACLs.. 158

Routers and Firewalls.. 159

Firewall 159

Host-based Firewalls... 159

Network-based Firewalls... 160

Firewall Rules.. 161

Web Application Firewall 161

Web Security Gateways and Appliances 162

Spam Filters... 163

Firewall Logs and Log Analysis.. 163

Load Balancers... 164

Exploring the Network Perimeter... 164

DMZ 164

Comparing Public and Private IP Addresses 165

Understanding NAT 166

Proxy Server... 166

Caching Content for Performance... 167

Using Content Filters to Restrict Access 167

Chapter 3 Exam Topic Review.. 168

Chapter 3 Practice Questions... 170

Chapter 3 Practice Question Answers.. 174

Chapter 4 Securing Your Network... 177

Understanding IDSs and IPSs.. 179

HIDS 180

NIDS 180

Detection Methods... 182

Signature Based... 182

Anomaly Based 182

Data Sources and Trends 183

Alarms, Alerts, and Trends.. 183
    IDS Threshold 184
IDS Responses.. 184
    Passive IDS 184
    Active IDS 184
IDS vs. IPS... 186
Securing Wireless Networks 188
    802.11 188
    Managing the Wireless Footprint 189
    Security Protocols.. 190
        WEP 190
        IV Attack 191
        WPA 192
        WPA2 192
        Personal and Enterprise Modes 193
        EAP, LEAP, and PEAP 194
        WTLS and ECC 194
    Other Security Concerns.. 195
        Change Default Administrator Password 195
        Enable MAC Filtering 195
        Disable SSID Broadcasting or Not 196
        Change Default SSID.. 197
    War Driving 198
    Rogue Access Points.. 198
    Interference 199
    Evil Twins.. 199
    Isolation Mode... 200
    Ad-Hoc Mode 200
    Bluetooth Wireless.. 200
        Discovery Mode... 201
        Bluesnarfing 201
        Bluejacking 201
        Smartphone Security... 202
Exploring Remote Access 202
    Dial-up RAS 203
    VPN 203
        Tunneling... 203
        Site-to-Site VPNs... 206
    RAS Authentication... 206
    Network Access Control 207
        Inspection and Control 207
        MAC Filtering.. 209
Chapter 4 Exam Topic Review... 209

Chapter 4 Practice Questions...212

Chapter 4 Practice Question Answers...217

Chapter 5 Securing Hosts and Data... 221

Implementing Host Security... 223

    Hardening Systems.. 223

        Disabling Unnecessary Services.. 223

        Eliminate Unneeded Applications... 224

    Using Baselines.. 224

        Security Baselines 224

        Configuration Baseline.. 226

        Performance Baselines and Baseline Reporting 227

    Understanding Imaging.. 228

Understanding Virtualization...230

    Reduced Footprint 231

    Increased Availability 232

    Isolation.. 233

    Virtualization Weakness 233

        VM Escape... 233

        Loss of Confidentiality... 234

        Loss of Availability 234

Implementing Patch Management 235

    Comparing Updates 236

    Deploying Patches 236

    Testing Patches.. 237

    Scheduling Patches..238

Understanding Change Management... 238

Protecting Data 239

    Data Categories.. 240

    Protecting Confidentiality with Encryption 241

        Software-based Encryption 241

        Hardware-based Encryption.. 242

        Hardware Security Module.. 244

    Data Leakage..245

        Data Loss Prevention 245

        Portable Storage Devices 246

    Protecting Mobile Devices 247

Understanding Cloud Computing 248

    Software as a Service.. 249

    Infrastructure as a Service 250

    Platform as a Service 250

    Drawbacks to Cloud Computing... 251

    Chapter 5 Exam Topic Review.. 251

    Chapter 5 Practice Questions... 254

Chapter 5 Practice Question Answers...259
Chapter 6 Understanding Malware and Social Engineering 263
Understanding Malware 264
    Viruses... 265
        Characteristics... 265
        Delivery of Viruses 265
        Virus Hoaxes... 266
    Worms... 267
    Trojan Horse.. 267
    Logic Bombs 269
    Rootkits 270
    Spam and Spam Filters 271
    Spyware.. 271
    Adware 272
    Backdoors 273
    Protection against Malware 273
        Antivirus Software 273
        Anti-spyware Software.. 275
        Privilege Escalation 275
        Trusted Operating System 275
Recognizing Social Engineering Tactics 276
    Education and Awareness Training 277
        Rogueware and Scareware... 277
        Phishing... 278
        Spear Phishing and Whaling 280
        Vishing 281
    Tailgating 281
    Dumpster Diving.. 282
    Impersonation 282
    Shoulder Surfing.. 282
Chapter 6 Exam Topic Review 283
Chapter 6 Practice Questions... 285
Chapter 6 Practice Question Answers.. 289
Chapter 7 Identifying Advanced Attacks 293
Analyzing Attacks... 294
    Denial-of-service... 294
        SYN Flood Attack.. 295
        Smurf Attack... 296
    Distributed Denial-of-service 297
    Botnet 297
    Spoofing... 298
    XMAS Attack 298
    Man-in-the-middle... 299

Replay 299

Web Browser Concerns 300

    Malicious add-ons 300

    Cookies 300

    Session Hijacking 300

    Header Manipulation 301

ARP Poisoning 301

    Man-in-the-Middle 302

    Denial-of-Service 303

    VLAN Segregation 303

Domain Name Kiting 303

Securing Applications 304

Basic Application Hardening Steps 304

    Follow Vendor Guidelines 304

    Changing Defaults and Disabling Unnecessary Accounts 305

    Eliminate Backdoors 305

Software Development Life Cycles 305

Performing Input Validation 306

Analyzing Server Attacks 307

Web Servers 308

    Buffer Overflows and Buffer Overflow Attacks 308

    SQL Queries and SQL Injection Attacks 309

    Cross-site Scripting 312

    Cross-site Request Forgery (XSRF) 313

    Directory Traversal/Command Injection 314

    LDAP Injection 314

    Fuzzing 314

Database Servers 315

Transitive Access and Client-side Attacks 315

E-mail Servers 316

DNS Servers 316

Chapter 7 Exam Topic Review 317

Chapter 7 Practice Questions 320

Chapter 7 Practice Question Answers 324

Chapter 8 Managing Risk 327

Threats, Vulnerabilities, and Risks 329

Threats 329

    Types of Threats 329

    Malicious Insider Threat 330

    Threat Modeling 330

Vulnerabilities 330

Risks 331

    Risk Management 331

Risk Assessment 332
Checking for Vulnerabilities... 336
   Anatomy of an Attack 336
      Identify IP Addresses of Targets 336
      Identify Open Ports with a Port Scanner 337
      Fingerprint System 337
      Identify Vulnerabilities 338
      Attack 338
      Putting it All Together 339
   Vulnerability Assessment.. 339
   Vulnerability Scanning.. 341
   Penetration Testing 342
      White, Gray, and Black Box Testing 344
      Obtaining Consent 345
Identifying Security Tools 345
   Protocol Analyzer (Sniffer)... 345
   Routine Audits 346
   User Rights and Permissions Review 347
   Password-cracking Tools 348
   Monitoring Logs 350
      Operating System Logs 350
      Other Logs 351
      Reviewing Logs 352
   OVAL 352
Chapter 8 Exam Topic Review.. 352
Chapter 8 Practice Questions... 355
Chapter 8 Practice Question Answers.. 360
Chapter 9 Preparing for Business Continuity 363
Designing Redundancy... 370
   Single Point of Failure 370
   Disk Redundancies.. 371
      RAID-0 372
      RAID-1 372
      RAID-5 372
      RAID-10.. 372
      Software vs. Hardware RAID 373
   Server Redundancy.. 373
      Failover Clusters.. 373
      Load Balancers.. 374
   Power Redundancies.. 375
      UPS 375
      Generators... 376
Protecting Data with Backups 376

Backup Types..377
    Full Backups 378
    Restoring a Full Backup...378
    Differential Backups 378
    Restoring a Full/Differential Backup Set 379
    Incremental Backups 379
    Restoring a Full/Incremental Backup Set 379
    Choosing Full/Incremental or Full/Differential 380
Testing Backups...380
Protecting Backups 381
Backup Policies 381
Comparing Business Continuity Elements...383
    Business Impact Analysis 383
    Recovery Time Objective...384
    Recovery Point Objective..385
    Mean Time Between Failure 385
    Mean Time to Restore...385
Continuity of Operations 385
    Hot Site 386
    Cold Site 387
    Warm Site..387
    Site Variations...388
    After the Disaster 388
Disaster Recovery 388
IT Contingency Planning...389
Succession Planning 390
BCP and DRP Testing 390
Environmental Controls 391
    Fire Suppression..391
    Heating, Ventilation, and Air Conditioning 392
    Hot and Cold Aisles 393
    HVAC and Fire...394
Failsafe/secure vs. Failopen 394
Shielding 394
    Shielding Cables 395
    Faraday Cage 395
    TEMPEST 396
Chapter 9 Exam Topic Review...396
Chapter 9 Practice Questions..398
Chapter 9 Practice Question Answers..403
Chapter 10 Understanding Cryptography 407
Introducing Cryptography Concepts...409
Providing Integrity with Hashing 409

MD5 410

SHA 410

HMAC 411

Hashing Files 411

Hashing Messages 413

Using HMAC 414

Other Hash Algorithms 415

    RIPEMD 415

    LANMAN and NTLM 416

Providing Confidentiality with Encryption 417

Symmetric Encryption 418

    Block vs. Stream Ciphers 419

    AES 420

    DES 420

    3DES 420

    RC4 421

    One-Time Pad 421

    Blowfish and TwoFish 422

Asymmetric Encryption 422

The Rayburn Box 423

    The Rayburn Box Used to Send Secrets 423

    The Rayburn Box Used for Authentication 424

    The Rayburn Box Demystified 424

Certificates 424

RSA 426

Diffie-Hellman 427

Elliptic Curve Cryptography 427

Steganography 427

Quantum Cryptography 428

SSL 429

TLS 429

Other Transport Encryption Protocols 430

Using Cryptographic Protocols 430

Protecting E-mail 431

    Signing E-mail with Digital Signatures 431

    Encrypting E-mail 433

    S/MIME 435

    PGP/GPG 435

Encrypting HTTPS Traffic with SSL and TLS 436

Exploring PKI Components 438

Certificate Authority 438

Certificate Trust Paths 439

    Trust Models 440

Self-signed Certificates 440
Registration 441
Revoking Certificates 441
Validating Certificates 442
Key Escrow 443
Recovery Agent 444
Chapter 10 Exam Topic Review 444
Chapter 10 Practice Questions 447
Chapter 10 Practice Question Answers 452
Chapter 11 Exploring Operational Security 457
Exploring Security Policies 458
Clean Desk Policy 459
Account Management Policies 460
User Privilege Policy 460
Require Administrators to Use Two Accounts 461
Account Disablement Policy 462
Change Management Policy 462
Portable Device Policies 463
Personnel Policies 464
Acceptable Use 464
Mandatory Vacations 465
Separation of Duties 465
Job Rotation 466
Security Awareness and Training 468
Data Policies 469
Information Classification 469
Data Labeling and Handling 469
Storage and Retention Policies 470
Personally Identifiable Information 471
Protecting PII 472
Privacy Policy 472
Social Networking Sites 473
P2P 473
Decommissioning Systems 475
Incident Response Policies 475
Containment 476
Incident Response Team 477
Basic Forensic Procedures 477
Order of Volatility 478
Capture Images 479
Take Hashes 480
Network Traffic and Logs 480
Chain of Custody 481

Capture Video...482

Record Time Offset 482

Screenshots...483

Witnesses 483

Track Man Hours and Expense 483

Chapter 11 Exam Topic Review 484

Chapter 11 Practice Questions 486

Chapter 11 Practice Question Answers 491

CompTIA Security+ Practice Exam..495

Security+ Practice Exam Answers 512

Appendix A—Acronym List..527

Introduction

Congratulations on your purchase of *CompTIA Security+: Get Certified, Get Ahead*. You are one step closer to becoming CompTIA Security+ certified. This certification has helped many individuals get ahead in their jobs and their careers, and it can help you get ahead, too.

It is a popular certification within the IT field. One IT hiring manager told me that if a resume doesn't include the Security+ certification (or a higher level security certification), he simply sets it aside. He won't even talk to applicants. That's not the same with all IT hiring managers, but it does help illustrate how important security is within the IT field.

Who This Book is For

If you're studying for the CompTIA Security+ exam and want to pass it on your first attempt, this book is for you. It covers 100 percent of the objectives identified by CompTIA in enough depth so that you'll be able to easily answer the exam questions.

The first target audience for this book is students in CompTIA Security+ classes. My goal is to give students a book they can use to study the relevant and important details of CompTIA Security+ in adequate depth for the challenging topics, but without the minutiae in topics that are clear for most IT professionals. I regularly taught from the first edition of this book, and I'll continue to teach using this edition. I also heard from instructors around the United States and in three other countries that used the first edition to help students master the topics and pass the Security+ exam the first time they took it.

This book is also for those people who can study on their own. If you're one of the people who can read a book and learn the material without sitting in a class, this book has what you need to take and pass the exam the first time.

Additionally, you can keep this book on your shelf (or in your Kindle) to remind yourself of important, relevant concepts. These concepts are important for security professionals and IT professionals in the real world.

Based on many conversations with students and readers of the previous version of this book, I know that many people use the Security+ certification as the first step in achieving other security certifications. For example, you may follow the Security+ with the ISC(2) SSCP or CISSP, or possibly the CompTIA CASP certification. If you plan to pursue any of these advanced security certifications, you'll find this book will help you lay a solid foundation of security knowledge. Learn this material, and you'll be a step ahead on the other exams.

About This Book

Over the past several years, I've taught literally hundreds of students, helping them to become CompTIA Security+ certified. During that time, I've learned what concepts are easy to grasp and what concepts need more explanation. I've developed handouts and analogies that help students grasp the elusive concepts.

Feedback from students was overwhelmingly positive—both in their comments to me and their successful pass rates after taking the certification exam. When the objectives changed in 2008, I rewrote my handouts as the first edition of this book. When the objectives changed again in 2011, I rewrote the book to reflect the new objectives.

This book has allowed me to reach a much larger audience and share security and IT-related information. Even if you aren't in one of the classes I teach, this book can help you learn the relevant material to successfully pass the exam.

How to Use This Book

When practicing for any certification exam, the following steps are a good recipe for success:

- **Review the objectives**. The objectives for the SY0-301 exam can be found in this introduction.
- **Learn the material related to the objectives**. This book covers all of the objectives, and the introduction includes a map showing which chapter (or chapters) covers each objective.
- **Take practice questions**. A key step when preparing for any certification exam is to make sure you can answer the exam questions. Yes, you need the knowledge, but you also must be able to read a question and pick the right answer. This simply takes practice.
- **Read and understand the explanations**. When preparing, you should make sure you know why the correct answers are correct and why the incorrect answers are incorrect. The explanations provide this information and are also worded to help you get other questions correct.

This book has over 450 practice test questions you can use to test your knowledge and your ability to correctly answer them. Every question has a detailed explanation to help you understand why the correct answers are correct and why the incorrect answers are incorrect.

You can find the practice questions in the following areas:

- **Assessment exam**. Use these questions at the beginning of the book to get a feel for what you know and what you need to study more.
- **End-of-chapter practice questions**. Each chapter has practice questions to help you test your comprehension of the material in the chapter.
- **End-of-book practice exam**. Use this as a practice exam to test your comprehension of the subject matter and readiness to take the actual exam.

It's OK if you do the practice questions in a different order. You may decide to tackle all the chapters in the book and then do the pre-assessment and post-assessment questions. That's fine. However, I strongly suggest you review all the questions in the book.

Remember This

Throughout the book, you'll see text boxes that highlight important information you should remember to successfully pass the exam. The surrounding content provides the additional information needed to fully understand these key points, and the text boxes summarize the important points.

These text boxes will look like this:

> ### Remember this
> I strongly encourage you to repeat the information in the text boxes to yourself as often as possible. The more you repeat the information, the more likely you are to remember it when you take the exam.

A tried-and-true method of repeating key information is to take notes when you're first studying the material and then rewrite the notes later. This will expose you to the material a minimum of three times.

Another method that students have told me has been successful for them is to use an MP3 player. Many MP3 players can record. Start your MP3 recorder and read the information in each text box for a chapter and the information in the Exam Topic Review section of each chapter. Save the MP3 file and regularly listen to it. This allows you to reaffirm the important information in your own voice.

You can play it while exercising, walking, or just about any time when it's not dangerous to listen to any MP3 file. You can even burn the MP3 files to a CD and play them back from a CD player.

If the MP3 method is successful for you, you can also record and listen to exam questions. Read the question, only the correct answer, and the first sentence or two of the explanation in each practice question.

If you don't have time to create your own MP3 recordings, check out the companion website (GetCertifiedGetAhead.com) for this book. You can purchase MP3 recordings there that you can download and use.

Vendor Neutral

CompTIA certifications are vendor neutral. In other words, certifications are not centered on any single vendor, such as Microsoft, Apple, or Linux. With that in mind, you don't need significantly deep knowledge of any of the operating systems, but don't be surprised if you see more questions about one OS over another simply because of market share.

In October 2011, Windows had about 90 percent market share of operating systems. Apple MACs were next with about 6 percent and iOS (for iPhones and iPads) had about 3 percent. Linux had about 1 percent. Surveys in 2004 and 2008 also showed Microsoft had about 90 percent market share, indicating it's staying relatively stable.

Since approximately 90 percent of systems you'll touch in a corporate environment are Microsoft based, don't be surprised to see some Microsoft-specific questions.

Web Resources

Check out http://GetCertifiedGetAhead.com for up-to-date details on the CompTIA Security+ exam. This site includes additional information related to the CompTIA Security+ exam and this book.

Although many people have spent a lot of time and energy trying to ensure that there are no errors in this book, occasionally they slip through. This site includes an errata page listing any errors we've discovered.

If you discover any errors, please let me know through the links on the website. I'd also love to hear about your success when you pass the exam. I'm constantly getting good news from readers and students who are successfully earning their certifications.

Last, I've found that many people find cryptography topics challenging, so I've posted some videos on YouTube (http://www.youtube.com/). As time allows, I'll post additional videos, and you can get a listing of all of them by searching on "Darril Gibson."

Assumptions

The CompTIA Security+ exam assumes you have at least two years of experience working with computers in a network. It also assumes you earned the Network+ certification, or at least have the equivalent knowledge. While writing this book, I have largely assumed the same thing.

However, I'm well aware that two years of experience in a network could mean many different things. Your two years of experience may expose you to different technologies than someone else's two years of experience.

When it's critical that you understand an underlying network concept in order to master the relevant exam material, I have often included the concept within the background information.

Set a Goal

Look at a calendar right now and determine the date forty-five days from today. This will be your target date to take this exam. Set this as your goal to complete studying the materials and to take the exam.

This target allows you to master about one and a half chapters per week. It may be that some of the chapters take you less time and some of the chapters take you more time. No problem. If you want to modify your target date later, do so. However, a recipe for success in almost any endeavor includes setting a goal.

When I teach CompTIA Security+ at a local university, I often help the students register for the exam on the first night. They pick a date close to the end of the course and register. I've found that when we do this, about 90 percent of the students take and pass the exam within one week after completing the course. On the other hand, when I didn't help the students register on the first night, more than half of them did not complete the exam in the same time frame. Setting a goal helps.

About the Exam

CompTIA first released the Security+ exam in 2002, and it has quickly grown in popularity. It revised the exam objectives in 2008 and again in 2011. The 2011 exam is numbered as SY0-301 (or JK0-018 for the academic version of the exam). SY0-101 (the original version of CompTIA Security+) was retired in July 2009, and SY0-201 will retire on December 31, 2011.

A summary of the details of the exam includes:

- **Number of questions:** 100
- **Time to complete questions:** 90 minutes (does not include time to complete pretest and posttest surveys)
- **Passing score:** 750
- **Grading criteria:** Scale of 100 to 900 (about 83 percent)
- **Question types:** Multiple choice
- **Exam format:** Traditional—can move back and forth to view previous questions
- **Exam prerequisites:** None required but Network+ is recommended
- **Exam test providers:** Prometric and Pearson Vue

Number of Questions and Duration

You have ninety minutes to complete one hundred questions. This gives you about one minute per question. Don't let this scare you; it's actually a good thing. With only about a minute to read and answer a question, you know the questions can't be very long.

Passing Score

A score of 750 is required to pass. This is on a scale of 100 to 900. If the exam is paid for and you don't get a single question correct, you still get a score of 100. If you get every testable question correct, you get a score of 900.

If all questions are equal, then you need to get eighty-four questions correct—a passing score of 750 divided by 900 equals .8333 or 83.33 percent. However, CompTIA doesn't say if all questions are scored equally or whether harder questions are weighted and worth more. A score of 83 percent is higher than many other certification exams, so you shouldn't underestimate the difficulty of this exam. However, many people regularly pass it and you can pass it, too. With this book, you will be well prepared.

Beta Questions

Your exam may have some beta questions. They aren't graded but instead are used to test the validity of the questions. If everyone gets a beta question correct, it's probably too easy. If everyone gets it incorrect, there's probably something wrong with the question. After enough people have tested a beta question, it's analyzed and may be added to the test bank or rewritten and retested.

The good news is that CompTIA doesn't grade the beta questions. However, you don't know what questions are beta and what questions are valid, so you need to treat every question equally.

Question Types

Expect the questions on the exam to be straightforward. For example, what's 5 x 5? Either you know the answer is 25 or you don't. The exam questions test your knowledge of the material, not necessarily your ability to dissect the question so that you can figure out what the question is really trying to ask.

I'm not saying the knowledge is simplistic, only that the questions will be worded so that you can easily understand what they are asking.

As a comparative example, Microsoft certification questions can be quite complex. Microsoft questions often aren't just testing your knowledge of the topic, but your ability to analyze the material and logically come to the right conclusion.

Here are two examples of questions—the first shows how Microsoft may word the question on a Microsoft certification exam, and the second shows how CompTIA may word it for the CompTIA Security+ exam.

- **Microsoft**. You are driving a bus from Chicago to Atlanta at 55 mph with twenty-two passengers. The bus is painted blue. At the same time, a train is traveling from Miami to Atlanta at 40 mph. The train has a yellow caboose. What color are the bus driver's eyes?
- **CompTIA Security+**. What color are your eyes?

Notice the first question adds a lot of superfluous information. Two pieces are critical to answering the first question. It starts by saying, "You are driving a bus…" and then ends by asking, "What color are the bus driver's eyes?" You're required to put the two together and weed through the irrelevant information to come to the correct answer.

The second question is straightforward. "What color are your eyes?" There's very little analysis required. Either you know it or you don't. This is what you can expect from most of the CompTIA Security+ questions.

Some of the CompTIA exam questions may have a little more detail than just a single sentence, but overall, expect them to be one- to two-sentence questions. They are only giving you about one minute for each question, and it's not intended to be a reading comprehension exam.

As an example, you may see a question like: "What port does HTTPS use?" In this case, you'd need to know that HTTPS uses port 443.

However, knowledge of expanded material could be tested by rewording it a little, such as: "What port needs to be opened to allow secure web server traffic?" In this case, you'd need to know that a web server uses HTTPS for secure web traffic, and HTTPS uses port 443.

You may also see questions that use phrases such as "best choice," "best description," or "most secure." In these examples, don't be surprised if you see two answers that could answer the question, while only one is the best choice. For example, which one of the following numbers is between 1 and 10 and is the highest: 1, 8, 14, 23. Clearly 1 and 8 are within 1 and 10, but 14 and 23 are not. However, only 8 is both within 1 and 10 and the highest.

Here is a more realistic, security-related question that shows this:

Question: You have discovered a wireless base station using the same SSID as your wireless network. No one in your organization installed this. What best describes this?

A. Rogue access point

B. IV attack

C. War driving

D. Evil twin

This is a rogue access point, since it isn't authorized. However, a *better* answer is that it is an evil twin (answer D) since it's a rogue access point with the same SSID as your production environment. When you see key words like "best," "most," or "highest," be careful not to jump on the first answer. There may be a more correct answer.

Exam Format

Questions are multiple-choice types where you choose one answer or multiple answers. When you need to choose multiple answers, the question may direct you to choose two, choose three, or choose all that apply.

You start at question 1 and go to question 100. During the process, you can mark any questions you want to review when you're done. Additionally, you can view previous questions if desired. For example, if you get to question 10 and then remember something that helps you answer question 5, you can go back and redo question 5.

Exam Prerequisites

All that is required for you to take the exam is money. Other than that, there are no enforced prerequisites.

However, to successfully pass the exam, you're expected to have at least two years of experience working with computers in a networking environment. If you have more than that, the exam materials will likely come easier to you. If you have less, the exam may be more difficult.

Exam Test Providers

You can take the exam at either a Pearson Vue or Prometric testing site. Some testing sites providing testing and nothing else. However, most testing sites are part of another company, such as a training company, college, or university. You can take an exam at the training company's testing site even if you haven't taken a course with them.

Both the Pearson Vue and the Prometric websites include search tools you can use to find a testing site close to you. Check them out at http://www.vue.com and http://prometric.com.

At this writing, the CompTIA Security+ exam is $266 if you purchase it at full price. However, you can usually purchase discount vouchers for less than the retail price. If you want to pay less for the exam, use Google and enter "Security+ test voucher." You'll get several links to companies that sell vouchers at a discount.

When you purchase the voucher, you get the voucher number, and you can use this number to register at a testing site. A word of caution: make sure you purchase a voucher for the right testing center. If you purchase a Pearson Vue voucher, you won't be able to use it at a Prometric testing center unless it is also a Pearson Vue testing center. Some testing centers support both Vue and Prometric, but you should check first.

Exam Domains

The exam objectives are divided into the following domains, or general topic areas. Additionally, CompTIA publishes the percentage of questions you can anticipate in any of the domains.

- **1.0 Network Security:** 21 percent of examination content
- **2.0 Compliance and Operational Security:** 18 percent of examination content
- **3.0 Threats and Vulnerabilities:** 21 percent of examination content
- **4.0 Application, Data, and Host Security:** 16 percent of examination content
- **5.0 Access Control and Identity Management:** 13 percent of examination content
- **6.0 Cryptography:** 11 percent of examination content

CompTIA publishes a listing of the objectives on its website. At this writing, this listing is accurate, but CompTIA includes the following disclaimers:

- *"The lists of examples provided in bulleted format below each objective are not exhaustive lists. Other examples of technologies, processes or tasks pertaining to each objective may also be included on the exam although not listed or covered in this objectives document."*
- *"The CompTIA Security+ Certification Exam Objectives are subject to change without notice."*

You can verify that the objectives haven't changed by checking on www.comptia.org. Additionally, you can check this book's companion site at http://GetCertifiedGetAhead.com for any up-to-date changes and additional materials to help you take and pass the exam.

Objective to Chapter Map

This following listing shows the SY0-301 objectives published by CompTIA. In parentheses following the objective, you can also see the chapter or chapter where the objective is covered within this book.

1.0 Network Security

1.1 Explain the security function and purpose of network devices and technologies (chapters 3, 4, 8, 9)

- Firewalls (chapter 3)
- Routers (chapter 3)
- Switches (chapter 3)
- Load balancers (chapters 3, 9)
- Proxies (chapter 3)

- Web security gateways (chapter 3)
- VPN concentrators (chapter 4)
- NIDS and NIPS (Behavior based, signature based, anomaly based, heuristic) (chapter 4)
- Protocol analyzers (chapter 8)
- Sniffers (chapter 8)
- Spam filter, all-in-one security appliances (chapter 3)
- Web application firewall vs. network firewall (chapter 3)
- URL filtering, content inspection, malware inspection (chapter 3)

1.2 Apply and implement secure network administration principles (chapters 1, 2, 3, 4, 7)
- Rule-based management (chapter 3)
- Firewall rules (chapter 3)
- VLAN management (chapter 3)
- Secure router configuration (chapter 3)
- Access control lists (chapter 3)
- Port security (chapter 3)
- 802.1x (chapters 1, 3, 4)
- Flood guards (chapters 3, 7)
- Loop protection (chapter 3)
- Implicit deny (chapters 1, 2, 3)
- Prevent network bridging by network separation (chapter 3)
- Log analysis (chapter 3)

1.3 Distinguish and differentiate network design elements and compounds (chapters 3, 4, 5)
- DMZ (chapter 3)
- Subnetting (chapter 3)
- VLAN (chapter 3)
- NAT (chapter 3)
- Remote Access (chapter 4)
- Telephony (chapter 4)
- NAC (chapter 4)
- Virtualization (chapter 5)
- Cloud computing (chapter 5)
  - Platform as a Service (chapter 5)
  - Software as a Service (chapter 5)
  - Infrastructure as a Service (chapter 5)

1.4 Implement and use common protocols (chapters 3, 4, 10)
- IPSec (chapters 3, 4)
- SNMP (chapter 3)
- SSH (chapter 3)
- DNS (chapter 3)

- TLS (chapters 3, 4, 10)
- SSL (chapters 3, 4, 10)
- TCP/IP (chapter 3)
- FTPS (chapter 3)
- HTTPS (chapters 3, 10)
- SFTP (chapter 3)
- SCP (chapter 3)
- ICMP (chapter 3)
- IPv4 vs. IPv6 (chapter 3)

1.5 Identify commonly used default network ports (chapter 3)
- FTP (chapter 3)
- SFTP (chapter 3)
- FTPS (chapter 3)
- TFTP (chapter 3)
- TELNET (chapter 3)
- HTTP (chapter 3)
- HTTPS (chapter 3)
- SCP (chapter 3)
- SSH (chapter 3)
- NetBIOS (chapter 3)

1.6 Implement wireless network in a secure manner (chapter 4)
- WPA (chapter 4)
- WPA2 (chapter 4)
- WEP (chapter 4)
- EAP (chapter 4)
- PEAP (chapter 4)
- LEAP (chapter 4)
- MAC filter (chapter 4)
- SSID broadcast (chapter 4)
- TKIP (chapter 4)
- CCMP (chapter 4)
- Antenna Placement (chapter 4)
- Power level controls (chapter 4)

2.0 Compliance and Operational Security
2.1 Explain risk-related concepts (chapters 2, 4, 5, 8, 11)
- Control types (chapter 2)
  - Technical (chapter 2)
  - Management (chapter 2)
  - Operational (chapter 2)
- False positives (chapter 4)

- Importance of policies in reducing risk (chapters 2, 11)
    - Privacy policy (chapter 11)
    - Acceptable use (chapter 11)
    - Security policy (chapter 11)
    - Mandatory vacations (chapter 11)
    - Job rotation (chapter 11)
    - Separation of duties (chapter 11)
    - Least privilege (chapters 2, 11)
- Risk calculation (chapter 8)
    - Likelihood (chapter 8)
    - ALE (chapter 8)
    - Impact (chapter 8)
- Quantitative vs. qualitative (chapter 8)
- Risk-avoidance, transference, acceptance, mitigation, deterrence (chapter 8)
- Risks associated to cloud computing and virtualization (chapter 5)

2.2 Carry out appropriate risk mitigation strategies (chapters 2, 5, 8, 9, 11)

- Implement security controls based on risk (chapter 2)
- Change management (chapter 5)
- Incident management (chapter 11)
- User rights and permissions reviews (chapters 8, 11)
- Perform routine audits (chapters 2, 8)
- Implement policies and procedures to prevent data loss or theft (chapters 5, 9, 11)

2.3 Execute appropriate incident response procedures (chapter 11)

- Basic forensic procedures (chapter 11)
    - Order of volatility (chapter 11)
    - Capture system image (chapter 11)
    - Network traffic and logs (chapter 11)
    - Capture video (chapter 11)
    - Record time offset (chapter 11)
    - Take hashes (chapter 11)
    - Screenshots (chapter 11)
    - Witnesses (chapter 11)
    - Track man hours and expense (chapter 11)
- Damage and loss control (chapter 11)
- Chain of custody (chapter 11)
- Incident response: first responder (chapter 11)

2.4 Explain the importance of security related awareness and training (chapters 1, 2, 4, 5, 6, 11)

- Security policy training and procedures (chapter 11)
- Personally identifiable information (chapter 11)

- Information classification: sensitivity of data (hard or soft) (chapter 11)
- Data labeling, handling, and disposal (chapter 11)
- Compliance with laws, best practices, and standards (chapter 11)
- User habits (chapters 1, 2, 5, 6, 11)
  - Password behaviors (chapter 1)
  - Data handling (chapter 11)
  - Clean desk policies (chapter 11)
  - Prevent tailgating (chapters 2, 6)
  - Personally owned devices (chapter 5, 11)
  - Threat awareness (chapters 4, 5, 6)
  - New viruses (chapter 6)
  - Phishing attacks (chapter 6)
  - Zero day exploits (chapters 4, 5, 6)
- Use of social networking and P2P (chapter 11)

2.5 Compare and contrast aspects of business continuity (chapter 9)
- Business impact analysis (chapter 9)
- Removing single points of failure (chapter 9)
- Business continuity planning and testing (chapter 9)
- Continuity of operations (chapter 9)
- Disaster recovery (chapter 9)
- IT contingency planning (chapter 9)
- Succession planning (chapter 9)

2.6 Explain the impact and proper use of environmental controls (chapters 2, 9)
- HVAC (chapter 9)
- Fire suppression (chapter 9)
- EMI shielding (chapter 9)
- Hot and cold aisles (chapter 9)
- Environmental monitoring (chapter 9)
- Temperature and humidity controls (chapter 9)
- Video monitoring (chapter 2)

2.7 Execute disaster recovery plans and procedures (chapter 9)
- Backup/backout contingency plans or policies (chapter 9)
- Backups, execution, and frequency (chapter 9)
- Redundancy and fault tolerance (chapter 9)
  - Hardware (chapter 9)
  - RAID (chapter 9)
  - Clustering (chapter 9)
  - Load balancing (chapter 9)
  - Servers (chapter 9)
- High availability (chapter 9)

- Cold site, hot site, warm site (chapter 9)
- Mean time to restore, mean time between failures, recovery time objectives, and recovery point objectives (chapter 9)

2.8 Exemplify the concepts of confidentiality, integrity, and availability (CIA) (chapters 1, 9, 11)

3.0 Threats and Vulnerabilities

3.1 Analyze and differentiate among types of malware (chapter 6)
- Adware (chapter 6)
- Virus (chapter 6)
- Worms (chapter 6)
- Spyware (chapter 6)
- Trojan (chapter 6)
- Rootkits (chapter 6)
- Backdoors (chapter 6)
- Logic bomb (chapter 6)
- Botnets (chapter 6)

3.2 Analyze and differentiate among types of attacks (chapters 6, 7, 8)
- Man-in-the-middle (chapter 7)
- DDoS (chapter 7)
- DoS (chapter 7)
- Replay (chapter 7)
- Smurf attack (chapter 7)
- Spoofing (chapter 7)
- Spam (chapter 7)
- Phishing (chapter 6)
- Spim (chapter 6)
- Vishing (chapter 6)
- Spear phishing (chapter 6)
- Xmas attack (chapter 7)
- Pharming (chapter 7)
- Privilege escalation (chapter 6)
- Malicious insider threat (chapter 8)
- DNS poisoning and ARP poisoning (chapter 7)
- Transitive access (chapter 7)
- Client-side attacks (chapter 7)

3.3 Analyze and differentiate among types of social engineering attacks (chapter 6)
- Shoulder surfing (chapter 6)
- Dumpster diving (chapter 6)
- Tailgating (chapter 6)

- Impersonation (chapter 6)
- Hoaxes (chapter 6)
- Whaling (chapter 6)
- Vishing (chapter 6)

3.4 Analyze and differentiate among types of wireless attacks (chapter 4)
- Rogue access points (chapter 4)
- Interference (chapter 4)
- Evil twin (chapter 4)
- War driving (chapter 4)
- Bluejacking (chapter 4)
- Bluesnarfing (chapter 4)
- War chalking (chapter 4)
- IV attack (chapter 4)
- Packet sniffing (chapter 4)

3.5 Analyze and differentiate among types of application attacks (chapters 4, 5, 7)
- Cross-site scripting (chapter 7)
- SQL injection (chapter 7)
- LDAP injection (chapter 7)
- XML injection (chapter 7)
- Directory traversal/command injection (chapter 7)
- Buffer overflow (chapter 7)
- Zero day (chapter 4, 5)
- Cookies and attachments (chapter 7)
- Malicious add-ons (chapter 7)
- Session hijacking (chapter 7)
- Header manipulation (chapter 7)

3.6 Analyze and differentiate among types of mitigation and deterrent techniques (chapters 2, 3, 4, 5, 6, 8, 9)
- Manual bypassing of electronic controls (chapters 3, 9)
  - Failsafe/secure vs. failopen (chapters 3, 9)
- Monitoring system logs (chapter 8)
  - Event logs (chapter 8)
  - Audit logs (chapter 8)
  - Security logs(chapter 8)
  - Access logs (chapter 8)
- Physical security (chapters 2, 6)
  - Hardware locks (chapter 2)
  - Mantraps (chapters 2, 6)
  - Video surveillance (chapters 2)
  - Fencing (chapter 2)
  - Proximity readers (chapter 2)

- Access list (chapter 2)
  - Hardening (chapter 5)
    - Disabling unnecessary services (chapter 5)
    - Protecting management interfaces and applications (chapter 5)
    - Password protection (chapters 1, 5)
    - Disabling unnecessary accounts (chapter 5)
  - Port security (chapters 3, 4)
    - MAC limiting and filtering (chapters 3, 4)
    - 802.1x (chapters 3, 4)
    - Disabling unused ports (chapters 3, 4)
  - Security posture (chapters 4, 5)
    - Initial baseline configuration (chapter 5)
    - Continuous security monitoring (chapter 4)
    - Remediation (chapter 4)

Reporting (chapter 4)
  - Alarms (chapter 4)
  - Alerts (chapter 4)
  - Trends (chapter 4)

Detection controls vs. prevention controls (chapters 2, 4)
  - IDS vs. IPS (chapter 4)
  - Camera vs. guard (chapter 2)

3.7 Implement assessment tools and techniques to discover security threats and vulnerabilities (chapters 3, 4, 8)
  - Vulnerability scanning and interpret results (chapter 8)
  - Tools (chapters 3, 4, 8)
    - Protocol analyzer (chapter 8)
    - Sniffer (chapter 8)
    - Vulnerability scanner (chapter 8)
    - Honeypots (chapter 4)
    - Honeynets (chapter 4)
    - Port scanner (chapters 3, 4, 8)
  - Risk calculations (chapter 8)
    - Threat vs. likelihood (chapter 8)
  - Assessment types (chapter 8)
    - Risk (chapter 8)
    - Threat (chapter 8)
    - Vulnerability (chapter 8)
  - Assessment technique (chapters 8)
    - Baseline reporting (chapter 8)
    - Code review (chapter 8)
    - Determine attack surface (chapter 8)
    - Architecture (chapter 8)
    - Design reviews (chapter 8)

3.8 Within the realm of vulnerability assessments, explain the proper use of penetration
   testing versus vulnerability scanning (chapter 8)
   - Penetration testing (chapter 8)
     - Verify a threat exists (chapter 8)
     - Bypass security controls (chapter 8)
     - Actively test security controls (chapter 8)
     - Exploiting vulnerabilities (chapter 8)
   - Vulnerability scanning (chapter 8)
     - Passively testing security controls (chapter 8)
     - Identify vulnerability (chapter 8)
     - Identify lack of security controls (chapter 8)
     - Identify common misconfiguration (chapter 8)
   - Black box (chapter 8)
   - White box (chapter 8)
   - Gray box (chapter 8)

4.0 Application, Data and Host Security

4.1 Explain the importance of application security (chapters 7, 8)
   - Fuzzing (chapters 7, 8)
   - Secure coding concepts (chapter 7)
     - Error and exception handling (chapter 7)
     - Input validation (chapter 7)
   - Cross-site scripting prevention (chapter 7)
   - Cross-site request forgery (XSRF) prevention (chapter 7)
   - Application configuration baseline (proper settings) (chapter 7)
   - Application hardening (chapter 7)
   - Application patch management (chapter 7)

4.2 Carry out appropriate procedures to establish host security (chapters 2, 4, 5, 6)
   - Operating system security and settings (chapter 5)
   - Anti-malware (chapter 6)
     - Antivirus (chapter 6)
     - Anti-spam (chapter 6)
     - Anti-spyware (chapter 6)
     - Pop-up blockers (chapter 6)
     - Host-based firewalls (chapter 6)
   - Patch management (chapter 5)
   - Hardware security (chapter 2)
     - Cable locks (chapter 2)
     - Safe (chapter 2)
     - Locking cabinets (chapter 2)

- Host software baselining (chapter 5)
- Mobile devices (chapters 4, 5)
  - Screen lock (chapter 5),
  - Strong password (chapters 4, 5)
  - Device encryption (chapters 4, 5
  - Remote wipe/sanitation (chapters 4, 5)
  - Voice encryption (chapters 4, 5)
  - GPS tracking (chapters 4, 5)
- Virtualization (chapter 5)

4.3 Explain the importance of data security (chapters 5, 10)
- Data Loss Prevention (DLP) (chapter 5)
- Data encryption (chapters 5, 10)
  - Full disk (chapter 5)
  - Database (chapters 5, 10)
  - Individual files (chapters 5, 10)
  - Removable media (chapters 5, 10)
  - Mobile devices (chapter 5)
- Hardware based encryption devices (chapter 5)
  - TPM (chapter 5)
  - HSM (chapter 5)
  - USB encryption (chapter 5)
  - Hard drive (chapter 5)
- Cloud computing (chapter 5)

5.0 Access Control and Identity Management

5.1 Explain the function and purpose of authentication services (chapter 1)
- RADIUS (chapter 1)
- TACACS (chapter 1)
- TACACS+ (chapter 1)
- Kerberos (chapter 1)
- LDAP (chapter 1)
- XTACACS (chapter 1)

5.2 Explain the fundamental concepts and best practices related to authentication, authorization, and access control (chapters 1, 2, 3, 11)
- Identification vs. authentication (chapter 1)
- Authentication (single factor) and authorization (chapter 1)
- Multifactor authentication (chapter 1)
- Biometrics (chapter 1)
- Tokens (chapter 1)
- Common access card (chapter 1)
- Personal identification verification card (chapter 1)
- Smart card (chapter 1)

- Least privilege (chapters 2, 11)
- Separation of duties (chapter 11)
- Single sign on (chapter 1)
- ACLs (chapters 1, 2)
- Access control (chapters 1, 2)
- Mandatory access control (chapter 2)
- Discretionary access control (chapter 2)
- Role/rule-based access control (chapter 2)
- Implicit deny (chapters 1, 2, 3)
- Time of day restrictions (chapter 2)
- Trusted OS (chapter 2)
- Mandatory vacations (chapter 11)
- Job rotation (chapter 11)

5.3 Implement appropriate security controls when performing account management (chapters 1, 2, 11)
- Mitigates issues associated with users with multiple account/roles (chapter 11)
- Account policy enforcement (chapters 1, 2)
  - Password complexity (chapters 1, 2)
  - Expiration (chapter 2)
  - Recovery (chapter 1)
  - Length (chapters 1, 2)
  - Disablement (chapter 2)
  - Lockout (chapter 1)
- Group based privileges (chapter 2)
- User assigned privileges (chapter 2)

6.0 Cryptography

6.1 Summarize general cryptography concepts (chapter 10)
- Symmetric vs. asymmetric (chapter 10)
- Fundamental differences and encryption methods (chapter 10)
  - Block vs. stream (chapter 10)
- Transport encryption (chapter 10)
- Non-repudiation (chapter 10)
- Hashing (chapter 10)
- Key escrow (chapter 10)
- Steganography (chapter 10)
- Digital signatures (chapter 10)
- Use of proven technologies (chapter 10)
- Elliptic curve and quantum cryptography (chapter 10)

6.2 Use and apply appropriate cryptographic tools and products (chapters 1, 2, 3, 4, 10)
WEP vs. WPA/WPA2 and preshared key (chapter 4)
- MD5 (chapter 10)

- SHA (chapter 10)
- RIPEMD (chapter 10)
- AES (chapter 10)
- DES (chapter 10)
- 3DES (chapter 10)
- HMAC (chapter 10)
- RSA (chapter 10)
- RC4 (chapter 10)
- One-time-pads (chapter 10)
- CHAP (chapter 1)
- PAP (chapter 1)
- NTLM (chapter 10)
- NTLMv2 (chapter 10)
- Blowfish (chapter 10)
- PGP/GPG (chapter 10)
- Whole disk encryption (chapter 5)
- TwoFish (chapter 10)
- Comparative strengths of algorithms (chapter 10)
- Use of algorithms with transport encryption (chapters 3, 4, 10)
  - SSL (chapters 3, 4, 10)
  - TLS (chapters 3, 4, 10)
  - IPSec (chapters 3, 4)
  - SSH (chapters 3, 4)
  - HTTPS (chapters 3, 4, 10)

6.3 Explain the core concepts of public key infrastructure (chapter 10)
- Certificate authorities and digital certificates (chapter 10)
  - CA (chapter 10)
  - CRLs (chapter 10)
- PKI (chapter 10)
- Recovery agent (chapter 10)
- Public key (chapter 10)
- Private key (chapter 10)
- Registration (chapter 10)
- Key escrow (chapter 10)
- Trust models (chapter 10)

6.4 Implement PKI, certificate management, and associated components (chapter 10)
- Certificate authorities and digital certificates (chapter 10)
  - CA (chapter 10)
  - CRLs (chapter 10)
- PKI (chapter 10)
- Recovery agent (chapter 10)

- Public key (chapter 10)
- Private keys (chapter 10)
- Registration (chapter 10)
- Key escrow (chapter 10)
- Trust models (chapter 10)

Recertification Requirements

The CompTIA Security+ certification was previously a lifetime certification. You took it once and you were certified for life. However, for anyone taking the exam after January 1, 2011, the certification expires after three years unless it is renewed.

You can renew the certification by either taking the next version of the exam or by enrolling in CompTIA's new Continuing Education (CE) program. You will be required to pay an annual fee of $49 and earn a minimum of fifty Continuing Education Units (CEUs). You can earn CEUs through a variety of activities. Some examples include presenting or teaching topics to others, attending training sessions, participating in industry events or seminars, or writing relevant articles, white papers, blogs, or books.

For full details, check out CompTIAs website: http://certification.comptia.org/getCertified/steps_to_certification/stayCertified.aspx.

CompTIA Security+ Assessment Exam

Use this assessment exam to test your knowledge of the topics before you start reading the book, and again before you take the live exam. An answer key with explanation is available at the end of the assessment exam.

1. You want to ensure that data can only be viewed by authorized users. What provides this assurance?
    A. Confidentiality
    B. Integrity
    C. Availability
    D. Authentication

2. A database administrator has just completed an update to a database using a script. Unfortunately, the script had an error and wrote incorrect data throughout the database. What has been lost?
    A. Confidentiality
    B. Integrity
    C. Availability
    D. Authentication

3. What does RAID-1 support?
    A. Authentication
    B. Availability
    C. Confidentiality
    D. Integrity

4. A user enters a username and a password and logs onto a system. What does this describe?
    A. Identification
    B. Authentication
    C. Authorization
    D. Availability

5. Your organization has configured an account policy that locks out a user accounts for thirty minutes if they enter the wrong password five times. What is this policy?
    A. Account lockout policy
    B. Account disablement policy
    C. Account continuance policy
    D. Password policy

6. Which of the following supports the use of one-time passwords?
    A. Proximity card
    B. Tokens
    C. CAC
    D. PIV

7. A user must swipe his finger on a fingerprint scanner to gain access to his laptop. What is being used for authentication?
    A. Something the user knows
    B. Something the user has
    C. Something the user wants
    D. Biometrics

8. Of the following choices, what qualifies as two-factor authentication?
    A. Fingerprints from both of a user's hands
    B. Two passwords
    C. A smart card and a PIN
    D. A token and a smart card

9. Which of the following choices is an example of authentication based on *something you have* and *something you are*?
    A. A username, password, and PIN
    B. A token and a fingerprint scan
    C. A token and a password
    D. A PIN and a fingerprint scan

10. Which of the following authentication protocols uses tickets?
    A. LDAP
    B. MD5
    C. SHA1
    D. Kerberos

11. Dawn logged on using her work account at 6:45 a.m. into a Kerberos realm. She was able to access network resources throughout the day with no problem. A crisis kept her at work late. However, she found that at about 7:30 p.m., she was no longer able to access a server she accessed earlier. Another worker working on the evening shift accessed the server without any problem. What is the likely problem?
    A. The server is down
    B. Her certificate has expired
    C. Her ticket has expired
    D. The server's certificate has expired

12. What is a primary difference between TACACS and TACACS+?
    A. TACACS can use either TCP or UDP ports 514 while TACACS+ uses only TCP port 514
    B. TACACS can use either TCP or UDP ports 49 while TACACS+ uses only TCP port 49
    C. TACACS+ can use either TCP or UDP ports 49 while TACACS uses only TCP port 49
    A. TACACS+ can use either TCP or UDP ports 514 while TACACS uses only TCP port 514

13. Sally is required to review security logs and maintain three servers within a network. Instead of giving her full access to all network resources, she is granted access only to the security logs and the three servers. Which of the following choices best identifies what is being used?
    A. MAC
    B. DAC
    C. RBAC
    D. Least privilege

14. An administrator wants to use user templates as a method of complying with the principle of least privilege. What access control model supports this process?
    A. Discretionary access control (DAC)
    B. Mandatory access control (MAC)
    C. Role-based access control (RBAC)
    D. Rule-based access control (RBAC)

15. What is the difference between rule-based and role-based access control?
    A. Rule-based access control is based on a set of approved instructions while role-based is based on job function
    B. Rule-based access control is based on job function while role-based is based on a set of approved instructions
    C. Rule-based access control uses labels to identify subjects and objects while role-based requires every object to have an owner
    D. They are both the same, and known as RBAC

16. You want to increase physical security for your server room. Which of the following provides the best protection?
    A. Limit access to only a single well-protected entrance
    B. Ensure that the server room has one door for entrance and one door for exit
    C. Ensure that access to the server is limited to only management
    D. Remove all physical access to the server room

17. Users in an organization are issued proximity cards that they use to access secure areas. Lately, users have begun trading their proximity cards so co-workers can access resources with someone else's card. What permits this misuse?
    A. A lack of authorization controls
    B. A lack of access controls
    C. Authentication verification without authorization
    D. Authorization verification without authentication

18. A security professional observes employees regularly tailgating others into a secure datacenter. What can prevent this?
   A. CCTV
   B. Mantrap
   C. Proximity card
   D. Cipher lock

19. An employee found a USB flash drive in the parking lot. What should the employee do with this?
   A. Look at the contents to determine the owner
   B. Destroy it
   C. Turn it into a security professional
   D. Take it home and insert it into a home computer

20. An employee has left the company to go back to school. Which of the following is considered a security best practice in this situation?
   A. Disable the account
   B. Set the account to expire in sixty days
   C. Set the password to expire
   D. Since the employee left on good terms, nothing needs to be done

21. You want to ensure that data remains in an encrypted format while it is transmitted over the Internet. Of the following choices, what can you use? (Choose all that apply.)
   A. SFTP, FTPS, TFTP, HTTPS, SSL, TLS
   B. SSH, SFTP, SSL, HTTP
   C. TLS, SSL, SSH, FTPS, SFTP,
   D. HTTPS, FTP, SSH, SSL

22. You want to configure traps on devices in your network. What would you use?
   A. A load balancer
   B. SNMP
   C. Default gateways
   D. SCP

23. What port does SCP use?
   A. 22
   B. 23
   C. 25
   D. 80

24. Of the following choices, what is the best choice to indicate the protocol(s) that use(s) port 22?
   A. SCP
   B. SCP and SSH
   C. SCP, TFTP, SQL, and SSH
   D. SCP, SFTP, and SSH

25. An administrator wants to determine what services and protocols are running on a remote system. Of the following choices, what is the best choice to achieve this goal?
   A. Go to the datacenter, log on, and inspect the system
   B. Perform a vulnerability assessment
   C. Perform an ICMP sweep
   D. Identify open ports on the system

26. You are examining open ports on a firewall and you see that port 500 is open. What is the likely reason?
   A. To support an L2TP VPN connection
   B. To support a PPTP VPN connection
   C. To support a TACACS+ VPN connection
   D. To support an IPsec VPN connection

27. Your organization has configured switches so that only devices with specific MAC addresses can connect to specific ports on the switches. The switch prevents any other devices from connecting. What is this?
   A. Content filtering
   B. Port security
   C. Load balancing
   D. Proxy caching

28. You are reviewing a firewall's ACL and see the following statement: **drop all**. What security principle does this enforce?
   A. Least privilege
   B. Integrity
   C. Availability
   D. Implicit deny

29. Firewalls include rules in an ACL. Which of the following would block network traffic that isn't in any of the previously defined rules?
   A. Explicit allow
   B. Implicit allow
   C. Explicit deny
   D. Implicit deny

30. An organization wants to hide addresses it uses on its internal network. What can assist with this goal?
- A. MAC filtering
- B. NAC
- C. NAT
- D. DMZ

31. Your network includes a device that examines network traffic and determines when the traffic is outside expected boundaries. What is this device?
- A. Anomaly-based HIDS
- B. Signature-based HIDS
- C. Anomaly-based NIDS
- D. Signature-based NIDS

32. Attackers frequently attack your organization, and administrators want to learn more about zero day attacks on the network. What can they use?
- A. Anomaly-based HIDS
- B. Signature-based HIDS
- C. Honeypot
- D. Signature-based NIDS

33. Users in your network are complaining that they are unable to download content from a specific website. Additionally, your IDS is recording multiple events on the network. What is a likely reason why users are unable to download this content?
- A. A load balancer is blocking content from the website
- B. The firewall is in failopen mode
- C. An evil twin is on the network
- D. NIPS is blocking content from the website

34. Attackers have launched multiple attacks against your network in recent weeks. While administrators have taken action to reduce the impact of the attacks, management wants to prevent these attacks. What can prevent ongoing network-based attacks?
- A. NIDS
- B. NIPS
- C. HIDS
- D. HIPS

35. Users that are further away from the WAP installed in your company's network are having trouble connecting. What can you check to increase the coverage of the WAP?
- A. SSID broadcasting
- B. Encryption method
- C. Verify Enterprise mode is used
- D. Power levels

36. You are configuring a secure wireless network that will use WPA2. Management wants to use a more secure method than PSKs. Of the following choices, what will you need?
    A. 802.11n
    B. CCMP
    C. AES
    D. RADIUS

37. You have discovered a counterfeit wireless station using the same SSID as your wireless network. What best describes this?
    A. Evil twin
    B. IV attack
    C. War driving
    D. Rogue access point

38. You are planning to complete a wireless audit. What should you check? (Choose all that apply.)
    A. Antenna placement
    B. Power levels
    C. Footprint
    D. Encryption
    E. Flood guards

39. Your organization wants to provide secure remote access to the internal network to over two hundred employees that are regularly on the road. What would they use?
    A. VPN concentrator
    B. Health agents
    C. Web application firewall
    D. Honeypot

40. What type of control is MAC filtering?
    A. Network access control
    B. Physical control
    C. Detective control
    D. Management control

41. Of the following choices, what can you do to protect a system from malicious software? (Choose two.)
    A. Disable unused services
    B. Disable the host-based firewall
    C. Keep a system up-to-date with current patches
    D. Install malware

42. An administrator is upgrading an application on a server. What would the administrator update when complete?
- A. Baseline
- B. The IaaS plan
- C. The HVAC system
- D. The hard drive hash

43. An administrator is deploying a service pack to several database servers. What would the administrator update when complete?
- A. The SaaS plan
- B. The patch management policy
- C. A chain of custody
- D. Configuration baseline

44. A virtual machine includes data on employees, including folders and files with payroll data. Management is concerned that an attacker can copy the virtual machine and access the data. What would you suggest to protect against this?
- A. Enable VM escape
- B. Disable VM escape
- C. Encrypt the files and folders
- D. Add a network-based DLP device

45. Of the following choices, what indicates the best choice to verify software changes on a system?
- A. Patch management
- B. A patch management policy
- C. Standardized images
- D. Performance baseline

46. A software vendor recently released several patches that apply to several of your servers. When should you apply these patches to the production servers?
- A. Immediately
- B. On the second Tuesday of each month
- C. Annually
- D. After testing

47. Sally stores a list of her passwords in a file on her computer's local hard drive. What can protect this data if her computer is lost or stolen?
- A. File level encryption
- B. DLP
- C. GPS
- D. Permissions

48. Of the following choices, what will store RSA keys?
    A. TPM and SSL
    B. TPM and HSM
    C. SSL and HSM
    D. CCMP and TKIP

49. Your organization has an existing server and you want to add a hardware device to provide encryption capabilities. What is the easiest way to accomplish this?
    A. TPM
    B. HSM
    C. DLP
    D. IaaS

50. Your organization issues laptop computers to employees. Employees use them while traveling, and frequently store sensitive data on these systems. What can you use to recover a laptop if an employee loses it?
    A. Encryption
    B. Remote wipe
    C. Remote lock
    D. GPS tracking

51. Your organization is considering using different cloud-based technologies. What security control is lost with these technologies?
    A. Backup capabilities
    B. Physical control of the data
    C. Operating system choice
    D. Access to the data

52. While surfing the Internet, a user sees a message indicating a malware infection and offering free antivirus software. The user downloads and installs the free antivirus software but then realizes it infected the system. Which of the following choices best explains what happened to the user's system?
    A. Social engineering
    B. Trojan
    C. Vishing
    D. Spim

53. What malware can hide its running processes to avoid detection?
    A. Worm
    B. Virus
    C. Rootkit
    D. Integrity checker

54. After browsing the Internet, a user notices the computer is running slowly. An antivirus scan with updated signatures doesn't report any problems. What is a likely cause?
   A. Known virus
   B. LDAP injection
   C. Zero day attack
   D. Spyware

55. Of the following choices, what can prevent malicious code from running on a computer?
   A. Antivirus software
   B. Host-based firewall
   C. Input validation
   D. Fuzzing

56. A security newsletter describes an attack where e-mails that look like they are from reputable companies are actually from attackers trying to get personal and financial information. What type of attack is this?
   A. Arrow phishing
   B. Phishing
   C. Bear phishing
   D. VolPing

57. An organization has purchased privacy screens for all users. What threat is it trying to mitigate?
   A. Password masking
   B. Vishing
   C. Shoulder surfing
   D. Dumpster diving

58. An investigation revealed that multiple computers within your network connected to an unknown server after business hours. These computers then launched an attack. What is the best explanation for this behavior?
   A. Botnet
   B. Malware
   C. Kiting
   D. Fuzzing

59. A user entered improper data into an application and the application crashed. What is missing in this application?
   A. Error handling
   B. Cross-site scripting
   C. Shredding
   D. Password masking

60. Which of the following is related to a buffer overflow attack?
    A. Flood guard
    B. Memory addressing
    C. HTML tags
    D. Whaling

61. A web developer wants to avoid data loss from SQL injection attacks. What should the developer include in web applications?
    A. Buffer overflows
    B. Input validation
    C. Output validation
    D. Fuzzing

62. An organization evaluated a marketing application and discovered that it required opening several ports on firewalls. They decided on purchasing a different marketing application. What risk management strategy did they use?
    A. Risk acceptance
    B. Risk avoidance
    C. Risk deterrence
    D. Risk transference

63. A security professional is performing a quantitative risk analysis. Of the following choices, what is most likely to be used in the assessment?
    A. Judgment
    B. Expert opinions
    C. Asset value
    D. Fuzzing

64. Management is deciding which controls to implement to reduce specific risks. They are basing their decisions on the result of an assessment that used cost. What type of assessment was completed?
    A. Quantitative
    B. Qualitative
    C. Vulnerability scan
    D. Penetration test

65. Your organization recently installed a new server hosting a database application. You want to test the server to determine if it has any known security issues. What would you use?
    A. Port scanner
    B. Vulnerability scanner
    C. IPS
    D. Firewall

66. Of the following choices, what best describes a goal of a vulnerability scan?
    A. Exploit weaknesses in security controls
    B. Identify baseline configuration of security controls
    C. Identify security control threats
    D. Identify lack of security controls

67. Of the following choices, what provides the best explanation for what a penetration test provides?
    A. Demonstration of security vulnerabilities
    B. Identification of security vulnerabilities
    C. Demonstration of system capabilities
    D. Identification of system capabilities

68. Security testers are performing a penetration test with some inside knowledge of the system. What type of test is this?
    A. Black box test
    B. White box test
    C. Gray box test
    D. Internal test

69. What does black hat indicate?
    A. A malicious attacker
    B. A tester working with zero knowledge of the tested system
    C. An application sending random data to an application
    D. Fuzzing

70. You are tasked with maintaining a file server. Which of the following should you periodically review to ensure the server's security configuration?
    A. User rights and permissions
    B. Evil twin capabilities
    C. PaaS capabilities
    D. Hard drive hash

71. A security administrator wants to verify that all users are following company policies for login. What can they use?
    A. Protocol analyzer
    B. Sniffer
    C. Password cracker
    D. User rights review

72. A recent attack modified logs on a server. In the future, you want to protect logs from compromise. What can you use?
    A. Change the logs to read only
    B. Archive the logs at least weekly
    C. Centralized log management
    D. Disable logging

73. Of the following choices, what can ensure availability of a server if half of its drives fail?
    A. Hardware RAID-0
    B. Hardware RAID-1
    C. Software RAID-0
    D. Software RAID-5

74. An organization is in a location at risk of hurricanes, which can cause extended power outages. What can the organization use to prepare for these power outages?
    A. UPS
    B. Generators
    C. HVAC system
    D. Hot and cold aisles

75. An organization has decided to create a warm site to house a redundant datacenter. What likely drove this decision?
    A. Vulnerability assessment
    B. Penetration test
    C. Annual test
    D. Business impact analysis

76. An organization completes backups for critical servers daily. The organization wants to minimize downtime if a disaster occurs. Where should a copy of the backups be stored?
    A. At any off-site location
    B. At a designated hot site
    C. At a designated warm site
    D. At a designated cold site

77. An organization is completing a business continuity plan for its datacenter. It determines that half of these servers must be operational within a day after a disaster. What would it use?
    A. Hot site
    B. Cold site
    C. Warm site
    D. Full backups

78. Of the following choices, what is included in a DRP?
    A. List of all computers
    B. Chain of custody
    C. Regular testing
    D. Digital signatures

79. Your organization is designing a large datacenter that will host several bays of servers. Which of the following choices will increase availability of the datacenter?
    A. Hot and cold aisles
    B. Mantrap
    C. Cameras
    D. Guards

80. You are evaluating the security and availability of a system. Availability is more important than security in the system. If it fails, what state should it fail in?
    A. It should fail open
    B. It should fail closed
    C. It should shut down
    D. It should be rebooted

81. An administrator wants to verify that a file has not been altered. What technology provides this capability?
    A. 3DES
    B. MD5
    C. RSA
    D. Blowfish

82. Which of the following converts passwords to all upper case and divides them into two seven-character strings?
    A. LANMAN
    B. AES
    C. RSA
    D. Kerberos

83. What type of encryption uses hard-copy printouts of keys?
    A. AES
    B. One-time pads
    C. RSA
    D. Diffie-Hellman

84. Of the following choices, what addresses key management?
    A. S/MIME
    B. PGP
    C. Diffie-Hellman
    D. RC4

85. What key encrypts the data sent between a web browser and a web server in an SSL session?
    A. Symmetric key
    B. Private key
    C. Public key
    D. Prime number key

86. Sally sent an encrypted e-mail with a digital signature to Joe. Of the following choices, what is involved in this process? (Choose all that apply.)
    A. Sally's private key verifies the digital signature
    B. Joe's public key decrypts the e-mail
    C. Sally's private key signs the e-mail
    D. Joe's public key encrypts the e-mail

87. What is a private key used for in a PKI?
    A. Encrypt the hash in a digital signature
    B. Decrypt the hash in a digital signature
    C. Encrypt data before sending it
    D. MD5

88. Of the following choices, what uses public and private keys for encryption and decryption of e-mail?
    A. CRL
    B. CA
    C. LANMAN
    D. PGP

89. Of the following choices, which are publically available? (Choose all that apply.)
    A. Certificate revocation list
    B. Certificate holding a public key matched to a private key
    C. Website certificate
    D. User passphrase

90. An organization has determined that data loss is unacceptable within its PKI. What can it implement?
    A. CRL
    B. CA
    C. Key escrow
    D. Trusted root certification authority store

91. Of the following choices, what is the most important security benefit of a clean desk policy?
    A. Prevents illnesses due to viruses and bacteria
    B. Presents a positive image to customers
    C. Ensures sensitive data and passwords are secured
    D. Increases integrity of data

92. A user requires read access to a business application. However, an administrator discovers the user can read, write, and delete data in the application. What policy is this violating?
    A. User privilege review
    B. Chain of custody
    C. User privilege policy
    D. Retention policy

93. An organization has implemented a mandatory vacation policy for security administrators. What is the organization's most likely goal?
    A. Reduce potential for privilege escalation
    B. Reinforce compliance with security policies
    C. Detect malicious actions by security administrators
    D. Ensure administrators have time for recreation

94. After a promotion, an administrator is not able to access some servers. However, the administrator was able to access the servers in the previous job. What policy is most likely causing this?
    A. Mandatory vacations policy
    B. Separation of duties policy
    C. Job rotation policy
    D. Single sign-on policy

95. A company provides employees with annual security awareness training. Of the following choices, what is the most likely reason the company is doing this?
    To minimize risk posed by users
    To reduce user compliance with security policies
    To eliminate risk posed by users
    To increase risk posed by users

96. A receptionist regularly answers the phone and answers queries for the company. Of the following choices, what identifies the biggest threat from this receptionist?
    A. Providing information on the website
    B. Providing information from a company sales brochure
    C. Providing contact information for a sales person
    D. Providing personal contact information

97. A security policy restricts the use of P2P software on any company system. Of the following choices, what is the easiest way an administrator can verify systems are not running this software?
    A. Protocol analyzer
    B. Penetration test
    C. Port scanner
    D. User rights review

98. An employee has been accused of stealing data using a personal laptop. A forensics investigation into the theft includes logs and protocol analyzer captures. What information will most accurately identify the computer used by the attacker?
    A. User logon name
    B. Computer name
    C. IP address
    D. MAC address

99. When would a security professional create a forensic hash of a drive?
    A. Before and after creating an image
    B. Before creating an image, after creating an image, and on the image
    C. Immediately before creating the chain of custody
    D. Immediately after disconnecting the computer from the network

100. An administrator collected a thumb drive as evidence and stored the drive on his desk for analysis the next day. Of the following choices, what incident response procedure did the forensic expert violate?
    A. Chain of custody
    B. Cleanliness policy
    C. Separation of duties
    D. Containment

Assessment Exam Answers

When checking your answers, take the time to read the explanation. Understanding the explanations will help ensure you're prepared for the live exam. The explanation also shows the chapter or chapters where you can get more detailed information on the topic.

1. **A.** Confidentiality prevents unauthorized disclosure and is enforced with access controls and encryption. Integrity provides assurances that data has not been modified and is enforced with hashing. Availability ensures systems are up and operational when needed and uses fault tolerance and redundancy methods. Authentication provides proof that users are who they claim to be. See chapter 1.

2. **B.** If an unauthorized or unintended change occurs to data, the data has lost integrity. Confidentiality prevents unauthorized disclosure and is enforced with access controls and encryption. Availability ensures systems are up and operational when needed and uses fault tolerance and redundancy methods. Authentication provides proof that users are who they claim to be. See chapter 1.

3. **B.** Redundant Array of Inexpensive Disks 1 (RAID-1) uses two disks to create a mirror of each, and it provides availability through fault tolerance. If a single drive fails, the system can tolerate the fault and continue to operate. Authentication provides proof of a user's identity. Confidentiality ensures that data is only viewable by authorized users. Integrity provides assurances that data has not been modified. See chapters 1 and 8.

4. **B.** Authentication occurs when an identity is verified. An entity claims an identity by presenting something like a username and proves the identity with an authentication mechanism such as a password. Authorization provides access to resources and occurs after authentication. Availability indicates that the system is up and operational when needed. See chapter 1.

5. **A.** An account lockout policy will force an account to be locked out after the wrong password is entered a set number of times (such as after five failed attempts). An account disablement policy specifies that accounts are disabled when no longer needed, such as after an employee leaves the company. There is no such thing as an account continuance policy. A password policy ensures strong passwords are used and users change their password regularly. See chapter 1.

6. **B.** A token (such as an RSA token) provides a rolling password for one-time use. A proximity card is *something you have* (or something a user has) as a factor of authentication, but it doesn't use one-time passwords. A CAC and a PIV are both specialized types of smart cards that include photo identification. See chapter 1.

7. **D.** A fingerprint scanner is using biometrics (in the *something the user is* factor of authentication). Biometrics are the most difficult for an attacker to falsify or forge since it represents a user based on personal characteristics. A password or PIN is an example of

something the user knows. A token or smart card is an example of something the user has. Something the user wants is not a valid factor of authentication. See chapter 1.

8. **C.** Two-factor authentication includes authentication from two of three factors (*something you know*, *something you have*, and *something you are*) and only a smart card (*something you have*) and a PIN (*something you know*) meet this requirement. Fingerprints from two hands use only biometrics (*something you are*), two passwords are two instances of *something you know*, and a token and smart card represent two instances of *something you have*. See chapter 1.

9. **B.** Token-based authentication is based on *something you have*, and a fingerprint scan is based on *something you are*. A username, password, and PIN all fall in under the *something you know* factor of authentication. A token and password are *something you have* and *something you know*. A PIN and a fingerprint scan are *something you know* and *something you are*. See chapter 1.

10. **D.** Kerberos is a network authentication protocol using tickets. The Lightweight Directory Access Protocol (LDAP) specifies formats and methods to query directories and is used to manage objects (such as users and computers) in an Active Directory domain. MD5 and SHA1 are hashing algorithms, not authentication protocols. See chapter 1.

11. **C.** Kerberos uses time-stamped tickets, and they often have a lifetime of ten or twelve hours. If the ticket is expired, the user won't be able to use it anymore without logging off and back on. Since another user is accessing the server, it is not down. A Kerberos realm uses tickets, not certificates, and there is no indication that certificates are being used. See chapter 1.

12. **B.** TACACS can use either TCP or UDP ports 49, while TACACS+ uses only TCP port 49. Port 514 is used for the UNIX-based syslog. See chapter 1.

13. **D.** The principle of least privilege is a technical control and ensures that users have only the rights and permissions needed to perform the job, and no more. MAC, DAC, and RBAC are access control models that include much more than just a single access control such as least privilege. See chapter 2.

14. **C.** Role-based access control (RBAC) allows an administrator to create a user template, add the user template to one or more groups based on roles, and then assign rights and permissions to the groups. Any user accounts created with this template will automatically have these permissions. The DAC model specifies that every object has an owner, and Windows systems use the DAC model by default for NTFS files and folders. The MAC model uses sensitivity labels. Rule-based access control is based on a set of approved instructions. See chapter 2.

15. **A.** Rule-based access control (RBAC) is based on a set of approved instructions configured as rules, while role-based uses roles (or groups) based on job functions. MAC uses labels to identify subjects and objects and DAC requires every object to have an owner. While both rule-based and role-based access controls share the same acronym (RBAC), they are not the same. See chapter 2.

16. **A.** One of the best examples of physical security for a server room is to ensure that access is limited to only a single well-protected entrance. Two doors (one for entrance and one for exit) requires security at both doors, and it is difficult to ensure that each is only used for an entrance or exit. More than one entrance and exit makes it harder to monitor access. Administrators need physical access to a server room, but management typically does not need physical access. See chapter 2.

17. **D.** The proximity card is being used without any type of authentication other than holding the proximity badge, which is granting authorization to resources without authenticating users; a solution would be to require authentication though a method other than the proximity badge prior to authorizing access, such as matching a PIN to the card. Authorization is being granted based on possession of the proximity cards so there are authorization and access controls; however, there isn't any authentication verification. See chapter 2.

18. **B.** A mantrap is highly effective at preventing unauthorized entry and can also be used to prevent tailgating. CCTV provides video surveillance and it can record unauthorized entry, but it can't prevent it. A proximity card is useful as an access control mechanism, but it won't prevent tailgating, so it isn't as useful as a mantrap. A cipher lock is a door access control, but it can't prevent tailgating. See chapter 2.

19. **C.** The USB flash drive should be turned in to a security professional. It's risky to plug it in to look at the contents or take it home, since it could have malware. While it may be safe to destroy it, a security professional can plug it into an isolated system to determine its contents and the owner. See chapter 2.

20. **A.** An account disablement policy would ensure that a terminated employee's account is disabled to revoke the employee's access. Setting an account to expire is useful for a temporary account, but in this situation, it would leave the account available for anyone to use for the next sixty days instead of immediately disabling it. Expiring the password forces the user to change the password at the next logon. It doesn't matter why employees leave a company; if they are no longer employed, the account should be disabled. See chapter 2.

21. **C.** Transport Layer Security (TLS), Secure Sockets Layer (SSL), Secure Shell (SSH), File Transfer Protocol Secure (FTPS), and Secure File Transfer Protocol (SFTP) can all encrypt data transmitted over the Internet. (Notice they all have an "S" in them.) TFTP, HTTP, and FTP are all unencrypted. See chapter 3.

22. **B.** The Simple Network Management Protocol (SNMP) uses device traps to send notifications, and it can monitor and manage network devices, such as routers or switches. A load balancer can optimize and distribute data workloads across multiple computers. A default gateway is an IP address on a router, and it provides a path to another network. SCP is based on SSH and copies files over a network in an encrypted format. See chapter 3.

23. **A.** Secure Copy (SCP) uses port 22, as do other protocols encrypted with Secure Shell (SSH), such as Secure File Transfer Protocol (SFTP). Telnet uses port 23. SMTP uses port 25. HTTP uses port 80. See chapter 3.

24. **D.** Secure Copy (SCP), Secure File Transfer Protocol (SFTP), and Secure Shell (SSH) all use port 22. While SCP alone, and SCP and SSH, both use port 22, answer D is the best choice since it shows more of the protocols using this port. TFTP uses port 69 and Microsoft's SQL server uses port 1433. See chapter 3.

25. **D.** Since many services and protocols use open ports, an administrator can identify running services on a system by determining what ports are open. Since the system is remote, it could be in another building or even another city, so going to the datacenter is not the best choice. While a vulnerability assessment will often include a port scan, it will do much more. An ICMP sweep (also called a host enumeration sweep) will identify servers on a network, but not individual services, protocols, or ports. See chapter 3.

26. **D.** Internet Protocol security (IPsec) virtual private network (VPN) connections use port 500 (often combined with protocol IDs 50 and/or 51 to identify IPsec) with the Internet Key Exchange (IKE) protocol. L2TP uses port 1701. PPTP uses port 1723. TACACS+ uses port 49. See chapters 3 and 4.

27. **B.** A version of port security maps specific end-device MAC addresses to specific ports on the switch and prevents any other devices from connecting. Web security gateways and all-in-one security appliances provide content filtering. A load balancer optimizes and distributes data loads across multiple computers or multiple networks. A proxy server provides content filtering and caching. See chapter 3.

28. **D.** A **drop all** or **deny any any** statement is placed at the end of an access control list (ACL) and enforces an implement deny strategy. Least privilege ensures users have only the access they need to perform their jobs and no more. Integrity provides assurances that data has not been modified, and availability ensures systems and data are up and operational when needed, but the **drop all** statement doesn't address either of these as directly as implicit deny. See chapter 3.

29. **D.** Most firewalls have an implicit deny statement (such as **drop all** or **deny any any**) at the end of an access control list (ACL) to block all traffic not previously allowed. An allow rule would not block traffic. An explicit deny rule explicitly blocks traffic defined in the rule only, not all other traffic. See chapter 3.

30. **C.** Network Address Translation (NAT) translates public IP addresses to private, private IP addresses back to public, and hides addresses on the internal network. Port security and network access control use MAC filtering to limit access. Network access control can inspect clients for health prior to allowing network access. A DMZ provides access to services (hosted on servers) from the Internet while providing a layer of protection for the internal network. See chapter 3.

31. **C.** An anomaly-based, network-based intrusion detection system (NIDS) compares current activity with a previously created baseline to detect abnormal activity. HIDS systems only monitor individual systems, not the network. Signature-based IDSs use signatures similar to antivirus software. See chapter 4.

32. **C.** A honeypot is a server designed to look valuable to an attacker and can help administrators learn about zero day exploits, or previously unknown attacks. HIDS protects host-based attacks and wouldn't help with network-based attacks. Signature-based tools would not have a signature for zero day attack since the attack method is unknown by definition. See chapter 4.

33. **D.** A network-based intrusion prevention system (NIPS) can detect and block malicious content, and both a NIPS and an intrusion detection system (IDS) can record the events. A load balancer can optimize and distribute data loads across multiple computers. Firewalls would normally fail in failsafe/failsecure (or closed) mode, blocking all traffic, but if it failed in failopen mode, it would allow all traffic. An evil twin is a rogue wireless access point with the same SSID as a live wireless access point. See chapter 4.

34. **B.** A network-based intrusion prevention system (NIPS) can detect and prevent ongoing network-based attacks. In contrast, a NIDS would only detect the activity, and this is likely what is alerting administrators to the attacks now. Host-based IDSs and IPSs detect malicious activity only on a host, not a network. See chapter 4.

35. **D.** You can increase coverage of a wireless access point (WAP) by increasing the power level and by adjusting the antenna placement. SSID broadcasting and encryption method does not affect the wireless coverage. Enterprise mode uses an 802.1X server for authentication and stronger security but does not affect the coverage of the WAP. See chapter 4.

36. **D.** WPA2 needs RADIUS to support WPA2 Enterprise mode. WPA2 personal mode uses a preshared key (PSK), and since management does not want to use PSKs, the solution requires Enterprise mode. 802.11n is a wireless standard. CCMP and AES provide strong encryption. However, using 802.11n, CCMP, or AES does not prevent the use of PSKs. See chapter 4.

37. **A.** An evil twin is a rogue (or counterfeit) access point with the same SSID as an authorized access point. An IV attack attempts to discover encryption keys to crack WEP. War driving is the practice of driving around looking for access points. A rogue access point is an unauthorized wireless station, but if it has the same SSID, it's best described as an evil twin. See chapter 4.

38. **A, B, C, D.** A wireless audit can check antenna placement, WAP power levels, WAP footprint, and encryption techniques. It also looks for rogue access points and unauthorized users, which are not listed in the answers. Flood guards can help prevent SYN flood attacks. See chapter 4.

39. **A.** VPN concentrators provide strong security and support large numbers of VPN clients. Health agents are required for network access control (NAC) solutions, but not required for all

remote access solutions. A web application firewall (WAF) is a firewall specifically designed to protect a web application, such as a web server, and not required for remote access. A honeypot is a server designed to look valuable to an attacker, can divert attacks, and can help organizations identify the latest unknown attacks. See chapter 4.

40. **A.** MAC filtering is a form of network access control (NAC). A physical control restricts physical access to buildings and hardware devices. A detective control such as a security audit detects when a vulnerability has been exploited. Management controls are primarily administrative in function, such as risk assessments or vulnerability assessments. See chapter 4.

41. **A, C.** You can protect a system from malicious software by disabling unused services and keeping a system up-to-date. Enabling the firewall, not disabling it, provides protection against attacks. Installing antivirus or anti-malware software, not installing malware, protects a system. See chapters 5 and 6.

42. **A.** A configuration baseline documents the configuration of a system and should be updated after modifying a system, such as after upgrading new software or installing a service pack. IaaS is a cloud-based technology that allows an organization to reduce its hardware footprint by outsourcing equipment requirements. HVAC provides heating and cooling, but doesn't need to be updated after upgrading an application. Incident response procedures use a hard drive hash to identify evidence tampering. See chapter 5.

43. **D.** A configuration baseline documents the configuration of a system and is updated after modifying a system, such as through a service pack or upgrading new software. SaaS is a cloud-based technology that provides applications such as web-based e-mail to users. A patch management policy defines how patches are tested and applied, including a timeline for deployment. A chain of custody validates the control of forensic evidence, such as a disk drive, during transport. See chapter 5.

44. **C.** You can encrypt files and folders on virtual machines to protect against loss of confidentiality just as you can on physical systems. VM escape is an attack run on virtual machines, allowing the attacker to access and control the physical host. You can't enable or disable VM escape, but you can keep a system patched and up to date to help protect against VM escape attacks. A DLP is a device that reduces the risk of employees e-mailing confidential information outside the organization. See chapters 1 and 5.

45. **A.** Patch management includes testing and deploying patches and verifying the software changes made by the patches. A patch management policy defines the patch management process, including a timeline for installing patches. Standardized images provide a secure baseline and include mandatory security configurations, and a performance baseline documents a system's performance. You can compare current systems with standardized images and performance baselines to identify differences, but just an image or a baseline will not verify the changes. See chapter 5.

46. D. You should apply patches to production servers after performing regression testing, and testing should be performed in a test environment that mirrors the production environment. Patches applied immediately may adversely affect production systems. Microsoft releases patches on the second Tuesday of each month, but patches still need to be tested. Applying patches annually leaves systems vulnerable to known threats between the updates. See chapter 5.

47. A. File level encryption can protect a single file against loss of confidentiality if a computer is lost or stolen. A DLP system can examine and analyze data to detect sensitive or confidential data. A GPS can help locate a lost or stolen computer but won't protect the individual file. Permissions provide a level of protection but can be bypassed if a computer is lost or stolen. See chapter 5.

48. B. A Trusted Platform Module (TPM) and a hardware security module (HSM) are hardware devices that store RSA keys, provide encryption and decryption services, and can assist with user authentication. SSL uses RSA keys, also called asymmetric keys, but it is a protocol and does not store RSA keys. CCMP is an improved wireless encryption protocol used with WPA2, while TKIP is an older wireless protocol used with WPA, but neither store RSA keys. See chapter 5.

49. B. A hardware security module (HSM) is a hardware device you can add to a server to provide encryption capabilities. A TPM is a chip embedded into a motherboard that also provides hardware encryption, but you can't easily add a TPM to an existing server. A DLP can reduce the risk of employees e-mailing confidential information outside the organization. Organizations use IaaS to rent access to hardware such as servers via the cloud to limit their hardware footprint and personnel costs. See chapter 5.

50. D. The goal in the question is to recover the laptop, and the only answer that helps recover it is Global Positioning System (GPS) tracking. If you want to protect the data in the event that the employee loses the laptop, full disk encryption is a good choice. If you want to erase all the data so that an attacker can't read it after the laptop is lost, you can use remote wipe. If you want to make it more difficult for an attacker to use the device, you can use remote lock to lock it with a different passcode. See chapter 5.

51. B. Since cloud computing stores data in unknown locations accessible via the Internet, you lose physical control of the data. Cloud computing providers often include backup services and customers can back up their data. Cloud computing does not limit operating system choices, and it does not result in a loss of data access. See chapter 5.

52. B. The user's system was infected with a Trojan commonly known as rogueware. The website tricked the user into installing the malware using a form of social engineering, and this would be the best answer if the question asked what happened to the user. Vishing is a form of phishing that uses recorded voice over the telephone. Spim is a form of spam using instant messaging (IM). See chapter 6.

53. **C.** Rootkits can hide their internal processes so that users can't easily detect them, and they are more difficult for antivirus software to detect. Worms and viruses do not hide their processes to avoid detection. A file integrity checker can detect files modified by rootkits, but it is not malware. See chapter 6.

54. **D.** Spyware can be installed without the user's knowledge; it can add processes and change settings, which can cause a system to run slower. A known virus would be detected by an antivirus scan with updated signatures, but not all antivirus software detects spyware. LDAP injection attempts to access Active Directory data in a domain. A zero day attack is an attack on an undisclosed vulnerability. See chapter 6.

55. **A.** Antivirus software can detect malware and prevent it from running on a computer. Firewalls can prevent intrusions but won't block software from running. Input validation checks input data and can help mitigate buffer overflow, SQL injection, and cross-site scripting attacks. Fuzzing sends pseudo-random data as input to an application in an attempt to crash or confuse it. See chapter 6.

56. **B.** Phishing is the practice of sending e-mail to users with the purpose of tricking them into revealing personal information, such as bank account information. There's no such thing as arrow phishing, but a spear phishing attack targets a specific person or specific groups of people, such as employees of a company. There's no such thing as bear phishing, but whaling is a phishing attack that targets high-level executives. There's no such thing as VoIPing, but vishing is a form of phishing that uses recorded voice over the telephone. See chapter 6.

57. **C.** Shoulder surfing can be mitigated with the use of privacy screens and password-protected screen savers. A password mask displays another character, such as an asterisk (*), to prevent shoulder surfing. Vishing is a form of phishing that uses recorded voice over the telephone and is not related to shoulder surfing. Dumpster divers search through trash looking for information, and shredding mitigates the threat. See chapter 6.

58. **A.** Computers within a botnet regularly check in with command and control servers for instructions and then follow instructions, which often include launching DDoS attacks. Some malware infects systems and joins them to a botnet, but not all malware follows this behavior. Kiting is the practice of repeatedly reserving domain names without paying for them. Fuzzing, or fuzz testing, sends invalid, unexpected, or random data to a system looking for vulnerabilities. See chapter 7.

59. **A.** Error handling routines are a part of input validation and can prevent application failures and many application attacks. Cross-site scripting is a type of attack that can be prevented with input validation. Organizations shred paper documents instead of throwing them away to mitigate dumpster diving attacks. Password masking helps prevent shoulder surfing attacks by displaying a character such as an asterisk instead of the password. See chapter 7.

60. **B.** A buffer overflow attack occurs when an attacker sends more data to an application than it can handle and overwrites memory locations. A flood guard is a security control that protects against SYN flood attacks. Cross-site scripting attacks use HTML or JavaScript tags. Whaling is a targeted phishing e-mail against a company executive, such as a CEO or president. See chapter 7.

61. **B.** Input validation checks the validity of data before using it can help prevent SQL injection, buffer overflow, and cross-site scripting attacks. Buffer overflows are a vulnerability that attackers can exploit. Only inputted data needs to be validated, not outputted data. Fuzzing, or fuzz testing, sends invalid, unexpected, or random data to a system to detect buffer overflow vulnerabilities. See chapter 7.

62. **B.** An organization can avoid a risk by not providing a service, using an application, or participating in a risky activity, and in this case, it used a different application to avoid the risk of the open ports. Organizations often accept a risk when the cost of the control exceeds the cost of the risk. Risk deterrence attempts to discourage attacks with preventative controls such as a security guard. Organizations can transfer a risk by purchasing insurance.See chapter 8.

63. **C.** A quantitative risk analysis uses cost and asset values. A qualitative risk assessment uses judgment based on expert opinions to categorize risks based on probability and impact. Fuzzing sends random data to an application and is sometimes used in black box testing, but it is not specific to any type of risk analysis.See chapter 8.

64. **A.** A quantitative risk analysis uses cost and asset values. A qualitative risk assessment uses judgment to categorize risks based on probability and impact. A vulnerability scan passively checks systems for vulnerabilities, and a penetration test will actively assess security controls to identify what can be exploited, but neither is an assessment based on cost.See chapter 8.

65. **B.** A vulnerability scanner checks systems for known security issues. A port scanner will identify open ports but won't identify security issues. An intrusion prevention system (IPS) is a preventative control used to detect and stop attacks. A firewall can prevent intrusions on a system but cannot identify security issues.See chapter 8.

66. **D.** Vulnerability scanning will passively test security controls to identify vulnerabilities and identify a lack of security controls. A penetration test will attempt to exploit weaknesses. Vulnerability scans look for common misconfigurations of security controls and can compare current configuration against a baseline, but they do not identify baseline configurations. A scan will not identify threats, only vulnerabilities. See chapter 8.

67. **A.** A penetration test demonstrates how security vulnerabilities can be exploited. A vulnerability test identifies security vulnerabilities but doesn't demonstrate how they can be exploited. A penetration test is not used to demonstrate or identify system capabilities. See chapter 8.

68. **C.** In gray box testing, the testers have some knowledge of the environment. In white box testing, testers have access to all of the system details. In a black box test, testers have zero knowledge of system details. Both internal testers and external testers can start with some inside knowledge of the tested system.See chapter 8.

69. **A.** Black hat identifies a malicious attacker performing criminal activities. Black box testers have zero knowledge of system details. A fuzzer sends random data to an application, and black box testing (not black hat) is sometimes referred to as fuzzing.See chapter 8.

70. **A.** Reviewing user rights and permissions is a form of a system audit, and it can help ensure a server's security configuration. An evil twin is a counterfeit wireless access point using the same SSID as a legitimate access point. Platform as a Service (PaaS) provides an easy-to-configure operating system as a cloud computing service. A hard drive hash is useful in forensics as part of an incident response and verifies that a hard drive has not been modified.See chapter 8.

71. **C.** A password cracker can verify users are creating strong passwords for their login account in compliance with a company policy (though it is more effective to use a password policy to require strong passwords). You can use a protocol analyzer (sniffer) to view headers and clear-text contents in IP packets, but login passwords wouldn't be passed across the network in clear text. Reviewing user rights and permissions is a form of a system audit, but it doesn't examine the password used for login.See chapter 8.

72. **C.** You can protect logs from compromise with centralized logging. If the logs are read only, the system will not be able to write log entries. Archiving is a good practice, but it won't protect the logs from compromise during the attack. If logging is disabled, logs won't have any data.See chapter 8.

73. **B.** RAID-1 (mirroring) includes two drives and will continue to operate if one of the drives (half the total) fail, and this is the same for both hardware RAID-1 and software RAID-1. RAID-0 does not provide fault tolerance. RAID-5 uses three or more drives. See chapter 9.

74. **B.** Generators can provide an alternate power source for extended power outages. An uninterruptible power supply (UPS) is a battery that provides temporary power for short-term outages or power fluctuations. An HVAC system provides heating and cooling. Hot and cold aisles regulate cooling to reduce cooling costs while also increasing availability.
See chapter 9.

75. **D.** A business impact analysis identifies critical functions and services and helps an organization make decisions related to business continuity, including alternate sites. A vulnerability assessment identifies and prioritizes weaknesses, but it doesn't identify critical functions. A penetration test is an active test that attempts to exploit vulnerabilities. Business continuity plans are often tested to validate them, but they would not identify critical functio
See chapter 9.

76. **B.** Between the choices, a hot site provides the minimum downtime if a disaster occurs. Storing a copy of the backups at the hot site helps ensure that the hot site servers can become operational with minimal downtime after a disaster at the primary location. Warm sites and cold sites will take longer to become operational.See chapter 9.

77. **C.** A warm site provides the capability to bring services back online within a day. A hot site brings services back online within minutes or possibly an hour. A cold site brings services back online as long as a few days after the outage. Backups will not provide an alternate location that can be used after a disaster.See chapter 9.

78. **C.** A disaster recovery plan (DRP) includes a testing element to validate the plan. A DRP will include a hierarchical list of *critical* systems but not a list of all systems. A chain of custody verifies forensic data is handled properly. Digital signatures provide authentication, integrity, and non-repudiation but are unrelated to a DRP. See chapter 9.

79. **A.** Hot and cold aisles regulate cooling to reduce cooling costs while also increasing availability. A mantrap can counter the social engineering tactic of tailgating, but it doesn't increase availability. Cameras and guards can provide access control, but do not directly increase availability.
See chapter 9.

80. **A.** If availability is more important than security, it should fail in an open state. If security is more important than availability, it should fail in a closed state. Different systems can achieve a closed state using different methods and they don't necessarily have to be shut down or rebooted.
See chapter 9.

81. **B.** Message Digest 5 (MD5) is a hashing algorithm that can ensure the integrity of data, including files. Triple Data Encryption Standard (3DES) and Blowfish are symmetric encryption (not hashing) algorithms. RSA is an asymmetric encryption algorithm.
See chapter 10.

82. **A.** The older LANMAN protocol stores passwords using a LM hash of the password by first dividing the password into two seven-character blocks, and then converting all lower case letters to upper case. AES is used for symmetric encryption, and RSA is used for asymmetric encryption. Kerberos is a network authentication protocol using tickets.

See chapter 10.

83. **B.** One-time pads are hard-copy printouts of keys in a pad of paper. Advanced Encryption Standard (AES) is a strong encryption algorithm that uses 128-bit, 192-bit, or 256-bit keys, but keys are not printed. RSA is a public key encryption method that creates keys based on prime

numbers. Diffie-Hellman provides a method to privately share a symmetric key between two parties, but keys aren't printed.See chapter 10.

84. **C.** Diffie-Hellman addresses key management and provides a method to privately share a symmetric key between two parties. Secure/Multipurpose Internet Mail Extensions (S/MIME) and Pretty Good Privacy (PGP) provide methods of digitally signing and encrypting e-mail. RC4 is a strong symmetric stream cipher used for encryption, not key management.See chapter 10.

85. **A.** SSL uses symmetric encryption to encrypt data in a browser session, so it uses a symmetric key. Asymmetric encryption using public and private keys is used to privately share the symmetric key. RSA uses prime numbers to create asymmetric keys, but there is no such thing as a prime number key.See chapter 10.

86. **C, D.** The sender's private key (Sally's private key) signs the e-mail and the recipient's public key (Joe's public key) encrypts the e-mail. In this case, Sally sent the e-mail so her private key signs it, and it is encrypted with Joe's public key. The sender's public key (not the private key) verifies the digital signature. The recipient's private key (not the public key) decrypts the e-mail. See chapter 10.

87. **A.** The sender's private key encrypts the e-mail hash in a digital signature. The sender's public key decrypts the e-mail hash in a digital signature. If data is encrypted with a private key, anyone with the public key (which is publically available) can decrypt it. Message Digest 5 (MD5) is a hashing algorithm that can ensure the integrity of data, but it doesn't use keys. While not included in the answers, a recipient's private key is used to decrypt data (not the digital signature) encrypted with the recipient's public key. See chapter 10.

88. **D.** Pretty Good Privacy (PGP) uses public and private keys for asymmetric encryption and decryption of e-mail. A certificate revocation list (CRL) identifies revoked certificates. A certificate authority (CA) publishes the CRL, but the CRL and CA do not encrypt or decrypt e-mail. LANMAN is an older protocol that stores passwords as a hash after converting all lower case letters to upper case and dividing the password into two seven-character blocks.See chapter 10.

89. **A, B, C.** A certificate revocation list (CRL) identifies revoked certificates and is publically available. Certificates include public keys and are publically available (though the matching private key is always kept private). Websites use certificates for authentication and encryption of HTTPS sessions, and they freely share the certificates. A user's passphrase (or password) should be kept private.See chapters 1 and 10.

90. **C.** A key escrow stores copies of user's private keys to ensure that the loss of the original key does not result in data loss. A certificate revocation list (CRL) identifies revoked certificates, and a certificate authority (CA) publishes the CRL, but neither address data loss. The trusted root certification authority store is a collection of certificates from trusted CAs.See chapter 10.

91. **C.** A clean desk policy requires users to organize their areas to reduce the risk of possible data theft and password compromise. Physical health issues are not security issues related to a clean desk policy. Not all employees necessarily interact with customers, but a clean desk policy still applies, requiring them to protect data. Integrity ensures data is not modified, but a clean desk policy helps ensure confidentiality by preventing unauthorized disclosure. See chapter 11.

92. **C.** A user privilege policy mandates that users only have the rights and permissions needed to perform their job and no more. A user privilege review will audit assigned rights and permissions to discover these types of violations. A chain of custody provides assurances that evidence collected after an incident has been controlled and handled properly after collection. Storage and retention policies identify how long it is retained. See chapter 11.

93. **C.** Mandatory vacation policies require employees to take time away from their job and help detect malicious activities. Dual accounts for administrators help prevent privilege escalation attacks but are unrelated to vacations. Regular security awareness training helps reinforce compliance with security policies. While vacations are valuable for recreation, this is not the goal. See chapter 11.

94. **B.** A separation of duties policy separates individual tasks of an overall function between different people. In this case, the administrator was likely promoted into a job that required separation from the access of the previous job. Mandatory vacation policies require employees to take time away from their job and help detect malicious activities. Job rotation policies require employees to change roles on a regular basis. Single sign-on (SSO) allows users to access multiple systems by providing credentials only once, so this wouldn't prevent access. See chapter 11.

95. **A.** Organizations provide security awareness training to minimize the risk posed by users. Training helps reinforce user compliance with security policies, not reduce compliance. It is not possible to eliminate risk and not desirable to increase the risk. See chapter 11.

96. **D.** Revealing personally identifiable information (PII) represents a significant threat, and organizations provide training to employees not to do so. It's acceptable to provide any type of publically available information, such as that on a website or in sales brochure. Salespeople want to be contacted, so giving out their contact information is acceptable, as long as its professional and not personal contract information. See chapter 11.

97. **C.** A port scanner can detect open ports used by peer-to-peer (P2P) software. A protocol analyzer can capture packets and view the contents, but it isn't the easiest way to detect P2P software. A user rights review audits assigned rights and permissions and will discover accounts with too many permissions and enabled accounts of previous employees. A penetration test will actively assess or test security controls, and while it may include a port scan, it does much more. See chapters 7 and 11.

98. **D.** The media access control (MAC) address is a hexadecimal number permanently assigned to a computer's network interface card. The user logon name identifies the user, but the question asks how to identify the computer. The user can change the name and IP address of the personal computer. See chapters 7 and 11.

99. **A.** The forensic hash of the drive verifies that the imaging process did not modify the drive and is performed before and after creating the image. Forensic hashing of an image provides assurances of image integrity, but this is different than creating a forensic image of the drive. A chain of custody provides assurances that evidence has been controlled and handled properly after collection, but is not directly related to creating the hash. You can isolate a computer from an attack by disconnecting the computer from the network, but this is unrelated to a forensic hash of a drive. See chapter 11.

100. **A.** A chain of custody provides assurances that evidence has been controlled and handled properly after collection, but if the drive was left on a desk, it was not controlled. A clean desk policy (not a cleanliness policy) would dictate keeping a desk clean of sensitive data, but this is not an incidence response procedure. A separation of duties policy separates individual tasks of an overall function between different people. The first response after identifying an incident is to isolate the problem, and removing the thumb drive may have isolated the problem, but leaving it uncontrolled is unrelated to containment. See chapter 11.

Chapter 1

Mastering the Basics of Security

CompTIA Security+ objectives covered in this chapter:

1.2 Apply and implement secure network administration principles
- 802.1x
- Implicit deny

2.4 Explain the importance of security related awareness and training
- User habits
- Password behaviors

2.8 Exemplify the concepts of confidentiality, integrity, and availability

3.6 Analyze and differentiate among types of mitigation and deterrent techniques
- Hardening
- Password protection

5.1 Explain the function and purpose of authentication services
- RADIUS
- TACACS
- TACACS+
- Kerberos
- LDAP
- XTACACS

5.2 Explain the fundamental concepts and best practices related to authentication, authorization, and access control
- Identification vs. authentication
- Authentication (single factor) and authorization
- Multifactor authentication
- Biometrics
- Tokens

- Common access card
- Personal identification verification card
- Smart card
- Single sign on
- ACLs
- Access control
- Implicit deny

5.3 Implement appropriate security controls when performing account management

- Account policy enforcement
  - Password complexity
  - Recovery
  - Length
  - Lockout

6.2 Use and apply appropriate cryptographic tools and products

- CHAP and PAP

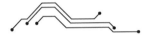

Before you dig into some of the details of security, you should have a solid understanding of core security principles. This chapter will present many of these core principles as an introduction. The second part of the chapter will cover authentication—how systems and users provide credentials to a system to verify their identity— including authentication used in remote access systems.

Exploring Core Security Principles

Security starts with several core principles that are integrated throughout an organization. These principles drive many security-related decisions at multiple levels. Understanding these basic concepts helps to give you a solid foundation in security.

Confidentiality, integrity, and availability together form the security triad. Each element is important to address in any security program. Additionally, several other core security principles, such as non-repudiation, defense in depth, and implicit deny, are addressed in any well-designed security program.

Confidentiality

Confidentiality helps prevent the unauthorized disclosure of data. It uses multiple methods, such as authentication combined with access controls, and cryptography. Authentication is presented later in this chapter, and access controls are covered in chapter 2.

Cryptography provides confidentiality by encrypting data. Many different encryption algorithms are available to provide confidentiality. Chapter 10 covers the relevant algorithms (such as AES and RSA) that you'll need to understand for the CompTIA Security+ exam.

Two of the key concepts related to confidentiality are:

- **Confidentiality ensures that data is only viewable by authorized users.** Unauthorized personnel are unable to access the information.
- **Encryption also enforces confidentiality**. You can use various encryption algorithms to encrypt or cipher the data to make it unreadable. If the encrypted data falls into the wrong hands, the unintended recipient will not be able to read it.

Many elements of security help to enforce confidentiality beyond encryption. These include elements such as authentication, access control methods, physical security, and permissions that combine to ensure only authorized personnel can access the data. This book presents all of these methods.

Remember this

Confidentiality ensures that data is only viewable by authorized users. If there is a risk of sensitive data falling into the wrong hands, it should be encrypted to make it unreadable. Any data should be protected with access controls to enforce confidentiality.

Integrity

Integrity provides assurances that data has not been modified, tampered with, or corrupted. Ideally, only authorized users modify data. However, there are times when unauthorized or unintended changes occur. This can be from unauthorized users, or through system or human errors. When this occurs, the data has lost integrity.

You can use hashing techniques to enforce integrity. Chapter 10 presents the relevant hashing algorithms, such as MD5, SHA, and HMAC. Briefly, a hash is simply a number created by executing a hashing algorithm against data such as a file or message. As long as the data never changes, the resulting hash will always be the same. By comparing hashes created at two different times, you can determine if the original data is still the same. If the hashes are the same, the data is the same. If the hashes are different, the data has changed.

For example, a simplistic hash of a message could be 123. The hash is created at the source and sent with the message. When the message is received, the received message is hashed. If the hash of the received message is 123 (the same as the hash of the sent message), data integrity is maintained. However, if the hash of the received message is 456, then you know that the message is not the same. Data integrity has been lost.

Hashes can be applied to messages such as e-mail, or any other type of data files. Some e-mail programs use a message authentication code (MAC) instead of a hash to verify integrity, but the underlying concept works the same way.

Acronyms

Don't you just love all of these acronyms? MD5, SHA, RAID. There are actually three different meanings of MAC within the context of CompTIA Security+:

1. Media access control (MAC) addresses that are the physical addresses assigned to NICs
2. Mandatory access control (MAC) model as one of the three access control models
3. Message authentication code (MAC) used for integrity similar to how a hash is used

If you're having trouble keeping them all straight, don't feel alone. All of the acronyms used within the book are spelled out with short descriptions in the acronym list at the back of this book.

Hashing techniques are also used to verify that integrity is maintained when files are downloaded or transferred. Some programs can automatically check hashes and determine if a file loses even a single bit during the download process. The program performing the download will detect it by comparing the source hash with the destination hash. If a program detects that the hashes are different, it knows that integrity has been lost and reports the problem to the user.

In other instances, a website administrator can calculate and post the hash of a file on the website. Users can manually calculate the hash of the file after downloading it and compare the calculated hash with the posted hash. For example, the md5sum.exe is freeware to calculate MD5 hashes, and sha1sum.exe is freeware to calculate SHA1 hashes. Chapter 10 shows how to do this in the "Providing Integrity with Hashing" section. If a virus infected a file on a file server, the hash on the infected file would be different from the hash on the original file (and the hash posted on the website).

It's also possible to lose data integrity through human error. For example, if a database administrator needs to modify a significant amount of data in a database, the administrator can write a script to perform a bulk update. However, if the script is faulty, it can corrupt the database, resulting in a loss of integrity.

Two key concepts related to integrity are as follows:

- **Integrity provides assurances that data has not modified, tampered with, or corrupted.** Loss of integrity indicates the data is different. Unauthorized users can change data, or the changes can occur through system or human errors.
- **Hashing verifies integrity**. A hash is simply a numeric value created by executing a hashing algorithm against a message or file. Hashes are created at the source and destination or at two different times (such as on the first and fifteenth of the month). If the hashes are the same, integrity is maintained. If the two hashes are different, data integrity has been lost.

> **Remember this**
>
> Integrity is used to verify that data has not been modified, and loss of integrity can occur through unauthorized or unintended changes. Hashing algorithms such as MD5, HMAC, or SHA1 can calculate hashes to verify integrity. A hash is simply a number created by applying the algorithm to a file or message at different times. The hashes are compared to each other to verify that integrity has been maintained.

Availability

Availability indicates that data and services are available when needed. For some companies, this simply means that the data and services must be available between 8 a.m. and 5 p.m., Monday through Friday. For other companies, this means they must be available twenty-four hours a day, seven days a week, 365 days a year.

Chapter 9 covers many fault tolerance and redundancy techniques in more depth. A common goal of fault tolerance and redundancy techniques is to remove single points of failure (SPOF). If an SPOF fails, the entire system can fail. For example, if a server has a single drive, the drive is an SPOF since its failure takes down the server.

From a broad perspective, availability includes:

- **Disk redundancies**. Fault-tolerant disks such as RAID-1 (mirroring) and RAID-5 (striping with parity) allow a system to continue to operate even if a disk fails.
- **Server redundancies**. Failover clusters can be implemented that will allow a service to continue to be provided even if a server fails. In a failover cluster, the service switches from the failed server in a cluster to an operational server in the same cluster. Virtualization (covered in chapter 5) can also increase availability of servers by reducing unplanned downtime.
- **Site redundancies**. If a site can no longer function due to a disaster, such as a fire, flood, hurricane, or earthquake, the site can move functionality to an alternate site. The alternate site can be a hot site (ready and available 24/7), a cold site (a location where equipment, data, and personnel can be moved to when needed), or a warm site (somewhere in the middle of a hot site and cold site).
- **Backups**. If important data is backed up, it can be restored when it is lost. Data can be lost due to corruption, deletion, application errors, human error, and even hungry gremlins that can randomly eat your data. If data backups do not exist, then when it is lost, it will be lost forever.
- **Alternate power**. Uninterruptible power supplies (UPSs) and power generators can provide power to key systems even if commercial power fails.
- **Cooling systems**. Heating, ventilation, and air-conditioning (HVAC) systems improve the availability of systems by reducing outages from overheating.

> ### Remember this
> Availability ensures that systems are up and operational when needed and often addresses single points of failure. You can increase availability by adding fault tolerance and redundancies such as RAID, clustering, backups, and generators. HVAC systems also increase availability.

Balancing CIA

It's possible to ensure the confidentiality, integrity, and availability of data equally. However, an organization may choose to prioritize the importance of one or two of these based on the goals of the organization, or the goals of a specific system. In other words, an organization can spend less money on ensuring confidentiality if confidentiality isn't as important.

One way of prioritizing these is with simple values such as low, medium, and high. For example, if a system holds proprietary secrets, confidentiality is of primary importance and the value of confidentiality is high. If the information is shared anonymously with the public, the importance of confidentiality is low. Medium indicates the confidentiality of the data has some importance to the organization.

As an example, imagine that you decided to host an online forum for users to share information about IT security-related concepts. Users can read data anonymously and post data after logging in. In this example, the importance of confidentiality is low, since anyone can read the data anonymously. You'd want to ensure the integrity and availability of the data, but it wouldn't be life shattering if data was modified or the site went down. The importance of integrity and availability is medium.

On the other hand, imagine an online gaming site that holds accounts for hundreds of thousands of users, including their credit card data. Users pay for the time they're online playing the game. If confidentiality of data is lost, customers will lose confidence in the company and may even sue. If the system data is not available when users want to play, users may not return. If users can modify other users' data, such as deleting their treasures, or the user's game data is not consistent, users could get frustrated and not return. In this example, the importance of confidentiality, availability, and integrity is equally high for all three. While this costs more to ensure, a data breach may result in higher losses for the online site in the end.

If you understand the concepts of confidentiality, integrity, and availability, and you understand the goals of a system, you should be able to match the concepts with the needs.

Non-repudiation

While non-repudiation isn't one of the core principles in the security triad, it is closely related and specifically mentioned in the objectives, making it an important core concept to understand. Non-repudiation provides proof of a person's identity and can be used to prevent individuals from denying they took a specific action.

In commerce, non-repudiation is commonly used with credit cards. If I buy something with a credit card and sign the receipt, I can't later deny making the purchase. My signature can be used to repudiate me if I deny making the purchase. In other words, my signature is used for non-repudiation.

Remember this

Non-repudiation is used to prevent entities from denying they took an action. Digitally signed e-mail prevents individuals from later denying they sent it. An audit log provides non-repudiation since audit log entries include who took an action in addition to what the action was, where the action took place, and when it occurred.

Some common examples of non-repudiation within computer systems are:

- **Using digital signatures to verify someone sent a message**. If I send you an e-mail that is signed with a digital signature, you know that I sent it and I can't later deny doing so. Chapter 10 will cover how digital signatures work in detail, but, as an introduction, digital signatures provide authentication, integrity, and non-repudiation.
- **Logging activity in an audit log.** Audit logs will log details such as who, what, when, and where. The "who" in the audit log provides non-repudiation.

Defense in Depth

Defense in depth refers to the security practice of implementing several layers of protection. You can't simply take a single action, such as implementing a firewall or installing antivirus software, and consider yourself protected. You must implement security at several different layers.

Remember this

Security is never "done." Instead, security and IT professionals constantly monitor, update, add to, and improve existing methods. A single layer of security is easily beatable. Defense in depth employs multiple layers to make it harder for attacks to exploit a system or network.

As an example, if I drive my car to a local Walmart, put a five-dollar bill on the dash, and leave the keys in the car and the car running, there is a very good chance the car will not be there when I come out of the store. On the other hand, if I ensure nothing of value is visible from the windows, the car is locked, and it has an alarm system and stickers on the windows advertising the alarm system, it's a lot less likely that my car will be stolen. Not impossible, but less likely.

You've probably heard this as "there is no silver bullet." If you want to kill a werewolf, you can load your gun with a single silver bullet and it will find its mark. The truth is that there is no such thing as a silver bullet. (Of course, there is no such thing as a werewolf either.)

Applied to computers, security must be implemented at every step, every phase, and every layer. IT professionals can never rest on their laurels with the thought they have done enough and no longer need to worry about security.

Implicit Deny

Implicit deny indicates that unless something is explicitly allowed, it is denied. Routers and firewalls often have access control lists (ACLs) that explicitly identify allowed traffic. If traffic doesn't meet any of the explicit rules in the ACL to allow it, the traffic is blocked.

For example, if you configured a firewall to allow HTTP or HTTPS traffic to a web server on ports 80 and 443 respectively, then the firewall would have explicit rules defined to allow this traffic to the server. However, if you didn't define any other rules, then all other traffic would be implicitly denied. For example, any SMTP traffic sent to this web server on port 25 would be implicitly denied since there isn't an explicit rule allowing the traffic.

This same concept applies to file and folder permission. For example, Microsoft's New Technology File System (NTFS) allows you to grant permissions such as Full Control, Read, and Modify. If Sally is granted Full Control permission to a file named Projects and she is the only person granted permission, then she would have full control. That's simple enough. However, what permissions does Bob have? Since Bob is not explicitly granted any permissions, he is implicitly denied all access to the file.

Introducing Basic Risk Concepts

One of the basic goals of implementing IT security is to reduce risk. Since risk is so important and so many chapters refer to elements of risk, it's worth providing a short introduction here.

Risk is the possibility or likelihood of a threat exploiting a vulnerability resulting in a loss. A threat is any circumstance or event that has the potential to compromise confidentiality, integrity, or availability. A vulnerability is a weakness. It can be a weakness in the hardware, software, the configuration, or even in the users operating the system.

Threats can come from inside an organization, such as from a disgruntled employee, or from outside the organization, such as an attacker from anywhere on the Internet. They can be natural, such as hurricanes, tsunamis, or tornadoes, or man-made, such as malware written by a criminal. Threats can be intentional, from attackers, or accidental, from employee mistakes or system errors.

Reducing risk is also known as risk mitigation. Risk mitigation reduces the chances that a threat will exploit a vulnerability. You reduce risks by implementing controls (also called countermeasures and safeguards), and many of the actions described throughout this book are different types of controls.

> **Remember this**
>
> Risk is the likelihood that a threat will exploit a vulnerability. Risk mitigation reduces the chances that a threat will exploit a vulnerability by implementing controls.

You can't prevent most threats. For example, you can't stop a tornado or prevent a criminal from writing malware. However, you can reduce risk by reducing vulnerabilities or by reducing the impact of the threat.

For example, access controls (starting with authentication) ensure that only authorized personnel have access to specific areas, systems, or data. If an employee does become disgruntled and wants to cause harm, access controls reduce the amount of potential harm by reducing what an employee can access. If a natural disaster hits, business continuity and disaster recovery plans help reduce the impact. Similarly, antivirus software prevents the impact of any malware by intercepting it before it causes any harm.

Exploring Authentication Concepts

Authentication proves an identity with some type of credential that is previously known by the authenticator. A user claims (or professes) an identity by presenting something like a username. Users then prove the professed identity with authentication, such as with a password. Authentication is not limited to users. It can also be used to prove the identity of a service, a process, a workstation, a server, or a network device.

At least two entities know the credentials. One entity presents the credentials, and the other entity verifies the credentials are accurate. For example, Sally knows her username and password, and an authenticating server knows her username and password. Sally presents her credentials to the authenticating server, and the server authenticates her. Mutual authentication occurs when both entities authenticate each other.

The importance of authentication cannot be understated. You can't have any type of access control if you can't identify a user. In other words, if everyone is anonymous, then everyone has the same access to all resources.

Comparing Identification, Authentication, and Authorization

It's important to realize the differences between identification, authentication, and authorization. When users type in their usernames, they are claiming or professing an identity. Users then provide authentication (such as with passwords) to prove their identity. However, just because users can prove their identity doesn't mean they'll automatically be granted access to everything. Authorization to resources is granted based on the user's proven identity.

Chapter 2 will present different access control models. However, the first step of access control is to implement some method of authentication, such as the use of complex passwords, smart cards, or biometrics.

> ### Remember this
> Identification occurs when a user claims an identity. Authentication occurs when the user proves the identity (such as with a password) and the credentials are verified. Authorization is granted to resources based on a proven identity.

Identity Proofing

Identity proofing is the process of verifying that people are who they claim to be prior to issuing them credentials, or later when individuals lose their credentials. Before credentials are issued, individuals are often required to show other forms of identification, such as a driver's license.

This may occur out of view of the IT person creating the account, but identity proofing still occurs. For example, HR personnel process new hires and ensure all their paperwork is in order, including their identification. Later, HR may simply introduce the new employee to an IT professional to create an account. This introduction by the HR person is all the identity proofing needed by the IT worker.

Identity Proofing for Verification

A second use of identity proofing is after issuing credentials. For example, when a user performs some critical activity (such as transferring money between bank accounts), the bank may verify the user's identity before transferring the funds. This is often done by having the user verify key information that third parties are highly unlikely to know, such as the name of a first pet.

If you've signed up for online banking recently, you've probably seen this. The bank gives you a list of questions, such as what is the name of your first pet, the name of your closest childhood friend, the middle name of your oldest or youngest sibling, etc. The idea is that an attacker wouldn't know these answers, and, therefore, the list works as an identity proofing method.

Many banks record information about the computer you use to access an online site. If you later use a different computer, or a computer with a different IP address, you may be prompted to answer one of the identity proofing questions. If attackers somehow steal your credentials and use them to access your bank account, the goal is that identity proofing will reduce the risk of their success. Asking attackers a question that they are less likely to be able to answer, such as what was the name of the street where you grew up, increases security.

In the past, identity proofing consisted of very few items, such as your birth date, Social Security number, and mother's maiden name. Because so many entities requested this information and didn't always protect it, it became easy for attackers to obtain this information and use it to steal identities. Many criminals have stolen identities from information visible on a renter's application.

Unfortunately, many banks have had security breaches compromising their databases (including your answers to the more personal questions). In other words, it's becoming less likely that these answers are known only by you, and they may not be valid as identity proofing tools for very long.

Self-service Password Reset Systems

An additional use of identity proofing is with password reset or password management systems. These systems provide automated password recovery and are extremely useful in systems with a large number of users. They can actually reduce the total cost of ownership of the system.

Instead of an IT professional spending valuable time resetting passwords, a self-service password reset or password retrieval system uses identity proofing to automate the process.

For example, some online systems include a link such as "Forgot Password." By clicking on this link, your password may be e-mailed to your previously given e-mail address, or an identity proofing system may be invoked. The identity proofing system will ask you questions that only you should know. Once you adequately prove your identity, you're given the opportunity to change your password to something different.

Of course, an online password reset system won't help a user that can't get online. Some organizations utilize password reset systems using the phone system. Users who have forgotten their passwords can call the password reset system and reset their password by using an identity proofing method such as a PIN (personal identification number).

Three Factors of Authentication

Authentication is often simplified as three types, or three factors, of authentication. Entities can authenticate with any one of these factors, and often two or more factors are combined to provide multifactor authentication. The three factors are:

- *Something you know* (such as username and password)
- *Something you have* (such as a smart card)
- *Something you are* (such as a fingerprint or other biometric identification)

Something You Know

The *something you know* authentication factor typically refers to a shared secret, such as a password, a username and password, or even a PIN. This factor is the least secure form of authentication. However, you can increase the security of a password.

> ### Remember this
> The first factor of authentication (*something you know*, such as a password or PIN) is the weakest factor. Passwords should be strong, changed regularly, never shared with another person, and stored in a safe if written down. Technical means (such as a technical password policy) should be used to ensure that users regularly change their passwords and don't use the same passwords.

Chapter 2 presents elements of a technical password policy in more depth. However, the following provides some general rules about passwords to ensure they are secure.

- **Passwords should be strong**. This means they are at least eight characters and include multiple character types, such as upper case, lower case, numbers, and symbols.
- **Passwords should be changed regularly**. Users should be forced to change their passwords on a regular basis by setting maximum password ages, or password expiration times.
- **Passwords should not be reused**. Password histories prevent users from using the same passwords repeatedly.
- **Default passwords should be changed**. If a system comes with a default password, that default password should be changed before the system is brought into service.
- **Passwords should not be written down**. If the password absolutely must be written down, store it in a safe (not just a safe place).
- **Passwords should not be shared**. Only one person should know the password to any single account. If an administrator resets a password, the password should be set to expire immediately. This requires users to reset the password the first time they log on.
- **Account lockout policies should be used**. If a user enters the wrong password too many times, an account lockout policy locks the account. This prevents password guessing attempts.

Strong Passwords

One method used to make passwords more secure is to require them to be strong. A strong password is at least eight characters in length, doesn't include words found in a dictionary or any part of a user's name, and combines three of the four following character types:

- Uppercase characters (twenty-six letters A-Z)
- Lowercase characters (twenty-six letters a-z)
- Numbers (ten numbers 0-9)
- Special characters (thirty-two printable characters, such as !, $, and *)

The combination of different characters in a password makes up the key space, and you can calculate the key space with the following formula: C^N (C^N). C is the number of possible characters used, and N is the length of the password. For example, a six-character password using only lower case letters (twenty-six possibilities) is calculated as 26^6 (26^6), or about 308 million possibilities. Change this to a ten-character password and the value is 26^10 (26^{10}), or about 141 trillion possibilities. While this looks like a high number of possibilities, there are password-cracking tools that can test as many as 2.8 billion passwords per second on desktop computers with a high-end graphics processor. One can crack a ten-character password using only lower case characters (141 trillion possibilities) in as little as thirteen hours.

However, if you use all ninety-four printable characters with the same six and ten character password lengths, the values change significantly: 94^6 (94^6) is about 689 billion possibilities, and 94^10 (94^{10})is about fifty-three quintillion. The ^ character in 94^6 indicates that 94 is raised to the sixth power.

You probably don't come across quintillion very often, but the order is million, billion, trillion, quadrillion, and then quintillion, or fifty-three followed by eighteen zeros. The password-cracking tool that cracks a lower case password in thirteen hours will take years to crack a ten-character using any of the ninety-four possible characters.

It's sometimes debated that if you make a password too complex, you make it less secure. Read that again. It is not a typo. More complexity equates to less security. This is because the more complex a password is, the less likely it is that the user will remember it, forcing the user to write it down. A password written on paper or in a file on a user's computer significantly reduces security. Instead, users are encouraged to use pass phrases. Instead of nonsensical strings of characters, a passphrase is a long string of characters that has meaning to the user.

Remember this

Strong passwords use a mix of character types with a minimum password length such as eight or ten characters. The key space of a password is calculated as C^N where C indicates the number of possible characters in the password, and the N indicates the password length.

A few examples of strong passphrases are IL0veSecurity+, IL0veThi$B00k, and IWi11P@$$. Note that these examples include uppercase letters, lowercase letters, one or more numbers, and one or more special characters. These passwords are also known as pass phrases since they are a combination of words that are easier to remember than a nonsensical string of characters such as 4*eiRS@<].

Strong passwords never include words that can be easily guessed, such as a user's name, words in a dictionary (for any language), or common key combinations.

Storing Passwords

Passwords should not be written down unless absolutely necessary. If they are written down, they should be stored in a safe. Note that this is not simply a "safe place."

Many users have simply written down their passwords on a Post-it note and stuck it to the bottom of their keyboard, thinking no one would ever look there. Hackers, crackers, attackers, and even curious fellow employees who have physical access to your system will think to look under a keyboard. At one place I worked, this was so prevalent that when a computer was disposed of, the computer sanitization checklist included checking under the keyboard.

Sharing Passwords

Only one person should know the password, and users should not share their passwords with anyone. This is a difficult message to ingrain in the minds of end users, resulting in many successful social engineering attempts.

Chapter 6 will cover social engineering in more depth, but, for now, just be aware that attackers often gain information just by asking. They can ask over the phone, in person, or via e-mail with increasingly sophisticated phishing attacks.

Social engineers use trickery and conniving to convince users to give out their passwords. If a user is trained by an administrator to believe that sometimes it's OK to share a password, when the social engineer goes into action, the user quickly may believe that this is one of those times. On the other hand, if a user consistently hears the message that passwords should *never* be shared, alarm bells will ring in the user's head when the social engineer tries to get a password.

Changing Passwords

In addition to being strong, passwords should also be changed regularly. In most networks, users are automatically required to change their passwords regularly through technical means.

I can tell you from experience that if users are not forced to change their passwords through technical means, they often simply don't. It doesn't matter how many reminders you give them. On the other hand, if a password policy locks out user accounts until users change their password, users will change them.

Resetting Passwords

It's not uncommon for users to occasionally forget their password. In many organizations, help-desk professionals or other administrators are tasked with resetting the password and letting the user know the new password.

Imagine a user calls the help desk and asks for a password reset. The help-desk professional changes the password and lets the user know the new password. However, at this point, there's a security problem. Two people know the password. The help-desk professional could use the password and impersonate the user, or the user could blame the help-desk professional for impersonating the user.

Instead, the help-desk pro should set the password to immediately expire. This requires the user to change the password immediately after logging on and maintains password integrity.

Password History

Passwords should not be reused. Forcing users to change their password is a good first step, but some users will change back and forth between two passwords that they constantly use and reuse.

A password history system can remember past passwords and prevent the user from reusing passwords that have been used before. It's common for password policy settings to remember the last twenty-four passwords used and prevent any of these twenty-four passwords from being used again. When a password history is used, a minimum password age setting is also used to prevent users from changing their passwords multiple times to get back to their original password. Chapter 2 covers how to implement password history with a minimum password age.

> ## Remember this
> Password history is combined with a minimum password age to prevent users from reusing the same passwords.

Account Lockout Policies

Accounts will typically have lockout policies preventing users from guessing the password. If the wrong password is entered a specific number of times (such as three or five times), then the account will be locked. Two key phrases associated with account lockout policies are:

- **Account lockout threshold**. This is the maximum number of times a wrong password can be entered. When the threshold is exceeded, the account is locked.
- **Account lockout duration**. This indicates how long an account will be locked. It could be set to thirty, indicating that once the account lockout threshold is reached, the account will be locked out for thirty minutes. After thirty minutes, the account will automatically be unlocked. If the duration is set to zero, the account will remain locked until an administrator unlocks it.

Change Defaults

In chapter 5, you'll learn the basics of hardening systems, including changing defaults, removing unnecessary protocols and services, and keeping the system up to date.

Many systems and devices have default passwords. A basic security practice is to change these defaults as soon as the system or device is installed. As an example, many wireless routers have default accounts named "admin" with a default password of "admin." If you don't change these defaults, someone can log in to your network and have full control of the router, even going so far as locking you out of your own network.

Changing defaults also includes changing the default name of the Administrator account, if possible. In many systems, the Administrator account can't be locked out through regular lockout policies, so an attacker can continue to try to guess the password of the Administrator account without risking being locked out. By changing the name of the Administrator account to something else, the attacker can't try to guess the password of the Administrator account since the account name is unknown. Some administrators go a step further and add a dummy user account named "administrator." This account has no permissions. If this account is discovered to be locked out, the administrator knows that someone was trying to guess the password.

Previous Logon Notification

A simple technique used to alert users when their account may have been compromised is to provide notification of when they last logged on. This is sometimes shortened to "previous logon notification."

As an example, consider Sally, who took Friday off last week. She was at work and logged in on Thursday. When she comes in to work on Monday, the system informs her that the last time she logged in was on Friday. If she's paying attention to this message, she'll realize that someone else logged into her account, meaning that her credentials are compromised.

The primary challenge with this system is that users will tend to ignore the notification. More than 99 percent of the time, the message will tell users what they already know. So, instead of reading the message, users tend to ignore it.

Importance of Training

Many users don't understand the value of their password, or the damage that can be done if they give it out. It's important that users are provided with adequate training on passwords if passwords are used within the organization. This includes both the creation of strong passwords and the importance of never giving out their passwords.

For example, the password "123456" frequently appears on lists as the most common password in use. The users that are creating this password very likely don't know that it's almost like using no password at all. They probably don't realize that they can significantly increase the password strength by using a simple pass phrase such as "ICanCountTo6." A little training can go a long way.

Something You Have

The *something you have* factor refers to something you can physically hold. The two common items in this category are smart cards and key fobs (such as those sold by RSA SecureID). Chapter 2 covers proximity cards, and, in some instances, these are included in the *something you have* factor of authentication.

- **Smart cards**. Smart cards are credit-card-size cards that have embedded certificates used for authentication. The smart card is inserted into a smart card reader similar to how a credit card is inserted into some credit card readers.
- **Tokens or Key fobs**. A token or key fob (sometimes simply called a fob) is an electronic device about the size of a remote key for a car. It has an LCD display that displays a number that is synced with a server.

> **Remember this**
>
> The second factor of authentication (*something you have*, such as a smart card, key fob, or proximity card) is commonly combined with *something you know*. Smart cards have embedded certificates issued by a Public Key Infrastructure (PKI). Both smart cards and key fobs provide a significant level of secure authentication, especially when used with another factor of authentication (multifactor authentication).

Smart Cards

Smart cards are credit-card-sized cards that have an embedded microchip and a certificate. Users insert the smart card into a smart card reader, which reads information on the card, including details from the certificate. The embedded certificate allows the use of a complex encryption key and provides much more secure authentication than is possible through the use of a simple password. The smart card provides confidentiality, integrity, authentication, and non-repudiation.

Requirements for a smart card are:

- **Embedded certificate**. A certificate is embedded in the smart card. The certificate holds a user's private key (which is only accessible to the user) and is matched with a public key (that is publicly available to others). The private key is used each time the user logs on to a network.
- **Public Key Infrastructure (PKI).** Chapter 10 will cover PKI in more depth, but in short, the PKI allows the issuance and management of certificates.

Smart cards are often used with another factor of authentication. For example, a user may also enter a PIN or username and password in addition to using the smart card.

CACs and PIVs

A common access card (CAC) is a specialized type of smart card used by the United States Department of Defense. In addition to including the capabilities of a smart card, it also includes a picture of a user and other readable information. Users can use the CAC as a form of photo identification to gain access into a secure location. For example, users can show their CAC to guards that are protecting access to secure areas. Once inside the secure area, the user can use the CAC as a smart card.

Similarly, a personal identity verification (PIV) card is a specialized type of smart card used by United States federal agencies. It also includes photo identification and provides confidentiality, integrity, authentication, and non-repudiation for the users, just as a CAC does.

> **Remember this**
>
> CACs and PIVs are specialized smart cards that include photo identification. They are used to gain access into secure locations, and can also be used to log onto computer systems.

Tokens or Key Fobs

Tokens are small objects you can carry around in your pocket or connect to a key chain. They include an LCD that displays a number that changes periodically, such as every sixty seconds, and the token is synced with a server that knows what the number will be at any moment. For example, at 9:01, the number displayed on the token may be 135792 and the server knows the number is 135792. At 9:02, the displayed number changes to something else and the server also knows the new number.

This number is a one-time use, rolling password. If attackers intercept the number, it is not useful for very long. For example, a shoulder surfing attacker may be able to look over someone's shoulder and read the number. However, the number will expire within the next sixty seconds and be replaced by another one-time password.

Users often use tokens to authenticate via a website. They enter the number displayed in the token along with their username and password. This provides multifactor authentication, since the user must have something (the token) and know something (the username and password).

RSA sells RSA Secure ID, a popular token used for authentication. You can Google "Secure ID picture" to view a picture of one of these tokens. While RSA tokens are popular, many other brands of tokens are available.

Something You Are

The third factor of authentication refers to *something you are*, which is identified through biometrics. Biometrics is considered the strongest form of authentication because it's the most difficult for an attacker to falsify. In comparison, passwords are the weakest form of authentication.

Biometrics is divided into two categories: physical biometrics and behavioral biometrics. Physical biometrics is based on physical traits of an individual. It includes:

- Fingerprint, thumbprint, or handprints
- Retinal scanners (scans the retina of one or both eyes)
- Iris scanners(scans the iris of one or both eyes)

Behavioral biometrics is based on behavioral traits of an individual. It includes:

- Voice recognition (based on speech patterns)
- Signature geometry (handwriting analysis)
- Key strokes on a keyboard

Just a few years ago, most people only saw examples of biometrics in the movies, but today, examples are frequently seen in day-to-day life. Some examples include:

- **Amusement parks**. Many amusement parks sell annual passes, but they don't want these passes shared with everyone in the neighborhood. Biometric hand scans are frequently used to authenticate someone as the owner of a pass. If someone else tries to use the pass, the hand scan fails.
- **Computers**. Many laptops and some keyboards include fingerprint scanners that can be used to unlock access to a computer.
- **USB flash drive**. Some USB flash drives include a fingerprint scanner. Often four fingerprints can be stored, allowing access to up to four people.
- **Police records**. The use of fingerprinting has been popular for decades, and more recently, programs have been created to automate the search for matching identities.

Remember this

The third factor of authentication (*something you are*, defined with biometrics) is considered the strongest method of authentication since it is the most difficult for an attacker to falsify. Physical biometrics (such as fingerprints) and behavioral biometrics (such as voice recognition) can be used to authenticate individuals.

While the use of DNA is possible in the future for authentication, it's unlikely it'll be used in the near term. Besides the lack of ability to identify DNA in a timely manner, most users will likely balk at having to prick their fingers to provide a blood sample to authenticate to a computer.

Biometrics can be very exact when the technology is implemented accurately. However, it is possible for a biometric sales company to take shortcuts and not implement it correctly, resulting in false readings. Two possible false readings are:

- **False acceptance.** This is when a biometric system incorrectly identifies an unauthorized user as an authorized user. The False Accept Rate (FAR, also known as a type 2 error) identifies the percentage of times false acceptance occurs.
- **False rejection**. This is when a biometric system incorrectly rejects an authorized user. The False Reject Rate (FRR, also known as a type 1 error) identifies the percentage of times false rejections occur.

True readings occur when the biometric system accurately accepts or rejects a user. For example, true acceptance is when the biometric system accurately determines a positive match. In contrast, true rejection occurs when the biometric system accurately determines a non-match.

Most biometric systems allow you to adjust the sensitivity of the system based on your needs. For example, if you want to ensure there is very little possibility of an unauthorized user being identified as an authorized user, you can set the sensitivity of the system very high. Similarly, if you want to ensure a system will rarely reject an authorized user, you can set the sensitivity very low.

You can determine the accuracy of a biometric system based on its crossover error rate (CER). The CER is the rate at which both the FAR and FRR are equal. A lower CER indicates a more accurate biometric system than one with a higher CER.

For example, Figure 1.1 shows a graph mapping the FAR, the FRR, and CER of a biometric system. You can see that the number of false acceptance errors decreases as the sensitivity is increased. In contrast, the number of false rejection errors increases as the sensitivity is increased. The CER is where both the FAR and FRR are equal.

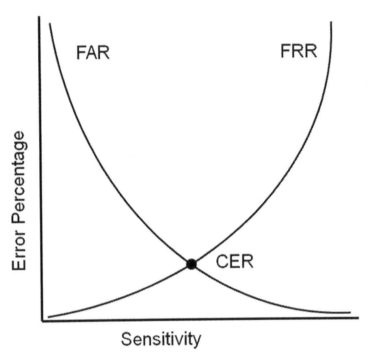

Figure 1.1: Identifying the crossover error rate (CER)

A local grocery store had problems with false acceptance. It allowed shoppers to register their debit cards with their fingerprints. Once the shoppers registered their debit cards, they could simply place one of their fingers in a fingerprint reader instead of swiping a debit card and entering a PIN. Then one day, all the fingerprint scanners disappeared. I later learned that the scanners were falsely accepting some users. Users who had not registered their debit cards tried the fingerprint scanners to pay for groceries, and it worked. The system instead charged someone else's bank account.

Amusement parks often have problems with false rejection later in the season. Families are often the biggest customers of these annual passes. Children often grow enough during the season that the handprint recorded for them early in the season no longer matches for them later in the season.

Multifactor Authentication

Multifactor authentication is the use of more than one factor of authentication. As mentioned previously, this is frequently done with smart cards and PINs, tokens and PINs, or even combining a smart card or token with usernames and passwords. In each of these cases, the user must have something and know something. It's also possible to combine biometrics with other factors of authentication. In highly secure environments, you may even see all three factors of authentication used.

It's worth noting that using two methods of authentication in the same factor is not multifactor authentication. For example, requiring users to use a password and a PIN (both in the *something you know* factor) is not multifactor authentication. Similarly, using a thumbprint and a retina scan is not multifactor authentication.

Exploring Authentication Services

Several other authentication services are available that fall outside the scope of the three previously described factors of authentication. The following section describes many of these services.

Kerberos

Kerberos is a network authentication mechanism used within Windows Active Directory domains and some UNIX environments known as realms. It was originally developed at MIT (the Massachusetts Institute of Technology) for UNIX systems and later released as an RFC. Kerberos provides mutual authentication that can help prevent man-in-the-middle attacks and uses tickets to help prevent replay attacks.

Kerberos includes several requirements in order for it to work properly. They are:

- **A method of issuing tickets used for authentication.** The Key Distribution Center (KDC) uses a complex process of issuing *ticket-granting tickets*, which are later presented to request tickets used to access objects. These tickets are sometimes referred to as tokens, but they are logical tokens, not a key-fob type of token discussed in the *something you have* factor of authentication.
- **Time synchronization**. Kerberos version 5 requires all systems to be synchronized and within five minutes of each other. The clock that provides the time synchronization is used to time-stamp tickets, ensuring they expire correctly. This helps prevent replay attacks. In a replay attack, a third party attempts to impersonate a client after intercepting data captured in a session. However, if an attacker intercepts a ticket, the time stamp limits the amount of time an attacker can use the ticket.
- **A database of subjects or users.** In a Microsoft environment, this is Active Directory, but it could be any database of users.

Remember this

Kerberos is a network authentication protocol within a Microsoft Windows Active Directory domain or a UNIX realm. It uses a database of objects such as Active Directory and a KDC to issue time-stamped tickets that expire after a certain period. Kerberos requires internal time synchronization and uses port 88.

When a user logs on with Kerberos, the KDC issues the user a ticket-granting ticket, which typically has a lifetime of ten hours to be useful for a single workday. When the user tries to access a resource, the ticket-granting ticket is presented as authentication, and the user is issued a ticket for the resource. However, if users stay logged on for an extended period (such as longer than ten hours), they may not be able to access resources after the ticket has expired. In this case, users may be prompted to provide a password to renew the ticket-granting ticket, or they may need to log off and back on to generate a new ticket-granting ticket.

Kerberos uses port 88 by default. As with any well-known ports, this can be changed to another port, but it's rare to change the port. Chapter 3 explains ports and their usage in more depth.

Additionally, Kerberos uses symmetric-key cryptography to prevent unauthorized disclosure and to ensure confidentiality. Chapter 10 will explain algorithms in more depth, but in short, symmetric-key cryptography uses a single key for both encryption and decryption of the same data.

In contrast, asymmetric encryption uses two keys: one key to encrypt and one key to decrypt. Asymmetric encryption requires a PKI to issue certificates. The two keys used in a PKI are a public key and a private key created as matched pairs. Information encrypted with the public key can only decrypted with the matching private key. Similarly, information encrypted with the private key can only decrypted with the matching public key.

As a memory trick, you may like to remember this: symmetric encryption uses one key. Asymmetric adds a syllable ("a"), and it also adds a key, using two keys.

LDAP

Lightweight Directory Access Protocol (LDAP) specifies formats and methods to query directories. In this context, a directory is a database of objects that provides a central access point, or location, to manage users, computers, and other directory objects.

As an example, Active Directory used in Windows environments uses LDAP. Active Directory is a directory of objects (such as users, computers, and groups), and it provides a single location for object management. Queries to Active Directory use the LDAP format.

LDAP is an extension of the X.500 standard that was used extensively by Novell and early Microsoft Exchange Server versions. LDAP v2 can be encrypted with SSL, and LDAP v3 can be encrypted with TLS.

The well-known ports used by LDAP are 389 for unencrypted transmissions, and 636 when encrypted with either SSL or TLS.

Mutual Authentication

Mutual authentication is accomplished when both entities in a session authenticate with each other prior to exchanging data. Chapter 7 will cover different types of attacks, including attacks where an attacker may try to impersonate a server. Mutual authentication provides assurances of the server's identity before the client transmits data. This reduces the risk of a client sending sensitive data to a rogue server.

Many current authentication processes commonly implement mutual authentication. For example, an improvement of MS-CHAPv2 over MS-CHAP is the implementation of mutual authentication.

Single Sign-on

Single sign-on (SSO) refers to the ability of a user to log on or access multiple systems by providing credentials only once. SSO increases security, since the user only needs to remember one set of credentials and is less likely to write them down. It's also much more convenient for users to access network resources if they only have to log on one time.

As an example, consider a user who needs to access multiple servers within a network to perform normal work. If SSO was not implemented, the user would need to know one set of credentials to log on locally, and another set of credentials for each of the servers. Many users would resort to writing these credentials down to remember them.

Alternatively, if a network has implemented SSO, the user would need to log on to the network once, and these credentials would be used during the entire logon session. Each time the user accesses a network resource, the SSO credentials are presented and used.

> ### Remember this
>
> Single sign-on enhances security by requiring users to use and remember only one set of credentials for authentication. Once signed on using SSO, this one set of credentials is used throughout a user's entire session. SSO can provide central authentication against a federated database for different operating systems.

SSO systems can connect authentication mechanisms from different operating systems (sometimes called nonhomogeneous operating systems). One common type is a federated identity management system, often integrated as a federated database. This federated database provides central authentication in a nonhomogeneous environment.

Federated indicates a group of independent entities joined together and treated as one while they still keep their own independence. For example, the United States is a federation of individual states. A federated identity links a user's credentials from different operating systems, but treats it as one identity.

Imagine two websites hosted by two different organizations. Normally a user would have to provide different credentials to access either website. However, if the organizations trust each other, they can use a federated identity management system. Users authenticate with one website and are not required to authenticate again when accessing the second website.

Many web-based portals use SSO. The user logs in to the portal once and the portal then passes proof of the users authentication to back end systems. As long as users have been authenticated by one organization, they are not required to authenticate again for the other organization.

IEEE 802.1X

The IEEE 802.1X protocol is a port-based authentication protocol. It provides authentication when a user connects to a specific access point, or, in this context, a logical port. Its primary purpose is to secure the authentication process prior to a client actually gaining access to a network. While 802.1X can be used in both wired and wireless networks, it is often closely associated with wireless networks.

The Institute of Electrical and Electronic Engineers (IEEE, often pronounced as "I Triple E") is an international organization that is actively involved in the development of many different protocol standards. Protocols and standards are created by the IEEE and prefaced with IEEE. For example, different wireless standards developed by the IEEE are IEEE 802.11a, 802.11b, 802.11g, and 802.11n.

Chapter 4 will cover wireless networks in more depth, but as an introduction, you can use 802.1x with wireless standards, such as Wi-Fi Protected Access (WPA) and Wi-Fi Protected Access v2 (WPA2). WPA and WPA2 both support Enterprise mode, which uses an 802.1x server for authentication. In Enterprise mode, wireless clients authenticate using their own username and password through an 802.1x server. This 802.1x server is integrated with a database of accounts, and if users don't provide valid credentials, they can't access the wireless network.

In contrast, many home wireless networks use Personal mode. In Personal mode, each wireless device uses a pre-shared key (PSK). Any user that has the PSK can access the wireless network. An 802.1x server is not needed.

IEEE 802.1X can be implemented as a Remote Authentication Dial-in User Service (RADIUS) server. RADIUS (explained later in this chapter) provides centralized authentication. When implemented with WPA or WPA2, it provides an added layer of protection by protecting the authentication portion of the wireless session from interception.

Remote Access Authentication

Remote Access Services (RAS) are used to provide access to an internal network from an outside source. Chapter 4 will cover RAS in more depth but this section covers different authentication mechanisms that can be used with RAS.

Clients access a RAS server via either dial-up or a virtual private network (VPN). A VPN allows a client to access a private network over a public network (such as the Internet).

Remote access methods are useful for personnel that need access to the private network from remote locations. However, no matter what method of remote access you use, you still need to ensure that only authorized clients can access your network remotely. Authorization begins with authentication, and there are multiple methods of authentication used with remote access.

The different authentication mechanisms that may be used with remote access services are:

- **PAP**. Password Authentication Protocol. Passwords are sent in clear text so PAP is rarely used today.
- **CHAP**. Challenge Handshake Authentication Protocol. CHAP uses a handshake process where the server challenges the client. The client then responds with appropriate authentication information.

- **MS-CHAP.** Microsoft's implementation of CHAP, which is used only by Microsoft clients.
- **MS-CHAPv2**. An improvement over MS-CHAP. A significant improvement of MS-CHAPv2 over MS-CHAP is the ability to perform mutual authentication.
- **RADIUS**. Remote Authentication Dial-In User Service. Radius provides a centralized method of authentication for multiple remote access services servers. RADIUS encrypts the password packets, but not the entire authentication process.
- **TACACS and XTACACS.** Terminal Access Controller Access-Control System (TACACS) is a remote authentication protocol that was commonly used in UNIX networks. Extended TACACS (XTACACS) is an improvement over TACACS developed by Cisco Systems and is proprietary to Cisco systems. Neither of these are commonly used today with most organizations using either RADIUS or TACACS+.
- **TACACS+.** Terminal Access Controller Access-Control System+ (TACACS) is an alternative to RADIUS and is proprietary to Cisco systems. A benefit of TACACS+ is that it can interact with Kerberos allowing it to work with a broader range of environments including Microsoft. Additionally, TACACS+ encrypts the entire authentication process (RADIUS encrypts only the password).

PAP

Password Authentication Protocol (PAP) is used with Point to Point Protocol (PPP) to authenticate clients. It replaced Serial Line Interface Protocol (SLIP) as a more efficient method of connecting to remote servers such as Internet Service Providers (ISPs). However, a significant weakness of PAP is that passwords are sent in clear text, presenting a significant security risk.

PPP is primarily used with dial-up connections. Believe it or not, there was a time when the thought of someone wiretapping a phone was rather remote. Because of this, security was an afterthought with PPP. Today, PPP would only be used as a last resort due to passwords being passed in clear text, or used with another protocol that provides encryption.

Throughout this book, you'll read that sending data across a line in clear text is a security risk. It's not just PPP that has this risk, but also FTP, SNMP, NetBIOS, and many other protocols. It's relatively easy for someone to download and use a free protocol analyzer (such as Wireshark) to capture packets. These packets can easily be analyzed with the protocol analyzer, and the data within the packets can be read. Protocol analyzers are commonly referred to as sniffers, and chapter 8 covers protocol analyzers in more depth.

CHAP

Challenge Handshake Authentication Protocol has often been used to authenticate users in the past. However, it is often replaced with more secure forms of authentication today. The goal of CHAP is to allow the client to pass credentials over a public network (such as a phone or the Internet) without allowing attackers to intercept the data and later use it in an attack.

The client and server both know a shared secret (similar to a password) used in the authentication process. However, the client doesn't send the shared secret over the network in plain text as PAP does. Instead, the client hashes it after combining it with a nonce (number used once) provided by the server. This handshake process is done when the client initially tries to connect to the server, and at different times during the connection.

MS-CHAP and MS-CHAPv2

Microsoft introduced Microsoft Challenge Handshake Authentication Protocol (MS-CHAP) as an improvement over CHAP for Microsoft clients. MS-CHAP supported clients as old as Windows 95. Later, Microsoft improved MS-CHAP with MS-CHAPv2.

A significant improvement of MS-CHAPv2 over MS-CHAP is the ability to perform mutual authentication. Not only does the client authenticate to the server, but the server also authenticates to the client. This provides added protection to ensure that the client doesn't send data to a server that may be impersonating the live remote access server.

RADIUS

Remote Authentication Dial-In User Service (RADIUS) is a centralized authentication service. Instead of each individual RAS server needing a separate database to identify who can authenticate, authentication requests are forwarded to a central RADIUS server.

One of the ways to visualize this is to think of a dial-up ISP, such as America Online (AOL). AOL provides dial-in services for just about any city in the United States. While anyone can dial in to an AOL server, only those with accounts in good standing will be authenticated and allowed access.

Imagine if you lived in Virginia Beach, Virginia. You could sign up for AOL, pay the required fee, and access the AOL service via a server in Virginia Beach. AOL could maintain a database on the server in Virginia Beach showing your account is in good standing.

However, what if you travel to Atlanta, Chicago, San Francisco, or somewhere else? Since you paid your fees, you would reasonably expect to be able to access AOL no matter where you traveled. If the databases were stored on individual servers then every single server in the United States would need to be updated. Similarly, if you cancelled your subscription, then every single server would need to be updated again. Clearly, this would take a lot of work.

Instead, AOL could use a centralized RADIUS server as shown in Figure 1.2.

This centralized RADIUS server would hold the database. Now if you tried to access AOL from any city, that AOL server would then contact the RADIUS server to check your account.

While this example with AOL works well to illustrate how RADIUS works, you don't need servers all over the country to take advantage of RADIUS. You could have as few as two or three RAS servers. Instead of having authentication databases on each server, you could configure a centralized RADIUS server.

RADIUS uses the UDP protocol, which uses a best-effort delivery mechanism. In contrast, TACACS+ uses TCP, which provides guaranteed delivery. Also, RADIUS only encrypts the password.

Remember this

MS-CHAPv2 is used to authenticate Microsoft clients and includes mutual authentication. TACACS+ is used by Cisco for authentication and can use Kerberos, allowing it to interact with a Microsoft environment. TACACS+ uses TCP, encrypts the entire authentication process, and uses multiple challenges and responses. RADIUS uses UDP and encrypts just the password.

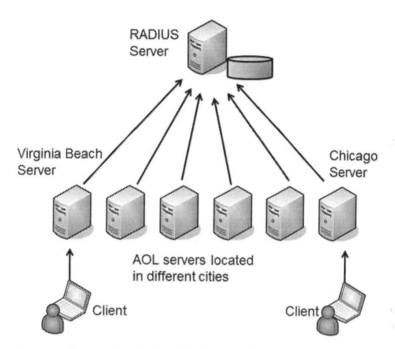

Figure 1.2: Remote Authentication Dial-In User Service (RADIUS)

TACACS/XTACACS

Terminal Access Controller Access-Control System (TACACS) and Extended TACACS (XTACACS) are older authentication protocols rarely used today. TACACS is a generic protocol and was commonly used on Cisco and UNIX systems. It uses UDP port 49 by default and is formally defined in RFC 1492. Cisco improved TACACS with XTACACS as a proprietary authentication protocol.

TACACS+

Terminal Access Controller Access-Control System+, or TACACS+, is Cisco's alternative to RADIUS. TACACS and XTACACS have been replaced with TACACS+ in most implementations, but you may still see TACACS in a legacy system. In addition to using TACACS+ for remote access, you can also use it for authentication with routers and other networked devices. While TACACS uses UDP port 49, TACACS+ uses TCP port 49 for increased reliability of the transmissions.

TACACS+ provides two important security benefits over RADIUS. First, it encrypts the entire authentication process, while RADIUS encrypts only the password. Second, TACACS+ uses multiple challenges and responses between the client and the server.

While TACACS+ is proprietary to Cisco, it can interact with Kerberos. This allows a Cisco RAS server (or VPN concentrator) to interact in a Microsoft Active Directory environment. As a reminder, Microsoft's Active Directory uses Kerberos for authentication.

TACACS+ is also used as an authentication service for network devices. In other words, you can use it to authenticate users before they are able to access a configuration page for a router or a switch. The network devices must be TACACS+ enabled, and a TACACS+ server provides the authentication services.

AAA Protocols

AAA protocols provide authentication, authorization, and accounting. Authentication verifies a user's identification. Authorization determines if a user should have access. Accounting tracks user access with logs.

As an example, RADIUS and TACACS+ are both considered AAA protocols because they provide all three services. They authenticate users who attempt remote access, determine if the user is authorized for remote access by checking a database, and then record the user's activity. TACACS+ uses multiple challenges and responses during a session. Kerberos is sometimes referred to as an AAA protocol, but it does not provide any accounting services.

Chapter 1 Exam Topic Review

When preparing for the exam, make sure you understand these key concepts covered in this chapter.

Core Security Principles

- Confidentiality ensures that data is only viewable by authorized users. Access controls and encryption protect the confidentiality of data.
- Integrity provides assurances that data has not been modified, tampered with, or corrupted through unauthorized or unintended changes. Data can be a message, a file, or data within a database. Hashing is one method of ensuring that integrity has not been lost.
- Availability ensures that data and services are available when needed. A common goal is to remove single points of failure (SPOF). Methods used to increase or maintain availability include fault tolerance, backups, virtualization, HVAC systems, and generators.
- Confidentiality, integrity, and availability are not treated equally in all situations. Organizations may prioritize confidentiality, integrity, or availability differently depending on their goals.

- Non-repudiation prevents entities from denying they took an action. Digital signatures and audit logs provide non-repudiation.
- Defense in depth employs multiple layers of security. Security and IT professionals constantly monitor, update, add to, and improve existing security controls.
- Implicit deny indicates that unless something is explicitly allowed, it is denied. Firewalls often use implicit deny by explicitly allowing some traffic and then implicitly denying all other traffic that is not identified. Anything not explicitly allowed is implicitly denied.

Basic Risk Concepts

- Risk is the possibility of a threat exploiting a vulnerability resulting in a loss.
- A threat is any circumstance or event that has the potential to compromise confidentiality, integrity, or availability.
- A vulnerability is a weakness. It can be a weakness in the hardware, software, the configuration, or users operating the system.
- Risk mitigation reduces risk by reducing the chances that a threat will exploit a vulnerability.
- Controls are actions taken to reduce risks. Examples include access controls (starting with authentication), business continuity plans, and antivirus software.

Authentication Concepts

Authentication allows entities to prove their identity by using credentials known to another entity. Authentication concepts covered in this chapter were:

- Identification occurs when a user professes or claims an identity, such as with a username.
- Authentication occurs when an entity provides proof of an identity (such as a password) and the proof is verified by a second entity.
- Authorization provides access to resources based on a proven identity.
- Three factors of authentication:
  - *Something you know* (such as a username and password)
  - *Something you have* (such as a smart card, CAC, PIV, or a token)
  - *Something you are* (using biometrics)
- The *something you know* factor typically refers to a shared secret, such as a password, a username and password, or even a personal identification number (PIN). This is the least secure form of authentication.
- Passwords should be strong and changed often. Complexity (or key space) is calculated as C^N (C^N) where C is the number of possible characters used and N is the length of the password. Using more character types increases the key space.
- Self-service password systems automate password recovery.
- Account lockout policies lock out an account after an incorrect password is entered too many times.
- Smart cards are credit-card-size cards that have embedded certificates used for authentication. They require a PKI to issue certificates.

- Common access cards (CACs) and personal identity verification (PIV) cards can be used as photo IDs and as smart cards.
- Tokens (or key fobs) display numbers in an LCD synchronized with a server. These numbers provide rolling one-time use passwords.
- Biometric methods are the most difficult to falsify. Physical methods include fingerprints and iris scans. Behavioral methods include voice recognition and signature geometry.
- Multifactor authentication employs two or more of the three factors. Multifactor authentication is stronger than any form of single-factor authentication.

Authentication Services

- Kerberos is a network authentication protocol using tickets issued by a KDC. If a ticket-granting ticket expires, the user may not be able to access resources. Kerberos is used in Microsoft Active Directory domains and in UNIX realms.
- Lightweight Directory Access Protocol (LDAP) specifies formats and methods to query directories. It provides a single point of management for objects, such as users and computers, in an Active Directory domain.
- Single sign-on (SSO) allows users to authenticate with a single user account and access multiple resources on a network without authenticating again. SSO can be used to provide central authentication with a federated database and use this authentication in an environment with different operating systems (nonhomogeneous environment).

Remote Access Authentication

Remote access authentication is used when a user accesses a private network from a remote location, such as with a dial-up connection or a VPN connection. The following authentication mechanisms used with remote access were covered in this chapter:

- PAP is rarely used, primarily because passwords are sent in clear text.
- CHAP uses a challenge response authentication process.
- MS-CHAP and MS-CHAPv2 are Microsoft's improvement over CHAP. CHAPv2 provides mutual authentication.
- RADIUS provides central authentication for multiple remote access services. RADIUS uses UDP and only encrypts the password during the authentication process.
- TACACS /XTACACS are two legacy protocols that are rarely used anymore. TACACS is generic, defined by RFC 1492, and uses UDP port 49. XTACACS is a Cisco systems proprietary improvement over TACACS.
- TACACS+ is used by some Cisco and UNIX remote access systems as an alternative to RADIUS. TACACS+ uses TCP, encrypts the entire authentication process, and supports multiple challenge and responses. TACACS+ uses TCP port 49.

Chapter 1 Practice Questions

1. You want to ensure that data is only viewable by authorized users. What security principle are you trying to enforce?
    - A. Confidentiality
    - B. Integrity
    - C. Availability
    - D. Authentication

2. Of the following choices, what is the best way to protect the confidentiality of data?
    - A. Authentication
    - B. Encryption
    - C. Hashing
    - D. PaaS

3. You want to ensure that data has not been changed between the time when it was sent and when it arrived at its destination. What provides this assurance?
    - A. Confidentiality
    - B. Integrity
    - C. Availability
    - D. Authentication

4. A database administrator is tasked with increasing the retail prices of all products in a database by 10 percent. The administrator writes a script performing a bulk update of the database and executes it. However, all retail prices are doubled (increased by 100 percent instead of 10 percent). What has been lost?
    - A. Confidentiality
    - B. Integrity
    - C. Hashing
    - D. Authentication

5. Your organization is addressing single points of failure as potential risks to security. What are they addressing?
    - A. Confidentiality
    - B. Integrity
    - C. Availability
    - D. Authentication

6. An organization hosts several bays of servers used to support a large online ecommerce business. Which one of the following choices would increase the availability of this datacenter?
   A. Encryption
   B. Hashing
   C. Generators
   D. Integrity

7. You are planning to host a free online forum for users to share IT security-related information with each other. Any user can anonymously view data. Users can post messages after logging in, but you do not want users to be able to modify other users' posts. What levels of confidentiality, integrity, and availability should you seek?
   A. Low confidentiality, low integrity, and low availability
   B. Medium confidentiality, low integrity, and high availability
   C. High confidentiality, low integrity, and low availability
   D. Low confidentiality, medium integrity, and medium availability

8. What is the purpose of risk mitigation?
   A. Reduce the chances that a threat will exploit a vulnerability
   B. Reduce the chances that a vulnerability will exploit a threat
   C. Eliminate risk
   D. Eliminate threats

9. What is completed when a user's password has been verified?
   A. Identification
   B. Authentication
   C. Authorization
   D. Access verification

10. Which of the following formulas represent the complexity of a password policy that requires users to use only upper and lower case letters with a length of eight characters?
    A. 52^8
    B. 26^8
    C. 8^52
    D. 8^26

11. Of the following choices, what password has a dissimilar key space than the others?
    A. Secur1tyIsFun
    B. Passw0rd
    C. ILOve$ecur1ty
    D. 4uBetutaOn

12. Robert lets you know that he is using his username as his password since it's easier to remember. You decide to inform the user that this isn't a secure password. What explanation would you include?
    A. The password wouldn't meet account lockout requirements
    B. The password is too hard to remember
    C. The password is not long enough
    D. The password is not complex

13. Your organization has implemented a self-service password reset system. What does this provide?
    A. Password policy
    B. Certificate reset
    C. Password recovery
    D. Previous logon notification

14. A user entered the incorrect password for his account three times in a row and can no longer log on because his account is disabled. What caused this?
    A. Password policy
    B. Account disablement policy
    C. Account complexity policy
    D. Account lockout policy

15. A user is issued a token with a number displayed in an LCD. What does this provide?
    A. Rolling password for one-time use
    B. Multifactor authentication
    C. CAC
    D. PIV

16. Which one of the following includes a photo and can be used as identification? (Choose all that apply.)
    A. CAC
    B. MAC
    C. DAC
    D. PIV

17. Which of the following is a behavioral biometric authentication model?
    A. Fingerprint
    B. Token
    C. Voice recognition
    D. Iris scan

18. Which of the following is an example of multifactor authentication?
    A. Smart card and token
    B. Smart card and PIN
    C. Thumbprint and voice recognition
    D. Password and PIN

19. Which of the following choices is an example of using multiple authentication factors?
    A. Fingerprint and retina scan
    B. Smart card and token
    C. Fingerprint and password
    D. A password and a PIN

20. Of the following choices, what provides the strongest authentication?
    A. Password
    B. Smart card
    C. Retina scan
    D. Multifactor authentication

21. What is used for authentication in a Microsoft Active Directory domain?
    A. RADIUS
    B. TACACS+
    C. Kerberos
    D. NIDS

22. Which of the following best describes the purpose of LDAP?
    A. A central point for user management
    B. Biometric authentication
    C. Prevent loss of confidentiality
    D. Prevent loss of integrity

23. A federated user database is used to provide central authentication via a web portal. What service does this database provide?
    A. SSO
    B. Multifactor authentication
    C. CAC
    D. DAC

24. Of the following protocols, which one does not encrypt the entire authentication process, but instead only encrypts the password in traffic between the client and server?
    A. RADIUS
    B. TACACS+
    C. XTACACS
    D. Token

25. Which one of the following AAA protocols uses multiple challenges and responses?
    A. CHAP
    B. RADIUS
    C. TACACS
    D. TACACS+

Chapter 1 Practice Question Answers

1. **A.** Confidentiality ensures that data is only viewable by authorized users and can be ensured with access controls and encryption. Integrity is enforced with hashing. Availability can be ensured with power and cooling systems, and various fault tolerance and redundancy techniques. Authentication proves a person's identity and is a first step in access control, but by itself it does not provide confidentiality.

2. **B.** Encryption protects the confidentiality of data. You can encrypt any type of data, including sensitive data stored on a server, a desktop, a mobile device, or within a database. Authentication proves a person's identity and is a first step in access control, but, by itself, it does not provide confidentiality. Hashing ensures the integrity of data. Platform as a Service (PaaS) provides an easy to configure operating system for on-demand cloud computing.

3. **B.** Integrity provides assurances that data has not been modified and is enforced with hashing. Confidentiality prevents unauthorized disclosure and is enforced with access controls and encryption. Availability ensures systems are up and operational when needed and uses fault tolerance and redundancy methods. Authentication provides proof that users are who they claim to be.

4. **B.** The database has lost integrity through an unintended change. Loss of confidentiality indicates that unauthorized users have accessed the database. Hashing can be used to verify integrity in some situations (though not in this scenario), but hashing would not be compromised. Authentication provides proof that users are who they claim to be.

5. **C.** By addressing a single point of failure (SPOF), you increase availability. An SPOF can be a drive, a server, power, cooling or any other item whose failure will cause the entire system to fail. Confidentiality is enforced with encryption, and integrity is enforced with hashing, Authentication provides proof of a user's identity.

6. **C.** Generators can provide power to a datacenter if the power fails, ensuring that the servers within the datacenter continue to operate. Encryption increases the confidentiality of data within the datacenter. Hashing verifies integrity.

7. **D.** Data can be viewed anonymously, so low confidentiality is acceptable. You do not want users to modify other users' posts, so integrity is medium. The site is free but you do want users to be able to access it when needed, so availability is medium.

8. **A.** Risk mitigation reduces the chances that a threat will exploit a vulnerability. Risk is the likelihood that a threat (such as an attacker) will exploit a vulnerability (any weakness). A vulnerability cannot exploit a threat. You cannot eliminate risk or eliminate threats.

9. **B.** A user is authenticated when the password is verified. The user claims an identity with a username. After authentication, users are authorized to access resources based on their identity, and auditing can verify what resources a user has accessed.

10. **A.** The correct formula is 52^8. The formula to calculate the complexity of a password is C^N, where C is the number of possible characters used and N is the length of the password. Since both uppercase (A-Z) and lowercase (a-z) characters are used, C is fifty-two, and the password has a stated length of eight characters.

11. **C.** IL0ve$ecur1ty has 13 characters with a mixture of all four character types (uppercase letters, lowercase letters, numbers, and symbols). This has a larger key space (more possibilities) than the other passwords. Secur1ty, Passw0rd, and 3uBetuta each use only three character types.

12. **D.** Strong passwords do not include any part of a username, and if just the username is used, the password would not be complex. Password characteristics are not related to account lockout (where a user account can be locked out after entering the wrong password too many times). A username as a password would not be difficult to remember. Users with long names could have extremely long passwords so they will likely meet length requirements.

13. **C.** A self-service password reset system allows users to recover passwords without administrative intervention. A password policy ensures that users create strong passwords and change them periodically. A password reset system does not reset certificates. A previous logon notification provides notification to users when they last logged on and can help them identify if someone else is using their account.

14. **D.** An account lockout policy will force an account to be locked out after the wrong password is entered a set number of times (such as after three failed attempts). A password policy ensures strong passwords are used and users change their password regularly. An account disablement policy refers to disabling inactive accounts, such as after an employee is terminated. A password policy ensures users create strong, complex passwords, but there is no such thing as an account complexity policy.

15. **A.** A token (such as an RSA token) provides a rolling password for one-time use. While it can be used with multifactor authentication (requiring the user to also enter other information such as a password), it doesn't provide multifactor authentication by itself. A CAC and a PIV are both specialized types of smart cards that include photo identification.

16. **A, D.** A common access card (CAC) and a personal identity verification (PIV) card both include photo identification and function as smart cards. MAC and DAC are access control models, not photo IDs.

17. **C.** Voice recognition is a form of behavioral biometric authentication. Biometrics are the most difficult for an attacker to falsify or forge, because they represent a user based on personal

characteristics. Fingerprints and iris scans are forms of physical biometric authentication. A token provides a rolling password for one-time use.

18. **B.** A smart card and PIN is an example of multifactor authentication since it uses methods from the *something you have* factor and *something you know* factor. A smart card and token are both in the *something you have* factor. Thumbprint and voice recognition are both in the *something you are* factor. A password and PIN are both in the *something you know* factor.

19. **C.** A fingerprint uses the *something you are* factor, and a password uses the *something you know* factor. All the other answers use examples from the same factor. A fingerprint and retina are both examples of the *something you are* factor. A smart card and token are both examples of the *something you have* factor. A password and a PIN are both examples of the *something you know* factor.

20. **D.** Multifactor authentication combines two or more other factors of authentication and is stronger than any authentication using a single factor. A password is *something you know*, a smart card is *something you have*, and a retina scan is based on *something you are*.

21. **C.** Kerberos is used as a network authentication protocol in Microsoft Active Directory domains and in UNIX realms. Kerberos uses tickets issued by a KDC. RADIUS and TACACS+ are central authentication services that also provide authorization and accounting. A network-based intrusion detection service (NIDS) attempts to detect intrusions on a network.

22. **A.** The Lightweight Directory Access Protocol (LDAP) specifies formats and methods to query directories and is used to manage objects (such as users and computers) in an Active Directory domain. LDAP is not associated with biometrics. While LDAP contributes indirectly to confidentiality and integrity, it is more accurate to say that LDAP is used as a central point for user management.

23. **A.** Single sign-on (SSO) can be used to provide central authentication with a federated database and use this authentication in a nonhomogeneous environment. Multifactor authentication uses authentication from two or more factors. A common access card (CAC) is a form of photo identification and also function as a smart card. DAC is an access control model.

24. **A.** Remote Authentication Dial-In User Service (RADIUS) will encrypt the password packets between a client and a server, but it does not encrypt the entire authentication process. Terminal Access Controller Access-Control System + (TACACS+) and Extended TACACS (XTACACS) both encrypt the entire logon process. A token uses a one-time rolling password, but it is not a protocol in itself.

25. **D.** TACACS+ uses multiple challenges and responses and is an authentication, authorization, and accounting (AAA) protocol. CHAP is not an AAA protocol. RADIUS and TACACS do not use multiple challenges and responses.

Chapter 2

Exploring Control Types and Methods

CompTIA Security+ objectives covered in this chapter:

1.2 Apply and implement secure network administration principles
- 802.1x
- Implicit deny

2.1 Explain risk related concepts
- Control types
  - Technical
  - Management
  - Operational
- Importance of policies in reducing risk
  - Least privilege

2.2 Carry out appropriate risk mitigation strategies
- Implement security controls based on risk
- Perform routine audits

2.4 Explain the importance of security related awareness and training
- User habits
  - Prevent tailgating

2.6 Explain the impact and proper use of environmental controls
- Video monitoring

3.6 Analyze and differentiate among types of mitigation and deterrent techniques
- Physical security
  - Hardware locks
  - Mantraps
  - Video surveillance
  - Fencing

- Proximity readers
- Access list
- Detection controls vs. prevention controls
  - Camera vs. guard

4.2 Carry out appropriate procedures to establish host security

- Hardware security
  - Cable locks
  - Safe
  - Locking cabinets

5.2 Explain the fundamental concepts and best practices related to authentication, authorization, and access control

- Least privilege
- ACLs
- Access control
- Mandatory access control
- Discretionary access control
- Role-/rule-based access control
- Implicit deny
- Time of day restrictions
- Trusted OS

5.3 Implement appropriate security controls when performing account management

- Account policy enforcement
  - Password complexity
  - Expiration
  - Length
  - Disablement
- Group based privileges
- User assigned privileges

Once you've ensured personnel have adequately identified themselves with authentication, you can now move to different methods to restrict or control access. This chapter will introduce basic control types and explain three common access control models (MAC, DAC, and RBAC). It also covers some common physical security and logical access controls.

Understanding Basic Control Types

Chapter 1 introduced the definitions of risk and risk mitigation. As a reminder, risk is the likelihood that a threat will exploit a vulnerability, resulting in a loss, and risk mitigation uses controls to reduce risk. Controls are also referred to as countermeasures or safeguards, referencing their ability to counter threats or provide safeguards to reduce vulnerabilities.

Objectives for the Security+ exam specifically identify the following three control types: technical, management, and operational. Controls are also identified based on their function. The three primary functions of controls are preventative, detective, and corrective.

NIST

The National Institute of Standards and Technology (NIST) is a part of the U.S. Department of Commerce, and it includes a Computer Security Division with the Information Technology Laboratory (ITL). The ITL publishes Special Publications (SPs) in the 800 series that are of general interest to the computer security community.

Many IT security professionals use these documents as references to design secure IT systems and networks. Additionally, many security-related certifications (beyond the Security+ certification) also reference the SP 800 documents both directly and indirectly.

For example, SP 800-53 revision three is titled "Recommended Security Controls for Federal Information Systems and Organizations." It includes three relatively short chapters providing an introduction to technical, management, and operational security controls followed with multiple appendixes providing a significant amount of depth on individual controls.

If you're interested in pursuing other security-related certifications or making IT security a career, the SP 800 documents are well worth your time. You can download SP 800-53 here: http://csrc.nist.gov/publications/nistpubs/800-53-Rev3/sp800-53-rev3-final_updated-errata_05-01-2010.pdf. If you want to view a listing of all SP 800 documents, check out this link: http://csrc.nist.gov/publications/PubsSPs.html.

NIST's SP 800-53 revision three provides a formal definition of security controls. They are "*the management, operational, and technical safeguards or countermeasures employed within an organizational information system to protect the confidentiality, integrity, and availability of the system and its information.*" Further, SP 800-53 also defines the controls in three classes as technical, management, and operational. This section provides an overview of the different classes or types of controls.

Technical Controls

A technical control is one that uses technology to reduce vulnerabilities. An administrator installs and configures a technical control, and the control then provides the protection automatically.

> ### Remember this
> Technical controls use technology to reduce vulnerabilities. Some examples include the principle of least privilege, antivirus software, IDSs, and firewalls.

Throughout this book, you'll come across several examples of technical controls. The following list provides a few examples.

- **Least Privilege**. The principle of least privilege is an example of a technical control. It specifies that individuals or processes are granted only the rights and permissions needed to perform their assigned tasks or functions, but no more. Least privilege is covered in greater depth in the "Understanding Logical Controls" section later in this chapter.
- **Antivirus software.** Once installed, the antivirus software provides protection against infection. Chapter 6 covers malicious software (malware) and antivirus software.
- **Intrusion detection systems (IDSs).** An IDS can monitor a network or host for intrusions and provide ongoing protection against various threats. Chapter 4 covers different types of IDSs.
- **Firewalls.** Firewalls restrict network traffic going in and out of a network. Chapter 3 covers firewalls in more depth.

Management Controls

Management controls are primarily administrative in function. They use planning and assessment methods to provide an ongoing review of the organization's ability to reduce and manage risk. Chapter 8 covers vulnerability assessments and penetration tests, which fall into this category.

For example, two common management controls are:

- **Risk assessments.** These help quantify and qualify risks within an organization so that they can focus on the serious risks. For example, a quantitative risk assessment uses cost and asset values to quantify risks based monetary values. A qualitative risk assessment uses judgments to categorize risks based on probability and impact.
- **Vulnerability assessments.** A vulnerability assessment attempts to discover current vulnerabilities. When necessary, additional controls are implemented to reduce the risk from these vulnerabilities.

Operational Controls

Operational controls help ensure that day-to-day operations of an organization comply with their overall security plan. Operational controls include the following families:

- **Awareness and training.** The importance of training to reduce risks cannot be overstated. Training helps users maintain password security, follow a clean desk policy, understand threats such as phishing and malware, and much more.
- **Configuration management.** Configuration management often uses baselines to ensure that systems start in a secure, hardened state. Change management helps ensure that changes don't result in unintended configuration errors. Chapter 5 covers change and configuration management in more detail.
- **Contingency planning.** Chapter 9 presents several different methods that help an organization plan and prepare for potential system outages. The goal is to reduce the overall impact on the organization if an outage occurs.
- **Media protection.** Media includes physical media such as USB flash drives, external and internal drives, and backup tapes.
- **Physical and environmental protection.** This includes physical controls such as cameras, door locks, and environmental controls such as heating and ventilation systems.

Controls Based on Functions

Many controls are identified based on their function as opposed to the type of control. The three primary functions of controls are preventative, detective, and corrective.

Preventative Controls

Preventative controls attempt to prevent an incident from occurring. The goal is to take steps to prevent the risk. Some examples include:

- **Security guards.** Guards act as a deterrent and provide a preventative security control. For example, an attacker may attempt social engineering to fool a receptionist, but is less likely to attempt these techniques, or succeed, when guards protect an access control point.
- **Change management.** Change management (introduced as an operational control) ensures that changes don't result in ad-hoc (or as-needed) configuration errors. In other words, instead of administrators making changes on the fly, they submit the change to a change management process. Chapter 5 covers change management in more depth.
- **Account disablement policy.** Most organizations ensure that user accounts are disabled when an employee is terminated. This ensures that these accounts are not used by the ex-employee or by anyone else. The "Account Management" section later in this chapter covers account disablement policies in more depth.
- **System hardening.** Chapter 5 covers different methods of ensuring that a system is more secure from its default configuration. This includes removing and disabling unneeded services and protocols, keeping the system up to date, and enabling firewalls.

> **Remember this**
>
> A preventative control attempts to prevent an incident from occurring. Security guards can prevent unauthorized personnel from entering a secure area. A change management control helps prevent outages from ad-hoc (or as-needed) configuration mistakes. An account disablement policy ensures that a terminated employee's account can't be used.

Detective Controls

Detective controls are designed to detect when a vulnerability has been exploited. A detective control can't predict when an incident will occur, and it can't prevent it. However, it can discover the event after it's occurred. Some examples of detective controls are:

- **Security audit**. Security audits can examine the security posture of an organization. For example, a password audit can determine if the password policy is ensuring the use of strong passwords. Similarly, a periodic review of user rights can detect if users have more permissions than they should.
- **Video surveillance**. A closed circuit television (CCTV) system can record activity and detect what occurred. It's worth noting that video surveillance can also be used as a preventative control since it can act as a deterrent.

> **Remember this**
>
> Detective controls can detect when a vulnerability has been exploited. Two examples are security audits and CCTV systems.

Corrective Controls

Corrective controls attempt to reverse the impact of an incident or problem after it has occurred. Some examples of corrective controls are:

- **Active IDS**. Active intrusion detection systems (IDSs) attempt to detect attacks and then modify the environment to block the attack from continuing. Chapter 4 covers IDSs in more depth.
- **Backups and system recovery**. When data is lost, a backup ensures that the data can be recovered. Similarly, when a system fails, system recovery procedures ensure it can be recovered. Chapter 9 covers backups and disaster recovery plans in more depth.

Exploring Access Control Models

If you've never studied access control models before, these topics might seem a little foreign to you. As models, they are largely theoretical and used in the design stage of defining access control methods. The in-depth knowledge laid out in these models helps the experts create the logical access control methods that IT professionals implement and maintain.

Most IT professionals implement and maintain security within the networks. They don't design them, so the details of the underlying theories aren't as important as knowing how to manage them. In other words, you don't need to know enough to write a master's thesis on these models.

You're probably familiar with some of these topics, but the terms *RBAC*, *DAC*, and *MAC* may be unfamiliar. By understanding a little more of the underlying design principles, you'll understand why some of the rules are important, and you'll be better prepared to ensure that security principles are followed. The models you'll learn are:

- Role-/rule-based access control (RBAC)
- Discretionary access control (DAC)
- Mandatory access control (MAC)

Often, when using any of the models, you'll run across the following terms:

- **Subjects**. Subjects are typically users or groups that will access an object. Occasionally, the subject may be a service that is using a service account to access an object.
- **Objects**. Objects are items such as files, folders, shares, and printers that are accessed by subjects.

Chapter 11 covers data classification in more depth, but it's common for an organization to classify its data as proprietary, private, classified, or public, similar to how the government classifies data as "Top Secret," "Secret," "Confidential," and "Unclassified." The data classification determines the level of protection that the data requires. The access control model (RBAC, DAC, or MAC) helps determine how the data is protected.

Role- and Rule-Based Access Control

Role-based access control (RBAC) uses roles to manage rights and permissions for users. This is useful for users within a specific department that perform the same job functions. An administrator creates the roles and then assigns specific rights and permissions to the roles (instead of to the users). When an administrator adds a user to a role, the user has all the rights and permissions of that role.

Rule-based access control (with the same acronym of RBAC) is based on a set of approved instructions configured on rules. A simple example is the rules of a router or firewall. These use access control lists as a set of rules that define what traffic is allowed or blocked. In some scenarios, rules are scripted in real time. For example, intrusion prevention systems can detect, and then modify rules to block traffic from an attacker.

For the purpose of this chapter, we'll focus on Role-Based Access Control, and for clarity, when the RBAC acronym is being used, it represents Role-Based Access Control.

> ### Remember this
>
> The RBAC model uses roles (often implemented as groups) to grant access by placing users into roles based on their assigned jobs, functions, or tasks. A user account is placed into a role, inheriting the rights and permissions of the role. Rule-based access control is based on a set of approved instructions, such as an access control list.

Using Roles Based on Jobs and Functions

An example of the RBAC model is Microsoft's Project Server. The Project Server can host multiple projects managed by different project managers. It includes the following roles:

- **Administrators**. Administrators have complete access and control over everything on the server, including all of the projects.
- **Executives**. Executives can access data from any project held on the server but don't have access to modify system settings on the server.
- **Project Managers**. Project managers have full control over their own projects but do not have any control over projects owned by other project managers.
- **Team Members**. Team members can typically report on work they are assigned and complete, but they have little access outside the scope of their assignments.

Microsoft's Project Server includes more roles, but you can see the point with these four. Each of these roles has rights and permissions assigned to it, and to give someone the associated privileges, you'd simply add the user's account to the role.

RBAC is also called hierarchy based or job based.

- **Hierarchy based**. In the Project Server example, you can see how top-level roles, such as the Administrators role, have significantly more permissions than lower-level roles such as the Team Members role. Roles may mimic the hierarchy of an organization.
- **Job, task, or function based**. The Project Server example also shows how the roles are centered on jobs or functions that users need to perform.

Establishing Access with Groups as Roles

Access is established in the RBAC model based on role membership, and roles are often implemented as groups. Each role has rights and permissions assigned, and you simply add the user to the role to grant appropriate access. Access based on roles, or groups, simplifies user administration.

One implementation of the RBAC model is Microsoft's built-in groups, and specially created groups that are available in both workstations and domains. For example, if you wanted to grant Sally full and complete control to a local system, you could add Sally's user account to the Administrators group. All the appropriate rights and permissions are already granted to the

Administrators group, so by adding Sally as a member of the group, she has the same rights and permissions. Similarly, you can grant other users the rights and permissions to perform backups and restores by adding their user account to the Backup Operators group.

Built-in groups (like the Administrators group and the Backup Operators group) have rights and permissions already assigned. It's also possible to make changes to the built-in groups, giving this model some flexibility. More often, additional groups are created that can be used to meet specific needs. For example, to separate the backup and restore responsibilities, you can create one group that can only back up data and another group that can only restore data.

Without using groups, you would have to individually assign all the specific rights and permissions for every user. This may work for one or two users but quickly becomes unmanageable with any significant number of users.

In Windows domains, groups are often created to correspond to departments of an organization. For example, Figure 2.1 shows how you can do this for users in the sales department. The users are added to the sales department, and then rights and permissions are assigned to the group. Any user added to this group will have the same rights and permissions assigned to the group. If you remove the user from the group, the user no longer has these rights and permissions.

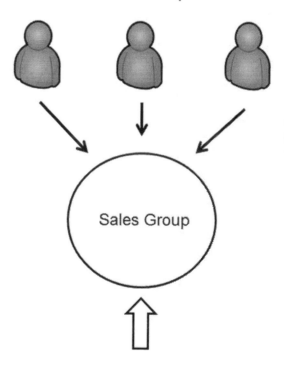

Figure 2.1: Establishing access with groups as roles

Administrators can use group membership to manage user accounts for any department. When a new employee is hired for a department, administrators create the account and place the account in the appropriate group. The new employee instantly has the appropriate level of access based on the rights and permissions assigned to the group.

> ### Remember this
>
> The use of roles, or groups, greatly simplifies user administration. Groups make it easier to grant appropriate permissions to new users, and they help enforce least privilege. The RBAC model can use user account templates to enforce the principle of least privilege. This ensures that new users are granted the access they need, and no more.

In contrast, if you assign permissions to users directly, they can be very difficult to manage. Imagine that people within the sales department need access to ten different resources (such as files, folders, and printers) within a network. When a new salesperson is hired, you need to manually assign permissions to these ten different resources requiring ten different administrative tasks. If you assigned the permissions to the sales group, you only need to add the user to the group once.

Groups provide another security benefit. Imagine that a user is promoted out of the sales department and now works in marketing. If you have a marketing group, you can place this user account into the marketing group and remove the account from the sales group. Removing the user from the sales group instantly removes all the rights and permissions from that group. However, if you're not using groups and assign permissions to users directly, you probably won't remember what resources were assigned to the user as a member of the sales department. Instead, the user will continue to have access to this sales data, violating the principle of least privilege.

Chapter 8 presents information on reviews of user rights and permissions as part of an auditing process. A routine user rights and permissions audit will detect when users have more rights and permissions than they need. However, using groups as part of a role-based access control model helps prevent the problem.

Using User Templates to Enforce Least Privilege

If you're using groups as part of a role-based access model, you can also use user templates. A user template is an account with basic settings that is copied to create new valid accounts. If the user template is a member of any groups, copies of the user template are also a member of these groups.

For example, you could create a user template for the sales department. This user account template is added to the appropriate groups, such as the sales group. When a new salesperson is hired, you can create a copy of the template, and the new salesperson would automatically be a member of the sales group (and any other groups determined appropriate for members of the sales department).

Discretionary Access Control

In the DAC model, every object (such as files and folders) has an owner, and the owner establishes access for the objects. Many operating systems, such as Windows and most UNIX-based systems, use the DAC model.

A common example of the DAC model is the New Technology File System (NTFS) used in Windows. NTFS provides security by allowing users and administrators to restrict access to files and folders with permissions. NTFS is based on the DAC model and the following section explains how it uses the DAC model.

Remember this

The DAC model specifies that every object has an owner, and the owner has full, explicit control of the object. Microsoft's NTFS uses the DAC model.

SIDs and DACLs

Each user is identified with a security identifier (SID), although you will rarely see it. A SID is a long string of characters that is meaningless to most of us and may look like this: S-1-5-21-3991871189-223218. Instead of the system displaying the SID, it will look up the name associated with the SID and display the name. Additionally, groups in Microsoft operating systems are identified with a SID.

Every object (such as a file or folder) includes a Discretionary Access Control List (DACL) that identifies who can access it in a system using the DAC model. The DACL is a list of Access Control Entries (ACEs). Each ACE is composed of a SID and the permission(s) granted to the SID.

Figure 2.2 shows an example of the DACL for a folder named Security+ Study Notes on a Windows 7 system. Each user or group account and its associated permissions make up an ACE.

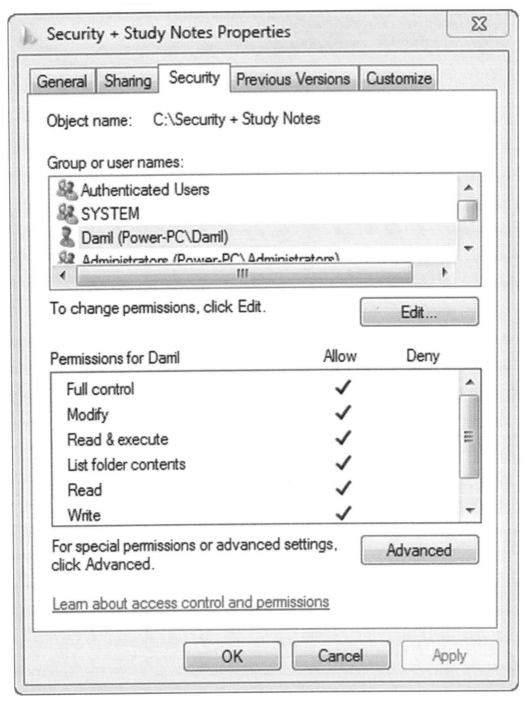

Figure 2.2: DACL in NTFS

You can view a DACL on a Microsoft system by following these steps:

1. Open Windows Explorer. One way is to press the Open Window+ E keys to launch Windows Explorer. The Open Window key is just to the left of the left Alt key on most keyboards.

2. Open up the C: drive to access the folders.
3. Right click any folder and select Properties.
4. Select the Security tab.
    a. You will see either user accounts, group accounts, or both. These accounts are actually held in the ACE as SIDs, but the system displays their names instead of the SID.
    b. Underneath the Group or User Names box, you will see the Permissions box showing the assigned permissions for the selected group or user. If you select a different group or user, you will see the permissions assigned to that group or user.

The Owner Establishes Access

If users create a file, they are designated as the owner and have explicit control over the file. As the owner, users can modify the permissions on the object by adding user or group accounts to the DACL and assigning the desired permissions.

The DAC model is significantly more flexible than the MAC model described in the next section. MAC has predefined access privileges, and the administrator is required to make the changes. With DAC, if you want to grant me access to a file you own, you simply make the change, and I have access.

Beware of Trojans

An inherent flaw associated with the DAC model is the susceptibility to Trojan horses. Chapter 6 will present malware in much more depth, but for this discussion, you should understand how Trojan horses work.

Trojan horses are executable files that masquerade as something useful but are actually malicious software. For example, Joe might decide to download and install a program that someone raved about. After installation, he decides it's not so great and forgets about it. However, the damage is done.

What really happened? When Joe installed the program, it also installed malicious software. Moreover, if Joe was logged on with administrative privileges when he installed it, the Trojan is able to run with these administrative privileges.

A common policy for anyone with an administrative account is to also have a regular user account. Most of the time, a user will be logged on with the regular account, and if that account is infected with some type of malware, it won't have the elevated permissions of an administrator.

Mandatory Access Control

The MAC model uses labels (sometimes referred to as sensitivity labels or security labels) to determine access. Both subjects (users) and objects (files or folders) are assigned labels. When the labels match, the appropriate permissions are granted.

SELinux (Security-Enhanced Linux) is one of the few operating systems that use the MAC model. SELinux is a trusted operating system platform that prevents malicious or suspicious code from executing on both Linux and UNIX systems.

Military units make wide use of this model to protect data. You may have seen movies where a folder is shown with a big red and black cover page with a label of "Top Secret." The cover page identifies the sensitivity label for the data contained within.

Only users who have a top secret label (a top secret clearance) and a need to know are granted access to the top secret folder. If users don't have a top secret clearance, they shouldn't be granted access.

Remember this

The MAC model uses sensitivity labels for users and data. SELinux (deployed in both Linux and UNIX platforms) is a trusted operating system platform using the MAC model that prevents malicious or suspicious code from executing on the system.

Labels and Lattice

The MAC model uses different levels of security to classify both the users and the data. These levels are defined in a lattice. The lattice can be a complex relationship between different ordered sets of multiple labels that define upper-level bounds and lower-level bounds.

You can think of a lattice like a trellis used to guide climbing plants like ivy or roses. The different levels of the trellis allow the plant to reach and climb to different levels. A lattice similarly has different levels, but these are defined as security levels such as "Top Secret," "Secret," and "Confidential" in the MAC model. Each level on the lattice identifies the start or end of a different security level, and the tiers between the levels identify the security boundaries.

Establishing Access

An administrator is responsible for establishing access, but only someone at a higher authority can define the access for subjects and objects.

Typically, a security professional identifies who is cleared for specific access and upgrades or downgrades an individual's access when needed. This person is also responsible for identifying privileges required to access different data. Note that the security professional does all this via paperwork and does not assign the rights and permissions on the computer. Instead, the administrator assigns the rights based on the direction of the security professional.

Multiple approval levels are usually involved in the decision-making process to determine what a user can access. For example, in the military an officer working in the security professional role would coordinate with higher-level entities. These higher-level entities actually approve or disapprove clearance requests.

Once an individual is formally granted access, a network administrator would be responsible for actually establishing access based on the clearances identified by the security professional. From the IT administrator's point of view, all the permissions and access privileges are predefined.

If someone needed different access, the administrator would forward the request to the security professional, who may approve or disapprove the request. On the other hand, the security professional may forward the request to higher entities based on established procedures. This process takes time and results in limited flexibility.

Understanding Physical Security Controls

Physical security includes all the elements employed to restrict physical access to buildings and hardware devices. This includes server rooms, datacenters, and individual devices such as servers, routers, and switches. It includes physical locks, access control mechanisms such as ID badges, and video monitoring.

Unlike the MAC, DAC, and RBAC models that are theoretical, physical security is physical in the sense that you can physically touch the different elements.

Access Controls

Access controls are used to control entry and exit at different boundary points. The different boundaries that can be controlled are:

- **Perimeter**. Military bases and many companies have a fence around the entire perimeter of the location, and access is often controlled at gates.
- **Building**. A building may have access controls to ensure that only authorized personnel are allowed in. Even when access isn't restricted, many buildings employ video cameras to monitor access.
- **Secure work areas**. Some companies restrict access to specific work areas where some type of classified or restricted access work is accomplished.
- **Server and network devices**. Servers and network devices such as routers and switches are normally stored in areas where only the appropriate IT personnel can access them. These spaces may be designated as server rooms or wiring closets. Providing additional physical security helps ensure they are not tampered with and ensures that illicit monitoring hardware, such as a sniffer, is not installed to capture traffic.

Door Access Systems

A door access system is one that only opens after some access control mechanism is used. It includes cipher locks and proximity cards.

An important consideration with door access systems is related to personnel security and fire. In the event of a fire, door access systems should allow personnel to exit the building without any form of authentication.

A basic step in physical security is to limit the number of access control points. If a datacenter has only one entrance and exit, it is much easier to monitor this single access point. You can control it with technical door locks, video surveillance, and guards. On the other hand, if the datacenter has two access points, you need another set of controls to control access.

> ### Remember this
> Door access systems include cipher locks and proximity cards. In the event of a fire, they should allow personnel to exit the building without any form of authentication. Access points to datacenters and server rooms should be limited to a single entrance and exit whenever possible.

Cipher Locks as a Door Access Systems

Cipher locks often have four or five buttons labeled with numbers. By pressing the numbers in a certain order, the lock is unlocked. For example, the cipher code could be 1, 3, 2, 4. By entering the code in the right order, you can gain access. Cipher locks can be electronic or manual. An electronic cipher lock automatically unlocks the door after the correct code is entered into a keypad. A manual cipher lock requires the user to turn a handle after entering the code.

To add complexity and reduce brute force attacks, many manual cipher locks include a code that requires two numbers entered at the same time. Instead of just 1, 3, 2, 4, the code could be 1/3 (entered at the same time), then 2, 4, 5.

Proximity Cards as a Door Access Systems

Proximity cards are small credit-card-sized cards that activate when they are in close proximity to a card reader. Many organizations use these for access points, such as the entry to a building or the entry to a controlled area within a building. The door uses an electronic lock that only unlocks when the user passes the proximity card in front of a card reader.

You've probably seen proximity card readers as credit card readers. You can see them at gasoline pumps and many fast-food restaurants. Instead of swiping the credit card, you can simply pass it in front of the reader (in close proximity to the reader), and the information on the card is read.

It's intriguing how this is accomplished. The card doesn't require its own power source. Instead, the electronics in the card include a capacitor and a coil that can accept a charge from the proximity card reader. When you pass the card close to the reader, the reader excites the coil and stores a charge in the capacitor. Once charged, the card will transmit information to the reader using a radio frequency. The information can be a simple signal to unlock the door, or it can include details on the user and record the user's access time in a database.

While a proximity card falls into the *something you have* factor of authentication, it should not be used without combining it with another factor such as a PIN. If users swap their cards, they will be granted access even though they haven't been authenticated. In other words, this results in authorization verification without authentication.

Proximity card technology can be used in:

- **Access points**. Access to rooms can be controlled with proximity cards and key pads requiring the user to have something and know something. Proximity cards are sometimes used with turnstiles to provide access for a single person at a time. These are the same type of turnstiles used as entry gates in subways, stadiums, and amusement parts.
- **Credit cards**. Many credit card readers at fast food restaurants and gas pumps use proximity card technology.
- **Mass transit entry points**. Cards can be sold with a set number of passes for bus or subway rides, or with an expiration date.

Remember this

Proximity cards are credit-card-sized access cards, and users pass the card near a proximity card reader. The card reader then reads data on the card. Proximity cards are used as access control in some areas to electronically unlock doors, and fall into the *something you have* factor of authentication. However, if users swap cards, it results in authorization verification without authentication. In other words, they are granted access (authorization) but their identity hasn't actually been proved (authentication).

As a side note, one of the worrisome issues related to these cards is that attackers can build or purchase systems that can read your credit cards if they operate as proximity cards. The attacker places the reader in a purse or bag and positions it close to your wallet or purse, perhaps by standing behind you in the elevator, a store, or a line. The electronics on the card would charge and then transmit without your knowledge. The collected information can be used later to make unauthorized purchases.

About the only way to prevent this is to wrap your credit cards in some type of shielding, like aluminum foil. I've heard of companies selling credit card shield protectors for as much as $29.95. Of course, you can make your own shield with a couple of well-placed pieces of aluminum foil in your wallet or purse.

Physical Access Control—ID Badges

Identification badges (ID badges) provide visual confirmation that someone is authorized in a certain area. ID badges will usually include information on the holder and a picture.

Building or secure area access points may be staffed with guards that check to ensure that everyone who enters has an ID badge. Additionally, within secure areas, users wear their ID badges so that others can see they are authorized within the area. Users clip the badge to their pocket or connect it to a lanyard that they wear around their neck.

You can also combine other electronic measures with an ID badges. For example, chapter 1 introduced common access cards (CACs), which are a combination of an ID badge and a smart card. Some badges work as proximity cards to automatically open doors by placing the badge in front of a reader. Other badges have a magnetic strip similar to a credit card that includes information on the user.

Physical Access Lists and Logs

Some organizations maintain physical access lists. Guards staff entry points, and if individuals are not on the list, they are not allowed in. Additionally, the guards can maintain physical access logs to show when employees enter or exit.

When access points include electronic measures such as proximity card readers that record information on users, access logs can verify exactly when someone enters or exits a building. When used for this purpose, the ID badges uniquely identify each holder to support accurate logging.

You can also use these logs to identify security vulnerabilities. For example, if a log shows that a user exited a building but does not show that the user entered the building, it indicates tailgating or piggybacking has occurred.

While these access logs are very useful, it's worth noting that video surveillance (covered later in this chapter) provides the most reliable proof of a person's location and activity. Someone may steal a proximity card, but they can't steal a person's likeness shown on a video.

Tailgating

Tailgating (also called piggybacking) occurs when one user follows closely behind another user without using credentials. For example, one user can open the door with a proximity card, and the second user follows without using a proximity card. If this often occurs with authorized users, it indicates the environment is susceptible to a social engineering attack where an unauthorized user follows closely behind an authorized user.

> ### Remember this
> Tailgating occurs when one user follows closely behind another user without using credentials. Mantraps and security guards are effective controls against tailgating.

As an example, an organization hired a security company to perform a vulnerability assessment. The company sent one of its top security professionals (an attractive woman) to see if she could get into the building. She saw that access to the building was controlled with proximity cards. She loaded herself up with a book bag and a laptop, ensuring her hands weren't free. She timed her approach carefully and followed closely behind an employee with a proximity card. She gave a friendly smile, and sure enough, the employee held the door open for her.

We're trained to be polite, not rude, and social engineers take advantage of this training. It's polite to hold a door open for a man or a woman that has their hands full. Many of us were trained that it's rude to slam the door in the face of someone following behind us. This is one of the many reasons why it's important to educate users on risks and vulnerabilities.

High traffic areas are the most susceptible to tailgating. Security guards can be an effective preventative measure at access points, but they need to be vigilant to ensure that tailgating does not occur.

Mantraps

A mantrap is a physical security mechanism designed to control access to a secure area through a buffer zone. Personnel use something like a proximity card to gain access, and the mantrap allows one person, and only one person, to pass through. Mantraps get their name due to their ability to lock a person between two areas, such as an open access area and a secure access area.

Mantraps are an effective deterrent against the social engineering tactic of tailgating or piggybacking. A tailgating attack is when a person who isn't authorized to enter an area follows closely behind someone who is authorized. The first person uses credentials, but the second person gains entry without credentials.

> ### *Remember this*
>
> Mantraps control the access between a secure area and a nonsecure area. They are very effective at preventing unauthorized access to sensitive areas of a building. They can prevent the social engineering tactic known as tailgating or piggybacking. Mantraps can be highly technical, including rooms made of bulletproof glass, or simplistic, similar to a turnstile used in subways.

Mantraps can be sophisticated or simple. A sophisticated mantrap is a room, or even a building, that creates a large buffer area between the secure area and the unsecured area. Access through the entry door and the exit door is tightly controlled, either through the use of guards or with an access card such as a proximity card. An example of a simple mantrap is a turnstile that can be locked before the turnstile turns completely through to the other side.

Security Guards

It's also possible to use security guards to control the access to secure spaces. Individuals can be required to show identity badges with a picture, such as a common access card (CAC), described in chapter 1. On the other hand, the security guard can just be there as a preventative control to ensure each person is using a proximity card to gain access and not tailgating behind another employee.

Video Surveillance (CCTV)

Security cameras are increasingly being used in the workplace and surrounding areas for video surveillance. Video surveillance is often referred to as closed-circuit television (CCTV) because it transmits signals from video cameras to monitors that are similar to TVs.

Video cameras are often used within a work environment to protect employees and enhance security in the workplace. In addition to monitoring, most video surveillance systems include a recording element, and they can verify if the company's equipment or data is being removed. By recording activity, it can be played back later for investigation and even prosecution.

Video surveillance provides the most reliable proof of a person's location and activity. Access logs provide a record, but it's possible to circumvent the security of an access log. For example, if I use your proximity card to gain access to a secure space, the log will indicate you entered, not me. In contrast, if the video shows that I entered the room at a certain time of day, the video can't be refuted.

> **Remember this**
> Video surveillance provides reliable proof of a person's location and activity. It can be used by an organization to verify if any equipment or data is being removed.

When using video surveillance in a work environment, it's important to respect privacy and to be aware of privacy laws. Some things to consider are:

- **Only record activity in public areas**. People have a reasonable expectation of privacy in certain areas, such as locker rooms or restrooms, and it is often illegal to record activity in these areas.
- **Notify employees of the surveillance**. If employees aren't notified of the surveillance, legal issues related to the video surveillance can arise. This is especially true if the recordings are used to take actions against the employee.
- **Do not record audio**. Recording audio is often illegal without the express consent of all parties being recorded. Many companies won't even sell surveillance cameras that record audio.

Camera Types

Multiple different camera types can be used depending on your needs. They include:

- **Wireless**. Wireless cameras have built-in transceivers that can be used to transmit the video to a wireless receiver, often up to seven hundred feet away. This is similar to how any wireless device such as a wireless laptop may connect to a wireless network. The benefit is that additional wiring isn't required. Additionally, while a wired connection can be cut to stop the recording, a wireless connection doesn't have any cable to cut.
- **Wired**. Wired cameras are more common and include the wiring to carry the video back to the recorder or display.
- **Low-light**. Low-light (or low-lux) cameras have the ability to record activity even in low-light conditions. This prevents someone from simply killing the lights to

prevent any video recording. Low-light cameras usually use either infrared or thermal technologies.

- **Color**. Most video cameras are color unless they are specifically designed to capture activity in low-light conditions. For regular lighting conditions, a color camera provides a better picture with no appreciable increase in cost.
- **Black and white**. Low-light cameras are generally black and white since both thermal and infrared technologies can't capture the color in low-light conditions.

Camera Positioning

When considering the use of video cameras, the basic question to ask is, "What do you want to record?" The answer will dictate where you'll place the camera. Cameras can be placed where they can monitor the entrances and exits of buildings or individual rooms. They can also be placed where they can monitor the activity of specific high-risk areas.

Some rooms may require the use of multiple cameras: one could record everyone who enters the room; another camera could record everyone who exits the room; and a third wide-angle camera could record all the activity within the room.

In addition to deciding how and where a camera is positioned, you can also consider whether the camera should be stationary or adjustable. Video surveillance cameras are classified as:

- **Fixed**. A fixed camera can only look at one area and doesn't include any zooming or repositioning ability.
- **PTZ**. Some cameras can pan (move left and right), tilt (move up and down), and zoom to get a closer or a wider view. Panning, tilting, zooming (PTZ) cameras are often used in public establishments with security personnel operating the cameras. PTZ cameras are more expensive than fixed cameras.

Physical Tokens

Chapter 1 included information on authentication. Tokens were described as key fobs or RSA tokens, such as those sold by RSA Secure ID. While these tokens are most often used for authentication with websites, they can also be used for access control.

As a reminder, these physical tokens have an LCD display that shows a number that regularly changes, such as every sixty seconds. This number is synchronized with a server that knows what the number on the token is at any time. The user enters the displayed number into the door access mechanism. As long as the number is correct, the door opens.

Hardware Locks

Of course, you can implement simple physical security to prevent access to secure areas. A hardware lock could be just like the locks you use to secure your home and belongings.

Hardware locks are frequently used in smaller companies that don't have the resources to employ advanced security systems. Server rooms and/or wiring closets are frequently just smaller rooms used to house servers and network devices, such as routers and switches. Hardware locks help prevent unauthorized access to these areas.

The number of laptops stolen during lunches at conferences is astronomical. Many people don't seem to know how common thefts are and often leave their laptops unprotected. Cable locks can secure a mobile computer, and even many desktop computers at work. If you've ever had a cable lock to secure your bicycle, you can envision one of these the same way. The user wraps the cable around a desk, table, or something heavy, and then plugs it into an opening in the laptop specifically created for this purpose. In order for the thief to steal the laptop, they either need to destroy the laptop to remove the lock or take the desk with the laptop.

Locked cabinets or safes help prevent the theft of smaller devices. For example, smaller devices such as external USB drives or USB flash drives aren't used continuously. When they aren't in use, a locked cabinet helps prevent their theft.

Understanding Logical Access Controls

Logical access control methods are implemented through technologies such as access control lists or Group Policy. They control access to the logical network as opposed to controlling access to the physical areas of a building or physical access to devices within the network.

The different methods used to provide logical access control include access control lists, Group Policy, and account management. Each of these topics is covered in this section.

Least Privilege

The principle of least privilege is an example of a technical control that uses access controls. Privileges are the rights and permissions assigned to users. Least privilege specifies that individuals and processes are granted only the rights and permissions needed to perform assigned tasks or functions, but no more. For example, if Joe needs to print to a printer, you should grant him print permission for that printer, but nothing else.

This principle also applies to administrators. Not every IT administrator needs full administrative rights on every device within the network. If an administrator only needs to be able to review logs and update specific network devices, the administrator should be given appropriate access to these logs and devices, and no more.

> **Remember this**
>
> The RBAC model uses roles (often implemented as groups) to grant access by placing users into roles based on their assigned jobs, functions, or tasks. A user account is placed into a role, inheriting the rights and permissions of the role. Rule-based access control is based on a set of approved instructions, such as an access control list.

A colleague shared an extreme example of how this principle was violated where he worked. He was the lone IT administrator, and no matter how much he asked for help, his boss was never able to get him additional staff. The company grew, and he found he was fielding many complaints because users didn't have the access they needed. He knew he needed to improve the administrative model with groups and roles, but he just didn't have enough time.

The users complained to his boss, who then put pressure on him. The boss's direction was simply: "Fix this problem!"

Ultimately, he put all the users into the Domain Admins group. In a Windows Active Directory domain, the Domain Admins group has full rights and permissions to do anything and everything in a domain. Suddenly, all the users had full privileges. This was the equivalent of lighting the fuse on a time bomb. It would only be a matter of time before users purposely or accidentally caused problems with their newfound permissions.

Ironically, his boss was happy because the users stopped complaining. I heard from him a couple of months later. One of the users found payroll data on the network and discovered the salaries of other employees. It spread through the company quickly and caused a significant amount of infighting. At that point, his boss's boss wasn't very happy.

It takes a little time and effort to implement role-based access control with groups, as described earlier in this chapter. However, it reduces overall administration and helps to implement the principle of least privilege.

Access Control Lists

Access control lists (ACLs) are used to specifically identify what is allowed and what is not allowed. An ACL can define what is allowed based on permissions or based on traffic.

ACLs typically operate using an implicit deny policy. For example, NTFS uses a DACL to identify who is allowed access to a file or a folder. Unless someone explicitly grants permission for a user to access the file (either directly through a user account or through group membership), permission is implicitly denied.

Routers also use ACLs. An ACL in a router is a list of rules that define what traffic is allowed. If the traffic meets the requirements of one of the rules, it is allowed. If it doesn't meet the requirements for any of the rules, the traffic is denied. This is often implemented with an explicit rule at the end of the list that denies all traffic not explicitly allowed. The last rule might look like "deny any any" to block all traffic not defined in other rules. In many routers, the rule is implied. In other words, even if the deny rule isn't added, the router will only route traffic identified in previous rules. Chapter 3 covers routers in more depth.

Group Policy

Windows domains use Group Policy to manage multiple users and computers in a domain. Group Policy allows an administrator to configure a setting once in a Group Policy object (GPO) and apply this setting to many users and computers within the domain. Group Policy is implemented on a domain controller in a domain, but can also be applied to individual computers.

Remember this

Group policy is implemented on a domain controller within a domain. Administrators use it to create password policies, lock down the GUI, configure host-based firewalls, and much more.

As an example, you may want to ensure that the firewall is configured a certain way or the graphical user interface (GUI) is secured on all the systems in your domain. You can configure a GPO, link the GPO to the domain, and the setting applies to all the computers in the domain. The magic of Group Policy is that it doesn't matter if you have five systems or five thousand systems. The policy still only needs to be set once to apply to all of them.

Group Policy can also be targeted to groups of users or computers. Active Directory allows you to organize user accounts and computer accounts into organizational units (OUs). You can then create a GPO and link it to the OU. This allows you to apply more specific settings to users and computers within an OU that don't apply to users and computers in another OU.

Using a Password Policy

Organizations commonly use a password policy to ensure that users create strong passwords and change them periodically. A password policy often starts as a written document. Administrators then enforce the password policy with a technical control. For example, in a Microsoft Active Directory domain, Group Policy is used to enforce a password policy for all users in the organization.

Figure 2.3 shows the password policy for a Windows domain and the following text explains these settings.

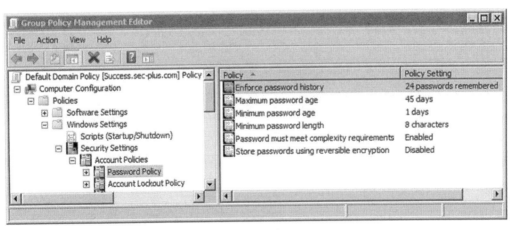

Figure 2.3: Password policy in Windows domain

- **Enforce password history**. Some users will change back and forth between two passwords that they constantly use and reuse. However, password history remembers past passwords and prevents the user from reusing previously used passwords. For example, setting this to twenty-four prevents users from reusing passwords until they've used twenty-four new passwords.

- **Maximum password age**. This setting defines when users must change their password. For example, if the maximum password age is set to forty-five, it expires on the forty-sixth day. Once the password expires, users can't log on until they change it.
- **Minimum password age**. The minimum password age defines how long a user must wait before changing the password again. If this were set to one day, the user wouldn't be able to change the password again until a day has passed. This is useful with a password history to prevent users from changing their password multiple times until they get back to the original password. If the password history is set to twenty-four and the minimum password age is set to one day, it'll take a user twenty-five days to get back to the original password. This is enough to discourage most users.
- **Minimum password length**. This setting enforces the character length of the password. It's common to require users to have passwords at least eight characters long, but some organizations require users to have passwords as long as fifteen characters.
- **Password must meet complexity requirements**. This setting requires users to have complex passwords that include at least three of the four character types (upper case, lower case, numbers, and special characters). You may remember from chapter 1 that you increase the key space (or complexity) of a password by using more character types.
- **Store passwords using reversible encryption**. Reversible encryption stores the password in such a way that the original password can be discovered. This is rarely enabled.

If an administrator creates the initial password for a user or resets the password, the administrator should set the password to expire immediately. This is the same as a password reaching its maximum age and forces the user to reset the password before logging on. If more than one person knows the credentials for an account, the credentials no longer uniquely identify the individual—someone else could log on with the same credentials, and even if the event is logged, you can't prove who did it.

Remember this

Password policies include several elements. The password history is used with the minimum password age to prevent users from changing their password. Maximum password age causes passwords to expire and requires users to change their passwords periodically. Minimum password length specifies the minimum number of characters in the password. Password complexity increases the key space, or complexity, of a password by requiring more character types.

Domain Password Policy

In Windows Server 2003 and 2008 domains, a single password policy applies to all users in the domain. It doesn't matter if the domain has five users or five thousand users. When an administrator sets the password policy, it applies to all users.

A drawback in a Windows Server 2003 domain is that the domain can have only one password policy. Windows Server 2008 added the capability to apply additional password policies to different groups. For example, a standard password policy could be applied to all users in the domain, and then a special password policy could be created requiring anyone in a group defined by the administrator to use a stronger password.

Device Policy

It's also possible to use Group Policy to enforce the restriction of portable devices in a network. Small devices such as flash drives and portable media players can easily become infected with viruses, and, once infected, those devices can insert the virus into a system.

When these small devices are inserted into a computer, the operating system detects the installation and can be configured to automatically run software on the device. Similarly, if a system is infected with malware, the malware can spread to the small device as soon as it's plugged in. Then, when the device is inserted into another system, the malware spreads to the other system.

If the malware includes a worm component, it can quickly spread through the network after the USB is inserted and the malware is installed on a single system. Many companies employ two protections against this threat, both of which can be enforced with Group Policy:

- **Disable Autorun**. Autorun causes an application to run as soon as a user inserts a device into a system. Malware adds a virus to the device and modifies the autorun.inf file to run this virus each time the user inserts the device. When Autorun is disabled, the executables identified in the autorun.inf file cannot execute by default.
- **Prevent the installation of small devices**. Administrators can prevent the installation of drivers such as for USB flash drives or MP3 players. This prevents systems from recognizing the devices and reduces the risks from these devices.
- **Detect the use of small devices**. You can enforce a written policy through automatic detection. As an example, one company told all employees via e-mail and logon banners that USB drives were expressly forbidden. Further, an executive stated publicly that the company took this rule very seriously and there would be serious consequences if anyone violated the rule. Within a week, an employee plugged in a USB drive, automatic detection detected it, and the employee was looking for another job the next day.

USB Flash Drives and Malware

A security professional was hired to perform a vulnerability assessment for a bank. She dropped multiple USB flash drives in the bank's parking lot before the bank opened and then dropped more inside the bank in areas accessible by bank employees.

Eventually, one of the employees found one of the flash drives and inserted it into his system. Bingo! Simply inserting the flash drive into the system exploited a vulnerability. The Start program on the flash drive (launched through Autorun) installed malware, including a keylogger that captured the employee's keystrokes and later e-mailed the captured data to the security professional performing the vulnerability assessment.

Employees finding these USB drives could have good intentions. Perhaps they want to return the USB flash drive to the owner, so decide to look on the flash drive to see if any data would identify the owner. However, the intentions of the employee don't really matter. The malware that is installed onto USB flash drives and the attackers behind the malware don't have good intentions.

This widely known example is a key reason why many organizations restrict the use of flash drives on company computers. It may be inconvenient, but it's also a sound layer of security. If employees find unattended USB drives, they should contact security professionals within the organization. These security professionals have the tools and expertise to examine the devices without risking exposure to the network.

Account Management

Account management is concerned with the creation, management, and disabling or termination of accounts. When the account is active, access control methods are used to control what the user can do. Additionally, administrators use access controls to control when and where users can log on.

Centralized and Decentralized Account Management

As a reminder, users have user accounts with passwords that they use to authenticate. The user knows the username and password, and an authentication server authenticates the user. User accounts can be managed in a centralized or decentralized environment.

- **Centralized**. All user accounts are stored in a central database (such as Active Directory in a Windows domain). A centralized user account database helps provide single sign-on since users only need to sign on once to the domain. Chapter 1 mentioned that Lightweight Directory Access Protocol (LDAP) is a protocol that supports centralized management. It provides a central location for user and other account management.
- **Decentralized**. User accounts are stored on each individual workstation or server. A user could have multiple accounts to access multiple systems. On Windows systems, the local database storing local user accounts is the Security Accounts Manager (SAM). The SAM provides a decentralized user account database.

Disabling and Deleting Accounts

Many organizations have account management policies (sometimes called account disablement policies) that specify what to do with accounts in different situations. In general, policies require administrators to disable inactive accounts. When the organization determines that the account is no longer needed, administrators delete it. For example, they may decide to keep inactive accounts for sixty or ninety days before deleting them.

Some of the contents of an account management policy include:

- **Terminated employee**. An account disablement policy specifies that accounts for ex-employees should be disabled. This ensures a terminated employee doesn't become a disgruntled ex-employee that wreaks havoc on the network. Note that "terminated" refers to both employees that resign and employees that are fired.
- **Leave of absence**. If an employee will be absent for an extended period of time, the account should be disabled while the employee is away.

Remember this

Account management will specify what to do with an account for employees on a leave of absence or terminated. An account disablement policy ensures that inactive accounts are disabled. This is useful to ensure that terminated employee accounts cannot be used. Normally, accounts are disabled so that access to account data is maintained until the company is sure it is no longer needed.

Time-of-day Restrictions

Time-of-day restrictions specify when users can actually log on to a computer. If a user tries to log in to the network outside the restricted time, access is denied.

Figure 2.4 shows the time-of-day restrictions for a user account in a Windows domain.

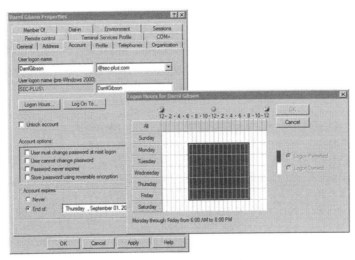

Figure 2.4: User account properties with time restrictions

As an example, a company may operate between 8 a.m. and 5 p.m. on a daily basis. Managers decide they don't want regular users logging in to the network except between 6 a.m. and 8 p.m. You could set time-of-day restrictions for user accounts, and if someone tried to log in outside the restricted time (such as at midnight), the logon attempt would be denied.

If users were working overtime on a project, they would not be logged off when the time restriction was reached. For example, if Sally were working late on a critical project, the system wouldn't log her off at 8 p.m. when the time restriction is reached. However, the time restriction would prevent her from creating any new network connections.

Account Expiration

It's possible to set user accounts to expire automatically. When the account expires, the system disables it, and the user is no longer able to log in using the account.

If you look back at figure 2.4, it shows the properties of an account. The Account Expires section is at the bottom of the page, and the account is set to expire on September 1. When September 1 arrives, the account is automatically disabled and the user will no longer be able to log on.

It's common to configure temporary accounts to expire. For example, an organization may hire a contractor for a ninety-day period to perform a specific job. An administrator creates an account for the contractor and sets it to expire in ninety days. If the contract is extended, it's a simple matter to change the expiration date and enable the account.

Account Access Review

It's possible to verify the time and date when any users log on or accesses a system within a network. This is referred to as an account login audit. Most systems don't have this enabled by default, but it is fairly easy to set it up.

Configuring logging of logon attempts is an important security step for system monitoring. When users first log on to their account, it's recorded as a logon action. Additionally, when users access a resource over the network (such as to a file server), it is also recorded as a logon action. Single sign-on is often enabled so users don't have to provide their credentials again, but it is still recorded as a logon action. Many organizations have centralized monitoring of logs to make this daunting task manageable.

> ### Remember this
> You can identify when a user logs on to a local system and when a user accesses a remote system by monitoring account logon events. Configuring account logon monitoring is an important security step for system monitoring.

You can identify if someone is trying to hack into an account by monitoring failed logon attempts. If a log shows fifty failed logon attempts followed by a success, it indicates someone successfully guessed the password for an account. Chapter 1 presented information related to account lockout policies where a system locks out an account after so many failed logon attempts. However, the administrator account cannot be locked out. If the name of the administrator account is not changed (a standard security practice) and someone tries to hack into it, an account login audit will capture the details.

You can identify specifically when a user accesses a remote system by monitoring logins on the remote system. This is very useful in a network and documents system access.

Chapter 8 covers logs in more depth, including security logs. As a brief introduction, security logs will record who took an action, what action they took, where they took it, and when they took it. In other words, if users access a file server over a network, the audit log entries would show the user identities, when they accessed the server, what server they accessed, and what computer they used to access the server. Users would not be able to refute the recorded action, since auditing provides non-repudiation.

Chapter 2 Exam Topic Review

When preparing for the exam, make sure you understand these key concepts covered in this chapter.

Basic Control Types

- A technical control is one that uses technology to reduce vulnerabilities. The principle of least privilege is a technical control.
- Management controls are primarily administrative and include items such as risk and vulnerability assessments.
- Operational controls help ensure that day-to-day operations of an organization comply with their overall security plan. Some examples include training, configuration management, and change management.
- Preventative controls attempt to prevent an incident from occurring. Examples include change management plans, security guards, account disablement policies, and user training.
- Detective controls can detect when a vulnerability has been exploited. Examples include security audits, such as a periodic review of user rights, and a CCTV system that can record and provide proof of a person's actions, such as theft of resources.
- Corrective controls attempt to reverse the impact of an incident or problem after it has occurred. Examples include active intrusion detection systems, backups, and system recovery plans.

Access Control Models

- The role based access control (RBAC) model uses roles (often implemented as groups) to grant access by placing users into roles based on their assigned jobs, functions, or tasks. Roles, or groups, simplify administration. RBAC supports the use of user templates to enforce least privilege.

- The rule based access control (RBAC) model is based on a set of approved instructions, such as access control list rules in a firewall.
- In the discretionary access control (DAC) model, every object has an owner. The owner has explicit access and establishes access for any other user. Microsoft's NTFS uses the DAC model, with every object having a Discretionary Access Control List (DACL). The DACL identifies who has access and what access they are granted. A major flaw of the DAC model is its susceptibility to Trojan horses.
- Mandatory access control (MAC) uses security or sensitivity labels to identify objects (what you'll secure) and subjects (users). The administrator establishes access based on predefined security labels that are typically defined with a lattice to specify the upper and lower security boundaries.

Physical Security Controls

- Cipher locks and proximity cards are two examples of systems that control access at a door. In the event of a fire, they should allow personnel to exit the building without any form of authentication. Datacenters and server rooms should have only a single entrance and exit.
- A proximity card can electronically unlock a door and helps prevent unauthorized personnel from entering a secure area. It falls into the *something you have* factor of authentication. If users swap cards, it results in authorization verification without authentication, since they are granted access without ever being authenticated.
- Security guards are a preventative physical security control, and they can prevent unauthorized personnel from entering a secure area.
- Closed-circuit television (CCTV) systems provide video surveillance. They provide reliable proof of a person's location and activity, and can be used by an organization to verify if any equipment or data is being removed.
- Tailgating (also called piggybacking) occurs when one user follows closely behind another user without using credentials. A mantrap can prevent tailgating. Security guards should be especially vigilant to watch for tailgating in high traffic areas.
- Physical security also includes basic locks on doors and cabinets. Locked cabinets can prevent the theft of unused resources. Cable locks secure mobile computers.

Logical Access Controls

- The principle of least privilege is a technical control that uses access controls. It specifies that individuals or processes are granted only the rights and permissions needed to perform assigned tasks or functions, but no more.
- Group policy manages users and computers in a domain, and it is implemented on a domain controller within a domain. Administrators use it to create password policies, lock down the GUI, configure host-based firewalls, and much more.
- Password policies provide a technical means to ensure users employ secure password practices.

- Password length specifies minimum number of characters.
- Password history remembers past passwords and prevents users from reusing passwords.
- Minimum password age is used with password history to prevent users from changing their password repeatedly to get back to the original password.
- Maximum password age or password expiration forces users to change their password periodically. When administrators reset user passwords, the password should be immediately expired.

- An account disablement policy ensures that inactive accounts are disabled. Accounts for employees that either resign or are terminated should be disabled. Temporary accounts should be set to automatically disable when possible.
- Time restrictions can prevent users from logging in or accessing network resources during specific hours.
- Account logon events include when a user logs on locally, and when the user accesses a resource such as a server over the network. These events are logged and can be monitored.

Chapter 2 Practice Questions

1. Of the following choices, what type of control is least privilege?
   A. Corrective
   B. Technical
   C. Detective
   D. Preventative

2. Of the following choices, what type of control is a vulnerability assessment?
   A. Corrective
   B. Management
   C. Detective
   D. Technical

3. Which of the following is a preventative control that can prevent outages due to ad-hoc configuration errors?
   A. Least privilege
   B. A periodic review of user rights
   C. Change management plan
   D. Security audit

4. Which of the following is a preventative control?
   A. Least privilege
   B. Security audit
   C. Security guard
   D. Periodic review of user rights

5. Your organization regularly performs routine security audits to assess the security posture. What type of control is this?
   A. Corrective
   B. Technical
   C. Detective
   D. Preventative

6. Of the following choices, what is a detective security control?
   A. Change management
   B. HVAC
   C. CCTV
   D. User training

7. An administrator is assigning access to users in different departments based on their job functions. What access control model is the administrator using?

    A. DAC
    B. MAC
    C. RBAC
    D. CAC

8. You manage user accounts for a sales department. You have created a sales user account template to comply with the principle of least privilege. What access control model are you following?

    A. DAC
    B. MAC
    C. RBAC
    D. DACL

9. Windows systems protect files and folders with New Technology File System (NTFS). What access control model does NTFS use?

    A. Mandatory access control (MAC)
    B. Discretionary access control (DAC)
    C. Rule-based access control (RBAC)
    D. Implicit allow

10. What is the purpose of a cipher lock system?

    A. Control door access with a keypad
    B. Control door access with a proximity card
    C. Control access to a laptop with biometrics
    D. Control access to laptop with a smart card

11. What can you use to electronically unlock a door for specific users?

    A. Token
    B. Proximity card
    C. Physical key
    D. Certificate

12. An organization wants to prevent unauthorized personnel from entering a secure workspace. Of the following choices, what can be used? (Choose two).

    A. Security guard
    B. Piggybacking
    C. CCTV
    D. Proximity cards

13. A company hosts a datacenter with highly sensitive data. Of the following choices, what can provide the best type of physical security to prevent unauthorized entry?
    A. Proximity card
    B. CCTV
    C. ID badges
    D. Mantrap

14. Two employees have entered a secure datacenter. However, only one employee provided credentials. How did the other employee gain entry?
    A. Mantrap
    B. HVAC
    C. Vishing
    D. Tailgating

15. Your organization has several portable USB drives that users are able to use to transfer large video files instead of copying them over the network. What should be used to prevent the theft of these drives when they are not being used?
    A. HSM
    B. TPM
    C. Video surveillance
    D. Locked cabinet

16. Your organization requires users to create passwords of at least ten characters for their user accounts. Which of the following is being enforced?
    A. Password length
    B. Password complexity
    C. Password masking
    D. Password history

17. Your password policy includes a password history. What else should be configured to ensure that users aren't able to easily reuse the same password?
    A. Maximum age
    B. Minimum age
    C. Password masking
    D. Password complexity

18. Your organization has a password policy that requires employees to change their passwords at least every forty-five days and prevents users from reusing any of their last five passwords. However, when forced to change their passwords, users are changing their passwords five more times to keep their original password. What can resolve this security vulnerability?
   - A. Modify the password policy to prevent users from changing the password until a day has passed
   - B. Modify the password policy to require users to change their password after a day has passed
   - C. Modify the password policy to remember the last twelve passwords
   - D. Modify the password policy to remember the last twenty-four passwords

19. A user has forgotten his password and calls the help desk for assistance. The help-desk professional will reset the password and tell the user the new password. What should the help desk professional configure to ensure the user immediately resets the password?
   - A. Password complexity
   - B. Password masking
   - C. Password history
   - D. Password expiration

20. Users in your network are required to change their passwords every sixty days. What is this an example of?
   - A. Password expiration requirement
   - B. Password history requirement
   - C. Password length requirement
   - D. Password strength requirement

21. Your company has hired a temporary contractor that needs a computer account for sixty days. You want to ensure the account is automatically disabled after sixty days. What feature would you use?
   - A. Account lockout
   - B. Account expiration
   - C. Deletion through automated scripting
   - D. Manual deletion

22. After an employee is terminated, what should be done to revoke the employee's access?
   - A. Expire the password
   - B. Lock out the account
   - C. Delete the account
   - D. Disable the account

23. Management wants to prevent users in the Marketing Department from logging onto network systems between 6 p.m. and 5 a.m. How can this be accomplished?

    A. Use time-of-day restrictions

    B. Account expiration

    C. Password expiration

    D. Implement a detective control

24. You have recently added a server to your network that will host data used and updated by employees. You want to monitor security events on the system. Of the following, what is the most important security event to monitor?

    A. Data modifications

    B. TCP connections

    C. UDP connections

    D. Account logon attempts

Chapter 2 Practice Question Answers

1. **B.** The principle of least privilege is a technical control and ensures that users have only the rights and permissions needed to perform the job, and no more. A corrective control attempts to reverse the effects of a problem. A detective control (such as a security audit) detects when a vulnerability has been exploited. A preventative control attempts to prevent an incident from occurring.

2. **B.** A vulnerability assessment is a management control and attempts to discover weaknesses in systems. A corrective control attempts to reverse the effects of a problem. A detective control (such as a security audit) detects when a vulnerability has been exploited. A technical control (such as the principle of least privilege) enforces security using technical means.

3. **C.** A change management strategy can prevent outages by ensuring that configuration changes aren't made on an as-needed (ad-hoc) basis, but instead are examined prior to making the change; change management is also known as an operational control. The principle of least privilege is a technical control and ensures that users have only the rights and permissions needed to perform the job, and no more. A security audit is a detective control and a periodic review of user rights is a specific type of detective control.

4. **C.** A security guard (armed or not armed) is a preventative physical security control. The principle of least privilege is a technical control and ensures that users have only the rights and permissions needed to perform the job, and no more. A security audit is a detective control and a periodic review of user rights is a specific type of detective control.

5. **C.** A security audit is a form of detective control, since it will detect when a vulnerability has been exploited after the fact. A corrective control attempts to reverse the effects of a problem. A technical control (such as the principle of least privilege) enforces security using technical means. A preventative control attempts to prevent an incident from occurring.

6. **C.** A closed-circuit television (CCTV) system can record activity and can detect what occurred as a detective security control. Change management is a preventative control. HVAC is an environmental control that is preventative. User training is preventative.

7. **C.** In a role-based access control (RBAC) model, roles are used to define rights and permissions for users. The DAC model specifies that every object has an owner, and the owner has full, explicit control of the object. The MAC model uses sensitivity labels for users and data. A CAC is an identification card that includes smart-card capabilities.

8. **C.** The role-based access control (RBAC) model can use groups (as roles) with a user account template assigned to a group to ensure new users are granted access only to what they need, and no more. The DAC model specifies that every object has an owner, and the owner has full,

explicit control of the object. The MAC model uses sensitivity labels for users and data. A DACL is an access control list used in the DAC model.

9. **B.** Windows systems use the discretionary access control (DAC) model by default for NTFS files and folders. The MAC model uses labels. Rule-based access control uses rules to determine access. There is no such access control model as implicit allow. However, implicit deny is commonly used as the last rule in a firewall to indicate that all traffic not explicitly allowed is implicitly denied.

10. **A.** A cipher lock system is a door access security method and only opens after a user has entered the correct code into the cipher lock. A proximity card uses a proximity card reader, not a cipher lock. Biometric readers (such as a fingerprint reader) and smart cards can be used as authentication for systems such as laptop systems.

11. **B.** Proximity cards are used as an additional access control in some areas to electronically unlock doors. A token (such as an RSA token) provides a rolling password for one-time use. A physical key does not electronically unlock a door. A certificate can be embedded in a smart card but, by itself, it would not electronically unlock a door.

12. **A, D.** Security guards and proximity cards are valid methods to prevent unauthorized personnel from entering a secure workspace, such as a secure datacenter. Piggybacking (also called tailgating) occurs when one user follows closely behind another user without using credentials; it can be prevented with a mantrap. A CCTV can detect if an unauthorized entry occurred and provide reliable proof of the entry, but it can't prevent it.

13. **D.** A mantrap is highly effective at preventing unauthorized entry and can also be used to prevent tailgating. A proximity card is useful as an access control mechanism, but it won't prevent tailgating so it isn't as useful as a mantrap. CCTV provides video surveillance, and it can record unauthorized entry, but it can't prevent it. ID badges are useful if the entry is staffed with security guards, but won't prevent unauthorized entry if used without security guards.

14. **D.** Tailgating (also called piggybacking) occurs when one user follows closely behind another user without using credentials. A mantrap prevents tailgating. A heating, ventilation, and air-conditioning (HVAC) system can increase availability by ensuring that equipment doesn't fail due to overheating. Vishing is a variant of phishing techniques and often combines social engineering tactics with Voice over IP (VoIP).

15. **D.** A locked cabinet should be used to help prevent the theft of unused assets. A hardware security module (HSM) is used to create and store encryption keys. A TPM is used for hardware encryption of entire drives. Video surveillance is useful to provide proof of someone entering or exiting a secure space, but is not needed to protect unused assets.

16. **A.** Requiring passwords of a specific number of characters is the password length element of a password policy. Password complexity requires the characters to be different types, such

as uppercase, lowercase, numbers, and special characters. Password masking displays a special character, such as *, when users type in their password, instead of showing the password in clear text. Password history prevents users from reusing passwords.

17. **B.** The minimum password age prevents users from changing the password again until some time has passed, such as one day. The maximum age forces users to periodically change their password, such as after sixty or ninety days. Password masking displays a special character, such as *, when users type in their password instead of showing the password in clear text. Password complexity ensures the password has a mixture of different character types and is sufficiently long.

18. **A.** Password policies have a minimum password age setting, and if set to one day it will prevent users from changing their passwords until a day has passed. Requiring users to change their passwords every day wouldn't resolve the problem and is not reasonable. The password history is currently set to remember the last five passwords. If you change the password history to remember the last twelve or twenty-four passwords, they can do the same thing described in the scenario to get back to their original password.

19. **D.** Password expiration should be configured so that the user is forced to change the password the first time he logs on. This ensures the help-desk professional doesn't know the user's password once the user logs on. Password complexity ensures the password has a mixture of different character types and is sufficiently long. Password masking displays a special character, such as *, when users type in their password instead of showing the password in clear text. Password history prevents users from reusing passwords.

20. **A.** A password policy can include a password expiration requirement (or a maximum age) that ensures that users change their passwords periodically, such as every sixty days or every ninety days. Password history prevents users from using previously used passwords. Password length ensures the password includes a minimum number of characters, such as at least eight characters. Password strength ensures the password uses a mixture of character types.

21. **B.** Most systems include a feature that allows you to set the expiration of an account when a preset deadline arrives. Account lockout locks out an account if an incorrect password is entered too many times. The scenario states you want to disable the account, not delete it.

22. **D.** An account disablement policy would ensure that a terminated employee's account is disabled to revoke the employee's access. Expiring the password forces the user to change the password at the next logon. An account lockout policy locks out an account if an incorrect password is entered too many times. The account may be needed to access the user's resources, so it is recommended to disable the account instead of deleting it.

23. **A.** Time-of-day restrictions can be used to prevent users from logging in at certain times, or even from making connections to network resources at certain times. Account expiration refers to when a temporary account is automatically disabled (such as expiring a temporary account after sixty days). Password expiration refers to the practice of setting a password to immediately expire after resetting it. A detective control won't prevent a user from logging on but can detect it after it occurred.

24. **D.** Of the choices, account logon attempts are the most important. Since the purpose of the system is to host data that is read and updated by employees, data modifications are not critical because they are expected to occur regularly. TCP and UDP are the primary protocols used when users connect to a server over a network, but it's not important from a security perspective to monitor these events.

Chapter 3

Understanding Basic Network Security

CompTIA Security+ objectives covered in this chapter:

1.1 Explain the security function and purpose of network devices and technologies
- Firewalls
- Routers
- Switches
- Load balancers
- Proxies
- Web security gateways
- Spam filter, all-in-one security appliance
- Web application firewall vs. network firewall
- URL filtering, content inspection, and malware inspection

1.2 Apply and implement secure network administration principles
- Rule-based management
- Firewall rules
- VLAN management
- Secure router configuration
- Access control lists
- Port security
- 802.1X
- Flood guards
- Loop protection
- Implicit deny
- Prevent network bridging by network separation
- Log analysis

1.3 Distinguish and differentiate network design elements and compounds

- DMZ
- Subnetting
- VLAN
- NAT

1.4 Implement and use common protocols

- IPsec
- SNMP
- SSH
- DNS
- TLS
- SSL
- TCP/IP
- FTPS
- HTTPS
- SFTP
- SCP
- ICMP
- IPv4 vs. IPv6

1.5 Identify commonly used default network ports

- FTP
- SFTP
- FTPS
- TFTP
- Telnet
- HTTP
- HTTPS
- SCP
- SSH
- NetBIOS

3.6 Analyze and differentiate among types of mitigation and deterrent techniques

- Port security
  - MAC limiting and filtering
  - 802.1x
  - Disabling unused ports

3.7 Implement assessment tools and techniques to discover security threats and vulnerabilities

- Tools
  - Port scanner

5.2 Explain the fundamental concepts and best practices related to authentication, authorization, and access control

- Implicit deny

6.2 Use and apply appropriate cryptographic tools and products

- Use of algorithms with transport encryption
  - SSL
  - TLS
  - IPsec
  - SSH
  - HTTPS

CompTIA expects prospective CompTIA Security+ exam takers to have at least two years of networking experience. However, even with that amount of experience, there are often gaps in an IT professional's or security professional's knowledge. For example, you may have spent a lot of time troubleshooting connectivity but rarely manipulated ACLs on a router or modified firewall rules. In this chapter, you'll review some basic network concepts and how they relate to network security. This includes common protocols, the use of logical ports, basic networking devices, the network perimeter, and some types of common transmission media.

Reviewing Basic Networking Concepts

Before you can tackle any of the relevant security issues on a network, you'll need a basic understanding of networking. This section isn't intended to teach you all of the relevant network topics, but instead review some of the basic concepts. As a reminder, CompTIA lists Network+ as a recommended prerequisite. While Network+ isn't required, the knowledge goes a long way in helping you pass the networking portion of the Security+ exam.

If any of these concepts are completely unfamiliar to you, you may need to pick up a networking book to review them. This section includes a very brief review of many of the different protocols and networking devices that have a relevance to security.

> ### *Remember this*
> Networking includes many acronyms, and you'll see a lot of them in this chapter. You can refer to the acronym list at the back of the book for a quick reminder of what each acronym represents, along with some key information on the acronym.

Protocols

Networking protocols provide the rules needed for computers to communicate with each other on a network. TCP/IP is a full suite of protocols used on the Internet and many internal networks. Some of the TCP/IP protocols, such as TCP, UDP, and IP, provide basic connectivity. Other protocols, such as HTTP and SMTP, support specific types of traffic, such as web traffic or e-mail. This section includes information on common networking protocols and application protocols.

Chapter 5 covers the different steps to harden or secure a server. One of the primary steps is to disable unneeded services and protocols. Before you can identify unneeded protocols, you need to understand them.

The next section covers logical ports, including the use of well-known ports. For example, the default port for HTTP is 80. Because ports are so important to IT security, I've listed the associated port for many of the protocols in this section.

Common TCP/IP Protocols

TCP/IP isn't a single protocol, but a full suite of protocols. Obviously, there isn't room in this book to teach the details of all the TCP/IP protocols. Instead, the purpose of this section is to remind you of, or possibly expose you to, some of the commonly used protocols.

If any of these protocols are completely new to you, you might like to do some additional research to ensure you understand the basics. I've grouped these protocols into the following sections:

- Basic connectivity protocols
- Encryption protocols
- Application protocols
- E-mail protocols
- Remote access protocols

Basic Connectivity Protocols

Some basic protocols used within the TCP/IP suite for basic connectivity and testing basic connectivity include:

- **TCP**. Transmission Control Protocol provides connection-oriented traffic (guaranteed delivery). TCP uses a three-way handshake, and Figure 3.1 shows the TCP handshake process. To start a TCP session, the client sends a SYN (synchronize) packet. The server responds with a SYN/ACK (synchronize/acknowledge) packet, and the client completes the third part of the handshake with an ACK packet. At this point, the connection is established.

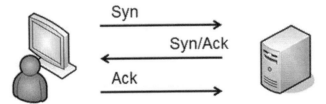

Figure 3.1: TCP handshake process

SYN Flood Attack

The SYN flood attack is a common denial-of-service (DoS) attack. In the SYN flood attack, the attacker sends multiple SYN packets but never completes the third part of the handshake. Instead, the attacker withholds the last ACK packet, leaving the server with several open sessions waiting to complete the handshake in each.

This is like a friend extending his hand to shake hands with you, you extending your hand in response, and then, at the last instant, he pulls his hand away. While you or I will probably stop extending our hand back to someone doing this, the server doesn't know any better and keeps answering every SYN packet with a SYN/ACK packet.

Each uncompleted session consumes resources on the server, and if the SYN flood attack continues, it can actually crash the server. Some servers reserve a certain number of resources for connections, and once the attack consumes these resources, the system blocks additional connections. Instead of crashing the server, the attack prevents legitimate users from connecting to the server.

An intrusion prevention system (IPS, covered in chapter 4) can detect a SYN lood attack and respond to block the attack. Additionally, many firewalls include a flood guard that can detect SYN flood attacks and take steps to close the open sessions.

- **UDP**. User Datagram Protocol provides connectionless sessions (without a three-way handshake). ICMP traffic and audio and video streaming use UDP. Many network-based denial-of-service (DoS) attacks use UDP. All TCP/IP traffic is either connection-oriented TCP traffic or connectionless UDP.

- **IP**. The Internet Protocol identifies hosts in a TCP/IP network and delivers traffic from one host to another using IP addresses. IPv4 uses 32-bit addresses represented in dotted decimal format, such as 192.168.1.100. IPv6 uses 128-bit addresses using hexadecimal code such as: FE80:0000:0000:0000:20D4:3FF7:003F:DE62

- **ARP**. Address Resolution Protocol resolves IP addresses to media access control (MAC) addresses. MACs are also called physical addresses, or hardware addresses. TCP/IP uses the IP address to get a packet to a destination network, but once it arrives on the destination network, it uses the MAC address to get it to the correct host. In other words, ARP is required once the packet reaches the destination subnet. ARP poisoning uses ARP packets to give clients false hardware address updates and can be used to redirect or interrupt network traffic.

- **ICMP**. Internet Control Message Protocol is used for testing basic connectivity and includes tools such as ping, pathping, and tracert. As an example, ping can check for basic connectivity between two systems. Many DoS attacks use ICMP. Because of how often ICMP is used in attacks, it has become common to block ICMP at firewalls and routers, which disables a ping response. Blocking ICMP prevents attackers from discovering devices in a network with a host enumeration sweep.

> **Remember this**
>
> Many DoS attacks use ICMP, so it is common to block ICMP at firewalls and routers. If ping fails, but other connectivity to a server succeeds, it indicates that ICMP is blocked.

Encryption Protocols

Any traffic sent across the wire in clear text is subject to sniffing attacks with a protocol analyzer. One way to protect against this vulnerability is to encrypt the data. Some protocols used to encrypt traffic include:

- **SSH**. Secure Shell can be used to encrypt a wide variety of traffic, such as Telnet, Secure Copy (SCP), and Secure File Transfer Protocol (SFTP). UNIX and Linux administrators often use SSH to remotely administer these systems. When traffic is encrypted with SSH, it uses port of 22.
- **SCP**. Secure Copy is based on SSH. Users can use SCP to copy encrypted files over a network. SCP uses port 22.

> **Remember this**
>
> SSH encrypts a wide variety of traffic and uses port 22 in each implementation. It encrypts FTP traffic (as SFTP) using port 22 instead of the FTP ports of 20 and 21. It encrypts Telnet traffic using port 22 (instead of the Telnet port of 23). SSH is also used with SCP to copy encrypted files over a network.

- **SSL**. The Secure Sockets Layer protocol secures HTTP traffic as HTTPS. SSL can also encrypt other types of traffic such as LDAP. SSL uses port 443 when encrypting HTTP, and port 636 when encrypting LDAP/SSL (LDAPS).
- **TLS**. Transport Layer Security protocol is the designated replacement for SSL. At this point, you can use TLS instead of SSL in just about any application. For example, TLS can encrypt HTTP traffic as HTTPS (on port 443), and LDAP traffic as LDAP/TLS (LDAPS) on port 636. Notice that LDAPS can use either SSL or TLS and both use port 636.
- **IPsec**. Internet Protocol security is used to encrypt IP traffic. It is native to IPv6 but also works with IPv4. IPsec encapsulates and encrypts IP packet payloads and uses tunnel mode to protect virtual private network (VPN) traffic. IPsec includes two components: Authentication Header (AH), identified by protocol ID number 51, and Encapsulating Security Payload (ESP), identified by protocol ID number 50.

> ### Remember this
>
> SSL and TLS encrypt traffic, including traffic over the Internet. IPsec includes ESP to provide payload encryption and AH to provide authentication and integrity. IPsec is built into IPv6 but can also work with IPv4.

Application Protocols

Many different applications protocols are used on the Internet and within an intranet. A common protocol that you probably use frequently is HTTP to access web pages on the Internet. Some of the more commonly used application protocols are:

- **HTTP**. Hypertext Transfer Protocol is used for web traffic on the Internet and in intranets. Web servers use HTTP to transmit web pages to client's web browsers. Hypertext Markup Language (HTML) is the common language used to display the web pages. HTTP uses port 80.
- **HTTPS**. HTTP Secure secures web traffic by transmitting it in an encrypted format. Web browsers commonly indicate that a secure session is using HTTPS by displaying a lock icon and with HTTPS in the URL. HTTPS is encrypted with either SSL or TLS and it uses port 443.
- **FTP**. File Transfer Protocol uploads and downloads files to and from an FTP server. By default, FTP transmits data in clear text, making it easy for an attacker to capture and read FTP data with a sniffer or protocol analyzer. FTP active mode uses port 20 for data and port 21 for control signals. FTP passive mode uses port 21 for control signals and a random port for data. FTP uses TCP.
- **SFTP**. Secure FTP is a secure implementation of FTP. It is an extension of Secure Shell (SSH) using SSH to transmit the files in an encrypted format. SFTP transmits data using port 22.
- **FTPS**. FTP Secure is an extension of FTP and uses SSL or TLS to encrypt FTP traffic. Some implementations of FTPS use ports 989 and 990.
- **TFTP**. Trivial File Transfer Protocol uses UDP and is used to transfer smaller amounts of data, such as when communicating with network devices. Many attacks have used TFTP, but it is not an essential protocol and can often be disabled. TFTP uses UDP port 69. In contrast, FTP uses TCP ports 20 and 21.

> ### Remember this
>
> HTTP and HTTPS use ports 80 and 443 and transmit data over the Internet in unencrypted and encrypted formats, respectively. FTP supports uploading and downloading files to and from an FTP server using ports 20 and 21. FTP uses TCP (ports 20 and 21) and TFTP uses UDP (ports 69). SFTP uses SSH to encrypt FTP traffic and uses port 22. FTPS uses SSL to encrypt FTP traffic.

- **Telnet**. Telnet is frequently used to connect to remote systems or network devices over a network. Telnet has a command line interface, and many administrators use Telnet to connect to routers and make configuration changes. Telnet transmits data in clear text, making it vulnerable to sniffing attacks, but you can use SSH to encrypt Telnet. Telnet uses port 23, or port 22 when encrypted with SSH.
- **SNMP**. Simple Network Management Protocol is used to monitor and manage network devices such as routers or switches. This includes using SNMP to modify the configuration of the devices or have network devices report status back to a central network management system. SNMP agents installed on devices send information to an SNMP manager via notifications known as traps (sometimes called device traps). The first version of SNMP had vulnerabilities, such as passing passwords across the network in clear text. SNMP v2 and SNMP v3 are much more secure. SNMP uses port 161.
- **DNS**. Domain Name System is a service that resolves host names to IP addresses on the Internet and internal networks. DNS servers host the DNS service and respond to DNS queries. DNS uses port 53.

Remember this

Telnet is often used to connect to network devices (such as routers) to make configuration changes. It uses port 23 and sends data in clear text. You can encrypt Telnet traffic with SSH, and it uses port 22 when encrypted with SSH. SNMP monitors and manages network devices such as routers or switches, and SNMP agents report information via notifications known as SNMP traps (also called SNMP device traps).

- **NetBIOS**. Network Basic Input/Output System is a name resolution service for NetBIOS names on internal networks. In contrast, DNS resolves host names on the Internet and internal networks. NetBIOS also includes session services for both TCP and UDP communication. NetBIOS uses ports 137 through 139.
- **LDAP**. Lightweight Directory Access Protocol is the language used to communicate with directories such as Microsoft's Active Directory or Novell's Netware Directory Services (NDS). LDAP provides a single location for object management and it uses port 389. LDAP can be encrypted with either TLS or SSL and uses port 636 when encrypted.
- **Kerberos**. Kerberos (presented in chapter 1) is the authentication protocol used in Windows domains and some UNIX environments. It uses a KDC to issue time-stamped tickets. Kerberos uses port 88.
- **Microsoft's SQL Server**. SQL server is a server application that hosts databases accessible from web servers and a wide array of applications. SQL server uses port 1433 by default.

- **Remote Administration, Terminal Services, or Remote Desktop Services**. Remote administration allows a client to remotely access another system. Microsoft previously called this Terminal Services and then renamed it in Server 2008 R2 to Remote Desktop Services. Microsoft's Remote Assistance allows one user to assist another user remotely. Microsoft's Remote Desktop Protocol (RDP) allows an administrator to remotely administer servers from desktop computers. Terminal Services (and Remote Desktop Services) uses port 3389. Additionally, remote assistance uses the same protocol and port.

Remember this

NetBIOS is used on internal servers and uses ports 137–139. Microsoft's SQL Server hosts databases and uses port 1433. Remote Desktop Services uses port 3389. SMTP is used to send e-mail and it uses port 25.

E-mail Protocols

Some common protocols used for e-mail include:

- **SMTP**. Simple Mail Transport Protocol transfers e-mail between clients and SMTP servers, and between SMTP servers. SMTP uses port 25.
- **POP3**. Post Office Protocol v3 transfers e-mails from servers down to clients. POP3 uses port 110.
- **IMAP4**. Internet Message Access Protocol is used to store e-mail on an e-mail server. IMAP4 allows a user to organize and manage e-mail in folders on the server. IMAP4 uses port 143.

Remote Access Protocols

Some common remote access and virtual private network (VPN) tunneling protocols include:

- **PPP**. Point-to-Point Protocol is used to create dial-up connections between a dial-up client and a remote access server, or between a dial-up client and an Internet Service Provider (ISP).
- **IPsec**. IPsec can be used as a remote access tunneling protocol to encrypt traffic going over the Internet. It uses the Internet Key Exchange (IKE) over port 500 to create a security association for the VPN.
- **PPTP**. Point-to-Point Tunneling Protocol is a tunneling protocol used with VPNs that has some known vulnerabilities. PPTP uses TCP port 1723.
- **L2TP**. Layer 2 Tunneling Protocol combines the strengths of Layer 2 Forwarding (L2F) and PPTP. L2TP is commonly used with IPsec for VPNs. Since NAT is not compatible

with IPsec, L2TP/IPsec can't go through a device running NAT. L2TP uses UDP port 1701.

- **RADIUS**. Remote Authentication Dial-In User Service provides central authentication to remote access clients. When an organization uses more than one remote access server, each remote access server can forward authentication requests to the central RADIUS server. RADIUS only encrypts passwords.
- **TACACS/XTACACS.** Terminal Access Controller Access-Control System and Extended TACACS are older network authentication protocols. TACACS is generic, and XTACACS is proprietary to Cisco. TACACS uses UDP port 49.
- **TACACS+**. TACACS+ is used as an alternative over RADIUS. Cisco VPN concentrators use TACACS+ and it encrypts the entire authentication process. It uses multiple challenge responses for authentication, authorization, and audit (AAA). TACACS+ has wider uses including as an authentication service for network devices. TACACS+ uses TCP port 49.

Remember this

IPsec uses port 500 for IPsec VPN connections. RADIUS only encrypts the password in the authentication process. TACACS+ encrypts the entire authentication process. TACACS+ uses multiple challenge responses for authentication, authorization, and audit. TACACS+ is also used as an authentication service for network devices. TACACS uses UDP and TACACS+ uses TCP.

IPv4 vs IPv6

IPv4 uses 32-bit IP addresses expressed in dotted decimal format. For example, the IPv4 IP address of 192.168.1.5 is four decimals separated by periods or dots. You can also express the address in binary form with 32 bits. While the number of IP addresses at first seemed inexhaustible, the Internet Assigned Numbers Authority (IANA) assigned the last block of IPv4 addresses in February 2011.

In contrast, IPv6 uses 128-bit IP addresses expressed in hexadecimal format. For example, the IPv6 IP address of FE80:0000:0000:0000:20D4:3FF7:003F:DE62 includes eight groups of four hexadecimal characters. Each hexadecimal character represents with four bits. IPv6 supports zero compression by substituting a string of zeros with two colons. For example, FE80::20D4:3FF7:003F:DE62 is the same as the previous IPv6 address in this paragraph.

IPv6 supports over 340 undecillion IP addresses. For context, the order is billion, trillion, quadrillion, quintillion, sextillion, septillion, octillion, nonillion, decillion, and undecillion. Everyone will have enough addresses to assign IP addresses to their computers, TVs, mobile phones, refrigerators, coffee makers, toasters, and anything else they may want to control remotely.

Another benefit of IPv6 over IPv4 is that it has more security built in. For example, the tunneling services provided by IPsec are built into IPv6 and work natively with it. In contrast, IPsec isn't native to IPv4 and it has some compatibility issues. For example, when IPsec passes through a device using Network Address Translation (NAT), NAT breaks IPsec. While there are ways to work around the issues, IPv6 doesn't have the same problems.

> ### Remember this
> IPv6 addresses include 128 bits. IPv6 is expressed as eight groups of four hexadecimal characters (numbers and letters), such as this: FE80: 0000:0000:0000: 20D4:3FF7:003F:DE62.

Subnetting

Subnetting divides a single range of IP addresses into several smaller ranges of IP addresses. This is often done to isolate traffic and increase efficiency. You don't need to know how to subnet for the CompTIA Security+ exam, but you should be familiar with the concept and how it can be used to isolate users onto different subnets. Additionally, you should be able to identify valid IP addresses for computers within a subnet.

As an example, you could have multiple users on a single Class C network. Some of the users may be running applications that stream audio and video across the network. A second group of users may regularly upload and download data via the Internet. A third group may upload and download files back and forth to servers on the network, and a fourth group could be users with just occasional access to the network. By subnetting a single Class C network into four smaller subnets, it isolates the traffic for each of these user groups.

Imagine that the original Class C network is 192.168.1.0 with a subnet mask of 255.255.255.0. It could hold 254 host addresses (192.168.1.1 through 192.168.1.254). You can subnet this into four smaller subnets with each one using a subnet mask of 255.255.255.192 as follows:

- **Subnet 1**. 192.168.1.1 through 192.168.1.62—use for streaming audio and video.
- **Subnet 2**. 192.168.1.65 through 192.168.1.126— use for upload and download of files on the Internet.
- **Subnet 3**. 192.168.1.129 through 192.168.1.190—use for upload and download of files to internal servers.
- **Subnet 4**. 192.168.1.193 through 192.168.1.254—use for regular users.

By dividing the network into the four subnets, you increase the efficiency by reducing collisions on each individual network. This effectively improves the performance of each subnet.

Subnetting and Availability

If a technician manually assigns a computer with an IP address outside of the subnet range, it loses availability. It will no longer be available on the network and it will lose availability to other resources on the network. While most computers aren't assigned addresses manually, many servers are and misconfiguration of a server's IP address has caused more than a few problems.

As an example, each host in Subnet 3 should have an IP address in the range of 192.168.1.129 through 192.168.1.190. If a technician assigns one of the servers in the subnet with an IP address of 192.168.1.10, it loses connectivity. This server will no longer be available to any users on the network. With this in mind, technicians should be able to look at an IP address and determine if it is valid for a subnet.

Take a look at the following four IP addresses, each with a subnet mask of 255.255.255.192. Are any of these on the same subnet?

- 192.168.1.50
- 192.168.1.100
- 192.168.1.165
- 192.168.1.189

Two IP addresses (192.168.1.165 and 192.168.1.189) are both on Subnet 3. You can determine this by looking at Subnet 3's range, shown previously (192.168.1.129 through 192.168.1.190). If someone used all four of these addresses for servers on Subnet 3, the first two servers wouldn't have network connectivity.

On the job, you may not always have a listing of IP address ranges handy. However, you will have a calculator. It's useful to know how to use it. Similarly, if you need a calculator on the Security+ exam, it will be available.

> ### Remember this
> You should be able to identify the subnet of IP addresses and verify which IP addresses have the same subnet. If needed, you will have access to a calculator you can use to convert decimal to binary.

Calculating Subnet IP Addresses with a Calculator

Imagine that you have the same four IP addresses (192.168.1.50, 192.168.1.100, 192.168.1.165, 192.168.1.189) with a subnet mask of 255.255.255.192. The challenge is identifying which two are on the same subnet. You need to convert the subnet mask and IP addresses to binary, and this section shows how to do that with a calculator.

The first three decimals (192.168.1) are the same in each IP address. However, the fourth decimal is different in each one, so you can focus on this last decimal for each (50, 100, 165, 189). Also, you only need to focus on the last decimal in the subnet mask (192). You start by converting each to binary.

Figure 3.2 shows two instances of a basic calculator using the Scientific view. On Windows 7, you'd use the Programmer view instead. It looks a little different on Windows 7 but it has the same functionality. In the top calculator in Figure 3.2, "Dec" is selected for decimal, and I've entered the decimal number 192. The bottom calculator shows the result after clicking "Bin" for binary. The calculator converts 192 from decimal to the binary value of 1100 0000. If you do this for each of the relevant decimal numbers, you get the results shown in Table 3.1

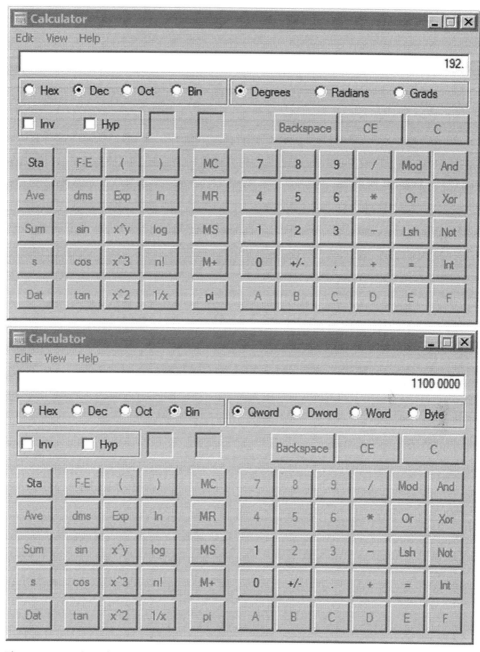

Figure 3.2: Using the calculator to convert decimal to binary

	Decimal	Without leading zeros	With leading zeros	First two bits
Subnet	192	1100 0000	<u>11</u>00 0000	11
IP	50	11 0010	<u>00</u>11 0010	00
IP	100	110 0100	<u>01</u>10 0110	01
IP	165	1010 0101	<u>10</u>10 0101	10
IP	189	1011 1101	<u>10</u>11 1101	10

Table 3.1: Results of converting decimal numbers to binary

When you convert decimal numbers to binary, it doesn't add leading zeros. However, each decimal in an IPv4 address is represented by eight bits, so you need to add enough leading zeros to show eight bits. Once you add the leading zeroes, you can identify the bits representing the subnet mask in each IP address.

As a reminder, the subnet mask is 255.255.255.192, and we are only focused on the last decimal (192). The table shows that the first two bits are a 1 in 192, so only these bits are used in the subnet mask for each of the IP addresses. You can see that the first two bits in 165 and 189 are both 10, so only these two IP addresses (192.168.1.165 and 192.168.1.189) are on the same subnet.

Imagine that the subnet mask is 255.255.255.224. Which of the four IP addresses are on the same subnet?

If you convert 224 to binary, it is 1110 0000. You can see that the first three bits are a 1. If you look back at Table 3.1, you can see the first three bits of 50 (001), 100 (011), 165 (101), and 189 (101). Only 165 and 189 have the same first three bits (101), so only these two are on the same subnet.

Admittedly, there is a lot more to subnetting. However, subnetting is a skill needed for the Network+ exam, which is a recommended prerequisite for Security+. I didn't attempt to teach it from scratch here, but instead showed a simple way to verify an IP address is accurate for a subnet. If you want to brush up on subnetting, try a Google search on "how to subnet."

Understanding and Identifying Ports

Ports are logical numbers used by TCP/IP to identify what service or application should handle data received by a system. Both TCP and UDP use ports with a total of 65,536 TCP ports (0 to 65,535) and 65,536 UDP ports (0 to 65,535). Administrators open ports on firewalls and routers to allow the associated protocol into or out of a network. For example, HTTP uses port 80, and an administrator allows HTTP traffic by opening port 80.

The Internet Assigned Numbers Authority (IANA) maintains a list of official port assignments that you can view here: http://www.iana.org/assignments/port-numbers. IANA divided the ports into three ranges as follows:

- **Well-known Ports: 0–1023**. IANA assigns port numbers to commonly used protocols in the well-known ports range.
- **Registered ports: 1024–49,151**. IANA registers these ports for companies as a convenience to the IT community. A single company may register a port for a proprietary use, or multiple companies may use the same port for a specific standard. As an example, Microsoft's SQL Server uses port 1433 for database servers, L2TP uses port 1701, and PPTP uses port 1723.
- **Dynamic and private ports: 49,152–65,535**. These ports are available for use by any application. Applications commonly use these ports to temporally map an application to a port. These are also called ephemeral ports, indicating that they are short lived.

While virtually all of the ports are subject to attack, most port attacks are against the well-known ports. Port scanners will often simply check to see if a well-known port is open. For example, SMTP uses the well-known port 25, so if port 25 is open, the system is likely running SMTP.

IT personnel who regularly work with routers and firewalls can readily tell you what protocol is associated with which well-known port, such as 20, 21, 22, 23, 25, 80, or 443. The reason is that they use these ports to allow or block traffic.

For example, an administrator can close port 23 to block all Telnet traffic into a network. The router then ignores traffic on port 23 instead of forwarding it. Similarly, an administrator can close port 1433 to block database traffic to a Microsoft SQL Server. On the other hand, the administrator can open port 25 to allow SMTP traffic.

While ports are second nature to the router and firewall administrators, they may not be so familiar to you. If you don't work with the ports often, you'll need to spend some extra time studying to ensure you're ready for the exam.

Well-Known Ports

There are 1024 well-known ports, but you don't need to know them all. However, at a minimum, you should know the ports listed in Table 3.2, which includes a few ports outside the well-known ports range.

Protocol	Port	Protocol	Port
FTP data port	20	NetBIOS	137-139
FTP control port	21	IMAP4	143
SFTP (using SSH)	22	SNMP	161
SSH, SCP	22	HTTPS	443
Telnet	23	LDAP	389
SMTP	25	IPsec (for VPN with IKE)	500
TACACS/TACACS+	49	LDAP/TLS	636
DNS	53	LDAP/SSL	636
TFTP	69	L2TP	1701
HTTP	80	PPTP	1723
Kerberos	88	Terminal Services	3389
POP3	110	Remote Desktop Services	3389

Table 3.2: Some commonly used well-known ports

Remember this

Ports are commonly used to allow or block traffic on routers and firewalls. By blocking a port (such as port 23 for Telnet) at a network firewall, it blocks all traffic into the network using this port. You don't need to memorize all 1024 well-known ports, but memorizing the ports in Table 3.2 will help you answer any Security+ questions related to ports.

When you take the Security+ exam, you can write down your own notes as soon as you start. Many successful test takers memorize the ports in this table and write down the table as their very first action when they start the exam. Later, when they come across a question that requires the knowledge of a port number, it's as simple as looking at their notes. If you don't know these ports now, practice writing this table from memory so you're ready when it's time for the live exam.

Combining the IP Address and the Port

At any moment, a computer could be receiving dozens of packets. Each of these packets includes a destination IP address and a destination port. TCP/IP uses the IP address to get the packet to the computer. The computer then uses the port number to get the packet to the correct service, protocol, or application that can process it.

For example, if the packet has a destination port of 80 (the well-known port for HTTP), the system passes the packet to the process handling HTTP. It wouldn't do much good to pass an SMTP e-mail packet to the HTTP service or send an HTTP request packet to the SMTP service.

IP Address Used to Locate Hosts

Imagine that the IP address of GetCertifiedGetAhead.com is 74.86.130.70, and the address assigned to your computer from your ISP is 70.160.136.100. TCP/IP uses these IP addresses to get the packets from your computer to the web server and the web server's answer back to your computer.

There's a lot more that occurs under the hood with TCP/IP (such as DNS, NAT, and ARP), but the main point is that the server's IP address is used to get the requesting packet from your computer to the server. The server gets the response packets back to your computer using your IP address (or the IP address of your NAT server).

Server Ports

Different protocols are enabled and running on a server. These protocols have well-known or registered port numbers, such as port 22 for SSH, 23 for Telnet, 80 for HTTP, 443 for HTTPS, and so on. When the system receives traffic with a destination of port 80, the system knows to send it to the service handling HTTP.

Any web browser knows that the well-known port for HTTP is 80. Even though you don't see port 80 in the URL, it is implied as http://GetCertifiedGetAhead.com:80. If you omit the port number, HTTP uses the well-known port number of 80 by default.

Popular web servers on the Internet include Apache and Internet Information Services (IIS). Apache is free and runs on UNIX or Linux systems, which are also free. Apache can also run on other platforms, such as Microsoft systems. IIS is included in Microsoft Server products, such as Windows Server 2003, Windows Server 2008, and 208 R2. All of these web servers use port 80 for HTTP. When the server receives a packet with a destination port of 80, the server sends the packet to web server application (Apache or IIS) that processes it and sends back a response.

Client Ports

TCP/IP works with the client operating system to maintain a table of client side ports. This table associates port numbers with different applications that are expecting return traffic. Client side ports start at port 49,152 and increment up to 65,535. If the system uses all the ports between 49,152 and 65,535 before being rebooted, it'll start over at 49,152. Some older operating systems (such as Windows XP) started at 1024 instead of 49,152.

When you use your web browser to request a page from a site, your system will record an unused client port number such as 49,152 in an internal table to handle the return traffic. When the web server returns the web page, it includes the client port as a destination port. When the client receives web page packets with a destination port of 49,152, it sends these packets to the web browser application. The browser processes the packets and displays the page.

Putting It All Together

The previous section described the different pieces, but understanding ports is extremely important, and often misunderstood. It's useful to put this together into a single description. Imagine that you decide to visit the website http://GetCertifiedGetAhead.com using Internet Explorer. You type the URL into the browser and the web page appears. Here are the details of what is happening.

Your computer creates a packet with source and destination IP addresses and source and destination ports. Figure 3.3 provides an overview of how this will look and the following text explains the process.

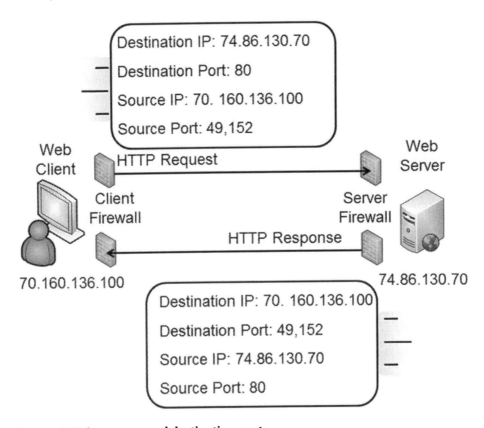

Figure 3.3: Using source and destination ports

The destination IP address is determined from a DNS lookup and is 74.86.130.70. Additionally, your computer will use its IP address as the source IP address. For this example, imagine your computer's IP address is 70.160.136.100.

Since the web server is serving web pages using HTTP and the well-known port is used, the destination port is 80. Your computer will identify an unused port in the dynamic and private ports range (a port number between 49,152 and 65,535) and map that port to the web browser. For this example, imagine it assigns 49,152 to the web browser. It uses this as the source port.

Comparing Ports and Protocol IDs

Ports and protocol identifiers (protocol IDs) are not the same thing, though they are often confused. well-known ports identify many services or protocols as discussed previously.

However, many protocols aren't identified by the port, but instead by the protocol ID. For example, within IPsec protocol ID 50 indicates the packet is an Encapsulating Security Payload (ESP) packet, and protocol ID 51 indicates it's an Authentication Header (AH) packet. Similarly, ICMP has a protocol ID of 1, TCP is 6, and UDP is 17.

You can use a protocol ID to block or allow traffic on routers and firewalls just as you can block or allow traffic based on the port. Note that it isn't accurate to say that you can allow IPsec ESP traffic by opening *port* 50. IANA lists port 50 as a Remote Mail Checking Protocol. However, you can allow IPsec traffic by allowing traffic using protocol ID 50.

Protocol analyzers (covered in greater depth in chapter 8) can capture and examine IP headers to determine the protocol ID and the port, as well as read any unencrypted data.

At this point, the packet has both destination and source data as follows:

- Destination IP address: 74.86.130.70 (the web server)
- Destination port: 80
- Source IP address: 70.160.136.100 (your computer)
- Source port: 49152

TCP/IP uses the IP address (74.86.130.70) to get the packet to the GetCertifiedGetAhead. com web server. When it reaches the web server, the server looks at the destination port (80) and determines that the packet needs to go to the web server program servicing HTTP. The web server creates the page and puts the data into one or more return packets. At this point, the source and destinations are swapped because the packet is coming from the server back to you.

- Destination IP address: 70.160.136.100 (your computer)
- Destination port: 49152
- Source IP address: 74.86.130.70 (the web server)
- Source port: 80

Again, TCP/IP uses the IP address to get the packets to the destination, which is your computer at this point. Once the packets reach your system, it sees that port 49,152 is the destination port. Since your system mapped this port to your web browser, it sends the packets to the web browser, which displays the web page.

The Importance of Ports in Security

Routers, and the routing component of firewalls, filter packets based on IP addresses, ports, and some protocols such as ICMP or IPsec. Since many protocols use well-known ports, you can control protocol traffic by allowing or blocking traffic based on the port.

In the previous example, the firewall must allow outgoing traffic on port 80. Firewalls automatically determine the client ports used for return traffic, and if they allow the outgoing traffic, they allow the return traffic. In other words, since the firewall allows the packet to the web server on port 80, it also allows the web page returning on the dynamic port of 49,152.

Note that the client firewall doesn't need to allow incoming traffic on port 80 for this to work. The web client isn't hosting a web server with HTTP, so the client firewall would block incoming traffic on port 80. However, the firewall that is filtering traffic to the web server needs to allow incoming traffic on port 80.

You can apply this same principle for any protocol and port. For example, if you want to allow SMTP traffic, you create a rule on the firewall to allow traffic on port 25. Similarly, if you want to block Telnet traffic, you ensure that the firewall blocks port 23.

IT professionals modifying ACLs on routers and firewalls commonly refer to this as opening a port to allow traffic or closing a port to block traffic.

Port Scanners

A port scanner is a tool used to query a host to determine which ports are open. System administrators use port scanners as part of an overall vulnerability assessment. It is also used as part of an attack, where an attacker tries to learn as much about a server as possible.

> ### Remember this
>
> A port scanner can help determine what services and protocols are running on a remote system by identifying open ports. Port scanners typically take further steps to verify the port is open.

The port scanner sends queries to ports of interest and analyzes the reply. If a server answers a query on a specific port, the associated service or protocol is likely running on the server. For example, if a server answers a query on port 25, it indicates that port 25 is open. More specifically, it indicates that the server is probably running SMTP. If port 80 is open, HTTP is probably running, and the server may be a web server such as Apache or Microsoft's Internet Information Services (IIS).

Even though it's not recommended for services to use ports other than the well-known ports for specific services, it is possible. Because of this, an open port doesn't definitively say the related service or protocol is running.

The attacker will use other methods for verification. For example, a fingerprinting attack will send specific protocol queries to the server and analyze the responses. These responses can verify that the service is running and will often include other details about the operating system, since different operating systems often respond differently to specific queries.

A common TCP port scan will send a TCP SYN packet to a specific port of a server as part of the TCP three-way handshake. If the server responds with a SYN/ACK packet, the scanner knows the port is open. However, instead of completing the three-way handshake, the scanner sends a RST packet to reset the connection and then repeats the process with a different port.

Understanding Basic Network Devices

Any network will include one or more network devices used to provide connectivity to the devices in the network. Any network can have various devices with different capabilities depending on the needs of the network.

When discussing the different devices, it's important to remember two primary methods of how TCP/IP traffic is addressed in IPv4.

- **Unicast**. One-to-one traffic. One host sends traffic to another host, using a destination IP address. Only the host with the destination IP address will process the packet.
- **Broadcast**. One-to-all traffic. One host sends traffic to all other hosts on the subnet, using a broadcast address such as 255.255.255.255. Every host that receives broadcast traffic will process it. Hubs and switches pass broadcast traffic between their ports, but routers do not pass broadcast traffic.

Hub

A hub has multiple physical ports used to provide basic connectivity to multiple computers. Hubs commonly have between four and thirty-two physical ports. In an Ethernet network, the hub would have multiple RJ-45 ports used to connect to NICs on the host computers using twisted pair cable. Most hubs are active, meaning they have power and will amplify the output to a set level.

Hubs have zero intelligence. Whatever goes in one port goes out all ports on the hub. This presents a security risk, because if an attacker installs a protocol analyzer (sniffer) on any computer connected to the hub, the sniffer will capture all the traffic passing through the hub.

As mentioned previously, any traffic sent across the wire in clear text is subject to sniffing attacks with a protocol analyzer. One way to protect against this is by encrypting the data. Another way of protecting against sniffing attacks is replace all hubs with switches to limit the amount of traffic that reaches any computer. Many companies specifically restrict the use of hubs in their networks to reduce the risk of sniffers capturing traffic. The following section describes how switches limit traffic to specific computers.

Switch

A switch has the ability to learn which computers are attached to each of its physical ports. It then uses this knowledge to create internal switched connections when two computers communicate with each other.

Comparing Ports and Ports

Note that a physical port used by a switch is completely different from the logical ports discussed previously. You plug cables into a physical port. A logical port is a number embedded in a packet and identifies services and protocols.

This is similar to minute (sixty seconds) and minute (tiny), or like the old joke about the meaning of *secure*. The Secretary of Defense directed members of different services to "secure that building." Navy personnel turned off the lights and locked the doors. The Army occupied the building and ensured no one could enter. The Marines attacked it, captured it, and set up defenses to hold it. The Air Force secured a two-year lease with an option to buy.

Consider Figure 3.4. When the switch turns on, it starts out without any knowledge other than knowing it has four physical ports. Imagine that the first traffic is the beginning of a TCP/IP conversation between Sally's computer and Joe's computer.

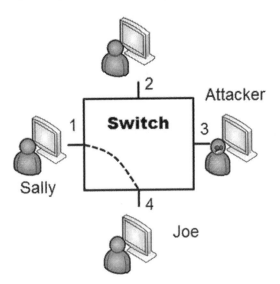

Figure 3.4: Switch

When Sally's computer sends the first packet, it includes the MAC address of the destination computer. However, since the switch doesn't know which port Joe's computer is connected to, it forwards this first packet to all, except the port where it was received (Sally's port).

Included in that first packet is the MAC address of Sally's computer. The switch logs this information into an internal table. The switch internally directs any future traffic addressed to Sally's MAC address to port 1, and port 1 only.

When Joe's computer receives the packet, it responds. Embedded in this return packet is the MAC address of Joe's computer. The switch captures Joe's MAC address and logs it with port

4 in the internal table. From here on, any unicast traffic between Sally's and Joe's computers is internally switched.

Switches will internally switch unicast traffic. However, switches pass broadcast traffic to all ports.

While a switch is valuable in a network to reduce traffic on subnets and increase efficiency, it also has an added security benefit.

Security Benefit of a Switch

Most of the previous discussion is basic networking, but what you really need to know is why it's relevant in security. If an attacker installed a sniffer on a computer attached to another port (such as port 3 in Figure 3.4), the sniffer would not capture all traffic going through the switch. If Sally and Joe are exchanging data on ports 1 and 4, none of the traffic reaches port 3. The sniffer can't capture traffic that doesn't reach the port.

This is the main *security* reason why organizations replace hubs with switches. The switch reduces the risk of an attacker capturing data with a sniffer.

Port Security

Port security limits the computers that can connect to ports on a switch. It includes restricting which devices can connect based on their MAC address, and disabling inactive ports. Port security includes restricting what computers can connect to any physical port based on the MAC address and disabling inactive ports.

In a simple implementation of port security, the switch remembers the first one or two MAC addresses that connect to the port. Any other MAC addresses associated with this port are blocked. Many switches also support manually configuring each port with a specific MAC address. This limits each port's connectivity to a specific device using this MAC address. This is much more labor intensive but provides a higher level of security.

If physical ports are not used, you can disable them on the switch to support basic port security. This prevents anyone from plugging in a laptop into an open RJ-45 wall jack, connecting to the switch, and accessing your network.

You can also use an IEEE 802.1X server for port-based authentication. IEEE 802.1X restricts unauthorized clients from connecting to the network until they authenticate via the 802.1X server.

> ### *Remember this*
> You can protect switches with port security by limiting the number of MAC addresses per port and by disabling unused ports. A more advanced implementation is to restrict each physical port to only a single specific MAC address. Physical security is also important to prevent access to a switch's console ports.

Physical Security of a Switch

Many switches have a console port that administrators can use to monitor all traffic. Unlike the normal ports that only see traffic specifically addressed to the port, the monitoring port will see all traffic into or out of the switch. This includes any unicast traffic the switch is internally switching between two regular ports. The monitoring port is useful for legitimate troubleshooting, but if the switch isn't protected with physical security, it can also be useful to an attacker.

Physical security protects a switch by keeping it in a secure area such as in a locked wiring closet. Physical security ensures that attackers don't have physical access to the switch and other network devices.

Loop Protection

In some situations, a network can develop a switching loop or bridge loop problem. This creates a broadcast storm, causing significant performance problems. For example, if a user connects two ports of a switch together with a cable, it creates a switching loop.

For many network administrators, this is trivial, since most current switches have Spanning Tree Protocol (STP) or the newer Rapid STP (RSTP) installed and enabled. STP and RSTP provide protection against switching loops. However, if these protocols are disabled, the switch is susceptible to loop problems.

The simple solution is to ensure that switches include loop protection such as STP or RSTP and that loop protection is enabled. The importance of this can't be overemphasized. A broadcast loop can disable a switch and seriously degrade performance of a network, affecting its availability.

> ### Remember this
>
> Loop protection such as STP or RSTP is necessary to protect against switching loop problems, such as those caused when two ports of a switch are connected together.

VLAN

A virtual LAN (VLAN) uses a switch to group several different computers into a virtual network. You can group the computers together based on departments, job function, or any other administrative need.

Normally, a router would group different computers onto different subnets, based on physical locations. All the computers in a routed segment are located in the same physical location, such as on a specific floor or wing of a building.

However, a single switch can create multiple VLANs to separate the computers based on logical needs rather than physical location. Additionally, the switch can easily be reconfigured to add or subtract computers from any VLAN if the need arises.

For example, a group of users who normally work in separate departments may begin work on a project that requires them to be on the same subnet. You can configure a switch to logically group these workers together, even if the computers are physically located on different floors or different wings of the building. When the project is over, you can simply reconfigure the switch to return the network to its original configuration.

Similarly, you can use a single switch with multiple VLANs to separate users. For example, if you want to separate the traffic between the HR department and the IT department, you can use a single switch with two VLANs. The VLANs logically separate all the computers between two different departments, even if the computers are located close to each other.

Because traffic can be isolated between computers in a VLAN, it provides security.

Remember this

You can create multiple VLANs with a single switch. A VLAN can logically group several different computers together, or logically separate computers, without regard to their physical location.

Prevent Network Bridging

Network bridging occurs when a single computer connects to a network with two separate connections at the same time. For example, many laptops include both wired connections and wireless transceivers. If the laptop connects with both connections, it creates a network bridge.

While two connections may seem beneficial, as though it will operate more efficiently, it doesn't work this way. Instead, it degrades performance for the user computer and for users on the connected networks.

One way of preventing network bridging problems is with network separation using VLANs. In other words, if clients access a network using wireless connections, network separation ensures they will only have access to network segments dedicated for wireless users. If clients connect using a wired connection, they will only have access to network segments dedicated to wired users.

Another solution is to ensure that users don't use both wired and wireless connections at the same time to avoid the problem. Unfortunately, you often can't depend on end users understanding the requirement, much less understanding the problems they'll cause by using network bridging.

Router

Routers connect multiple network segments together into a single network and route traffic between the segments. As an example, the Internet is effectively a single network hosting billions of computers. Routers route the traffic from segment to segment.

Since routers don't pass broadcasts, they effectively reduce traffic on any single segment. Segments separated by routers are sometimes referred to as broadcast domains. If a network has too many computers on a single segment, broadcasts can result in excessive collisions and reduce network performance. Moving computers to a different segment separated by a router can significantly improve overall performance.

Cisco routers are popular, but many other brands exist. Most routers are physical devices, and physical routers are the most efficient. However, it's also possible to add routing software to computers with more than one NIC. For example, Windows Server products (such as Windows Server 2008 and 2008 R2) can function as routers by adding additional services.

Routers and ACLs

Access control lists (ACLs) are rules implemented on a router (and on firewalls) to identify what traffic is allowed and what traffic is denied. Rules within the ACLs provide rule-based management for the router and control inbound and outbound traffic.

ACLs on routers provide basic packet filtering. As mentioned in the "Understanding and Identifying Ports" section in this chapter, routers can filter packets based on IP addresses, ports, and some protocols, such as ICMP or IPsec, based on the protocol identifiers.

- **IP addresses and networks**. You can add a rule in the ACL to block access from any single computer based on the IP address. If you want to block traffic from one subnet to another, you can use a rule to block traffic using the subnet IDs. For example, the sales department may be in the 192.168.1.0/24 network and the accounting department may be in the 192.168.5.0/24 network. You can ensure traffic from these two departments stays separate with an ACL on a router.

- **Ports**. You can filter traffic based on logical ports. For example, if you want to block HTTP traffic, you can create a rule to block traffic on port 80. Note that you can choose to block incoming traffic, outgoing traffic, or both. In other words, it's possible to allow outgoing HTTP traffic while blocking incoming HTTP traffic.

- **Protocol identifiers**. Many protocols are identified by their protocol IDs. For example, ICMP uses a protocol ID of 1 and many DoS attacks use ICMP. You can block all ICMP traffic (and the attacks that use it) by blocking traffic using this protocol ID. Many automated IPSs dynamically block ICMP traffic in response to attacks. Similarly, you can restrict traffic to only packets encrypted with IPsec ESP using a rule that allows traffic using protocol ID 50, but blocks all other traffic.

Remember this

Routers and packet-filtering firewalls perform basic filtering with an access control list (ACL). ACLs identify what traffic is allowed and what traffic is blocked. An ACL can control traffic based on networks, subnets, IP addresses, ports, and some protocols (using the protocol ID).

Routers and Firewalls

Administrators often create ACLs on boundary routers (between the internal network and the Internet) using an implicit deny philosophy. In other words, the router blocks all traffic (implicitly denies the traffic) unless a rule in the ACL explicitly allows the traffic.

Early firewalls provided basic packet filtering using this approach. While firewalls are much more advanced today, most firewalls include this basic packet filtering capability. These rules within the ACLs provide rule-based management of the firewall. The implicit deny rule provides a secure starting point for a firewall policy.

Firewall

A firewall filters traffic between networks and can filter both incoming and outgoing traffic. In other words, a firewall can ensure only specific types of traffic are allowed into your network and only specific types of traffic are allowed out of your network.

The purpose of a firewall in a network is similar to a firewall in a car. The firewall in a car is located between the engine and passenger compartment. If a fire starts in the engine compartment, the firewall will provide a layer of protection for passengers in the passenger compartment. Similarly, a firewall in a network will try to keep the bad traffic (often in the form of attackers) out of the network.

Of course, an engine has a lot of moving parts that can do damage to us if we accidentally reach into it while it's running. The firewall in a car protects passengers from touching any of those moving parts. Similarly, a network can also block users from going to places that an administrator deems dangerous. For example, uneducated users could inadvertently download damaging files, but many firewalls can block potentially malicious downloads.

Firewalls start with a basic routing capability for packet filtering. More advanced firewalls go beyond simple packet filtering and include content filtering provided by many web security gateways and appliances.

A firewall can be host-based or network-based. The following text describes both.

Host-based Firewalls

A host-based firewall monitors traffic going in and out of a single host, such as a server or a workstation. It monitors traffic passing through the NIC and can prevent intrusions into the computer via the NIC. Many operating systems include software-based firewalls used as host-based firewalls. For example, Microsoft has included a host-based firewall on operating systems since Windows XP. Additionally, many third-party host-based firewalls are available.

Figure 3.5 shows the host-based Windows Firewall on Windows 7. Notice that you can configure inbound rules to allow or restrict inbound traffic and outbound rules to allow or restrict outbound traffic. The connection security rules provide additional capabilities, such as configuring an IPsec connection in tunneling or transport mode to encrypt the traffic.

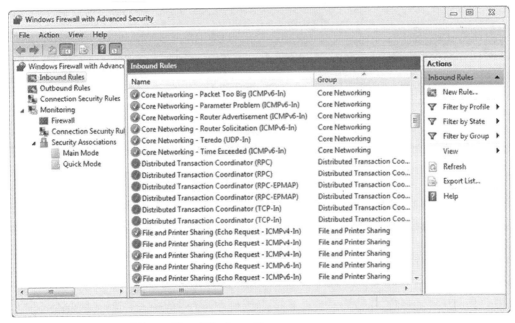

Figure 3.5: Personal firewall on Windows 7

Personal firewalls provide valuable protection for systems against unwanted intrusions. Many organizations use personal firewalls on each system in addition to network firewalls as part of an overall defense-in-depth strategy.

It's especially important to use personal firewalls when accessing the Internet in a public place. Free Wi-Fi Internet access is often available in public places such as airports, hotels, and many fast-food establishments, such as Starbucks and even McDonald's. However, connecting to a public Wi-Fi hotspot without the personal firewall enabled is risky, and never recommended.

> ### Remember this
> Host-based firewalls provide protection for individual hosts such as servers or workstations. A host-based firewall provides intrusion protection for the host. Network-based firewalls are often dedicated servers or appliances and provide protection for the network.

Network-based Firewalls

A network-based firewall controls traffic going in and out of a network. It does this by filtering traffic based on firewall rules and allows only authorized traffic to pass through it. Most organizations include at least one network-based firewall at the boundary between their internal network and the Internet.

The network-based firewall is usually a dedicated system with additional software installed to monitor, filter, and log traffic. For example, a popular network-based firewall used in many larger environments is Sidewinder. This is a dedicated server with proprietary firewall software installed. A network-based firewall would have two or more network interface cards (NICs) and all traffic passes through the firewall. Many network-based firewalls are dedicated servers or appliances.

Firewall Rules

Firewalls use rules implemented as ACLs to identify allowed and blocked traffic. This is similar to how a router uses rules. Most firewalls use an implicit deny strategy as introduced in Chapter 1. As a reminder, an implicit deny strategy blocks all traffic that is not explicitly allowed.

For example, a firewall may want to allow HTTP (port 80), HTTPS (port 443), and SMTP (port 25) traffic. You identify this traffic with firewall rules created in an access control list (ACL). While different firewalls have different formats, the following examples show one set of formatting you may run across.

- Allow TCP 80
- Allow TCP 443
- Allow TCP 25
- Deny any any

Notice that in this example, the format of each rule is Allow (or Deny), the protocol (such as TCP, UDP, or any), and the port (such as 80, 443, 25, or any). The **deny any any** rule is always placed last in the firewall's ACL, and in some firewalls it's listed as **deny all**, or **drop all**. This rule blocks any traffic not previously defined. Many firewalls will implement the **deny any any** rule even if the administrator doesn't include it.

> ### *Remember this*
>
> Firewalls use a **deny any any**, **deny any**, or a **drop all** statement at the end of the ACL to enforce an implicit deny strategy. The statement forces the firewall to block any traffic that wasn't previously allowed in the ACL. The implicit deny strategy provides a secure starting point for a firewall.

Web Application Firewall

A web application firewall (WAF) is a firewall specifically designed to protect a web application, such as a web server. In other words, it's placed between a server hosting a web application and a client. It can be a stand-alone appliance, or software added to another device.

As an example, an organization may host an ecommerce website to generate revenue. The web server will be placed within a DMZ (discussed later in this chapter), but due to the data that the web server handles, it needs more protection. A successful buffer overflow attack may be able to take the web server down or allow an attacker to access or manipulate valuable data.

Chapter 7 covers different types of attacks, including buffer overflow attacks. But as an example, many buffer overflow attacks start with a series of no operation (NOOP) commands called a NOOP sled or a NOOP ramp. The WAF inspects the contents of traffic to the web server, can detect this malicious content, and block it.

Note that you wouldn't use a WAF in place of a network-based firewall. Instead, it provides an added layer of protection for the web application in addition to the network-based firewall.

Web Security Gateways and Appliances

Many vendors have added features to firewalls to provide advanced content filtering within a single unified security solution. Some common names for these unified solutions include web security gateways and all-in-one security appliances.

Similar to a washer or dryer appliance you may have at your home, these appliances have dedicated jobs and are often easy to use. You simply plug them in and follow some basic steps for usage.

These security gateways can protect against multiple threats. This includes threats from malicious software (malware) coming in as an e-mail attachment, malicious code embedded in web browser pages, and spam. They usually include other firewall capabilities, but their real strength is in content filtering.

Many content filters actively monitor data streams by inspecting the packets in search of malicious code or behaviors. For example, e-mail may contain malicious attachments. By inspecting all the packets associated with an e-mail and its attachments, a content filter can detect the malicious content and filter it. Many web security gateways and appliances can filter traffic based on:

- **Content inspection—attachments**. Malware often comes into a network via spam, or malicious web pages. A content filter can screen incoming data for known malicious files and block them. Organizations often scan for malware at e-mail servers and at individual systems as part of a defense-in-depth solution.
- **Content inspection—spam**. Unsolicited e-mail can frequently clog a user's in-box. Many content filters can identify and filter out some known spam. It's also common to filter out spam at the e-mail server and at a user's system.
- **Content inspection—streaming data**. Streaming audio and video files (such as streaming radio) can consume a significant amount of network bandwidth. Some organizations block streaming data to prevent network degradation.
- **URL filtering**. Many websites are known to be malicious, and it's possible to block access to them based on the URL. This works similar to how proxy servers (covered later in this section) filter URLs.
- **Certificate inspection**. Many appliances can check certificates to ensure they are trusted, not expired, and not revoked. Chapter 10 covers certificates in more depth, but, in short, certificate authorities (CAs) issue certificates. If the CA is trusted, the certificate is trusted. The appliance can query the CA for a copy of the certificate revocation list (CRL) to determine if the CA revoked the certificate. If the certificate fails any checks, the appliance blocks access to the site.

> ### Remember this
> Web security gateways and all-in-one security appliances can filter content. These single devices provide a unified security solution. Different vendors include different capabilities, but most will monitor data streams in search of malicious code.

Spam Filters

Unwanted or unsolicited e-mail (spam) makes up between 80 percent and 92 percent of all Internet e-mail, depending on what study you quote. Some spam is harmless advertisements, while much more is malicious. Spam can include malicious links, malicious code, or malicious attachments. And if only one of ten e-mails is valid, it can waste a lot of your time.

While many all-in-one appliances and web security gateways include spam filtering, you can also purchase dedicated spam filter appliances. All e-mail passes through the spam-filtering appliance before going to the company's e-mail server.

The spam filter attempts to identify spam and then filters it out. This e-mail doesn't reach the e-mail server, but instead is kept on the spam-filtering appliance for review by an administrator, if desired. Additionally, e-mail servers usually include spam filters, and user e-mail programs include additional spam filters.

The challenge with most spam filters is to filter out only spam and never filter out actual e-mail. For example, a company wouldn't want a spam filter to filter out an e-mail from a customer trying to buy something. Because of this, most spam filters err on the side of allowing spam through rather than potentially marking valid e-mail as spam. However, the science behind spam filtering has gotten progressively better.

Firewall Logs and Log Analysis

In addition to filtering traffic, most firewalls have logs you can use to monitor traffic. Firewalls typically allow you to log all allowed traffic, all blocked traffic, or both. A firewall log is often the first place that an administrator might check to investigate a possible intrusion.

Scripts and applications automate the process of reviewing logs. As an example, intrusion detection systems frequently use firewall logs as a source of raw data to help identify intrusions. No matter how the logs are reviewed though, they will include valuable information that might signal an attack, or help an administrator create an audit trail of an attack.

As a simple example, a port scan attack will query different logical ports of an IP address to see what ports are open. Based on what ports are open, the attacker can determine what services or protocols may be running on the server. For example, if port 25 provides a response back to the scanner, it indicates this port is open. Since SMTP uses port 25, this system is very likely running SMTP and may be an e-mail server. The attacker will then send other packets to gather more information. If logging is enabled on the firewall, all of this activity is recorded and it can be used to thwart the attack.

Load Balancers

A load balancer can optimize and distribute data loads across multiple computers or multiple networks. For example, if an organization hosts a popular website, it can use multiple servers hosting the same website in a web farm. Load balancing software distributes traffic equally among all the servers in the web farm.

Exploring the Network Perimeter

Most networks have Internet connectivity, but it's rare to connect a network directly to the Internet. Instead, the perimeter divides the internal network (sometimes called the intranet) with the Internet. When an organization needs to host servers accessible via the Internet, they will typically place these servers in a demilitarized zone.

DMZ

The demilitarized zone (DMZ) is a buffered zone between a private network and the Internet. Attackers seek out servers on the Internet, so any server placed directly on the Internet has the highest amount of risk. However, the DMZ provides a layer of protection for these Internet-facing servers.

As an example, Figure 3.6 shows a common network configuration with a DMZ. The DMZ is the area between the two firewalls (FW1 and FW2) and hosts servers accessible from the Internet. Many DMZs have two firewalls creating a buffer zone between the Internet and the internal network, as shown in Figure 3.6, though other configurations are possible.

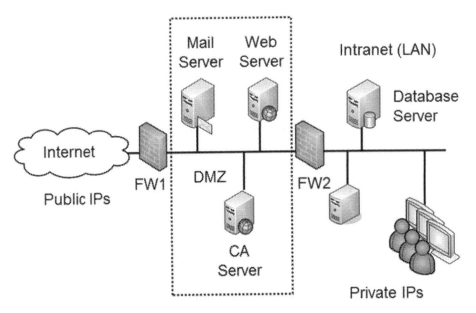

Figure 3.6: Network with DMZ

In this configuration, one firewall separates the DMZ from the Internet. The second firewall separates the DMZ from the internal network. Each firewall includes detailed rules designed to filter traffic and protect both the internal network and the public servers. One way of saying this is that the DMZ provides access to the services hosted in the DMZ, while segmenting access to the internal network.

For example, FW1 can have rules to allow traffic to the servers in the DMZ, but block unsolicited traffic to FW2. The mail server would send and receive e-mail to other e-mail servers on the Internet through port 25 of FW1, and also send and receive e-mail to internal clients through port 25 on FW2. The web server hosts web pages to any Internet users through ports 80 and 443 on FW1, but FW2 blocks these ports. The CA server validates certificates for Internet clients by answering through FW1.

Notice in Figure 3.6 that the intranet includes a database server. The web server may use this to create web pages for an e-commerce site. It could hold product data, customer data, and much more. FW2 allows traffic between the web server (and only the web server) and the database server on port 1433. All other Internet traffic to the database server is blocked.

The DMZ can host any Internet-facing server, not just those shown in the figure. Other examples include FTP servers used for uploading and downloading files and virtual private network (VPN) servers used for providing remote access.

Remember this

A DMZ is a buffer zone between the Internet and an internal network. It allows access to services while segmenting access to the internal network. In other words, Internet clients can access the services hosted on servers in the DMZ, but the DMZ provides a layer of protection for the internal network.

Comparing Public and Private IP Addresses

All Internet IP addresses are public IP addresses, and internal networks use private IP addresses. Both IPv4 and IPv6 use public and private IP addresses, but I'll limit this discussion to IPv4. While the details between IPv4 and IPv6 are different, the overall concepts of public IP addresses and private IP addresses are the same.

Public IP addresses are tightly controlled. You can't just use any public IP address. Instead, you must either purchase or rent it. ISPs purchase entire ranges of IP addresses and issue them to customers. If you access the Internet from home, you are very likely receiving a public IP address from an ISP.

RFC 1918 specifies the following private address ranges:

- **10.x.y.z**. (10.0.0.1 through 10.255.255.254)
- **172.16.y.z–172.31.y.z**. (172.16.0.1 through 172.31.255.254)
- **192.168.y.z**. (192.168.0.1 through 192.168.255.254)

Private IP addresses are not used on the Internet. Routers on the Internet include rules to drop any traffic that is coming from or going to a private IP address.

Understanding NAT

Network Address Translation (NAT) is a protocol that translates public IP addresses to private IP addresses and private addresses back to public. You'll often see NAT enabled on an Internet-facing firewall.

If you run a network at your home (such as a wireless network), the router that connects to the Internet is very likely running NAT. Some of the benefits of NAT include:

- **Public IP addresses don't need to be purchased for all clients**. A home or company network can include multiple computers that can access the Internet through one router running NAT. Larger companies requiring more bandwidth may use more than one public IP address.
- **NAT hides computers from the Internet**. Computers with private IP addresses are isolated and hidden from the Internet. NAT provides a layer of protection to these private computers because they aren't as easy to attack and exploit from the Internet.

> **Remember this**
>
> NAT translates public IP addresses to private IP addresses, and private IP addresses back to public. It also hides addresses on the internal network.

One of the drawbacks to NAT is that it is not compatible with IPsec. You can use IPsec to create VPN tunnels and use it with L2TP to encrypt VPN traffic. While there are ways of getting around NAT's incompatibility with IPsec, if your design includes IPsec going through NAT, you'll need to look at it closely.

NAT can be either static NAT or dynamic NAT.

- **Static NAT**. Static NAT uses a single public IP address in a one-to-one mapping. It maps a single private IP address with a single public IP address.
- **Dynamic NAT**. Dynamic NAT uses multiple public IP addresses in a one-to-many mapping. Dynamic NAT decides which public IP address to use based on load. For example, if several users are using the connection on one public IP address, NAT maps the next request to a less used public IP address.

Proxy Server

Many networks use proxy servers to forward requests for services (such as HTTP or HTTPS) from clients. They can improve performance by caching content and can restrict users' access to inappropriate websites by filtering content. A proxy server is located on the edge of the network bordering the Internet and the intranet, as shown in Figure 3.7.

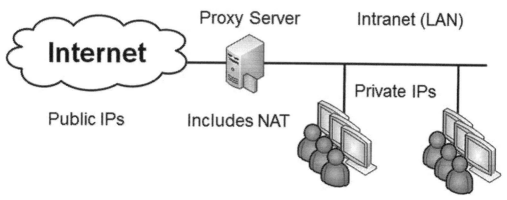

Figure 3.7: Proxy server

All internal clients send requests through the proxy server. The proxy accepts the request, retrieves the content from the Internet, and then returns the data to the client. Most proxy servers only act as a proxy for HTTP and HTTPS. However, proxy servers can also proxy other Internet protocols, such as FTP.

> ### Remember this
> A proxy server forwards requests for services from a client. It provides caching to improve performance and reduce Internet bandwidth usage. Proxy servers can filter content based on URLs and can log sites visited by any users.

Caching Content for Performance

The proxy server increases the performance of Internet requests by caching each result received from the Internet. Any data that is in the proxy server's cache doesn't need to be retrieved from the Internet again to fulfill another client's request.

In this context, *cache* simply means "temporary storage." Cache could be a dedicated area of RAM, or, in some examples, it could also be an area on a high-performance disk subsystem.

As an example, if Sally retrieves a web page from GetCertifiedGetAhead.com, the proxy server would store the result in cache. If Bob later requests the same page, the proxy server retrieves the page from cache and sends it to Bob. This reduces the amount of Internet bandwidth used for web browsing, since the page doesn't need to be retrieved again.

Using Content Filters to Restrict Access

Proxy servers can also restrict what users can access with the use of content filters. A proxy server content filter will examine the requested URL and choose to allow the request or deny the request.

Many third-party companies sell subscription lists for content filtering. These sites scour the Internet for websites and categorize the sites based on what companies typically want to block.

Categories may include anonymizers, pornography, gambling, web-based e-mail, and warez sites. Anonymizers are sites that give the illusion of privacy on the Internet. Employees sometimes try to use anonymizers to bypass proxy servers, but a proxy server will usually detect, block, and log these attempts. Web-based e-mail bypasses the security controls on internal e-mail servers, so many organizations block them. Warez sites often host pirated software, movies, MP3 files, and hacking tools.

The subscription list can be loaded into the proxy server, and whenever a user attempts to access a site on the content filter block list, the proxy blocks the request. Often, the proxy server presents users with a warning page when they try to access a restricted page. Many organizations use this page to remind users of a corporate acceptable usage policy, and some provide reminders that the proxy server is monitoring their online activity.

Proxy servers include logs that record each site visited by a user. These logs can be helpful to identify frequently visited sites and to monitor a user's web browsing activities.

Content filters are not restricted to only proxy servers. Web security gateways (mentioned earlier in the chapter) use content filters. Mail servers perform content filtering to block certain attachments that may include malware. Additionally, operating systems such as Windows 7 include parental controls that perform basic content filtering.

Chapter 3 Exam Topic Review

When preparing for the exam, make sure you understand these key concepts covered in this chapter.

Basic Networking Concepts

- Encryption protocols include SSH, FTPS, SFTP, SCP, IPsec, SSL, and TLS.
- IPsec includes ESP and AH, and can encrypt IP packet payloads. IPsec works in both tunnel and transport modes.
- SSH, SFTP (with SSH), and SCP all use port 22.
- FTP is used to upload and download files. It can be secured with SFTP (an extension of SSH), or FTPS (using SSL). FTP uses port 20 for data and port 21 for control.
- SNMP is used to monitor and configure network devices and uses notification messages known as traps. SNMP uses port 161.
- Telnet uses port 23. When encrypted with SSH, it uses port 22.
- HTTP uses port 80 and HTTPS uses port 443.
- NetBIOS uses ports 137 - 139.
- SMTP uses port 25.
- SQL Server uses port 1433.
- Remote Desktop Services uses port 3389.
- IPv6 uses 128-bit addresses and is displayed as eight groups of four hexadecimal characters.
- A port scanner scans systems for open ports and attempts to discover what services and protocols are running.

Basic Network Devices

- Switches are used for network connectivity and map MAC addresses to ports.
- Loop protection protects against switching loop problems, such as when a user connects two switch ports together with a cable. STP and RSTP are commonly enabled on switches to protect against switching loops.
- Port security limits access to switch ports. It includes limiting the number of MAC addresses per port and disabling unused ports. You can also manually map each port to a specific MAC address or group of addresses.
- VLANs can logically separate computers or logically group computers regardless of their physical location.
- A host-based firewall helps protect a single system from intrusions.
- A network-based firewall controls traffic going in and out of a network.
- A firewall controls traffic between networks using rules within an ACL. The ACL can block traffic based on ports, IP addresses, subnets, and some protocols.
- Most firewalls use an implicit deny strategy where all traffic not explicitly allowed is blocked. This can be implemented with a **deny all**, or **deny any any** rule at the end of the ACL.
- A web security gateway performs content filtering (including filtering for malicious attachments, malicious code, blocked URLs, and more).
- A load balancer can optimize and distribute data loads across multiple computers.

Network Perimeter

- A DMZ provides a layer of protection for servers that are accessible from the Internet.
- NAT translates public IP addresses to private IP addresses, private back to public, and hides IP addresses on the internal network from users on the Internet.
- A proxy server forwards requests for services from a client. It can filter requests based on URLs, cache content, and record user's Internet activity.

Chapter 3 Practice Questions

1. Which of the following protocols is a file transfer protocol using SSH?
    A. SFTP
    B. TFTP
    C. SICMP
    D. CCMP

2. Of the following choices, which one provides the most security for FTP?
    A. FTP active mode
    B. FTPS
    C. TFTP
    D. SCP

3. Of the following choices, what is a benefit of IPsec?
    A. MAC filtering
    B. Flood guard
    C. Load balancing
    D. Payload encryption

4. What protocol is used to monitor and configure network devices?
    A. ICMP
    B. SFTP
    C. SNMP
    D. DNS

5. Which of the following is an IPv6 address?
    A. 192.168.1.100
    B. 192.168.1.100 /128
    C. FE80:20D4:3FF7:003F:DE62
    D. FE80:0000:0000:0000:20D4:3FF7:003F:DE62

6. Which of the following IP addresses are on the same subnet? (Choose all that apply.)
    A. 192.168.1.50, 255.255.255.192
    B. 192.168.1.100, 255.255.255.192
    C. 192.168.1.165, 255.255.255.192
    D. 192.168.1.189, 255.255.255.192

7. An administrator decides to block Telnet access to an internal network from any remote device on the Internet. Which of the following is the best choice to accomplish this?
   - A. Block port 22 at the host firewall
   - B. Block port 22 on internal routers
   - C. Block port 23 at the network firewall
   - D. Block port 23 on internal routers

8. What port does SFTP use?
   - A. 22
   - B. 23
   - C. 443
   - D. 1443

9. What ports do HTTP and HTTPS use?
   - A. 20 and 21
   - B. 22 and 25
   - C. 80 and 443
   - D. 80 and 1433

10. What port does SMTP use?
   - A. 22
   - B. 25
   - C. 110
   - D. 143

11. Of the following choices, what ports are used by NetBIOS? (Choose two.)
   - A. 80
   - B. 137
   - C. 139
   - D. 3389

12. Your organization uses switches for connectivity. Of the following choices, what will protect the switch?
   - A. Disable unused MAC addresses
   - B. Disable unused ports
   - C. Disable unused IPv4 addresses
   - D. Disable unused IPv6 addresses

13. A user plugged a cable into two RJ-45 wall jacks connected to unused ports on a switch. In a short period, this disrupted the overall network performance. What should you do to protect against this problem in the future?

    A. Enable loop protection on the switch

    B. Disable port security

    C. Use a VLAN

    D. Create DMZ

14. What can you use to logically separate computers in two different departments within a company?

    A. A hub

    B. A VLAN

    C. NAT

    D. A flood guard

15. Most firewalls have a default rule placed at the end of the firewall's ACL. Which of the following is the most likely default rule?

    A. Deny any any

    B. Deny ICMP all

    C. Allow all all

    D. Allow TCP all

16. Of the following choices, what best describes a method of managing the flow of network traffic by allowing or denying traffic based on ports, protocols, and addresses?

    A. Implicit deny

    B. Firewall rules

    C. Proxy server content filter

    D. Firewall logs

17. Of the following choices, what represents the best choice to prevent intrusions on an individual computer?

    A. HIDS

    B. NIDS

    C. Host-based firewall

    D. Network-based firewalls

18. Your network includes a subnet that hosts accounting servers with sensitive data. You want to ensure that users in the Marketing Department (on a separate subnet) cannot access these servers. Of the following choices, what would be the easiest to achieve the goal?

    A. Enable load balancing

    B. Enable port security

    C. Use an ACL

    D. Add a host-based firewall to each server

19. Of the following choices, what controls traffic between networks?
    A. A firewall
    B. Load balancer
    C. VPN concentrator
    D. Protocol analyzer

20. An organization has a web security gateway installed. What function is this performing?
    A. MAC filtering
    B. Caching content
    C. Hiding internal IP addresses
    D. Content filtering

21. Your organization hosts a large website served by multiple servers. They need to optimize the workload and distribute it equally among all the servers. What should they use?
    A. Proxy server
    B. Load balancer
    C. Web security gateway
    D. Security appliance

22. Of the following choices, what can be used to allow access to specific services from the Internet while protecting access to an internal network?
    A. SSH
    B. Implicit deny
    C. DMZ
    D. Port security

23. Of the following choices, what hides the IP addresses of computers inside a network from computers outside the network?
    A. Web security gateway
    B. Replacing all hubs with switches
    C. WAF
    D. NAT

24. Of the following choices, what is the best choice for a device to filter and cache content from web pages?
    A. Web security gateway
    B. VPN concentrator
    C. Proxy server
    D. MAC filtering

Chapter 3 Practice Question Answers

1. **A.** Secure FTP (SFTP) is a secure implementation of FTP, an extension of Secure Shell (SSH), and transmits data using port 22. Trivial FTP is a form of FTP using UDP to transmit smaller amounts of data than FTP. ICMP is a diagnostic protocol used by tools such as ping, but there is no such thing as SICMP. CCMP is an encryption protocol used with wireless networks.

2. **B.** File Transfer Protocol Secure (FTPS) uses SSL to secure FTP transmissions. FTP can work in active or passive mode, but this only affects how the ports are used, not the security. TFTP is a trivial form of FTP and doesn't provide security. SCP uses SSH to copy files over a network and isn't related to FTP.

3. **D.** Internet Protocol security (IPsec) includes Encapsulating Security Payload (ESP), which can encrypt the IP packet payload. Port security and network access control can use MAC filtering. A flood guard protects against SYN flood attacks, and a load balancer can optimize and distribute data loads across multiple computers, but neither are related to IPsec.

4. **C.** Simple Network Management Protocol (SNMP) can monitor and manage network devices such as routers or switches and uses device traps. Diagnostic tools such as ping use ICMP, and many firewalls block ICMP traffic. SFTP is a secure form of FTP used to upload and download files. DNS resolves host names to IP addresses.

5. **D.** An IPv6 address uses 128-bit IP addresses and includes eight groups of four hexadecimal characters. IPv4 (not IPv6) uses the dotted decimal format with decimals separated by dots. A double colon indicates zero compression, when less than eight groups are shown, but if omitted the address isn't valid.

6. **C, D.** Both 192.168.1.165 and 192.168.1.189 are on the same subnet since bits 25 and 26 are the same (10). Bits 25 and 26 are 00 for 192.168.1.50, and 01 for 192.168.1.100 so these two are on different subnets from the any of the other IP addresses.

7. **C.** You can block all telnet traffic into the network by blocking port 23 on the network firewall. Port 22 is used for SSH, SCP or SFTP, not Telnet (unless Telnet is encrypted with SSH). Additionally, blocking it at the host firewall only blocks it to the host, not the network. It's easier to block the port once at the firewall rather than block the port on all internal routers. Additionally, the scenario states that the goal is to block access from the Internet, but Telnet may be authorized internally.

8. **A.** Secure File Transfer Protocol (SFTP) uses port 22, as do other protocols encrypted with Secure Shell (SSH) such as Secure Copy (SCP). Telnet uses port 23. HTTPS uses port 443. Microsoft's SQL Server uses port 1443.

9. **C.** Hypertext Transfer Protocol (HTTP) uses port 80 and HTTP Secure (HTTPS) uses port 443, and they are both used to transfer web pages. FTP uses ports 20 and 21. Microsoft's SQL server uses port 1433. SFTP and SCP use port 22. SMTP uses port 25.

10. **B.** Simple Mail Transfer Protocol (SMTP) uses port 25. SCP, TFTP, and SSH all use port 22. POP3 uses port 110. IMAP4 uses port 143.

11. **B, C.** NetBIOS uses ports 137, 138, and 139. HTTP uses port 80, and remote desktop services uses port 3389.

12. **B.** Disabling unused ports is a part of basic port security. While switches can associate MAC addresses associated with ports, it's not possible to disable unused MAC addresses on the switch. Switches track traffic based on MAC addresses, not IP addresses.

13. **A.** Loop protection such as Spanning Tree Protocol (STP) protects against the switching loop problem described in the scenario. While disabling unused ports may help against this problem, you do this by implementing port security, not disabling port security. A DMZ is used to host Internet facing servers and isn't relevant in this situation. VLANs can logically separate computers using the same switch but do not prevent switching loops.

14. **B.** A virtual local area network (VLAN) can group several different computers into a virtual network, or logically separate the computers in two different departments. A hub doesn't have any intelligence and can't separate the computers. NAT translates private IP addresses to public IP addresses, and public back to private. A flood guard protects against SYN flood attacks.

15. **A.** A **deny any any** or **drop all** statement is placed at the end of an ACL and enforces an implicit deny strategy. While many firewalls include a rule to deny ICMP traffic (such as pings or ICMP sweeps), it isn't a default rule and wouldn't be placed last. An **allow all all** rule allows all protocol traffic that wasn't previously blocked but is rarely (if ever) used in a firewall. Similarly, it's rare to allow all TCP traffic on any port. Instead, a firewall uses an implicit deny principle by specifying what is allowed, and blocking everything else.

16. **B.** Firewalls use firewall rules (or rules within an ACL) to identify what traffic is allowed and what traffic is denied, and a basic packet filtering firewall can filter traffic based on ports, protocols, and addresses. Firewalls use implicit deny to block all traffic not previously allowed, but this more accurately describes what is blocked rather describing the entire flow of traffic. A proxy server content filter can filter traffic based on content (such as URLs), but can't allow or deny traffic based on ports or protocols. Firewall logs are useful to determine what traffic a firewall has allowed or blocked but do not allow or deny traffic themselves.

17. **C.** A host-based firewall can help prevent intrusions on individual computers such as a server or desktop computer. A host-based intrusion detection system (HIDS) and a network-based

intrusion detection system (NIDS) can *detect* intrusions, not *prevent* them. A network-based firewall is used to monitor and control traffic on a network, not just an individual system.

18. **C.** An access control list (ACL) on a router can block access to the subnet from another subnet. A load balancer can optimize and distribute data loads across multiple computers or multiple networks, but it doesn't isolate traffic. Disabling unused ports is a part of basic port security and wouldn't separate subnet traffic. A host-based firewall can protect against intrusions on individual systems and could block the traffic, but you'd have to enable it on every server, as opposed to creating a single rule in an ACL.

19. **A.** A firewall controls traffic between networks using rules within an ACL. A load balancer can optimize and distribute data loads across multiple computers. A VPN concentrator provides access to an internal network from a public network such as the Internet. A protocol analyzer (a sniffer) is used to view headers and clear-text contents in IP packets, but it can't control the traffic.

20. **D.** A web security gateway performs content filtering (including filtering for malicious attachments, malicious code, blocked URLs, and more). Port security and network access control use MAC filtering to limit access. A proxy server caches content. NAT translates public IP addresses to private IP addresses, private back to public, and can hide addresses on the internal network.

21. **B.** A load balancer can optimize and distribute data loads across multiple computers or multiple networks. A proxy server provides content filtering and caching. Web security gateways and all-in-one security appliances provide content filtering, but not load balancing.

22. **C.** A demilitarized zone (DMZ) can provide access to services (hosted on servers) from the Internet while providing a layer of protection for the internal network. SSH encrypts traffic such as Telnet, SCP, and SFTP over port 22, but it can't control access. Implicit deny blocks all traffic not explicitly allowed. Port security enhances switch security and includes disabling unused ports.

23. **D.** Network Address Translation (NAT) translates public IP addresses to private IP addresses, and private back to public, and hides addresses on the internal network. A Web security gateway performs content filtering, including filtering for malicious attachments, malicious code, blocked URLs, and more. Replacing hubs with switches improves network performance and adds security, but doesn't hide addresses outside of a network. A WAF is an additional firewall designed to protect a web application.

24. **C.** A proxy server includes the ability to filter and cache content from web pages. A web security gateway can filter web-based content, but it doesn't always have caching capabilities. A VPN concentrator provides access to VPN clients. MAC filtering can be used with port security on a switch, but doesn't filter web page content.

Chapter 4

Securing Your Network

CompTIA Security+ objectives covered in this chapter:

1.1 Explain the security function and purpose of network devices and technologies

- VPN concentrators
- NIDS and NIPS (behavior based, signature based, anomaly based, heuristic)

1.2 Apply and implement secure network administration principles

- 802.1x

1.3 Distinguish and differentiate network design elements and compounds

- Remote access
- Telephony
- NAC

1.4 Implement and use common protocols

- IPsec
- TLS
- SSL

1.6 Implement wireless network in a secure manner

- WPA
- WPA2
- WEP
- EAP
- PEAP
- LEAP
- MAC filter
- SSID broadcast

- TKIP
- CCMP
- Antenna placement
- Power level controls

2.1 Explain risk related concepts

- False positives

2.4 Explain the importance of security related awareness and training

- Threat awareness
  - Zero days exploits

3.4 Analyze and differentiate among types of wireless attacks

- Rogue access points
- Interference
- Evil twin
- War driving
- Bluejacking
- Bluesnarfing
- War chalking
- IV attack
- Packet sniffing

3.5 Analyze and differentiate among types of application attacks

- Zero day

3.6 Analyze and differentiate among types of mitigation and deterrent techniques

- Port security
  - MAC limiting and filtering
  - 802.1x
  - Disabling unused ports
- Security posture
  - Continuous security monitoring
  - Remediation
- Reporting
  - Alarms
  - Alerts
  - Trends
- Detection controls vs. prevention controls
  - IDS vs. IPS

3.7 Implement assessment tools and techniques to discover security threats and vulnerabilities

- Tools
  - Honeypots
  - Honeynets
  - Port scanner

4.2 Carry out appropriate procedures to establish host security
- Mobile devices
  - Screen lock
  - Strong password
  - Device encryption
  - Remote wipe/sanitation
  - Voice encryption
  - GPS tracking

6.2 Use and apply appropriate cryptographic tools and products
- WEP vs. WPA/WPA2 and preshared key
- Use of algorithms with transport encryption
  - SSL
  - TLS
  - IPsec
  - SSH
  - HTTPS

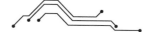

In this chapter, you'll learn about some more advanced network security concepts. Topics include intrusion detection and prevention systems (IDSs and IPSs), methods used to secure wireless networks, and remote access technologies.

Understanding IDSs and IPSs

Intrusion detection systems (IDSs) help detect attacks on systems and networks. Intrusion prevention systems (IPSs) stop attacks in progress by detecting and blocking attacks on systems and networks. While some active IDSs can also take steps to block attacks, not all IDSs are active. This section presents IDSs first, and then wraps up with some information on IPSs and compares the two.

> ### Remember this
> An IDS is a detective control that attempts to detect attacks after they occur. In contrast, a firewall is a preventative control that attempts to prevent the attacks before they occur. An IPS is a preventative control that will stop an attack in progress.

The primary types of IDSs you'll see are host-based IDSs (HIDSs) and network-based IDSs (NIDSs). Each of these IDSs detect attacks either through predefined attack signatures or by detecting anomalies. Once an attack occurs, an IDS can respond either passively or actively. An IPS responds actively to prevent the attack.

The following items summarize the important concepts related to IDSs and IPSs.

- A HIDS is installed on individual servers and workstations.
- A NIDS is installed on network devices such as routers and firewalls.
- Signature-based (or definition-based) monitoring detects attacks based on known attack patterns.
- Anomaly-based (also called behavior-based or heuristics-based) monitoring detects attacks by first identifying normal operation through a baseline. It then then compares current operations against the baseline to detect abnormal behavior.
- A passive IDS will log an alert. It may also inform personnel of the alert.
- An active IDS will log and possibly inform personnel of the alert, and also take action to change the environment.
- An IPS is similar to an active IDS with one distinctive difference. An IPS is always placed in line with the traffic so it can prevent the attack from reaching the network.

HIDS

A host-based intrusion detection system (HIDS) is additional software installed on a system such as a workstation or server. It provides protection to the individual host and can protect critical operating system files. The primary goal of any IDS is to monitor traffic. For a HIDS, this traffic passes through the network interface card (NIC).

Many host-based IDSs have expanded to monitor application activity on the system. As one example, you can install a HIDS on different Internet-facing servers such as web servers, mail servers, and database servers. In addition to monitoring the network traffic reaching the servers, the HIDS can also monitor the server applications.

> ### Remember this
> A host-based IDS (HIDS) is additional software on a workstation or server. It can detect attacks on the local system. The HIDS protects local resources on the host such as the operating system files.

Some organizations install a HIDS on every workstation as an extra layer of protection, similar to how most organizations install antivirus protection on every workstation. Just as the HIDS on a server is used primarily to monitor network traffic, a workstation HIDS is primarily used to monitor network traffic reaching the workstation. However, a HIDS may also monitor some applications and can protect local resources such as operating system files.

NIDS

A network-based intrusion detection system (NIDS) monitors activity on the network. An administrator installs NIDSs sensors on network devices such as routers and firewalls. These sensors gather information and report to a central monitoring server hosting a NIDS console.

A NIDS is not able to detect anomalies on individual systems or workstations unless the anomaly causes a significant difference in network traffic. Additionally, a NIDS is unable to decrypt encrypted traffic. In other words, it can only monitor and assess threats on the network from traffic sent in plain text or non-encrypted traffic.

Figure 4.1 shows an example of a NIDS configuration. In the figure, sensors are located before the firewall, after the firewall, and on routers. These sensors monitor network traffic on subnets within the network and report back to the NIDS console. If an attacker launched an attack on the network (such as a smurf attack, described in Chapter 7), the NIDS will detect it.

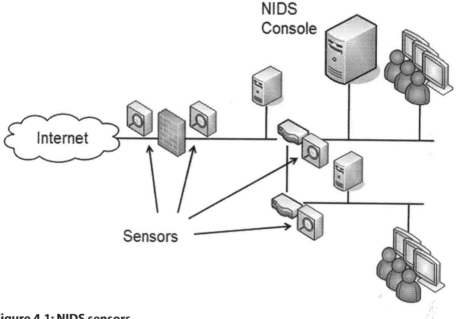

Figure 4.1: NIDS sensors

The decision on where you want to place the sensors depends on what you want to measure. For example, the sensor on the Internet side of the firewall will see all the traffic. However, the sensor on the internal side of the firewall will only see traffic that has passed by the firewall. In other words, the firewall will filter some attacks, and the internal sensor won't see them.

If you want to see all attacks on your network, put a sensor on the Internet side. If you only want to see what gets through, put sensors internally only. If you want to see both, put sensors in both places.

Remember this

A network-based IDS (NIDS) is installed on network devices, such as routers or firewalls, to monitor network traffic. It can detect network-based attacks such as smurf attacks. A NIDS cannot monitor encrypted traffic and cannot monitor traffic on individual hosts.

Detection Methods

An IDS can only detect an attack. It cannot prevent them. In contrast, an IPS prevents attacks by detecting them and stopping them before they reach the target. An attack is any attempt to compromise confidentiality, integrity, or availability.

The two primary methods of detection are signature based and anomaly based. Any type of IDS (HIDS or NIDS) can detect attacks based on signatures, anomalies, or both. The HIDS will monitor the network traffic reaching its NIC, and the NIDS will monitor the traffic on the network.

Signature Based

Signature-based IDSs (also called definition based) use a database of known attack patterns. For example, tools are available for an attacker to launch a SYN flood attack (described in chapter 3) on a server by simply entering the IP address of the system to attack. The tool will then flood the attacked system with SYN packets but never complete the TCP handshake with the ACK packets.

Since this is a recognized attack, it has a known pattern of successive SYN packets from one IP to another IP. The traffic does not include matching ACK packets, resulting in a steadily increasing number of open sessions.

> ### Remember this
>
> Signature-based IDSs (also called definition based) use a database of predefined traffic patterns. IDS vendors regularly release signature file updates as they learn about and document new attack patterns. A signature-based IDS is the most basic form of detection and the easiest to implement.

The IDS can detect these patterns when the signature database includes the attack definitions. The process is very similar to what antivirus software uses to detect malware. You need to update both IDS signatures and antivirus definitions on a regular basis to protect against current threats.

Anomaly Based

Anomaly-based detection (also called heuristic or behavior-based detection) first identifies normal operation or normal behavior. It does this by creating a performance baseline under normal operating conditions.

The IDS constantly compares current behavior against the baseline. When the IDS detects abnormal activity (outside normal boundaries as identified in the baseline), it gives an alert indicating a potential attack.

Anomaly-based detection is similar to how heuristic-based antivirus software works. While the internal methods are different, both examine activity and make decisions that are outside the scope of a signature or definition database.

Any time significant changes are made to a system or network that cause normal behavior to change, the baseline should be recreated. Otherwise, the IDS will constantly alert on what is now normal behavior.

Remember this

Anomaly-based IDSs (also called behavior based) start with a performance baseline of normal behavior. The IDS compares network traffic against this baseline, and when traffic differs significantly outside the expected boundaries, the IDS will give an alert. If the network environment is updated or changed, the IDS requires a new baseline to identify the new normal.

Data Sources and Trends

Any type of IDS will use various raw data sources to collect information on activity. This includes a wide variety of logs, such as firewall logs, system logs, and application logs. These logs can be analyzed to provide insight on trends. These trends can detect a pattern of attacks and provide insight into how to better protect a network.

Many IDSs have the capability to monitor logs in real time. Each time a system records a log entry, the IDS examines the log to determine if it is an item of interest or not. Other IDSs will periodically poll relevant logs and scan new entries looking for items of interest.

Alarms, Alerts, and Trends

Alarms and alerts are the same thing and they indicate that an IDS has detected an event of interest. An alert is not necessarily an attack. Alerts occur when activity reaches a threshold indicating a potential attack. The goal is to set the threshold of an alert to a level low enough so that you are always informed when an attack occurs and high enough so that you do not get too many false positives.

Consider the classic SYN flood attack, where the attacker withholds the third part of the TCP handshake. A host will send a SYN packet and a server will respond with a SYN/ACK packet. However, instead of completing the handshake with an ACK packet, the attacking host never sends the ACK, but continues to send more SYN packets. This leaves the server with open connections that can ultimately disrupt services.

It is possible for the third packet of a single TCP handshake to never reach a server during normal operation. A host system could start the handshake process but not complete it due to network issues or some other minor problem. This isn't an attack and shouldn't cause an alert.

However, if the same IP address initiated over one thousand TCP sessions in less than sixty seconds and never completed any of the sessions, it is clear this is an attack. Some number between one and one thousand would be set as the threshold to signal an alert.

IDS Threshold

When setting the threshold, the IDS administrator will try to balance the risks of an attack against the risks of false positives.

Most administrators want to know if their system is under attack. That's the primary purpose of the IDS. However, an IDS that constantly cries "Wolf!" will be ignored when the real wolf attacks. It's important to set the threshold low enough to reduce the number of false positives, but high enough to alert on any actual attacks.

There is no perfect number for the threshold. Administrators adjust thresholds in different networks based on the network's activity level and personal preferences of security administrators.

IDS Responses

An IDS will respond after detecting an attack, and the response can be either passive or active. A passive response primarily consists of logging and notifying personnel, while an active response will also change the environment to block the attack.

Passive IDS

A passive IDS will log the attack and may also raise an alert to notify someone. Most IDSs are passive by default. The notification can come in many forms, including:

- **A pop-up window**. A dialog box can appear notifying the user of the event.
- **A central monitor**. Some large organizations use central monitors to display events of interest.
- **An e-mail**. The IDS can send an e-mail to a user or group. Many e-mail systems can forward these to portable devices such as BlackBerry devices or mobile phones.
- **A page or text message**. Many e-mail servers can accept e-mail and forward it to a phone system to send a page or text message.

Active IDS

An active IDS will log and notify personnel just as a passive IDS will, but it can also change the environment to thwart or block the attack. An active IDS can:

- Modify ACLs on firewalls to block offending traffic
- Close processes on a system that were caused by the attack
- Divert the attack to a safe environment
- Consider the SYN flood attack, where an attack floods a system with SYN packets but never completes the three-way TCP handshake with the ACK packet.
- The attack is often coming from a specific IP address. The IDS can modify access control lists on a router or firewall to block all traffic from this IP address. The attacker initiated TCP sessions consume resources on the server until they're closed. The active IDS can close all of these sessions to free up resources.
- It's also possible to divert the attack to a honeypot or honeynet.

Diverting to a Honeypot

A honeypot is a sweet-looking server—at least it's intended to look sweet to the attacker, similar to how honey looks sweet to a bear. It's actually a server that is left open or appears to have been sloppily locked down, allowing an attacker relatively easy access. The intent is for the server to look like an easy target so that the attacker spends his time in the honeypot instead of in a live network. In short, the honeypot diverts the attacker away from the live network.

As an example, a honeypot could be an FTP server that has minimal protection that an attacker can easily bypass. If the server is left completely open without any security, it may look too suspicious to experienced attackers, and they may simply avoid it.

Honeypots are often used as a tool to gather intelligence on the attacker. Attackers are constantly modifying their methods to take advantage of different types of attacks. Some sophisticated attackers discover vulnerabilities before a patch is released (also known as a zero day exploit, or zero day vulnerability).

A zero day vulnerability is usually defined as one that is unknown to the vendor. However, in some usage, administrators define a zero day exploit as one where the vendor has not released a patch. In other words, the vendor may know about the vulnerability but has not written, tested, and released a patch to close the vulnerability yet.

In both cases, the vulnerability exists and systems are unprotected. If attackers discover the vulnerabilities, they exploit them. On the other hand, if security professionals have a honeypot, they may be able to observe attackers launching zero day vulnerability attacks.

Honeypots never hold any data that is valuable to the organization. The data may appear to be valuable to an attacker, but its disclosure is harmless. Honeypots have two primary goals:

- **Divert attackers from the live network**. As long as an attacker is spending time in the honeypot, he is not attacking live resources.
- **Allow observation of an attacker**. While an attacker is in the honeypot, security professionals are able to observe the attack and learn from the attacker's methodologies. Honeypots can also help security professionals learn about zero day exploits, or previously unknown attacks.

Remember this

A honeypot is used to divert an attacker from a live network and/or allow IT administrators an opportunity to observe methodologies used in an attack. Honeypots can be useful to observe zero day exploits (previously unknown attacks).

Sun Tzu famously wrote in *The Art of War*, "All warfare is based on deception," and "Know your enemies." Security professionals on the front lines of network and system attacks recognize that these attacks mimic warfare in many ways, and they are sometimes referred to as cyber warfare. Honeypots and honeynets are extra tools that security professionals use in the war.

Honeynets

A honeynet is a group of virtual servers contained within a single physical server. The honeynet mimics the functionality of a live network.

As an example, you can use a single powerful server with a significant amount of RAM and processing power. This server could host multiple virtual servers, where each virtual server is running an operating system and applications. A physical server hosting six virtual servers will appear as seven systems on a subnet. An attacker looking in will not be able to determine if the servers are physical or virtual.

The purpose of this virtual network is to attract the attention of an attacker, similar to how a single honeypot tries to attract the attention of an attacker. As long as the attacker is in the honeynet, the live network isn't being attacked, and administrators can observe the attackers actions.

Counterattacks

An active response IDS would rarely perform a counterattack against the attacker. Some network security professionals specialize in attacks or counterattacks, but regular administrators should avoid them.

Consider basic human nature. If one person bumps into another in a crowd, the second person could simply ignore it or give a smile and a nod indicating "no problem," and the event is over. On the other hand, if the response is an aggressive push accompanied by some loud words, the event escalates. It can turn ugly quickly.

Consider some basic facts about attackers today.

- **Attackers are professionals**. Attackers aren't just bored teenagers passing their time away like Matthew Broderick in the movie *War Games*. Most attackers today are professional attackers, similar to how you might consider a seasoned car thief as a professional car thief. They are often very good at what they do. Attackers' skills steadily increase, and their tools are becoming more and more sophisticated.
- **Attackers have unlimited time**. Attackers usually have the luxury of spending 100 percent of their time on attack strategies and methodologies. Compare this to network administrators, who have a host of other duties and rarely can spend 100 percent of their time on security.

Many administrators certainly have the expertise to investigate an attack, trace an IP address back, and launch a counterattack. However, just because you can doesn't mean you should. The attacker will likely detect the counterattack and escalate the attack. Instead of moving on from your network, the attacker may take your attack personally and consider it a lifelong mission to cripple your network.

It's also highly likely that the attacking IP address is not the actual attacker. Very often, the attacker will hijack the machines of unwitting users and launch attack from their systems. If you counterattack, you may be attacking the wrong computer.

IDS vs. IPS

Intrusion prevention systems (IPSs) are an extension of IDSs. Just as you can have both a HIDS and a NIDS, you can also have a HIPS or a NIPS, but a NIPS is more common. There are two primary distinctions of an IPS.

- All IPSs will detect and block attacks, while only *active* IDSs will detect and block attacks. A passive IDS only detects attacks and logs or records them.
- An IPS is in line with the traffic. In other words, all traffic passes through the IPS and the IPS can block malicious traffic.

As an example, Figure 4.2 shows the location of a network-based IPS (NIPS).All traffic flows through the IPS giving it an opportunity to inspect incoming traffic. The NIPS blocks malicious traffic by detecting and preventing the attacks.

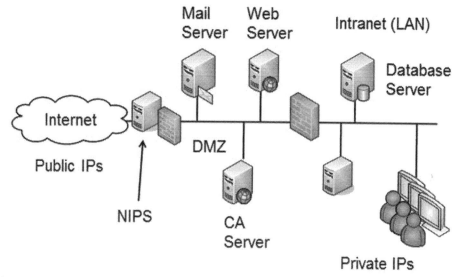

Figure 4.2: NIPS used to detect and prevent attacks

An IPS has the capability of actively monitoring data streams looking for malicious behavior. Chapter 3 discussed content filters and how web security gateways use them to inspect packet contents to detect malicious code. An IPS can also inspect these packets looking for malicious behaviors and prevent them as they are occurring. For example, if an attacker is using a port scanner to detect open ports on a system, the IPS can detect the activity and take action to block it. In some cases, the IPS simply drops the packets to stop them before they reach the network.

In contrast, a NIDS has sensors that monitor and report the traffic. An active NIDS can take steps to block an attack, but it's only after the attack has started. The in-line configuration of the IPS allows an IPS to perform much quicker than an IDS.

Remember this

An intrusion prevention system (IPS) is a preventative control. It is similar to an active IDS except that it's placed in line with traffic. An IPS can actively monitor data streams, detect malicious content, and stop attacks in progress.

Securing Wireless Networks

Wireless local area networks (WLANs) have become quite popular in recent years, especially in home networks. A wireless network is easy to set up and can quickly connect several computers without the need to run cables.

The significant challenge with wireless networks is security. Wireless security has improved over the years, but wireless networks are still susceptible to vulnerabilities, so it's important to understand the basics of security when setting up a wireless network.

Figure 4.3 shows a typical home wireless network. Users share a single connection to the Internet through an Internet service provider (ISP). This connection can be a regular modem, a broadband cable modem, or another method.

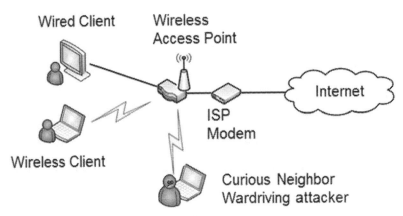

Figure 4.3: Typical home wireless network

A wireless access point (WAP) connects to the modem to share Internet access and connects all the computers in the network. Most WAPs include physical ports for wired access and a wireless transceiver for wireless clients. In other words, some users can connect with regular twisted pair cable, and other users can connect using wireless transmissions. When used as shown in Figure 4.3, the WAP also includes extra capabilities such as routing, network address translation (NAT), and more.

Since wireless networks broadcast on known frequency bands, other wireless users can often see a wireless network. This can be a curious neighbor or a dedicated war driver, driving through your neighborhood looking for open wireless networks to attack.

WAPs with routing capabilities are commonly called wireless routers. However, not all WAPs are wireless routers. Many corporate networks use WAPs simply to bridge wireless clients to the wired network.

802.11

IEEE 802.11 is a group of several protocols that define the standards for wireless networks. Table 4.1 shows some of the common wireless standards, their maximum throughput, and operating frequencies.

IEEE Standard	Maximum Bandwidth	Operating Frequencies
802.11a	54 Mbit/s	5 GHz
802.11b	11 Mbit/s	2.4 GHz
802.11g	54 Mbit/s	2.4 GHz
802.11n	600 Mbit/s	2.4 GHz and 5 GHz

Table 4.1: Wireless standards

Not every connection to a WAP will achieve the maximum throughput. Instead, the client and WAP negotiate the highest throughput they can achieve without errors. A wireless device in the same room as the WAP will be quicker than a wireless device separated by space, walls, and floors.

Additionally, wireless devices don't operate on exactly 2.5 GHz or 5 GHz. Instead, wireless transmissions use multiple channels within these bands. For the Security+ exam, it's not critical to know the details of wireless transmission bands, but you should understand that the signals are transmitted over the air, and the frequencies are known. An attacker with a wireless receiver (such as a simple laptop) and a protocol analyzer (a sniffer) can easily detect and capture wireless transmissions.

Managing the Wireless Footprint

A significant vulnerability of wireless networks is that they broadcast traffic over the air. The area where wireless devices can receive wireless transmissions is the wireless network's footprint. Anyone within the footprint of the transmitter can tune to the correct frequency and access the transmissions.

Administrators have competing goals with the footprint. Users want easy access to the WAP, so they prefer a large footprint with strong signals. However, the stronger the signal is, the easier it is for an attacker to eavesdrop and capture network traffic. From a security perspective, the goal is to limit the footprint to prevent attackers from accessing the wireless network from external locations such as a parking lot.

If you want to reduce the footprint, you can reduce the power output of the WAP. The amount of power used by the WAP determines how far it transmits. Use less power and you'll have a weaker signal and a smaller footprint. Of course, the tradeoff is reduced performance for authorized users. If the signal is weak, the negotiated speed is slower. Some users farther away from the WAP may not be able to connect at all.

Another method to reduce the footprint is to modify the placement of the WAP's antenna. For example, walls (especially walls with metal in them) can interfere with wireless signals. By placing the WAP behind a metal wall, you may be able to prevent the signal from going too far beyond this wall.

Additionally, you can modify the position of the antennas. For example, if you position the antennas vertically (straight up and down), the signals will radiate outwards increasing the footprint. However, if you position the antennas horizontally (parallel with the horizon or the floor) the signal radiates up and down more than it radiates outward. This is useful when transmitting a signal between floors of a building, and it also reduces the footprint outside the building.

> **Remember this**
> Increasing the power level of a WAP increases the wireless coverage of the WAP. You can limit the range of wireless signals by decreasing the power levels of the WAP, and by moving or positioning the wireless antenna.

Decreasing the footprint isn't always successful to thwart eavesdroppers. Most common wireless devices use omnidirectional antennas to receive a wireless signal from any direction. However, an attacker can create a unidirectional antenna that can receive wireless traffic from a specific direction. For example, attackers create simple cantennas (antennas using a can) to capture signals from a specific direction. They connect the wireless receiver to one end of an empty can and simply point the can toward a wireless network. By pointing the cantenna in different directions, they can home in on the exact location of a wireless network. Additionally, they can eavesdrop on wireless conversations even though they are well outside the normal footprint.

Security Protocols

Since wireless networks broadcast over the air, anyone who has a wireless transceiver can intercept the transmissions. You can secure wireless networks with several different steps, but the most important step is to implement a security protocol. As an introduction, the available security protocols are:

- **WEP**. Considered compromised and should not be used
- **WPA**. Considered compromised, but stronger with AES (instead of TKIP)
- **WPA2**. Current standard and provides best security when used in Enterprise mode (with an 802.1X or RADIUS server)

WEP

Wired Equivalent Privacy (WEP) was the original security protocol used to secure wireless networks. As the name implies, the goal was to provide the same level of privacy and security within a wireless network as you'd have in a wired network.

Unfortunately, WEP has significant vulnerabilities, and tools are widely available to break into WEP-protected networks. Due to the widely published vulnerabilities of WEP, it was deprecated in 2004. WPA was identified as an interim replacement, and WPA2 is a permanent replacement.

Chapter 10 will cover encryption in greater depth, but an important concept is that most encryption methods use both an algorithm and a key. Encryption algorithms are widely known, but the keys should be kept secret and changed regularly.

WEP uses the RC4 stream cipher for encryption of transmitted data. An important implementation rule with any stream cipher is that encryption keys should never be reused. A single key can encrypt and decrypt data, but if encryption always uses the same key to decrypt and decrypt the data, it becomes relatively easy for an attacker to crack the key and read the data. Even if the encryption reuses a key just once, it increases the ability of an attacker to crack it.

The following section describes one of the ways attackers exploit this weakness in WEP.

IV Attack

One method of creating different keys is with an initialization vector (IV). The IV provides randomization of the keys to help ensure that keys are not reused. Unfortunately, WEP uses a relatively small IV, and the result is that WEP regularly reuses the same keys. Because of this, attackers can use an IV attack to discover the keys and read the data.

While RC4 is very strong and used successfully elsewhere (such as in SSL), the small IV used in WEP made it quite easy for attackers to crack it. Attackers have off-the-shelf software they can use to capture, analyze, and decrypt WEP traffic within a couple of minutes.

The keys used in WEP are derived from the WEP key (or passphrase) entered into the WAP and the wireless devices. WEP then uses an initialization vector (IV), transmitted in plain text, to create the keys used for RC4.

As an example, imagine the passphrase is Ip@$$ed. WEP combines Ip@$$ed with an IV to create a key, and then encrypts the packet with this key. Of course, the other side needs to be able to decrypt the packet. WEP includes the IV in plain text. Both entities already know the passphrase, so it isn't included. When the other system receives the packet, it combines the IV included in the packet with the passphrase to decrypt the packet.

Unfortunately, with a small IV the number of possible keys is limited. The result is that WEP will eventually reuse encryption keys. Once WEP reuses the key, it becomes easy to crack and decrypt the data.

In many IV attacks, the attacker uses packet injection techniques to add additional packets into the data stream. The WAP responds with more packets, increasing the probability that it will reuse a key. An IV attack using packet injection decreases the time it takes to crack a WEP key to a very short time, sometimes less than a minute.

Remember this

WEP is weak and should not be used. It has several problems including the misuse of encryption keys with the otherwise secure RC4 symmetric encryption protocol. In an IV attack, the attacker uses packet injection, increasing the number of packets to analyze, and discovers the encryption key.

WPA

Wi-Fi Protected Access (WPA) was an intermediate replacement for WEP. It provided an immediate solution to the weaknesses of WEP without requiring users to upgrade their hardware. Even when WPA replaced WEP, its developers recognized that WPA wasn't solid enough to last for an extended period. Instead, WPA improved wireless security by giving users an alternative to WEP with existing hardware while the developers worked on creating the stronger WPA2 protocol.

When first released, WPA used RC4 stream encryption with Temporal Key Integrity Protocol (TKIP). This is the same RC4 that WEP implemented incorrectly resulting in vulnerabilities. However, TKIP implemented it correctly and did a better job of managing the encryption keys. Even though TKIP helped correct several of WEPs flaws, it was ultimately cracked.

Later implementations of WPA can use Advanced Encryption Standard (AES) instead of TKIP. Chapter 10 presents in AES in more depth, but in short, it is a very strong and efficient encryption algorithm. Many applications beyond WPA2 use AES to provide secure encryption and ensure confidentiality.

A benefit of TKIP is that it didn't require new hardware. WEP users could upgrade software and/or firmware and implement WPA with TKIP without the need to replace the hardware. Newer hardware supports WPA2, so the usage of WPA and TKIP is waning. However, you may still see some legacy hardware using WEP, WPA, and TKIP. Several people have been successful at cracking WPA with TKIP, so whenever possible, it's best to upgrade WPA to WPA2, or at least upgrade TKIP to AES.

WPA2

Wi-Fi Protected Access v2 (WPA2) is the permanent replacement for WEP and WPA. WPA2 (also known as IEEE 802.11i) uses stronger cryptography than both WEP and WPA. The Wi-Fi Alliance requires all devices carrying its WI-FI CERTIFIED logo to meet WPA2 standards.

WPA2 supports Counter Mode with Cipher Block Chaining Message Authentication Code Protocol (CCMP), which is based on AES. In contrast, the first implementation of WPA used TKIP with RC4, and later implementations used AES. WPA2 also uses much more secure methods of managing the encryption keys.

> ### Remember this
>
> WPA provided an immediate replacement for WEP, and it didn't require the replacement of hardware. WPA2 is a permanent replacement of WEP and is recommended for use instead of WEP or WPA. WPA2 supports CCMP (based on AES), which is much stronger than the older TKIP protocol.

While WPA2 provides significant security improvements over previous wireless encryptions, some enterprises need stronger security. Another step you can take is to enable authentication with Enterprise mode.

Personal and Enterprise Modes

Both WPA and WPA2 operate in either Personal or Enterprise modes, and Enterprise mode provides additional security by adding authentication. As a reminder, authentication (presented in chapter 1) proves a user's identity with the use of credentials such as a username and password.

Personal mode uses a preshared key (PSK) and is rather simple to implement. You simply enter the same PSK in each of the wireless devices as you enter in the WAP. In this way, anyone with the PSK can access the wireless network. WPA-PSK or WPA2-PSK indicates Personal mode.

However, each of these users access the network anonymously, since a single PSK used by all users does not provide unique identification. In contrast, if users have usernames and passwords, the usernames provides identification of the users, and the passwords provide proof that the users are who they claim to be.

Enterprise mode (also called 802.1X mode) uses an 802.1X server (introduced in chapter 1) to provide authentication. In a wireless network, it acts like a RADIUS server, providing central authentication for the wireless clients. 802.1X servers can use multiple methods of authentication from simple usernames and passwords, to extensible authentication protocols (EAP) such as LEAP and PEAP.

Wireless authentication systems are more advanced than most home networks need, but many larger organizations use them. In other words, most home networks will use Personal mode while many organizations will use Enterprise mode to increase security. A combination of both a security protocol such as WPA2 and an 802.1X authentication server significantly reduces the chance of a successful access attack against a wireless system. Even WPA Enterprise using AES provides stronger security than WPA2-PSK.

> ### Remember this
> Personal mode (or WPA-PSK and WPA2-PSK) uses a preshared key and does not provide individual authentication. WPA/WPA2 Enterprise mode is more secure than Personal mode, and it provides strong authentication. Enterprise mode uses an 802.1X server (implemented as a RADIUS server) to add authentication.

Similarly, some hotels and resorts use pay-as-you-go Wi-Fi access. For example, some Las Vegas hotels and Walt Disney resorts have wireless access for $15 per day. If you choose to pay for this service, you create an account with a username and password. To access the wireless network, you authenticate with these credentials.

What Wireless Security Are You Using?

What wireless security are you using? WEP, WPA, WPA2, or nothing at all?
I frequently ask this question when teaching CompTIA Security+ classes. Many students simply don't know, and this question often starts a lot of whispering among students, as some realize they may not even be using WEP.

The next day many of the students report their findings, and it's common to hear that they've upgraded security on their wireless networks. You can upgrade many WAPs and wireless NICs to support WPA and WPA2 if they don't already support it. However, hardware on some older wireless NICs will only support WPA.

How about you? What wireless security are you using? If you don't know, check. The single most important step you can take to secure your wireless network is to upgrade to WPA2. Go ahead. Dig out the manual for your wireless access point or wireless router and check it out now.

EAP, LEAP, and PEAP

The Extensible Authentication Protocol (EAP) is an authentication framework that provides general guidance for authentication methods. Different EAP standards are often used for authentication in both wireless networks and remote access solutions. While there are multiple implementations of EAP, the primary methods you should know about for the Security+ exam are Lightweight EAP (LEAP) and Protected EAP (PEAP).

Cisco created LEAP using a modified version of the Challenge Handshake Authentication Protocol (CHAP) presented in chapter 1. It was effective in its early days but is no longer secure. Cisco recommends using stronger protocols, such as PEAP.

PEAP provides an extra layer of protection for EAP. The EAP designers assumed that EAP would be used with a secure channel, but in practice that wasn't always the case. PEAP encapsulates and encrypts the EAP conversation in a Transport Layer Security (TLS) tunnel. Since TLS requires a certificate, PEAP-TLS requires a certification authority to issue certificates. Chapter 3 introduced TLS, and chapter 10 presents additional information on TLS.

WTLS and ECC

Two other security protocols you may run across are Wireless Transport Layer Security (WTLS) and elliptic curve cryptography (ECC). Many smaller wireless devices use WTLS or ECC.

Smaller wireless devices such as PDAs and cell phones don't have the same processing power as servers and desktop computers and can't easily handle the processing requirements of advanced security protocols such as WPA2.

However, WTLS and ECC provide protection for the smaller devices without requiring a significant amount of processing power.

- **WTLS**. WTLS is a wireless implementation of TLS.
- **ECC**. ECC elegantly exploits a field of mathematics that can use a formula to create a curve and another formula to identify one or more points on the curve. ECC uses the points on the curve to create the encryption key.

Other Security Concerns

The use of WPA2, and especially WPA2 Enterprise, clearly provides the highest level of security for a wireless network. However, you can take some additional steps to secure a wireless network.

The settings described in this section are normally accessible via a group of web pages hosted on your wireless router. You can often access these web pages with your web browser and entering either http://192.168.0.1 or http://192.168.1.1 to access the home page.

Change Default Administrator Password

Many WAPs come with a default Administrator account of "admin," and default passwords of "admin." Some even ship with blank passwords. The defaults are documented in the instruction manual, and most manuals stress changing the password, but, quite simply, the password does not always get changed.

If the default password isn't changed, anyone who can access your WAP can log in and modify the configuration. Additionally, anyone with access to the Internet can easily download instruction manuals for the popular WAPs to identify the default administrator names and passwords. As an example, http://portforward.com/ has lists of usernames and passwords for a wide assortment of routers.

An attacker can easily bypass an otherwise secure wireless network if the administrator password is not changed. The attacker can log in and simply turn off security. Unless you go back into the WAP configuration, you may never know this feature has been turned off.

> ### *Remember this*
>
> Wireless access points and wireless routers have default Administrator accounts and default passwords. The default password of any device should be changed as soon as it is placed into service.

Enable MAC Filtering

An additional step you can take to provide a small measure of security to a wireless network is to enable media access control (MAC) filtering. As a reminder, the MAC address (also called a physical address) is a 48-bit address used to identify network interface cards (NICs). You will usually see the MAC address displayed as six pairs of hexadecimal characters such as 00-16-EA-DD-A6-60. Every network interface card (NIC) including wireless adapters has a MAC address.

MAC filtering is a form of network access control. It's used with port security on switches (covered in chapter 3) and you can also use it to restrict access to wireless networks.

For example, Figure 4.4 shows the MAC filter on a Cisco WAP. In the figure, you can see that the system is set to Permit PCs Selected Below to Access the Wireless Network. The MAC 01 through MAC 04 text boxes include MAC addresses of four devices.

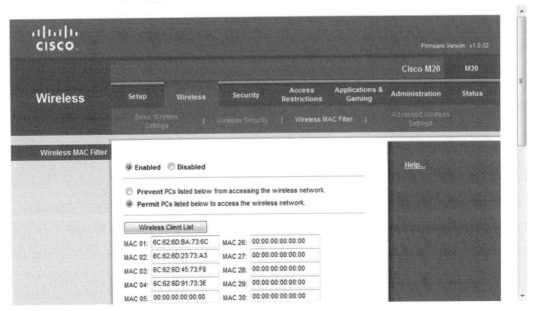

Figure 4.4: MAC filter on a WAP

Theoretically, MAC addresses are unique. With this in mind, the MAC filter in Figure 4.4 limits access to only the four devices with these MAC addresses. This may sound secure, but an attacker with a wireless sniffer can easily detect allowed MAC addresses in a wireless network. Additionally, it's very easy to change a MAC address. An attacker can change the original MAC to impersonate one of the allowed MAC addresses. This impersonation is a form of spoofing.

Many operating systems include built-in functionality to change a NIC's MAC address. For example, in Windows 7 you can access the NIC's properties from Device Manager, click the Advanced tab, and configure the Network Address setting with a new MAC.

Remember this

MAC filtering can restrict access to a wireless network to specific clients. However, an attacker can use a sniffer to discover allowed MAC addresses and circumvent this form of network access control. It's relatively simple for an attacker to spoof a MAC address.

Disable SSID Broadcasting or Not

One of the goals of 802.11 wireless networks is ease of use. The designers wanted wireless computers to be able to easily find each other and work together. They were successful with this goal. Unfortunately, attackers can also easily find your networks. Wireless networks are identified by a service set identifier (SSID), which is simply the name of the wireless network. By default, WAPs broadcast the SSID in clear text, making it easy to locate wireless networks.

At some point years ago, someone stated that the SSID was a password (not true!), and many IT professionals latched onto the idea that you can increase security by disabling the SSID broadcast. Others say that the SSID has nothing to do with security and disabling the broadcast reduces usability but does not increase security.

As background, WAPs must regularly send out a beacon frame to ensure interoperability with other devices in the wireless network. This beacon frame includes the SSID, and if the SSID broadcast is disabled, the SSID entry is blank. However, even if SSID broadcast is disabled, the WAP includes the SSID in Probe responses sent in response to Probe requests from authorized wireless clients. Because of this, it's easy for an attacker with a wireless sniffer to listen for the Probe responses and detect the SSID.

In other words, disabling the SSID makes it a *little* more difficult for attackers to find your network, but not much. It's almost like locking the front door of your house, but leaving the key in the lock.

Steve Riley wrote in a security blog titled "Myth vs. reality: Wireless SSIDs" that disabling the SSID for security "is a myth that needs to be forcibly dragged out behind the woodshed, strangled until it wheezes its last labored breath, then shot several times for good measure." In case it isn't clear, Mr. Riley is in the camp that says you should not disable the SSID. For the record, I agree with him.

For the Security+ exam, you should know that it is possible to disable the SSID broadcast. However, an attacker with a wireless sniffer can easily discover the SSID even if SSID broadcast is disabled.

Remember this

The service set identifier (SSID) identifies the name of the wireless network. You should change the SSID from the default name. Disabling SSID broadcast can hide the network from casual users, but an attacker can easily discover it with a wireless sniffer.

Change Default SSID

Many WAPs come with default SSIDs. For example, the default SSID of some older Linksys WAPs is "Linksys" or "linksys-g." Some newer WAPs force you to enter the name of the SSID when you first install it and do not include a default. From a defense-in-depth perspective, it's a good idea change the name of the SSID if a default is used. It simply gives attackers less information.

For example, if a war driver sees a wireless network with a SSID of Linksys, the attacker has a good idea that the network is using a Linksys WAP. If the attacker knows about specific weaknesses with this WAP, he can start attacking. On the other hand, a WAP with a SSID of "Success" doesn't give the attacker any clues about the WAP.

War Driving

War driving is the practice of looking for a wireless network. While war driving is more common in cars, you can just as easily do it by walking around in a large city. Attackers use war driving to discover wireless networks that they can exploit and often use directional antennas (cantennas) to detect wireless networks with weak signals.

Administrators sometimes use war driving as part of a wireless audit. A wireless audit is a detective control and examines the signal footprint, antenna placement, and encryption of wireless traffic. These audits are useful at detecting weaknesses in wireless networks. For example, administrators can sometimes detect the existence of rogue access points and evil twins by war driving, and determine when their WAPs footprint extends too far.

Remember this

Administrators use war driving techniques as part of a wireless audit. A wireless audit checks a wireless signal footprint, power levels, antenna placement, and encryption of wireless traffic. Wireless audits using war driving can detect rogue access points and identify unauthorized users.

Many current operating systems include software to identify wireless networks. For example, Microsoft's Windows 7 includes tools that allow you to view details about wireless networks in range of the system. The software shows the SSID of the network, signal strength, and the security protocol used (such as WEP, WPA, or WPA2).

Occasionally people use war chalking to publically mark wireless networks. These are simple marks written in chalk, or painted on a wall as graffiti. For example two parentheses marks placed back to back as)(indicate an open Wi-Fi network, and an open circle with a W in the middle indicates a Wi-Fi network using WEP.

Rogue Access Points

Generically, you can think of a rogue as a scoundrel, crook, or a villain. A rogue access point is a WAP placed within a network by someone with some type of attack in mind. Clearly, if a rogue is a crook or villain, then rogue access points are not an administrator's friend. You may also see them called counterfeit access points, which is also a clear indication they aren't legitimate.

Attackers may connect a rogue access point to network devices in wireless closets that lack adequate physical security. This access point acts as a sniffer to capture traffic passing through the wired network device, and then broadcasts the traffic using the wireless capability of the WAP. The attacker can then capture the traffic from the parking lot.

Additionally, attackers may be able to use the rogue access point to connect into the wired network. This works the same way that regular users can connect to a wired network via a wireless network. The difference is that the attacker configures all the security for the counterfeit access point and can use it for malicious purposes.

> ### Remember this
>
> Rogue (or counterfeit) access points are malicious. An evil twin is a rogue access point using the same SSID as a legitimate access point. While a secure WAP will block unauthorized users, a rogue access point provides access to unauthorized users.

If you discover an unauthorized WAP, you should disconnect it as quickly as possible. A basic first step to take when you discover any attack is to contain or isolate the threat. By simply unplugging an Ethernet cable, you can stop any attacks from an unauthorized WAP.

Often, administrators will use war driving tools to scan their networks for rogue access points. This can help identify the physical location of access points, since the signal will get stronger as the administrator gets closer. Some sophisticated war driving tools include directional antennas (such as cantennas) that an administrator (or an attacker) can use to locate a WAP.

Interference

Attackers can transmit noise or another radio signal on the same frequency used by a wireless network. This interferes with the wireless transmissions and can seriously degrade performance. Interference attacks like this are commonly called jamming.

In some cases, you can increase the power levels of the WAP to overcome the attack. However, it's worth remembering that as you increase the power level, you increase the wireless footprint and become more susceptible to war driving attacks.

Another method of overcoming the attack is to use different wireless channels. Each wireless standard has several channels you can use, and if one channel is too noisy, you can use another one. While this is useful to overcome interference in home networks, it won't be as effective to combat an interference attack. If you switch channels, the attacker can also switch channels.

Evil Twins

An evil twin is a rogue access point with the same SSID as a legitimate access point. For example, many public places such as coffee shops, hotels, and airports include free Wi-Fi as a service. An attacker can set up a WAP using the same SSID as the public Wi-Fi network, and many unsuspecting users will connect to this evil twin.

Once a user connects to an evil twin, wireless traffic goes through the evil twin instead of the legitimate WAP. Often, the attacker presents bogus login pages to users in an attempt to capture usernames and passwords. Other times, they simply capture traffic from the connection, such as e-mail or text entered into a web page, and analyze it to detect sensitive information they can exploit.

While it may sound complex to set this up, it's actually rather easy. Attackers can configure a laptop that has a wireless access card as a WAP. With it running, the attackers look just like any other user in a coffee shop or airport waiting area. They'll have their laptop open and appear to be working (just like you perhaps), and you'll have no idea they are trying to steal your credentials or other personal data that you send over the Internet via the evil twin.

Isolation Mode

If you want to prevent wireless clients from communicating with each other, you can enable isolation mode on the WAP. Clients are able to connect to the WAP, but isolation mode segments or isolates each wireless user.

While you probably won't see isolation mode in a corporate network, many public hotspots use it. It provides a level of security for the customers but does not prevent someone from hosting an evil twin.

> **Remember this**
>
> Isolation mode is used in an access point (AP) to prevent clients from connecting to each other. Public networks sometimes use this to protect wireless clients.

Ad-Hoc Mode

Wireless networks can operate in one of two modes: infrastructure mode and ad-hoc mode. Infrastructure mode uses a WAP and all devices connect through the WAP. In ad-hoc (or as-needed) mode, wireless devices connect to each other without a WAP. For example, if two users have wireless laptops, they can create an ad-hoc wireless network to connect the two computers.

One of the risks when using ad-hoc mode is that any user that accesses your computer using this mode has the same rights and permissions you have. In other words, if you log on as an administrator, anyone in the ad-hoc network has access to your computer with administrator permissions. If you do use an ad-hoc network, it's best to log on as a user with limited rights and permissions before creating it.

Bluetooth Wireless

Bluetooth is a short-range wireless system used in personal area networks (PANs) or a network of devices close to a single person. Bluetooth devices include smartphones, personal digital assistants (PDAs), and computer devices.

The range of Bluetooth was originally designed for about three meters (about ten feet), but the range is often farther, and ultimately extends beyond a person's personal space. Attackers have found that attacks on these networks are possible. Two common attacks are bluesnarfing and bluejacking. Both attacks are much easier when Bluetooth devices remain in discovery mode.

Discovery Mode

When Bluetooth devices are first configured, they are configured in discovery mode. Bluetooth devices use MAC addresses, and in discovery mode the Bluetooth device broadcasts its MAC address, allowing other devices to see it and connect to it. This is required when pairing Bluetooth devices.

For example, if you had a cell phone and an earpiece that both supported Bluetooth, you would use discovery mode to pair the two devices. You could then keep the cell phone in your pocket or purse, but still carry on a conversation through the earpiece.

One of the risks with Bluetooth occurs when a Bluetooth device is left in discovery mode. Just as you can pair an earpiece with your cell phone, an attacker can pair a Bluetooth-enabled laptop with your cell phone if it's left in discovery mode. With the right software, the attacker can then launch bluesnarfing and bluejacking attacks (described in the next sections).

While there are improvements in Bluetooth devices, such as using PINs or passwords, it's still important to change the devices from discovery mode to nondiscovery mode after pairing them. While in nondiscovery mode, the device doesn't broadcast information about itself. Additionally, many devices add encryption to the communication process when in nondiscovery mode.

Bluesnarfing

Bluesnarfing is any unauthorized access to or theft of information from a Bluetooth connection. A bluesnarfing attack can access information such as e-mail, contact lists, calendars, and text messages.

A bluesnarfing attack can exploit any Bluetooth device that is powered on and in discovery mode. Users with a Linux system and Bluetooth capabilities can launch an attack with just a few commands using tools like hcitool and obexftp.

Remember this

Bluesnarfing is the unauthorized access to or theft of information from a Bluetooth device. Bluejacking is the unauthorized sending of text messages from a Bluetooth device.

Bluejacking

Bluejacking is the practice of sending text messages over someone else's Bluetooth device without the user's permission or knowledge. A bluejacking message may only be text, but it can also include sound on some Bluetooth devices.

Often the user won't have any idea that the message has been sent. Attackers have used bluejacking to send advertising via someone's Bluetooth device, but it can also be much more malicious in nature.

Imagine your device is bluejacked. If someone sends a threatening text message to a political figure, guess who it will be traced back to? You! If sound and text can be sent, it's only a short leap for someone to figure out how to send malware. If someone releases the next I Love You virus via your Bluetooth device, guess who the authorities will track the release of this virus back to? You again!

Clearly, the best defense for Bluetooth devices is to ensure the device stays in nondiscovery mode.

Smartphone Security

Many smartphones include security capabilities such as data encryption, remote wipe capabilities, and password protection.

Data encryption of a smartphone's data protects it against loss of confidentiality if the phone is lost. It's also possible to use voice encryption with some phones to help prevent the interception of your conversations.

Remote wipe capabilities are useful if the phone is lost. The owner can send a remote wipe signal to the phone to delete all the data on the phone. This also deletes any cached data, such as cached online banking passwords, and provides a complete sanitization of the device, ensuring that all valuable data is removed.

Password protection prevents someone from easily accessing the phone and the data it contains. Passwords should be strong. You probably won't keep the thief out of your system for very long, but you can slow someone down, giving the owner enough time to send a remote wipe signal before the thief accesses the data.

A Global Positioning System (GPS) pinpoints the location of the phone. Many phones include GPS applications that you can run on another computer. If you lose your phone, GPS can help you find it. Who knows? You may find that it just fell through the cushions in your couch. This is useful to know before you send a remote wipe signal.

It's worth mentioning that a bluesnarfing attack bypasses most of a mobile phone's security. The attacker accesses the device remotely bypassing the password protection. In many cases, the attacker views encrypted data in an unencrypted format, just as the user does.

> ### Remember this
> Smartphone security includes device encryption to protect the data, password protection to help prevent unauthorized access, and remote wipe capabilities to delete all data on a lost phone. A bluesnarfing attack bypasses password protection and data encryption.

Exploring Remote Access

Remote access is the group of technologies that allow users to access an internal network from remote locations. Remote Access Service (RAS) provides access through dial-up or virtual private networks (VPNs).

Several components come together to form a successful RAS solution. They include:

- **Access method**. Users can access a RAS server through dial-up or a VPN.
- **Authentication**. Remote access requires secure authentication methods since users may connect over unsecure lines.

- **Access control**. Once a user is authenticated, network access control helps determine if the user is authorized and inspects the client for health based on preconfigured conditions.

Dial-up RAS

Dial-up RAS uses phones and modems. Both the client and server need access to phone lines, and each must have a modem. Dial-up RAS allows the client to have access to a remote network over a POTS (plain old telephone system).

As a simple example, I was a traveling trainer for many years. While I was on the road, I was able to dial in to the RAS server using a laptop with a modem anytime I needed access to the company network. Once I connected, I could access resources on the network similar to how I could access the resources if I was at my desk at work—just not as quickly, since I was using a 56K dial-up modem.

The client has a modem and access to a phone line and can dial directly into the RAS server. The RAS server also has a modem and access to a phone line. Once connected, the RAS server provides access to the internal network.

The primary protocol used for dial-up access is Point-to-Point Protocol (PPP). When it was developed, tapping phone lines was considered rare, so PPP didn't include much security. However, PPP is often combined with other protocols to enhance security of the connection.

Dial-up remote access includes telephony technologies—the use of telephone technologies to connect computers. Telephony also includes combining the use of computers and telephone technologies to provide voice-over IP.

Long-distance phone costs can make dial-up cost prohibitive. VPNs provide better security than a dial-up solution and can reduce phone costs.

VPN

A virtual private network (VPN) allows a connection to a private network over a public network. The public network is most commonly the Internet, but it can also be a semi-private leased line from a telecommunications company. Since the telecommunications company will often lease access to one physical line to several companies, the leased line is not truly private.

Access over a public network is a core concern with VPNs. Different tunneling protocols encapsulate and encrypt the traffic to protect the data from unauthorized disclosure.

Tunneling

Figure 4.5 shows an example of how a tunneling protocol would work with a VPN. The figure shows the VPN server between two firewalls (configured as a DMZ). The firewalls provide some protection for the VPN server and the private network. The VPN server is reachable through a public IP address, making it accessible from any other host on the Internet. Of course, the firewall access control lists would need to include rules allowing the traffic. The ports you open are dependent on the tunneling protocols used for the VPN.

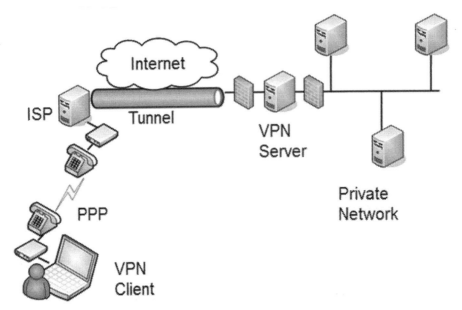

Figure 4.5: Tunneling to a VPN server

In large organizations, the VPN server is a VPN concentrator. A VPN concentrator includes all the services needed by a VPN server, including strong encryption and authentication techniques, and supports a large number of clients.

> ### Remember this
> VPN concentrators provide strong security and support large numbers of VPN clients. A firewall access control list (ACL) includes rules allowing VPN traffic and the ports you open are dependent on the tunneling protocol. A common protocol used for tunneling through the Internet is IPsec using port 500 for IKE. Other tunneling protocols include PPTP (on port 1723), L2TP (on port 1701), and SSTP (on port 443).

Clients can use PPP to dial up to a local Internet Service Provider (ISP) and receive a public IP address. If clients already had a public IP address, such as through a broadband always-on connection, they wouldn't need to use a dial-up connection.

Once connected to the Internet with a public IP address, clients use a tunneling protocol to create a protected tunnel through the Internet to the VPN server. The following bullets provide a summary of common tunneling protocols used by VPNs:

- **IPsec**. You can use IPsec as a tunneling protocol by itself or as an encryption protocol for other tunneling protocols. It uses Internet Key Exchange (IKE) over port 500 to create the secure channel. IPsec has compatibility issues with devices using network address translation (NAT).

- **PPTP**. Many Microsoft implementations used Point-to-Point Tunneling Protocol. PPTP uses Microsoft's Point-to-Point Encryption to create the secure channel. PPTP has known vulnerabilities. PPTP uses TCP port 1723.
- **L2TP**. Cisco and Microsoft joined forces to create the Layer 2 Tunneling Protocol. L2TP does not encrypt the tunnel itself but often uses IPsec for encryption (as L2TP/IPsec). L2TP uses UDP port 1701.
- **SSTP**. Secure Socket Tunneling Protocol encrypts VPN traffic using SSL over port 443. Using port 443 provides a lot of flexibility for many administrators and rarely requires opening additional firewall ports. It is a useful alternative when the VPN tunnel must go through a device using NAT, and IPsec is not feasible.

IPsec as a Tunneling Protocol

Chapter 3 introduced IPsec as a method of encrypting traffic on the wire. IPsec can be used in either transport mode (where only the payload is encrypted) or in tunnel mode (where the entire IP packet is encrypted). IPsec uses tunnel mode when used with VPNs and it uses transport mode within a private network.

IPsec uses Internet Key Exchange (IKE) over port 500 to authenticate clients in the IPsec conversation. IKE creates security associations (SAs) for the VPN and uses these to set up a secure channel between the client and the VPN server.

As a reminder, IPsec can use Authentication Header (AH) alone for authentication and integrity, or Encapsulating Security Payload (ESP) to encrypt the data and provide confidentiality, authentication, and integrity. An important security consideration when transporting data over the Internet is confidentiality, so IPsec uses ESP in tunnel mode when used with VPNs.

Remember this

IPsec includes Encapsulating Security Payload (ESP) to provide confidentiality, integrity, and authentication for VPN traffic. IPsec uses tunnel mode for VPN traffic (instead of transport mode) and can be identified based on the protocol ID of 50 for ESP. IPsec (and other tunneling protocols) can be used to create a site-to-site tunnel between two physical locations of a business, such as the main office, and a remote office.

L2TP and IPsec

While it is possible to use L2TP to create a tunnel between devices, L2TP doesn't include any encryption, so it does not provide confidentiality of the data. However, you can combine IPsec with L2TP (as L2TP/IPsec) to provide security for the VPN tunnel. IPsec provides security in two ways:

- **Authentication**. IPsec includes an Authentication Header (AH) to allow each of the hosts in the IPsec conversation to authenticate with each other before exchanging data. AH uses protocol ID number 51.

- **Encryption**. IPsec includes Encapsulating Security Payload (ESP) to encrypt the data and provide confidentiality. ESP uses protocol ID number 50.

The term *protocol ID number* may look like a typo, but it isn't. AH and ESP are identified with protocol ID numbers, not port numbers. Chapter 3 presented routers and firewalls. You may remember that a basic packet-filtering firewall can filter packets based on IP addresses, ports, and some protocols, such as ICMP and IPsec. Packet filters use the protocol ID numbers to identify AH and ESP traffic.

In contrast, L2TP uses UDP port 1701. A packet-filtering firewall would use UDP port 1701 to identify L2TP traffic, and protocol IDs 50 and 51 to identify IPsec traffic.

NAT and IPsec

IPsec and Network Address Translation (NAT) are not compatible with each other. NAT manipulates the IP header of the packets when it translates the IP addresses. This change causes the receiving end of the VPN tunnel to discard the packet as invalid.

If the path to the VPN server is through a device using NAT, you need to look for alternatives. NAT Traversal (NAT-T) is one possible choice, or you could use another tunneling protocol, such as SSTP.

Site-to-Site VPNs

A site-to-site, or gateway-to-gateway, VPN includes two VPN servers that act as gateways for multiple clients to access a remote network over a public connection. Each of the VPN servers acts as a gateway for multiple users in the different networks.

For example, an organization can have two locations. One is its headquarters, and the other is a remote office. It can use two VPN servers to act as gateways to connect the two sites together.

A benefit of the site-to-site model is that it connects both networks without requiring additional steps on the part of the user. Users in the remote office can connect to servers in the headquarters location as easily as if the servers were in the remote office. Connecting to the remote server may be slower than connecting to a local server, but otherwise it's transparent to end users.

In contrast, in a host-to-site, or host-to-gateway, model, the end user makes the direct connection to the VPN server and is very much aware of the process.

RAS Authentication

Chapter 1 presented authentication, including the different mechanisms used with remote access authentication. To connect the two topics, it's worth a short review of the authentication mechanisms used with RAS.

- **CHAP**. Challenge Handshake Authentication Protocol introduced a challenge-response mechanism for authentication. Many other more current methods are used in place of CHAP today.
- **MS-CHAPv2**. Microsoft improved CHAP with MS-CHAP and MS-CHAPv2. The significant improvement MS-CHAPv2 provided was mutual authentication, requiring

both the client and the server to authenticate to each other before sharing data. You can integrate MS-CHAPv2 with other authentication methods such as EAP, PEAP, and more.

- **RADIUS**. Remote Authentication Dial-In User Service uses a central server for authentication when multiple RAS or VPN servers are used. A weakness with RADIUS is that it only encrypts the password and not the entire authentication process.
- **TACACS+**. Many Cisco VPN concentrators use TACACS+ as a replacement for RADIUS. TACACS+ encrypts the entire client-server negotiation process, while RADIUS only encrypts the password. Additionally, TACACS+ uses multiple challenges and responses.

Network Access Control

Allowing access to your private network can expose your network to a significant number of risks from the clients. If an employee VPNs into the network with a computer infected with malware, this computer can then infect other computers on the internal network. Network access control (NAC) methods can inspect clients and prevent them from accessing the network if they don't pass the inspection.

Most administrators have complete control over computers in their network. For example, they can ensure the clients have up-to-date antivirus software installed, operating systems have current patches applied, and their firewalls are enabled. However, administrators don't have complete control of computers employees use at home or on the road.

NAC provides a measure of control for these other computers. It ensures that clients meet predetermined characteristics prior to accessing a network. NAC systems often use *health* as a metaphor indicating that a client meets these predetermined characteristics. Just as doctors can quarantine patients with certain illnesses, NAC can quarantine or isolate unhealthy clients that don't meet the predefined NAC conditions.

Network access control includes the following components:

- **Inspection and control**. NAC inspects clients to ensure they meet specific predefined health conditions, such as being up-to-date and are running antivirus software. NAC grants access to healthy clients, but restricts network access to clients not meeting predefined conditions.
- **Authentication**. Clients provide credentials for authentication when they try to connect. Based on the proven identity, the NAC can grant or block access.

Inspection and Control

Many NAC systems can inspect any client that attempts to access a network. Administrators set predefined conditions for healthy clients, and those that meet these preset conditions can access the network. The NAC system isolates computers that don't meet the conditions. Common health conditions checked by a NAC are:

- Up-to-date antivirus software, including updated signature definitions
- Up-to-date operating system, including current patches and fixes
- Firewall enabled on the client

NAC clients have authentication agents (sometimes called health agents) installed on them. These agents are applications or services that periodically check different conditions on the computer and document the status in a statement of health. When a client connects to a NAC-controlled network, the NAC system queries the client's authentication agent. The user is prompted for credentials, and the agent also provides the statement of health.

- However, if the client isn't running the necessary authentication agent, it won't be prompted for credentials and will never gain access to the network.
- Consider Figure 4.6. When a VPN client accesses the network, the VPN server queries the NAC health server to determine required health conditions. The VPN server also queries the client for a statement of the client's health. As long as the client meets all health requirements, NAC allows the client to access the network.

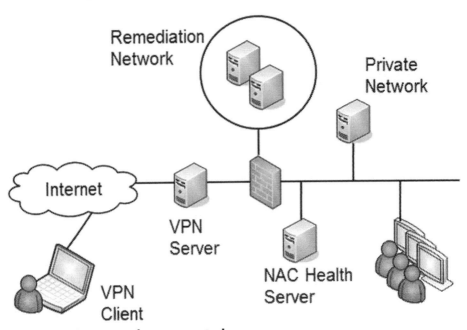

Figure 4.6: Using network access control

However, if a client doesn't meet the health conditions mandated by the NAC server, the VPN server redirects the client to a remediation network (also called a quarantine network). The remediation network includes resources the client can use to get healthy. For example, it would include current approved patches, antivirus software, and updated virus signatures. The client can use these resources to improve its health and then try to access the network again.

While NAC can inspect the health of VPN clients, you can also use it to inspect the health of internal clients. For example, internal computers may occasionally miss patches and be vulnerable. NAC will detect the unpatched system and quarantine it. If you use this feature, it's important that the detection is accurate. In at least one situation, the NAC identified healthy clients as unhealthy and prevented these healthy systems from accessing the network.

Similarly, your organization may allow visitors or employees to plug in their mobile computers to live wall jacks for connectivity, or connect to a wireless network. NAC inspects the clients, and if they don't meet health conditions, they may be granted Internet access through the network but remain isolated from any other network activity.

> ### Remember this
> Network access control (NAC) includes methods (such as health agents) to inspect clients for health. NAC can restrict access of unhealthy clients to a remediation network. You can use NAC for VPN clients and for internal clients. MAC filtering is a form of NAC.

MAC Filtering

As mentioned in the Securing Wireless Networks section of this chapter, MAC filtering is a form of network access control. You can restrict access to any network using the MAC address. As an example, chapter 3 discussed port security. You can map the MAC address to specific physical ports on a switch to control what devices have access.

Additionally, you can configure a NAC system to restrict access to any network based on the MAC address. For example, you can use it to predefine what clients can connect to a network with a VPN.

It's worth stressing that MAC filtering is not an effective control in a wireless network since it attackers can easily circumvent it. Attackers can eavesdrop on wireless transmissions and then spoof allowed MAC addresses. However, MAC filtering is more effective in nonwireless networks since it is more difficult for an attacker to discover authorized MACs.

Chapter 4 Exam Topic Review

When preparing for the exam, make sure you understand these key concepts covered in this chapter.

IDSs and IPSs

- An intrusion detection system (IDS) is a detective control and detects activity after it occurs.
- A host-based IDS (HIDS) can detect attacks on local systems such as workstations and servers. The HIDS protects local resources on the host such as the operating system files.
- A network-based IDS (NIDS) detects attacks on networks such as smurf attacks.
- A signature-based IDS uses signatures to detect known attacks.
- An anomaly-based (also called heuristic or behavior-based) IDS requires a baseline and detects attacks based on anomalies or when traffic is outside expected boundaries.

- A honeypot is a server designed to look valuable to an attacker, can divert malicious attacks, and can help administrators learn about zero day exploits, or previously unknown attacks.
- An intrusion prevention system (IPS) is similar to an active IDS except that it's placed in line with the traffic, and can stop attacks in progress. An IPS can actively monitor data streams, detect malicious content, and mitigate the effect of malicious activity.

Wireless Networks

- The power level and antenna placement of a wireless access point (WAP) affects the footprint. You can increase the footprint by increasing power levels and reduce the footprint by reducing power levels, or modify the footprint by modifying the placement of the antenna.
- WEP is an older, insecure wireless protocol. It implemented RC4 incorrectly using a small initialization vector (IV). IV attacks can easily crack the encryption key. WEP should not be used.
- WPA was an initial improvement over WEP, and WPA2 is a permanent improvement over WEP. WPA2 should be used whenever possible.
- WPA and WPA2 support the older, compromised TKIP encryption, but the newer CCMP encryption based on AES is more secure.
- WPA/WPA2 Personal mode uses a preshared key (PSK). It is easy to implement and is used in many smaller wireless networks.
- WPA/WPA2 Enterprise mode is more secure than Personal mode since it adds authentication. It uses an 802.1X authentication server (often implemented as RADIUS server) to provide authentication.
- You can restrict what devices can connect to a WAP by using MAC filtering. However, an attacker with a wireless sniffer can circumvent this security.
- Disabling the SSID (the network name) prevents easy discovery of a WAP. However, an attacker with a wireless sniffer can easily determine the SSID even if SSID broadcasting is disabled.
- A rogue access point is an authorized WAP. Attackers can use them to capture data on your network. Unauthorized users can access your network via a rogue access point.
- An evil twin is a rogue access point using the same SSID as an authorized WAP.
- A wireless audit checks WAP power levels, antenna placement, wireless footprint, and encryption techniques. It will often include war driving techniques and can detect rogue access points.
- WAPs in hotspots often use isolation mode to segment, or separate, wireless users from each other.
- Bluejacking involves sending unsolicited messages to a phone. Bluesnarfing involves accessing data on a phone.
- You can protect mobile devices with encryption of data, password protection, and remote wipe capabilities. Remote wipe removes all the data from a lost phone.

Remote Access

- VPNs provide remote access to mobile users to a corporate network. Firewall ACLs include rules to allow VPN traffic based on the tunneling protocol.
- VPN concentrators provide secure remote access to a large number of remote users.
- IPsec is a common tunneling protocol used with VPNs. It can secure traffic in a site-to-site tunnel and from clients to the VPN. IPsec uses tunnel mode for VPNs. ESP encrypts VPN traffic and provides confidentiality, integrity, and authentication.
- Firewalls identify IPsec ESP traffic with protocol ID 50, and AH traffic with protocol ID 51. IKE creates the security association for the IPsec tunnel and uses port 500.
- Other tunneling protocols include SSTP (using SSL over port 443), L2TP (over port 1701), and PPTP (over port 1723).
- NAC inspects clients for specific health conditions and can redirect access to a remediation network for unhealthy clients.
- NAC can be used with VPN clients, and with internal clients. MAC filtering is a form of network access control.

Chapter 4 Practice Questions

1. What can an administrator use to detect malicious activity after it occurred?
   - A. Firewall
   - B. Sniffer
   - C. Port scanner
   - D. IDS

2. Of the following choices, what would detect compromises on a local server?
   - A. HIDS
   - B. NIPS
   - C. Firewall
   - D. Protocol analyzer

3. Of the following choices, what represents the best choice for a system to detect attacks on a network, but not block them?
   - A. NIDS
   - B. NIPS
   - C. HIDS
   - D. HIPS

4. Your organization is using a NIDS. The NIDS vendor regularly provides updates for the NIDS to detect known attacks. What type of NIDS is this?
   - A. Anomaly-based
   - B. Signature-based
   - C. Prevention-based
   - D. Honey-based

5. You are preparing to deploy an anomaly-based detection system to monitor network activity. What would you create first?
   - A. Flood guards
   - B. Signatures
   - C. Baseline
   - D. Honeypot

6. Of the following choices, what can you use to divert malicious attacks on your network away from valuable resources to relatively worthless resources?

    A. IDS

    B. Proxy server

    C. Web application firewall

    D. Honeypot

7. Of the following choices, what best describes the function of an IPS?

    A. Detect attacks

    B. Stop attacks in progress

    C. Prevent attackers from attacking

    D. Notify appropriate personnel of attacks

8. Of the following choices, what provides active protection for an operating system?

    A. NIDS

    B. NIPS

    C. HIDS

    D. HIPS

9. Of the following choices, what most accurately describes a NIPS?

    A. Detects and takes action against threats

    B. Provides notification of threats

    C. Detects and eliminates threats

    D. Identifies zero day vulnerabilities

10. You've recently completed a wireless audit and realize that the wireless signal from your company's WAP reaches the parking lot. What can you do to ensure that the signal doesn't reach outside your building?

    A. Increase the WAP's power level

    B. Decrease the WAP's power level

    C. Enable SSID broadcasting

    D. Disable SSID broadcasting

11. Which one of the following secure protocols did WEP implement incorrectly, allowing attackers to crack it?

    A. SSL

    B. RC4

    C. CCMP

    D. AES

12. Your organization is designing an 802.11n network and wants to use the strongest security. What would you recommend?

    A. FTPS

    B. SSL

    C. WEP

    D. WPA2

13. Which of the following authentication mechanisms can provide centralized authentication for a wireless network?

    A. WPA2

    B. RADIUS

    C. Multifactor authentication

    D. Kerberos

14. You want to ensure that only specific wireless clients can access your wireless networks. Of the following choices, what provides the best solution?

    A. MAC filtering

    B. Content filtering

    C. NAT

    D. NIPS

15. You recently completed a wireless audit of your company's wireless network. You've identified several unknown devices connected to the network and realize they are devices owned by company employees. What can you use to prevent these devices from connecting?

    A. MAC filtering

    B. Enable SSID broadcast

    C. Enable isolation mode on the WAP

    D. Reduce the power levels on the WAP

16. What can you do to prevent the easy discovery of a WAP?

    A. Enable MAC filtering

    B. Disable SSID broadcast

    C. Enable SSID broadcast

    D. Enable 802.1X authentication

17. While troubleshooting a problem with a WAP in your organization, you discover a rogue access point with the same SSID as the organization's WAP. What is this second access point?

    A. IDS

    B. War chalking

    C. Evil twin

    D. Packet sniffer

18. You want to identify the physical location of a rogue access point you discovered in the footprint of your company. What would you use?
    A. Bluesnarfing
    B. Bluejacking
    C. War chalking
    D. War driving

19. You are hosting a wireless hotspot, and you want to segment wireless users from each other. What should you use?
    A. Personal mode
    B. Enterprise mode
    C. Isolation mode
    D. WEP

20. Which of the following best describes bluejacking?
    A. Bluejacking involves accessing data on a phone.
    B. Bluejacking involves checking a WAPs antenna placement, power levels, and encryption techniques.
    C. Bluejacking involves sending unsolicited messages to a phone.
    D. Bluejacking involves a rogue access point with the same SSID as your production WAP.

21. Someone stole an executive's smartphone, and the phone includes sensitive data. What should you do to prevent the thief from reading the data?
    A. Password protect the phone
    B. Encrypt the data on the phone
    C. Use remote wipe
    D. Track the location of the phone

22. You are deploying a remote access server for your organization. Employees will use this to access the network while on the road. Of the following choices, what must you configure?
    A. NAC
    B. ACLs
    C. MACs
    D. NAT-T

23. Your organization is creating a site-to-site VPN tunnel between the main business location and a remote office. What can it use to create the tunnel?
    A. WPA2-Enterprise
    B. RADIUS
    C. NAC
    D. IPsec

24. You are planning to deploy a VPN with IPsec. Users will use the VPN to access corporate resources while they are on the road. How should you use IPsec?

    A. With AH in tunnel mode

    B. With AH in transport mode

    C. With ESP in tunnel mode

    D. With ESP in transport mode

25. An employee connects to the corporate network using a VPN. However, the client is not able to access internal resources, but instead receives a warning indicating their system is not up to date with current patches. What is causing this behavior?

    A. The VPN is using IPsec

    B. The VPN is not using IPsec

    C. NAC is disabled on the network and remediation must take place before the client can access internal resources

    D. NAC is enabled on the network and remediation must take place before the client can access internal resources

Chapter 4 Practice Question Answers

1. **D.** An intrusion detection system (IDS) detects malicious activity after it has occurred. A firewall attempts to prevent attacks. A sniffer can capture and analyze packets to read data or inspect IP headers. A port scanner looks for open ports on a system to determine running services and protocols.

2. **A.** A host-based intrusion detection system (HIDS) can detect attacks (including successful attacks resulting in compromises) on local systems such as workstations and servers. A NIPS detects and mitigates attacks on a network, not local systems. A firewall attempts to prevent attacks not detect them. A protocol analyzer can capture and analyze packets, but it will not detect attacks.

3. **A.** A network-based intrusion detection system (NIDS) will detect attacks, but will not necessarily block them (unless it is an active NIDS). In contrast, a network-based intrusion prevention system will detect and block attacks. Host-based systems (HIDS and HIPS) provide protection for hosts, not networks.

4. **B.** Signature-based, network-based intrusion detection systems (NIDS) use signatures similar to antivirus software which are downloaded regularly as updates. An anomaly-based (also called heuristic or behavior-based) detection system compares current activity with a previously created baseline to detect any anomalies or changes. An IPS is prevention based, but an IDS is detection based. There is no such thing as honey based.

5. **C.** An anomaly-based (also called heuristic or behavior-based) detection system compares current activity with a previously created baseline to detect any anomalies or changes. Flood guards help protect against SYN flood attacks. Signature-based systems use signatures similar to antivirus software. A honeypot is a server designed to look valuable to an attacker and can divert attacks.

6. **D.** A honeypot can divert malicious attacks to a harmless area of your network, away from production servers. An IDS can detect attacks, but only an active IDS (or an IPS) will take action, and it usually blocks the attack instead of diverting it. A proxy server can filter and cache content from web pages, but doesn't divert attacks. A web application firewall (WAF) is an additional firewall designed to protect a web application.

7. **B.** The primary purpose of an intrusion prevention system (IPS) is to stop attacks in progress. While an IPS detects attacks just as an IDS does, a distinguishing factor between an IDS and an IPS is that an IPS can also stop attacks in progress. It's not possible to prevent attackers from attacking, but an IPS can reduce the impact they have on a system. Both IDSs and IPSs provide notifications.

8. **D.** A host-based intrusion prevention system (HIPS) provides active protection for an individual host, including its operating system. In contrast, HIDS is passive by default. Network based IDSs and IPSs monitor and protect network traffic.

9. **A.** A network-based intrusion prevention system (NIPS) attempts to detect and mitigate threats by taking action to block them. While a NIPS does provide notification, a distinguishing difference between a NIDS and a NIPS is that a NIPS takes action to stop the attack. Threats can't be eliminated. An anomaly-based IDS or IPS may be able to identify zero day vulnerabilities, though honeypots are used more often to detect zero day vulnerabilities.

10. **B.** You can decrease the wireless access point's (WAP's) power level to reduce the footprint and ensure the WAP's signal doesn't reach outside the parking lot (or reposition the WAP's antenna). Increasing the WAP's power level increases the footprint. SSID broadcasting won't have an impact on the footprint.

11. **B.** Wired Equivalent Privacy (WEP) implemented RC4 with small initialization vectors (IVs), allowing an IV attack to discover the key. SSL uses RC4 successfully to encrypt and decrypt traffic, but WEP does not use SSL. CCMP is a strong encryption protocol based on AES that overcomes problems with TKIP, and WEP did not use CCMP. AES is a strong encryption standard. WEP did not use AES.

12. **D.** Wi-Fi Protected Access version 2 (WPA2) provides the strongest security for an 802.11n (wireless) network of the given choices. FTPS secures FTP traffic with SSL. SSL encrypts other types of traffic, but not wireless network traffic. WEP is weak and should not be used.

13. **B.** Remote Authentication Dial-in user Service (RADIUS) can provide centralized authentication for wireless networks as an 802.1X server in Enterprise mode. WPA2 provides security for a wireless network. Multifactor authentication uses two or more factors of authentication but does not provide centralized authentication. Kerberos provides authentication in Microsoft networks.

14. **A.** MAC filtering allows you to restrict access to the wireless networks to devices with specified MAC addresses (though an attacker can circumvent this method). Content filtering can filter traffic for malware and more, but it doesn't restrict clients. NAT translates IP addresses and can hide internal private IP addresses, but it doesn't restrict access. NIPS can detect and block attacks but not filter wireless clients.

15. **A.** MAC filtering can restrict the devices' connectivity based on their MAC address and prevent the employees' devices from connecting. Enabling SSID broadcast won't prevent the devices from connecting. Isolation mode prevents wireless users from connecting to each other, not the WAP. Reducing the power levels reduces access for all devices, not just the employee owned devices.

16. **B.** You can disable SSID broadcasts to prevent the easy discovery of a WAP, but attackers can still locate the wireless network with a sniffer. MAC filtering can restrict what devices can connect, but attackers can circumvent this method, too. Enabling the SSID broadcast makes the WAP easier to discover. 802.1X authentication uses a RADIUS server to add security but doesn't prevent the easy discovery of a WAP.

17. **C.** An evil twin is a rogue (or counterfeit) access point with the same SSID as an authorized wireless access point (WAP). An IDS detects malicious activity after it has occurred, but is unrelated to WAPs. War chalking is the practice of drawing symbols in public places to identify wireless networks. While the evil twin is very likely capturing traffic with packet sniffing, an evil twin is not a packet sniffer.

18. **D.** War driving is the practice of looking for a wireless network, and administrators sometimes use war driving as part of a wireless audit to locate rogue access points. Bluesnarfing involves accessing data on a phone. Bluejacking involves sending unsolicited messages to a phone. War chalking identifies publically accessible wireless networks with symbols written in chalk or painted on a wall as graffiti.

19. **C.** Isolation mode on a WAP segments wireless users from each other and is commonly used in hotspots. Personal mode uses a PSK and Enterprise mode uses an 802.1X authentication server to increase security. WEP is a weak encryption algorithm and not recommended for use.

20. **C.** Bluejacking involves sending unsolicited messages to a phone. Bluesnarfing involves accessing data on a phone. A wireless audit involves checking a WAPs antenna placement, power levels, and encryption techniques. An evil twin is a rogue access point with the same SSID as an authorized WAP.

21. **C.** Remote wipe capabilities can send a remote wipe signal to the phone to delete all the data on the phone, including any cached data. The phone is lost, so it's too late to password protect or encrypt the data now if these steps weren't completed previously. While tracking the phone may be useful, it doesn't prevent the thief from reading the data.

22. **B.** Access control lists within a firewall must include rules to open the appropriate ports. NAC increases security and can filter traffic based on MAC addresses, but neither is required for remote access. NAT-T can circumvent problems related to IPsec usage, but it is not requirement for all remote access.

23. **D.** IPsec is one of many tunneling protocols the organization can use to create a VPN tunnel. WPA2-Enterprise is a secure wireless protocol that includes authentication using an 802.1X server (often implemented as RADIUS). RADIUS provides authentication but doesn't create a tunnel. NAC provides security for clients, such as inspecting them for health, but doesn't create the tunnel.

24. **C.** Encapsulating Security Payload (ESP) in tunnel mode encapsulates the entire IP packets and provides confidentiality, integrity, and authentication. AH only provides integrity and authentication. Transport mode doesn't encrypt the entire IP packets and is used internally within a private network, not with a VPN.

25. **D.** Network access control (NAC) inspects clients for specific health conditions and can redirect access to a remediation network for unhealthy clients. NAC is not dependent on the tunneling protocol (such as IPsec). The warning would not appear if NAC was disabled.

Chapter 5

Securing Hosts and Data

CompTIA Security+ objectives covered in this chapter:

1.3 Distinguish and differentiate network design elements and compounds

- Virtualization
- Cloud computing
  - Platform as a Service
  - Software as a Service
  - Infrastructure as a Service

2.1 Explain risk-related concepts

- Risks associated to cloud computing and virtualization

2.2 Carry out appropriate risk mitigation strategies

- Change management
- Implement policies and procedures to prevent data loss or theft

2.4 Explain the importance of security-related awareness and training

- User habits
  - Personally owned devices
- Threat awareness
  - Zero days exploits

3.5 Analyze and differentiate among types of application attacks

- Zero day

3.6 Analyze and differentiate among types of mitigation and deterrent techniques

- Hardening
  - Disabling unnecessary services
  - Protecting management interfaces and applications

- Password protection
- Disabling unnecessary accounts
- Security posture (initial baseline configuration)

4.2 Carry out appropriate procedures to establish host security

- Operating system security and settings
- Patch management
- Host software baselining
- Virtualization
- Mobile devices
  - Screen lock
  - Strong password
  - Device encryption
  - Remote wipe/sanitation
  - Voice encryption
  - GPS tracking

4.3 Explain the importance of data security

- Data Loss Prevention (DLP)
- Data encryption
  - Full disk
  - Database
  - Individual files
  - Removable media
  - Mobile devices
- Hardware-based encryption devices
  - TPM
  - HSM
  - USB encryption
  - Hard drive
- Cloud computing

6.2 Use and apply appropriate cryptographic tools and products

- Whole disk encryption

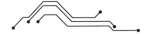

In this chapter, you'll learn about different methods used to secure hosts, such as servers, workstations, and other computing devices. Steps include disabling unnecessary services and keeping them up to date. Data is one of the most valuable resources of any organization and organizations take steps to protect data, prevent data leakage, and prevent the loss of confidentiality.

Implementing Host Security

Hosts are any servers, workstations, or other computing devices. In an ideal world, they start in a secure state. Unfortunately, it's not an ideal world, and administrators need to be proactive to secure hosts before deployment and keep them secure after deployment.

This section outlines several steps used to secure hosts, starting with basic hardening methods. Many organizations use different types of baselines, such as security baselines, configuration baselines, and performance baselines, to assist in the hardening process. Additionally, many organizations use imaging technologies to create standardized images with mandatory security settings.

Hardening Systems

Hardening is the practice of making a system or application more secure from its default installation. This section covers steps to harden the operating system, and chapter 7 covers information related to application hardening.

Key steps to harden a server or workstation include:

- Protecting passwords
- Disabling unnecessary services
- Disabling unneeded applications
- Protecting management interfaces and applications

Chapters 1 and 2 explored the different steps used to protect passwords, including the use of password policies to ensure users follow secure password practices. This section will explore the other items in this list. Additional hardening steps covered later in this chapter include keeping systems up-to-date with patch management and controlling the configuration with change management controls.

Disabling Unnecessary Services

A core principle associated with hardening a system includes removing all unnecessary services. If a service is not running on a system, attackers cannot attack it. For example, an expert on exploiting FTP vulnerabilities will be unsuccessful using these techniques on a server that is not running the FTP service. It doesn't matter how vulnerable a service is. If it's not running, it can't be attacked.

When you disable a service, you often remove access to the associated protocol. For example, if you disable the FTP service, you disable the FTP protocol. Some protocols, such as TCP, UDP, IP, and ARP, are necessary for connectivity within a TCP/IP network. Other protocols, such as HTTP, SMTP, and FTP, are optional application protocols and only run to support the underlying service.

Disabling unnecessary services and removing unneeded protocols provides several key benefits, including the following:

- **Provides protection against zero day attacks**. A zero day attack is an attack on an undisclosed vulnerability. Some attackers know about the vulnerability, but it is not public knowledge, and the vendor has not released a patch. By limiting the services and protocols running on a system, you limit vulnerabilities against zero day attacks.

- **Reduces risks associated with open ports**. If an attacker does a port scan, the port scan fails on the associated port fail. For example, disabling the FTP service on a server causes a port scan on ports 20 and 21 to fail even if these ports are open on a firewall.

Remember this

Disabling unused services is a key step in protecting systems from attacks such as zero day attacks, malware, or risks associated with open ports. This is an important step for both operating system hardening and application hardening.

Eliminate Unneeded Applications

In addition to disabling unnecessary services to reduce vulnerabilities, it's important to uninstall unneeded software. Software frequently has bugs and vulnerabilities. While patching software will frequently close these vulnerabilities, you can eliminate these vulnerabilities by simply eliminating unneeded applications.

Years ago, I was working at a small training company. One of the servers had a default installation of Windows. We were using the server as a file server, but since it wasn't hardened from the default installation, it was also running Internet Information Services (IIS), Microsoft's web server.

At some point, attackers released the Nimda virus that exploited a vulnerability with IIS. Microsoft released a patch for IIS, but since IIS was installed by default and we weren't using it, we also weren't managing it. Ultimately, the Nimda virus found our server, and the worm component of Nimda quickly infected our network. If the IIS software hadn't been installed, the server would not have been vulnerable to the attack.

Using Baselines

A baseline is a known starting point. In the context of host security, you can use baselines to provide known starting points for host systems. This section covers three types of baselines.

- Security baseline
- Configuration baseline
- Performance baseline

Security Baselines

A security baseline is a secure starting point for an operating system. The first step in creating the security baseline is creating a written security policy. Once the organization creates the security policy, administrators use different methods, such as Group Policy, security templates, or imaging, to deploy the baseline. Later, they can check existing systems against the security baseline to verify the system is still secure.

For example, imagine that your organization's security policy mandates that users should not be able to install software. Administrators deploy systems enforcing this policy. Later, they can check existing systems to ensure that users cannot install software and the original security baseline is still intact.

An organization will typically have several security baselines. For example, end-user operating systems use one baseline, generic servers use another baseline, and specialty servers use other baselines.

Each operating system is different, so there isn't a standard checklist that identifies how to lock down all operating systems. However, there is a place to check—the vendor's documentation. If you're trying to secure an operating system or an application running on the operating system, check the documentation. This documentation often includes valuable information with easy-to-follow steps.

Some vendors include tools to help create a security baseline. For example, Microsoft Server operating systems include the Security Configuration Wizard (SCW). SCW leads administrators through a series of questions about a system and then creates an Extensible Markup Language (XML) database file that includes a wide assortment of security settings. Administrators can import these settings into a Group Policy object to apply them.

Enforcing Security Baselines with Group Policy

Microsoft domains use Group Policy to standardize the configuration of systems. An administrator can create and apply a Group Policy object (GPO) to configure all the systems in the domain, or target specific systems.

The magic of Group Policy is that an administrator can configure a single setting within a GPO and apply it to multiple users or computers with very little effort. A GPO works the same way whether it's being applied to five systems or five thousand. Group Policy is applied when a computer starts up and when a user logs on. The system periodically checks for any changes to Group Policy and automatically applies them.

Another benefit of Group Policy is that it regularly reapplies security settings. If a problem or attack compromises a system, this process helps keep the Group Policy security settings in place.

Using Security Templates

GPOs have so many capabilities that it's difficult for any single administrator to learn and know all the possible security settings. However, you can use preconfigured security templates to address many different security needs. Additionally, you can modify any of the security templates to meet specific needs. For example, if your organization has strict security guidelines for systems, you can use security templates to configure the settings and apply them consistently across the organization.

Remember this

You can use Group Policy and security templates to standardize system configuration and security settings. These methods allow you to enforce strict company guidelines when deploying computers and reapply security settings to multiple computers.

Security templates provide a secure starting point for systems to enforce a security baseline. You can use them to deploy multiple security settings to individual computers and to multiple computers through a GPO.

Security templates include the following sections:

- **Account Policies**. This includes password and lockout policy settings.
- **Local Policies**. You can control many user rights with settings in this section.
- **System Services**. You can use this to disable any unnecessary services.
- **Software Restrictions**. You can control what software can be installed on a system and what software can run on a system.
- **Restricted Groups**. You can control any group with this setting. For example, you can use this to control which users are in the Administrators group.

Configuration Baseline

A configuration baseline documents the configuration of a system. This includes all the system configuration settings, such as printer configuration, application settings, and TCP/IP settings. It may also include a host software baseline, which lists all software installed on the system.

The differences between a configuration baseline and a security baseline can be a little fuzzy. The security baseline settings are strictly security related. The configuration baseline settings ensure consistent operation of the system. However, since the configuration baseline contributes to improved availability of a system, which is part of the security triad, it also contributes to overall security.

An important consideration with a configuration baseline is keeping it up to date. Administrators should update the configuration baseline after changing or modifying the system. This includes after installing new software, deploying service packs, or modifying any other system configuration settings.

Remember this

Configuration baselines document system configuration and should be updated when the system is updated. This includes after installing new software, deploying service packs, or modifying any system configuration settings.

It's also important to maintain the integrity of the configuration baseline. The change management section later in this chapter covers the importance of managing changes to prevent unintended outages.

Performance Baselines and Baseline Reporting

A performance baseline identifies the overall performance of a system at a point in time. If performance deteriorates later, administrators can compare the current performance against the baseline report. The differences between the current measurements and the baseline help an administrator differentiate between normal performance and actual problems.

The baseline report includes information on usage of basic system hardware resources, such as the processor, memory, disk, and network interface card (NIC). It also includes additional system data, such as logs to show normal behavior.

As an example, Performance Monitor is a tool used within Windows systems to create performance baseline reports. A performance baseline report will capture snapshots of key metrics every thirty minutes throughout a seven-day period. These snapshots will give a good picture of a system's performance during peak performance times and slack times. An administrator can later compare current performance with the baseline to identify any differences.

Figure 5.1 shows Performance Monitor with a dynamic system performance report displayed. The report includes multiple sections, titled System Performance Report, Summary, Diagnostic Results, CPU, Network, Disk, Memory, and Report Statistics, and in the figure, the Summary and Diagnostic Results are expanded. An administrator can expand any of the other sections by clicking the down arrow on the far right of the section title.

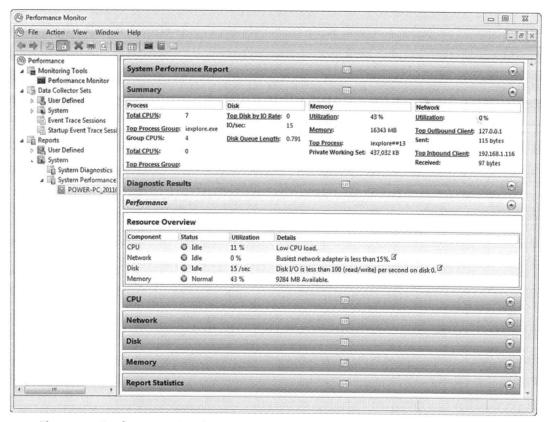

Figure 5.1: Performance Monitor

> ### Remember this
> Baseline reporting documents normal system performance. Administrators compare current performance against a baseline report to determine abnormal activity.

As an example, imagine that you are asked to troubleshoot the performance of a server because it's running slow. During your investigation, you discover that the system has an average of twenty active SSH sessions and the processor utilization averages at about 50 percent.

Is this normal? Is the system under attack? If you have a baseline report, you can compare the current activity with the baseline report to determine normal behavior. The performance baseline report will often provide you the answers. However, if you don't have a performance baseline report, you may spend a lot of time and effort investigating normal performance that is unrelated to any problem.

As a comparison, chapter 4 presented baselines in the context of anomaly-based intrusion detection systems (IDSs). As a reminder, the anomaly-based IDS starts by creating a baseline and then compares current behavior against the baseline. Without a baseline, the anomaly-based IDS cannot detect anomalies. Similarly, without a security or configuration baseline, you can't detect changes.

Understanding Imaging

One of the most common methods of deploying secure hosts is with images. An image is a snapshot of a single system that administrators deploy to multiple other systems. Imaging has become an important security practice for many organizations. Figure 5.2 and the following text identify the overall process of capturing and deploying an image.

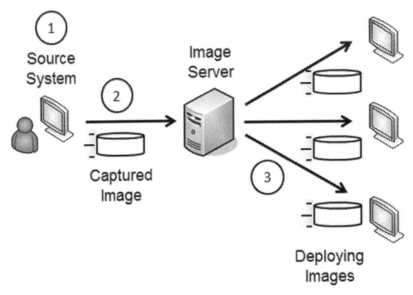

Figure 5.2: Capturing and deploying images

1. Administrators start with a blank source system. They install and configure the operating system, install and configure any desired applications, and modify security settings. They perform extensive testing to ensure the system works as desired and that it is secure.

2. Next, administrators capture the image. Symantec's Ghost is a popular imaging application, and Windows Server 2008 includes free tools many organizations use to capture and deploy images. The captured image is simply a file that can be stored on a server or copied to external media, such as a DVD or external USB drive.

3. In step 3, administrators deploy the image to multiple systems. The image installs the same configuration on the target systems as the original source system.

Administrators will often take a significant amount of time to configure and test the source system. They follow the same hardening practices discussed earlier and often use security and configuration baselines. If they're deploying the image to just a few systems, they may create the image in just a few hours. However, if they're deploying it to thousands of systems, they may take weeks or months to create and test the image. Once the image is created, image deployment is very quick and requires little administrative effort.

Imaging provides two important benefits.

- **Secure starting point.** The image includes mandated security configurations for the system. Personnel who deploy the system don't need to remember or follow extensive checklists to ensure that new systems are set up with all the detailed configuration and security settings. The deployed image retains all the settings of the original image. Administrators will still configure some settings, such as the computer name, after deploying the image.

- **Reduced costs**. Deploying imaged systems reduces the overall maintenance costs and improves reliability. Support personnel don't need to learn multiple different end-user system environments to assist end users. Instead, they learn just one. When troubleshooting, support personnel spend their time focused on helping the end user rather than trying to learn the system configuration. Managers understand this as reducing the total cost of ownership (TCO) for systems.

Many virtualization tools include the ability to convert an image to a virtual system. In other words, once you create the image, you can deploy it to either a physical system or a virtual system. From a security perspective, there is no difference how you deploy it. If you've locked down the image for deployment to a physical system, you've locked it down for deployment to a virtual system.

Remember this

Standardized images include mandatory security configurations. This ensures the system starts in a secure state and reduces overall costs. There is no difference in the security requirements for images deployed to physical computers, or as virtual systems.

Imaging isn't limited to only desktop computers. You can image any system, including servers. For example, consider an organization that maintains fifty database servers in a large datacenter. The organization can use imaging to deploy new servers or as part of its disaster recovery plan to restore failed servers. It is much quicker to deploy an image to rebuild a failed server than it is to rebuild a server from scratch. As long as the images are kept up to date, this also helps ensure the recovered server starts in a secure state.

U.S. Government Configuration Baseline (USGCB)

The U.S. government has been using standard images for many years. This started as a Standard Desktop Core Configuration (SDCC) with the U.S. Air Force and morphed into the Federal Desktop Core Configuration (FDCC) mandated by Office of Management and Budget (OMB) for all federal agencies. The current version is the USGCB, which is also mandated by OMB.

Before using these images, many agencies were repeating common security errors. Smaller agencies without extensive IT or security experience deployed systems without locking them down. Even when government security professionals knew about common attacks and how to protect systems, the smaller agencies didn't have the expertise or manpower to implement the fixes.

However, agencies are now consistently deploying new systems in a secure state. The images include the mandated security settings and do not require extensive security knowledge or expertise to deploy. Of course, this isn't the only security measure the agencies take, but it does provide a good start.

Understanding Virtualization

Virtualization is a technology that has been gaining a lot of popularity in recent years. Virtualization allows you to host one or more virtual systems, or virtual machines (VMs), on a single physical system. Organizations are using virtualization more and more to reduce costs. They sometimes use them to host honeypots or honeynets, described in chapter 4.

Different virtual machines can run different operating systems. For example, a VM could be running Microsoft, Linux, UNIX, or just about any other operating system needed by the organization.

Admittedly, you'll need to beef up the core resources of the physical system, which is also called the host. It needs multiple processors, massive amounts of RAM, more hard drive space, and one or more fast network cards. However, the cost of the hardware for a single system is much less than you'd pay for multiple separate systems. It also requires less electricity, less cooling, and less space.

Several virtualization technologies currently exist, including VMware, Microsoft's Hyper-V, Window's Virtual PC (VPC), and Sun's VirtualBox. VMware has been around the longest as a server product, and it's specifically designed to host multiple machines in a production environment. Microsoft's Hyper-V is a direct competitor with VMware.

Microsoft's VPC and Sun's VirtualBox are free and run on desktop systems such as Windows 7. You can use them to create simple test environments that include multiple systems within an isolated virtual network. VPC does not support 64-bit operation systems as virtual hosts, but Sun's VirtualBox does support 64-bit hosts.

It's worth pointing out that virtual machines are simply files. These files certainly have some complexity, but they are just files. As an example, Figure 5.3 shows Microsoft's Hyper-V Manager running on a Windows Server 2008 R2 system, along with Windows Explorer. In the figure, I've selected the Win7 VM in Hyper-V and browsed to the folder holding all of the VM files in Windows Explorer. You can see the Win7 virtual hard disk (VHD) and other folders associated with the VM. It's relatively easy to export these files from one server and import them to another server.

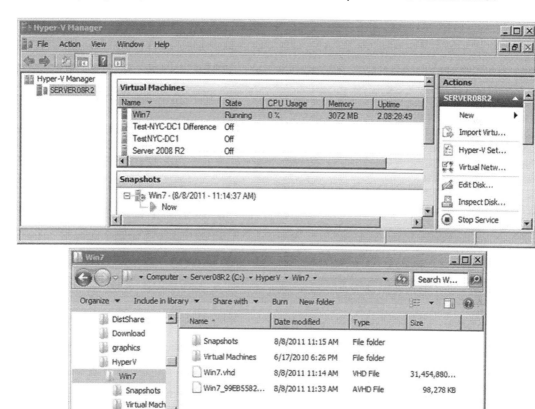

Figure 5.3: Microsoft's Hyper-V Manager

The figure also shows a Snapshots section in Hyper-V Manager. Administrators can take a snapshot of a system at any time. They can later revert the VM to the exact state it was in when the snapshot was taken.

Reduced Footprint

The amount of physical space IT systems require and the amount of power they consume is sometimes referred to as their footprint. In this context, *footprint* is referring to an environmental footprint. For example, a carbon footprint refers to the total amount of carbon dioxide emitted due to the consumption of fossil fuels.

If an organization uses fewer physical servers, it reduces its footprint. A reduced footprint results in fewer wasted resources. Additionally, it can improve physical security, since the organization has less physical hardware to protect.

It's worth noting that many organizations have underutilized servers. For example, a server may be running at less than 10 percent utilization, resulting in a significant amount of wasted resources. Not only is the extra processing power of these servers wasted, but all of the power and air to cool the servers is also wasted. This is one of the main drivers for physical to virtual (p2v) projects. For example, one company I know of did a survey and found that 80 percent of their servers were operating at less than 10 percent utilization. By virtualizing the servers, the company was able to save money on heating, ventilation, and cooling (HVAC) and server equipment.

Compare the deployment of five servers. If an organization installs five virtual servers on a single physical server instead of five, it saves on multiple fronts. The hardware costs less, takes up less space, consumes less power, and requires less cooling.

Similarly, if an organization converts a large datacenter from primarily physical servers to virtual servers, it can significantly reduce its datacenter's footprint. For example, it may be able to reduce the size of a large datacenter from twenty rows of bays to just four rows.

Remember this

Virtualization reduces the footprint of an organization's server room or datacenter and helps eliminate wasted resources. It also helps reduce the amount of physical equipment, reducing overall physical security requirements.

Increased Availability

Virtualization management software has improved over the years. Whether you're using VMware's virtualization products or Microsoft's Hyper-V technology, you have tools that allow you to easily manage multiple physical servers hosting these virtual servers. Overall, this provides increased availability by reducing unplanned downtime for the virtual servers.

As mentioned previously, VMs are files. Just as you can copy a couple of text files from one system to another, you can also copy the VM files from one host to another.

For example, if one of your physical servers becomes overloaded, you can move virtual servers off the overloaded system to another physical server. Some virtual server management software makes this as simple as dragging and dropping the virtual servers from one host to another.

It's also easy to restore a failed virtual server. If you create a backup of the virtual server files and the original server fails, you simply restore the files. You can measure the amount of time it takes to restore a virtual server in minutes. In contrast, rebuilding a physical server can take hours.

Most virtual management software also supports snapshots. For example, Figure 5.3 shown earlier showed that a snapshot was taken of the Win7 VM. This can be very useful when testing updates. You can take a snapshot of a system prior to the update. If the update causes undesired results, you simply restore the snapshot and, as the saying goes, "it's like it never happened."

Isolation

Organizations usually configure online virtual servers so that they can communicate with other virtual and physical systems on the network. They use virtual network interface cards (NICs), and virtual networks for connectivity. However, it's also possible to configure the virtual systems so that they are completely isolated.

For example, you can isolate a virtual server so that it can't communicate with any other virtual or physical systems. In this way, it works just like a single system without a NIC. You can also group several virtual servers in their own virtual network so that they can communicate with each other but are isolated from hosts on the physical network.

Many security professionals use a virtual system or virtual network to test and investigate malicious software (malware). Malware released in an isolated environment presents minimal risk to the hardware and host operating system. Unfortunately, some malware is able to detect that it is running in a virtual environment. In some cases, malware developers have written code to change the behavior of the malware when it discovers it is running in a virtual environment.

Remember this

Security professionals use virtual systems to perform research on threats such as viruses. The virtual system remains isolated, preventing risk of contamination to the production environment.

Virtualization Weakness

Despite the strengths of virtualization technologies, you should understand some weaknesses. Many people consider virtual machine escape (VM escape) to be the most serious threat to virtual system security. Loss of confidentiality and loss of availability can also be a concern.

VM Escape

VM escape is an attack that allows an attacker to access the host system from within the virtual system. The host system runs an application or process called a hypervisor to manage the virtual systems. In some situations, the attacker can run code on the virtual system and interact with the hypervisor.

Most virtual systems run on a physical server with elevated privileges, similar to administrator privileges. A successful VM escape attack often gives the attacker unlimited control over the host system and each virtual system within the host.

When vendors discover VM escape vulnerabilities, they write and release patches. Just as with any patches, it is important to test and install these patches as soon as possible. This includes keeping both the physical and the virtual servers patched.

Remember this

VM escape is an attack that allows an attacker to access the host system from within the virtual system. If successful, it allows the attacker to control the physical host server and all other virtual servers on the physical server. Keeping both virtual and physical systems up to date with current patches protects them against known vulnerabilities, including VM escape.

Loss of Confidentiality

As a reminder, each virtual system or virtual machine is just one or more files. While this makes it easy to manage and move virtual machines, it also makes them easy to steal.

It's worth pointing out that a virtual machine includes the operating system and data, just as a physical system would have both the operating system and data on its physical drives. For example, a virtual machine can include a database with credit card data, company financial records, or any type of proprietary data.

With this in mind, consider an administrator that has turned to the dark side and become a malicious insider. The insider has access to the systems and can easily copy the virtual machine, take it home, and launch it on another physical server. At this point, the attacker has access to the system and the data.

You may remember from chapter 1 that one of the primary methods of protecting against loss of confidentiality is with encryption. Virtual systems support encryption just as physical systems do. If any of the data is important, you can protect it with encryption.

Loss of Availability

Another weakness associated with virtualization is that the host operating system becomes a single point of failure. If a physical server is hosting five virtual servers, and it fails, the five virtual servers also fail.

One way to overcome this weakness for critical servers is to use clustering technologies. Chapter 9 covers clustering in more depth, but, in short, a failover cluster ensures that a service provided by a critical server continues to operate even if a server fails. The failover clustering service switches from a failed server in a cluster to an operational server in the same cluster.

As a simple example, imagine that you have are hosting five virtual database servers on one physical server. You can mirror this configuration on another physical server with the same five virtual servers. If one physical server fails, the other server takes over.

> **Remember this**
>
> You can protect against loss of confidentiality on virtual machines by encrypting files and folders, just as you can encrypt them on a physical system. You can protect against loss of availability on virtual machines using redundancy and failover technologies.

Implementing Patch Management

Software is not secure. There. I said it. As someone who has written a few programs over the years, it's not easy to say. In a perfect world, extensive testing would discover all the bugs, exploits, and vulnerabilities that cause so many problems.

However, since operating systems and applications include millions of lines of code, testing simply doesn't find all the problems. Instead, most companies make a best effort to test software before releasing it. Later, as problems crop up, companies write and release patches or updates. Administrators must apply these patches to keep their systems up to date and protected against known vulnerabilities.

Patch management is a hardening procedure that ensures that systems and applications stay up to date with current patches. This is one of the most efficient ways to reduce operating system and application vulnerabilities, since it protects systems from known vulnerabilities. Patch management includes a group of methodologies and includes the process of identifying, downloading, testing, deploying, and verifying patches.

> **Remember this**
>
> Patch management is one of the most efficient methods of reducing known operating system and application vulnerabilities. It includes testing, deploying, and verifying changes made by patches.

As an example, bugs have been discovered in many web browsers that allow drive-by downloads. In other words, all the user has to do is visit a specially crafted web page and the web page will download and install malicious software. This happens without the user's knowledge or approval. The attacker will send an e-mail as spam that includes a link to the malicious website, and encourage the user to click it. One click and the user's system is infected. In contrast, if these bugs are patched, the drive-by downloads fail. Unpatched systems remain vulnerable to known attacks.

Comparing Updates

You will often see all updates referred to as patches. For example, patch management includes managing the deployment of patches, hotfixes, and service packs. There are some differences, though.

A patch is a small piece of code used to correct a single bug or vulnerability discovered in an operating system or application. Think of a bicycle tire. When the tire gets a puncture and goes flat, you don't replace the entire tire, but instead apply a small patch to fix it. This is similar to a patch applied to operating systems or applications that use a small piece of code to correct a problem. Of course, if you don't apply a patch, the problem remains. A bicycle tire will remain flat. An unpatched system remains vulnerable.

Hotfixes are similar to patches. In general, a hotfix is a patch that you can apply without rebooting the system. Vendors sometimes release hotfixes to address an immediate threat.

A service pack is a collection of patches and fixes and may include additional features. The primary purpose of the service pack is to make it easier to apply a large number of patches and fixes to a system to bring it up to date.

Deploying Patches

Small users and organizations sometimes configure systems to automatically download and install patches. Many other organizations take control of the process and use servers to control patch deployments.

Figure 5.4 and the following text shows the overall process of patch management when an organization takes control of the process.

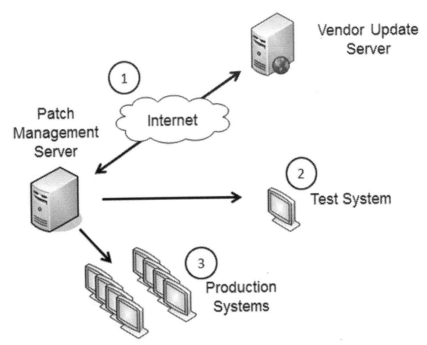

Figure 5.4: Downloading, testing, and deploying patches

In general, patch management involves the following tasks:

- When vendors release patches, administrators connect to the vendor's update server, identify patches they need, and download them.
- Administrators deploy the patches to one or more test systems. These systems mirror the configuration of the production environment. If a patch causes a problem, it does not affect production systems.
- Administrators then deploy patches to appropriate systems. Patch management software often includes a verification component so that it can verify patch deployments. Similarly many vulnerability-scanning tools (covered in chapter 8) check system vulnerabilities to known attacks by verifying patches. Network access control tools verify patches and quarantine or isolate unpatched clients.

Occasionally, systems may block patches. Verification actions will discover the problem, but it's important to investigate why a patch is blocked and correct the problem. As a simple example, the configuration of a host-based firewall could block the patches. Obviously, if this is the case, you can reconfigure the firewall to allow the patches.

Testing Patches

Patches can fix one problem but create others, so the importance of testing patches cannot be overstated. Consider the worst-case scenario. In some unfortunate situations, systems shut down and never work again. If this happens to your home computer, it is inconvenient. However, if one thousand computers within an organization stop working one day, it can be catastrophic.

Instead of deploying patches as soon as they are released, many organizations first examine them to determine if they're needed, and then test relevant patches. The goal of testing is to ensure that a patch does not introduce new problems.

In order for testing to be realistic, you need to install the patch on systems that mirror the production environment. In other words, if all the users have new computers, it won't do any good to test a patch on an older system.

Regression testing is a specific type of testing used to detect any new errors (or regressions). In regression testing, administrators run a series of known tests on a system and compare the results with tests run before applying the patch.

> ### Remember this
> Organizations test patches in a test environment that mirrors the production environment. Regression testing verifies that a patch has not introduced new errors.

Scheduling Patches

Many organizations have patch management policies. These policies document the process of patching systems and often provide a timeline for patching.

As an example, Microsoft releases most of its patches on the second Tuesday of the month, which is also called Patch Tuesday. IT departments can plan on this release and immediately begin evaluating the patches, testing relevant patches, and deploying them. Microsoft will sometimes release an out-of-band (OOB) patch that is released right away, but it only does this for critical vulnerabilities.

Other operating systems, such as UNIX and Linux, don't currently release patches on a schedule, but they still release patches. Administrators can sign up for notifications about patches and plan their timeline based on these notifications.

Exploit Wednesday

Immediately after Microsoft releases patches on Patch Tuesday, many attackers go to work. They read as much as they can find about the patches, download the patches, and analyze them. They attempt to reverse engineer the patches to determine exactly what the patch is fixing.

Next, the attackers write their own code to exploit the vulnerability on unpatched systems. They often have exploits attacking systems the very next day—Exploit Wednesday. Since many organizations take more than a single day to test the patch before applying it, this gives the attackers time to attack unpatched systems.

Additionally, some attackers discover unknown exploits before Patch Tuesday. If they exploit the vulnerability immediately, Microsoft may detect the vulnerability and fix it on Patch Tuesday. Instead, attackers sometimes wait until Patch Tuesday, verify the exploit remains unpatched, and then begin attacking. This gives them a full month to exploit systems before a patch is available.

Understanding Change Management

The worst enemies of many networks have been unrestrained administrators. A well-meaning administrator can make what appears to be a minor change to fix one problem, only to cause a major problem somewhere else. A misconfiguration can take down a server, disable a network, stop -e-mail communications, and even stop all network traffic for an entire enterprise.

For example, I once saw a major outage occur when an administrator was troubleshooting a printer problem. After modifying the printer's IP address, the printer began to work. Sounds like a success, doesn't it? Unfortunately, the new IP address was the same IP address assigned to a DNS server, and it created an IP address conflict. The conflict prevented the DNS server from resolving names to IP addresses. This resulted in a major network outage until another administrator discovered and corrected the problem.

These self-inflicted disasters were relatively common in the early days of IT. They still occur today, but organizations with mature change management processes in place have fewer of these problems.

Change management defines the process for any type of system modifications or upgrades. It provides two key goals:

- Ensure changes to IT systems do not result in unintended outages
- Provide an accounting structure or method to document all changes

---

Remember this

Change management defines the process and accounting structure for handling modifications and upgrades. The goals are to reduce unintended outages and provide documentation for all changes.

When a change management program is in place, administrators are discouraged from making ad-hoc, or as-needed, configuration changes. In other words, they don't immediately make a change as soon as they identify a potential need for the change. This includes making any type of configuration changes to systems, applications, patches, or any other change. Instead, they follow the change management process before making a change.

Experts from different areas of an organization examine change requests and can either approve or postpone them. The process usually approves simple changes quickly. A formal change review board regularly reviews postponed requests and can approve, modify, or reject the change.

This entire process provides documentation for approved changes. For example, some automated change management systems create accounting logs for all change requests. The system tracks the request from its beginning until implementation. Administrators use this documentation for configuration management and disaster recovery. If a modified system fails, change and configuration management documentation identifies how to return the system to its pre-failure state.

Protecting Data

Data is one of the most valuable resources any organization manages, second only to its people. However, there are countless stories of how organizations lose control of their data, resulting in substantial losses. Here are a few examples.

- **March 2011:** Attackers hacked into Epsilon, an e-mail marketing company. Attackers harvested hundreds of millions of customer e-mail addresses used by several well-known companies, such as BestBuy, TiVo, Capital One, Citi, and more. This affected the reputations of Epsilon and the companies using its services.

- **April 2011:** The MidState Medical Center in Connecticut admitted losing a hard drive that contained personally identifiable information (PII) on over ninety-three thousand patients. It offered to pay for identity protection for all of the patients.
- **April 2011:** Attackers breached Sony's PlayStation Network. The attack compromised more than seventy-seven million customer records, and Sony spent about $171 million as a direct response. Most analysts consider this $171 million just a down payment and believe losses will be much higher.
- **June 2011:** The National Health Services (NHS) in the United Kingdom admitted losing a laptop with medical records of over eight million patients.

It's important to realize that these examples are not unique. You can pick any month of any recent year and find multiple examples. Losing control of data directly affects the reputation, and often the bottom line, of an organization. The importance of taking steps to protect valuable data cannot be overstated.

Chapter 11 covers security policies that an organization can implement to protect data. The security policy helps an organization classify and label its data. This section presents many of the security controls an organization can use to protect data based on the requirements set within a data security policy.

Data Categories

You will frequently see data categorized based on how it is used or stored. The most common terms are data at rest, data in motion, and data in use.

- **Data at rest** is any stored data. This includes data on hard drives, mobile phones, USB flash drives, external drives, and backups. Data can be stored as individual files or full databases. The best way to protect data at rest from an attacker is to encrypt it.
- **Data in motion**, also called data in transit, is any data traveling over a network. Data Loss Prevention (DLP) techniques are effective at analyzing and detecting sensitive data sent over a network. You can also encrypt traffic sent over the network using encryption protocols such as IPsec, SSH, or SFTP.
- **Data in use** is a less-used term, and it refers to any data that resides in temporary memory. Applications retrieve stored data, process it, and may either save it back to storage or send it over a network. The application is responsible for protecting data in use.

Remember this

The best way to protect data against loss of confidentiality is with encryption. This is especially important for data at rest on any type of mobile storage device such as on a USB flash drive, an external USB hard drive, drives within laptops, or storage on any other mobile system. Encryption also protects data in transit using protocols such as IPsec, SSH, and SFTP.

Protecting Confidentiality with Encryption

As mentioned in chapter 1, one of the primary ways you can prevent the loss of confidentiality is by encrypting data. This includes encrypting data at rest and data in motion. It is much more difficult for an attacker to view encrypted data than it is if the data is stored as plain text.

You can use other tools to restrict access to data, but this isn't always effective. For example, consider Microsoft's New Technology File System (NTFS). You can use NTFS to set permissions on files and folders to restrict access. However, if a thief steals a laptop with NTFS protected files, it's a simple matter to access them. The thief simply moves the drive to another system as an extra drive, logs on as the administrator, and takes ownership of the files. Encryption isn't as easy to bypass.

Software-based Encryption

Many operating systems support file and folder level encryption. Linux systems support GNU privacy guard (gpg), which is a command-line tool used to encrypt and decrypt files with a password. Microsoft's NTFS includes Encrypting File System (EFS), available in Windows Explorer. Users can right-click any file or folder, select Advanced, and select Encrypt Contents to Secure Data as shown in Figure 5.5. An attacker will have a much more difficult time accessing these encrypted files.

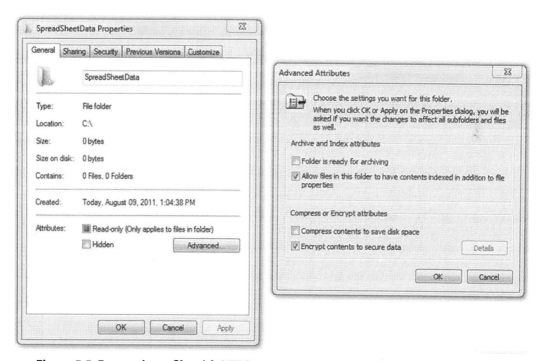

Figure 5.5: Encrypting a file with NTFS

A benefit of file and folder encryption is that you can encrypt individual files that need protection. For example, a server may store files used by users throughout the company. Access controls provide a first level of protection for these files, but administrators may be able to bypass the access controls. Imagine that the company stored payroll data on the server and they want to ensure that a malicious insider with administrative privileges can't access the data. By using file encryption, it provides an additional level of protection.

As another example, some people store passwords in a file on their computer. After all, it's not a good idea to use the same password for Facebook as you use for online banking, and it can be difficult to remember them all. File level protection for a password file helps protect this file if the system is lost or stolen.

Remember this

File and folder level protection can protect individual files. This can be useful to protect data against users with elevated permissions, such as administrators, and to protect individual sensitive files, such as files with passwords. USB encryption programs protect the confidentiality of data on USB flash drives.

Another form of software-based encryption is with an application. For example, many database application programs such as Oracle Database or Microsoft's SQL Server include the ability to encrypt data held within a database. While it's possible to encrypt the entire database, it's more common to encrypt specific data elements. For example, a database table can include columns used to hold credit card data, such as the number, expiration date, and security code. The database can encrypt the sensitive data in these columns, but not waste valuable processing power encrypting data that isn't sensitive, such as order numbers or order dates.

Hardware-based Encryption

While software-based encryption is useful, the drawback is that it can take extra processing power and time. It isn't as useful when a large quantity of data, such as an entire disk, needs to be encrypted, or when performance is a concern.

You can use hardware-based encryption devices, such as a Trusted Platform Module or a hardware security module, for better performance. A significant benefit of hardware encryption is that it is much quicker than software encryption.

However, one of the drawbacks with many hardware-based drive encryption solutions is a lack of management software. Administrators can encrypt systems on a case-by-case basis, but large scale deployments of systems with encrypted drives is labor intensive. This is one of the reasons hardware-based drive encryption has seen slower deployment.

Remember this

Hardware encryption is much quicker than software encryption. However, hardware-based drive encryption is slower to deploy due to a lack of management software. Two common methods of hardware encryption are with a Trusted Platform Module (TPM) and a hardware security module (HSM). Both store RSA keys used with asymmetric encryption.

Table 5.1 provides an overview of these hardware encryption devices, and the following sections explore them in greater depth. Both use strong asymmetric encryption and provide a secure method of storing encryption keys.

Characteristics	TPM	HSM
Hardware	Chip in motherboard (included with many laptops)	Removable or external hardware device, (purchased separately)
Uses	Full disk encryption (for laptops and some servers)	High-end mission-critical servers (SSL accelerators, high availability clusters, certificate authorities)
Authentication	Performs platform authentication (verifies drive not moved)	Performs application authentication (only used by authorized applications)
Encryption Keys	RSA key burned into chip when created and can generate other keys	Stores RSA keys, asymmetric encryption keys and can generate keys

Table 5.1: A comparison of TPM and HSM features

Trusted Platform Module

A Trusted Platform Module (TPM) is a hardware chip on the computer's motherboard that stores cryptographic keys used for encryption. Many laptop computers include a TPM, but if the system doesn't include a TPM, it is not feasible to add one. Once enabled, the TPM provides full disk encryption capabilities. It keeps hard drives locked, or sealed, until the system completes a system verification or authentication process.

The TPM includes a unique RSA key burned into it, which is used for asymmetric encryption. Additionally, the TPM can generate, store, and protect other keys used in the encryption and decryption process.

Remember this

A Trusted Platform Module (TPM) is a hardware chip on the motherboard included on many newer laptops. A TPM includes a unique RSA asymmetric key, and it can generate and store other keys used for encryption, decryption, and authentication. TPM provides full disk encryption.

If the system includes a TPM, you use the operating system to enable it. For example, Microsoft's Windows 7 and Windows Server 2008 include BitLocker that you can enable for systems that include the TPM. Once enabled, TPM keeps the hard drive locked until platform verification and user authentication processes are complete.

BitLocker uses the TPM to detect tampering of any critical operating system files or processes as part of the platform verification process. Additionally, users provide authentication, such as with a smart card, a password, or personal identification number (PIN). The user inserts a USB flash drive with a startup key into the system, or provides a PIN in order for the operating system to start. If these steps don't pass, the drive remains locked.

If a thief steals the system, the drive remains locked and protected. An attacker wouldn't have authentication credentials, so he can't access the drive using a normal boot-up process. If the attacker tries to modify the operating system to bypass security controls, the TPM detects the tampering and keeps the drive locked. If a thief moves the drive to another system, the drive remains locked since the TPM isn't available.

Hardware Security Module

A hardware security module (HSM) is a security device you can add to a system to manage, generate, and securely store cryptographic keys. High performance HSMs are external devices connected to a network using TCP/IP. Smaller HSMs come as expansion cards you install within a server, or as devices you plug into computer ports.

One of the noteworthy differences between an HSM and a TPM is that HSMs are removable or external devices. In comparison, a TPM is a chip embedded into the motherboard. You can easily add an HSM to a system or a network, but if a system didn't ship with a TPM, it's not feasible to add one later. Both HSMs and TPMs provide secure encryption capabilities by storing and using RSA keys.

The following list shows some common usages of HSMs:

- **High-speed SSL sessions**. High-volume e-commerce sites using SSL, such as with HTTPS, often need the benefit of hardware encryption provided by an HSM. These sites use SSL accelerators with HSMs for performance, and the HSMs provide a secure method of storing keys and digital certificates needed in SSL sessions.

- **Mission-critical systems**. HSMs provide high-speed services in high availability clusters. Chapter 9 presents clusters in more depth, but, in short, a cluster includes redundant servers or devices and continues to provide a service even if a single device fails. You can cluster multiple HSMs and if a single HSM fails, the overall service continues to operate.

- **Certification authorities (CAs).** Many CAs use HSMs to create, store, and manage public key infrastructure (PKI) key pairs used in asymmetric encryption. Chapter 10 discusses CAs, PKIs, and asymmetric key pairs in more depth.

Remember this

A hardware security module (HSM) is a removable or external device that can generate, store, and manage RSA keys used in asymmetric encryption. High-volume e-commerce sites use HSMs to increase the performance of SSL sessions. High-availability clusters needing encryption services can use clustered HSMs.

Data Leakage

Another danger with data comes from data leakage. Just as a leak in one of your car's tires can let air out leaving you with a flat tire, data can leak out of a company, leaving the company with flat financial performance. Worse, the data leakage can result in losses, reversing the company's profits.

Data Loss Prevention

Data Loss Prevention (DLP) techniques examine and inspect data looking for unauthorized data transmissions. You may also see it as data leak prevention. A DLP system can be network-based to inspect data in motion, storage-based to inspect data at rest, or endpoint-based to inspect data in use. The most common is a network-based DLP.

Chapter 3 discussed different types of content files used in web application firewalls, web security gateways, and appliances. Most of these are monitoring incoming data streams looking for malicious code. However, a network-based DLP will monitor outgoing data looking for sensitive data, specified by an administrator.

DLPs will scan the text of all e-mails and the content of any attached files, including documents, spreadsheets, presentations, and databases. Even if a user compresses a file as a zip file before sending it, the DLP examines the contents by simply unzipping it.

> ### *Remember this*
> A network-based Data Loss Prevention (DLP) system can examine and analyze network traffic. It can detect if confidential company data or any PII data is included in e-mail and reduce the risk of internal users e-mailing sensitive data outside the organization.

As an example, I know of one organization that routinely scans all outgoing e-mails looking for personally identifiable information (PII), such as Social Security numbers. The network-based DLP includes a mask to identify Social Security numbers as a string of numbers in the following format: ###-##-####. If an e-mail or an attachment includes this string of numbers, the DLP detects it, blocks the e-mail, and sends an alert to a security administrator.

Many organizations classify and label data using terms such as "Classified," "Confidential," "Private," and "Sensitive." It is easy to include these search terms in the DLP application, or any other terms considered important by the organization. Network-based DLPs are not limited to scanning only e-mail. Many can scan the content of other traffic, such as FTP and HTTP traffic.

Portable Storage Devices

Portable storage devices refers to any storage system that you can attach to a computer and easily copy data. It primarily refers to USB hard drives and USB flash drives.

- A USB hard drive has all the same hardware and moving parts (such as platters and heads) as an internal drive.
- A USB flash drive isn't actually a hard drive but is instead nonvolatile memory. It uses solid-state memory to store data without the need to keep it powered on. People commonly call these thumb drives.

You can easily copy data onto a USB device and carry it with you. This is useful when working with data, but also results in data leakage. They combine high volume and transfer speeds with ease of concealment. For example, employees can easily copy entire databases, including patient medical data, customer credit card numbers, and much more onto these devices. Even if the employee isn't copying the data for malicious purposes, data on most portable devices isn't encrypted and can easily fall into the wrong hands.

As another example, foreigners have purchased many USB flash drives at flea market type bazaars outside of United States installations overseas. These drives included a significant amount of personal information on personnel stationed at the base. I doubt that people intentionally gave the USB away with the data on it. Instead, they copied the data onto the drive, didn't protect it, and it was lost or stolen.

The biggest single way to reduce data leakage risks with portable storage devices is with encryption. Many tools are now available that provide full disk encryption for these devices. This includes full encryption of removable USB drives and external hard drives. Even if the device is lost, the encryption makes it much less likely that an attacker will access the data.

For example, TrueCrypt is available on Linux and many other operating systems. It performs whole disk encryption for USB drives to protect the confidentiality of data if the device is lost. Users can access the data with a password, and TrueCrypt will decrypt and encrypt data on the fly without any other user intervention.

Many full disk encryption programs require the user to enter a password or pass phrase to unlock and access the data. It's worth stating the obvious. The password or key should not be stored with the device. This is like writing your PIN on the back of your debit card.

Another issue when users are able to copy data onto portable devices is loss of control. Operating systems often have file and folder permissions, but a USB flash drive is typically formatted with a basic file system such as FAT32 that does not include permissions.

As an example, consider a developer that wants to test an application using realistic customer data such as credit card numbers. Most developers know better than to test an application in a production system. However, they may be tempted to copy data from a production environment to a test environment. Once the customer data is in the test environment, the production system no longer controls it and can fall into the wrong hands.

Protecting Mobile Devices

Chapter 4 presented several methods that can protect smartphones. These same methods are available for most mobile devices such as laptops and tablets. You can encrypt the data on the devices, locate them with a Global Positioning System (GPS), and send a remote wipe command to erase all the data and sanitize the drive. Some devices allow you to create a new screen lock passcode to prevent a thief from using the stolen device.

As an example, Apple's iPhones and iPads support MobileMe. You can use MobileMe to locate devices with GPS, send messages to the device, such as "Please, return my iPad," lock it with a new passcode, or send a remote wipe signal. Figure 5.6 shows a screenshot of MobileMe used to locate an iPad.

Figure 5.6: Using MobileMe

I expanded the map to show more states, but you can easily home in on the exact street location. With just a few clicks and keystrokes, you can send a message to the iPad, lock it, and wipe the data.

> ## Remember this
> You can protect mobile devices such as laptops, tablets, or smartphones with several methods. Full disk encryption protects the data on the device if it is lost. Global Positioning System (GPS) tracking can help you locate a lost device. Remote wipe, or remote sanitize, erases all data on lost devices.

It's worthwhile mentioning that while GPS can be an effective tool to help you locate and recover a system, it can also be a vulnerability. An attacker may be able to use GPS to track the location of an individual that owns a mobile device. Because of this, many users disable GPS tracking.

Understanding Cloud Computing

Cloud computing is one of those catchy terms that has captured our imagination. It just sounds cool. "To the cloud...." You can use cloud-computing technologies to host hardware, such as servers, and to host data.

Even though the phrase "cloud computing" is relatively new, the concept isn't. In short, cloud computing simply refers to accessing computing resources via a different location than your local computer. In most situations today, you're accessing these resources through the Internet.

As an example, if you use web-based e-mail such as Gmail, you're using cloud computing. More specifically, the web-based mail is a Software as a Service cloud computing service. You know that you're accessing your e-mail via the Internet, but you really don't know where the physical server hosting your account is located. It could be in a datacenter in the middle of Virginia, tucked away in Utah, or just about anywhere else in the world.

Cloud computing is very useful for heavily utilized systems and networks. As an example, consider the biggest shopping day in the United States—black Friday, the day after Thanksgiving, when retailers go into the black. Several years ago, Amazon.com had so much traffic during the Thanksgiving weekend that its servers could barely handle it. The company learned its lesson, though. The next year, it used cloud computing to rent access to servers specifically for the Thanksgiving weekend, and, despite increased sales, it didn't have any problems.

As many great innovators do, Amazon didn't look on this situation as a problem, but rather an opportunity. If it needed cloud computing for its heavily utilized system, other companies probably had the same need. Amazon now hosts cloud services to other organizations via its Amazon Elastic Compute Cloud (Amazon EC2) service. Interestingly, Amazon EC2 combines virtualization with cloud computing. When customers rent servers, they are able to create their own virtual machines and configure them as needed. Providing access to a computing platform via the cloud is also known as Platform as a Service (Paas).

There are three specific cloud-computing services mentioned in the Security+ exam you should understand: Software as a Service (SaaS), Infrastructure as a Service (IaaS), and Platform as a Service (PaaS). The following sections describe these and include some of the drawbacks to cloud computing.

> ### Remember this
>
> Cloud computing is provided by cloud providers and is very useful for heavily utilized systems and networks. Software as a Service (SaaS) is used for web-based applications. Infrastructure as a Service (IaaS) is also known as Hardware as a Service. Platform as a Service (PaaS) provides easy-to-configure operating systems.

Software as a Service

Software as a Service (SaaS) includes any software or application provided to users over a network such as the Internet. Internet users access the SaaS applications with a web browser. It usually doesn't matter which web browser or operating system a SaaS customer uses. They could be using Internet Explorer, Chrome, Firefox, or just about any web browser.

As mentioned previously, web-based e-mail is an example of SaaS. This includes Gmail, Yahoo! Mail, and others. The service provides all the components of e-mail to users via a simple web browser.

If you have a Gmail account, you can also use Google docs, another example of a SaaS. Google Docs provides access to several SaaS applications, allowing users to open text documents, spreadsheets, presentations, drawings, and PDF files through a web browser.

A talented developer named Lee Graham and I teamed up to create CertApps.com to create study materials. He's an Apple guy running a Mac while I'm a Microsoft guy running Windows, and we live in different states. However, we post and share documents through Google docs and despite different locations and different applications running on our individual systems, we're able to easily collaborate. One risk is that our data is hosted on Google docs, and if attackers hack into Google docs, our data may be compromised.

> ### Remember this
>
> Applications such as web-based e-mail provided over the Internet are Software as a Service (SaaS) cloud-based technologies. Internet users access SaaS applications with a web browser. Data hosted in the cloud presents a security concern.

Infrastructure as a Service

Infrastructure as a Service (IaaS) allows an organization to outsource its equipment requirements, including the hardware and all of its support operations. The IaaS service provider owns the equipment, houses it in its datacenter, and performs all of the required maintenance. The customer essentially rents access to the equipment and often pays on a per-use basis.

You can also think of IaaS as Hardware as a Service (HaaS). In other words, instead of purchasing all of the hardware, and infrastructure to support the hardware, you can rent the hardware through the cloud. This can be very useful for a small company that needs the benefits of advanced servers, but lacks the budget to support them.

For example, imagine that a small company would like to deploy a new service to its Internet customers that requires an expensive database solution. A little research shows that it will need new servers to host the database, and it'll also need to hire additional administrators to install, manage, and maintain the servers.

On the other hand, if the company rents access to the server via the cloud as an IaaS solution, someone else manages the hardware. All the company needs to do is remotely manage its database. Additionally, if the venture doesn't work out, the company simply stops renting access to the servers, limiting its losses.

> **Remember this**
>
> Infrastructure as a Service (IaaS) is also known as Hardware as a Service. Organizations can limit their hardware footprint and personnel costs by renting access to hardware such as servers. The IaaS provider maintains the server.

IaaS can also be useful if an organization is finding it difficult to manage and maintain servers in its own datacenter. By outsourcing its requirements, the company limits its hardware footprint. It can do this instead of, or in addition to, virtualizing some of its servers. With IaaS, it needs fewer servers in its datacenter and fewer resources such as power, HVAC, and personnel to manage the servers.

Notice the subtle difference between IaaS benefits and virtualization benefits. Both allow you to reduce the hardware footprint. However, IaaS allows you to outsource the housing and maintenance of the servers, while you will still own, house, and maintain, virtualized servers.

Platform as a Service

Platform as a Service (Paas) provides customers with a computing platform they can use to configure and manipulate as needed. It provides the customer with an easy-to-configure operating system, combined with on-demand computing.

As mentioned previously, the Amazon EC2 service provides PaaS to customers. Customers are able to rent their own virtual machines and configure them as needed. Customers can even use these virtual machines to deploy their own cloud-based applications, providing an SaaS solution to other customers.

> ### Remember this
>
> Platform as a Service (PaaS) provides cloud-computing customers with an easy-to-configure operating system, combined with on-demand computing.

Drawbacks to Cloud Computing

Many cloud-computing solutions are blended. They combine data and operating systems, located in the cloud. While this can provide benefits since you reduce your own datacenter's footprint, it also presents risks.

One of the primary drawbacks to cloud computing is that you lose physical control of your data. You often won't even know where the data is stored. Employees at the cloud datacenter can easily steal your data, and you may not know it until the thief has exploited the data. It's also possible for employees to make mistakes that suddenly grant access to your data to anyone.

As an example, consider a glitch that occurred at Dropbox in June 2011. Dropbox is a cloud storage site used by about twenty-five million customers to store files such as documents, videos, and photos. After an update to their site, visitors could use any password to access accounts. Obviously, that wasn't the intent of the update. The company's official statement was that the glitch impacted only 1 percent of its customers, but 1 percent of twenty-five million people is still a lot of people.

Many security professionals say that the only data you should put in the cloud is data you're willing to give away. After all, that's exactly what you may be doing.

Chapter 5 Exam Topic Review

When preparing for the exam, make sure you understand these key concepts covered in this chapter.

Host Security

- Disable unnecessary services. This protects systems from zero day attacks, malware, and risks from open ports.
- Group Policy and security templates standardize system configuration and security settings for multiple systems.
- Configuration baselines document system configuration and should be updated when systems are modified.
- Baseline reporting documents normal behavior of a system. You can compare current performance against a baseline to detect abnormal behavior.
- Standardized images increase security by including mandated security configurations, and they reduce overall costs. Virtualized server images have the same logical security requirements as physical servers.

Virtualization

- Virtualization helps reduce costs, reduce an organization's footprint, and eliminate wasted resources. Additionally, less physical equipment results in reduced physical security requirements.
- Security researchers use virtual systems to test and investigate malware in isolated virtual systems, reducing risks to production environments.
- VM escape is an attack that allows an attacker to access the host system from within the virtual system. The best protection is keeping systems up to date.

Patch Management

- Patch management combats operating system vulnerabilities by keeping systems up to date with current patches. It includes testing, deploying, and verifying changes made by patches.
- Patches are tested before deployment in a test environment that mirrors the production environment. Regression testing verifies that a patch doesn't introduce problems.
- A patch management policy provides guidance on patch management. This documents the process and provides a timeline.

Change Management

- Change management helps reduce unintended outages from changes.
- Change management defines the process for making changes, and provides the accounting structure or method to document the changes.

Protecting Data

- Encryption is the primary method of protecting data against loss of confidentiality.
- Whole disk, or full disk, encryption provides confidentiality for entire drives such as USB flash drives, USB hard drives, and drives in mobile systems.
- File and folder level encryption provides confidentiality for individual files.
- Hardware encryption is faster and more efficient than software encryption.
- A Trusted Platform Module (TPM) is a chip in a motherboard included with many laptops. TPMs store RSA encryption keys and support full disk encryption.
- A hardware security module (HSM) is a removable or external device used for encryption. An HSM generates and stores RSA encryption keys and can be integrated with servers to provide hardware encryption. High performance servers, such as those with SSL accelerators or in clustered environments, use HSMs.
- Copying live data from a production environment to a test environment risks the compromise of the data.

- Network-based Data Loss Prevention (DLP) devices reduce the risk of data leakage. They can analyze outgoing data, such as e-mails, and detect when employees send out confidential company data.
- You can protect data on portable devices with whole drive encryption and erase data on lost devices with remote wipe.
- Global Positioning System (GPS) tracking can locate lost devices. Some people consider GPS a risk for the user and disable it.

Cloud Computing

- Provider clouds provide increased capabilities for heavily utilized systems and networks.
- Software as a Service (SaaS) includes web-based applications such as web-based e-mail.
- Infrastructure as a Service (IaaS) provides hardware resources via the cloud. It can help an organization limit the size of their hardware footprint and reduce personnel costs.
- Platform as a Service (PaaS) provides an easy-to-configure operating system and on-demand computing for customers.
- Physical control of data is a key security control an organization loses with cloud computing.

Chapter 5 Practice Questions

1. Your organization wants to reduce threats from zero day vulnerabilities. Of the following choices, what provides the best solution?
   A. Opening ports on a server's firewall
   B. Disabling unnecessary services
   C. Keep systems up to date with current patches
   D. Keep systems up to date with current service packs

2. Of the following choices, what could you use to deploy baseline security configurations to multiple systems?
   A. IDS
   B. Security template
   C. Change management
   D. Performance baseline

3. An administrator wants to prevent users from installing software. Of the following choices, what is the easiest way to accomplish this?
   A. Manually remove administrative rights
   B. Implement port scanners
   C. Use a security template
   D. Implement a job rotation policy

4. You are troubleshooting a server that users claim is running slow. You notice that the server frequently has about twenty active SSH sessions. What can you use to determine if this is normal behavior?
   A. Vendor documentation
   B. Security template
   C. Baseline report
   D. Imaging

5. Your organization is considering deploying multiple servers using a standardized image. Of the following choices, what best describes the security benefit of this plan?
   A. The image can include unnecessary protocols
   B. The image provides fault tolerance as a RAID 5
   C. It eliminates Trojans
   D. The image can include mandated security configurations

6. Management is reviewing a hardware inventory in a datacenter. They realize that many of the servers are underutilized resulting in wasted resources. What can they do to improve the situation?

    A. Implement virtualization

    B. Implement VM escape

    C. Increase the datacenter footprint

    D. Add TPMs

7. What type of attack starts on a virtual system but can affect the physical host?

    A. TPM

    B. DLP

    C. VM escape

    D. VMware

8. An organization is considering using virtualization in their datacenter. What benefits will this provide? (Choose all that apply.)

    A. Increased footprint

    B. Decreased footprint

    C. Reduction in physical equipment needing security

    D. Elimination of VM escape attacks

9. You have created an image for a database server that you plan to deploy to five physical servers. At the last minute, management decides to deploy these as virtual servers. What additional security steps do you need to take with these virtual images before deploying them?

    A. None

    B. Lock down the virtual images

    C. Install virtual antivirus software

    D. Install virtual patches

10. Of the following choices, what indicates the best method of reducing operating system vulnerabilities?

    A. Whole disk encryption

    B. Patch management

    C. Trusted Platform Module

    D. File level encryption

11. Of the following choices, what would you use in a patch management process?

    A. VM escape

    B. TPM

    C. Penetration testing

    D. Regression testing

12. An organization recently suffered a significant outage due to attacks on unpatched systems. Investigation showed that administrators did not have a clear idea of when they should apply the patches. What can they do to prevent a reoccurrence of this problem?
    A. Apply all patches immediately
    B. Apply the missing patches on the attacked systems immediately
    C. Test the patches with regression testing in a test environment mirroring the production environment
    D. Create a patch management policy

13. Of the following choices, what best identifies the purpose of a change management program?
    A. It defines the process and accounting structure for handling system modifications
    B. It provides a method of defining a timeline for installing patches
    C. It is a primary method of protecting against loss of confidentiality
    D. It reduces the footprint of a datacenter

14. Your organization wants to prevent unintended outages caused from changes to systems. What could it use?
    A. Patch management
    B. Regression testing
    C. Change management
    D. Security template

15. A file server within a network hosts files that employees throughout the company regularly access. Management wants to ensure that some personnel files on this server are not accessible by administrators. What provides the best protection?
    A. Remove administrative access to the server
    B. Protect the files with permissions
    C. Use file encryption
    D. Use full disk encryption

16. You organization is considering purchasing new computers that include hardware encryption capabilities. What benefit does this provide?
    A. It is faster than software encryption
    B. It does not require a TPM
    C. It does not require an HSM
    D. Reduced confidentiality

17. Your organization recently purchased several new laptop computers for employees. You're asked to encrypt the laptop's hard drives without purchasing any additional hardware. What would you use?
    A. TPM
    B. HSM
    C. VM escape
    D. DLP

18. Your organization is considering the purchase of new computers. A security professional stresses that these devices should include TPMs. What benefit does a TPM provide? (Choose all that apply.)

 A. It uses hardware encryption, which is quicker than software encryption

 B. It uses software encryption, which is quicker than hardware encryption

 C. It includes an HSM file system

 D. It stores RSA keys

19. Of the following choices, what is the best choice to provide encryption services in a clustered environment?

 A. Virtual servers

 B. SaaS provider

 C. HSM

 D. TPM

20. What functions does an HSM include?

 A. Reduces the risk of employees e-mailing confidential information outside the organization

 B. Provides webmail to clients

 C. Provides full drive encryption

 D. Generates and store keys

21. Employees regularly send e-mail in and out of the company. The company suspects that some employees are sending out confidential data, and it wants to take steps to reduce this risk. What can it use?

 A. HSM

 B. TPM

 C. A network-based DLP

 D. Port scanner

22. Your organization wants to prevent losses due to data leakage on portable devices. What provides the best protection?

 A. Smart cards

 B. Full disk encryption

 C. Permissions

 D. SSH

23. What technology can an organization use to assist with computing requirements in heavily utilized systems?

 A. ISP

 B. DLP

 C. Cloud computing

 D. Remote wipe

24. Employees in your organization access web-based e-mail using cloud-based technologies. What type of technology is this?
    A. IaaS
    B. PaaS
    C. SaaS
    D. Network-based DLP

25. Of the following choices, what is the best explanation of what a PaaS provides to customers?
    A. Web-based applications provided over the Internet.
    B. A device that reduces the risk of employees e-mailing confidential information outside the organization
    C. Protection against VM escape attacks
    D. An easy-to-configure operating system and on-demand computing capabilities

Chapter 5 Practice Question Answers

1. **B.** Disabling unnecessary services helps reduce threats, including threats from zero day vulnerabilities. It also reduces the threat from open ports on a firewall if the associated services are disabled, but opening ports won't reduce threats. Keeping systems up to date with patches and service packs protects against known vulnerabilities and is certainly a good practice. However, by definition there aren't any patches or service packs available for zero day vulnerabilities.

2. **B.** You can use security templates to deploy baseline security configurations to multiple systems. An IDS can detect malicious activity after it occurs. A performance baseline identifies the overall performance of a system at a point in time. A change management system helps ensure that changes don't result in unintended outages through a change, and includes the ability to document changes.

3. **C.** You can use a security template to restrict user rights and control group membership so that users don't have rights to install software. Manually removing administrative rights is possible, but it requires you to touch every system and isn't as easy as using a security template. A port scanner can help determine what services and protocols are running on a remote system by identifying open ports. A job rotation policy rotates employees through different positions and can help prevent fraud.

4. **C.** Baseline reports document normal behavior of a system, and you can compare current activity against the baseline report to determine what is different or abnormal. Vendor documentation identifies methods of locking down an operating system or application but won't document baseline activity. You can use security templates to deploy the same security settings to multiple systems. Images include mandated security configurations but don't show normal operation.

5. **D.** One of the benefits of an image used as a baseline is that it includes mandated security configurations to the operating system. It's common to remove unnecessary protocols on an image, not include them. RAID provides fault tolerance and increases availability for disk drives, but a standardized image is unrelated to RAID. Trojans are a type of malware that look useful to the user but are malicious.

6. **A.** Virtualization can reduce the number of physical servers used by an organization, reduce the datacenter's footprint, and eliminate wasted resources. VM escape is an attack run on virtual machines allowing the attacker to access and control the physical host. Virtualization decreases the datacenter's footprint, but increasing it will result in more wasted resources. A TPM is a hardware chip that stores encryption keys and provides full disk encryption, but it doesn't reduce wasted resources.

7. **C.** A VM escape attack runs on a virtual system and, if successful, allows the attacker to control the physical host server and all other virtual servers on the physical server. A TPM is a hardware chip that stores encryption keys and provides full disk encryption. A DLP is a device that reduces the risk of employees e-mailing confidential information outside the organization. VMware is a popular virtualization application.

8. **B, C.** Virtualization can reduce the footprint of a datacenter, eliminate wasted resources, and result in less physical equipment needing physical security. Virtualization reduces the footprint, not increases it. Virtual systems are susceptible to VM escape attacks if they aren't kept patched.

9. **A.** Virtual servers have the same security requirements as physical servers, so additional security steps are not required. The original image should include security settings and antivirus software, and should be up to date with current patches. Virtual servers use the same patches as physical systems and do not use virtual patches.

10. **B.** Patch management is the most efficient way to combat operating system vulnerabilities. Whole disk encryption protects the confidentiality of data on a system and is useful in mobile devices, but doesn't directly reduce operating system vulnerabilities. A Trusted Platform Module supports whole disk encryption. File level encryption can prevent users, including administrators, from accessing specific files.

11. **D.** Regression testing verifies that a patch has not introduced new errors. VM escape is an attack run on a virtual machine allowing the attacker to access physical host system. A TPM is a hardware chip that is included on the motherboard of many laptops, and it stores encryption keys used for full drive encryption. Penetration tests actively test security controls by attempting to exploit vulnerabilities and can cause system instability.

12. **D.** A patch management policy defines a timeline for installing patches and can help solve this problem. Patches should be tested before applying them, instead of applying them immediately. It's appropriate to identify missing patches on these systems and test them with regression testing, but this only solves the immediate issue and won't prevent a reoccurrence of the problem.

13. **A.** A change management system defines the process and accounting structure for system modifications. A patch management policy defines a timeline for installing patches, but change management isn't restricted to only applying patches. Encryption and access controls protect against loss of confidentiality. Virtualization and cloud computing can reduce the footprint of a datacenter.

14. **C.** A change management system helps prevent unintended outages from unauthorized changes and provides a method of documenting all changes. Patch management ensures that systems are up to date with current patches. Regression testing verifies that a patch has not introduced new errors. You can use security templates to deploy multiple systems using the same settings.

15. **C.** File level encryption is a security control that provides an additional layer of protection and can prevent administrators from accessing specific files. Administrators need access to a server to manage and maintain it, so it's not feasible to remove administrative access. Permissions provide access control, but an administrator can bypass permissions. Full disk encryption is appropriate for removable storage or mobile devices, but not to protect individual files on a server.

16. **A.** A significant benefit of hardware encryption over software encryption is that it is faster. Hardware encryption methods can use a TPM or an HSM, but the absence of either isn't a benefit of hardware encryption. Encryption helps ensure confidentiality, not reduce it.

17. **A.** A Trusted Platform Module (TPM) is included in many new laptops, provides a mechanism for vendors to perform hard drive encryption, and does not require purchasing additional hardware. An HSM is a removable hardware device and is not included with laptops, so it requires an additional purchase. A VM escape attack runs on a virtual system, and if successful, it allows the attacker to control the physical host server and all other virtual servers on the physical server. A network-based Data Loss Protection (DLP) system can examine and analyze network traffic and detect if confidential company data is included.

18. **A, D.** A Trusted Platform Module (TPM) is a hardware chip that stores RSA encryption keys and uses hardware encryption, which is quicker than software encryption. A TPM does not use software encryption. An HSM is a removable hardware device that uses hardware encryption, but it does not have a file system and TPM does not provide HSM as a benefit.

19. **C.** A hardware security module (HSM) is a removable or external device that provides encryption services and can be used in a clustered environment. You may be able to configure virtual servers to provide encryption services in a clustered environment, but they will not be as efficient as the hardware-based encryption provided by an HSM. A SaaS provider provides software or applications, such as webmail, via the cloud. A TPM is a chip on the motherboard of a computer, and while it does provide full disk encryption services, it can't be used in a clustered environment.

20. **D.** A hardware security module (HSM) is a removable device that can generate and store RSA keys used for asymmetric encryption and decryption. A Data Loss Protection (DLP) device is a device that can reduce the risk of employees e-mailing confidential information outside the organization. A TPM provides full drive encryption and is included in many laptops. SaaS provides software or applications, such as webmail, via the cloud.

21. **C.** A network-based Data Loss Prevention (DLP) system can examine and analyze network traffic and detect if confidential company data is included. An HSM is a removable hardware device that stores RSA keys and provides encryption services. A TPM is a hardware chip that is included on the motherboard of many laptops, and it stores encryption keys used for full drive encryption. A port scanner looks for open ports on a system to determine running services and protocols.

22. **B.** Encryption, including full disk encryption, provides the best protection against data leakage on portable devices, and any data at rest. Smart cards provide authentication but won't protect data on a portable device if it falls into the wrong hands. Permissions provide access controls while a device is within a network, but an attacker can remove a portable device and bypass permissions. SSH is a good encryption protocol for data in transit, but not data at rest stored on a portable device.

23. **C.** Cloud computing is very useful for heavily utilized systems and networks, and cloud providers provide the services. An ISP provides access to the Internet. A network-based DLP can examine and analyze network traffic and detect if confidential company data is included. Remote wipe can erase data on lost mobile devices, such as mobile phones.

24. **C.** Applications such as web-based e-mail provided over the Internet are Software as a Service (SaaS) cloud-based technologies. Organizations use IaaS to rent access to hardware such as servers to limit their hardware footprint and personnel costs. PaaS provides cloud customers with an easy-to-configure operating system, and on-demand computing capabilities. A DLP is a device that reduces the risk of employees e-mailing confidential information outside the organization.

25. **D.** Platform as a Service (PaaS) provides cloud customers with an easy-to-configure operating system and on-demand computing capabilities. Applications such as web-based e-mail provided over the Internet are Software as a Service (SaaS) cloud-based technologies. A network-based DLP is a device that reduces the risk of employees e-mailing confidential information outside the organization. Keeping systems up to date protects virtual systems from VM escape attacks, but PaaS does not provide this protection.

Chapter 6

Understanding Malware and Social Engineering

CompTIA Security+ objectives covered in this chapter:

2.4 Explain the importance of security related awareness and training

- User habits
  - Prevent tailgating
- Threat awareness
  - New viruses
  - Phishing attacks
  - Zero day exploits

3.1 Analyze and differentiate among types of malware

- Adware
- Virus
- Worms
- Spyware
- Trojan
- Rootkits
- Backdoors
- Logic bomb
- Botnets

3.2 Analyze and differentiate among types of attacks

- Spam
- Phishing
- Spim

- Vishing
- Spear phishing
- Privilege escalation

3.3 Analyze and differentiate among types of social engineering attacks

- Shoulder surfing
- Dumpster diving
- Tailgating
- Impersonation
- Hoaxes
- Whaling
- Vishing

3.6 Analyze and differentiate among types of mitigation and deterrent techniques

- Physical security
  - Mantraps

4.2 Carry out appropriate procedures to establish host security

- Anti-malware
  - Antivirus
  - Anti-spam
  - Anti-spyware
  - Pop-up blockers
  - Host-based firewalls

Malicious software and social engineering are two common threats that any organization will face. Within IT security, these are relatively easy to prevent. However, that doesn't reduce their importance. The damage can be extensive if an organization ignores these threats.

Understanding Malware

Malicious software (malware) is a wide range of different software that has malicious intent. Malware is not software that you would knowingly purchase or download and install. Instead, it is installed onto your system through devious means. Infected systems give various symptoms, such as running slower, starting unknown processes, sending out e-mail without user action, random reboots, and more.

The term *virus* is sometimes erroneously used to describe all types of malware. Actually, a virus is a specific type of malware, and malware includes many other types of malicious software, including not just viruses, but also worms, Trojans (or Trojan horses), logic bombs, rootkits, and spyware.

Viruses

A virus is a set of malicious code that attaches itself to a host application. The host application must be executed to run, and when the host application is executed, the malicious code executes. The virus will try to find other host applications to infect with the malicious code. At some point, the virus will activate and deliver its payload, such as causing damage or delivering a message.

Typically, the payload of a virus is damaging. It may delete files, cause random reboots, or enable backdoors that attackers can use to remotely access a system. Some older viruses merely displayed a message at some point, such as "Legalize Marijuana!" and many viruses today join computers to botnets.

Most viruses won't cause damage immediately. Instead, they give the virus time to replicate or distribute other malware. Note that not all malware needs user interaction to run. As an example, worms are self-replicating and do not need user interaction.

A user will often unknowingly execute the virus, but other times, an operating system will automatically execute it after user interaction. For example, when a user plugs in an infected USB, the system can execute the virus infecting the system.

Characteristics

Viruses have specific characteristics. These include:

- **Replication mechanism**. For a virus to survive, it must replicate. When the program hosting the virus runs, the virus looks for other host applications to infect.
- **Activation mechanism**. This is the point in time when the malware executes the objective. There is usually a time lag between replication and activation to give the virus time to replicate.
- **Objective mechanism**. The objective is the damage or the payload the virus seeks to inflict or deliver. Objectives could be to make the hard drive unbootable, connect to a botnet command and control server to download additional malware, or just about anything else the attacker can conceive.

Delivery of Viruses

Viruses are delivered from system to system through a variety of methods, but they are most often spread through the Internet. Spammers often include viruses as attachments or include links to malicious websites. They use different techniques to encourage users to execute the virus on their systems or click a link. Many links take the user to a malicious website that will automatically install malware on a user's system as soon as a user visits.

USB drives are a very popular method of delivering viruses. Systems automatically detect a USB drive as soon as a user plugs it in. Malware on an infected USB flash drive will often infect the computer when a user plugs it in, and the infected system will then infect any other USB drives that a user plugs in.

> ## *Operation Buckshot Yankee*
>
> William Lynn, a U.S. Deputy Secretary of Defense wrote an article in the Foreign Affairs magazine that demonstrates the risk from USB drives. He indicated that this incident marked a turning point in the U.S. cyber defense strategy.
>
> In 2008, the U.S. military suffered a significant data breach that they traced back to a USB flash drive. Apparently, a foreign intelligence agency developed malware and installed it on a USB drive. Someone, though no one seems to be saying who, inserted the USB drive into a military laptop somewhere in the Middle East. The malware quickly infected the system.
>
> The malware continued to operate silently on the mobile system and ultimately infected the U.S. Central Command's network, including both classified and unclassified systems. Reports indicate that attackers were able to transfer data from the network to foreign servers. Ultimately, the U.S. military discovered the malware and launched Operation Buckshot Yankee. They cleaned the systems of the virus and investigated the incident. It is clear that this was a major incident, even though it started from malware on a single USB drive.
>
> I was working on a U.S. base in 2008 when a new rule came out that banned the use of all removable USB flash drives. There was no mention of Operation Buckshot Yankee at the time, but it was clear that they were serious about enforcing the rule. I know of one contractor that ignored the rule, plugged in a USB flash drive, and had an opportunity to upgrade his resume the next day. He was fired.

Virus Hoaxes

A virus hoax is a message, often circulated through e-mail, that tells of impending doom from a virus that simply does not exist. Users may be encouraged to delete files or change their system configuration.

An example is the teddy bear virus (jdbgmgr.exe), which is not a virus at all. The victim may receive an e-mail that says this virus lies in a sleeping state for fourteen days and then it will destroy the user's system. However, if you can find and delete this file now, the e-mail explains, you will protect your system. It then gives instructions on how to find the file (which has an icon of a little bear). The program is a Java Debug Manager, which is important to some users. However, if users follow the steps in the message, they lose some system capability.

More serious virus hoaxes have the potential to be as damaging as a real virus. If users are convinced to delete important files, they may make their systems unusable. Additionally, they waste help-desk personnel's time due to needless calls about the hoax or support calls if users damaged their systems in response to the hoax.

There are several resources you can check to determine if a virus threat is valid or a hoax. They include:

- **Antivirus vendor sites**. Sites such as Symantec and McAfee regularly post information on emerging threats and virus hoaxes. They have their own search engines, and other Internet search engines will often take you to the right page.

- **Urban legend sites**. Sites like Snopes.com separate the truth from fiction and have pages dedicated to viruses and virus hoaxes.

Worms

A worm is self-replicating malware that travels throughout a network without the assistance of a host application or user interaction. A worm resides in memory and is able to use different transport protocols to travel over the network.

Remember this

Worms are self-replicating. They can travel through a network without user interaction. In comparison, viruses must be executed.

One of the significant problems caused by worms is that they consume network bandwidth. Worms can replicate themselves hundreds of times and spread to all the systems in the network. Each infected system tries to locate and infect other systems on the network, and performance can slow to a crawl.

Trojan Horse

A Trojan, also called a Trojan horse, looks like something beneficial, but it's actually something malicious. Trojan horses are named after the infamous horse from the Trojan War.

In Greek mythology, the Achaeans tried to sack the city of Troy for several years, but they simply couldn't penetrate the city's defenses. At some point, someone got the idea of building a huge wooden horse and convincing the people of Troy that it was a gift from the gods. Warriors hid inside, and the horse was rolled up to the gates.

The people of Troy partied all day and all night celebrating their good fortune, but when the city slept, the warriors climbed down from the horse and opened the gates. The rest of the warriors flooded in. What the Greek warriors couldn't do for years, the Trojan horse helped them do in a single day.

In computers, a Trojan horse can come as pirated software, a cool screen saver, a useful utility, a game, or something else that users may be enticed to download and try. As an example, a keygen is an application that illegally creates license keys or product keys for applications. Software pirates sometimes download and run a keygen to create a license key and enable the full version of a product. However, keygens often include malware, so when the pirates run the keygen, they also install malware.

As mentioned previously, you can also infect a system by plugging in an infected USB flash drive. In this case, the attacker can install the Trojan onto several USB drives and leave them lying around. Someone picks one up, plugs it in, and the system is infected. The system then infects other USBs, which infect other systems.

> ## Remember this
>
> A Trojan (or Trojan horse) appears to be something useful but instead is something malicious. Users may download pirated software, rogueware, or games that includes a Trojan and infects their system. Trojans also infect systems via USB drives.

One method that has become popular in recent years is rogueware, also known as scareware. This is a type of Trojan that masquerades as a free antivirus program. When a user visits a site, a message on the web page or a popup appears indicating it detected malware on the user's system. The user is encouraged to download and install free antivirus software. Users that take the bait actually download and install malware.

Figure 6.1 is an example of rogueware. This is *not Microsoft* Security Essentials, a free antivirus program offered by Microsoft. However, the criminals are using *Security Essentials* in the name to trick users. Some rogueware targets Mac OS X users and is called MacDefender, Mac Security, or MacProtector.

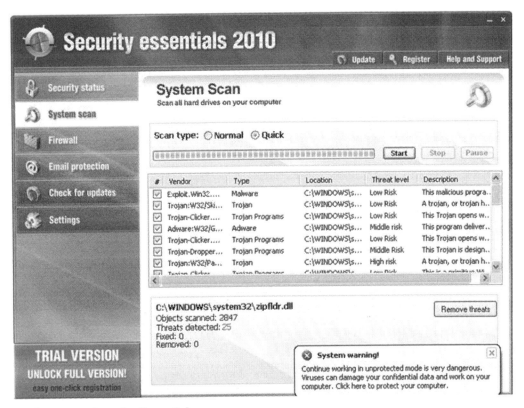

Figure 6.1: Security Essentials rogueware

I downloaded this and installed it on a clean installation of Windows 7 in a virtual machine to ensure it was isolated. After the "system scan," it detected twenty-five threats and popped up an official System Warning. In reality, it didn't actually scan for real malware, and it will always reports dozens of bogus infections.

Before the download, the user is told that this is free antivirus software. However, if the user clicks on the Remove Threats button, the program informs the user that this is only the trial version, and the trial version won't remove any threats. However, for the small fee of $79.95, users can unlock the full version to remove the threats. Many people pay. Panda security reported that criminals took in an average of $34 million a month in 2008.

Some rogueware installs additional malicious components. For example, it can join the computer to a botnet, or allow the attacker to take remote control of the infected system.

Logic Bombs

A logic bomb is a string of code embedded into an application or script that will execute in response to an event. The event may be a specific date or time, when a user launches a specific program, or any event the programmer decides on.

There's an often repeated story about a company that decided it had to lay off an engineer due to an economic downturn. His bosses didn't see him doing much, so they thought they could do without him. Within a couple of weeks after he left, they started having all sorts of computer problems they just couldn't resolve.

They called him back, and within a couple of weeks, everything was fine. A few months later, they determined they had to lay him off again. You guessed it. Within a couple of weeks, things went haywire again.

The engineer had programmed a logic bomb that executed when the payroll program ran. It checked for his name on the payroll, and when it was there, things were fine, but when his name wasn't there, ka-boom!—the logic bomb exploded.

> ### Remember this
>
> A logic bomb executes in response to an event, such as when a specific application is executed or a specific time arrives. Malicious insiders plant logic bombs.

A more recent example of a logic bomb occurred in 2008 when Fannie Mae terminated a UNIX engineer. Its account management policy did not revoke his elevated system privileges right away, and he became a malicious insider for a short period. He wrote and installed malicious code set to run at 9 a.m. on January 31, 2009. If the script hadn't been detected, it would have deleted data and backups for about four thousand servers, changed passwords, and shut them down.

Rootkits

A rootkit is a group of programs (or, in rare instances, a single program) that hides the fact that the system has been infected or compromised by malicious code. A user may suspect something is wrong, but antivirus scans and other checks may indicate everything is fine since the rootkit hides its running processes to avoid detection.

In addition to modifying the internal operating system processes, rootkits will often modify system files such as the registry. In some cases, the rootkit modifies system access, such as removing users' administrative access.

Rootkits have system level access to systems. This is sometimes called root level access, or kernel level access, indicating that they have the same level of access as the operating system. Rootkits use hooked processes, or hooking techniques to intercept calls to the operating system. In this context, hooking refers to intercepting system level function calls, events, or messages. The rootkit installs the hooks into memory and uses them to control the system's behavior.

Antivirus software often makes calls to the operating system that could detect malware, but the rootkit prevents the antivirus software from making these calls. This is why antivirus software will sometimes report everything is OK. However, antivirus software can often detect the hooked processes by examining the contents of the systems random access memory (RAM).

> **Remember this**
>
> Rootkits have system level or kernel access and can modify system files and system access. Rootkits hide their running processes to avoid detection with hooking techniques. A file integrity checker can detect files modified by a rootkit and an inspection of RAM can discover hooked processes.

Some antivirus scanners and host-based intrusion detection systems (HIDS) use file integrity checkers to detect modified files. Chapter 10 covers hashing in more depth, and it provides a good example of how a file integrity checker works using a command line program called md5sum.

In short, a hash is simply a number calculated with a hashing algorithm. As long as the file is the same, the hashing algorithm will always create the same hash. A file integrity checker calculates hashes on system files as a baseline. It then periodically recalculates the hashes on these files and compares them with the hashes in the baseline. If the hashes are ever different, it indicates the system files have been modified. When an antivirus scanner or HIDS detects a modified file, it will send an alert indicating a possible rootkit infection.

Another method used to detect rootkits is to boot into safe mode, or have the system scanned before it boots, but even this isn't always successful.

It's important to remember that rootkits are very difficult to detect, since they can hide so much of their activity. A clean bill of health by a malware scanner may not be valid.

The Trojan.Popureb/E rootkit is an example of a rootkit. Among other things, it overwrites the hard drive's master boot record (MBR), where code is stored to start the operating system.

The code on the MBR starts before the operating system boots and it remains invisible to the operating system and security software. Even when antivirus software detects the rootkit, the rootkit protects itself. It prevents any attempts to overwrite the MBR by changing write operations to read operations, though it reports that the write operation completed.

Spam and Spam Filters

Spam is unwanted or unsolicited e-mail, and spam filters attempt to block spam. Chapter 3 covered spam filters used on web security gateways and all-in-one appliances. Within the context of malware and attacks, it's important to mention spam, since a great deal of spam is malicious.

Attackers have included malicious attachments and malicious code within e-mails for many years. Most spam filters and antivirus software can detect this type of malware. More recently, spam attacks have included malicious links. If users click on a link in a malicious e-mail, it can take them to a specially crafted website that can download malware onto their system without their knowledge. Social engineering tactics include the various types of phishing attacks that use spam.

Spam filters are useful on end-user machines in addition to network-based filters. This is especially true when employees are traveling and don't have the benefit of network-based spam filters.

Remember this

Spam filters can block unsolicited e-mails. Network-based spam filters reduce spam entering a network, and end-user spam filters further restrict spam. Traveling employees benefit from spam filters on mobile systems in addition to antivirus software and host-based firewalls.

Spim is a form of spam using instant messaging (IM). It targets instant messaging users, such as those using Yahoo! Messenger or Windows Live Messenger. Many IM services support the use of whitelists, where users identify who they'll receive messengers from and the IM system blocks all other messages.

Spyware

Spyware is software installed on users' systems without their awareness or consent. Its purpose is often to take some level of control over the user's computer to learn information and send this information to a third party. If spyware can access a user's private data, it results in a loss of confidentiality.

Some examples of spyware activity are changing a user's home page, redirecting web browsers, and installing additional software, such as search engines. In some situations, these changes can slow a system down, resulting in poorer performance. These examples are rather harmless compared to what more malicious spyware (called privacy-invasive software) may do.

Privacy-invasive software tries to separate users from their money using data-harvesting techniques. It attempts to gather information to impersonate users, empty bank accounts, and steal identities. For example, some spyware includes keyloggers used to capture keystrokes. The keystrokes are stored in a file, and the spyware periodically sends the file to the attacker. In some instances, the spyware allows the attacker to take control of the user's system remotely.

Spyware is often included with other software like a Trojan. The user installs one application but unknowingly gets some extras. Spyware can also infect a system in a drive-by download. The user simply visits a malicious website that includes code to automatically download and install the spyware onto the user's system.

There are many anti-spyware programs available. Additionally, most antivirus software includes the ability to block spyware.

Remember this

Spyware can access a user's private data and result in loss of confidentiality. Spyware often results in a system running slower. Dedicated anti-spyware software is available, and some antivirus software protects against spyware.

Adware

When adware first emerged, its intent was usually to learn a user's habits for the purpose of targeted advertising. As the practice of gathering information on users became more malicious, more people began to call it spyware. However, some adware still exists.

A common type of adware is pop-ups. For example, while you are visiting a site, another browser window will appear, or pop up, with an advertisement. These pop-up windows aren't malicious but instead just annoying. Newer web browsers and many web browser add-ins known as pop-up blockers are commonly used to block pop-up ads.

Sometimes pop-ups can be helpful. As a legitimate example, my online bank has rate information that I can view. When I click on this link, it pops up another window showing current rate information without taking me away from the current page I'm viewing. Most pop-up blockers allow you to list URLs that allow pop-ups, but block all pop-ups that aren't on the allowed list.

However, in the hands of attackers or aggressive advertisers, pop-ups can be quite annoying and downright harassing. At their height, pop-ups were sometimes responding to Windows close events by launching five more pop-ups.

The term *adware* is sometimes still used to identify software that is free but includes advertisements. The user is well aware that the advertisements appear, and they can purchase a version of the software that does not include the ads. All of this is aboveboard without any intention of misleading the user.

Remember this

Pop-ups are annoying windows that appear while browsing. The most effective protection against unwanted adware is the use of pop-up blockers in web browsers. Many pop-up blockers support lists of URLs that allow pop-ups.

Backdoors

A backdoor provides another way of accessing a system, similar to how a backdoor in a house provides another method of entry. Malware such as Trojans often install backdoors on systems to bypass normal authentication methods. In many cases, this allows an attacker to access a system remotely.

Protection against Malware

Malware is a significant threat that administrators must address in a network. It's common to have a multipronged defense to protect against malware. This includes:

- **Mail servers**. A common method of delivering viruses today is through e-mail as attachments. Organizations prevent many malware infections by scanning all e-mail for malicious attachments. Instead of forwarding the suspicious content, the software strips the attachment, and the user receives an e-mail text with an explanation of what was removed and why.
- **All systems**. All workstations and servers also have antivirus software installed. Servers may have additional specialized antivirus software installed. Workstations may also have anti-spyware software installed.
- **Boundaries or firewalls**. Many networks include antivirus tools that monitor network traffic through the firewall. For example, web security gateways and all-in-one appliances inspect network traffic to reduce the risk of users downloading and installing malicious software. Chapter 3 covered web security gateways and appliances.

Antivirus Software

Antivirus software is specifically designed to detect and remove different types of malware. Notice that the lines have blurred a little. While the term *virus* refers to some malware, antivirus software will detect more than just viruses. Malware detected by antivirus software includes viruses, Trojans, worms, rootkits, spyware, and adware. However, there are some rootkits that escape detection by hiding themselves, and antivirus software doesn't always look for spyware and adware.

Most antivirus software provides real-time protection and can perform both scheduled and manual scans. The real-time protection continuously monitors the system. For example, when a user downloads or opens a file, antivirus software scans it. Scheduled scans occur regularly, such as once a week. If users or technicians detect suspicious activity, they can perform manual scans to check the system.

Antivirus software detects viruses using either signature-based detection or heuristic-based detection.

Remember this

Antivirus software detects and removes malware such as viruses, Trojans, and worms. Signature-based antivirus software detects known malware based on signature definitions. Heuristic-based software detects previously unknown malware based on behavior.

Signature-based Detection

Viruses and other malware have known patterns. Signature files (also called data definition files) define the patterns and the antivirus software scans files for matching patterns. When the antivirus matches a pattern in a file, it reports it as an infection and takes action, such as deleting or quarantining the file.

A quarantined virus is not harmful to the system while it is in quarantine, but it's still available for analysis. As an example, a security professional could release a quarantined virus into an unprotected but isolated virtual environment for research and study.

New viruses are constantly being released, so it's important to regularly update signature definition files. Most antivirus software includes the ability to automate the process of checking and downloading updated signature definition files.

Heuristic-based Detection

Some antivirus software includes heuristic-based detection. Heuristic-based detection attempts to detect viruses that were previously unknown and do not have signatures.

Heuristic-based detection is similar to anomaly-based detection used with intrusion detection systems (IDSs) as discussed in chapter 4. Both methods detect suspicious behavior that can't be detected by signature-based detection alone. However, heuristic-based analysis for malware performs the analysis quite differently than anomaly-based detection does for an IDS.

You may remember that anomaly-based detection starts by creating a baseline of normal behavior and then compares it to current behavior. Heuristic-based analysis runs questionable code in a virtualized environment specifically designed to protect the live environment, but observe the behavior of the questionable code. Most viruses engage in "viral activities"—actions that can be harmful, but rarely performed by legitimate programs. The heuristic-based analysis detects these viral activities.

Additionally, some heuristic analysis programs will attempt to reverse-engineer the suspect program to read the actual source code. This is also known as decompiling the program.

Anti-spyware Software

Anti-spyware software has emerged as a separate application that targets spyware. It is common today for a system to have both antivirus software and anti-spyware software installed.

Some of the lines between spyware and malware have become blurry, especially since some spyware is so malicious. Because of this, many antivirus software programs may catch some spyware, and anti-spyware software may catch some malware.

Several anti-spyware programs are available free of charge including:

- Lavasoft's Ad-Aware
- Microsoft's Windows Defender
- Spybot—Search and Destroy

Privilege Escalation

Privilege escalation occurs when a user or process accesses elevated rights and permissions. When attackers first compromise a system, they often only have minimal privileges. However, privilege escalation tactics allow them to get more and more privileges.

For example, imagine hacker Harry is attacking a web server over the Internet. He only has guest or anonymous access to the system initially, and he can't do much with this access. He uses different techniques during the attack to gain more and more privileges. If he can escalate his privileges high enough, he will have full administrative or root access to the system.

Malware frequently tries to gain access to elevated privileges through the logged on user. For example, if a user logs on with administrative privileges, the malware can elevate its privileges through the user account.

Many organizations require administrators to have two accounts. They use one account for regular use and one for administrative use. The only time they would log on with the administrator account is when they are performing administrative work. This reduces the time the administrative account is used and reduces the potential for privilege escalation.

Trusted Operating System

Chapter 2 mentioned trusted operating systems in the context of the mandatory access control (MAC) model. A trusted operating system provides multilevel security and meets specific criteria for security. One of the benefits of a trusted operating system is its ability to prevent malware from executing on the system.

Security-Enhanced Linux (SELinux) is an example of a trusted operating system. The United States National Security Agency (NSA) originally created it by adding patches and utilities to Linux. SELinux features have since been integrated into version 2.6 of the Linux kernel.

> ### Remember this
> SELinux is an example of a trusted operating system that can prevent malicious or suspicious code from executing on a computer.

Recognizing Social Engineering Tactics

Social engineering is the practice of using social tactics to gain information. It's often low-tech and encourages individuals to do something they wouldn't normally do, or cause them to reveal some piece of information, such as user credentials.

Some of the individual methods and techniques include:

- Flattery and conning
- Assuming a position of authority
- Encouraging someone to perform a risky action
- Encouraging someone to reveal sensitive information
- Impersonating someone, such as an authorized technician
- Tailgating or closely following authorized personnel without providing credentials

> **Remember this**
>
> Social engineering uses social tactics to trick users into giving up information or performing actions they wouldn't normally take. Social engineering attacks can occur in person, over the phone, while surfing the Internet, and via e-mail.

In the movie *Catch Me If You Can*, Leonardo DiCaprio played Frank Abagnale Jr., an effective con artist. He learned some deep secrets about different fields by conning and flattering people into telling him. He then combined all he learned to impersonate pilots and doctors and perform some sophisticated forgery.

Social engineers con people in person, as Frank Abagnale Jr. did, and they use other methods as well. They may use the phone, e-mail with phishing tactics, and even use some trickery on websites, such as fooling someone into installing rogueware.

As an example of a social engineer using the phone, consider this scenario. Sally is busy working and receives a call from hacker Harry, who identifies himself as a member of the IT department.

Hacker Harry: "Hi, Sally. I just wanted to remind you, we'll be taking your computer down for the upgrade today, and it'll be down for a few hours."

Sally: "Wait. I didn't hear anything about this. I need my computer to finish a project today."

Hacker Harry: "You should have gotten the e-mail. I'm sorry, but I have to get the last few computers updated today."

Sally: "Isn't there any other way? I really need my computer."

Hacker Harry: "Well…it is possible to upgrade it over the network while you're still working. We don't normally do it that way because we need the user's password to do it."

Sally: "If I can still work on my computer, please do it that way."

Hacker Harry: "OK, Sally. Don't tell anyone I'm doing this for you, but if you give me your username and password, I'll do this over the network."

This is certainly a realistic scenario, and many end users will give out their passwords unless training and security awareness education repeatedly repeat the mantra: "*Never* give out your password."

Education and Awareness Training

The single best protection against social engineering attacks is education and awareness training. Many users simply aren't aware of the multiple methods that attackers regularly employ. However, once they understand the risks and methods used by social engineers, they are less likely to fall prey to social engineering attacks.

Many organizations have training and awareness programs designed to help users understand the risks. Some common methods include formal classes, short informal training sessions, posters, newsletters, logon banners, and e-mails.

The following sections cover many of the common social engineering tactics. Security professionals that understand the risks are better able to educate others.

Rogueware and Scareware

Many attacks combine different types of attack methods. For example, rogueware or scareware, described in the Trojan horse section, uses social engineering tactics to trick or scare users. Admittedly, this is a more sophisticated form of social engineering, but it provides an excellent example of how attackers keep changing their tactics.

Attackers try to trick users into thinking their system is infected and encourage them to download free antivirus software. However, the download is actually a Trojan horse. For example, Figure 6.2 shows a pop-up that appeared on a malicious website.

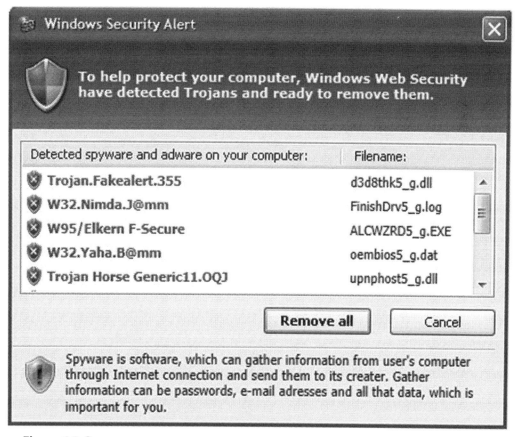

Figure 6.2: Rogueware pop-up

Clicking Remove All starts the download. However, what do you think should happen if a user clicks Cancel, or the X in the top right corner? You'd think that either of these actions would close the pop-up. However, attackers commonly program the pop-up so that any choice starts the download. The only way to safely dismiss these pop-ups is by launching Task Manager and stopping the application from there.

> ### Remember this
> Rogueware/scareware uses social engineering tactics to trick users into installing Trojan horse malware onto their systems.

Phishing

Phishing is the practice of sending e-mail to users with the purpose of tricking them into revealing personal information or clicking on a link. A phishing attack will often send the user to a malicious website that appears to the user as a legitimate site.

The classic example is where a user receives an e-mail that looks like it came from eBay, PayPal, a bank, or some other well-known company. The "phisher" doesn't know if the recipient has an account at the company, just as a fisherman doesn't know if any fish are in the water where he casts his line. However, if the attacker sends out enough e-mails, the odds are good that someone who receives the e-mail has an account.

The e-mail may look like this:

```
"We have noticed suspicious activity on your account.
To protect your privacy, we will suspend your account unless
you are able to log in and validate your credentials. Click
here to validate your account and prevent it from being
locked out."
```

The e-mail often includes the same graphics that you would find on the vendor's website or an actual e-mail from the vendor. While it may look genuine, it simply isn't.

> ### Remember this
> Phishing is the practice of sending e-mail to users with the purpose of tricking them into revealing sensitive or personal information (such as bank account information) or clicking on a link. Links within e-mail can also lead unsuspecting users to install malware.

Legitimate companies simply do not ask you to revalidate your credentials via e-mail. If you go directly to the site, you may be asked to provide additional information to prove your identity beyond your credentials, but legitimate companies don't send e-mails asking you to follow a link requesting you to input your credentials to validate them.

Phishing to Install Malware

One phishing e-mail looked like it was from a news organization with headlines of several recent news events. However, if the user clicked it, a dialog box popped up indicating that the user's version of Adobe Flash was older than was needed to view the story, and gave the question, "Would you like to upgrade your version of Adobe Flash?" If the user clicked Yes, Flash wasn't upgraded, but instead malware was installed.

Another e-mail had the subject line as "We have hijacked your baby" and the following content:

> "You must pay once to us $50,000. The details we will send later. We have attached photo of your family."

The English seems off, and the receiver may not even have a baby, making this look bogus to most people right away. However, curiosity about the photo is all the attackers seek. If the user tries to open the photo, it installs malware.

Sometimes the e-mail only requires the user to click a link. Attackers can create malicious websites and as soon as a user visits, a drive-by download installs malware on their system.

Remember, a common method of malware delivery is through e-mail. Phishing is one more technique attackers have added to their arsenal.

Phishing to Validate E-mail Addresses

A simple method used to validate e-mail addresses is the use of beacons. A beacon is a link included in the e-mail that links to an image stored on an Internet server. The link includes unique code that identifies the receiver's e-mail address.

In order for the e-mail application to display the image, it must retrieve the image from the Internet server. When the server hosting the image receives the request, it logs the user's e-mail address, indicating it's valid. This is one of the reasons that most e-mail programs won't display images by default.

Phishing to Get Money

The classic Nigerian scam (also called a 419 scam) is alive and well. You receive an e-mail from someone claiming a relative or someone else has millions of dollars. Unfortunately, the sender can't get the money without your help. The e-mail says that if you help retrieve the money, you'll get a substantial portion of the money for your troubles.

This scam often requires the victim to pay a small sum of money with the promise of a large sum of money. However, the large sum never appears. Instead the attackers come up with reasons why more and more money is needed. In many cases, the scammers request access to your bank account to deposit your share, but instead they use it to empty your bank account.

There are countless variations. Lottery scams inform e-mail recipients they won. Victims sometimes have to pay small fees to release the funds or provide bank information to get the money deposited. They soon learn there is no prize.

In check fraud, victims are convinced to cash a check and keep a portion of the proceeds for their time. The check is a bogus cashier's check, and banks often release the money immediately. However, when the check bounces, the victim is responsible for the entire amount. A student in a recent Security+ class I taught showed me a $4,500 check he received along with a letter. He was invited to work as a mystery shopper for Western Union. He could keep $450 and send the rest via Western Union and report on their service. He believed this was the result of answering an email about being a mystery shopper. He didn't cash the check.

A report released in 2010 by Ultrascan Advanced Global Investigations provided some interesting statistics that prove people are still being hooked by these scams. Scammers have received over $41 billion overall, including $9.3 billion in 2009.

Spear Phishing and Whaling

Spear phishing is a targeted form of phishing. Instead of sending the e-mail out to everyone indiscriminately, a spear phishing attack attempts to target specific groups of users, or even a single user. Whaling is a form of spear phishing that attempts to target high-level executives.

A spear phishing attack may target employees within a single company or customers of a specific company. Chapter 5 mentioned an attack on Epsilon (an e-mail marketing company) where attackers harvested hundreds of millions of customer e-mail addresses from specific companies like Capital One and Citi. The attackers can use these e-mails in a spear phishing attack to known customers.

Las Vegas casinos refer to the big spenders as whales, and they are willing to spend extra time and effort to bring them into their casinos. Attackers consider high-level executives the whales, and attackers are willing to take extra effort to catch a whale since the payoff can be so great.

> ### Remember this
> A spear phishing attack attempts to target specific groups of users, or even a single user. It could target employees within a company or customers of a company. Whaling targets high-level executives.

As an example, attackers singled out as many as twenty thousand senior corporate executives in a fine-tuned phishing attack in 2008. The e-mails looked like official subpoenas requiring the recipient to appear before a federal grand jury and included the executive's full name and other details, such as their company name and phone number. The e-mails also included a link for more details about the subpoena. If the executives clicked the link, it took them to a website that indicated they needed a browser add-on to read the document. If they approved this install, they actually installed a keylogger and malware. The keylogger recorded all their keystrokes to a file, and the malware gave the attackers remote access to the executive's systems.

Similar whale attacks have masqueraded as complaints from the Better Business Bureau or the Justice Department. Executives are sensitive to issues that may affect the company's profit, and these attacks get their attention.

Vishing

Vishing attacks use the phone system to trick users into giving up personal and financial information. It often uses Voice over IP (VoIP) technology and tries to trick the user similar to other phishing attacks. When the attack uses VoIP, it can spoof the caller ID, making it appear as though the call came from the actual company.

In one form, a person receives a phone message indicating they need to call about one of their credit cards, and the message provides a phone number. In another form, the person receives an e-mail with the same information.

If the person calls, an automated recording gives some vague excuse about a policy and then prompts the user to verify their identity. One by one, the recording prompts the user for information like name, birthday, Social Security number, credit card number, expiration date, and so on. Once the person provides the information, the recording indicates the account is verified. What really happened, though, is that the person just gave up some important data to a crook.

> ### *Remember this*
> Vishing is a form of phishing that uses the phone system or VoIP. The user is encouraged to call a number and an automated recording prompts the user to provide personal and financial information.

Tailgating

Tailgating (sometimes called piggybacking) is the practice of one person following closely behind another without showing credentials. For example, if Joe uses a badge to gain access to a secure building and Sally follows closely behind Joe without using a badge, Sally is tailgating.

Employees often do this as a matter of convenience and courtesy. Instead of shutting the door on the person following closely behind, they often hold the door open for the person. However, this bypasses the access control, and if employees tailgate, it's very easy for a non-employee to slip in behind someone else. Often, all it takes is a friendly smile.

Chapter 2 introduced tailgating in the context of physical security controls. As a reminder, mantraps and security guards provide the best prevention for tailgating. A simple mantrap can be a turnstile similar to those used in subways or bus stations. Imagine two men trying to go through a turnstile like this together. It's just not likely. Security guards can check the credentials of each person, and they won't be fooled by a smile as easily.

Dumpster Diving

Dumpster diving is searching through trash to gain information from discarded documents. Many organizations either shred or burn paper instead of throwing it away.

For example, old copies of company directories can be valuable to attackers. They may identify the names, phone numbers, and titles of key people within the organization. Attackers may be able to use this information in a whaling attack against executives or social engineering attack against anyone in the organization. An attacker can exploit any document that contains detailed employee or customer information, and can often find value in seemingly useless printouts and notes.

On a personal basis, preapproved credit applications or blank checks issued by credit card companies can be quite valuable to someone attempting to gain money or steal identities. Documentation with any type of personally identifiable information (PII) should be shredded or burned.

> **Remember this**
>
> Dumpster divers search through trash looking for information. Shredding papers instead of throwing them away mitigates this threat.

Impersonation

Some social engineers often attempt to impersonate others. The goal is often to convince an authorized user to provide some information or help them defeat a security control.

As an example, an attacker can impersonate a repair technician to gain access to a server room or telecommunications closet. After gaining access, the attacker can install hardware such as a rogue access point to capture data and send it wirelessly to an outside collection point. Identity verification methods are useful to prevent the success of impersonation attacks.

Shoulder Surfing

Shoulder surfing is simply looking over the shoulder of someone to gain information. The goal is to gain unauthorized information by casual observation, and it's likely to occur within an office environment. This can be to learn credentials, such as a username and password, or a PIN used for a smart card or debit card.

Users can use privacy screens to limit what other people can see on computer monitors. Privacy screens limit the view, preventing someone from viewing the content unless they are right in front of the computer. Password-protected screen savers ensure that a screen locks if a user walks away.

Many applications use password masking to reduce the threat. A password mask displays another character, such as an asterisk (*), instead of the actual character as the user types in the password or PIN.

> ### Remember this
>
> Shoulder surfing is likely to occur within an office without needing any technical tools. A social engineer can gain unauthorized information just by looking over someone's shoulder. You can mitigate shoulder surfing with privacy screens and password masking.

Chapter 6 Exam Topic Review

When preparing for the exam, make sure you understand these key concepts covered in this chapter.

Malware

- A worm is self-replicating, unlike a virus, which must be executed.
- A Trojan appears to be one thing, such as pirated software or free antivirus software, but is something malicious. Trojans also infect systems through USB flash drives.
- A logic bomb executes in response to an event, such as a day, time, or a condition. Malicious insiders plant logic bombs into existing systems.
- Rootkits take root level or kernel level control of a system. They hide their processes to avoid detection. They can remove user privileges and modify system files.
- A file integrity checker can detect files modified by a rootkit and an inspection of RAM can discover hooked processes.
- Spam frequently includes malicious attachments and malicious links. Anti-spam software can block unsolicited e-mail.
- Spyware is software installed on user systems without their knowledge or consent. It can result in the loss of confidentiality as it steals secrets, and can cause systems to run slow. Anti-spyware software, and some antivirus software, can detect spyware.
- Antivirus software can detect and block different types of malware, such as worms, viruses, and Trojans. Antivirus software uses signatures to detect known malware.

Social Engineering

- Social engineering is the practice of using social tactics to gain information or trick users into performing an action they wouldn't normally take.
- Phishing is the practice of sending e-mail to users with the purpose of tricking them into revealing sensitive information or clicking on a link.

- Spear phishing attacks target specific groups of users or even a single user.
- Whaling is a phishing attack that targets high-level executives.
- Vishing is a form of phishing that uses recorded voice over the telephone and often uses Voice over IP (VoIP).
- Tailgating, also called piggybacking, is the practice of one person following closely behind another without showing credentials. Mantraps help prevent tailgating, and security guards should watch for tailgating in high traffic areas.
- Dumpster divers search through trash looking for information, and document shredding reduces the risk of dumpster diving.
- Shoulder surfing is an attempt to gain unauthorized information through casual observation, such as looking over someone's shoulder. You can mitigate shoulder surfing with privacy screens and password masking.

Chapter 6 Practice Questions

1. What is the difference between a worm and a virus?
   - A. A worm is self-replicating but a virus isn't self-replicating
   - B. A virus is self-replicating but a worm isn't self-replicating
   - C. A virus runs in response to an event such as a date, but a worm runs on its own schedule
   - D. A worm runs in response to an event such as a date, but a virus runs on its own schedule

2. After downloading pirated software, a user notices the computer is running very slowly and antivirus software is detecting malware. What likely happened?
   - A. The user installed a Trojan
   - B. The user installed a worm
   - C. The user installed a logic bomb
   - D. The user installed a botnet

3. What type of malware do users inadvertently install with USB thumb drives?
   - A. Spam
   - B. Trojans
   - C. Buffer overflow
   - D. Logic bomb

4. At 9 a.m. on January 31, an administrator starts receiving alerts from monitoring systems indicating problems with servers in the datacenter. He discovers that all servers are unreachable. Of the following choices, what is the most likely cause?
   - A. Logic bomb
   - B. XSRF attack
   - C. Buffer overflow
   - D. Rootkit

5. An employee has added malicious code into the company's personnel system. The code verifies the employment status of the employee once a month. If the check shows the person is no longer an active employee, it launches attacks on internal servers. What type of code is this?
   - A. Botnet
   - B. Logic bomb
   - C. Trojan
   - D. Adware

6. A process running on a system has system level access to the operating system kernel. Investigation shows that it has modified system files. What best describes this behavior?
   - A. Rootkit
   - B. Worm
   - C. Cross-site scripting
   - D. Adware

7. Where would a security specialist look for a hooked process?
   A. Rootkit
   B. Disk
   C. RAM
   D. Firewall log

8. A file integrity checker on a database server detected several modified system files. What could cause this?
   A. Spam
   B. Buffer overflow
   C. Logic bomb
   D. Rootkit

9. What can you use to block unsolicited e-mail?
   A. Spam filter
   B. Rootkit
   C. Spyware
   D. Antivirus software

10. What can reduce unwanted e-mail that contains advertisements?
    A. Anti-spam software
    B. Antivirus software
    C. File integrity checkers
    D. Botnet software

11. A user's system has spyware installed. What is the most likely result?
    A. Loss of root level access
    B. Loss of confidentiality
    C. Loss of integrity
    D. Loss of anonymity on the Internet

12. Additional windows are appearing when a user surfs the Internet. These aren't malicious, but the user wants them to stop. What can stop this behavior?
    A. Antivirus software
    B. Host-based firewall
    C. Pop-up blocker
    D. Input validation

13. What type of signature-based monitoring can detect and remove known worms and Trojans?
    A. Anti-spyware
    B. NIDS
    C. NIPS
    D. Antivirus

14. A user's computer has recently been slower than normal and has been sending out e-mail without user interaction. Of the following choices, what is the best choice to resolve this issue?
    A. Botnet software
    B. Anti-spam software
    C. Anti-spyware software
    D. Antivirus software

15. While surfing the Internet, a user sees a message indicating a malware infection and offering free antivirus software. The user downloads the free antivirus software but realizes it infected this system. Which of the following choices best explains what happened to the user?
    A. Social engineering
    B. Trojan
    C. Vishing
    D. Spim

16. An attacker wants to obtain bank account information from a user. Which of the following methods do attackers use?
    A. Tailgating
    B. Fuzzing
    C. Password masking
    D. Phishing

17. Of the following choices, what best represents an attack against specific employees of a company?
    A. Phishing
    B. Vishing
    C. Spim
    D. Spear phishing

18. Attackers sent a targeted e-mail attack to the president of a company. What best describes this attack?
    A. Phishing
    B. Spam
    C. Whaling
    D. Botnet

19. Bob reported receiving a message from his bank prompting him to call back about a credit card. When he called back, an automated recording prompted him to provide personal information to verify his identity and then provide details about his bank and credit card accounts. What type of attack is this?
    A. Phishing
    B. Whaling
    C. Vishing
    D. VoIP

20. An organization regularly shreds paper instead of throwing it away. What are they trying to prevent?

    A. Losses due to dumpster diving

    B. Losses due to data classification

    C. Losses due to data classification labeling

    D. Losses due to P2P

21. A person is trying to gain unauthorized information through casual observation. What type of attack is this?

    A. Tailgating

    B. Whaling

    C. Dumpster diving

    D. Shoulder surfing

22. A web application developer is suggesting using password masking in the application. What is the developer trying to prevent?

    A. Buffer overflow attacks

    B. Shoulder surfing

    C. SQL injection

    D. Cross-site scripting

Chapter 6 Practice Question Answers

1. **A.** A worm is self-replicating. Viruses are not self-replicating but require user interaction to run. A logic bomb runs in response to an event such as a date, but worms and viruses do not run in response to events.

2. **A.** A Trojan appears to be something useful but instead includes something malicious and in this case, the pirated software included malware. Worms are self-replicating. Logic bombs execute in response to an event such as time. A user may join a botnet such as after visiting a malicious website, but a user does not install a botnet.

3. **B.** Users can unknowingly transfer and install Trojan horse malware onto their systems with USB thumb drives. Spam is unwanted e-mail filtered with anti-spam software. A buffer overflow occurs when a system receives unexpected data or more data than program can handle. A logic bomb is a program or code snippet that executes in response to an event, such as a specific time or date.

4. **A.** A logic bomb is a program or code snippet that executes in response to an event, such as a specific time or date, and since all the servers are affected at the same time, this is the most likely cause. An XSRF occurs when an attacker tricks a user into performing an action on a website. A buffer overflow attack occurs when an attacker sends more data to a single system than it can handle and overwrites memory locations, and would not affect all servers at the same time. A rootkit provide attackers with system or kernel access on a single system and can modify file system operations for a single system.

5. **B.** A logic bomb is a program or code snippet that executes in response to an event and can execute after checking for a condition. A botnet is group of computers controlled through command and control software, and commonly launches DDoS attacks. A Trojan appears to be something useful but instead includes something malicious, but the code in this question is strictly malicious. Adware may open and close windows with advertisements and pop-up blockers can block it.

6. A. Rootkits provide attackers with system level (or kernel) access and can modify file system operations. A worm is self-replicating malware but wouldn't typically have system level access. Cross-site scripting allows an attacker to inject malicious code into a website's HTML pages. Adware may open and close windows with advertisements, but wouldn't modify administrative access.

7. **C.** Processes (including hooked processes) are stored and run from random access memory (RAM), so experts look in RAM for hooked processes. A rootkit commonly uses a hooked process, but examining files in the rootkit would not identify a hooked process. Rootkit files would be stored on the drive but not hooked processes. A firewall log can record firewall activity but it wouldn't include information on hooked processes.

8. **D.** Rootkits have system level (or kernel) access and can modify system files (detectable with host-based intrusion detection systems or antivirus software file integrity checkers). Spam is unwanted e-mail and doesn't modify system files. A buffer overflow occurs when a vulnerable application receives unexpected data that it can't handle, but it isn't necessarily an attack. A logic bomb is a program or code snippet that executes in response to an event, such as a specific time or date.

9. **A.** A spam filter filters out, or blocks, unsolicited e-mail (spam). A rootkit is malicious software with kernel level access that hides its processes to prevent detection. Spyware is software installed on users' systems without their awareness or consent. Antivirus software can detect viruses, worms, and Trojan horses.

10. **A.** Anti-spam software can filter out unwanted or unsolicited e-mail (also called spam). Antivirus software detects and blocks malware such as viruses, worms, and Trojans. File integrity checks can detect if a rootkit modified system files. A botnet is a network of multiple computers and attackers use them to send spam and attack other systems.

11. **B.** Spyware collects user data and results in the loss of confidentiality. A rootkit may remove a user's root level access. Spyware rarely disables systems or modifies data, so integrity is not lost, though spyware may slow a system down. There is no such thing as anonymity on the Internet, with or without spyware.

12. **C.** Pop-up windows are windows that appear while browsing, and a pop-up blocker blocks them. Antivirus software can detect and remove many types of malware but cannot block pop-ups. Firewalls can block intrusions but can't block pop-ups. Input validation checks input data and can help mitigate buffer overflow, SQL injection, and cross-site scripting attacks.

13. **D.** Antivirus software monitors a system and can detect and remove known malware (including worms and Trojans) based on signatures. Anti-spyware detects spyware, and while it can detect some types of malware, it isn't as reliable as antivirus software to detect malware. Intrusion detection and prevention systems do not remove malware such as worms and Trojans, though they may detect network activity from a worm.

14. **D.** Antivirus software can resolve many types of malware infections and this activity indicates an infection possibly related to a botnet. Botnet software is malware that joins a computer to a botnet and does not resolve problems, but causes them. Anti-spam software can block spam coming in but wouldn't remove malware or block e-mails going out. Anti-spyware software detects spyware, and some malware but isn't as good a choice as antivirus software.

15. **A.** The user was tricked by the website using a sophisticated form of social engineering. The system, not the user, was infected with a Trojan commonly known as rogueware or scareware. Vishing is a form of phishing that uses recorded voice over the telephone. Spim is a form of spam using instant messaging (IM).

16. **D.** Phishing is the practice of sending e-mail to users with the purpose of tricking them into revealing personal information (such as bank account information). Tailgating occurs when one user follows closely behind another user without using credentials, and mantraps help prevent tailgating. Fuzzing, or fuzz testing, sends invalid, unexpected, or random data to a system to detect buffer overflow vulnerabilities. Password masking displays a special character, such as an asterisk (*), instead of the password to prevent shoulder surfing.

17. **D.** A spear phishing attack targets a specific person or specific groups of people such as employees of a company. Phishing sends e-mail to users with the purpose of tricking them into revealing personal information, such as bank account information, but it doesn't target specific employees of a company. Vishing is a form of phishing that uses recorded voice over the telephone. Spim is a form of spam using instant messaging (IM).

18. **C.** Whaling is a phishing attack that targets high-level executives. Phishing sends e-mail to users with the purpose of tricking them into revealing personal information (such as bank account information), but it doesn't target users. Spam is unsolicited e-mail. Phishing and whaling attacks are sent as spam, but spam itself isn't a targeted attack. A botnet is a group of computers joined to a network, and criminals control them with command and control servers.

19. **C.** Vishing is a form of phishing that uses recorded voice over the telephone. Phishing sends e-mail to users with the purpose of tricking them into revealing personal information (such as bank account information). Whaling is a phishing attack that targets high-level executives. Vishing attacks often use Voice over IP (VoIP), but VoIP isn't an attack.

20. **A.** Dumpster divers search through trash looking for information, and shredding mitigates the threat. Data classification helps protect sensitive data by ensuring users understand the value of data. Data labeling ensures that users know what data they are handling and processing. Peer-to-peer (P2P) and file sharing applications cause data leakage, and port scanners can detect P2P applications.

21. **D.** Shoulder surfing is an attempt to gain unauthorized information through casual observation, such as looking over someone's shoulder, and password masking helps mitigate the risk. Tailgating is the practice of one person following closely behind another without showing credentials, and mantraps help prevent tailgating. Whaling is a phishing attack that targets high-level executives. Dumpster divers search through trash looking for information and shredding documents can mitigate their success.

22. **B.** Password masking displays a special character, such as an asterisk (*), instead of the password to prevent shoulder surfing. Input validation checks input data and can help mitigate buffer overflow, SQL injection, and cross-site scripting attacks.

Chapter 7

Identifying Advanced Attacks

CompTIA Security+ objectives covered in this chapter:

1.2 Apply and implement secure network administration principles
- Flood guards

3.2 Analyze and differentiate among types of attacks
- Man-in-the-middle
- DDoS
- DoS
- Replay
- Smurf attack
- Spoofing
- Xmas attack
- Pharming
- DNS poisoning and ARP poisoning
- Transitive access
- Client-side attacks

3.5 Analyze and differentiate among types of application attacks
- Cross-site scripting
- SQL injection
- LDAP injection
- XML injection
- Directory traversal/command injection
- Buffer overflow
- Cookies and attachments
- Malicious add-ons
- Session hijacking
- Header manipulation

4.1 Explain the importance of application security

- Fuzzing
- Secure coding concepts
  - Error and exception handling
  - Input validation
- Cross-site scripting prevention
- Cross-site request forgery (XSRF) prevention
- Application configuration baseline (proper settings)
- Application hardening
- Application patch management

If there's one thing that's abundant in the IT world, it is attacks and attackers. Attackers lurk almost everywhere. If you have computer systems, you can't escape them. However, you can be proactive in identifying the different types of attacks and take steps to prevent them, or at least prevent their effectiveness. This chapter covers a wide assortment of attacks from different sources and provides some insight into preventing many of them.

Analyzing Attacks

While malware is a significant threat to protect against, several other attacks also present risks to systems and networks. In this section, you'll learn about many of these other attacks.

It's important to realize that effective countermeasures exist for all of the attacks listed in this book. However, attackers are actively working on beating the countermeasures. As they do, security professionals create additional countermeasures and the attackers try to beat them. The battle continues daily.

The goal in this section is to become aware of many of the well-known attacks. By understanding these, you'll be better prepared to comprehend the improved attacks as they emerge, and the improved countermeasures.

Denial-of-service

A denial-of-service (DoS) attack is an attack intended to make a computer's resources or services unavailable to users. In other words, it prevents a server from operating or responding to normal requests. DoS attacks come from a single attacker.

There are many different types of DoS attacks, including SYN flood, smurf, and buffer overflow attacks. The "Web Servers" section later in this chapter covers buffer overflow attacks.

> ### Remember this
>
> A denial-of-service (DoS) attack is an attack from a single source that attempts to disrupt the services provided by another system. Examples include SYN flood, smurf, and some buffer overflow attacks.

SYN Flood Attack

The SYN flood attack is a common DoS attack used against servers on the Internet. They are easy for attackers to launch, difficult to stop, and can cause significant problems. The SYN flood attack disrupts the TCP handshake process and can prevent legitimate clients from connecting.

Chapter 3 explained how TCP sessions use a three-way handshake when establishing a session. As a reminder, two systems normally start a TCP session by exchanging three packets in a TCP handshake. For example, when a client establishes a session with a server it will take the following steps:

1. The client sends a SYN packet to the server.
2. The server responds with a SYN/ACK packet.
3. The client completes the handshake by sending an ACK packet. After establishing the session, the two systems exchange data.

However, in a SYN flood attack, the attacker never completes the handshake by sending the ACK packet. Additionally, the attacker sends a barrage of SYN packets, leaving the server with multiple half-open connections. Figure 7.1 shows an example of the start of a SYN flood attack.

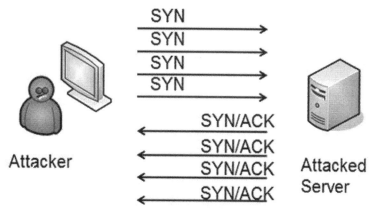

Figure 7.1: SYN flood attack

In some cases, these half-open connections can consume a server's resources while it is waiting for the third packet, and it can actually crash. More often though, the server will limit the number of these half-open connections. Once the limit is reached, the server won't accept any new connections blocking connections from legitimate users.

Flood guards use a variety of different methods to protect against SYN flood attacks. Many firewalls and intrusion detection systems include flood guards, which are simply techniques to limit the success of a SYN flood attack. Additionally, some vendors sell dedicated flood guard appliances dedicated to detecting and blocking these attacks.

One method of detecting and blocking these attacks is by identifying the source IP address. If a single source IP address is initiating these half-open connections, but never completing them, a flood guard can block all traffic from this IP. However, attackers now commonly spoof the source IP address in each SYN flood packet.

Some flood guards limit the number of half-open connections. Once the threshold is reached, all other connections are blocked. While this protects the server, it can also potentially block legitimate clients.

Another method is to dynamically adjust the time a system waits for the third packet. For example, the system may normally wait seventy-five seconds for an ACK after sending the SYN/ACK packet. After sensing a barrage of SYN packets, it can reduce the time it waits for the ACK.

Remember this

A SYN flood attack disrupts the TCP initiation process by withholding the third packet of the TCP three-way handshake. Flood guards protect against SYN flood attacks.

There is a lot more depth to SYN flood attacks and methods, such as flood guards, used to mitigate them. Additionally, attacks and mitigation techniques continue to evolve. If you're interested in digging deeper, check out RFC 4987, "TCP SYN Flooding Attacks and Common Mitigations" here: http://tools.ietf.org/html/rfc4987.

Smurf Attack

A smurf attack spoofs the source address of a broadcast ping packet to flood a victim with ping replies. It's worthwhile to break this down.

- **A ping is normally unicast—one computer to one computer**. A ping sends ICMP echo requests to one computer, and the receiving computer responds with ICMP echo responses.
- **The smurf attack sends the ping out as a broadcast**. In a broadcast, one computer sends the packet to all other computers in the subnet.
- **The smurf attack spoofs the source IP**. If the source IP address isn't changed, the computer sending out the broadcast ping will get flooded with the ICMP replies. Instead, the smurf attack substitutes the source IP with the IP address of the victim, and the victim gets flooded with these ICMP replies.

The rumor that a smurf attack is one where attackers send out little blue packets that report back to a Papa Smurf is simply not true.

Distributed Denial-of-service

A distributed denial-of-service (DDoS) attack is similar to a denial-of-service attack except that it includes multiple attacking computers. In other words, a DoS attack is launched from one computer, but a DDoS attack is launched from two or more computers. These attacking computers are often part of a botnet and can be thousands of computers scattered around the world.

DDoS attacks often include sustained, abnormally high network traffic on the network interface card of the attacked computer. Other system resource usage (such as the processor and memory usage) will also be abnormally high. If administrators have a performance baseline (discussed in chapter 5) showing normal performance, they can compare current performance against the baseline to detect a DDoS.

Remember this

A distributed denial-of-service (DDoS) attack includes multiple computers attacking a single target. DDoS attacks typically include sustained, abnormally high network traffic. A performance baseline helps administrators detect a DDoS.

Botnet

A botnet combines the words *robot* and *network*. It includes multiple computers that act as software robots and function together in a network (such as the Internet), often for malicious purposes. The computers in a botnet are called zombies and they will do the bidding of whoever controls the botnet.

Bot herders are criminals that manage botnets. They attempt to infect as many computers as possible and control them through one or more servers running command and control software. The infected computers periodically check in with the command and control servers, receive direction, and then go to work. The user is often unaware of the activity.

A firewall placed between the Internet and an internal network can log all network activity, including botnet activity. Reviewing these logs can show that multiple computers are frequently communicating to the same unknown remote server.

Additionally, you can use tools on the infected computer such as netstat to detect unidentified outbound connections. Netstat is a command-line tool that shows network connections and it's available on Windows, UNIX, and Linux systems. The basic command is **netstat -a** to show all active connections.

Most computers join a botnet through malware infection. For example, a user could download pirated software with a Trojan or click a malicious link, resulting in a drive-by download, and join the system to a botnet. Of course, the primary protection is to have antivirus software with up-to-date definitions in addition to keeping systems up to date with current patches.

Botnets previously used Internet Relay Chat (IRC) channels for communication. However, most organizations hosting IRC networks have taken steps to block this traffic, so the use of IRC channels isn't as common today.

> **Remember this**
> A botnet is group of computers called zombies controlled through a command and control server. Attackers use malware to join computers to botnets. Zombies regularly check in with the command and control server and can launch DDoS attacks against other victims. Botnet activity often includes hundreds of outbound connections. Some botnets use Internet Relay Chat (IRC) channels.

As an example, Coreflood malware is a Trojan horse that opens a backdoor on the compromised computer. Criminals took advantage of the vulnerability and created the Coreflood botnet. Experts don't exactly know how much these criminals stole, but estimates range between $10 million and $100 million. Authorities shut down the Coreflood botnet in April 2011, and its command and control servers managed about 2.3 million computers at that time.

Infecting 2.3 million computers and stealing tens of millions of dollars draws a lot of attention. However, many botnets manage fewer than fifty thousand computers and fly under the radar of many authorities. The result is the same for the victims, though. It doesn't matter if victims are robbed by a huge botnet or a smaller botnet; they have still been robbed.

Botnet herders sometimes maintain complete control over their botnets. Other times, they rent access out to others to use as desired. Some of the instructions sent by the command and control servers include:

- Download additional malware, adware, or spyware such as key loggers
- Launch a distributed denial-of-service attack
- Send spam e-mail

Spoofing

Spoofing occurs when one person or entity impersonates or masquerades as someone or something else. Many different types of attacks use spoofing.

For example, chapter 4 mentioned how wireless attackers can bypass MAC filtering by spoofing the MAC address of authorized systems. The smurf attack (mentioned earlier in this chapter) spoofs the source IP address by replacing the original address with the IP address of the victim.

E-mail spoofing occurs when someone changes the "From" address in an e-mail to make it appear as though the e-mail is coming from someone else. The e-mail may come from an attacker, but the spoofed address attempts to hide the attacker's identity and make the e-mail look valid. This is actually easy to do with most e-mail software.

XMAS Attack

The Xmas attack, also called a Christmas tree attack, is a type of port scan. Chapter 3 introduced port scans; as a reminder, a port scan attempts to learn what ports are open on a system. Based on what ports are open, the port scanner can detect what services and protocols are running on a system. For example, if port 80 is open, it's very likely that the HTTP protocol is running since the well-known port for HTTP is port 80.

However, the Xmas attack goes a step further. It has several bits set in the packet header and is reminiscent of lights lit in a Christmas tree. As least someone thought it looked like a Christmas tree and decided to name it a Christmas tree attack, or Xmas attack.

More importantly, it sets specific flags within the TCP header of packets. Different operating systems respond to these flags in specific ways. Attackers can analyze the response and determine the operating system of the remote system in addition to what ports are open. In many cases, the attacker can even determine the version of responding system.

The Xmas attack is often used as reconnaissance in an overall attack. It doesn't cause damage itself. However, attackers use the information they gain from the Xmas attack to launch other attacks.

Man-in-the-middle

A man-in-the-middle (MITM) attack is a form of active interception or active eavesdropping. It uses a separate computer that accepts traffic from each party in a conversation and forwards the traffic between the two. The two computers are unaware of the MITM computer, and it can interrupt the traffic at will or insert malicious code.

For example, imagine that Sally and Joe are exchanging information with their two computers over a network. If hacker Harry can launch a MITM attack from a third computer, he will be able to intercept all traffic. Sally and Joe still receive all the information so they are unaware of the attack. However, hacker Harry also receives all the information. Since the MITM computer can control the entire conversation, it is easy to insert malicious code and send it to the computers.

The ARP Poisoning section later in this chapter shows how ARP poisoning can be used to launch a MITM attack.

Kerberos helps prevent man-in-the-middle attacks with mutual authentication. It doesn't allow a malicious system to insert itself in the middle of the conversation without the knowledge of the other two systems.

Remember this
A man-in-the-middle attack is a form of active interception allowing an attacker to intercept traffic and insert malicious code sent to other clients. Kerberos provides mutual authentication and helps prevent man-in-the-middle attacks.

Replay

A replay attack is one where an attacker replays data that was already part of a communication session. In a replay attack, a third party attempts to impersonate a client that is involved in the original session.

As an example, Sally and Joe may initiate a session with each other. During the communication, each client authenticates with the other by passing authentication credentials to the other system. Hacker Harry intercepts all the data, including the credentials, and later initiates a conversation with Sally pretending to be Joe. When Sally challenges hacker Harry, he sends Joe's credentials. Kerberos, covered in chapter 1, helps prevent replay attacks with time-stamped tickets.

Web Browser Concerns

Users surf the Internet with web browsers. In the context of security, there are some issues related to web browsers that cause some problems. Some of the concerns related to web browsers include malicious add-ons, cookies, and session hijacking attacks.

Malicious add-ons

Many web browsers support add-ons to enhance the capability of the browser. For example, you can install the Adobe PDF reader add-on into a browser to automatically open PDF files within the browser window. Similarly, some add-ons include pop-up blockers to prevent these pop-ups from appearing.

While many add-ons are helpful, some are malicious. As an example, the Mozilla Sniffer add-on added malicious capabilities to the Firefox browser. After installation, it intercepted the user's login data submitted to any website and sent it to a remote location, presumably managed by attackers. The add-on was only available for a short time as an experimental add-on, but was downloaded and installed by at least 1,800 users. Users should be cautious when installing new add-ons.

Cookies

A cookie is a text file stored on a user's computer used for multiple purposes, including tracking a user's activity. Websites regularly write cookies on user systems to help remember the user and enhance the user experience.

As an example, Amazon makes frequent use of cookies. When I visit the site and look at different products, it tracks my activity and places ads on the website based on my previous searches or purchases. In most cases, only the website can read the cookie. However, cross-site scripting attacks (described later in this chapter) allow attackers to read cookies.

Some web developers store sensitive data, such as usernames or passwords, in cookies. If an attacker can read the cookie, he may have access to sensitive data. Additionally, cookies include a session ID that can identify the user session when the user logs on, and this session ID can be used in a session hijacking attack.

Session Hijacking

When a user logs onto a website, the website often returns a cookie with the session ID. In many cases, this cookie is stored on the user's system and remains active. If the user closes the session and returns to the website, the website reads the cookie and automatically logs the user on.

In a session hijacking attack, the attacker learns the user's session ID and uses it to impersonate the user. The web server doesn't know the difference between the original user and the attacker, since it is only identifying the user based on the session ID.

Attackers can read cookies installed on systems through cross-site scripting attacks, or with a sniffer if they are on the same network. Once they have the session ID, they can use header manipulation to hijack the session.

> ### Remember this
>
> If an attacker can discover a user's session ID, the attacker can impersonate the user in a session hijacking attack. Attackers can read cookies using cross-site scripting attacks.

Header Manipulation

TCP/IP packages data into packets before sending them over a network, and attackers can manipulate the headers of these packets to modify behavior.

In some cases of header manipulation, the attacker modifies flags within the packet. A flag is simply a bit that is set to a 1 or a 0, often indicating true or false. In other cases of header manipulation, the attacker modifies data within the packet, such as the session ID. Many programs are available to attackers, making it relatively easy to modify these headers.

In a session hijacking attack, the attacker inserts the session ID of the original user into the header. If the web server uses this session ID to automatically log the user on, the attacker has access to the user's account.

Many websites use dual authentication to prevent an attacker from taking malicious action with the session ID. For example, Amazon will use the session ID to identify the user and enhance the browsing experience, but if the user makes a purchase, Amazon requires the user to authenticate again.

> ### Remember this
>
> Header manipulation attacks modify flags and other data within packets. Session hijacking uses header manipulation to insert session IDs into a packet and impersonate a user. Cross-site scripting and cross-site request forgery (XSRF) attacks use header manipulation to steal cookies.

ARP Poisoning

Address Resolution Protocol (ARP) poisoning is an attack that misleads computers or switches about the actual MAC address of a system. The MAC address is the physical address, or hardware address, assigned to the network interface card (NIC). ARP resolves the IP addresses of systems to their hardware address and stores the result in ARP cache.

TCP/IP uses the IP address to get a packet to a destination network. Once the packet arrives on the destination network, it uses the MAC address to get it to the correct host. ARP uses two primary messages.

- **ARP request**. The ARP request broadcasts the IP address and essentially asks, "Who has this IP address?"
- **ARP reply**. The computer with the IP address in the ARP request responds with its MAC address. The computer that sent the ARP request will cache the MAC address for the IP. In many operating systems, all computers that hear the ARP reply will also cache the MAC address.

A vulnerability with ARP is that it is very trusting. It will believe any ARP reply packet. Attackers can easily create ARP reply packets with spoofed or bogus MAC addresses, and poison the ARP cache on systems in the network. Two possible attacks from ARP poisoning are a man-in-the-middle attack, and a DoS attack.

Man-in-the-Middle

In a man-in-the-middle attack, an attacker can redirect network traffic, and in some cases insert malicious code. Consider Figure 7.2. Normally, traffic from the user to the Internet will go through the switch directly to the router, as shown in the top of Figure 7.2. However, after poisoning the ARP cache of the victim, traffic is redirected to the attacker.

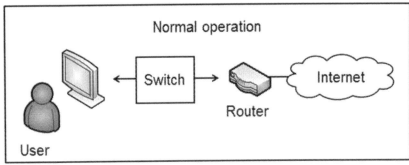

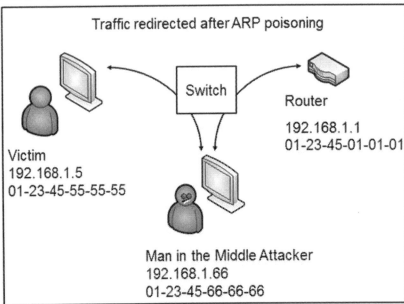

Figure 7.2: ARP poisoning used to redirect traffic

The victim's ARP cache should include this entry to send data to the router
- 192.168.168.1.1, 01-23-45-01-01-01

However, after poisoning the ARP cache, it includes this entry:
- 192.168.168.1.1, 01-23-45-66-66-66

The victim now sends all traffic destined for the router to the attacker. The attacker captures the data for analysis later. It also uses another method such as IP forwarding to send the traffic to the router so that the victim is unaware of the attack.

> ### Remember this
> ARP poisoning can redirect traffic through an attacker's system by sending false MAC address updates. VLAN segregation helps prevent the scope of ARP poisoning attacks within a network.

Denial-of-Service

An attacker can also use ARP poisoning in a DoS attack. For example, an attacker can send an ARP reply with a bogus MAC address for the default gateway. The default gateway is the IP address of a router connection that provides a path out of the network. If all of the computers cache a bogus MAC for the default gateway, none of them can reach it, and it stops all traffic out of the network.

VLAN Segregation

It's important to realize that ARP traffic is broadcast. This limits the scope of an ARP poisoning attack to broadcast domains. Routers do not pass broadcast traffic, and virtual local area networks (VLANs) do not broadcast traffic.

Chapter 3 presented information on VLANs, including how they can be used to logically group several different computers together, or logically separate computers. It's also possible to use VLAN segregation to help prevent the scope of ARP poisoning attacks within a network.

Domain Name Kiting

Domain name kiting (also called domain kiting or just kiting) is the practice of repeatedly registering a domain name and then deleting it before five days have passed. The domain name is free for the first five days, so by canceling it, the name is free. It can then be registered for another five days for free.

> ### Remember this
> Domain name kiting is a tactic used to reserve domain names without paying for them. Attackers sometimes use several small companies to repeatedly reserve domain names without paying for them.

The purpose of the free period is to allow domain tasting. Domain tasting allows potential purchasers to perform some basic testing to check for traffic to the domain name. If the domain name generates traffic, it will likely be able to generate revenue from advertising.

Domain tasting was never intended to be used repeatedly for the same domain name. Due to the abuse of domain name kiting, some registrars have begun charging minimal fees to cancel a domain name and discourage domain name kiting.

Securing Applications

Applications often provide a method for attackers to generate attacks. While applications on desktops need to be secured, in the context of Security+ the focus is more on server applications, such as web server applications hosted on the Internet.

Chapter 5 presented many of the concepts used to harden operating systems, such as disabling unnecessary services and keeping systems up to date. Server-hosted applications require the same steps. If a service isn't needed by an application, it should be disabled. As vendors release patches for applications, they should be tested and applied to keep the applications up to date.

You can also take additional application hardening steps. Application hardening applies to server applications that an organization develops in-house, such as web-based applications. It also applies to applications an organization purchases, such as database server applications. Internet-facing applications are highly susceptible to attacks, and if they aren't hardened, attackers will quickly identify the vulnerabilities and attack.

Basic Application Hardening Steps

When an organization purchases an application, it can take several basic steps to ensure the application starts in a secure state. This includes following the vendor guidelines and changing defaults.

Follow Vendor Guidelines

An important first step when hardening an application is to read the directions. The vendor documentation and guidelines include important details on steps you can take to secure them, but they're only useful when someone reads them and applies the knowledge.

Many vendors approach application development with a goal of usability over security. The application will be easy to set up and configure, but it may have gaping security holes. Other vendors value security over usability. It's secure when you install it, but it may not work as desired.

Interestingly, it's only when applications value security over usability that administrators are forced to read the documentation. If security settings prevent the application from working as desired, they have to dig into the documentation to modify the settings. On the other hand, if they install it and it works (even if it has gaping security holes), they may be called away to fight another crisis before checking the documentation for security issues.

> **Remember this**
>
> Application hardening starts by hardening the server hosting the application, using standard hardening practices such as disabling unnecessary services, disabling default accounts, and changing passwords. Vendor documentation is often the best source for steps to harden an application.

Changing Defaults and Disabling Unnecessary Accounts

Many applications come with default accounts, and default passwords for key accounts. A basic principle in hardening systems and applications is to change these defaults before deploying them.

For example, database server applications include default database accounts and sometimes use blank or default passwords. These default accounts should be disabled if they aren't used. If they are used, the accounts should have strong passwords.

Similarly, many wireless devices come with predefined accounts and passwords used in the application. For example, some Linksys wireless routers come with an Administrator account named "admin" and a password of "admin." Unless this password is changed, an attacker can easily break into the network and cause considerable damage.

Eliminate Backdoors

Some applications also include backdoors. A backdoor is access point to an application or service that bypasses normal security mechanisms. Developers use backdoors for legitimate purposes to view the internal workings of an application or for ease of administration. However, the use of backdoors is strongly discouraged in the final released version.

Some malware will open backdoors with the express purpose of later exploiting the system. If a backdoor exists, expect attackers to locate and exploit it.

Software Development Life Cycles

If an organization develops applications in-house, it often implements models to manage the process. In the early days of software development, coders started with notes on napkins and started hammering away on the keyboards writing code. As time went on, professional developers and managers realized there must be a better way. They developed many different models and tools to help manage the process.

Several software development life cycle (SDLC) models are in use by different organizations. Some examples of SDLC models are Waterfall, Spiral, V-Shaped, and the Rapid Application Model. While detailed steps of each of these models are beyond the scope of the Security+ exam and this book, you should know that developers use software development models. Some of the common goals of these models are:

- **Requirements and design identification.** The development team identifies the application requirements and ensures that they are incorporated into the application design. This avoids a "code and fix" practice that can waste a lot of development time.
- **Secure code review**. At multiple stages of code development, someone is reviewing the code for security. This ensures that developers follow secure coding concepts throughout the project. In other words, security is not an afterthought, but coders are conscious about application hardening throughout the process. Code review is the most thorough way to discover software vulnerabilities.
- **Testing.** Testing ensures that the application meets the original requirements, modules of the code interact with each other correctly, and the code acts as expected and is secure. Testing can often detect bugs that attackers may be able to exploit.

The most effective method of testing an application before it goes live is the use of black box testing from a third party. Chapter 8 covers vulnerability assessments including black box, white box, and gray box testing. In short, black box testers have zero knowledge, white box testers have full knowledge, and gray box testers have some knowledge. Chapter 8 discusses how they test a network, but they can also test individual applications.

Remember this

Software development requires a secure code review at multiple stages of code development. A code review is the most thorough way to discover software vulnerabilities. The most effective method of testing is third-party black box testing.

Third-party black box testers hammer away at an application attempting to break or exploit it. They aren't influenced by any inside knowledge about the application or by internal issues such as company politics. Experts in this field know the tricks attackers commonly use and the vulnerabilities often left open by coders.

Of course, it is more expensive to hire external experts than it is to perform internal testing. Even though black box testing from a third party is the most effective testing method, it isn't always the first choice.

Performing Input Validation

One of the most important security steps that developers should take is to include input validation. Input validation is the practice of checking data for validity before using it.

Error handling routines are a part of input validation, and they ensure that an application can handle an error gracefully. They catch errors and provide user-friendly feedback. When an application doesn't catch an error, it provides debugging information. The debugging information is useful for a developer to identify the error, but it can also be valuable to an attacker.

Attackers can analyze the errors to determine details about the system. For example, if an application is unable to connect with a database, the returned error can let the attacker know exactly what type of database the system is running. This indirectly lets the attacker know what types of commands the system will accept.

Input validation also prevents an attacker from sending malicious code that an application will use by either sanitizing the input to remove malicious code or rejecting the input. The lack of input validation is one of the most common security issues on web-based applications. It allows many different types of attacks, such as buffer overflow, SQL injection, and cross-site scripting attacks (covered in the next section).

For example, if an application is expecting a user to enter a text string of no more than fifteen characters, an input validation check verifies that the data is no more than fifteen characters. If the entry is longer, it's ignored and the user is given an error. If it includes invalid characters such as less-than or greater-than characters (< or >) used in HTML-based attacks, the application doesn't use it, and the attack fails.

Consider a web form that includes a text box for a first name. You can logically expect a valid first name to have only letters, and no more than twenty-five letters. The developer uses input validation techniques to ensure that the name entered by the user meets this validity check. If a user enters other data, such as numbers, semicolons, or HTML code, it will fail the validity check.

Similarly, an application may expect to receive a number within a certain range, such as between one and one thousand. The application checks the number to ensure it is within that range. The validation check identifies data outside the range as invalid and the application does not use it.

Remember this

Input validation verifies the validity of inputted data before using it. It uses error-handling routines to prevent improper input from crashing an application and providing information to attackers. The lack of input validation is one of the most common security issues on web-based applications. When input validation is not used, web applications are more susceptible to buffer overflow, SQL injection, and cross-site scripting attacks.

You've probably seen input validation checks and error handling routines in use if you've ever filled out a form on a web page. If you didn't fill out all the required text boxes, or if you entered invalid data into one or more of the boxes, the web site didn't crash. Instead, it redisplayed the page and showed an error. Websites often use a red asterisk next to text boxes with missing or invalid data.

Analyzing Server Attacks

Many attacks are specific to certain types of servers. For example, web servers are highly susceptible to buffer overflow attacks, since they commonly accept data from users. However, an e-mail server rarely has a problem with buffer overflow attacks, but is susceptible to open relay attacks. This section covers many of the common attacks related to different types of servers.

Web Servers

Web servers most commonly host websites accessible on the Internet, but they can also serve pages within an internal network. Organizations place web servers within a DMZ to provide a layer of protection.

The two primary applications used for web servers are:

- **Apache**. Apache is the most popular web server used on the Internet. It's free and can run on UNIX, Linux, and Windows systems.
- **Internet Information Services (IIS)**. IIS is Microsoft's web server, and it's included free with any Windows server product.

Establishing a web presence is almost a requirement for organizations today, and users expect fancy websites with dynamic pages that are easy to use. While many applications make it easy to create websites, they don't always include security. This often results in many websites being highly susceptible to attacks. The following section identifies many common attacks on websites.

Buffer Overflows and Buffer Overflow Attacks

A buffer overflow occurs when an application receives more input, or different input, than it expects. The result is an error that exposes system memory that would otherwise be protected and inaccessible. Normally, an application will have access only to a specific area of memory, called a buffer. The buffer overflow allows access to memory locations beyond the application's buffer, enabling an attacker to write malicious code into this area of memory.

As an example, an application may be expecting to receive a string of fifteen characters. If input validation is not used and it receives sixteen characters instead of fifteen, the sixteenth character can cause a buffer overflow and expose system memory.

The buffer overflow exposes a vulnerability, but it doesn't necessarily cause damage by itself. However, once attackers discover the vulnerability, they exploit it and overwrite memory locations with their own code. If the attacker uses the buffer overflow to crash the system or disrupt its services, it is a DoS attack.

More often, the attacker's goal is to insert malicious code in a location that the system will execute. It's not easy for an attacker to know the exact memory location where the malicious code is stored, making it difficult to get the computer to execute it. However, an attacker can make educated guesses to get close.

A popular method that makes guessing easier is with no operation (NOOP or NOP, and pronounced as no-op) commands, written as a NOOP slide or NOOP sled. The attacker writes a long string of NOOP instructions into memory, followed by malicious code. When a computer is executing code from memory and it comes to a NOOP, it just goes to the next memory location. With a long string of NOOPs, the computer simply slides through all of them until it gets to the last one and then executes the code in the next instruction. If the attacker can get the computer to execute code from a memory location anywhere in the NOOP slide, the system will execute the attacker's malicious code.

The malicious code varies. In some instances, the attackers write code to spread a worm through the web server's network. In other cases, the code modifies the web application so that the web application tries to infect every user that visits the website with other malware. The attack possibilities are almost endless.

> ### *Remember this*
> Buffer overflows occur when an application receives unexpected data, exposing system memory. A buffer overflow attack often writes a large number of NOOP instructions as a NOOP sled into memory, followed with malicious code. Attacks can be from data manually entered into an application or from a script, such as JavaScript. Using input validation and keeping a system up to date are two primary prevention methods against buffer overflow attacks.

A buffer overflow attack includes several different elements, but they happen all at once. The attacker sends a single string of data to the application. The first part of the string causes the buffer overflow. The next part of the string is a long string of NOOPs followed by the attacker's malicious code, stored in the attacked system's memory. Last, the malicious code goes to work.

In some cases, an attacker is able to write a malicious script to discover buffer overflow vulnerabilities. For example, the attacker could use JavaScript to send random data to another service on the same system.

While error handling routines and input validation go a long way to prevent buffer overflows, they don't prevent them all. Attackers occasionally discover a bug allowing them to send a specific string of data to an application causing a buffer overflow. When vendors discover buffer overflow vulnerabilities, they are usually quick to release a patch or hotfix. From an administrator's perspective, the solution is easy. Keep the systems up to date with current patches.

SQL Queries and SQL Injection Attacks

SQL (pronounced as "sequel" or "es-que-el") is a structured query language used to communicate with databases. SQL statements read, insert, update, and delete data to and from a database. Many websites use SQL statements to interact with a database providing users with dynamic content.

The following sections identify how SQL queries work, how an attacker can launch a SQL injection attack, and protections against SQL injection attacks.

SQL Queries

As a simple example of a website that uses SQL queries, think of Amazon.com. When you enter a search term and click Go (as shown in Figure 7.3), the web application creates a SQL query, sends it to a database server, and formats the results into a web page that it sends back to you.

Figure 7.3: Web page querying a database with SQL

In the example, I selected the Books category and entered **Darril Gibson**. The result shows a list of books authored by Darril Gibson available for sale on Amazon. The query sent to the database from the Amazon web application may look like this:

Select * From Books Where Author = 'Darril Gibson'

The * is a wildcard and returns all columns in a table. Notice that the query includes the search term entered into the web page form (Darril Gibson) and encloses the search term in single quotes. If the website simply plugs the search term into the select statement, surrounded by single quotes it will work, but it's also highly susceptible to SQL injection attacks.

SQL Injection Attack

In a SQL injection attack, the attacker enters additional data into the web page form to generate different SQL statements. SQL query languages use a semi colon (;) to indicate the end of the SQL line and use two dashes (--) as an ignored comment. With this knowledge, the attacker could enter different information into the form like this:

Darril Gibson'; Select * From Customers;--

If the web application plugged this string of data directly into the select statement surrounded by the same single quotes, it would look like this:

Select * From Books Where Author = 'Darril Gibson';

Select * From Customers;

--'

The first line retrieves data from the database, just as before. However, the semicolon signals the end of the line and the database will accept another command. The next line reads all the data in the Customers table, which can give the attacker access to names, credit card data, and more. The last line comments out the second single quote to prevent a SQL error.

In many cases, a SQL injection attack starts by sending improperly formatted SQL statements to the system to generate errors. Proper error handling prevents the attacker from gaining information from these errors, though. Instead of showing the errors to the user, many websites simply present a generic error web page that doesn't provide any details.

If the application doesn't include error-handling routines, these errors provide details about the type of database the application is using, such as an Oracle, Microsoft SQL Server, or MySQL database. Different databases format SQL statements slightly differently, but once the attacker learns the database brand, it's a simple matter to format the SQL statements required by that brand. The attacker then follows with SQL statements to access the database and may allow the attacker to read, modify, delete, and/or corrupt data.

This attack won't work against Amazon (please don't try it) because it is using secure coding principles. I don't have access to its code, but I'd bet it is using input validation and SQL-based stored procedures.

> ### Remember this
> Attackers use SQL injection attacks on unprotected web pages to access databases. SQL queries provide the attacker with information about the database and allow the attacker to read and modify the data. Input validation and stored procedures reduce the risk of SQL injection attacks.

Protecting Against SQL Injection Attacks

As mentioned previously, input validation provides strong protection against SQL injection attacks. Before using the data entered into a web form, the web application verifies that the data is valid.

Additionally, database developers often use stored procedures with dynamic web pages. A stored procedure is a group of SQL statements that execute as a whole, similar to a mini-program. A parameterized stored procedure accepts data as an input called a parameter. Instead of copying the user's input directly into a select statement, the input is passed to the stored procedure as a parameter. The stored procedure performs data validation, but it also handles the parameter (the inputted data) differently and prevents a SQL injection attack.

Consider the previous example searching for a book by an author where an attacker entered the following text: **Darril Gibson'; Select * From Customers;--**. The web application passes this search string to a stored procedure. The stored procedure then uses the entire search string in a select statement like this:

Select * From Books Where Author = "Darril Gibson'; Select * From Customers;-- ".

In this case, the text entered by the user is interpreted as harmless text rather than malicious SQL statements.

Depending on how well the database server is locked down (or not), SQL injection attacks may allow the attacker to access the structure of the database, all the data, and even modify data. In some cases, attackers have modified the price of products from several hundred dollars to just a few dollars, purchased several, and then returned the price to normal.

XML Injection

Many databases use extensible markup language (XML) for inputting or exporting data. XML provides formatting rules to describe the data. For example, here's an XML tag for a name: <name>Darril Gibson</name>. The data is "Darril Gibson" and the XML tags (<name> and </name>) describe the data as a name.

Additionally, databases use XPath as a query language for XML data. If an application accepts XML data without input validation and without stored procedures, it is susceptible to an XML injection attack similar to a SQL injection attack. The attacker can insert additional data to create XPath statements to retrieve or modify data.

Cross-site Scripting

Cross-site scripting (XSS) is another web application vulnerability developers need to understand. It allows attackers to embed HTML or JavaScript code into a web site or an e-mail. When an innocent user visits the attacked web site or clicks a link in the e-mail, the code runs on the user's system. In many cases, the attacker is able to read cookies on the end user's system.

HTML code uses tags surrounded by the less-than or greater-than (< or >) characters. For example, images are placed within a web page with the <img> tag. These tags support many additional options and commands that developers use to create feature-rich web pages. However, attackers can manipulate these tags to run malicious code. Attackers often embed cross-scripting code into comments on blog pages or forums when the page allows users to include HTML tags.

As an example, a bug in Twitter's website resulted in a cross-site scripting problem in 2010. A malicious Twitter user discovered the bug and embedded JavaScript code into a tweet. When innocent users opened a web page that included the malicious tweet, the code ran on their systems. In this case, the malicious code used the onMouseOver event. When users hovered their mouse over the tweet, it did two things. It retweeted the tweet, sending it out to all of the user's followers. It also launched a pop-up window displaying content from a hard-core Japanese pornography website.

While this attack was more embarrassing to Twitter than harmful to end users, many other cross-site scripting attacks are malicious. They can allow attackers to redirect users to other websites, steal cookies off a user's system, read passwords from a web browser's cache, and more. If a website stored private data in a user's cookie, such as a username and password, an attacker can use a cross-site scripting attack to retrieve this information.

In some cases, attackers modify a website with a cross-site scripting attack and then spam an e-mail with the link. If a user clicks the link, the web page launches and runs the malicious code on the user's system. In other cases they embed an HTML image object or a JavaScript image tag in the e-mail. Users can prevent the attack by not clicking links provided in e-mail, especially from unknown sources.

However, the primary protection against cross-site scripting attacks must happen at the web application. The best protection against cross-site scripting is for web developers to use input validation to detect and block the use of HTML tags and JavaScript tags. Tags are embedded within the < and > characters so it's possible to block these tags by rejecting any text that includes them.

> ### *Remember this*
> Cross-site scripting allows an attacker to redirect users to malicious websites and steal cookies. E-mail can include an embedded HTML image object or a JavaScript image tag as part of a malicious cross-site scripting attack. Websites prevent cross-site scripting attacks with input validation to detect and block input that include HTML and JavaScript tags. Many sites prevent the use of < and > characters to block cross-site scripting.

Cross-site Request Forgery (XSRF)

Cross-site request forgery (XSRF) is an attack where an attacker tricks a user into performing an action on a website. The attacker creates a specially crafted HTML link and the user performs the action without realizing it.

As an innocent example of how HTML links create action, consider this html link: http://www.google.com/search?q=Success. If a user clicks on the link, it works just as if the user browsed to Google and entered Success as a search term. The ?q=Success part of the query causes the action.

Many websites use the same type of HTML queries to perform actions. For example, imagine a website that supports user profiles. If users wanted to change profile information, they could log onto the site, make the change, and click a button. The website may use a link like this to perform the action:

http://sec-plus.com/Edit?action=set&key=email&value=you@home.com

Attackers use this knowledge to create a malicious link. For example, the following link could change the e-mail address in the user profile, redirecting the user's e-mail to the attacker:

http://sec-plus.com/Edit?action=set&key=email&value=hacker@hackersrs.com

While this shows one possibility, there are many more. If a website supports any action via an HTML link, an attack is possible. This includes changing passwords, making purchases, transferring money, and much more.

Websites typically won't allow these actions without users first logging on. However, if users have logged on before, authentication information is stored on their system either in a cookie or in the web browser's cache. Some websites automatically use this information to log users on as soon as they visit. In some cases, the XSRF attack allows the attacker to access the user's password.

Users should be educated on the risks related to links from sources they don't recognize. Phishing e-mails (covered in chapter 6) often include malicious links that look innocent enough to users, but can cause significant harm. If a user doesn't click the link, they don't launch the XSRF attack.

However, just as with cross-site scripting, the primary burden of protection from XSRF falls on the website developers. Developers need to be aware of XSRF attacks and the different methods used to protect against them. One method is to use dual authentication and force the user to manually enter credentials prior to performing actions. Another method is to expire the cookie after a short period, such as after ten minutes, preventing automatic log on for the user.

> ### Remember this
> Cross-site request forgery (XSRF) scripting causes users to perform actions on websites without their knowledge. In some cases, it allows an attacker to steal cookies and harvest passwords.

Directory Traversal/Command Injection

In some cases, attackers are able to inject operating system commands into an application using web page forms or text boxes. Any web page that accepts input from users is a potential threat. Directory traversal is a specific type of command injection attack that attempts to access a file by including the full directory path, or traversing the directory structure.

For example, in UNIX systems, the passwd file includes user login information, and it is stored in the /etc directory with a full directory path of /etc/passwd. Attackers can use commands such as **../../etc/passwd** or **/etc/passwd** to read the file. Similarly, they could use a remove directory command (such as **rm -rf**) command to delete a directory including all files and subdirectories. Input validation can prevent directory traversal.

> ### Remember this
> Command injection attacks attempt to run operating system commands from within an application. Directory traversal is a specific type of command that attempts to access files on a system.

LDAP Injection

Chapter 3 introduced Lightweight Directory Application Protocol (LDAP). As a reminder, this is the primary protocol used to communicate with Active Directory in a Microsoft system. In some cases, attackers are able to use LDAP injection attacks to query and modify account information in Active Directory with LDAP commands.

Fuzzing

Fuzzing (or fuzz testing) uses a computer program to send random data to an application. In some cases, the random data can actually crash the program or provide unexpected results indicating a vulnerability. Security professionals use fuzz testing to test systems for vulnerabilities they can correct while attackers use fuzz testing to identify vulnerabilities they can exploit.

Sometimes attackers will write a fuzz testing script to run on the attacked system instead of sending the data over the network. For example, an attacker can use JavaScript to send random data to another service on the same system. In some cases, this discovers a string of code that can cause a buffer overflow. If an attacker discovers a string of data that can crash a web server, they can use it as a DoS attack. A limitation of fuzz testing is that can usually only find simple faults.

> **Remember this**
>
> Fuzzing sends random strings of data to applications looking for vulnerabilities. Attackers use fuzz testing to detect strings of data that can be used in a buffer overflow attack.

Database Servers

Database servers host database applications. For example, Oracle Database and Microsoft's SQL Server are server applications you can install on a server to host one or more databases.

Web servers frequently use database servers as back-end servers. In other words, the web servers provide the front end that users access for web pages. The database server is hidden from the users behind a firewall and only accessible to the web server.

For example, Figure 7.4 shows a common configuration for a web server and database server. Users access the web server in the DMZ. Ports 80 and 443 are open in FW1 to allow HTTP and HTTPS traffic. When necessary, the web server queries the database server through port 1443 on FW2. In this case, the two firewalls provide a layer of protection for the database since Internet users cannot access the database server directly.

Figure 7.4: Protected database server

An organization may think that by placing its database server behind the second firewall, it is protected, and that's all it needs to do. It would be wrong. If the web server doesn't use input validation, attackers can use SQL injection to access data on the database server. SQL injection is an example of using transitive access to attack a server through a client side attack.

Transitive Access and Client-side Attacks

Transitive relationships refer to trusts. For example, if Sally trusts Bob, and Bob trusts Maria, than a transitive trust means that Sally trusts Maria. Of course, this isn't always true with people, and Sally may be a little upset with Bob if he shares her secrets with Maria.

Similarly, just because a database server trusts a web server and will answer its queries, that doesn't mean that it trusts all of the web server's clients. However, an attacker can use transitive access to reach the database server through the web server.

As an example, consider the database server that is behind two firewalls, shown previously in Figure 7.4. On the surface, it looks like attackers from the Internet cannot access this database server. However, they can access it through client-side attacks using transitive access. The web server accepts connections from Internet clients, and the database server accepts connections from the web server. If a web application isn't using input validation and stored procedures, an attacker can use transitive access to launch a SQL injection attack.

Notice that the attacker is using a client application such as a web browser. Client-side attacks take advantage of transitive access when direct attacks are not possible. In this scenario, the attacker is unlikely to be able to breach both firewalls and access the database server directly. However, with the client-side attack, the attacker can still attack the database server.

Of course, if the web application on the web server uses secure coding principles, such as input validation and stored procedures, the attacker will fail.

E-mail Servers

E-mail servers send and receive e-mail on the Internet and internal networks. The three primary protocols used by e-mail servers are Simple Mail Transport Protocol (SMTP), Post Office Protocol v3 (POP3), and Internet Message Access Protocol v4 (IMAP4).

As mentioned previously, malware and spam pass through e-mail servers. Many e-mail servers include both antivirus and anti-spyware software to filter out both malware and spam as a basic protection.

E-mail servers send e-mail to other e-mail servers using a process called SMTP relay, which can present a risk. Organizations normally restrict the SMTP relay process so that e-mail servers will only accept e-mail from specific e-mail servers. Authorized e-mail servers authenticate with each other before relaying e-mail back and forth, and they block all e-mail from unauthorized servers.

In contrast, an anonymous open relay doesn't use any type of authentication. It will forward e-mail received from any system, even spammers. Most e-mail servers disable anonymous open relay by default, but if an administrator accidentally enables it, spammers can use the server to forward spam.

DNS Servers

Domain Name System (DNS) servers provide name resolution. Specifically, DNS resolves names to IP addresses. This eliminates the need for you and me to have to remember the IP address for websites. Instead, we simply type the name into the browser, and it connects. Part of the process is a query to DNS for the IP address.

The name resolution results are stored in a memory location known as cache. For example, when DNS resolves google.com to an IP address, the results are stored in the system memory. The next time google.com needs to be resolved, the system uses the cached results, instead of repeatedly querying DNS. End-user computers store results in their computer's cache. When a DNS server queries another DNS server, it stores the results in its cache.

DNS also provides reverse lookups. In a reverse lookup, a client sends an IP address to a DNS server with a request to resolve it to a name. Some applications use this as a rudimentary security mechanism to detect spoofing.

For example, an attacker may try to spoof the computer's identity by using a different name during a session. However, the TCP/IP packets in the session include the IP address of the masquerading system and a reverse lookup will show the system's actual name. If the names are different, it shows suspicious activity. Reverse lookups are not 100 percent reliable because reverse lookup records are optional on DNS servers. However, they are useful when they're available.

> ### Remember this
> DNS poisoning attacks attempt to corrupt cached DNS data, including both forward and reverse lookup results. A pharming attack redirects a website's traffic to another website.

The two primary attacks against a DNS server are:

- **DNS poisoning.** This attack attempts to modify or corrupt cached DNS results. Attacks may modify regular name to IP address results and reverse lookup results.
- **Pharming**. A pharming attack is a specific type of DNS poisoning attack that redirects a website's traffic to another website.

Chapter 7 Exam Topic Review

When preparing for the exam, make sure you understand these key concepts covered in this chapter.

Attacks

- A DoS attack is an attack launched from a single system and attempts to disrupt services. Examples include SYN flood (mitigated with flood guards), smurf, and some buffer overflow attacks.
- DDoS attacks are DoS attacks from multiple computers. Systems experience sustained, abnormally high network traffic. Administrators use performance baselines to help detect DDoS attacks.
- Botnets are groups of computers (called zombies) controlled with command and control servers, and they frequently launch DDoS attacks. A computer can join a botnet after a malware infection, and suspicious activity includes hundreds of outbound connections. Some botnets communicate via IRC.

- An Xmas attack is a specific type of port scan used by many scanners. It analyzes returned packets to identify the operating system and other details about the scanned system.
- Man-in-the-middle attacks are a form of active interception. They can intercept traffic and insert malicious code into network conversations. Kerberos provides mutual authentication and helps prevent man-in-the-middle attacks.
- In a session hijacking attack, the attacker impersonates the user in a browsing session, using the user's session ID. Attackers use header manipulation to modify flags and data within packets.
- An ARP poisoning attack can redirect traffic by sending false hardware address (MAC address) updates. VLAN segregation helps prevent ARP poisoning attacks across a network.
- Domain name kiting reserves domain names for short periods to avoid paying.

Securing Applications

- Application hardening starts by hardening the operating system. It includes basics such as disabling unnecessary services, disabling default accounts, and changing default passwords.
- Vendor documentation provides important information on hardening steps for off-the-shelf applications.
- In-house developed software should include code review and testing steps. Code review is the most thorough way to discover software vulnerabilities. The most effective method of application testing is third-party black box testing.
- Error handling routines within an application can prevent application failures and many application attacks.
- Input validation checks input data, such as data entered into web page forms. It can help mitigate buffer overflow, SQL injection, and cross-site scripting attacks.

Server Attacks

- Buffer overflows occur when an application receives unexpected data it can't handle and exposes access to system memory.
- Buffer overflow attacks exploit buffer overflow vulnerabilities. A common method uses NOOP instructions or NOOP sleds. Two primary protection methods against buffer overflow attacks are input validation and keeping a system up to date.
- SQL injection attacks provide information about a database and can allow an attacker to read and modify data within a database from a web page. Input validation and stored procedures provide the best protection.
- Cross-site scripting allows an attacker to redirect users to malicious websites and steal cookies. It uses HTML and JavaScript tags with < and > characters.
- Cross-site request forgery (XSRF) causes users to perform actions on websites without their knowledge and allows attackers to steal cookies and harvest passwords.

- Command injection attacks run operating system commands. Directory traversal is a type of command injection attack where an attack attempts to access files stored on the system.
- Fuzzing, or fuzz testing, sends random data to applications to detect vulnerabilities.
- DNS poisoning modifies data in DNS cache from forward or reverse lookups. Pharming redirects website traffic to another website.

Chapter 7 Practice Questions

1. An attacker enters a string of data in a web application's input form and crashes it. What type of attack is this?
    A. DoS
    B. DDoS
    C. Man-in-the-middle
    D. Header manipulation

2. What will protect against a SYN attack?
    A. Input validation
    B. Error handling
    C. Flood guard
    D. Cross-site scripting

3. What can an administrator use to detect a DDoS attack?
    A. Privilege escalation
    B. Performance baseline
    C. Web form sanitization
    D. Antivirus software

4. A user browsing the Internet notices erratic behavior right before the user's system crashes. After rebooting, the system is slow, and the user detects hundreds of outbound connections. What likely occurred?
    A. The system has become a botnet
    B. The system is hosting a botnet
    C. The system is spamming other users
    D. The system has joined a botnet

5. A computer is regularly communicating with an unknown IRC server and sending traffic without user interaction. What is likely causing this?
    A. Buffer overflow
    B. Cross-site scripting
    C. Botnet
    D. Rootkit

6. Of the following choices, what uses a command and control server?
    A. DoS attacks
    B. Trojans
    C. Man-in-the -middle attacks
    D. Botnet

7. Of the following choices, what type of attack can intercept traffic and insert malicious code into a network conversation?
    A. Spim
    B. Xmas attack
    C. LDAP injection
    D. Man-in-the-middle

8. What can a header manipulation attack modify?
    A. Flags
    B. Buffers
    C. Databases
    D. Signature definitions

9. An attacker is sending false hardware address updates to a system, causing the system to redirect traffic to an attacker. What type of attack is this?
    A. IRC
    B. ARP poisoning
    C. Xmas attack
    D. DNS poisoning

10. What can mitigate ARP poisoning attacks in a network?
    A. Disable unused ports on a switch
    B. Man-in-the-middle
    C. DMZ
    D. VLAN segregation

11. You manage a server hosting a third-party database application. You want to ensure that the application is secure and all unnecessary services are disabled. What should you perform?
    A. Secure code review
    B. Application hardening
    C. White box testing
    D. Black box testing

12. Of the following choices, what is a step used to harden a database application?
    A. Enabling all services
    B. Disabling default accounts and changing default passwords
    C. Disabling SQL
    D. Disabling stored procedures

13. An organization develops its own software. Of the following choices, what is a security practice that should be included in the process?
   A. Check vendor documentation
   B. SDLC Waterfall model
   C. Code review
   D. Enabling command injection

14. An attacker is entering incorrect data into a form on a web page. The result shows the attacker the type of database used by the website and provides hints on what SQL statements the database accepts. What can prevent this?
   A. Error handling
   B. Antivirus software
   C. Anti-spam software
   D. Flood guards

15. Your organization hosts several websites accessible on the Internet and is conducting a security review of these sites. Of the following choices, what is the most common security issue for web-based applications?
   A. Input validation
   B. Phishing
   C. Whaling
   D. Social engineering

16. An IDS detected a NOOP sled. What kind of attack does this indicate?
   A. Input validation
   B. SQL injection
   C. Cross-site scripting
   D. Buffer overflow

17. A web-based application expects a user to enter eight characters into a text box. However, the application allows a user to copy more than eight characters into the text box. What is a potential vulnerability for this application?
   A. Input validation
   B. Buffer overflow
   C. SYN flood
   D. Flood guard

18. Of the following choices, what can help prevent SQL injection attacks?
   A. Output validation
   B. NOOP sleds
   C. Stored procedures
   D. Antivirus software

19. A web developer wants to prevent cross-site scripting. What should the developer do?
    A. Use input validation to remove hypertext
    B. Use input validation to remove cookies
    C. Use input validation to SQL statements
    D. Use input validation to overflow buffers

20. A website prevents users from using the less-than character (<) when entering data into forms. What is it trying to prevent?
    A. Logic bomb
    B. Cross-site scripting
    C. Fuzzing
    D. SQL injection

21. While analyzing an application log, you discover several entries where a user has entered the following command into a web-based form: ../etc/passwd. What does this indicate?
    A. Fuzzing
    B. Kiting
    C. Command injection attack
    D. DoS

Chapter 7 Practice Question Answers

1. **A.** The question describes a buffer overflow attack, which can be used as a denial-of-service (DoS) attack. A DDoS attack comes from multiple computers. A man-in-the-middle attack can interrupt network traffic and insert malicious code into a session, but it doesn't attack applications. A header manipulation manipulates flags and data in packets.

2. **C.** Flood guards help protect against SYN flood attacks. Input validation checks input data and can help mitigate buffer overflow, SQL injection, and cross-site scripting attacks. Error handling routines are a part of input validation and can prevent application failures and many application attacks. Cross-site scripting is an attack that uses HTML or JavaScript tags.

3. **B.** A performance baseline can help detect a distributed denial-of-service (DDoS) by showing differences in performance. Malware uses privilege escalation to gain more rights and permissions after compromising a system. Web form sanitization (or input validation) can prevent injection attacks, but won't detect a DDoS attack. Antivirus software can detect viruses, worms, and Trojan horses, but not DDoS attacks.

4. **D.** This describes a drive by download that downloads malware onto a user's system after visiting a web site, and joins it to a botnet (indicated by the hundreds of outbound connections). A botnet is composed of multiple systems, not a single system and criminals (known as bot herders) control the systems in the botnet. Botnets members can spam (and attack) others but the symptoms don't indicate that this what is happening.

5. **C.** Botnets control computers in the botnet and can use Internet Relay Chat (IRC) messages. A buffer overflow occurs when a system receives unexpected data, such as a string of NOOP instructions. Cross-site scripting allows an attacker to inject malicious code into a website's HTML pages. Rootkits provide attackers with system level access and can modify file system operations, but don't use IRC.

6. **D.** Criminals control botnets through command and control software running on Internet servers. Botnets frequently launch DDoS attacks from each system, but not DoS attacks from a single system. A Trojan is malware that appears to be something useful but instead includes something malicious. A man-in-the-middle attack can intercept traffic and insert malicious code but it doesn't use a command and control server.

7. **D.** A man-in-the-middle attack can intercept traffic and insert malicious code, but Kerberos helps prevent man-in-the-middle attacks with mutual authentication. Spim attacks send messages over instant messaging channels but can't intercept traffic. A Xmas attack is a port scan attack where an attacker attempts to detect the operating system of the scanned system. LDAP injection is an attack used against Active Directory based systems.

8. **A.** A header manipulation modifies flags and data in a packet and can launch a session hijacking attack. Buffer overflow attacks can modify memory buffers. SQL injection attacks can modify databases. Antivirus software requires up-to-date signature definitions, but header manipulation does not modify these.

9. **B.** Hardware addresses are MAC addresses, and an ARP poisoning attack misleads computers or switches about the actual MAC address of a system and can redirect traffic. Botnets sometimes communicate via IRC channels, but IRC channels don't send false updates to a switch. An Xmas attack is a port scan where an attacker attempts to detect the operating system of the scanned system. DNS poisoning attacks corrupt name resolution data used to resolve names to IP addresses.

10. **D.** Address Resolution Protocol (ARP) poisoning attacks modify the hardware addresses in ARP cache to redirect traffic, and virtual local area network (VLAN) segregation can limit the scope of these attacks. Disabling unused physical ports on a switch is a good security practice, but it doesn't prevent ARP poisoning attacks. A man-in-the middle attack can interrupt traffic and insert malicious code, and ARP poisoning is one way to launch a man-in-the middle attack. A DMZ provides access to services from Internet clients while segmenting access to an internal network.

11. **B.** Application hardening ensures that a system is secure and includes basics such as disabling unnecessary services and checking vendor documentation. The developer should perform secure code reviews and test the application before releasing it, but these aren't steps for the customer of the application. In other words, the developer should have already performed these steps. Applications developed in-house (not third-party applications) require secure code reviews, and third party black box testing is the most effective method of application testing.

12. **B.** Application hardening (including hardening database applications) includes disabling default accounts and changing default passwords. Application hardening includes disabling unnecessary services, not enabling all of them. SQL is the language used to communicate with most databases, so it shouldn't be disabled in a database application. Stored procedures increase performance, can help prevent SQL injection attacks, and shouldn't be disabled.

13. **C.** Secure software development includes security at each stage of development, including code reviews for security. Vendor documentation for purchased software is an important application-hardening step, but in-house developed software wouldn't have vendor documentation during development. Using an SDLC model helps an organization manage the development process, but there is nothing in the question to indicate that the Waterfall model should be used. Attacks use command injection, and applications should block command injection.

14. **A.** Error handling will return a generic error web page rather than a detailed error that can provide an attacker with valuable information to launch a SQL injection attack. Antivirus software can detect malware, such as viruses and worms, and prevent it from running on a computer. Anti-spam software can filter out unwanted or unsolicited e-mail (also called spam). Flood guards can prevent SYN flood attacks.

15. **A.** Input validation checks input data, but because so many sites do not use it, they are vulnerable to buffer overflow, SQL injection, and cross-site scripting attacks. Phishing is the practice of sending e-mail to users with the purpose of tricking them into revealing personal information (such as bank account information). Whaling is a phishing attack that targets high-level executives. Social engineering is the practice of using social tactics to encourage a person to do something or reveal some piece of information.

16. **D.** Many buffer overflow attacks use a string of no-operation commands as a NOOP sled, and while input validation prevents a buffer overflow attack, an intrusion detection system (IDS) can detect them. Input validation checks input data and can help mitigate buffer overflow, SQL injection, and cross-site scripting attacks. SQL injection attacks use SQL statements. Cross-site scripting attacks use HTML or JavaScript tags.

17. **B.** A buffer overflow occurs when an application receives more data than it expects and can expose system memory. Input validation checks input data and can help mitigate buffer overflow, SQL injection, and cross-site scripting attacks. A SYN flood attack withholds the third packet in a TCP handshake, and a flood guard is a security control that protects against SYN flood attacks.

18. **C.** Stored procedures help prevent SQL injection attacks by interpreting and validating inputted data rather than just using it in a SQL statement. Input validation (not output validation) is another method used to prevent SQL injection attacks. Many buffer overflow attacks use a string of no-operation commands (NOOP sled). Antivirus software protects against malware but not SQL injection attacks.

19. **A.** Web developers reduce cross-site scripting attacks with input validation and filter out hypertext and JavaScript tags (using < and > characters). Cookies are text files used by the website. SQL injection attacks use SQL statements and input validation helps prevent SQL injection attacks. Input validation can prevent buffer overflows, reducing buffer overflow attacks.

20. **B.** Web developers reduce cross-site scripting attacks with input validation and filtering out hypertext and JavaScript tags (using < and > characters). A logic bomb is a program or code snippet that executes in response to an event, such as a specific time or date. Fuzzing sends pseudo-random data as input to an application in an attempt to crash or confuse it. Input validation blocks SQL injection attacks but SQL statements aren't blocked by blocking the < character.

21. **C.** A command injection attack is any attempt to inject commands into an application such as a web-based form, and, in this case, the attack is attempting to retrieve password information with directory traversal. Fuzzing, or fuzz testing, sends invalid, unexpected, or random data to a system and can detect buffer overflow vulnerabilities. Kiting is the practice of repeatedly reserving domain names without paying for them. A DDoS attack is launched from multiple computers and results in loss of services.

Chapter 8

Managing Risk

CompTIA Security+ objectives covered in this chapter:

1.1 Explain the security function and purpose of network devices and technologies
- Protocol analyzers
- Sniffers

2.1 Explain risk related concepts
- Risk calculation
  - Likelihood
  - ALE
  - Impact
- Quantitative vs. qualitative
- Risk-avoidance, transference, acceptance, mitigation, and deterrence

2.2 Carry out appropriate risk mitigation strategies
- User rights and permissions reviews
- Perform routine audits

3.2 Analyze and differentiate among types of attacks
  - Malicious insider threat

3.6 Analyze and differentiate among types of mitigation and deterrent techniques
- Monitoring system logs
  - Event logs
  - Audit logs
  - Security logs
  - Access logs

3.7 Implement assessment tools and techniques to discover security threats and vulnerabilities

- Vulnerability scanning and interpret results
- Tools
  - Protocol analyzer
  - Sniffer
  - Vulnerability scanner
  - Port scanner
- Risk calculations
  - Threat vs. likelihood
- Assessment types
  - Risk
  - Threat
  - Vulnerability
- Assessment technique
  - Baseline reporting
  - Code review
  - Determine attack surface
  - Architecture
  - Design reviews

3.8 Within the realm of vulnerability assessments, explain the proper use of penetration testing versus vulnerability scanning

- Penetration testing
  - Verify a threat exists
  - Bypass security controls
  - Actively test security controls
  - Exploiting vulnerabilities
- Vulnerability scanning
  - Passively testing security controls
  - Identify vulnerability
  - Identify lack of security controls
  - Identify common misconfiguration
- Black box
- White box
- Gray box

4.1 Explain the importance of application security

- Fuzzing

As a security professional, you need to be aware of the different security issues associated with threats, vulnerabilities, and risks, and the tools available to combat them. This chapter covers the following concepts.

- Threats, vulnerabilities, and risks
- How to check for vulnerabilities
- Security tools

Threats, Vulnerabilities, and Risks

There's a direct relationship between threats, vulnerabilities, and risks within the context of security. You can't fully understand one without understanding the others. In this section, I've used a variety of sources to provide accurate definitions of these terms, including the United States National Institute of Standards and Technology (NIST).

The Information Technology Laboratory (ITL) at NIST has published a significant number of well-researched documents on computer security, including the Special Publication 800 series (SP 800 series). The SP 800 series includes research, guidelines, and guides resulting from the collaboration of industry, government, and academic organizations.

If you want to dig deeper into any of these topics, the SP 800 series is a great place to continue your research: http://csrc.nist.gov/publications/PubsSPs.html.

Threats

A threat is a potential danger. Within the realm of CompTIA Security+, a threat is any circumstance or event that can compromise the confidentiality, integrity, or availability of data or a system.

Types of Threats

Threats come in different forms.

- **Natural threats**. This could include hurricanes, floods, tornados, earthquakes, landsides, electrical storms, and other similar events. On a less drastic scale, a natural threat could also mean hardware failure.
- **Malicious human threats**. Attackers regularly launch different types of attacks, including network attacks, system attacks, and the release of malware.
- **Accidental human threats**. Users can accidentally delete or corrupt data, or accidentally access data that they shouldn't be able to access. Even administrators can unintentionally cause system outages. The common cause is by a well-meaning administrator making a configuration change to fix one problem but inadvertently causing another one.
- **Environmental threats**. This includes long-term power failure, which could lead to chemical spills, pollution, or other possible threats to the environment.

Different locations have different threats. When evaluating threats, it's important to consider the likelihood of the threat. For example, I live in Virginia Beach, Virginia, and while we're concerned about the natural threat of hurricanes during the hurricane season, we aren't very concerned about earthquakes. However, my sister, who lives in San Francisco, helps companies prepare for risks associated with earthquakes there, but she spends very little time or energy considering the risks of a hurricane in San Francisco.

Malicious Insider Threat

A malicious insider is anyone that has legitimate access to an organization's internal resources, but exploits this access for personal gain or damage against the company. This person's actions can compromise confidentiality, integrity, and availability.

Malicious insiders have a diverse set of motivations. For example, some malicious insiders are driven by greed and simply want to enhance their finances, while others want to take revenge on the company. They may steal files that include valuable data, install or run malicious scripts, redirect funds to their personal accounts, or take any of countless other actions.

Most employees are overwhelmingly honest, but a single malicious insider can launch a successful attack and cause significant damage to the company. Because of this, most organizations implement basic controls to prevent potential problems.

For example, the principle of least privilege ensures that employees have only the rights and permissions to perform their assigned tasks and functions, but no more. Chapter 11 discusses other policies such as job rotation, separation of duties, and mandatory vacations. Combined, these policies help prevent damage from malicious insiders,

Threat Modeling

Threat modeling is a process that helps an organization identify and categorize threats. It attempts to predict the threats against a system or application along with the likelihood and potential impact from these threats. Once the organization identifies and prioritizes threats, it identifies security controls to protect against the most serious threats.

Organizations have limited resources so it's not possible to protect against all threats. However, threat modeling improves the security posture of any system or application by ensuring that the resources aren't squandered on low-priority threats.

Vulnerabilities

A vulnerability is a flaw or weakness in software or hardware, or a weakness in a process that could be exploited, resulting in a security breach. Just because a vulnerability exists doesn't mean it *will* be exploited, only that it *can* be exploited.

Examples of vulnerabilities include:

- **Lack of updates**. If systems aren't kept up to date with patches, hotfixes, and service packs, they are vulnerable to bugs and flaws in the software.
- **Default configurations**. If defaults aren't changed in hardware and software configurations, they are susceptible to attacks. Similarly, default usernames and passwords are susceptible to attacks if they aren't changed.
- **Lack of malware protection or updated definitions**. If antivirus and anti-spyware protection isn't used and kept up to date, systems are vulnerable to malware attacks.

- **No firewall**. If personal and network firewalls aren't enabled or configured properly, systems are more vulnerable to network and Internet-based attacks.
- **Lack of organizational policies**. If job separation, mandatory vacations, and job rotation policies aren't implemented, an organization may be more susceptible to fraud and collusion from employees. These policies are covered in chapter 11.

Not all vulnerabilities are exploited. For example, a user may install a wireless router using the defaults. It is highly vulnerable to an attack, but that doesn't mean that an attacker will discover it and attack. In other words, just because the wireless router has never been attacked, it doesn't mean that it isn't vulnerable. At any moment, a war driving attacker can drive by and exploit the vulnerability.

Risks

A risk is the likelihood that a threat will exploit a vulnerability. A vulnerability is a weakness, and a threat is a potential danger. The result is a negative impact on the organization. Impact refers to the magnitude of harm that can be caused if a threat exercises a vulnerability.

For example, a system without up-to-date antivirus software is vulnerable to malware. Malware written by malicious attackers is the threat. The likelihood that the malware will reach a vulnerable system represents the risk. Depending on what the malware does, the impact may be an unbootable computer, loss of data, or a remote-controlled computer that has joined a botnet.

However, the likelihood of a risk occurring isn't 100 percent. An isolated system without Internet access, network connectivity, or USB ports has a low likelihood of malware infection. The likelihood will significantly increase for an Internet-connected system, and it will increase even more if a user visits risky websites and downloads and installs unverified files.

It's important to realize that you can't eliminate risk. Sure, you can avoid IT risks completely by unplugging your computer and burying it. However, it's not very useful. Instead, users and organizations practice risk management to reduce the risks.

You probably practice risk management every day. Driving or walking down roads and streets can be a very dangerous activity. Car-sized bullets are speeding back and forth, representing significant risks to anyone else on the road. However, you mitigate these risks with caution and vigilance. The same occurs with computers and networks. An organization mitigates risks using different types of security controls.

Risk Management

Risk management is the practice of identifying, monitoring, and limiting risks to a manageable level. It doesn't eliminate risks, but instead identifies methods to limit or mitigate them. The amount of risk that remains after managing risk is residual risk.

The primary goal of risk management is to reduce risk to a level that the organization will accept. Senior management is ultimately responsible for residual risk—the amount of risk that remains after mitigating risk. Management must choose a level of acceptable risk based on their organizational goals. They decide what resources (such as money, hardware, and time) to dedicate to mitigate the risk.

There are multiple risk management methods available to an organization. They include:

- **Risk avoidance**. An organization can avoid a risk by not providing a service or not participating in a risky activity. For example, an organization may evaluate an application that requires multiple open ports on the firewall that it considers too risky. It can avoid the risk by purchasing another application.
- **Risk transference**. The organization transfers the risk to another entity. The most common method is by purchasing insurance. Another method is by outsourcing, or contracting a third party.
- **Risk acceptance**. When the cost of a control outweighs a risk, an organization will often accept the risk. For example, spending $100 in hardware locks to secure a $15 mouse doesn't make sense. Instead, the organization accepts the risk of someone stealing the mouse. Similarly, even after implementing controls, some risk remains, and the organization accepts this residual risk.
- **Risk mitigation**. The organization implements controls to reduce the risk. These controls may reduce the vulnerabilities or reduce the impact of the threat. For example, up-to-date antivirus software mitigates the risks of malware.
- **Risk deterrence**. An organization can deter a risk by implementing some security controls. For example, a security guard mitigates the risk of tailgating, and cameras can mitigate risks associated with theft.

Some security professionals identify the first four methods of risk management but don't include risk deterrence. Instead, they include deterrence methods within the risk mitigation category. However, the Security+ objectives list these five.

Remember this

It is not possible to eliminate risk, but you can take steps to manage it. An organization can avoid a risk by not providing a service or not participating in a risky activity. Insurance transfers the risk to another entity. You can mitigate risk by implementing controls. When the cost of the controls exceeds the cost of the risk, many organizations accept the risk.

Risk Assessment

A risk assessment, or risk analysis, is an important task in risk management. It quantifies or qualifies risks based on different values or judgments. A risk assessment starts by first identifying assets and asset values. This helps an organization focus on the high value assets and avoid wasting time on low value assets. It then identifies threats and vulnerabilities, prioritizes them, and makes recommendations on what controls to implement. It can identify the impact of potential threats and identify the potential harm.

A risk assessment is a point-in-time assessment, or a snapshot. In other words, it assesses the risks based on current conditions such as current threats, vulnerabilities, and existing controls. For example, consider a library computer that has up-to-date antivirus protection and cannot access the Internet. Based on these conditions, the risks are low. However, if administrators connect the system to the Internet, or fail to keep the antivirus software up to date, the risk increases.

It's common to perform risk assessments on new systems or applications. For example, if an organization is considering adding a new service or application that can increase revenue, it will often perform a risk assessment. This helps it determine if the potential risks may offset the potential gains.

Risk assessments use quantitative measurements or qualitative measurements. Quantitative measurements use numbers, such as a monetary figure representing cost and asset values. Qualitative measurements use judgments. Both methods have the same core goal of helping management make educated decisions based on priorities.

Quantitative Risk Assessment

A quantitative risk assessment measures the risk using a specific monetary amount. This monetary amount makes it easier to prioritize risks. For example, a risk with a potential loss of $30,000 is much more important than a risk with a potential loss of $1,000.

The asset value is an important element in a quantitative risk assessment. It may include the revenue value or replacement value of an asset. A web server may generate $10,000 in revenue per hour. If the web server fails, the company will lose $10,000 in direct sales each hour it's down, plus the cost to repair it. It can also result in the loss of future business if customers take their business elsewhere. In contrast, the failure of a library workstation may cost a maximum of $1,000 to replace it.

One quantitative model uses the following values to determine risks:

- **Single loss expectancy (SLE)**. The SLE is the cost of any single loss.
- **Annualized rate of occurrence (ARO)**. The ARO indicates how many times the loss will occur annually.
- **Annualized loss expectancy (ALE)**. The ALE is the SLE x ARO.

Imagine that employees at your company lose, on average, one laptop a month. Thieves have stolen them when employees left them in conference rooms during lunch, while they were on location at customer locations, and from employees' homes.

Now, imagine that you're able to identify the average cost of these laptops, including the hardware, software, and data, as $2,000 each. This assumes employees do not store entire databases of customer information or other sensitive data on the systems, which can easily result in much higher costs.

A security professional can use the following model to determine the annual losses.

- **SLE**—$2,000 for each laptop.
- **ARO**—Employees lose about one laptop a month, so the ARO is 12.
- **ALE**—$2,000 x 12 = $24,000.

Managers can now make educated decisions on what controls to use. For example, the organization could purchase hardware locks to secure the laptops. These locks work similar to bicycle locks and allow employees to wrap the cable around a piece of furniture and connect into the laptop. A thief needs to either destroy the laptop to remove the lock or take the furniture with them when stealing the laptop.

It's reasonable to estimate that these locks will reduce the number of lost or stolen laptops from twelve a year to only two a year. This changes the ALE from $24,000 to only $4,000 (saving $20,000 a year). If the cost to purchase these locks for all laptops is $1,000, this is a sound fiscal decision. The manager is spending $1,000 to save $20,000.

However, if the cost to mitigate the threat exceeds the ALE, it doesn't make fiscal sense. For example, the company could choose to implement several different controls, such as hardware locks, biometric authentication, LoJack for Laptops, and more, at a cost of $30,000 per year.

Even if a laptop is never stolen again, the company is spending $30,000 to save $24,000, resulting in a higher net loss—they're losing $6,000 more a year. Admittedly, a company could choose to factor in other values, such as the sensitivity of data on the laptops, and make a judgment to purchase these controls. However, if they're using a quantitative risk assessment, these values would need to be expressed in monetary terms.

Remember this

A quantitative risk assessment uses specific monetary amounts to identify cost and asset values.

Qualitative Risk Assessment

A qualitative risk assessment uses judgment to categorize risks based on probability and impact. Probability is the likelihood that an event will occur, and impact is the negative result of the event.

Notice that this is much different from the exact numbers provided by a quantitative assessment that uses costs. You can think of quantitative as using a quantity or a number, while qualitative is related to quality, which is often a matter of judgment.

Some qualitative risk assessments use surveys or focus groups. They canvass experts to provide their best judgments and then tabulate the results. For example, a survey may ask the experts to rate the probability and impact of risks associated with a web server selling products on the Internet and a library workstation without Internet access. The experts would use words such as "low," "medium," and "high" to rate them.

They could rate the probability of a web server being attacked as high, and if the attack takes the web server out of service, the impact is also high. On the other hand, the probability of a library workstation being attacked is low, and, even though a library patron may be inconvenienced, the impact is also low.

It's common to assign numbers to these judgments. For example, you can use terms such as low, medium, and high, and assign values of 1, 5, and 10, respectively. The experts assign a probability and impact of each risk using low, medium, and high, and when tabulating the results, you change the words to numbers. This makes it a little easier to calculate the results.

In the web server and library computer examples, you can calculate the risk by multiplying the probability and the impact.

- **Web server**. High probability and high impact: 10 x 10 = 100
- **Library computer**. Low probability and low impact: 1 x 1 = 1

Management can look at these numbers and easily determine how to allocate resources to protect against the risks. They would allocate more resources to protect the web server than the library computer.

One of the challenges with a qualitative risk assessment is gaining consensus on the probability and impact. Unlike monetary values that you can validate with facts, probability and impact are often subject to debate.

Remember this

A qualitative risk assessment uses judgment to categorize risks based on probability and impact.

Documenting the Assessment

The final phase of the risk assessment is the report. This identifies the risks discovered during the assessment and the recommended controls. As a simple example, a risk assessment on a database-enabled web application may discover that it's susceptible to SQL injection attacks. The risk assessment will then recommend rewriting the web application with input validation techniques or stored procedures to protect the database.

Management uses this to decide which controls to implement and which controls to accept. In many cases, a final report documents the managerial decisions. Of course, management can decide not to implement a control, but instead accept a risk.

Think how valuable this report will be for an attacker. They won't need to dig to identify vulnerabilities or controls. Instead, the report lists all the details. Even when management approves controls to correct the vulnerabilities, it may take some time to implement them. Because of this, the results of a risk assessment are highly protected. Normally, only executive management and security professionals will have access to these reports.

Remember this

Risk assessments help an organization evaluate threats and vulnerabilities against new and existing systems. Risk assessment results should be protected and only accessible to management and security professionals.

Checking for Vulnerabilities

Vulnerabilities are weaknesses, and by reducing vulnerabilities, you can reduce risks. That sounds simple enough. However, how do you identify the vulnerabilities that present the greatest risks? Common methods are with vulnerability assessments, vulnerability scans, and penetration tests.

To understand how these are used, it's worthwhile understanding how attackers may look for targets. The following section outlines common attack methods, followed by some details on vulnerability assessments, vulnerability scans, and penetration tests.

Anatomy of an Attack

From a defensive perspective, it's valuable to understand how attackers operate. Many penetration testers use similar methodologies, so you can also apply this knowledge to penetration testing. While there is no single definition that identifies all attackers, one thing is clear: attackers are sophisticated and clever. They should not be underestimated.

Imagine an organization that has unlimited funds to launch attacks. They could be government employees employed by another country, or they could be a group of criminals. They may be trying to steal secrets or steal some of the millions of dollars that attackers are pocketing from businesses and individuals monthly. How will they go about it?

They often combine reconnaissance with fingerprinting to identify targets. Reconnaissance provides a big-picture view of a network, including the IP addresses of a target network. Fingerprinting then homes in on individual systems to provide details of each. Some of the attackers may be experts on reconnaissance, while others are experts on different elements of fingerprinting. Once they identify their targets, attackers use this information to launch an attack.

Here is one possibility of how these attackers may work.

Identify IP Addresses of Targets

One group in this organization identifies IP addresses of live systems as potential targets. For example, they may be interested in government or military systems in a specific area, or a certain company operating in a specific city.

IP addresses are assigned geographically, so this is a little easier than it may seem. You've probably been surfing the Internet and seen advertisements for your city, even though the web page isn't local. The advertisement identifies your location based on your IP address and targets the ad. Attackers have access to the same information as the advertisers. As an example, check out the website http://www.geobytes.com/iplocator.htm, which shows you detailed information on any IP address.

Once they identify a geographical range of IP addresses, attackers can use an ICMP sweep or host enumeration sweep to identify systems that are operational in that range. This is similar to sending a ping to each IP address in that range, and tools that perform ICMP sweeps are commonly called ping scanners. As mentioned in chapter 3, it's possible to block ICMP at firewalls to reduce the success of ICMP sweeps.

Identify Open Ports with a Port Scanner

The next group in the organization takes the list of IP addresses and identifies open ports on each system. Chapter 3 covered ports in greater depth and introduced port scanners. As a reminder, many protocols use well-known ports. For example, Telnet uses port 23 and HTTP uses port 80. If a port scanner detects port 80 is open, it's likely that the HTTP protocol is running and it may be a web server.

Additionally, ports also identify applications running on a system. For example, peer-to-peer (P2P) software, used for file sharing, uses specific ports for communications with other peers on the Internet. A port scan can discover these ports, and detect P2P software running on a system.

Each open port represents a potential attack vector, so by identifying open ports, attackers can determine the attack surface. As a reminder, you can reduce the attack surface by disabling all unused services and removing all unneeded protocols. This is a key step in hardening a system, or making it more secure from the default configuration.

Many vulnerability-scanning tools like Nmap, Netcat, and Nessus include port scanning abilities and scan systems to determine open ports. Security professionals use these tools for vulnerability scans within their networks, but attackers can use these same tools. These tools have more capabilities than just scanning for open ports. They can also fingerprint the system.

Fingerprint System

Attackers also attempt to fingerprint the system to identify details of the operating system. For example, is this a Linux system or a Windows system?

Chapter 7 introduced the Xmas attack as a specific type of port scan. It analyzes the returned packets to identify the operating system of the target system, and sometimes even the version of the operating system, in addition to identifying open ports.

Similarly, scanners send additional queries to the system's open ports. For example, if port 25 is open, indicating it's running SMTP, it will send SMTP queries to the system and analyze the response. These queries provide verification that the protocol is running and include additional details on the system. Similarly, HTTP queries can identify if it's a Windows Internet Information Services (IIS) web server or an Apache web server running on a Linux system.

Chapter 4 presented intrusion detection and intrusion prevention systems. These can reduce the success of port scanning and fingerprinting scans.

> ### *Remember this*
> Vulnerability tools like Nmap, Netcat, and Nessus can perform port scans to determine open ports and perform advanced analysis to fingerprint systems. An Xmas attack is a specific type of port scan that analyzes the returned packets to determine the operating system and other details about the scanned system.

Identify Vulnerabilities

At this stage, attackers know the IP address of live systems, what operating systems they're running, and what protocols they're running. This information is passed to the appropriate experts. For example, some attackers may be expert at attacking IIS web servers and Windows systems, while others are expert at attacking Apache web servers and Linux or UNIX systems.

If it's a web server, attackers may check to see if input validation is used. If not, it may be susceptible to buffer overflow, SQL injection, or cross-site scripting attacks. If it's an e-mail server, it may be susceptible to anonymous relay attacks. If it's an application server with known default accounts and passwords, the attacker checks to see if the defaults are still available. Chapter 7 presented information on each of these attacks.

Many vulnerability scanners can easily check for current patches. If a system is not patched, it's susceptible to known vulnerabilities. Again, vulnerability scanners such as Nmap and Netcat can identify vulnerabilities, and both security professionals and attackers can use them.

Attack

Attackers now have a list of systems and their vulnerabilities. They may have attack tools they can run immediately to exploit vulnerable systems. Other times, experts may write code to exploit a new vulnerability. However, you can bet that they will attack.

The reconnaissance and fingerprinting stages may take days, weeks, or months. Some attacks are quick after some detailed planning, while other attacks will linger as long as the attacker is undetected or until the attacker has completed the mission.

For example, when attackers extract or exfiltrate data, they often get in and get out as soon as possible. This often requires them to use privilege escalation tactics to gain elevated rights and permissions to access the data. Escalating their privileges is likely to sound an alarm. Once they're detected, they can expect to be blocked, so they must get as much data as possible, as quickly as possible. However, sometimes the attacks are undetected, and they can continue the attacks for days.

It's also worth pointing out that attackers often launch attacks through other systems. They take control of remote computers through different types of malware and launch the attacks through these systems. It is difficult, though not impossible, to track these attacks back to the actual source.

As the last step in the attack, many attackers will attempt to erase or modify the logs. The goal is to remove traces of their attack.

> ### Remember this
> Attackers use privilege escalation tactics during data exfiltration attacks after they gain access to a system. Privilege escalation gives attackers elevated rights and permissions to access data.

Putting it All Together

Is it possible that governments have dedicated teams working together to identify exploitable vulnerabilities? Absolutely. Is it possible that criminals have the ability to organize their efforts to identify targets of opportunity? Count on it.

These types of groups are commonly called an Advanced Persistent Threat (APT). An APT is a group such as this that has both the capability and intent to launch these types of attacks.

Cyber warfare and cybercrime are similar to spying and espionage. Espionage is the process of gathering multiple innocuous details that form the individual pieces of a much larger picture. Just as the pieces of a jigsaw puzzle eventually come together to complete a picture, the individual details of any system come together to fingerprint it. Security professionals need to be aggressive at closing all the holes to limit the amount of information that is available to any attacker.

Of course, some criminals don't have large organizations. A handful of attackers can combine their skills to identify a niche or specialty. They could become expert at SQL injection attacks and only need to look for websites without input validation. They could exploit a specific vulnerability to manage a botnet. The possibilities are endless.

However, security professionals can't afford to protect against niches only. Security professionals must protect against all attacks.

Vulnerability Assessment

The overall goal of a vulnerability assessment is to identify vulnerabilities or weaknesses. These weaknesses can be within a system, a network, or an organization. Vulnerability assessments are part of an overall risk management plan. They help identify vulnerabilities for high value resources, or vulnerabilities that can result in severe losses.

Vulnerability assessments can include information from a wide variety of sources. This includes reviewing documentation such as security policies, logs, interviews with personnel, and system testing. Assessments often use vulnerability scans and penetration tests, covered in more depth later in this chapter.

A vulnerability assessment will often perform the following high-level steps:

- Identify assets and capabilities
- Prioritize assets based on value
- Identify vulnerabilities and prioritize them based on severity
- Recommend controls to mitigate serious vulnerabilities

Remember this

Vulnerability assessments identify vulnerabilities or weaknesses within a system, network, or organization. They organize results based on the severity of the vulnerabilities and value of the assets.

Many organizations perform vulnerability assessments internally. Organizations also occasionally hire external security professionals to complete external assessments.

Vulnerability assessments are broader than just vulnerability scans. A vulnerability scanner like Nmap can discover technical vulnerabilities, but an organization can have vulnerabilities that go beyond technical controls.

A vulnerability assessment can also check for nontechnical vulnerabilities. For example, chapter 2 mentioned tailgating, where an employee can follow closely behind another employee without using credentials. One employee uses a proximity card to open a door and other employees follow. If employees are tailgating, can an attacker do the same? Theoretically, yes, but in some cases, management wants more than theory. A vulnerability assessment can include a test to see if a visitor can access secure spaces without credentials.

Similarly, employees may be susceptible to social engineering attacks. An attacker may use low-tech methods to trick employees into revealing sensitive information. Educated employees will often recognize these techniques, but even if a company provides training, it doesn't necessarily mean that the employees are educated. A vulnerability assessment can verify what training was effective and sometimes identify which employees represent the highest risks.

For example, users should not give their password out to anyone, and many organizations regularly remind users of this security practice. However, will users give out their password?

I remember one vulnerability assessment within a bank. The testers drafted an official-looking e-mail explaining a fictitious problem, but linked it to an actual internal server migration. The e-mail indicated that due to the migration, there was a problem with the accounts and users would lose access unless they provided their password. Despite training less than a month earlier on the importance of not giving out passwords, over 35 percent of the employees provided their password.

Other assessment methods include:

- **Baseline reporting**. Chapter 5 presented information on baselines, including security baselines and configuration baselines. Many vulnerability assessment tools can compare current security and configuration data with a baseline to detect changes. These changes, especially if they aren't authorized, can introduce vulnerabilities.

- **Code review**. Chapter 7 discussed the software development life cycle (SDLC) and the importance of code review. A code review goes line by line through the code and is one of the most thorough methods to discover vulnerabilities.

- **Architecture review**. An architecture review examines the layout of the network looking for potential vulnerabilities. For example, an architecture review may discover that a database server is located within a DMZ and is accessible from the Internet. The review can recommend moving the database server behind an additional firewall.

- **Design reviews**. A design review examines any design looking for vulnerabilities. It can include the physical layout of a building, the interaction with an application, or the layout of the network. Security is easier to implement early in the design stage than it is to implement later.

Vulnerability Scanning

A vulnerability scanner is a management control used by security administrators and attackers to identify which systems are susceptible to attacks. It identifies a wide range of weaknesses and known security issues that attackers can exploit. As mentioned previously, some common vulnerability scanners are Nmap, Netcat, and Nessus. They combine the features of many different tools into a single package.

Many vulnerability scans include the following elements:

- Passively test security controls
- Identify vulnerability
- Identify lack of security controls
- Identify common misconfiguration

An important point about a vulnerability scan is that it does not attempt to exploit any vulnerabilities. Instead, a vulnerability scan is a passive attempt to identify weaknesses. Security administrators then assess the vulnerabilities to determine which ones to mitigate. In contrast, a penetration test is an active test that will attempt to exploit vulnerabilities.

Some of the vulnerabilities discovered by a vulnerability scan include:

- **Security and configuration errors**. This can check the system against a configuration or security baseline to identify unauthorized changes.
- **Patches and updates**. While many patch management tools include the ability to verify systems are patched, the vulnerability scanner provides an additional check to detect unpatched systems.
- **Open ports**. Open ports can signal a vulnerability if the services associated with these ports aren't actively managed.
- **Weak passwords**. Many scanners include a password cracker that can discover weak passwords or verify that users are creating strong passwords in compliance with a company policy. It is more efficient to use a technical password policy to require and enforce the use of strong passwords. However, if this isn't possible, administrators use a separate password cracker to discover weak passwords.
- **Default accounts and passwords**. Operating systems and applications can have default user names and passwords. Basic operating system and application hardening steps should remove the defaults, and a scan can discover the weakness if they weren't hardened. For example, some SQL database systems allow the sa (system administrator) account to be enabled with a blank password. Scanners such as Nessus will detect this.
- **Sensitive data**. Some scanners include Data Loss Prevention (DLP) techniques to detect sensitive data sent over the network. For example, a DLP system can scan data looking for patterns such as Social Security numbers or key words that identify classified or proprietary data.

In some cases, vulnerability scanners can detect issues that aren't detectable through other means. In one example, something was corrupting a user's data. The administrator restored it and even updated patches. However, a short time later, something corrupted the data again. After running a vulnerability scan on the system, the administrator discovered a vulnerable port opened on the system, and then discovered an attack coming through the port.

Administrators can scan specific systems or an entire network. For example, many organizations perform periodic scans on the entire network to detect vulnerabilities. If an administrator makes an unauthorized change resulting in a vulnerability, the scan can detect it. Similarly, if a rebuilt system is missing some key security settings, the scan will detect them. It's also possible to scan a new system before or right after it's deployed.

> **Remember this**
>
> Vulnerability scans are an effective tool to identify systems that are susceptible to an attack. Vulnerability scanning will passively test security controls to identify vulnerabilities, a lack of security controls, and common misconfigurations. It does not attempt to exploit vulnerabilities.

Many tools are available to help with vulnerability assessments. Some of the tools used by administrators are the same tools used by attackers. If an attacker can find security holes with any available tool, an administrator should also be aware of these holes.

> **Passive vs. Active**
>
> Throughout this section, I'm stressing that vulnerability scanning is passive, while penetration testing is active. In this context, passive doesn't mean that a vulnerability scanner isn't doing anything. It certainly is probing systems to identify vulnerabilities and other problems. However, it is does not take any action to exploit these vulnerabilities.
>
> When preparing for any exam, including the Security+ exam, it's worthwhile looking at the objectives. These objectives specifically use the word passively, and passive verbs, in the context of vulnerability scanning. They also use the word actively, and active verbs in the context of penetration testing.
>
> That doesn't mean that you can feel free to run a vulnerability scanner on any network since it is passive. If your actions are discovered, you can easily be identified as an attacker, and face legal action.

Penetration Testing

A penetration test (sometimes called a pentest) actively assesses deployed security controls within a system or network. It starts with a vulnerability scan but takes it a step further and actually tries to exploit the vulnerability by simulating or performing an attack.

An organization may perform a penetration test to demonstrate the actual security vulnerabilities within a system. This can help the organization determine the impact of a threat against a system. In other words, it helps an organization determine the extent of damage that an attacker could inflict by exploiting a vulnerability.

Although it's not as common, it's also possible to perform a penetration test to determine how an organization will respond to a compromised system. This allows an organization to demonstrate security vulnerabilities and flaws in policy implementation. For example, many organizations may have perfect policies on paper. However, if employees aren't consistently following the policies, a penetration test can accurately demonstrate the flaws.

Remember this

A penetration test is an active test that can assess deployed security controls, identify the ability of employees to respond, and determine the impact of a threat. It starts with a vulnerability scan and then tries to exploit vulnerabilities by actually attacking or simulating an attack.

Many penetration tests include the following elements:

- Verify a threat exists
- Bypass security controls
- Actively test security controls
- Exploit vulnerabilities

For example, an organization could hire an external tester to test the security of a web application. A first step could check for a SQL injection vulnerability and, once it's verified, launch a SQL injection attack to harvest user credentials from a database. The attacker can then use these credentials to exploit other areas of the system. If the database included credentials of elevated accounts, the attacker can use these for privilege escalation and exploit other system vulnerabilities.

Since a pentest can exploit vulnerabilities, it has the potential to disrupt actual operations and cause system instability. Because of this, it's important to strictly define boundaries for the test. Ideally, the penetration test will stop right before performing an exploit that can cause damage or result in an outage. However, some tests result in unexpected results.

For example, consider fuzzing or fuzz testing (covered in chapter 7). As a reminder, fuzzing sends pseudo-random data to an application to see if the random data can crash the application, or to detect unhandled errors. The tester won't know if a fuzz test will crash an application until it's run.

Organizations sometimes perform penetration tests on a test system rather than the live system. For example, an organization may be hosting a web application accessible on the Internet. Instead of performing the test on the live server and affecting customers, they configure another server with the same web application. If a penetration test cripples the test server, it will accurately demonstrate security vulnerabilities, but it won't affect customers.

White, Gray, and Black Box Testing

It's common to identify testing based on the level of knowledge the testers have prior to starting the test. These testers could be internal employees, or external security professionals working for a third-party organization to perform the test.

- **Black box testing**. Testers have zero knowledge of the environment prior to the test. Instead, they approach the test with the same knowledge as an attacker. Black box testers often use fuzzing to check for application vulnerabilities.
- **White box testing**. Testers have full knowledge of the environment. For example, they would have access to product documentation, source code, and possibly even login details.
- **Gray box testing**. Testers have some knowledge of the environment but do not have access to all documentation or data.

Fuzzing implies black box testing, since fuzzing doesn't require any prior knowledge of the application. It can be an effective way to identify vulnerabilities within an application when the testers don't have access to source code. This is not to say that white box or gray box testers can't use fuzzing, but it is more commonly used by black box testers.

However, a limitation with fuzz testing is that it can only detect simple faults, and it isn't as effective as a code review to detect application vulnerabilities.

> ## *Remember this*
>
> Black box testers have zero prior knowledge of the system prior to a penetration test. White box testers have full knowledge, and gray box testers have some knowledge. Black box testers often use fuzzing.

You may also come across the terms "black hat," "white hat," and "gray hat." These aren't referring to testers but instead to different types of attackers. They are reminiscent of the Wild West, where you could easily identify the good guys and the bad guys by the color of their hat. Black hat identifies a malicious attacker performing criminal activities. White hat identifies a security professional working within the law. Gray hat identifies individuals that may have good intentions but their activities may cross ethical lines. For example, an activist, sometimes called a hacktivist, may use attack methods to further a cause, but not for personal gain.

Hackers and crackers are terms you may also come across. Originally, a hacker indicated someone proficient with computers that wanted to share knowledge with others. They weren't malicious. In contrast, a cracker was a proficient hacker that used the knowledge for malicious purposes. However, English is a living language that continues to evolve and the media consistently uses the term hacker to identify malicious attackers. Throughout this book, I've avoided the controversy and instead just use the term "attacker."

Obtaining Consent

It's important to obtain consent of the system owner before starting a penetration test. In most cases, this consent is in writing. If it isn't in writing, many security professionals won't perform the test. A penetration test without consent is an attack. An organization may perceive a well-meaning administrator doing an unauthorized penetration test as a black hat or gray hat attacker, and this administrator may soon be out of a job.

Many organizations use a written rules-of-engagement document when hiring outside security professionals to perform the test. The rules-of-engagement document identifies the boundaries of the penetration test. If testing does result in an outage even though the testers followed the rules of engagement, repercussions are less likely. For example, if the rules of engagement allow fuzzing and it crashes a system, the testers aren't at fault.

Remember this

It's important to obtain consent of the system owner prior to starting a penetration test, because it can cause system instability. Without consent, the penetration test may be perceived as a black hat malicious attack. A rules-of-engagement document identifies limits of the test.

Identifying Security Tools

Several tools are available for use by security professionals and attackers alike. Vulnerability scanners were discussed at length earlier in this chapter, including their use as ping scanners and port scanners. However, other tools are available. This section discusses routine audits, protocol analyzers, and password crackers.

Protocol Analyzer (Sniffer)

A protocol analyzer can capture and analyze packets on a network. The process of using a protocol analyzer is sometimes referred to as sniffing or using a sniffer. Both administrators and attackers can use a protocol analyzer to view IP headers and examine packets. For example, administrators can use a protocol analyzer to determine if applications are sending data in clear text.

Wireshark is a free protocol analyzer anyone can download from the Internet and use. Figure 8.1 shows Wireshark after it captured packets transmitted over the network. It includes about 150 packets and has packet 121 selected in the top pane. The middle pane shows details from this packet with the Internet Protocol Version 4 header information partially expanded. The bottom pane shows the entire contents of the packet displayed in hexadecimal and ASCII characters.

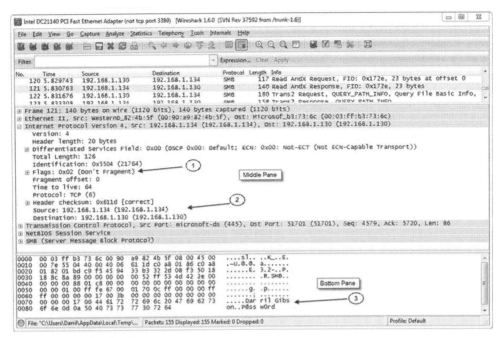

Figure 8.1: Wireshark capture

Notice that you can view the username and password (Darril P@ssw0rd) in the bottom pane (arrow 3) because it was sent in clear text. However, if an application encrypted the data before sending it across the network, it would not be readable.

While it can be tedious to analyze a packet capture, there is a lot of additional information in the middle pane available for anyone willing to take the time. Occasionally, attackers manipulate flags (arrow 1) within the headers for different types of attacks, and the protocol analyzer allows you to verify header manipulation attacks. You can also see the source and destination IP addresses (arrow 2) within the IP header field. The Ethernet II section can be expanded to show the media access control (MAC) addresses of the source and destination computers.

Remember this

You can use a protocol analyzer to capture, display, and analyze packets sent over a network. You can view unencrypted network traffic, such as passwords sent in clear text, and examine IP headers.

Routine Audits

Many organizations perform routine audits to help identify risks. An audit provides an independent and objective examination of processes and procedures. It can help an organization determine its security posture and verify that the organization is following its policies. Internal personnel or external auditors can conduct audits.

As an example, a security policy may state that when an employee leaves the company, an administrator must disable the employee's account. This prevents the ex-employee or someone else from using the account. This can prevent attacks such as the one at Fannie Mae (discussed in chapter 6) where the employee installed a logic bomb after learning he lost his job.

If the audit discovers that accounts are not disabled, the organization then takes steps to identify and correct the problem. Is a written policy in place? Do appropriate personnel know their responsibilities in relation to the policy? For example, if a single administrator is tasked with disabling accounts, but the administrator isn't informed of employee terminations until days later, there's no way the administrator will disable the accounts immediately. In this case, many organizations coordinate exit interviews with security personnel and disable the account during the interview.

For example, an organization may have an account disablement or expiration policy that requires disabling accounts when an employee leaves the organization. An audit verifies that ex-employee accounts are disabled. Similarly, an organization may have a policy requiring administrators to have two accounts—a regular user account and an administrator account. They use the normal account for regular work and use the administrative account only when doing administrative tasks. An audit of this policy verifies that administrators are following the policy.

Chapter 8 covered vulnerability assessments and penetration tests. Auditors may use these tools to verify that the steps a company has taken to mitigate risks are successful. For example, the security policy may dictate that all systems should be kept up to date with patches. A vulnerability scan can detect unpatched systems that are not in compliance with the policy.

User Rights and Permissions Review

A user rights and permissions review is a type of audit. It identifies the privileges (rights and permissions) granted to users and compares these against what is needed by the users. This can detect two common problems: permission bloat and inactive accounts.

Permission bloat occurs when a user is granted more and more permissions due to changing job requirements, but unneeded permissions are never removed. For example, imagine Nicole is working in the human resources (HR) department, so she has access to HR data. Later, she transfers to the sales department and is granted additional access to sales data. However, her access to HR data is never removed, even though she doesn't need it to perform her job in the sales department.

At a minimum, accounts should be disabled when users leave the company. Many organizations later delete the accounts after determining they aren't needed. However, if a process isn't in place to disable accounts, the accounts remain enabled. Ex-employees may still be able to use it, or they may share their passwords with other employees who can use it.

> **Remember this**
>
> Routine audits help an organization ensure they are following their policies. A user rights and permissions review ensures that inactive accounts are either disabled or deleted. It also ensures that users have only the access they need and no more.

Password-cracking Tools

Password-cracking tools can discover, recover, or bypass passwords used for authentication on systems and networks, and for different types of files. System administrators use them to identify weak passwords or recover data protected with passwords. Attackers use these tools to crack passwords to hack into a system or open password-protected files.

Many password crackers are called password recovery tools. In other words, they're advertised as a tool that users and administrators can use to recover lost or forgotten passwords. Many allow the user to learn the original password, and some allow the user to change the password. Password crackers can sniff the network to recover passwords sent over the network, identify cached passwords, crack encrypted passwords, and discover passwords used to password-protect files.

For example, archive programs such as RAR and WinZIP support password protection. A user can create an archive of sensitive files and password-protect them, providing a sense of security, but are the files secure? You could use a password cracker to determine if you can crack the password and access the data. If you can, an attacker can.

Password cracking involves different methods, such as comparative analysis, brute force, and cryptanalysis. In a dictionary attack, the cracker tries all the words in a dictionary of common words. This dictionary often includes common passwords such as 123456 and letmein. Complex passwords that mix uppercase, lowercase, numbers, and special characters can normally beat this type of attack, because these words won't be in the dictionary.

A brute force attack attempts all possible character combinations. Complex passwords of at least eight characters thwart a brute force attack, since it takes too long for it to succeed.

Cryptanalysis attacks exploit vulnerabilities with the cryptography used to protect the password. For example, L0phtcrack exploits the weak cryptographic methods used by LANMAN passwords. Chapter 10 presents information on LANMAN, including its vulnerabilities.

Hash attacks will attack the hash of a password instead of the password. Chapter 1 introduced hashing and, as a reminder, a hash is simply a number created with a hashing algorithm such as MD5 or SHA1. A system can use a hashing algorithm such as MD5 or SHA1 to create a hash of a password. Instead of sending the password over the network, or storing the password on the system, a system sends or stores the hash. When hashes are used, the password cracker attempts to identify the actual password using the hash.

This can be very time consuming, but rainbow tables speed up the process by using precalculated lookup tables. A rainbow table is a huge database of hashes created from hashing different character combinations. A password cracker can compare an intercepted hash with hashes in the rainbow table to discover the original password.

It helps to review the process of how comparative analysis works in a password attack without a rainbow table.

1. The attacker intercepts or discovers the hash of the original password.
2. The attacker guesses a password.
3. The attacker hashes the guess.
4. The attacker compares the original password hash with the guessed password hash. If they are the same, the attacker knows the password.
5. If they aren't the same, the attacker repeats steps 2 through 4 until a match is found.

In a rainbow table attack, the rainbow table includes precalculated hashes in a lookup table. Some rainbow tables are as large as 160 GB in size and they include hashes for every possible combination of characters up to eight characters in length. Larger rainbow tables are also available.

When the rainbow table is used, the password cracker doesn't need to take the time-consuming and processor-intensive step of hashing a guessed password (step 3). Instead, the password cracker simply compares the original password hash against all the hashes in the lookup table. If a match occurs, the attacker has the original password (or at least text that can reproduce the hash of the original password).

Remember this

Password-cracking tools can check the security of password-protected files. Attackers use rainbow tables to crack weak passwords.

Admittedly, this is a simplistic explanation of a rainbow table attack, but it is adequate if you don't plan on writing the algorithm to create your own rainbow table attack software.

Rainbow table attacks are successful against hashes of plain-text passwords. Passwords that are hashed with random bits, known as a salt, prevent this attack. Additionally, encrypting and then hashing the password will defeat a rainbow table attack.

Many password-cracking tools are available. Password crackers use different forms of comparative analysis to discover or crack a password. Some of the popular password crackers are:

- **John the Ripper**—Can crack passwords on multiple platforms. It's often used to detect weak passwords.
- **Cain and Abel**—Commonly used to discover passwords on Windows systems; can sniff the network and use dictionary, brute force, and cryptanalysis attacks.
- **Ophcrack**—Used to crack passwords on Windows systems through the use of rainbow tables.
- **Airsnort**—Can discover WEP keys used on 802.11 wireless networks.
- **Aircrack**—Used for both WEP and WPA cracking on 802.11 wireless networks.
- **L0phtCrack**—Can crack passwords on older Windows systems.

Monitoring Logs

Logs have the capability to record what happened, when it happened, where it happened, and who did it. One of the primary purposes of logging is to allow someone, such as an administrator or security professional, to identify exactly what happened and when.

With this in mind, it's tempting to set up logging to record every event and provide as much detail as possible—most logs support a verbose mode that will log additional details. However, a limiting factor is the amount of disk space available. Additionally, when logging is enabled, there is an implied responsibility to review the logs. The more you choose to log, the more you may have to review.

Operating System Logs

Operating systems have basic logs that record events. For example, Windows systems have several common logs that record what happened on a Windows computer system. All of these logs are viewable in the Event Viewer, and Figure 8.2 shows the Event Viewer from a Windows 7 system.

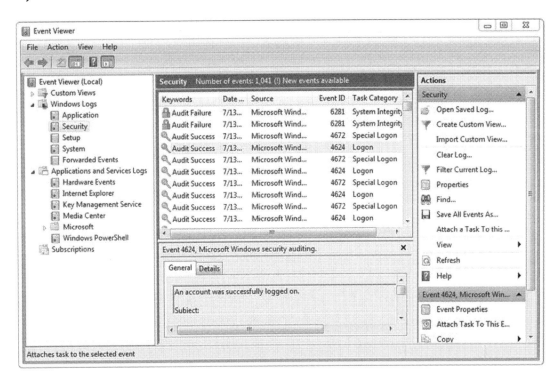

Figure 8.2: Event Viewer

There is a wealth of logs that you can view from Event Viewer, but the important logs from a security perspective are:

- **Security**. The Security log records auditable events, such as when a user logs on or off, or when a user accesses a resource. Some auditing is enabled by default in some systems, but administrators can add additional auditing. The Security log will record details such as who did something, when he did it, what he did, and where.

- **Application**. The Application log records events recorded by applications or programs running on the system. Any application has the capability of recording errors in the Application log.
- **System**. The operating system uses the System log to record events related to the functioning of the operating system. This can include when it starts, when it shuts down, information on services starting and stopping, drivers loading or failing, or any other system component event deemed important by the system developers.

If a system is attacked, you may be able to learn details of the attack by reviewing the operating system logs. Depending on the type of the attack, any of the operating system logs may be useful.

> ### Remember this
>
> Windows logs continuously record information that can be useful in troubleshooting and gaining information on attacks. The Security log records auditable events such as when a user logs on or off, or when a user accesses a resource. The system log includes system events such as when services start and stop. Logs stored in a central location provide protection against attacks.

The Security log includes entries for audited events, such as when someone logs on or off, or accesses a file. Audited events are recorded as success or failure. Success indicates an audited event completed successfully, such as a user successfully logging on or successfully deleting a file. Failure indicates that a user tried to perform an action but failed, such as failing to log on or trying to delete a file but receiving a permission error instead.

Other Logs

In addition to the basic operating system logs, many other logs are available to provide additional information.

- **Firewall logs**. Firewall logs can log all traffic that is blocked or allowed. You can check firewall logs to detect intrusions or attacks, such as port sniffing attacks, or simply to record traffic through the firewall.
- **Antivirus logs**. Antivirus logs will log all antivirus activity including when scans were run and if any malware was detected. These logs will also identify if malware was removed or quarantined.
- **Application logs**. Many server applications include logging capabilities within the application. For example, database applications such as Microsoft SQL Server or Oracle Database include logs to record performance and user activity.
- **Performance logs**. Performance logs can monitor system performance and give an alert when preset performance thresholds are exceeded.

Reviewing Logs

Logs provide the ability to review activity, but ironically, this is often the most overlooked step in the auditing process. Often, administrators only dig into the logs when a symptom appears. Unfortunately, symptoms often don't appear until a problem has snowballed out of control.

Many third-party programs are available that can automate the review of logs for large organizations. For example, NetIQ has a full suite of applications that monitor multiple computers and servers in a network. When an event occurs, NetIQ examines the event to determine if it is an event of interest. If so, it triggers a programmed response, such as sending an e-mail to a group of administrators.

Another benefit of a third-party program like this is that it provides centralized log management. If a system is attacked and compromised, the logs stored on the log server are retained. As a reminder, attackers often try to erase or modify logs after the attack. Centralized log management reduces the success of these attempts.

OVAL

The Open Vulnerability and Assessment Language (OVAL) is an international standard used to rate the exposure of vulnerabilities. The goal is to standardize the assessment process and reporting used by vulnerability scanners and assessment tools. The National Cyber Security Division of the United States Department of Homeland Security funds OVAL research.

OVAL isn't a vulnerability assessment tool itself. Instead, it's a standard used by vulnerability assessment tools. As a standard, it helps ensure that information reported by different tools provides similar information. OVAL standardizes three steps in the assessment process:

1. Collecting system characteristics and configuration information of a system
2. Analyzing the system to determine the current state
3. Reporting the results

Chapter 8 Exam Topic Review

When preparing for the exam, make sure you understand these key concepts covered in this chapter.

Threats, Vulnerabilities, and Risks

- A threat is a potential danger that can compromise confidentiality, integrity, or availability of data or a system. A vulnerability is a weakness. A risk is the likelihood that a threat will exploit a vulnerability.
- Risk management attempts to reduce risk to a level that an organization is able to accept. Senior management is responsible for managing risk and the losses associated from residual risk.

- You cannot eliminate risk. Risk management methods include risk avoidance, transference, acceptance, mitigation, and deterrence. You avoid a risk by not providing a service or participating in a risky activity. Purchasing insurance transfers the risk to another entity. Security controls mitigate or reduce a risk. Some controls such as security guards deter a risk.
- Quantitative risk assessments use numbers, such as costs and asset values. The single loss expectancy (SLE) is the cost of any single loss. The annualized rate of occurrence (ARO) indicates how many times the loss will occur annually. The annualized loss expectancy (ALE) is calculated as SLE x ARO.
- Qualitative risk assessments use judgments to prioritize risks based on probability and impact. These judgments provide a subjective ranking.
- Risk assessment results are sensitive. Only executives and security professionals should be granted access to risk assessment reports.

Checking for Vulnerabilities

- Vulnerability scanners passively test security controls to identify vulnerabilities, a lack of security controls, and common misconfigurations. They are effective at discovering systems susceptible to an attack without exploiting the systems. A vulnerability scan will not negatively affect normal operations or user activity.
- Nmap, Netcat, and Nessus are three common vulnerability scanners. They can detect open ports, identify security and configuration errors, identify missing patches, discover weak passwords, and more.
- A penetration test is an active test that attempts to exploit discovered vulnerabilities. It starts with a vulnerability scan and then bypasses or actively tests security controls to exploit vulnerabilities. Since it can compromise a system, it can test how well employees respond to a compromised system.
- A significant difference between a vulnerability scan and a penetration test is that a vulnerability scan is passive, and a penetration test is active. The vulnerability scan identifies the vulnerabilities and the penetration test demonstrates the result of exploiting the vulnerabilities.
- Data exfiltration tests attempt to extract data from a system. They will normally attempt privilege escalation after gaining access to a system.
- In black box testing, testers perform a penetration test with zero prior knowledge of the environment. White box testing indicates that the testers have full knowledge of the environment including documentation and source code for tested applications. Gray box testing indicates some knowledge of the environment.
- Black box testing often uses fuzzing to test applications. Fuzzing sends random data to an application and can interfere with operations but it can only detect simple faults.
- Black hat indicates a malicious attacker, while white hat identifies a security professional working within the law.
- Penetration testers should gain consent prior to starting a penetration test. A rules-of-engagement document identifies the boundaries of the test.

Security Tools

- Routine audits help an organization verify they are following their own policies.
- A user rights and permission review is a system audit. It verifies that users have appropriate privileges and no more. It also verifies that inactive accounts are disabled.
- Protocol analyzers (sniffers) can capture and analyze data sent over a network. You can examine IP headers in the packet. You can also read any data sent in clear text to identify data sent across the network. Attackers can use these to capture passwords sent in clear text.
- A password cracker can discover, recover, or bypass passwords. This includes passwords sent over the network, passwords used for authentication, passwords used to secure files such as WinZip archives, and more.
- Security logs track logon and logoff activity on systems. System logs identify when services start and stop.
- Centralized log management protects logs when systems are attacked or compromised.

Chapter 8 Practice Questions

1. An organization has purchased fire insurance to manage the risk of a potential fire. What method are they using?
    A. Risk acceptance
    B. Risk avoidance
    C. Risk deterrence
    D. Risk mitigation
    E. Risk transference

2. What is included in a risk assessment? (Choose three.)
    A. Threats
    B. Vulnerabilities
    C. Asset values
    D. Recommendations to eliminate risk

3. Which of the following statements are true regarding risk assessments? (Choose two.)
    A. A quantitative risk assessment uses hard numbers.
    B. A qualitative risk assessment uses hard numbers.
    C. A qualitative risk assessment uses a subjective ranking.
    D. A quantitative risk assessment uses a subjective ranking.

4. A security professional is performing a qualitative risk analysis. Of the following choices, what will most likely to be used in the assessment?
    A. Cost
    B. Judgment
    C. ALE
    D. Hard numbers

5. An organization recently completed a risk assessment. Who should be granted access to the report?
    A. All employees
    B. Security professionals only
    C. Executive management only
    D. Security professionals and executive management

6. A security administrator is performing a vulnerability assessment. Which of the following actions would be included?
    A. Implement a password policy
    B. Delete unused accounts
    C. Organize data based on severity and asset value
    D. Remove system rights for users that don't need them

7. An organization has released an application. Of the following choices, what is the most thorough way to discover vulnerabilities with the application?

    A. Fuzzing

    B. OVAL comparison

    C. Rainbow table

    D. Code review

8. You are trying to determine what systems on your network are most susceptible to an attack. What tool would you use?

    A. Port scanner

    B. SQL injection

    C. Header manipulation

    D. Vulnerability scanner

9. A security administrator used a tool to discover security issues but did not exploit them. What best describes this action?

    A. Penetration test

    B. Vulnerability scan

    C. Protocol analysis

    D. Port scan

10. An administrator needs to test the security of a network without affecting normal operations. What can the administrator use?

    A. Internal penetration test

    B. External penetration test

    C. Vulnerability scanner

    D. Protocol analyzer

11. A security administrator wants to scan the network for a wide range of potential security and configuration issues. What tool provides this service?

    A. Fuzzer

    B. Protocol analyzer

    C. Port scanner

    D. Vulnerability scanner

12. Which of the following tools can perform a port scan? (Choose all that apply.)

    A. Nmap

    B. Netcat

    C. Wireshark

    D. Netstat

13. A security professional is performing a penetration test on a system. Of the following choices, what identifies the best description of what this will accomplish?
    A. Passively detect vulnerabilities
    B. Actively assess security controls
    C. Identify lack of security controls
    D. Identify common misconfiguration

14. An organization is hiring a security firm to perform vulnerability testing. What should it define before the testing?
    A. Rules of engagement
    B. Information given to the black box testers
    C. Vulnerabilities
    D. Existing security controls

15. An organization wants to test how well employees can respond to a compromised system. Of the following choices, what identifies the best choice to test the response?
    A. Vulnerability scan
    B. White hat test
    C. Black hat test
    D. Penetration test

16. Testers have access to product documentation and source code for an application that they are using in a vulnerability test. What type of test is this?
    A. Black box
    B. White box
    C. Black hat
    D. White hat

17. A tester is fuzzing an application. What is another name for this?
    A. Black box testing
    B. White box testing
    C. Gray box testing
    D. Black hat testing

18. Of the following choices, what is an example of a system audit?
    A. Separation of duties
    B. User rights and permissions review
    C. Whaling
    D. Smurf review

19. After a recent security incident, a security administrator discovered someone used an enabled account of an ex-employee to access data in the Sales Department. What should be done to prevent this in the future?

    A. Modify the security policy to disable all accounts in the Sales Department

    B. Vulnerability scans

    C. Port scans

    D. User access review

20. What can you use to examine IP headers in a data packet?

    A. Protocol analyzer

    B. Port scanner

    C. Vulnerability scanner

    D. Penetration tester

21. What can you use to examine text transmitted over a network by an application?

    A. Honeypot

    B. Honeynet

    C. Protocol analyzer

    D. Vulnerability scanner

22. An administrator suspects that a computer is sending out large amounts of sensitive data to an external system. What tool can the administrator use to verify this?

    A. Rainbow table

    B. Protocol analyzer

    C. Password cracker

    D. Port scanner

23. An administrator suspects that a web application is sending database credentials across the network in clear text. What can the administrator use to verify this?

    A. SQL injection

    B. Protocol analyzer

    C. A network-based DLP

    D. Password cracker

24. Sally used WinZip to create an archive of several sensitive documents on an upcoming merger, and she password-protected the archive file. Of the following choices, what is the best way to test the security of the archive file?

    A. Rainbow table

    B. Vulnerability scanner

    C. Password cracker

    D. Sniffer

25. You want to check a log to determine when a user logged on and off of a system. What log would you check?

   A. System
   B. Application
   C. Firewall
   D. Security

Chapter 8 Practice Question Answers

1. **E.** Purchasing insurance is a common method of risk transference. Organizations often accept a risk when the cost of the control exceeds the cost of the risk. An organization can avoid a risk by not providing a service or not participating in a risky activity. Risk deterrence attempts to discourage attacks with preventative controls such as a security guard. Risk mitigation reduces risks through internal controls.

2. **A, B, C.** A risk assessment identifies assets, asset values, threats, and vulnerabilities. It prioritizes the results and makes recommendations on what controls to implement. Risk cannot be eliminated.

3. **A, C.** A quantitative risk assessment uses hard numbers (such as costs) and a qualitative risk assessment uses a subjective ranking based on judgments. A qualitative risk assessment does not use hard numbers and a quantitative risk assessment does not use subjective rankings.

4. **B.** A qualitative risk assessment uses judgment to categorize risks based on probability and impact. A quantitative risk assessment uses hard numbers such as costs and asset values. A quantitative risk assessment uses annual loss expectancy (ALE).

5. **D.** Executive management needs access to the report to approve controls. and security professionals need access to the report to implement the controls. The report has sensitive data and should not be released to all employees.

6. **C.** The vulnerability assessment is prioritized based on the severity of the vulnerabilities and their ability to affect the high value asset items. A vulnerability assessment checks for the existence of security controls such as a password policy and can include a user rights and access review to identify unused accounts, or accounts with unneeded permissions. However, a vulnerability assessment identifies these issues, but does not make changes.

7. **D.** A code review is a line-by-line examination of the code to discover vulnerabilities and is the most thorough of the choices. Fuzzing sends random data to an application to identify vulnerabilities, but it will generally only find simple problems and isn't as thorough as a code review. The Open Vulnerability and Assessment Language (OVAL) is an international standard used to rate the exposure of vulnerabilities, but doesn't discover them. A rainbow table is a lookup table used to crack weak passwords.

8. **D.** A vulnerability scanner can scan systems for vulnerabilities and determine which ones are most susceptible to an attack. A port scanner scans a system for open ports and helps identify what services are running. SQL injection is a narrow attack on databases, but it would not check all systems. Attackers can manipulate headers in TCP packets for specific attacks, but this isn't as useful as a vulnerability scanner.

9. **B.** A vulnerability scan attempts to discover vulnerabilities but does not exploit them. A penetration test actively tests security controls by trying to exploit vulnerabilities. A protocol analyzer can capture and analyze IP packets but isn't as useful as a vulnerability scanner to discover security issues. A port scanner will identify open ports but won't identify security issues.

10. **C.** A vulnerability scanner will test the security of the network without affecting users. A penetration test (external or internal) is active and can affect users. A protocol analyzer can capture and analyze IP packets but won't test the security of a network.

11. **D.** A vulnerability scanner is a management control that can identify a wide range of security and configuration issues. A fuzzer is an active tool that sends random data to a system and can potentially result in an outage. A protocol analyzer can capture and analyze IP packets, and a port scanner can identify open ports. However, the question is asking for a tool that can scan the network for a wide range of issues, and vulnerability scanners can do more than either a protocol analyzer or a port scanner.

12. **A, B.** Nmap and Netcat are two tools that can perform port scans and vulnerability scans. Wireshark is a protocol analyzer and can view headers and clear-text contents in IP packets. Netstat is a command-line tool that identifies open connections.

13. **B.** A penetration test will actively assess or test security controls. A vulnerability scan is passive and detects vulnerabilities, identifies a lack of security controls, and identifies common misconfigurations but it stops there. Further, the three incorrect answers are specifically listed under vulnerability scanning in the objectives. While a penetration test starts with a passive vulnerability scan, it goes a step further to actively test the controls.

14. **A.** A rules-of-engagement document identifies boundaries of a test and expectations of the testers, and it provides consent for the testers to perform the test. Black box testers are not given any knowledge prior to the test. The test will help identify vulnerabilities so these aren't defined before the test. It's not required to tell the testers what security controls are in place.

15. **D.** A penetration test will exploit vulnerabilities and will test employees' ability to respond to a compromised system. A vulnerability scan will identify vulnerabilities but not exploit them, so employees won't need to respond. White hat refers to a security professional working within the law, and black hat refers to a malicious attacker, but these aren't tests. Black box testing, white box testing, and gray box testing (not included in the answers) are forms of penetration testing.

16. **B.** In white box testing, testers have access to all of the system details. In a black box test, testers have zero knowledge of system details. Black hat identifies a malicious attacker, while white hat identifies a security professional working within the bounds of the law.

17. **A.** Fuzzing sends random data to an application and is sometimes referred to as black box testing. White box and gray box testing have some knowledge of the application and can test the

application with specific data rather than random data. Black hat refers to a malicious attacker not a tester, though a black hat attacker can use a fuzzer.

18. **B.** Reviewing user rights and permissions is an example of a system audit. Separation of duties prevents any one person or entity from completing all the functions of a critical or sensitive process, and helps to prevent fraud, theft, and errors. Whaling is a form of phishing that targets high-level executives. Smurf is a type of attack that can be detected with a NIDS.

19. **D.** A user rights and access review will detect inactive accounts and accounts with more permissions than they require. Normally, a security policy will direct that accounts are disabled or deleted when an employee leaves, but isn't appropriate to disable all accounts for a department. Neither vulnerability scans nor port scans can detect if an account is for a current or previous employee.

20. **A.** You can use a protocol analyzer (sniffer) to view headers and clear-text contents in IP packets. A port scanner can detect open ports. A vulnerability scanner will passively identify vulnerabilities and a penetration will actively try to exploit vulnerabilities, and even though some may examine IP headers, not all of them do.

21. **C.** You can use a protocol analyzer (sniffer) to view headers and clear-text contents in IP packets. A honeypot is a system used to divert an attacker from a live network, and a honeynet is a group of honeypots. A vulnerability scanner will passively identify vulnerabilities but doesn't always include the ability examine transmitted text.

22. **B.** A protocol analyzer can capture packets and view the contents, including data sent across the network. A rainbow table is a lookup table used by password crackers, and a password cracker cracks passwords. A port scanner identifies open ports on a system.

23. **B.** A protocol analyzer can capture packets and view the contents, including credentials sent across the network in clear text. SQL injection is an attack against a database through an application that isn't using input validation. A network-based Data Loss Prevention (DLP) system can examine and analyze e-mail and detect if confidential company data is included. A password cracker cracks passwords that are protected, not that are sent in clear text.

24. **C.** A password cracker can attempt to crack the password of a password-protected file and is the best choice here. Some password crackers use a rainbow table, but it can't be used by itself. A vulnerability scanner can scan for vulnerabilities, but it won't necessarily be able to check for a password used to protect an archive file. You can use a sniffer (protocol analyzer) to view headers and clear-text contents in IP packets.

25. **D.** The Security log records auditable events such as user logons and logoffs. The System log records system such as when a service stops and starts. The Application log records events from individual applications. A firewall log can record what traffic is passed and what traffic is blocked.

Chapter 9

Preparing for Business Continuity

CompTIA Security+ objectives covered in this chapter:

1.1 Explain the security function and purpose of network devices and technologies

- Load balancers

2.2 Carry out appropriate risk mitigation strategies

- Implement policies and procedures to prevent data loss or theft

2.5 Compare and contrast aspects of business continuity

- Business impact analysis
- Removing single points of failure
- Business continuity planning and testing
- Continuity of operations
- Disaster recovery
- IT contingency planning
- Succession planning

2.6 Explain the impact and proper use of environmental controls

- HVAC
- Fire suppression
- EMI shielding
- Hot and cold aisles
- Environmental monitoring
- Temperature and humidity controls

2.7 Execute disaster recovery plans and procedures

- Backup/backout contingency plans or policies
- Backups, execution, and frequency
- Redundancy and fault tolerance
  - Hardware
  - RAID

- - Clustering
  - Load balancing
  - Servers
- High availability
- Cold site, hot site, warm site
- Mean time to restore, mean time between failures, recovery time objectives, and recovery point objectives

2.8 Exemplify the concepts of confidentiality, integrity, and availability (CIA)

3.6 Analyze and differentiate among types of mitigation and deterrent techniques

- Manual bypassing of electronic controls (failsafe/secure vs. failopen)

While you can't prevent some disasters, such as hurricanes or floods, you can prevent catastrophic failures by taking preventative steps. You can identify single points of failure, implement redundancy solutions, and perform backups. Many organizations use formal business continuity and disaster recovery plans to prepare for potential disasters. This chapter covers these concepts and some key environmental controls.

Designing Redundancy

One of the constants with computers, subsystems, and networks is that they will fail. It's one of the few things you can count on. It's not a matter of if they will fail, but when. However, by designing redundancy into your systems and networks, you can increase the reliability of your systems even when they fail. By increasing reliability, you increase one of the core security goals: availability.

Redundancy adds duplication to critical system components and networks and provides fault tolerance. If a critical component has a fault, the duplication provided by the redundancy allows the service to continue as if a fault never occurred. In other words, a system with fault tolerance can suffer a fault, but it can tolerate it and continue to operate. Organizations often add redundancies to eliminate single points of failure.

You can add redundancies at multiple levels:

- Disk redundancies using RAID
- Server redundancies by adding failover clusters
- Power redundancies by adding generators or UPS
- Site redundancies by adding hot, cold, or warm sites

Single Point of Failure

A single point of failure is a component within a system that can cause the entire system to fail if the component fails. When designing redundancies, an organization will examine different components to determine if they are a single point of failure. If so, they take steps to provide a redundancy or fault tolerance capability. The goal is to increase reliability and availability of the systems.

Some examples of single points of failure include:

- **Disk**. If a server uses a single drive, the system will crash if the single drive fails. Redundant Array of Independent Disks (RAID) provides fault tolerance for hard drives.
- **Server**. If a server provides a critical service and its failure halts the service, it is a single point of failure. Failover clusters (discussed later in this chapter) provide fault tolerance for critical servers.
- **Power**. If an organization only has one source of power for critical systems, the power is a single point of failure. However, elements such as uninterrupted power supplies (UPS) and power generators provide fault tolerance for power outages.

While IT personnel recognize the risks with single points of failure, they often overlook them until a disaster occurs. However, tools such as business continuity plans (covered later in this chapter) help an organization identify critical services and address single points of failure.

> ### Remember this
>
> A single point of failure is any component whose failure results in the failure of an entire system. Elements such as RAID, failover clustering, UPS, and generators remove many single points of failure. Single points of failure are often overlooked until a disaster occurs.

Disk Redundancies

Any system has four primary resources: processor, memory, disk, and the network interface. Of these, the disk is the slowest and most susceptible to failure. Because of this, administrators often upgrade disk subsystems to improve their performance and redundancy.

Redundant Array of Independent (or Inexpensive) Disks (RAID) subsystems provide fault tolerance for disks and increase the system availability. Even if a disk fails, most RAID subsystems can tolerate the failure and the system will continue to operate. RAID systems are becoming much more affordable as the price of drives steadily falls and disk capacity steadily increases.

> ### Remember this
>
> RAID subsystems, such as RAID-1 and RAID-5, provide increased availability for systems. RAID-1 uses two disks as a mirror. RAID-5 uses three or more disks using striping with parity.

RAID-0

RAID-0 (striping) is somewhat of a misnomer, since it doesn't provide any redundancy or fault tolerance. It includes two or more physical disks. Files stored on a RAID-0 array are spread across each of the disks.

The benefit of a RAID-0 is increased read and write performance. Because a file is spread across multiple physical disks, the different parts of the file can be read from or written to each of the disks at the same time. If you have three 500 GB drives used in a RAID-0, you have 1500 GB (1.5 TB) of storage space.

RAID-1

RAID-1 (mirroring) uses two disks. Data written to one disk is also written to the other disk. If one of the disks fails, the other disk still has all the data, so the system can continue to operate without any data loss. With this in mind, if you mirror all the drives in a system, you can actually lose half of the drives and continue to operate.

You can add an additional disk controller to a RAID-1 configuration to remove the disk controller as a single point of failure. In other words, each of the disks also has its own disk controller. Adding a second disk controller to a mirror is called disk duplexing.

If you have two 500 GB drives used in a RAID-1, you have 500 GB of storage space. The other 500 GB of storage space is dedicated to the fault-tolerant, mirrored volume.

RAID-5

A RAID-5 is three or more disks that are striped together similar to RAID-0. However, the equivalent of one drive includes parity information. This parity information is striped across each of the drives in a RAID-5 and is used for fault tolerance.

If one of the drives fails, the system can read the information on the remaining drives and determine what the actual data should be. If two of the drives fail in a RAID-5, the data is lost.

If you have three 500 GB drives used in a RAID-5, you have 1000 GB of storage space and 500 GB of space dedicated to parity. The equivalent of one drive (500 GB in this example) is dedicated to fault tolerance. If you striped five 500 GB drives in a RAID-5, you'd have 2000 GB of data storage space and 500 GB of parity space. Using the minimum of three drives, you lose 33 percent of your drives space. Using five drives you only lose 20 percent of your drive space. The more drives you have in a RAID 5 configuration, the more efficient it becomes in terms of available drive space.

RAID-10

A RAID-10 configuration combines the features of mirroring (RAID-1) and striping (RAID-0). RAID-10 is sometimes called RAID 1+0. A variation is RAID-01 or RAID 0+1 that also combines the features of mirroring and striping but implements the drives a little differently.

Software vs. Hardware RAID

Hardware RAID configurations are significantly better than software RAID. In hardware RAID, dedicated hardware manages the disks in the RAID removing the load from the operating system. In contrast, the operating system manages the disks in the RAID array in software RAID. Hardware RAID systems provide better overall performance and often include extra features.

For example, a hardware RAID may include five physical disks using three in an active RAID-5 configuration and two as online spares. If one of the active disks in the RAID-5 fails, the RAID will continue to operate, since a RAID-5 can tolerate the failure.

However, a hardware RAID can logically take the failed disk out of the configuration, add one of the online spares into the configuration, and rebuild the array. All of this happens without any administrator intervention. Hardware RAID systems are often hot swappable, allowing you to swap out the failed drive without powering the system down.

Server Redundancy

For some services, it's desirable to achieve 99.999 percent uptime, called five nines. This provides an extremely high level of availability. It equates to less than six minutes of downtime a year: $60 \times 24 \times 365 \times .00001 = 5.256$ minutes. Failover clusters are a key component used to achieve five nines.

While five nines is achievable, it's often expensive. However, if the potential cost of an outage is high, the high cost of the redundant technologies is justified. For example, some websites generate a significant amount of revenue, and every minute a website is unavailable represents lost money. High-capacity failover clusters ensure the service is always available even if a server fails.

Failover Clusters

The primary purpose of a failover cluster is to provide high availability for a service offered by a server. Failover clusters use two or more servers in a cluster configuration, and the servers are referred to as nodes. At least one server or node is active and at least one is inactive. If an active node fails, the inactive node can take over the load without interruption to clients.

> ### Remember this
> Failover clusters provide high availability for servers. They can remove a server as a single point of failure.

Consider Figure 9.1, which shows a two-node failover cluster. Both nodes are individual servers, and they both have access to external data storage used by the active server. Additionally, the two nodes have a monitoring connection to each other used to check the health or heartbeat of each other.

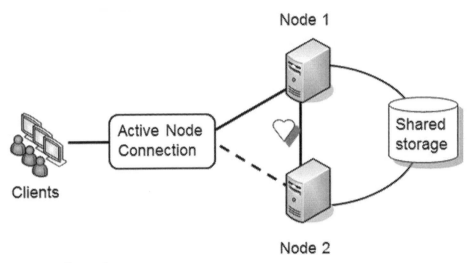

Figure 9.1: Failover cluster

Imagine that Node 1 is the active node. When any of the clients connect, the cluster software (installed on both nodes) ensures that the clients connect to the active node. If Node 1 fails, Node 2 senses the failure through the heartbeat connection and configures itself as the active node. Since both nodes have access to the shared storage, there is no loss of data for the client. Clients may notice a momentary hiccup or pause, but the service continues.

You may notice that the shared storage in Figure 9.1 represents a single point of failure. It's not uncommon for this to be a robust hardware RAID-5. This ensures that even if a hard drive in the shared storage fails, the service will continue.

Cluster configurations can include many more nodes than just two. Nodes need to have close to identical hardware and are often quite expensive. However, if a company truly needs to achieve 99.999 percent uptime, it's worth the expense.

Load Balancers

Chapter 3 introduced load balancers. As a reminder, a load balancer optimizes and distributes loads across multiple servers or networks. When servers are load balanced, it's called a load-balanced cluster.

The term *load balancer* makes it sound like it's a piece of hardware, but a load balancer can be hardware or software. A hardware-based load balancer accepts traffic and directs it to servers based on factors such as processor utilization and the number of current connections to the server. A software-based load balancer uses software running on each of the servers in the load-balanced cluster to balance the load.

Load balancing primarily provides scalability, but it also contributes to high availability. Scalability refers to the ability of a service to serve more clients without any decrease in performance. Availability ensures that systems are up and operational when needed

Consider a web server that can serve one hundred clients per minute, but if more than one hundred clients connect at a time, performance degrades. You need to either scale up or scale out to serve more clients. You scale the server up by adding additional resources, such as processors and memory, and you scale out by adding additional servers in a load balancer.

Some load balancers simply send new clients to the servers in a round-robin fashion. The load balancer sends the first client to Server 1, the second client to Server 2, and so on. Other load balancers will automatically detect the load on individual servers and send new clients to the least used server.

An added benefit of many load balancers is that they can detect when a server fails. If a server stops responding, the load balancing software no longer sends clients to this server. This contributes to overall high availability for the load balancer.

Power Redundancies

Power is a critical utility to consider when reviewing any disaster preparedness plan. For highly critical systems, you can use uninterruptible power supplies and generators to provide fault tolerance and high availability.

UPS

An uninterruptible power supply (UPS) is a battery or bank of batteries used as a backup in case of primary power failure. The UPS plugs into the wall and receives power from the commercial source, as shown in Figure 9.2. The commercial power keeps the batteries charged and electronics within the UPS system provides power to external systems.

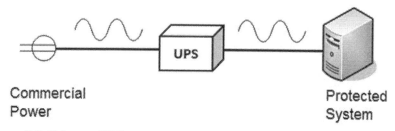

Commercial Power

Protected System

Figure 9.2: Using an UPS system

During normal operation, commercial power provides power to the system through the UPS. When commercial power fails, the UPS will continue to provide power. One of the benefits of an UPS system is that it can protect against power fluctuations. Even if commercial power has momentary fluctuations, external systems aren't affected because they receive their power directly from the UPS.

> **Remember this**
>
> An uninterruptible power supply (UPS) provides fault tolerance for power and can protect against power fluctuations. UPS provides short-term power. Generators provide long-term power in extended outages.

Common UPS systems provide power for ten to fifteen minutes after a power outage. They aren't meant to provide longer-term power. Instead, the goal is to provide power until one of the following events occurs:

- **The supported system has enough time to shut down**. For example, a ten-minute UPS may send a shutdown signal to a system after power has been lost for five minutes. The system now has five minutes to perform an orderly shutdown.
- **Generators have enough time to power up and stabilize**. Both UPS and generators support critical systems. The UPS provides short-term power, and the generator provides long-term power.
- **Commercial power returns**. An UPS provides fault tolerance for short outages and momentary power fluctuations. When commercial power returns, it will recharge the batteries to get them back to full potential.

Generators

For critical systems that need long-term power, generators can be used and diesel generators are common. It isn't feasible to keep the generators running all the time due to fuel costs. Instead, they are started when power fails. Since it takes time for a generator to rev up to full power and stabilize, it cannot provide AC power immediately. An UPS will power critical systems until the generators stabilize.

In some cases, generators automatically turn on when power is lost. In other cases, technicians power up the generators manually. Some systems exist that can sense when the generator is stabilized and automatically switch over to generator power. Once the generator power stabilizes, power is switched from UPS to the generators.

Protecting Data with Backups

Backups are copies of data created to ensure that if the original data is lost or corrupted, it can be restored. Maybe I should restate that. Backups are copies of data created to ensure that *when* the original data is lost or corrupted, it can be restored.

The truth is, if you work with computers long enough, you will lose data. The difference between a major catastrophe and a minor inconvenience is the existence of a backup.

It's important to realize that redundancy and backups are not the same thing. Protecting data with a RAID-1 or RAID-5 does not negate the need for backups. If a fire destroys a server, it also destroys the data on the RAID. Without a backup, all of the data is gone. An effective backup strategy includes some type of off-site storage of the backups. If a fire destroys a building and all the backups are in the building, the data is destroyed. Forever.

A Backup Horror Story

A friend of mine did consulting for small businesses and was once hired to help a small business owner recover some lost data. The owner had been growing his business for about five years and had just about everything related to his business (client lists, billing information, proposals, agreements, and more) on one system. This system crashed.

The consultant tried to restore information from the disk but couldn't restore any data. The business owner panicked, knowing he simply needed the information. If he couldn't get the data back, his business might fail.

Although it's expensive, it is possible to have a clean-room facility take a hard drive apart and read the data at the bit level to restore at least some of the data. At this point, the owner was willing to try anything, so he paid the high price and they sent the disk to a recovery facility. Unfortunately, the disk suffered a catastrophic failure, and they weren't able to retrieve any meaningful data even in the clean room.

My friend visited the owner to relay the bad news. He said that when he left, the owner had his head in his hands and was literally crying. The business he had built for five years was close to ruins without much chance for recovery.

The worst part of this story is that it's repeated over and over with many different people in many different environments. As an example of a larger scale disaster, MegaPetCo was a small chain of pet stores enjoying success when a single failure bankrupted them in 2009. An administrator accidentally performed a bulk update that deleted all data in their primary database. There were zero backups. Within a few months, they filed for bankruptcy, closed all their stores, and laid off several hundred employees.

Too many people don't recognize the importance of backups until they've lost their data. Unfortunately, by then, it's too late.

Backup Types

Backup utilities support several different types of backups. While third-party backup programs can be quite sophisticated in what they do and how they do it, you should have a solid understanding of the basics.

The most common media used for backups is tape. Tapes store more data and are cheaper than other media, though some organizations use disks for backups. However, the type of media doesn't affect the backup type.

The following backup types are the most common:

- **Full backups**. A full (or normal backup) backs up all the selected data.
- **Differential backup**. This backs up all the data that has changed since the last full backup.
- **Incremental backup**. This backs up all data that has changed since the last full or incremental backup.

Full Backups

A full backup will back up all data specified in the backup. For example, you could have several folders on the D: drive. If you specify these folders in the backup program, the backup program will back up all the data in these folders.

While it's possible to do a full backup on a daily basis, this is not done very often. This is because of two limiting factors:

- **Time**. A full backup can take several hours to complete and can interrupt with operations. However, administrators don't always have unlimited time to do backups and other maintenance. For example, if a system is online 24/7, administrators may need to limit the amount of time for full backups to early Sunday morning to minimize the impact on users.
- **Money**. Backups need to be stored on some type of media, such as tape or hard drives. Daily full backups require more media, and the cost can be prohibitive.

Instead, organizations often combine full backups with differential or incremental backups. However, every backup strategy must start with a full backup.

Restoring a Full Backup

A full backup is the easiest and quickest to restore. You only need to restore the single full backup and you're done. If you store backups on tapes, you only need to restore a single tape. However, most organizations need to balance time and money and use either a full/differential or full/incremental backup strategy.

Remember this

If you have unlimited time and money, the full backup alone provides the fastest recovery time. Full/differential and full/incremental strategies reduce the amount of time and resources needed for backups.

Differential Backups

A differential backup strategy starts with a full backup. After the full backup, differential backups back up data that has changed or is different since the last full backup.

For example, a full/differential strategy could start with a full backup on Sunday night. On Monday night, a differential backup would back up all files that changed since the last full backup on Sunday. On Tuesday night, the differential backup would again back up all the files that changed since the last full backup. This repeats until Sunday, when another full backup starts the process again. As the week progresses, the differential backup steadily grows in size.

Restoring a Full/Differential Backup Set

Assume for a moment that each of the backups was stored on different tapes. If the system crashed on Wednesday morning, how many tapes would you need to recover the data?

The answer is two. You would first recover the full backup from Sunday. Since the differential backup on Tuesday night includes all the files that changed after the last full backup, you would restore that tape to restore all the changes up to Tuesday night.

Incremental Backups

An incremental backup strategy starts with a full backup. After the full backup, incremental backups then back up data that has changed since the last backup.

As an example, a full/incremental strategy could start with a full backup on Sunday night. On Monday night, an incremental backup would back up all the files that changed since the last full backup. On Tuesday night, the incremental backup would back up all files that changed since the incremental backup on Monday night. Similarly, the Wednesday night backup would back up all files that changed since the last incremental backup on Tuesday night. This repeats until Sunday when another full backup starts the process again. As the week progresses, the incremental backups stay about the same size.

Restoring a Full/Incremental Backup Set

Assume for a moment that each of the backups were stored on different tapes. If the system crashed on Thursday morning, how many tapes would you need to recover the data?

The answer is four. You would first need to recover the full backup from Sunday. Since the incremental backups would be backing up different data each day of the week, each of the incremental backups must be restored and in the right order.

Sometimes, people mistakenly think the last incremental backup would have all the relevant data. This isn't true if more than one incremental backup was done.

For example, if you worked on a single project file each day of the week, then only the last incremental backup would hold the most recent copy of this file. However, what if you compiled a report every Monday but didn't touch it again until the following Monday? Only the incremental backup from Monday would include the most recent copy. An incremental backup from Tuesday or another day of the week wouldn't include the report.

Choosing Full/Incremental or Full/Differential

A logical question is, "Why are there so many choices for backups?" The answer is that there are different needs within an organization.

For example, imagine two organizations that perform daily backups to minimize losses. They each do a full backup on Sunday, but are now trying to determine if they should use a full/incremental or a full/differential strategy.

The first organization doesn't have much time to perform maintenance throughout the week. In this case, the backup administrator needs to minimize the amount of time required to complete backups during the week. An incremental backup only backs up the data that has changed since the last backup. In other words, it includes changes only from a single day. In contrast, a differential backup includes all the changes since the last full backup. Backing up the changes from a single day will take less time than backing up changes from multiple days, so a full/incremental backup is the best choice.

In the second organization, recovery of failed systems is more important. If a failure requires restoring data, the recovery time needs to be minimized. A full/differential is the best choice in this situation because it only requires the restoration of two backups, the full and the most recent differential backup. In contrast, a full/incremental can require the restoration of several different backups, depending on when the failure occurs.

Testing Backups

I've heard many horror stories where personnel are regularly performing backups thinking all is well. Ultimately, something happens and they need to restore some data. Unfortunately, they discover that none of the backups holds valid data. People have been going through the motions, but something in the process is flawed.

The only way to validate a backup is to do a test restore. Performing a test restore is nothing more than restoring the data from a backup and verifying its integrity. If you want to verify you can restore the entire backup, you perform a full restore of the backup. If you want to verify that you can restore individual files, you can perform a test restore of individual files. It's common to restore data to a different location other than the original source location, but in such a way that the data can be validated.

As a simple example, an administrator can retrieve a random backup and attempt to restore it. There are two possible outcomes of this test, and both are good.

- **The test succeeds**. Excellent! You know that the backup process works. You don't necessarily know that every backup tape is valid, but at least you know that the process is sound and at least some of your backups work.
- **The test fails**. Excellent! You know there's a problem that you can fix before a crisis. If this was discovered after an actual data loss, you wouldn't be able to fix it in time, but now you can.

An additional benefit of doing regular test restores is that it allows administrators to become familiar with the process. The first time they do a restore shouldn't be in the middle of a crisis with several high-level managers peering over their shoulders.

> ### *Remember this*
> Test restores are the best way to test the integrity of a company's backup data. You can verify that a backup can be recovered in its entirety by performing a full restore as a test. You can verify that individual files can be restored by restoring just the target files.

Protecting Backups

If data is important enough to be backed up, it's important enough to protect. Backup media should be protected at the same level as the data that it holds. In other words, if proprietary data enjoys the highest level of protection within an organization, than backups of this data should also have the highest level of protection.

Protecting backups includes:

- **Storage**. Backups should be protected when stored. This includes clear labeling to identify the data and physical security protection to prevent others from easily accessing it.
- **Transfer**. Data should be protected any time it is transferred from one location to another. This is especially true when transferring a copy of the backup to a separate geographical location.
- **Destruction**. When the backups are no longer needed, they should be adequately destroyed. This can be accomplished by degaussing the media, shredding or burning the media, or scrubbing the media by repeatedly writing varying patterns of 1s and 0s onto the media.

Backup Policies

Ask a manager this question: "How much data are you willing to lose?" The answer is often, "None!" However, the cost to backup and save all data forever can be astronomical. Faced with the bill, the manager is likely to reconsider.

I often consider a pain factor. If I lost some data, how painful would it be? If it's more pain than I want, I ensure the data is backed up. Organizations can use the same philosophy. If they lost some data, what is the impact? Some data is critical while other data would barely be missed if it was lost.

Many organizations create a backup policy to answer critical questions related to backups. The backup policy is a written document and will often include the following details:

- **Data to backup**. This identifies data important enough to back up. When this isn't identified, administrators or technicians have to make individual decisions on what data is important. Their decisions may not match management's value of the data.

- **Off-site backups**. A copy of a backup should be stored in a separate geographical location. This protects against a disaster such as a fire or flood. Even if a disaster destroys the site, they will still have another copy of the critical data.
- **Label media**. Media labels identify the data and the date of the backup. When data needs to be restored, the administrator should be able to quickly identify the backup that holds the data that needs to be restored.
- **Testing**. The policy identifies how often to test backups and the level of testing. For example, the policy may dictate full test restores to ensure that tape backups can be recovered in their entirety.
- **Retention requirements**. How long data is held directly relates to how many tapes the organization must purchase. Laws or regulations may require retention of some data for several years and the organization can choose to limit retention of other data. Some organizations limit the amount of data they keep to reduce potential exposure to future legal proceedings. For example, a court order could direct administrators to comb through e-mail for an investigation. The time spent will be significantly different if the organization kept archives of e-mail from the past year or if it kept archives for the past ten years.
- **Execution and frequency of backups**. The business impact analysis (covered later in this chapter) helps an organization identify backup frequency by identifying Recovery Time Objectives and Recovery Point Objectives. This also helps determine the backup strategy, such as a full/incremental or full/differential strategy.
- **Protect backups**. Backup media is handled with the same level of protection as the original data. If an attacker gets a copy of a backup, it's a simple matter to restore it and access all the data.
- **Disposing of media**. Backup media such as tapes holds a significant amount of information. Organizations often require the sanitation or destruction of tapes at the end of their life cycle. For example, you can erase all the data on a tape by degaussing it. A degausser is essentially a large magnet that makes the data unreadable. It's also possible to burn or shred tapes.

A key point here is that the backup policy identifies policy decisions related to backups. Without a policy, these important decisions may never be addressed. The organization may not maintain off-site backups. They may not label backups. They may never test backups. All of this adds up to a catastrophe waiting to happen.

Remember this

Best practices associated with backups include storing a copy off-site for retention purposes, labeling the media, performing test restores, and destroying the media when it is no longer usable.

Comparing Business Continuity Elements

Business continuity planning helps an organization predict and plan for potential outages of critical services or functions. The goal is to ensure that critical business operations continue and the organization can survive the outage. Organizations often create a business continuity plan (BCP). This plan includes disaster recovery elements that provide the steps used to return critical functions to operation after an outage.

Disasters and outages can come from many sources including:

- Fires
- Attacks
- Power outages
- Data loss from any cause
- Hardware and software failures
- Natural disasters, such as hurricanes, floods, tornadoes, and earthquakes

Addressing all of these possible sources takes a lot of time and effort. The goal is to predict the relevant disasters, their impact, and recovery strategies to mitigate them. The overall process of business continuity planning generally takes the following steps:

1. Complete a business impact analysis
2. Develop recovery strategies
3. Develop recovery plans
4. Test recovery plans
5. Update plans

You aren't required to know the details of all these steps for the Security+ exam, but you should have a general idea of the process. The following sections provide an overview of the relevant topics.

Business Impact Analysis

A business impact analysis (BIA) is an important part of a BCP. It helps an organization identify critical functions and services provided by the organization that it simply could not do without. If critical functions and services fail and can't be restored quickly, it's very possible that the organization will not survive the disaster.

For example, if a disaster such as a hurricane hit, what services must the organization restore to stay in business. Imagine a financial institution. It may decide that customers must have uninterrupted access to account data through an online site. If customers can't access their funds online, they may lose faith with the company and leave in droves.

On the other hand, the company may decide that it doesn't need the ability to accept and process loan applications right away. Loan processing is still important to the company's bottom line, but a delay will not seriously affect its ability to stay in business. In this case, the online site is a critical function but applications used for loan applications are not critical.

> ### Remember this
> The BIA identifies critical business or mission requirements. The BIA includes elements such as Recovery Time Objectives and Recovery Point Objectives, but it doesn't identify solutions. Information in the BIA helps an organization develop the BCP and drives decisions to create redundancies such as failover clusters or alternate sites.

The time to make these decisions is not during a crisis. Instead, the organization completes a BIA in advance. The BIA involves collecting information from throughout the organization and documenting the results. This documentation identifies core business or mission requirements. The BIA does not make recommendations on solutions. However, it provides management with valuable information so that they can focus on critical business functions. It helps them address some of the following questions:

- What assets should be included in recovery plans?
- What business functions must continue to operate?
- Are alternate sites required?
- What data should be backed up?
- Are backup utilities (such as water, heat, gas for generators, and so on) needed?

The BIA will often identify Recovery Time Objectives, Recovery Point Objectives, Mean Time Between Failure, and Mean Time to Restore for the evaluated systems. This information helps an organization identify various contingency plans and policies.

For example, the results of the BIA may help managers within an organization realize they cannot afford a disaster within their datacenter. To address the risk, they may decide to create a warm site to house a redundant datacenter in a separate geographical location. If the primary site fails, they can continue to operate with the warm site. The "Continuity of Operations" section later in this chapter covers alternate sites.

Recovery Time Objective

The Recovery Time Objective (RTO) identifies the maximum amount of time it can take to restore a system after an outage. Many BIAs identify the maximum acceptable outage or maximum tolerable outage time for critical services or business functions. If an outage lasts longer than this maximum time, the impact is unacceptable to the organization.

For example, imagine an organization that sells products via a website generating $10,000 in revenue an hour. It may decide that the maximum acceptable outage for the web server is five minutes. With this in mind, the RTO is five minutes, indicating any outage must be limited to less than five minutes.

On the other hand, the organization may have a database server used by internal employees. While the database server may be valuable, it is not critical. Management may decide they can accept an outage up to twenty-four hours, dictating an RTO less than twenty-four hours.

> ### *Remember this*
> A Recovery Time Objective identifies the maximum amount of time it can take to restore a system after an outage. A Recovery Point Objective identifies a point in time where data loss is acceptable. When these are identified, they are included in a BIA.

Recovery Point Objective

A Recovery Point Objective (RPO) identifies a point in time where data loss is acceptable. As an example, a server may host archived data that has very few changes on a weekly basis. Management may decide that some data loss is acceptable, but they always want to be able recover data from at least the previous week. In this case, the RPO is one week.

With an RPO of one week, administrators would ensure that they have at least weekly backups. In the event of a failure, they will be able to restore recent backups and meet the RPO.

In some cases, the RPO is up to the minute of the failure. For example, any data loss from an online database recording customer transactions may be unacceptable. In this case, the organization can use a variety of techniques to ensure the data can be restored up to the moment of failure.

Mean Time Between Failure

The Mean Time Between Failure (MTBF) provides a measure of a system's reliability and is usually represented in hours. More specifically, the MTBF identifies the average (the arithmetic mean) time between failures. Higher MTBF numbers indicate a higher reliability of a product or system.

A BIA will attempt to identify the MTBF for critical systems to predict potential outages. This can help an organization focus on improving failure rates for systems with low MTBFs.

Mean Time to Restore

The Mean Time to Restore (MTTR) identifies the average (the arithmetic mean) time it takes to restore a failed system. In some cases, people interpret MTTR as the mean time to repair, and both mean essentially the same thing.

Organizations that have maintenance contracts often specify the MTTR as a part of the contract. The supplier agrees that it will, on average, restore a failed system within the MTTR time. Sometimes it may take a little longer and sometimes it may be a little quicker. However, the MTTR does not provide a guarantee that it will restore the system within the MTTR.

Continuity of Operations

A Continuity of Operations Plan (COOP) is an important element of a BCP. It focuses on restoring critical business functions at an alternate location after a critical outage. For example, if a hurricane or other disaster prevents the company from operating in one location, a COOP site allows them to continue to provide critical services at an alternate location. Many organizations plan for using a COOP site for as long as thirty days after relocating.

> ### Remember this
> A Continuity of Operations Plan (COOP) site provides an alternate location for operations after a critical outage. The most common sites are hot, cold, and warm sites.

In this context, a site is an alternate location. It could be office space within a building, an entire building, or even a group of buildings. The three primary types of alternate sites are:

- Hot site
- Cold site
- Warm site

As a rule of thumb, you'd use a hot site when you need to be operational within sixty minutes, or a cold site if you must be operational within a few days. For periods between these two extremes, you'd use a warm site. The following sections provide more details on these sites.

Hot Site

A hot site would be up and operational twenty-four hours a day, seven days a week and would be able to take over functionality from the primary site quickly after failure at the primary site. It would include all the equipment, software, and communications capabilities of the primary site, and all the data would be up to date. In many cases, copies of backup tapes are stored at the hot site as the off-site location.

In many cases, a hot site is another active business location that has the capability to assume operations during a disaster. For example, a financial institution could have locations in two separate cities. The second location provides noncritical support services, but also includes all the resources necessary to assume the functions of the first location.

Some definitions of hot sites indicate they can take over instantaneously, though this isn't consistent. In most cases, it takes a little bit of time to transfer operations to the hot site, and this can take anywhere from a few minutes to an hour.

Clearly, a hot site is the most effective disaster recovery solution for high availability requirements. If an organization must keep critical systems with high availability requirements, the hot site is the best choice. However, a hot site is the most expensive to maintain and keep up to date.

> ### *Remember this*
> A hot site includes personnel, equipment, software, and communications capabilities of the primary site with all the data up to date. A hot site can take over for a failed primary site within an hour. It is the most effective disaster recovery solution for an alternate site, but it is also the most expensive to maintain.

Cold Site

A cold site requires power and connectivity but not much else. Generally, if it has a roof, electricity, running water, and Internet access, you're good to go. The organization brings all the equipment, software, and data to the site when it activates it as a COOP.

I often take my dogs for a walk at a local army base and occasionally see soldiers activate an extreme example of a cold site. On some weekends, one or more of the fields is empty. Other weekends, soldiers have transformed a field into a complete operational site with tents, antennas, cables, generators, and porta-potties.

Since the army has several buildings on the base, they don't need to operate in the middle of fields, but what they're really doing is testing their ability to stand up a cold site wherever they want. If they can do it in the field, they can do it in the middle of a desert.

A cold site is the cheapest to maintain, but it is also the most difficult to test.

> ### *Remember this*
> A cold site will have power and connectivity needed for COOP activation, but little else. Cold sites are the least expensive and the hardest to test. A warm site is a compromise between a hot site and a cold site.

Warm Site

You can think of a warm site as the Goldilocks solution—not too hot and not too cold, but just right. Hot sites are generally too expensive for most organizations, and cold sites generally take too long to configure for full operation. However, the warm site provides a compromise that an organization can tailor to meet its needs.

For example, an organization can place all the necessary hardware at the warm site location but not include up-to-date data. If a disaster occurs, the organization can copy the data to the warm site and take over operations. This is only one example, but there are many different possibilities of warm site configurations.

Site Variations

While hot, cold, and warm sites are the most common, you may also come across two additional alternate site types: mobile and mirrored.

A mobile site is a self-contained transportable unit with all the equipment needed for specific requirements. For example, you can outfit a semi-trailer with everything needed for operations, including a satellite dish for connectivity. Trucks, trains, or ships haul it to a destination and it only needs power to start operating.

Mirrored sites are identical to the primary location and provide 100 percent availability. They use real-time transfers to instantly send modifications to the primary location to the mirrored site. While a hot site can be up and operational within an hour, the mirrored site is always up and operational.

After the Disaster

After the disaster has passed, you will want to return all the functions to the primary site. As a best practice, the least critical functions are returned to the primary site first. Remember, the critical functions are operational at the alternate site and can stay there as long as necessary.

If a site has just gone through a disaster, it's very likely that all the problems haven't been discovered yet. By enabling the least critical functions first, undiscovered problems will appear and can be resolved without significantly affecting critical business functions.

Disaster Recovery

Disaster recovery is a part of an overall business continuity plan. Often the organization will use the business impact analysis to identify the critical business functions and then develop disaster recovery strategies and disaster recovery plans (DRPs) to address the systems hosting these functions.

In some cases, an organization will have multiple DRPs within a BCP, and in other cases, the organization will have a single DRP. For example, it's possible to have individual DRPs that identify the steps to recover individual critical servers, and other DRPS that detail the recovery steps after different types of disasters such as hurricanes or tornadoes. A smaller organization may have a single DRP that simply identifies all the steps used to respond to any disruption.

A DRP or a BCP will include a hierarchical list of critical systems. This list identifies what systems to restore after a disaster and in what order. For example, should a server hosting an online website be restored first, or a server hosting an internal application? The answer is dependent on how the organization values and uses these servers.

If the DRP doesn't prioritize the systems, individuals restoring the systems will use their own judgment, which may not meet the overall needs of the organization. For example, Nicky New Guy may not realize that a web server is generating $50,000 an hour in revenue but does know that he's responsible for keeping a generic file server operational. Without an ordered list of critical systems, he may spend his time restoring the file server and not the web server.

This hierarchical list is valuable when using alternate sites such as warm or cold sites, too. When the organization needs to move operations to an alternate site, they want the most important systems and functions restored first.

Similarly, the DRP often prioritizes the services to restore after an outage. As a rule, critical business functions and security services are restored first. Support services are restored last.

> ### Remember this
>
> A disaster recovery plan (DRP) includes a hierarchical list of critical systems and often prioritizes services to restore after an outage. Testing validates the plan. Recovered systems are tested before returning them to operation, and this can include a comparison to baselines. The final phase of disaster recovery includes a review to identify any lessons learned and may include an update of the plan.

The different phases of a disaster recovery process typically include the following steps:

- **Activation**. Some disasters, such as earthquakes or tornadoes, occur without much warning, and a disaster plan is activated after the disaster. Other disasters, such as hurricanes, provide a warning, and the plan is activated when the disaster is imminent.
- **Implement contingencies**. If the recovery plan requires implementation of an alternate site, critical functions are moved to these sites. If the disaster destroyed onsite backups, this step retrieves the off-site backups from the off-site location.
- **Recovery**. After the disaster has passed, the organization begins recovering critical systems. The DRP documents which systems to recover and includes detailed steps on how to recover them. This also includes reviewing change management documentation to ensure that recovered systems include approved changes.
- **Testing recovered systems**. Before bringing systems online, administrators will test and verify them. This may include comparing the restored system to a performance baseline to verify functionality.
- **Documentation and review**. The final phase of disaster recovery includes a review of the disaster, sometimes called an after-action review. This often includes a lessons-learned review to identify what went right and what went wrong. The organization will often update the plan after a disaster to incorporate any lessons learned.

IT Contingency Planning

Information Technology (IT) contingency planning is focused on recovery for IT systems only. From a broader perspective, a BCP looks at the entire organization and can include one or more DRPs. A DRP provides steps and procedures to return one or more systems to operation after a major disruption or outage and may involve moving operations to a different location. IT contingency planning works on a smaller scale and examines single systems only.

Notice there is a little overlap here. A DRP can document steps and procedures to return a single system to operation, just as an IT contingency plan can. For a small organization, there isn't any real distinction between the two. However, for a large organization, the IT contingency plan provides a little more manageability for the process. Instead of creating a massive DRP that does everything, it can create a DRP with multiple IT contingency plans.

Succession Planning

Succession planning means different things depending on the context. From a purely business perspective, succession planning identifies people within the company that can fill leadership positions. The goal is to ensure the business can continue to thrive even if key leaders within the company leave.

Within the context of business continuity and disaster preparedness, succession planning can indicate the need to identify a hierarchical chain of command. For example, the cost to activate a warm site may be substantial, so a BCP may dictate that only the CEO can decide when to activate the warm site. However, what does the organization do if the CEO is vacationing in Las Vegas or is otherwise unreachable? The BCP can provide an order of succession used during a disaster to ensure that someone has the authority to make decisions.

A less-used meaning of succession planning refers to a hierarchical list of critical systems. As mentioned previously, this list is often included in either a DRP or a BCP and identifies what systems to restore and in what order. The need for this list is very important, but it isn't always referred to as succession planning.

BCP and DRP Testing

Business continuity plans and disaster recovery plans often include testing. Testing validates that the plan works as desired and will often include testing redundancies and backups. There are several different types of testing used with BCPs and DRPs.

A desktop or tabletop exercise is a paper test. Participants sit in a conference room and talk through a scenario. As each stage of the incident is introduced, the participants identify what they'll do based on the plan. This often reveals flaws within the plan and validates the process of the plan.

In a simulation, the participants go through the steps in a controlled manner without affecting the actual system. For example, a simulation can start by indicating that a server failed. Participants then follow the steps to rebuild the server on a test system.

A full-blown test goes through all the steps of the plan. In addition to verifying that the test works, this also shows the amount of time it will take to execute the plan.

Some of the common elements of testing include:

- **Server restoration**. A simple disaster recovery exercise rebuilds a server. Participants follow the steps to rebuild a server using a test system.

- **Server redundancy**. If a server is within a failover cluster, you can test the cluster by taking a primary node offline. Another node within the cluster should automatically assume the role of this offline node.
- **Alternate sites**. You can test an alternate site (hot, cold, or warm) by moving some of the functionality to the alternate site and ensuring the alternate site works as desired. This is very simple with a hot site but extremely difficult with a cold site.
- **Backups**. Backups are tested by restoring the data from the backup. For example, you can verify that you can recover all the data on a tape backup by performing a full restore to an alternate location. If you can't restore the backup, you know you have a problem with the backup strategy. The good news is that you know you have the problem and don't have a crisis since it was just a test.

> ## Remember this
>
> You can validate business continuity plans and disaster recovery plans through testing. Plans are tested regularly, such as once a year or once a quarter, depending on the plan. A disaster recovery exercise can check the steps to restore a server, activate an alternate site, or any other element of the plan.

Environmental Controls

Environmental controls primarily include fire-suppression and HVAC equipment. In some secure environments, a Faraday cage can prevent data from emanating outside an enclosure.

While environmental controls may not seem security related, they can affect the availability of data. Remember, the security triad includes confidentiality, integrity, and availability. If adequate environmental controls aren't maintained, you will very likely lose availability of data and/or services.

Fire Suppression

You can fight fires with individual fire extinguishers, with fixed systems, or both. Most organizations included fixed systems to control fires and place portable fire extinguishers around the organization. A fixed system can detect a fire and automatically activate to extinguish the fire. Individuals use portable fire extinguishers to suppress small fires.

The different components of a fire are:

- Heat
- Oxygen
- Fuel
- Chain reaction creating the fire

The following are the primary methods of suppressing fires:

- **Remove the heat**. This is often done with water or chemical agents.
- **Remove the oxygen**. This is often done by displacing the oxygen with another gas, such as carbon dioxide (CO_2). This is a common method of fighting electrical fires since it is harmless to electrical equipment.
- **Remove the fuel**. Remove what is burning. Fire-suppression methods don't fight a fire this way, but of course once the material is burned, the fire will extinguish.
- **Disrupt the chain reaction**. Some chemicals can disrupt the chain reaction of some fires to stop them.

The class of fire often determines what element of the fire you will try to remove or disrupt. Within the United States, fires are categorized in one of the following fire classes:

- **Class A—Ordinary combustibles**. These include wood, paper, cloth, rubber, trash, and plastics.
- **Class B—Flammable liquids**. These include gasoline, propane, solvents, oil, paint, lacquers, and other synthetics or oil-based products.
- **Class C—Electrical equipment**. This includes computers, wiring, controls, motors, and appliances. The CompTIA Security+ exam is computer-centric, so you should especially understand that a Class C fire is from electrical equipment. You should not fight Class C fires with water or water-based materials, such as foam, because the water is conductive and can pose significant risks to personnel.
- **Class D—Combustible metals**. This includes metals such as magnesium, lithium, titanium, and sodium. Once they start to burn, they are much more difficult to extinguish than other materials.

You can extinguish a Class A fire with water to remove the heat. However, water will make things much worse if you use it on any of the other classes. For example, using water on live equipment will actually pose a risk, since electricity can travel up the stream and shock you. Additionally, water will damage electrical equipment.

Heating, Ventilation, and Air Conditioning

Heating, ventilation, and air-conditioning (HVAC) systems are important physical security controls that improve the availability of systems. Quite simply, computers and other electronic equipment don't like to get too hot, too cold, or wet. If systems overheat, the chips can actually burn themselves out.

The amount of air conditioning needed to cool a massive datacenter is much greater than you need to cool your home. If your home air conditioner fails in the middle of summer, you may be a little uncomfortable for a while, but if the datacenter HVAC system fails, it can result in loss of availability, and a substantial loss of money.

I worked in several environments where we had a policy of shutting down all electronics when the room temperature reached a certain threshold. When we didn't follow the policy, the systems often developed problems due to the heat and ended up out of commission for a lot longer than the AC.

Most servers aren't in cases like a typical desktop computer. Instead, they are housed in rack-mountable cases. These rack-mountable servers are installed in equipment cabinets (also called racks or bays) about the size of tall refrigerators. A large datacenter will have multiple cabinets lined up beside each other in multiple rows.

These cabinets usually have locking doors in the front and rear for physical security. The doors are perforated with cold air coming in the front, passing over and through the servers to keep them cool, and warmer air exiting out the rear. Additionally, a server room has raised flooring with air conditioning pumping through the space under the raised floor.

Hot and Cold Aisles

Hot and cold aisles help regulate the cooling in datacenters with multiple rows of cabinets. The back of all the cabinets in one row will face the back of all the cabinets in an adjacent row. Since the hot air exits out the back of the cabinet, the aisle with the backs facing each other is the hot aisle.

Similarly, the front of the cabinets in one row is facing the front of the cabinets in the adjacent row. Cool air is pumped through the floor to this cool aisle using perforated floor tiles in the raised flowing. This is the cold aisle. In some designs, cool air is also pumped through the base of the cabinets. This depends on the design of the cabinets and the needs of the equipment.

Consider what happens if all the cabinets had their front facing the same way without a hot/cold aisle design. The hot air pumping out the back of one row of cabinets would be sent to the front of the cabinets behind them. The front row would have very cold air coming in the front, but other rows would have warmer air coming in the front.

Of course, an HVAC also includes a thermostat as a temperature control and humidity control. The thermostat ensures that the air temperature is controlled and maintained. Similarly, humidity controls ensure that the humidity is controlled. High humidity can cause condensation on the equipment and computers just don't like water. Low humidity allows a higher incidence of electrostatic discharge (ESD).

> ### *Remember this*
> HVAC systems increase availability by regulating airflow within datacenters and server rooms. Hot and cold aisles are a method used to regulate the cooling. Temperature control systems use thermostats to ensure a relatively constant temperature. Humidity controls reduce the potential for static discharges, and damage from condensation. HVAC systems should be integrated with the fire alarm systems and either have dampers or the ability to be turned off in the event of a fire.

HVAC and Fire

HVAC systems are often integrated with fire alarm systems to help prevent a fire from spreading. One of the core elements of a fire is oxygen. If the HVAC system continues to operate normally when a fire is detected, it will continue to pump oxygen to feed the fire. When the HVAC system is integrated with the fire alarm system, it controls the airflow to help prevent the rapid spread of the fire. Many current HVAC systems have dampers that can control airflow to specific areas of a building. Other HVAC systems will automatically turn off when a fire is detected.

Failsafe/secure vs. Failopen

Many times, it's important to consider the state of a system if it fails. You can often force a system to fail in an open state, or to fail in a safe or secure state. The terms "failsafe," "fail secure," and "fail closed" all mean the same thing. The state you choose is often dependent on the needs of the organization.

For example, you may have a system that requires high availability, but security isn't as important. If it fails, you would want it to fail in an open state so that it remains available.

Consider an exit door secured with a proximity card. Normally, employees open the door with the proximity card and the system records their exit. The proximity card provides security but you need the exit to remain highly available.

What happens if a fire starts and power to the building is lost? The proximity card reader won't work, and if the door can't open, employees will be trapped. In this case, you would want the proximity card reader to fail in the failopen state so that personnel can get out. The value of personnel safety is always paramount.

On the other hand, consider a firewall used to provide security for a network. In this case, security is more important than availability. For example, if a firewall ACL became corrupt, you would want it to fail in a failsafe or secure mode. Essentially, it would block all traffic and continue to provide security for the network.

> ### **Remember this**
>
> If availability is more important than security, the system should fail in an open state. If security is more important than availability, the system should fail in a closed or secure state.

Shielding

Shielding can be used to prevent electromagnetic interference (EMI) and radio frequency interference (RFI) from corrupting signals. It will also protect against unwanted emissions and help prevent an attacker from capturing network traffic.

While you may see EMI and RFI in the same category as EMI/RFI, they are different. EMI comes from different types of motors, power lines, and even fluorescent lights. RFI comes from RF sources such as AM or FM transmitters. However, shielding used to block interference from both EMI and RFI sources is often referred to as simply EMI shielding.

Attackers often use different types of eavesdropping methods to capture network traffic. If the data is emanating outside of the wire or outside of an enclosure, they may be able to capture and read the data. EMI shielding fulfills the dual purpose of keeping interference out and preventing attackers from capturing network traffic.

It's worth mentioning that physical security is also important. Experienced technicians can cut a twisted pair cable and add a splitter within five minutes. I recently taught a Security+ class to some Verizon FIOS technicians, and they said they can do the same thing with a fiber cable within ten minutes.

Shielding Cables

Twisted pair (CAT 5, CAT 5E, or CAT6) cable comes in both shielded twisted pair (STP) and unshielded twisted pair (USP) versions. The shielding helps prevent an attacker from capturing network traffic and helps block interference from corrupting the data.

When data travels along a copper wire (such as twisted pair), it creates an induction field around the wire. If you have the right tools, you can simply place the tool around the wire and capture the signal. The shielding in STP cable blocks this.

Fiber-optic cable is not susceptible to this type of attack. Signals travel along a fiber-optic cable as light pulses, and they do not create an induction field.

> ### Remember this
> You can prevent someone from capturing network traffic by using EMI shielding. EMI shielding prevents outside interference sources from corrupting data and prevents data from emanating outside the cable.

Faraday Cage

A Faraday cage is a room that prevents signals from emanating beyond the room. It includes electrical features that cause RF signals that reach the boundary of the room to be reflected back, preventing signal emanation outside the Faraday cage.

In addition to preventing signals from emanating outside the room, a Faraday cage also provides shielding to prevent outside interference such as EMI and RFI from entering the room.

At a very basic level, some elevators act as a Faraday cage (though I seriously doubt the designers were striving to do so). You may have stepped into an elevator and found that your cell phone stopped receiving and transmitting signals. The metal shielding around the elevator prevents signals from emanating out or signals such as the cell phone tower signal from entering the elevator.

On a smaller scale, electrical devices such as computers are shielded to prevent signals from emanating out and interference from getting in.

TEMPEST

TEMPEST is a government program that has been around for several decades to measure emanations from different devices. Devices placed within Faraday cages or built with a Faraday-like enclosure cannot emanate signals outside the enclosure. TEMPEST measurements ensure that sensitive signals cannot be captured and exploited.

The word TEMPEST is not an acronym but instead a code name created by the U.S. government. However, I do like one of the acronyms that someone created and posted on the web—Tiny ElectroMagnetic Particles Emitting Secret Things.

Chapter 9 Exam Topic Review

When preparing for the exam, make sure you understand these key concepts covered in this chapter.

Redundancy

- A single point of failure is any component that can cause the entire system to fail if it fails.
- RAID-1 and RAID-5 disk subsystems provide fault tolerance and increase availability. RAID-1 (mirroring) uses two disks, and RAID-5 uses three or more disks.
- Failover clusters remove a server as a single point of failure. If one node in a cluster fails, another node can take over.
- An UPS system provides fault tolerance for power fluctuations and provides short-term power for systems during power outages. Generators provide long-term power for systems during extended power outages.

Backups

- Backup strategies include full, full/differential, and full/incremental. A full backup strategy alone allows the quickest recovery time.
- Test restores verify the integrity of backups. A test restore of a full backup verifies a backup can be restored in its entirety.
- A copy of backups should be kept off-site.
- Backups should be labeled to identify the contents.

Business Continuity Elements

- A business impact analysis (BIA) is part of a business continuity plan (BCP) and it identifies critical business functions based on business requirements.

- The BIA identifies the Recovery Point Objectives (RPOs) and Recovery Time Objectives (RTOs). RPOs and RTOs drive recovery strategies.
- Continuity of operations (COOP) sites provide alternate locations to operate critical business functions after a major disaster.
- A hot site includes everything needed to be operational within sixty minutes. It is the most effective recovery solution and the most expensive. A cold site has power and connectivity requirements and little else. It is the cheapest to maintain. A warm site is a compromise between a hot site and a cold site.
- Disaster recovery planning is part of overall business continuity planning. A disaster recovery plan (DRP) includes the steps to return one or more systems to full operation.
- BCPs or DRPs include a hierarchical list of critical systems identifying the order of restoration.
- Periodic testing validates BCPs and DRPs. Disaster recovery exercises validate the steps to restore individual systems, activate alternate sites, and other actions documented within a DRP. Functionality of restored systems are validated by comparing against baselines.
- The last phase of a DRP includes a review of lessons learned and may require a rewrite or update of the plan.

Environmental Controls

- Heating, ventilation, and air-conditioning (HVAC) systems control airflow for datacenters and server rooms.
- Hot and cold aisles are often used with temperature control systems to regulate cooling, and increase the availability of the systems. Humidity controls reduce potential damage from static discharge.
- HVAC systems should be integrated with fire control systems to prevent a fire from spreading.
- If security is more important than availability, a system should be designed to fail in a closed state. If availability is more important than security, a system should be designed to fail in an open state.
- EMI shielding prevents data loss in twisted pair cables (such as CAT 5, 5E, and CAT 6).

Chapter 9 Practice Questions

1. An organization is not actively involved in business continuity planning. What is it likely to overlook until a disaster results in a major outage?
    A. Data encryption
    B. Single points of failure
    C. Vulnerability scans
    D. Penetration tests

2. Which of the following provides fault tolerance through disk mirroring?
    A. RAID-0
    B. RAID-1
    C. RAID-5
    D. Clustering

3. An administrator is improving the availability of a server and needs to ensure that a hard drive failure does not result in the failure of the server. What will support this goal? (Choose all that apply.)
    A. Hardware RAID-0
    B. Hardware RAID-1
    C. Software RAID-1
    D. Software RAID-5

4. What can remove a server as a single point of failure?
    A. RAID-1
    B. Mirroring
    C. Clustering
    D. UPS

5. Several servers in your server room are connected to an UPS. What does this provide?
    A. Continuity of operations
    B. Disaster recovery
    C. Fault tolerance
    D. Long term power if commercial power fails

6. What helps ensure availability in the event of an extended power outage?
    A. UPS
    B. Failover clusters
    C. RAID
    D. Generators

7. You need to implement a backup strategy that allows the fastest recovery of data. What provides the best solution?

    A. A full backup daily

    B. A full/differential strategy

    C. A full/incremental strategy

    D. A differential/incremental strategy

8. An organization regularly performs backups of critical systems. Where should it keep a copy of the backups for retention?

    A. Off-site

    B. With the backed up systems

    C. On a mirrored drive of the backed up system

    D. On a cluster

9. An organization wants to verify that a tape backup can be restored in its entirety. What should it do?

    A. Perform test restores of random files on the backup

    B. Perform test restores of the full backup

    C. Copy the backup to the hot site

    D. Copy the backup to the cold site

10. Of the following choices, what identifies RPOs and RTOs?

    A. Failover clusters

    B. BIA

    C. RAID

    D. DRP

11. An organization is creating a business continuity plan (BCP). What will identify business requirements used in the development of the plan?

    A. BIA

    B. RPO

    C. RTO

    D. HSM

12. A business impact analysis (BIA) determined that a critical business function has a Recovery Time Objective (RTO) of an hour. What site will meet this objective?

    A. Hot site

    B. Cold site

    C. Warm site

    D. RTO site

13. Which of the following continuity-of-operations solutions is the most expensive?
    A. Hot site
    B. Cold site
    C. Warm site
    D. Clustered site

14. An organization is considering an alternate location as part of its business continuity plan. It wants to identify a solution that provides a balance between cost and recovery time. What will it choose?
    A. Hot site
    B. Cold site
    C. Warm site
    D. Mirrored site

15. Of the following choices, what is needed in a cold site used for continuity of operations?
    A. Power and connectivity
    B. All required equipment
    C. All required equipment with up-to-date patches
    D. All required equipment with up-to-date patches and data

16. An organization is performing a disaster recovery exercise. Of the following choices, what is likely to be included?
    A. Test server restoration
    B. Picking a hot, warm, or cold site
    C. Creation of BIA
    D. Determination of the failsafe state

17. An organization implemented a disaster recovery plan in response to a hurricane. What is the last step in the disaster recovery process?
    A. Activation
    B. Recover systems
    C. Test systems
    D. Review

18. An administrator used a disaster recovery plan to rebuild a critical server after an attack. Of the following choices, how can the administrator verify the system's functionality?
    A. Perform a review of the recovery process
    B. Install approved changes
    C. Compare the system's performance against a performance baseline
    D. Removed antivirus software

19. A critical system failed. Of the following choices, what would an organization implement to restore it?
    A. BIA
    B. DRP
    C. COOP
    D. RAID

20. How can an organization validate a BCP?
    A. With a BIA
    B. With a hot site
    C. With testing
    D. With a hierarchical list of critical systems

21. Your building is researching the costs and functionality of fire alarm systems for a new building. What capability should the system include to prevent a fire from spreading?
    A. Integration with a temperature control system
    B. Integration with a CCTV
    C. Integration with an HVAC system
    D. Integration with proximity card readers

22. An organization designed its datacenter with hot and cold aisles. Of the following choices, what is not a valid purpose of hot and cold aisles?
    A. Regulate cooling
    B. Increase availability
    C. Reduce cooling costs
    D. Fire suppression

23. Your organization hosts several bays of servers within a server room. What environmental control within the datacenter requires a thermostat?
    A. Temperature control
    B. Hot and cold aisles
    C. Humidity control
    D. Generators

24. An organization hosts several bays of servers used to support a large online ecommerce business. It wants to ensure that customer data hosted within the datacenter is protected, and it implements several access controls, including an HVAC system. What does the HVAC system help protect?
    A. Access
    B. Availability
    C. Confidentiality
    D. Integrity

25. You are evaluating the security and availability of a system. Security is more important than availability in the system. If it fails, what state should it fail in?
   A. It should fail open
   B. It should fail closed
   C. It should shut down
   D. It should be rebooted

26. Of the following choices, what is the best choice to help prevent someone from capturing network traffic?
   A. EMI shielding
   B. Use hubs instead of switches
   C. Ensure that SNMP traps are set
   D. Hot and cold aisles

Chapter 9 Practice Question Answers

1. **B.** Single points of failure are often overlooked until a disaster occurs. Business continuity planning helps an organization plan for disasters and continuity of operations but it does not include data encryption, vulnerability scans, or penetration tests.

2. **B.** RAID-1 uses two disks and is also known as disk mirroring. RAID-0 does not provide fault tolerance. RAID-5 uses three or more disks and is known as striping with parity. Clustering provides fault tolerance to servers, not disks.

3. **B, C, D.** RAID-1 and RAID-5 provide fault tolerance for disk subsystems and will increase availability. While hardware RAID is quicker than software RAID, both will provide fault tolerance. RAID-0 increases performance but it does not provide fault tolerance.

4. **C.** Failover clustering removes a server as a single point of failure by including additional servers that can take over the service if the server fails. RAID-1 (also called mirroring) removes a drive (not a server) as a single point of failure. UPS provides fault tolerance for power failures.

5. **C.** An uninterrupted power supply (UPS) provides fault tolerance and allows the servers to continue to operate for a short period even if commercial power fails. Continuity of operations (COOP) focuses on restoring critical functions at an alternate site such as a hot, warm, or cold site. Disaster recovery restores systems after a recovery is not the same as fault tolerance. Generators (not UPS) provide long-term power if commercial power fails.

6. **D.** Generators provide long-term power if commercial power fails. An uninterrupted power supply (UPS) provides fault tolerance for a short period. RAID increases availability for disk systems, and failover clusters remove servers as a single point of failure, but neither will help in an extended power outage.

7. **A.** The fastest strategy is a full backup every day of the week because a failure only requires restoring a single tape. A full/differential strategy will reduce the time required to do backups after the full and would require only two tapes to restore. A full/incremental strategy minimizes the time required to do backups but usually requires restoring more tapes, resulting in a longer recovery time. All backup strategies must include a full so a differential/incremental strategy will not work.

8. **A.** A copy of backups should be kept in an off-site location for retention purposes. If the backups are kept with the backed up systems or on system drives, they can be destroyed if the system is destroyed, such as in a fire. A cluster provides fault tolerance for a server but the servers are commonly located in the same place.

9. **B.** The only way to verify the entire tape can be restored is to restore the entire backup. Randomly restoring an individual file does not verify the entire backup tape. While an organization may store an off-site backup of tapes at a hot site, this won't verify the tape. Cold sites would not have any systems or data, so backups would not be copied there.

10. **B.** A business impact analysis (BIA) identifies the Recovery Point Objectives (RPOs) and Recovery Time Objectives (RTOs). Failover clusters reduce the likelihood of a single point of failure when a server fails, and a Redundant Array of Independent Disks (RAID) increases availability for hard drives. A disaster recovery plan (DRP) helps an organization prepare for potential disasters and includes a hierarchical list of critical systems.

11. **A.** A business impact analysis (BIA) identifies critical business functions and requirements and is created as part of the BCP. Recovery Point Objectives (RPOs) and Recovery Time Objectives (RTOs) are part of the BIA. A hardware security module (HSM) is a removable or external device that provides encryption services, but it does not identify security requirements.

12. **A.** A hot site includes all the elements to bring a critical function operational the quickest and will meet the RTO objective of ensuring a function is restored within an hour. A cold site takes the longest to restore. Because the RPO is one hour (sixty minutes), the site must be operational in fifty-nine minutes or less, and a warm site will take longer than this to become operational. The Recovery Time Objective (RTO) is related to the BIA, but there is no such thing as an RTO site.

13. **A.** Hot sites are the most expensive. Cold sites are the least expensive. There is no such thing as a clustered site.

14. **C.** A warm site is a cross between a hot site (which has everything needed for operations) and a cold site (which only has power and connectivity). A mirrored site is identical to the primary location and provides 100 percent availability.

15. **A.** A cold site will have power and connectivity but little else. A hot site will have all the required equipment with up-to-date patches, up-to-date data, and personnel.

16. **A.** A simple disaster recovery exercise rebuilds a server to validate the steps. The disaster recovery plan (DRP) documents the alternate site choice, but an exercise doesn't pick this location. The business impact analysis (BIA) identifies the Recovery Point Objectives (RPOs) and Recovery Time Objectives (RTOs) used in the DRP, but it would be created before testing the plan. The failure state is dependent on availability and security requirements and not determined during a disaster recovery exercise.

17. **D.** The final phase of a disaster recovery includes a review to identify lessons learned and possibly update the disaster recovery plan (DRP). In general, the order of the phases is activation, implement contingencies, recovery, testing (including comparing them against baselines), and review.

18. **C.** The functionality can be verified by comparing the system's performance against a performance baseline. The last phase of disaster recovery is a review, but this won't verify the system's functionality. The recovery should include installing approved changes and updates, but this doesn't verify functionality. Antivirus software should not be removed.

19. **B.** An organization would implement a disaster recovery plan (DRP) to restore a critical system after a disruption or failure. A business impact analysis (BIA) identifies the Recovery Point Objectives (RPOs) and Recovery Time Objectives (RTOs). A continuity of operations (COOP) site is an alternate site such as a hot, warm, or cold site. Redundant array of independent disks (RAID) is used to increase availability of disk subsystems.

20. **C.** Business continuity plans (BCPs) and disaster recovery plans (DRPs) are validated through testing, such as an annual or semiannual test. A business impact analysis (BIA) identifies critical business functions using elements such as Recovery Point Objectives and Recovery Time Objectives. A hot site is an alternate location ready for operation within an hour, but not all BCPs require alternate locations. A DRP will include a hierarchical list of critical systems, but the list doesn't validate a BCP.

21. **C.** A fire alarm system should be integrated with an HVAC system so that the HVAC system can control airflow when a fire is detected. An HVAC includes a thermostat to regulate temperature, but this is for normal operation unrelated to fire prevention. A CCTV can detect if an unauthorized entry occurred and provide reliable proof of the entry, but is not related to fire. Proximity cards can help prevent unauthorized personnel from entering a secure datacenter.

22. **D.** Hot and cold aisles do not suppress fires. They regulate cooling in datacenters, reducing cooling costs. If the datacenter temperature is adequately controlled in a datacenter, it reduces outages due to overheating and increases availability.

23. **A.** A thermostat ensures that the temperature within a server room or datacenter is controlled and regulated. Hot and cold aisles are a design principle used to regulate cooling in datacenters, reducing cooling costs. A thermostat can't regulate humidity, though a moisture control system is often used to maintain humidity. Generators are used as an alternative power source.

24. **B.** A heating, ventilation, and air-conditioning (HVAC) system can increase availability by ensuring that equipment doesn't fail due to overheating. An HVAC system doesn't contribute to access control. Confidentiality ensures that data is only viewable by authorized users and can be ensured with access controls or encryption. Integrity provides assurances that data has not been modified, tampered with, or corrupted.

25. **B.** If security is more important than availability, it should fail in a closed state. If availability is more important than security, it should fail in an open state. Different systems can achieve a closed state using different methods, and they don't necessarily have to be shut down or rebooted.

26. **A.** Electromagnetic interference (EMI) shielding can protect a signal from interference from outside sources, and it can help prevent an attacker from capturing network traffic without tapping into the cable. Switches are an improvement over hubs (not hubs instead of switches) when trying to protect against an attacker capturing network traffic. SNMP traps can provide notifications from SNMP agents to SNMP servers related to the monitoring of network devices, but do not limit data captures. Hot and cold aisles regulate airflow in datacenters.

Chapter 10

Understanding Cryptography

CompTIA Security+ objectives covered in this chapter:

1.4 Implement and use common protocols
- TLS
- SSL
- HTTPS

4.3 Explain the importance of data security
- Data encryption
- Database
- Individual files
- Removable media

6.1 Summarize general cryptography concepts
- Symmetric vs. asymmetric
- Fundamental differences and encryption methods
  - Block vs. stream
- Transport encryption
- Non-repudiation
- Hashing
- Key escrow
- Steganography
- Digital signatures
- Use of proven technologies
- Elliptic curve and quantum cryptography

6.2 Use and apply appropriate cryptographic tools and products
- MD5
- SHA
- RIPEMD
- AES

- DES
- 3DES
- HMAC
- RSA
- RC4
- One-time pads
- NTLM
- NTLMv2
- Blowfish
- PGP/GPG
- TwoFish
- Comparative strengths of algorithms

6.3 Explain the core concepts of public key infrastructure

- Certificate authorities and digital certificates
  - CA
  - CRLs
- PKI
- Recovery agent
- Public key
- Private key
- Registration
- Key escrow
- Trust models

6.4 Implement PKI, certificate management, and associated components

- Certificate authorities and digital certificates
  - CA
  - CRLs
- PKI
- Recovery agent
- Public key
- Private keys
- Registration
- Key escrow
- Trust models

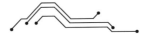

While cryptography is only 11 percent of the exam, you may find that many of these topics aren't as familiar to you as other topics, and you may have to spend more than 15 percent of your study time here. When tackling these topics, don't lose sight of the basics outlined in the very first section of the chapter—"Introducing Cryptography Concepts." This section provides an overview, and the rest of the chapter provides details explaining various cryptographic protocols.

Introducing Cryptography Concepts

Cryptography has several important concepts that you need to grasp for the Security+ exam, but they are often topics that are new to many IT professionals. Confidentiality and integrity were introduced as part of the security triad in Chapter 1—confidentiality, integrity, and availability.

This chapter covers the details of confidentiality and integrity along with some other important cryptography topics. As an overview, the following are the core cryptography concepts:

- **Integrity** provides assurances that data has not been modified. Hashing ensures that data has retained integrity.
  - A **hash** is a number derived from performing a calculation on data, such as a message or file. If the data is unchanged, the hash will always be the same no matter how many times the hash is calculated.
  - **Common hashing algorithms** include MD5, SHA, and HMAC. Each algorithm creates a fixed size string of bits to represent a number. For example, MD5 creates a hash of 128 bits.
- **Confidentiality** ensures that data is only viewable by authorized users. Encryption protects the confidentiality of data.
  - **Encryption** ciphers data to make it unreadable if intercepted. Encryption normally includes an algorithm and a key.
  - **Symmetric encryption** uses the same key to encrypt and decrypt data.
  - **Asymmetric encryption** uses two keys (public and private) created as a matched pair. Anything encrypted with the public key can only be decrypted with the matching private key. Anything encrypted with the private key can only be decrypted with the matching public key.
- **Authentication** validates an identity.
- **Non-repudiation** prevents a party from denying an action.
- **Digital signatures** provide authentication, non-repudiation, and integrity. Users sign e-mails with a digital signature, which is a hash of an e-mail message encrypted with the sender's private key. Only the sender's public key can decrypt the hash, providing verification it was encrypted with the sender's private key.

Providing Integrity with Hashing

You can verify integrity with hashing. Hashing is an algorithm performed on data such as a file or message to produce a number called a hash (sometimes called a checksum). The hash is used to verify that data is not modified, tampered with, or corrupted. In other words, you can verify the data has maintained integrity.

A key point about a hash is that no matter how many times you execute the hashing algorithm against the data, the hash will always be the same as long as the data is the same.

Hashes are created at least twice so that they can be compared. For example, you can create a hash on a message at the source before sending it, and then again at the destination. If the hashes are the same, you know that the message has not lost integrity.

Two common hashing algorithms are Message Digest 5 (MD5) and Secure Hash Algorithm (SHA).

Remember this

Hashing provides integrity for data such as e-mail, downloaded files, and files stored on a disk. A hash is a number created with a hashing algorithm. Message Digest 5 (MD5) and the Secure Hash Algorithm (SHA) family are popular hashing algorithms.

MD5

Message Digest 5 (MD5) is a common hashing algorithm that produces a 128-bit hash. Hashes are commonly shown in hexadecimal format instead of a stream of ones and zeros. For example, MD5 hashes are displayed as thirty-two hexadecimal characters instead of 128 bits.

Many applications use MD5 to verify the integrity of files. This includes e-mail, files stored on disks, files downloaded from the Internet, executable files, and more. The Hashing Files section shows how you can manually calculate hashes.

SHA

Secure Hash Algorithm (SHA) is another hashing algorithm. There are several variations of SHA grouped into three families: SHA-0, SHA-1, SHA-2, and SHA-3.

- SHA-0 is not used.
- SHA-1 is an updated version that creates 160-bit hashes. This is similar to the MD5 hash except that it creates 160-bit hashes instead of 128-bit hashes.
- SHA-2 improved SHA-1 to overcome potential weaknesses. It includes four versions: SHA-224, SHA-256, SHA-384, and SHA-512. The numbers represent the number of bits in the hash. For example, SHA-256 creates 256-bit hashes.
- SHA-3 is currently in development. The National Institute of Standards and Technology (NIST) is evaluating several potential versions in a NIST hash function competition, and it's expected to pick the winner in 2012.

Just as MD5 is used to verify the integrity of files, SHA also verifies file integrity. As an example, it's rare for executable files to be modified. However, some malware modifies executable files by adding malicious code into the file. Rootkits will often modify system level files.

Some HIDS and antivirus software capture hashes of files on a system when they first scan it and include valid hashes of system files in signature definition files. When they scan a system again, they can capture hashes of executable and system files and compare them to known good hashes. If the hashes are different for an executable or system file, it indicates the file has been modified, and it may have been modified by malware.

HMAC

Another method used to provide integrity is with a Hash-based Message Authentication Code (HMAC). An HMAC is a fixed length string of bits similar to other hashing algorithms such as MD5 and SHA-1 (known as HMAC-MD5 and HMAC-SHA1). However, HMAC also uses a shared secret key to add some randomness to the result and only the sender and receiver know the secret key.

For example, imagine that one server is sending a message to another server using HMAC-MD5. It starts by first creating a hash of a message with MD5 and then uses a secret key to complete another calculation on the hash. The server then sends the message and the HMAC-MD5 hash to the second server. The second server performs the same calculations and compares the received HMAC-MD5 hash with its result. Just as with any other hash comparison, if the two hashes are the same, the message retained integrity, but if the hashes are different, the message lost integrity.

The HMAC provides both integrity and authenticity of messages. The MD5 portion of the hash provides integrity just as MD5 does. However, since only the server and receiver know the secret key, if the receiver can calculate the same HMAC-MD5 hash as the sender, it knows that the sender used the same key. If an attacker was trying to impersonate the sender, the message wouldn't pass this authenticity check since the attacker wouldn't have the secret key.

Hashing Files

Many applications calculate and compare hashes automatically without any user intervention. For example, digital signatures (described later) use hashes within e-mail, and e-mail applications automatically create and compare the hashes.

Additionally, there are several applications you can use to manually calculate hashes. As an example, md5sum.exe is a free program anyone can use to take hashes of files. A Google search on "download md5sum" will show several locations. It runs the MD5 hashing algorithm against a file to create the hash.

Figure 10.1 shows the result of running md5sum. In the figure, I first used the **dir** command to list the two files in the directory (installer_r12-windows.exe and md5sum.exe). I then ran **md5sum** against the installer file three times. Each time, md5sum created the same hash (displayed as a hexadecimal number): *367f0ed4ecd70aefc290d1f7dcb578ab*.

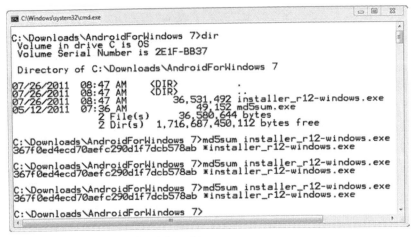

Figure 10.1: Calculating a hash with md5sum

The installer_r12-windows.exe file is an installation file for the Android Software Development Kit (SDK) that I downloaded from the Android Developers website. Figure 10.2 shows a partial screenshot of the page. Notice that the website includes an MD5 Checksum column. Before posting the files to the website, an administrator used a program (such as md5sum) to calculate the hash of the file and posted the hash in the MD5 Checksum column.

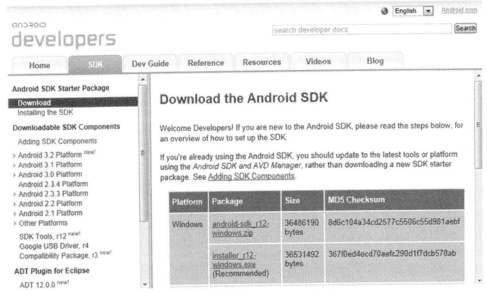

Figure 10.2: Android website page with posted MD5 checksum

I can compare the hash created with md5sum (in Figure 10.1) with the hash posted on the website (in Figure 10.2). Since both hashes are the same, I know that the file I downloaded is the same as the file posted on the website.

On the other hand, if md5sum created a different hash than the one posted on the website, I'd know that the file has lost integrity. I wouldn't necessarily know why the file lost integrity. It may have been infected with a virus or lost a bit or two during the transfer. However, I do know that the integrity of the file is lost and should not be trusted.

It's worth pointing out that hashes are one-way functions. In other words, you can calculate a hash on a file or a message, but you can't use the hash to reproduce the original data. The hashing algorithms always create a fixed-size bit string regardless of the size of the original data.

As an example, the MD5 hash from the message "I will pass the Security+ exam" is: *5384128261CF2EEA6D90ADACE48CD41B*. However, you can't look at the hash and determine the message or even that it is a message.

The hashes shown in Figures 9.1 and 9.2 were calculated on a 35 MB executable file. However, the hash doesn't give a clue about the size of the file, the type of the file, or anything else. It could just as easily be a single sentence message, a 10 KB e-mail, a 7 GB database file, or anything else.

Remember this

Hashing algorithms always provide a fixed size bit-string regardless of the size of the hashed data. By comparing the hashes at two different times, you can verify integrity of the data.

The File Checksum Integrity Verifier (FCIV) is another free command-prompt utility that computes and verifies cryptographic hash values of files with support for MD5 and SHA-1 cryptographic hash values. If you're interested, you can read about it and download it from here. http://support.microsoft.com/kb/841290.

Hashing Messages

Hashing provides integrity for messages. It provides assurance to someone receiving a message that the message has not been modified.

Imagine that Sally is sending a message to Joe as shown in Figure 10.3. The message is "The price is $75." This message is not secret, so there is no need to encrypt it. However, we do want to provide integrity, so this explanation is focused only on hashing.

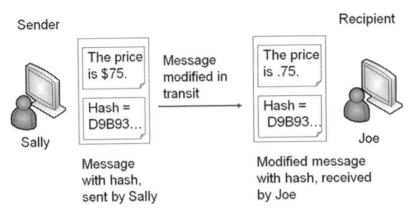

Figure 10.3: Simplified hash process

An application on Sally's computer calculates the MD5 hash as *D9B93C99B62646ABD06C887039053F56*. In the figure, I've shortened the full hash down to just the first five characters of *"D9B93."* Sally then sends both the message and the hash to Joe.

In this example, something has modified the message before it reaches Joe. When Joe receives the message and the original hash, the message is now "The price is .75." Note that the message is modified in transit, but the hash is *not* modified.

A program on Joe's computer calculates the MD5 hash on the received message as *564294439E1617F5628A3E3EB75643FE*. It then compares the received hash with the calculated hash.

- Hash created on Sally's computer, and received by Joe's computer:
  D9B93C99B62646ABD06C887039053F56
- Hash created on Joe's computer:
  564294439E1617F5628A3E3EB75643FE

Clearly, the hashes are different, so you know the message has lost integrity. The program on Joe's computer would report the discrepancy. Joe doesn't know what caused the problem. It could have been a malicious attacker changing the message, or it could have been a technical problem. However, Joe does know the received message isn't the same as the sent message and he shouldn't trust it.

Using HMAC

You may have noticed a problem in the explanation of the hashed message. If an attacker can change the message, why can't the attacker change the hash, too? In other words, if Hacker Harry changed the message to "The price is .75," he could also calculate the hash on the modified message and replace the original hash with the modified hash. Here's the result:

- Hash created on Sally's computer:
  D9B93C99B62646ABD06C887039053F56
- Modified hash inserted by attacker after modifying the message:
  564294439E1617F5628A3E3EB75643FE
- Hash created on Joe's computer:
  564294439E1617F5628A3E3EB75643FE

The calculated hash on the modified message would be the same as the received hash. This erroneously indicates that the message maintained integrity. HMAC helps solve this problem.

With HMAC, both Sally and Joe would know the same secret key and use it to create an HMAC-MD5 hash instead of just an MD5 hash. Figure 10.4 shows the result.

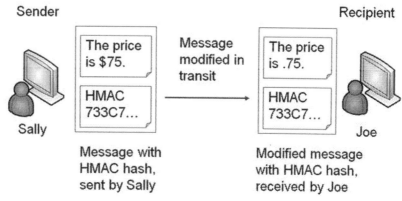

Figure 10.4: Using HMAC

Sally is still sending the same message. The MD5 hash is: *D9B93C99B62646ABD06C887039053F56*. However, after applying the HMAC secret key, the HMAC-MD5 hash is: *733C70A54A13744D5C2C9C4BA3B15034*.

In Figure 10.4, I've shortened this to only the first five characters: *733C7*. An attacker can modify the message in transit just as before. However, the attacker doesn't know the secret key so he can't calculate the HMAC hash.

Joe's computer calculates the HMAC-MD5 hash on the received message using the shared secret key. It then compares the calculated hash with the hash received from Sally.

- HMAC-MD5 hash created on Sally's computer:
  733C70A54A13744D5C2C9C4BA3B15034
- HMAC-MD5 hash created on Joe's computer:
  1B4FF0F6C04434BF97F1E3DDD4B6C137

Again, we can see that the hashes are different and the message has lost integrity. If the messages weren't modified, the HMAC-MD5 hash would be the same.

Other Hash Algorithms

MD5 and SHA are the most popular hashing algorithms in use today. However, the Security+ objectives mention other hashing algorithms that aren't used as often. The following sections describe these other hashing algorithms.

RIPEMD

RACE Integrity Primitives Evaluation Message Digest (RIPEMD) is another hash function. Different versions create different size hashes. RIPEMD-160 creates 160-bit fixed size hashes. Other versions create hash sizes of 128 bits, 256 bits, and 320 bits.

LANMAN and NTLM

Older Microsoft systems used hashing algorithms to secure passwords. While the protocols were primarily used for authentication, they are relevant here due to how they used hashing.

LANMAN

LAN Manager (LANMAN) is a very old authentication protocol used to provide backward compatibility to Windows 95, 98, and ME clients. LANMAN has significant weaknesses with how it stores the password.

Even though LANMAN is very old, some legacy services and software applications still use LANMAN. Additionally, some newer authentication protocols will still store passwords in the LANMAN format if the password is less than fifteen characters long. LANMAN cannot handle passwords of fifteen characters or more.

LANMAN performs a hashing algorithm on passwords that makes it easy for password-cracking tools, such as L0phtCrack, to discover the actual password. The LANMAN passwords are always stored as fourteen characters. If the password is less than fourteen characters, it pads the password with trailing spaces. It then converts all lower case characters to upper case and creates a hash on each of seven-character strings. The two hashes are stored locally as a single string.

If the password is only seven characters long, the resulting hash on the trailing seven spaces would always be: AAD3B435B51404EE. If the entire password is blank, it becomes two sets of seven spaces. The hash of the entire password is then two sets of AAD3B435B51404EE, or AAD3B435B51404EEAAD3B435B51404EE.

However, even if the password is more than seven characters long, it doesn't take L0phtCrack long to successfully crack the password, because it only needs to work on seven characters at a time. L0phtCrack guesses different one to seven character combinations and compares the hash of the guessed password with the hash of the stored password.

If at all possible, LANMAN should be disabled on all computers within a network. It is disabled in Windows Vista, Windows 7, Windows Server 2008, and Windows Server 2008 R2 by default.

Remember this

The LANMAN protocol stores passwords using an LM hash of the password. It first divides the password into two seven-character blocks, and then converts all lower case letters to upper case.

NTLM

Microsoft introduced New Technology LAN Manager (NTLM) as an improvement over LANMAN. There are two versions of NTLM: NTLM (or NTLMv1) and NTLMv2.

NTLMv1 uses an MD4 hash of the user's password, and for backward compatibility it also uses the LANMAN hash if the password is fourteen characters or less. Both LANMAN and MD4 are considered compromised, resulting in known vulnerabilities with NTLMv1 today.

Microsoft improved NTLMv1 with NTLMv2. NTLMv2 uses a completely different process and uses the more secure MD5 algorithm. NTLMv2 is significantly complex, making it infeasible to crack using current technologies.

While NTLMv1 and NTLMv2 provide improvements over LANMAN, a significant vulnerability exists in systems before Windows Vista such as Windows XP and Windows Server 2003. Specifically, LANMAN is still enabled by default on older systems. When it is enabled, these systems use the LANMAN hash for backward compatibility, in addition to the more secure NTLMv2.

Many networks impose policies requiring administrator passwords to be fifteen characters or more. This fifteen-character requirement overcomes the LANMAN vulnerability because LANMAN cannot create hashes of passwords with more than fourteen characters. If an organization doesn't need the LANMAN passwords for backward compatibility, they can disable it. This article provides details on how to do so: http://support.microsoft.com/kb/299656.

Providing Confidentiality with Encryption

Encryption provides confidentiality and prevents unauthorized disclosure of data. Encrypted data is in a cipher text format that is unreadable. Attackers can't read encrypted traffic sent over a network, or encrypted data stored on a system. In contrast, if data is sent in clear text, an attacker can capture and read the data using a protocol analyzer.

The two primary encryption methods are symmetric and asymmetric. Symmetric encryption encrypts and decrypts data with the same key. Asymmetric encryption encrypts and decrypts data using a matched key pair of a public key and a private key.

These encryption methods include two elements:

- **Algorithm.** The algorithm performs mathematical calculations on data. The algorithm is always the same.
- **Key.** The key is a number that provides variability for the encryption. It is either kept private and/or changed frequently.

Remember this

Encryption provides confidentiality and helps ensure that data is viewable only by authorized users. This applies to any type of data, including data at rest, such as data stored in a database, or data in motion sent over a network. Two basic components of encryption are algorithms and keys.

Symmetric Encryption

Symmetric encryption uses the same key to encrypt and decrypt data. In other words, if you encrypt data with a key of three, you decrypt it with the same key of three. Symmetric encryption is also called secret-key encryption or session-key encryption.

As a simple example, when I was a child, a friend and I used to pass encoded messages back and forth to each other. Our algorithm was:

- **Encryption algorithm**: Move __X__ spaces forward to encrypt.
- **Decryption algorithm**: Move __X__ spaces backward to decrypt.

On the way to school, we would identify the key (X) we would use that day. For example, we may have used the key of three one day. If I wanted to encrypt a message, I would move each character three spaces forward, and he would decrypt the message by moving three spaces backward.

Imagine the message "PASS" needs to be sent.

- Three characters past "P" is "S"—Start at P (Q, R, **S**)
- Three characters past "A" is "D"—Start at A (B, C, **D**)
- Three characters past "S" is "V"—Start at S (T, U, **V**)
- Three characters past "S" is "V"—Start at S (T, U, **V**)

The encrypted message is SDVV. My friend decrypted it by moving backwards three spaces and learning that "PASS" is the original message.

This shows how symmetric encryption uses the same key for encryption and decryption. If I encrypted the message with a key of three, my friend wouldn't be able to decrypt it with anything but a key of three. It also helps to demonstrate an algorithm and a key, though it is admittedly simple. Most algorithms and keys are much more complex. For example, the Advanced Encryption Standard (AES) symmetric algorithm typically uses 128-bit keys but can use keys with 256 bits.

Sophisticated symmetric encryption techniques use the same components of an algorithm and a key. Imagine two servers sending encrypted traffic back and forth to each other using AES symmetric encryption. They both use the same AES algorithm and the same key for this data. The data is encrypted on one server with AES and a key, sent over the wire or other transmission medium, and the same key is used to decrypt it on the other server. Similarly, if a database includes encrypted data, the key used to encrypt data is the same key used to decrypt data.

However, symmetric encryption doesn't use the same key to encrypt and decrypt all data. For example, my friend and I used a different key each day. On the way to school, we decided on a key to use for that day. The next day, we picked a different key. If someone cracked our code yesterday, they couldn't easily crack our code today.

Symmetric encryption algorithms change keys much more often than once a day. For example, imagine an algorithm uses a key of 123 to encrypt a project file. It could then use a key of 456 to encrypt a spreadsheet file. The key of 123 can only decrypt the project file and the key of 456 can only decrypt the spreadsheet file.

On the other hand, if symmetric encryption always used the same key of 123, it would add vulnerabilities. First, when keys are reused, the encryption is easier to crack. Second, once the key is cracked, all data encrypted with this key is compromised. If attackers discover the key of

123, not only would they have access to the project file, but they would also have access to the spreadsheet file and any other data encrypted with this same key.

> ## *Remember this*
>
> Symmetric encryption uses the same key to encrypt and decrypt data. For example, when transmitting encrypted data, symmetric encryption algorithms use the same key to encrypt and decrypt data at both ends of the transmission media. Symmetric encryption is much more efficient at encrypting large amounts of data than asymmetric encryption.

Block vs. Stream Ciphers

Most symmetric algorithms use either a block cipher or a stream cipher. They are both symmetric, so they both use the same key to encrypt or decrypt data. However, they divide data in different ways.

A block cipher encrypts data in specific sized blocks, such as 64-bit blocks or 128-bit blocks. The block cipher divides large files or messages into these blocks and then encrypts each individual block separately.

Stream ciphers encrypt data as a stream of bits rather than dividing it into blocks. An important principle when using a stream cipher is that encryption keys should never be reused. If a key is reused, it is easier to crack the encryption.

For example, chapter 4 introduced Wired Equivalent Privacy (WEP) and initialization vector (IV) attacks. WEP uses the RC4 stream cipher for symmetric encryption. RC4 is a secure algorithm when it's implemented correctly, but WEP did not follow the important stream cipher principle of never reusing keys. If wireless systems generate enough traffic, WEP reuses keys for RC4. Attackers discovered they could use packet injection techniques to increase the number of packets on a wireless network, detect the duplicate keys, and crack the encryption.

> ## *Comparing Symmetric Encryption to a Door Key*
>
> Occasionally, security professionals compare symmetric keys to a house key, and this analogy helps some people understand symmetric encryption a little better. For example, imagine Sally moves into a new home. She'll receive a single key that she can use to lock and unlock her home. Of course, Sally can't use this key to unlock her neighbor's home.
>
> Later, Sally marries Joe, and Joe moves into Sally's home. Sally can create a copy of her house key and give it to Joe. Joe can now use that copy of the key to lock and unlock the house. By sharing copies of the same key, it doesn't matter whether Sally or Joe is the one who locks the door; they can both unlock it.
>
> Similarly, symmetric encryption uses a single key to encrypt and decrypt data. If a copy of the symmetric key is shared, others that have the key can also encrypt and decrypt data.

AES

The Advanced Encryption Standard (AES) is a strong symmetric block cipher. The National Institute of Standards and Technology (NIST) adopted AES from the Rijndael encryption algorithm after a lengthy evaluation of several different algorithms. NIST is a United States agency that develops and promotes standards. They spent about five years conducting a review of fifteen different symmetric algorithms and identified AES as the best of the fifteen.

AES can use key sizes of 128 bits, 192 bits, or 256 bits and it's sometimes referred to as AES-128, AES-192, or AES-256 to identify how many bits are used in the key. When more bits are used, it makes it more difficult to discover the key. AES-128 provides strong protection but AES-256 provides stronger protection.

Because of its strengths, AES has been adopted in a wide assortment of applications. For example, many applications that encrypt data on USB drives use AES. Some of the strengths of AES are:

- **Fast**. AES uses elegant mathematical formulas and only requires one pass to encrypt and decrypt data. In contrast, 3DES requires multiple passes to encrypt and decrypt data.
- **Efficient**. AES is less resource intensive than other encryption algorithms such as 3DES. AES encrypts and decrypts quickly even when ciphering data on small devices, such as USB flash drives.
- **Strong**. AES provides strong encryption of data providing a high level of confidentiality.

> **Remember this**
>
> AES is a strong symmetric algorithm that uses 128-bit, 192-bit, or 256-bit keys. DES uses only 56-bit keys and should not be used today.

DES

Data Encryption Standard (DES) was widely used for many years, dating back to the 1970s. However, it uses a relatively small key of only 56 bits and can be broken with brute force attacks. In the '70s, the technology required to break 56-bit encryption wasn't easily available, but with the advances in computer technology, a 56-bit key is now considered trivial. DES should not be used today.

3DES

3DES (pronounced as Triple DES) is a symmetric block cipher designed as an improvement over the known weaknesses of DES. In basic terms, it encrypts data using the DES algorithm in three separate passes and uses multiple keys.

While 3DES is a strong algorithm, it isn't used as often as AES today. AES is much less resource intensive. However, if hardware doesn't support AES, 3DES is a suitable alternative. 3DES uses key sizes of 56 bits, 112 bits, or 168 bits.

Remember this

3DES was originally designed as a replacement for DES. It uses multiple keys and multiple passes and is not as efficient as AES. However, 3DES is still used in some applications, such as when hardware doesn't support AES.

RC4

Ron Rivest invented several versions of RC, which are sometimes referred to as Ron's Code or Rivest's Cipher. The most commonly used version is RC4 (also called ARC4), which is a strong symmetric stream cipher.

It's worthwhile pointing out that this is the same RC4 used in WEP. WEPs vulnerabilities weren't because it used RC4, but instead because it did not follow a basic rule of a stream cipher: don't reuse keys.

However, just because WEP uses RC4 and WEP is weak, it does not mean that RC4 is weak. RC4 is strong, and widely used. For example, Secure Sockets Layer (SSL) uses RC4 for symmetric encryption in HTTPS connections, and helps secure millions of web connections daily. If RC4 was weak, it wouldn't be used with HTTPS.

One-Time Pad

The one-time pad cipher has been around since 1917, and many consider it to be one of the most secure algorithms, though it is labor intensive. The one-time pad is a hardcopy printout of keys in a pad of paper. Each piece of paper in the pad has a single key along with a serial number that identifies the page. Spies have used these with miniature pads of paper so small it requires a magnifying glass to read the keys.

As an example, imagine Sally and Joe are two spies and they want to be able to share secrets with each other. They both have identical pads. Sally can create a message and encrypt it with a key from one of the pages in her pad. She includes the serial number of the page and sends the encrypted message and the serial number to Joe. She then destroys the page she used to create the message.

Joe receives the message with the serial number and he locates the page in his one-time pad. He uses the key on the page to decrypt the message, and after decrypting the message, Joe destroys the key.

One-time pads require following some basic principles for security. The keys must be random, and the key must be the same length as the plain text message. Users must destroy the key after using them once and never reuse a key. Additionally, there should only be two copies of a one-time pad.

Remember this

One-time pads are hardcopy printouts of keys in a pad of paper. Keys are distributed in these printed pads and keys are destroyed after a single use.

One-time pads have been adapted into some computer applications. For example, a token or fob (described in chapter 1) is in the *something you have* factor of authentication and makes use of one-time use, rolling passwords similar to one-time pads. As a reminder, users have a token that displays a number on an LCD display. This number changes regularly, such as every sixty seconds. The fob is synchronized with a server that will know the displayed number at any point in time.

Blowfish and TwoFish

Blowfish is a strong symmetric block cipher that is still widely used today. Bruce Schneier (a widely respected voice in IT security) designed Blowfish as a general purpose algorithm to replace DES.

TwoFish was related to Blowfish and was one of the finalist algorithms evaluated by NIST for AES. However, another algorithm (Rijndael) was selected over Blowfish as AES.

Asymmetric Encryption

Asymmetric encryption uses two keys in a matched pair to encrypt and decrypt data—a public key and a private key. There are several important points to remember with these keys:

- If the *public* key encrypts information, only the matching *private* key can decrypt the same information.
- If the *private* key encrypts information, only the matching *public* key can decrypt the same information.
- Private keys are always kept private and never shared.
- Public keys are freely shared by embedding them in a certificate.

Remember this

Only a private key can decrypt information encrypted with a matching public key. Only a public key can decrypt information encrypted with a matching private key.

While asymmetric encryption is very strong, it is also very resource intensive. It takes a significant amount of processing power to encrypt and decrypt data, especially when compared to symmetric encryption. Most cryptographic protocols that use asymmetric encryption only use it to privately share a symmetric key. They then use symmetric encryption to encrypt and decrypt data because symmetric encryption is so much more efficient.

Some protocols that use asymmetric cryptography include:

- SSL and TLS
- RSA and Diffie Hellman
- S/MIME and PGP/GPG
- Elliptic curve cryptography

Some of the more advanced topics related to asymmetric encryption become harder to understand if you don't understand the relationship of matched public and private key pairs. However, since you can't actually see these keys, the concepts are hard to grasp for some people. The Rayburn box demonstrates how you can use physical keys for the same purposes as these public and private keys.

The Rayburn Box

I often talk about the Rayburn box in the classroom to help people understand the usage of public and private keys. A Rayburn box is a lockbox that allows people to securely transfer items over long distances. It has two keys. One key can lock the box but can't unlock it. The other key can unlock the box but can't lock it.

Both keys are matched to one box and won't work with other boxes.

- Only one copy of one key exists—think of it as the private key.
- Multiple copies of the other key exist, and copies are freely made and distributed—think of this as the public key.

The box comes in two different versions. In one version, it's used to send secrets in a confidential manner to prevent unauthorized disclosure. In the other version, it's used to send messages with authentication so you know the sender actually sent the message and that the message wasn't modified in transit.

The Rayburn Box Used to Send Secrets

Imagine that I wanted you to send some proprietary information and a working model of a new invention to me. Obviously, we wouldn't want anyone else to be able to access the information or the working model. I could send you the empty open box with a copy of the key used to lock it.

You place everything in the box and then lock it with the key I've sent with the box. This key can't unlock the box, so even if other people had copies of the key I sent to you, they couldn't use their key to unlock the box. When I receive the box from you, I can unlock it with the only key that will unlock it.

This is similar to how public and private keys are used to send encrypted data over the Internet to ensure confidentiality. The public key encrypts information. After information has been encrypted with the public key, it can only be decrypted with the private key, and the private key always stays private. The "Encrypting HTTPS Traffic with SSL and TLS" section later in this chapter shows this process in more depth.

The Rayburn Box Used for Authentication

With a little rekeying of the box, it can be used to send messages while giving assurances that the message was actually sent by me. In this context, the message isn't secret and doesn't need to be protected; it's only important that you know the message was sent by me.

When used this way, the Rayburn box is keyed so that the private key will lock the box but can't unlock it. Remember, there is only one private key, and it stays private. Multiple copies of the public key exist, and they are freely given out and available. The public key can unlock the box but can't lock it.

Imagine that you and I are allies in a battle. I want to give you a message of "SY0-301," which tells you to launch a specific attack at a specific time. We don't care if someone reads this message since it's a code. Instead, we want you to be assured that the message came from me.

I write the message, place it in the box, and lock it with my private key. When you receive it, you can unlock it with the public key. Since the public key opens it, you know this is my box and it was locked with my private key—you know the message was sent by me.

If someone intercepted the box and opened it with the public key, it couldn't be locked again with the public key, so you'd receive an open box. This doesn't prove it was sent by me. The only way you know that it was sent by me is if it is locked when you receive it and you can unlock it with the public key.

This is similar to how public and private keys are used for digital signatures. Digital signatures are explained in more depth later in this chapter, but, in short, I could send you a message digitally signed with my private key. If you can decrypt the digital signature with my matching public key, you know it was encrypted, or signed, with my private key. Since only one copy of the private key exists, and I'm the only person that can access it, you know I sent the message.

The Rayburn Box Demystified

Before you try to find a Rayburn box, let me clear something up. The Rayburn box is just a figment of my imagination. Rayburn is my middle name.

I haven't discovered a real-world example of how public/private keys work, so I've created the Rayburn box as a metaphor to help people visualize how public/private keys work. Feel free to build one if you want.

Certificates

A key element of asymmetric encryption is a certificate. A certificate is a digital document that includes the public key and information on the owner of the certificate. Certificate authorities (CAs) issue and manage certificates. CAs are explored in greater depth later in this chapter.

Certificates are used for a variety of purposes, including:

- Encryption
- Authentication
- Digital signatures

Remember this

Certificates are an important part of asymmetric encryption. Certificates include public keys along with details on the owner of the certificate and on the CA that issued the certificate. Certificate owners share their public key by sharing a copy of their certificate.

Figure 10.5 shows a sample certificate with the public key selected. Users and applications share the certificate file to share the public key. They do not share the private key.

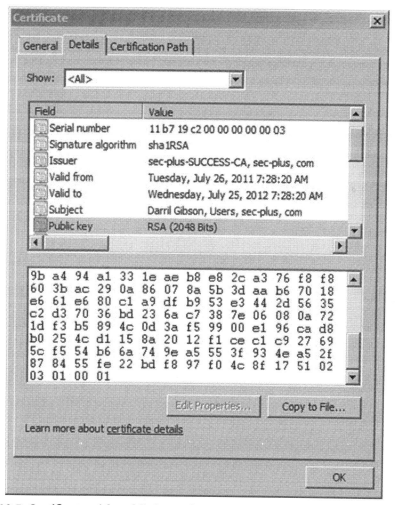

Figure 10.5: Certificate with public key selected

Notice that there is much more information in the certificate than just the public key. Some of it is visible in the figure, but there is more. Common elements within a certificate include:

- **Serial number**. The serial number uniquely identifies the certificate. The CA uses this serial number to validate a certificate. If the CA revokes the certificate, they publish this serial number in a certification revocation list (CRL).
- **Issuer**. This identifies the CA that issued the certificate.
- **Validity dates**. Certificates include "Valid From" and "Valid To" dates. This allows a certificate to expire.
- **Subject**. This identifies the owner of the certificate. In the figure, it identifies a user. A certificate from a website includes its website address.
- **Public key**. RSA asymmetric encryption uses the public key in combination with the matching private key.
- **Usage.** Some certificates are only for encryption or authentication, while other certificates support multiple usages.

RSA

Ron Rivest, Adi Shamir, and Leonard Adleman developed RSA, and it is named from the first letters of their last names (RSA). Asymmetric encryption methods use RSA, and it is widely used on the Internet and elsewhere due to its strong security.

For example, e-mail applications often use RSA to privately share a symmetric key between two systems. The application uses the recipient's public key to encrypt a symmetric key, and the recipient's private key decrypts it. This process is explained in the "Protecting E-mail" section later in this chapter. Chapter 5 introduced Trusted Platform Modules (TPMs) and hardware security modules (HSMs) used for hardware encryption. TPMs and HSMs provide secure storage for RSA keys.

RSA uses the mathematical properties of prime numbers to generate secure public and private keys. Specifically, RSA relies on the fact that the product of two large prime numbers can't be easily factored. The math is complex and intriguing to mathematicians, but you don't have to understand the math to understand that RSA is secure.

For example, researchers published a paper in 2010 identifying how long it took to factor a 232-digit number (768 bits). They wrote that it took them about two and a half years using hundreds of systems. They estimated that if a single 2.2 GHz computer was used, it would take fifteen hundred years to complete. RSA is used on the Internet as one of the protections for credit card transactions. It's safe to say that today's credit card information won't be of much value in fifteen hundred years.

RSA uses at least 1024-bit keys today. RSA Security (a company that frequently tests the security of RSA) recommends using key sizes of at least 2048 bits long, and 3072-bit keys are on the horizon.

> ### Remember this
>
> RSA is widely used to protect Internet traffic, including e-mail. It relies on the mathematical properties of prime numbers when creating public and private keys. These keys are commonly used with asymmetric encryption to privately share a symmetric key. Diffie-Hellman addresses key management and provides another method to privately share a symmetric key between two parties.

Diffie-Hellman

Diffie-Hellman is a key exchange algorithm used to privately share a symmetric key between two parties. Once the two parties know the symmetric key, they use symmetric encryption to encrypt the data.

The Diffie-Hellman scheme was first published in 1976 by Whitfield Diffie and Martin Hellman. Interestingly, Malcolm J. Williamson secretly created a similar algorithm while working in a British intelligence agency. It is widely believed that the work of these three provided the basis for public-key cryptography.

Elliptic Curve Cryptography

Elliptic curve cryptography (ECC) is commonly used with small wireless devices since it doesn't take much processing power to achieve the desired security. It uses mathematical equations to formulate an elliptical curve. It then graphs points on the curve to create keys. This is mathematically easier and requires less processing power, while also being more difficult to crack.

The math behind ECC is quite complex, but a simple fact helps to illustrate the strength of ECC. In 2005, the U.S. National Security Agency (NSA) announced approval of ECC for digital signatures and Diffie-Hellman key agreements. If the NSA has endorsed and approved ECC, you can bet that it is well tested and strong.

> ### Remember this
>
> Elliptic curve cryptography is commonly used with small wireless devices. It uses smaller key sizes and requires less processing power than many other encryption methods

Steganography

Steganography hides data inside other data, or, as some people have said, it hides data in plain sight. The goal is to hide the data in such a way that no one suspects there is a hidden message. It doesn't actually encrypt the data, so it can't be classified as either symmetric or asymmetric. However, it can effectively hide information, so it is included with encryption topics.

Some common examples of steganography are:

- **In images or sound files**. It's possible to manipulate bits within an image or sound file. The files appear normal. However, if people know the file includes a message, they can easily retrieve it.
- **In writing**. A simplistic form of steganography simply reduces the font size so small that it looks like a dot, colon, or dash. It would be easy to overlook the text. However, if someone knows the text is there, it is equally easy to expand the text to read it.

Remember this

Steganography is the practice of hiding data within data, such as hiding data within a file or reducing the size of a font so that the data looks like a dot or dash. Security professionals use hashing to detect changes in files that may indicate the use of steganography.

One method of embedding data in large files is modifying the least significant bit in some bytes. When the least significant bit of different bytes are modified, the changes are so small that they are difficult to detect. For example, an image file may look exactly the same to you or me. However, there are changes.

Imagine if a terrorist in one country wanted to communicate with terrorist cells in another country. They could use steganography by posting graphics to a web page. For example, the web page may include a picture of a tree as a graphic file. When they want to send a message, they modify the graphic to include the message and post the modified graphic to the site. This looks like the same tree. However, if their contacts know to look for a message, they can download the graphics file and decode it.

Security professionals use hashing to detect steganography. If a single bit of a file is modified, the hashing algorithm creates a different hash. By regularly taking the hashes of different files and comparing them to previous hashes, it's easy to detect when a file has been modified.

Quantum Cryptography

Quantum cryptography is based on quantum physics and photons, the smallest measure of light. Some applications use quantum cryptography to transmit an encryption key as a series of photons.

Normally a photon will spin and emit light in all directions, similar to how a light bulb emits light in all directions. In quantum cryptography, photons are modified so that they spin and emit light in a single direction, such as up and down or side to side. It's then possible to assign a value for the direction.

For example, if the photon emits light up and down, it's a one. If it emits light side to side, it's a zero. It's then possible to convert a stream of photons into an encryption key. Two parties exchange photon streams identifying and validating the key.

There's much more involved in this photon conversation, but I'm going to skip the quantum physics. However, there is one more important element. When a photon is read or measured, it will change direction. If a third party reads any of the photons in the stream, it will be obvious to the two parties trying to exchange the key. When the two parties realize someone is eavesdropping, they won't exchange secure data until the third party is removed.

SSL

Secure Sockets Layer (SSL) is an encryption protocol used to encrypt Internet traffic. For example, HTTPS uses SSL in secure web browser sessions. It can also encrypt other transmissions. For example, File Transport Protocol Secure (FTPS) uses SSL to encrypt transmissions.

SSL provides certificate-based authentication and encrypts data with a combination of both symmetric and asymmetric encryption during a session. It uses asymmetric encryption to privately share a session key, and symmetric encryption to encrypt data displayed on the web page and transmitted during the session.

Netscape created SSL for its web browser and updated it to version SSL 3.0. This was before organizations such as the Internet Engineering Task Force (IETF) created and maintained standards. Netscape's success waned and there wasn't a standardization process to update SSL, even though all web browsers were using it. The IETF created TLS to standardize improvements with SSL.

TLS

Transport Layer Security (TLS) is a replacement for SSL and is widely used in many different applications. The IETF has updated and published several TLS documents specifying the standard. TLS 1.0 was based on SSL 3.0 and is referred to as SSL 3.1. Similarly, each update to TLS indicated it was an update to SSL. For example, TLS 1.1 is called SSL 3.2 and TLS 1.2 is called SSL 3.3.

Just like SSL, TLS provides certificate-based authentication and uses both asymmetric and symmetric encryption. It uses asymmetric encryption to privately share a symmetric key and uses symmetric encryption to encrypt data in the web session. The "Encrypting HTTPS Traffic with SSL and TLS" section later in this chapter shows this process.

Many other applications use TLS. For example, chapter 4 introduced the Extensible Authentication Protocol (EAP) in the context of increasing wireless security by adding authentication. Protected EAP (PEAP) uses TLS (PEAP-TLS) to encrypt the authentication process between two systems. TLS can encrypt other traffic such as FTP and SMTP just as SSL does.

It's important to remember that TLS and SSL require certificates. Certificate authorities (CAs) issue and manage certificates, so a CA is required to support TLS and SSL. These CAs can be internal or third-party external CAs.

> ## Remember this
>
> TLS is the replacement for SSL. Both TLS and SSL require certificates issued by certificate authorities (CAs). For example, PEAP-TLS uses TLS to encrypt the authentication process and PEAP-TLS requires a CA to issue certificates. HTTPS uses a combination of symmetric and asymmetric encryption to encrypt HTTPS sessions.

Other Transport Encryption Protocols

Other transport encryption protocols were covered earlier in this book. As a reminder, they are:

- **IPsec**. Chapters 3 and 4 presented IPsec. It can encrypt data in tunnel mode with VPNs such as with L2TP/IPsec. It can also encrypt data in transport mode between two systems. An Authentication Header (AH) provides authentication and integrity. Encapsulating Security Payload (ESP) provides confidentiality, integrity, and authentication. AH uses protocol ID 51 and ESP uses protocol ID 50.
- **SSH**. Chapter 3 presented Secure Shell. It's used to encrypt a wide assortment of traffic such as Secure File Transport Protocol (SFTP), Secure Copy (SCP), and Telnet. SSH uses port 22.
- **HTTPS**. Chapter 3 presented HTTP Secure. HTTPS uses either SSL or TLS to encrypt web traffic over port 443.

Using Cryptographic Protocols

With a basic understanding of hashing, symmetric encryption, and asymmetric encryption, it's easier to grasp how cryptography is used. Many applications use a combination of these methods, and it's important to understand how they're intertwined.

When describing public and private keys earlier, I stressed that one key encrypts and the other key decrypts. A common question I often hear is "which one encrypts and which one decrypts." The answer depends on what you're trying to accomplish. The following sections describe the details, but, as an overview, these are the important points related to these keys:

- E-mail digital signatures
  - The *sender's private key* encrypts (or signs).
  - The *sender's public key* decrypts.
- E-mail encryption
  - The *recipient's public key* encrypts.
  - The *recipient's private key* decrypts.
- Website encryption
  - The *website's public key* encrypts (a symmetric key).
  - The *website's private key* decrypts (a symmetric key).
  - The *symmetric key* encrypts data in the website session.

E-mail and website encryption commonly use a combination of both asymmetric and symmetric encryption. They use asymmetric encryption to privately share a symmetric key. Symmetric encryption encrypts the data.

> ### Remember this
> Knowing which key encrypts and which key decrypts will help you answer many questions. For example, just by knowing that a private key is encrypting, you know that it is being used for a digital signature.

Protecting E-mail

Cryptography provides two primary security methods you can use with e-mail: digital signatures and encryption. These are separate processes, but you can digitally sign and encrypt the same e-mail.

Signing E-mail with Digital Signatures

Digital signatures are similar in concept to handwritten signatures on printed documents that identify individuals, but they provide more security benefits. A digital signature is an encrypted hash of a message, encrypted with the sender's private key. If the recipient of a digitally signed e-mail can decrypt the hash, it provides the following three security benefits:

- **Authentication**. This identifies the sender of the e-mail. E-mail recipients have assurances the e-mail actually came from who it appears to be coming from. For example, if an executive digitally signs an e-mail, recipients know it came from the executive and not from an attacker impersonating the executive.
- **Non-repudiation**. The sender cannot later deny sending the message. This is sometimes required with online transactions. For example, imagine if Harry sends an order to sell stocks using a digitally signed e-mail. If the stocks increase after his sale completes, he can't deny the transaction.
- **Integrity**. This provides assurances that the message has not been modified or corrupted. Recipients know that the message they received is the same as the sent message.

Digital signatures are much easier to grasp if you understand some other cryptography concepts discussed in this chapter. As a short review, these concepts are:

- **Hashing**. Digital signatures start by creating a hash of the message. A hash is simply a number created by performing an algorithm on the message.
- **Certificates**. Digital signatures need certificates, and certificates include the sender's public key.
- **Public/private keys**. In a digital signature, the sender uses the sender's private key to encrypt the hash of the message. The recipient uses the sender's public key to decrypt the hash of the message.

Figure 10.6 shows an overview of this process. In the figure, Sally is sending a message to Joe with a digital signature. Note that the message "I passed" is not secret. If it was, Sally would encrypt it, which is a completely separate process. The focus in this explanation is only the digital signature.

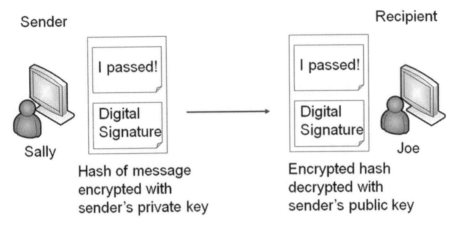

Figure 10.6: Digital signature process

Sally creates her message in an e-mail program, such as Microsoft Outlook. Once Microsoft Outlook is configured, all she has to do is click a button to digitally sign the message. Here is what happens when she clicks the button.

- The application hashes the message.
- The application retrieves Sally's private key and encrypts the hash using this private key.
- The application sends both the encrypted hash and the unencrypted message to Joe.

When Joe's system receives the message, it verifies the digital signature using the following steps:

1. Joe's system retrieves Sally's public key, which is in Sally's public certificate. In some situations, Sally may have sent Joe a copy of her certificate with her public key. In domain environments, Joe's system can automatically retrieve Sally's certificate from a network location.
2. The e-mail application on Joe's system decrypts the encrypted hash with Sally's public key.
3. The application calculates the hash on the received message.
4. The application compares the decrypted hash with the calculated hash.

If the calculated hash of the received message is the same as the encrypted hash of the digital signature, it validates several important checks:

- **Authentication**. Sally sent the message. The public key can only decrypt something encrypted with the private key, and only Sally has the private key. If the decryption succeeded, Sally's private key must have encrypted the hash. On the other hand, if another key was used to encrypt the hash, Sally's public key could not decrypt it. In this case, Joe will see an error indicating a problem with the digital signature.

- **Non-repudiation**. Sally cannot later deny sending the message. Only Sally has her private key and if the public key decrypted the hash, the hash must have been encrypted with her private key. Non-repudiation is valuable in online transactions.
- **Integrity**. Since the hash on the sent message matches the hash of the received message, the message has maintained integrity. It hasn't been modified.

Remember this

A digital signature is an encrypted hash of a message. The sender's private key encrypts the hash of the message to create the digital signature. The recipient decrypts the hash with the sender's public key, and, if successful, it provides authentication, non-repudiation, and integrity. Authentication identifies the sender. Integrity verifies the message has not been modified. Non-repudiation is used with online transactions and prevents the sender from later denying they sent the e-mail.

At this point, you might be thinking, if we do all of this, why not just encrypt the message, too? The answer is resources. It doesn't take much to encrypt 256 bits in a SHA-256 hash, but it would take quite a bit more to encrypt a lengthy e-mail and its attachments. However, if you need to ensure confidentiality of the e-mail, you can encrypt it.

Encrypting E-mail

There are times when you want to ensure that e-mail messages are only readable by authorized users. You can encrypt e-mail and just as any other time encryption is used, encrypting an e-mail provides confidentiality.

Encrypting E-mail with Only Asymmetric Encryption

Imagine that Sally wants to send an encrypted message to Joe. The following steps provide a simplified explanation of the process if only asymmetric encryption is used.

1. Sally retrieves a copy of Joe's certificate that contains his public key.
2. Sally encrypts the e-mail with Joe's public key.
3. Sally sends the encrypted e-mail to Joe.
4. Joe decrypts the e-mail with his private key.

This works since only Joe has access to his private key. If attackers intercepted the e-mail, they couldn't decrypt it without Joe's private key. With this in mind, it's important to remember that when you're encrypting e-mail contents, the recipient's public key encrypts and the recipient's private key decrypts. The sender's keys are not involved in this process. In contrast, a digital signature only uses the sender's keys but not the recipient's keys.

> ### *Remember this*
>
> The recipient's public key encrypts when encrypting an e-mail message. The recipient uses the recipient's private key to decrypt an encrypted e-mail message. In most cases, the public key doesn't actually encrypt the message, but instead encrypts a symmetric key used to encrypt the e-mail. The recipient then uses the private key to decrypt the symmetric key, and then uses the symmetric key to decrypt the e-mail.

Encrypting E-mail with Asymmetric and Symmetric Encryption

The previous description provides a simplistic explanation of e-mail encryption used by some e-mail applications. However, most e-mail applications combine both asymmetric and symmetric encryption. You may remember from earlier in this chapter that asymmetric encryption is slow and inefficient, but symmetric encryption is very quick.

Instead of using only symmetric encryption, most e-mail applications use asymmetric encryption to privately share a session key. They then use symmetric encryption to encrypt the data. For example, imagine that Sally is sending Joe an encrypted message. The following steps (shown in Figure 10.7) show the process:

1. Sally identifies a symmetric key to encrypt her e-mail. For this example, assume it's a simplistic symmetric key of 53, though a symmetric algorithm like AES would use 128-bit or larger keys.

2. Sally encrypts the e-mail contents with the symmetric key of 53.

3. Sally retrieves a copy of Joe's certificate that contains his public key. She uses Joe's public key to encrypt the symmetric key of 53.

4. Sally sends the encrypted e-mail and the encrypted symmetric key to Joe.

5. Joe decrypts the symmetric key with his private key. He then decrypts the e-mail with the decrypted symmetric key.

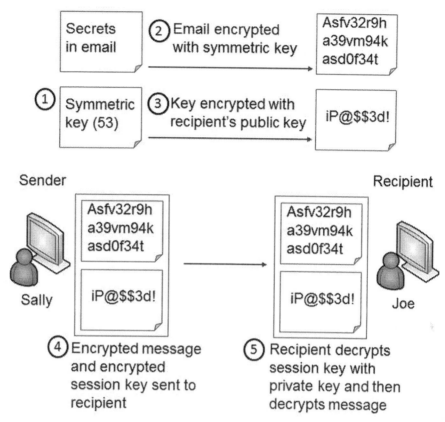

Figure 10.7: Encrypting e-mail

Unauthorized users that intercept the e-mail sent by Sally won't be able to read it since it's encrypted with the symmetric key. Additionally, they can't read the symmetric key since it's encrypted with Joe's public key, and only Joe's private key can decrypt it.

S/MIME

Secure/Multipurpose Internet Mail Extensions (S/MIME) is one of the most popular standards used to digitally sign and encrypt e-mail. Most e-mail applications that support encryption and digital signatures use S/MIME standards.

S/MIME uses RSA for asymmetric encryption and AES for symmetric encryption. It can encrypt e-mail at rest (stored on a drive) and in transit (data sent over the network). Since S/MIME uses RSA for asymmetric encryption, it requires a PKI to distribute and manage certificates.

PGP/GPG

Pretty Good Privacy (PGP) is a method used to secure e-mail communication. It can encrypt, decrypt, and digitally sign e-mail. Phillip Zimmerman designed PGP in 1991, and it has gone through many changes and improvements over the years and has been bought and sold by many different companies. Symantec Corporation purchased it in June 2010.

OpenPGP is a PGP based standard created to avoid any conflict with existing licensing. In other words, users have no obligation to pay licensing fees to use it. Some versions of PGP follow S/MIME standards. Other versions follow OpenPGP standards. GNU Privacy Guard (GPG) is free software that is based on the OpenPGP standard.

Each of the PGP versions use the RSA algorithm and public and private keys for encryption and decryption. Just like S/MIME, PGP uses both asymmetric and symmetric encryption.

> **Remember this**
>
> Both S/MIME and PGP use the RSA algorithm, and use public and private keys for encryption and decryption. They depend on a Public Key Infrastructure (PKI) for certificates. They can digitally sign and encrypt e-mail, including the encryption of e-mail at rest (stored on a drive) and in transit (data sent over the network).

Encrypting HTTPS Traffic with SSL and TLS

HTTP Secure (HTTPS) is commonly used on the Internet to secure web traffic. HTTPS can use either SSL or TLS to encrypt the traffic, and both use asymmetric and symmetric encryption. If you're able to grasp the basics of how HTTPS combines both asymmetric and symmetric encryption, you'll have what you need to know for most protocols that use both encryptions.

Since asymmetric encryption isn't efficient to encrypt large amounts of data, symmetric encryption is used to encrypt the session data. However, both the client and the server must know what this symmetric key is before they can use it. They can't whisper it to each other over the Internet. That's like an actor on TV using a loud whisper, or stage whisper, to share a secret. Millions of TV viewers can also hear the secret.

Instead, HTTPS uses asymmetric encryption to securely transmit a symmetric key. It then uses the symmetric key with symmetric encryption to encrypt all the data in the HTTPS session.

Figure 10.8 and the following steps show the overall process of establishing and using an HTTPS session. As you read these steps, try to keep these two important concepts in mind:

- SSL and TLS use *asymmetric* encryption to securely share the symmetric key.
- SSL and TLS use *symmetric* encryption to encrypt the session data.

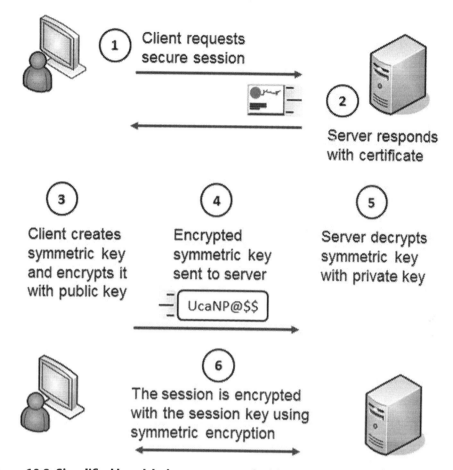

Figure 10.8: Simplified handshake process used with HTTPS

1. The client begins the process by requesting an HTTPS session. This could be by entering an HTTPS address in the URL or by clicking on an HTTPS link.
2. The server responds by sending the server's certificate. The certificate includes the server's public key. The matching private key is on the server and only accessible by the server.
3. The client creates a symmetric key and encrypts it with the server's public key.
    As an example, imagine that the symmetric key is 53 (though in reality it would be much more complex). The client encrypts the session key of 53 using the web server's public key creating cipher text of UcaNP@$$.
    This symmetric key will be used to encrypt data in the HTTPS session so it is sometimes called a session key.
4. The client sends the encrypted session key (UcaNP@$$) to the web server. Only the server's private key can decrypt this. If attackers intercept the encrypted key, they won't be able to decrypt it since they don't have access to the server's private key.
5. The server receives the encrypted session key and decrypts it with the server's private key. At this point, both the client and the server know the session key.

6. All of the session data is encrypted with this symmetric key using symmetric encryption.

The amazing thing to me is that this happens so quickly. If a web server takes as long as five seconds, many of us wonder why it's taking so long. However, a lot is happening to establish this session.

> **Remember this**
>
> SSL and TLS use both asymmetric and symmetric encryption in secure web sessions. The website's public key encrypts a symmetric key, and the symmetric key encrypts data within the web session.

Users can verify a session is encrypted with HTTPS using one of these methods. They can ensure the URL includes HTTPS (instead of just HTTP), or verify that the web browser is displaying an icon of a lock, indicating it's secure.

Exploring PKI Components

A Public Key Infrastructure (PKI) is a group of technologies used to request, create, manage, store, distribute, and revoke digital certificates. Asymmetric encryption depends on the use of certificates for a variety of purposes, such as protecting e-mail and protecting Internet traffic with SSL and TLS. For example, HTTPS sessions protect Internet credit card transactions, and these transactions depend on a PKI.

A primary benefit of a PKI is that it allows two people or entities to communicate securely without knowing each other previously. In other words, it allows them to communicate securely through an insecure public medium such as the Internet.

For example, you can establish a secure session with Amazon.com even if you've never done so before. Amazon purchased a certificate from VeriSign. As shown in the "Encrypting HTTPS Traffic with SSL and TLS" section previously, the certificate provides the ability to establish a secure session.

A key element in a PKI is a certificate authority.

> **Remember this**
>
> A PKI includes all the components required for certificates. It allows two entities to privately share symmetric keys without any prior communication.

Certificate Authority

A certificate authority (CA, pronounced cah) issues, manages, validates, and revokes certificates. CAs can be very large, such as VeriSign, a public CA. A CA can also be very small, such as a single service running on a server in a domain.

Public CAs make money by selling certificates. For this to work, the public CA must be trusted. Certificates issued by the CA are trusted as long as the CA is trusted.

This is similar to how a driver's license is trusted. The department of motor vehicles (DMV) issues driver's licenses after validating a person's identity. If you want to cash a check, you may present your driver's license to prove your identity. Businesses trust the DMV, so they trust the driver's license. On the other hand, if you purchased an ID from Gibson's Instant IDs, businesses may not trust it.

While we may trust the DMV, why would a computer trust a CA? The answer is based on the certificate trust path.

Certificate Trust Paths

CAs are trusted by placing a copy of their root certificate into a trusted root CA store. The root certificate is the first certificate created by the CA that identifies it, and the store is just a collection of these root certificates. If the CAs root certificate is placed in this store, all certificates issued by this CA are trusted.

Figure 10.9 shows the Trusted Root Certification Authority store from Internet Explorer. You can see that there are many certificates from many different CAs. VeriSign is a popular CA, so I scrolled down to show root certificates from VeriSign.

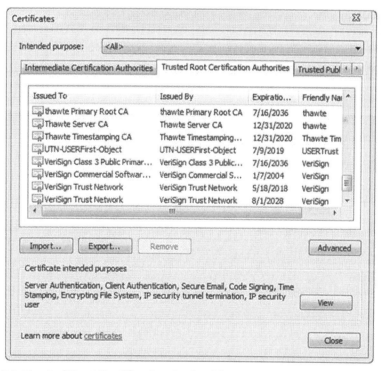

Figure 10.9: Trusted Root Certification Authorities

Public CAs such as VeriSign negotiate with web browser developers to have their certificates included with the web browser. This way, any certificates that they sell to businesses are automatically trusted.

> **Remember this**
> A CA issues, manages, validates, and revokes certificates. Root certificates of trusted CAs are stored in the trusted root certification authority store. All certificates issued by trusted CAs are trusted. Web browsers display errors when a site uses an untrusted certificate.

Trust Models

The most common trust model is the hierarchical trust model. In this model, the public CA creates the first CA, known as the root CA. If the organization is large, it can create child CAs. A large trust chain works like this:

- The root CA issues certificates to intermediate CAs.
- Intermediate CAs issue certificates to child CAs.
- Child CAs issue certificates to devices or end users.

In a small organization, the root CA can simply issue certificates to the devices and end users. It's not necessary to have intermediate and child CAs.

Another type of trust model is a web of trust, sometimes used with PGP and GPG. A web of trust uses self-signed certificates, and a third party vouches for these certificates. For example, if five of your friends trust a certificate, you can trust the certificate. If the third party is a reliable source, the web of trust provides a secure alternative. However, if the third party does not adequately verify certificates, it can result in the use of certificates that shouldn't be trusted.

Self-signed Certificates

It is possible to create a CA and use self-signed certificates. For example, an administrator can use Active Directory Certificate Services (AD CS) on Windows Server 2008 to create a CA and issue certificates to company-owned web servers. AD CS is built into Windows Server 2008, so this is certainly cheaper than purchasing a certificate from a public CA.

However, certificates issued by this CA will not be trusted by default. If a user connects to this web server and establishes an HTTPS session, the web browser will show an error. Depending on the web browser, it may indicate that the issuer of a certificate (the CA) is not recognized or indicate that the site's certificate is not trusted. The error is often accompanied with warning icons and other notes encouraging the users not to continue.

This is not acceptable for an e-commerce website. Imagine if Sally has her credit card in hand ready to buy a product, and then sees errors indicating trust problems. She very likely won't continue.

If only employees use this website, they could ignore the errors and click through to establish the connection. However, this may breed complacency. When they go to a public site and see this same type of error, they may ignore the error and continue.

Instead, an administrator can copy the CA's root certificate to the trusted root certification authority store for employee computers. Web browsers will then trust the certificate from the company website, eliminating the errors.

Registration

Users and systems request certificates from a CA using a registration process. In some cases, a user enters information manually into a website form. In other cases, they send a specifically formatted file to the CA. Within a domain, the system handles much of the process automatically.

As an example, imagine I wanted to purchase a certificate for GetCertifiedGetAhead.com for secure HTTPS sessions. I would first create a public and private key pair. Many programs are available to automate this process. I would then put together a request for the certificate including the purpose of the certificate, information about the website, the public key, and me. I then send the request to the CA. The CA validates my identity and creates a certificate with the public key. The validation process is different based on the usage of the certificate. In some cases, it includes extensive checking, and in other cases, verification comes from the credit card I use to pay.

I can then register this certificate with my website along with the private key. Any time someone initiates a secure HTTPS connection, the website sends the certificate with the public key and the TLS/SSL session creates the session.

In large organizations, a registration authority (RA) can assist the CA by collecting registration information. The RA never issues certificates. Instead, it only assists in the registration process.

Revoking Certificates

Normally, certificates will expire based on the Valid From and Valid To dates. However, there are some instances when a CA will revoke a certificate before it expires.

For example, if a private key is publically available, the key pair is compromised. It no longer provides adequate security since the private key is no longer private. Similarly, if the CA itself is compromised through a security breach, certificates issued by the CA may be compromised, so the CA can revoke certificates.

In general, any time a CA does not want anyone to use a certificate, the CA revokes it. While the most common reasons are due to compromise of a key or the CA, there are others. A CA can use any of the following reasons when revoking a certificate:

- Key Compromise
- CA Compromise
- Change of Affiliation
- Superseded
- Cease of Operation
- Certificate Hold

CAs use certification revocation lists (CRL, pronounced crill) to revoke a certificate. The CRL is a version 2 certificate that includes a list of revoked certificates by serial number. For example,

Figure 10.10 shows a copy of a CRL. Figure 10.5 (shown earlier) showed a screenshot of a certificate from a CA that I created for this chapter. In Figure 10.10, I revoked this certificate. If you compare the serial numbers, you can see that they're the same.

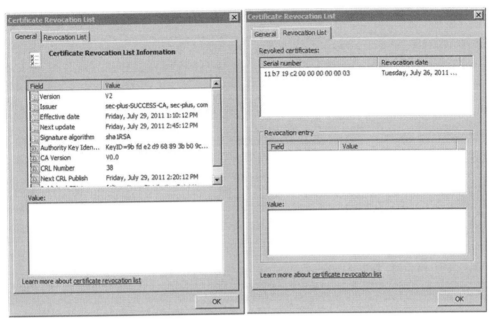

Figure 10.10: Certificate revocation list

> ### Remember this
>
> CAs revoke certificates when the key is compromised or the CA is compromised. The certificate revocation list (CRL) includes a list of revoked certificates. The CRL is publically available.

Validating Certificates

Clients routinely validate certificates through the CA. By validating the certificate, the client is able to verify that the certificate can be trusted and verify that it hasn't been revoked. A common method is by requesting a copy of the CRL.

Figure 10.11 shows the process of validating a certificate.

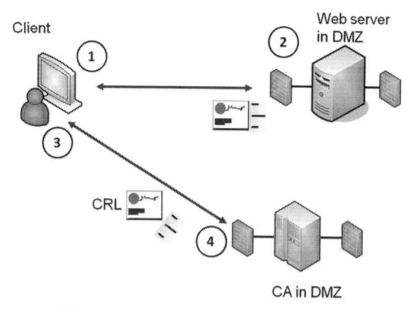

Figure 10.11: Validating a certificate

1. The client initiates the HTTPS session.
2. The server responds with a copy of the certificate that includes the public key.
3. The client queries the CA for a copy of the CRL.
4. The CA responds with a copy of the CRL.

The client then checks the serial number of the certificate against the list of serial numbers in the CRL. If the certificate is revoked for any reason, the application will give an error message to the user.

Notice that the CA and the web server are both protected within demilitarized zones (DMZs). As mentioned in Chapter 3, a DMZ is a buffered zone between an internal network and the Internet. The DMZ provides a layer of protection for Internet facing servers, but servers in the DMZ are available on the Internet.

Another method of validating a certificate is with the Online Certificate Status Protocol (OCSP). OCSP allows the client to query the CA with the serial number of the certificate. The CA then responds with an answer of "healthy," "revoked," or "unknown." A response of "unknown" could indicate the certificate is a forgery.

Key Escrow

Key escrow is the process of placing a copy of a private key in a safe environment. This is useful for recovery. If the original is lost, the organization retrieves the copy of the key to access the data. Key escrow isn't required, but if an organization determines that data loss is unacceptable, it will implement a key escrow process.

In some cases, an organization provides a copy of the key to a third party. Another method is to designate employees within the organization that will be responsible for key escrow. These employees maintain and protect copies of the key, and if the original key is lost, they check out a copy of the key to an administrator or user.

> **Remember this**
>
> A key escrow maintains a copy of a private key for recovery in the event the original is lost. An organization often uses key escrow if loss of encrypted data is unacceptable. Even if users lose access to their original private key, the organization will still be able to access the encrypted data using a key from key escrow.

Recovery Agent

A key recovery agent is a designated individual who can recover or restore cryptographic keys. In the context of a PKI, a recovery agent can recover private keys to access encrypted data. The recovery agent may be a security professional, administrator, or anyone designated by the company.

In some cases, the recovery agent can recover encrypted data using a different key. For example, Microsoft's BitLocker supports encryption of entire drives. It's possible to add a data recovery agent field when creating a BitLocker encrypted drive. In this case, BitLocker uses two keys. The user has one key and uses it to unlock the drive during day-to-day use. The second key is only accessible by the recovery agent and used for recovery purposes if the original key is lost or becomes inaccessible.

Chapter 10 Exam Topic Review

When preparing for the exam, make sure you understand these key concepts covered in this chapter.

Providing Integrity with Hashing

- Hashing provides integrity by verifying that data has not been modified or corrupted. Hashing can provide integrity for e-mail, files stored on drives, and files downloaded from the Internet.
- A hash is a number, and hashing algorithms create a fixed-size string of bits (such as 128 bits or 256 bits) regardless of the size of the hashed data.
- MD5 is a hashing algorithm creating 128 bit fixed-size keys. SHA is a family of hashing algorithms. SHA-1 creates 160-bit hashes and SHA-256 creates 256-bit hashes.
- LANMAN is an older hashing algorithm that stores passwords by first dividing the password into two seven-character blocks, and then converting all lower case letters to upper case. NTLMv1 superseded LANMAN, and NTLMv2 superseded NTLMv1.

Providing Confidentiality with Encryption

- Confidentiality ensures that data is only viewable by authorized users. Encryption provides confidentiality of data, including data at rest (any type of data stored on disk) and data in motion (any type of transmitted data).
- Two basic components of encryption are an algorithm and a key.
- Symmetric encryption uses the same key to encrypt and decrypt data. Transmitted data uses the same key at both ends of the transmission media for encryption and decryption. Data at rest uses the same key to encrypt and decrypt data.
- AES is a popular symmetric encryption algorithm, and it uses 128, 192, or 256 bits for the key.
- DES is an older, weak, symmetric encryption algorithm using 56-bit keys.
- 3DES was created as an improvement over DES. 3DES uses multiple keys and multiple cryptographic passes using the DES algorithm. AES is preferred today, but 3DES is used when hardware doesn't support AES.
- A one-time pad is a hardcopy printout of encryption keys on individual pieces of paper within a pad of paper.
- Asymmetric encryption uses public and private keys as matched pairs.
  - If the public key encrypted information, only the matching private key can decrypt it.
  - If the private key encrypted information, only the matching public key can decrypt it.
  - Private keys are always kept private and never shared.
  - Public keys are freely shared by embedding them in a certificate.
- RSA is a popular asymmetric algorithm. Many cryptographic protocols use RSA to secure data such as e-mail and data transmitted over the Internet. RSA uses prime numbers to generate public and private keys.
- Diffie-Hellman addresses key management and provides a method to privately share a symmetric key between two parties.
- Elliptic curve cryptography is an encryption technology commonly used with small wireless devices. It uses smaller key sizes and requires less processing power than traditional encryption methods.
- Steganography is the practice of hiding data within a file. A simple way is by reducing the font of text so small that it looks like a dot or a dash. A more sophisticated method is by modifying bits within a file. Capturing and comparing hashes of files can discover steganography attempts.
- TLS is the replacement for SSL, and many other applications use TLS. It requires certificates issued from a CA. PEAP-TLS uses TLS for the authentication process.

Using Cryptographic Protocols

- When using digital signatures with e-mail:
  - The sender's private key encrypts (or signs).
  - The sender's public key decrypts.

- A digital signature provides authentication (verified identification) of the sender, non-repudiation, and integrity of the message.
    - Senders create a digital signature by hashing a message and encrypting the hash with the sender's private key.
    - Recipients decrypt the digital signature with the sender's matching public key.
- When encrypting e-mail:
    - The recipient's public key encrypts.
    - The recipient's private key decrypts.
    - Many e-mail applications use the public key to encrypt a symmetric key, and then use the symmetric key to encrypt the e-mail contents.
- When encrypting website traffic with SSL or TLS:
    - The website's public key encrypts a symmetric key.
    - The website's private key decrypts the symmetric key.
    - The symmetric key encrypts data in the session.
- S/MIME and PGP secure e-mail with encryption and digital signatures. They both use RSA, certificates, and depend on a PKI. They can encrypt e-mail at rest (stored on a drive) and in transit (sent over the network).

PKI Components

- A Public Key Infrastructure (PKI) is a group of technologies used to request, create, manage, store, distribute, and revoke digital certificates. A PKI allows two entities to privately share symmetric keys without any prior communication.
- A CA issues, manages, validates, and revokes certificates.
- Root certificates of trusted CAs are stored in the trusted root certification authority store. If a CAs root certificate is not in the trusted store, web users will see errors indicating the certificate is not trusted or the CA is not recognized.
- CAs revoke certificates when the private key is compromised or the CA is compromised. A CRL identifies revoked certificates as a list of certificate serial numbers.
- The CA publishes the CRL, making it available to anyone. Web browsers can check certificates they receive from a web server against a copy of the CRL to determine if a received certificate is revoked.
- A key escrow stores a copy of private keys used within a PKI. If a original private key is lost or inaccessible, the copy is retrieved from escrow preventing data loss.
- PKI recovery agents can recover data secured with a private key, or recover a private key, depending on how the recovery agent is configured.

Chapter 10 Practice Questions

1. What will always create a fixed-size string of bits regardless of the size of the original data? (Choose all that apply.)
   - A. MD5
   - B. SHA
   - C. One-time pad
   - D. CRL

2. Of the following choices, what can ensure the integrity of e-mail messages?
   - A. MD5
   - B. AES
   - C. TwoFish
   - D. RSA

3. What are two basic components of encryption?
   - A. Algorithms and keys
   - B. CAs and CRLs
   - C. Certificates and private keys
   - D. Public keys and session keys

4. A system encrypts data prior to transmitting it over a network, and the system on the other end of the transmission media decrypts it. If the systems are using a symmetric encryption algorithm for encryption and decryption, which of the following statements is true?
   - A. A symmetric encryption algorithm uses the same key to encrypt and decrypt data at both ends of the transmission media
   - B. A symmetric encryption algorithm uses different keys to encrypt and decrypt data at both ends of the transmission media
   - C. A symmetric encryption algorithm does not use keys to encrypt and decrypt data at both ends of the transmission media
   - D. A symmetric encryption algorithm is an insecure method used to encrypt data transmitted over transmission media

5. Which of the following is an encryption algorithm that uses 128-bit keys?
   - A. DES
   - B. AES
   - C. 3DES
   - D. MD5

6. Which of the following uses 56-bit keys for encryption?
    E. AES
    F. DES
    G. MD5
    H. SHA

7. Which of the following is an encryption algorithm that uses multiple keys and encrypts data multiple times?
    A. DES
    B. AES
    C. 3DES
    D. MD5

8. Which of the following statements accurately describes the relationship between keys in a PKI?
    A. Data encrypted with a public key can only be decrypted with the matching private key
    B. Data encrypted with a public key can only be decrypted with the matching public key
    C. Data encrypted with a private key can only be decrypted with the matching private key
    D. The public key always encrypts and the private key always decrypts

9. Which encryption algorithm uses prime numbers to generate keys?
    A. RSA
    B. SHA
    C. S/MIME
    D. PGP

10. Of the following choices, what is an encryption algorithm that is commonly used in small portable devices, such as mobile phones?
    A. Steganography
    B. 3DES
    C. PGP
    D. Elliptic curve

11. A website includes graphic files. A security professional is comparing the hash of a graphic file captured last week with the hash of what appears to be the same graphic file today. What is the security professional looking for?
    A. CRL
    B. Steganography
    C. Key
    D. Digital signature

12. Which of the following protocols requires a CA for authentication?
    A. FTP
    B. PEAP-TLS
    C. AES
    D. PKI

13. An organization wants to verify the identity of anyone sending e-mails. The solution should also verify integrity of the e-mails. What can it use?
    A. AES
    B. Encryption
    C. CRL
    D. Digital signatures

14. Sally is sending an e-mail, and she encrypted a portion of the e-mail with her private key. What can this provide?
    A. Confidentiality
    B. Validation of her certificate
    C. Non-repudiation
    D. One-time pad

15. Sally is sending data to Joe. She uses asymmetric encryption to encrypt the data to ensure that only Joe can decrypt it. What key does Sally use to encrypt the data?
    A. Sally's public key
    B. Sally's private key
    C. Joe's public key
    D. Joe's private key

16. A user visits an e-commerce website and initiates a secure connection. What type of key does the website provide to the user?
    A. Symmetric key
    B. Private key
    C. Public key
    D. MD5 key

17. Of the following choices, what can you use to encrypt e-mail?
    A. HMAC
    B. RIPEMD
    C. PII
    D. S/MIME

18. Sally and Joe decide to use PGP to exchange secure e-mail. What should Sally provide to Joe so that Joe can encrypt e-mail before sending it to her?

    A. Her private key

    B. Her public key

    C. Her recovery key

    D. Her steganography key

19. Two systems need to establish a secure session between each other without any prior communication. What is needed to support this?

    A. Symmetric encryption

    B. PKI

    C. AES

    D. MD5

20. What entity verifies the authenticity of certificates?

    A. CRILL

    B. Digital signature

    C. CA

    D. Recovery agent

21. A user browses to a website and sees this message: "The site's certificate is not trusted." What is a likely reason?

    A. The CA's root certificate is in the trusted root certification authority store

    B. The certificate is listed in the CRL

    C. The CA is not a trusted root CA

    D. The certificate is not in the CRL

22. Which of the following choices are valid reasons to revoke a certificate holding a key? (Choose all that apply.)

    A. Key compromise

    B. CA compromise

    C. Loss of data

    D. Database breach

23. An organization wants to ensure that it does not use compromised certificates. What should it check?

    A. Trusted root certification authorities store

    B. Key escrow

    C. CRL

    D. RSA

24. A company is using a key escrow for its PKI. What does this provide?
    A. It maintains a copy of a private key for recovery purposes
    B. It maintains a copy of a public key for recovery purposes
    C. It provides a copy of revoked certificates
    D. It provides a digital signature

25. What can a PKI recovery agent recover?
    A. Public key
    B. CRL
    C. Private key
    D. MD5 key

26. Sally encrypted a project file with her public key. Later, an administrator accidentally deleted her account that had exclusive access to her private key. Can this project file be retrieved?
    A. No. If the private key is lost, the data cannot be retrieved.
    B. Yes. The public key can decrypt the file.
    C. Yes, if a copy of her public key is stored in escrow.
    D. Yes, if the organization uses a recovery agent.

Chapter 10 Practice Question Answers

1. **A, B.** Message Digest 5 (MD5) and Secure Hash Algorithm (SHA) are both hashing algorithm that create hashes of a fixed length. MD5 creates a 128-bit hash and SHA-256 creates a 256-bit hash. One-time pads are hardcopy printouts of keys in a pad of paper. A certificate revocation list (CRL) is a list of revoked certificates.

2. **A.** Message Digest 5 (MD5) is a hashing algorithm that can ensure the integrity of data, including e-mail messages. Advanced Encryption Standard (AES) and TwoFish are symmetric encryption algorithms, not hashing algorithms. RSA is an asymmetric encryption algorithm based on prime numbers.

3. **A.** Two basic components of encryption are algorithms and keys. Certificate authorities (CAs), certificates, and certificate revocation lists (CRLs) only apply to asymmetric encryption, not other types of encryption. Keys are only one element of encryption and can't encrypt data without an algorithm.

4. **A.** Symmetric encryption uses the same key to encrypt and decrypt data at both ends of a transmission medium. Asymmetric encryption uses two keys for encryption and decryption. Both symmetric and asymmetric encryption use keys. Symmetric encryption is commonly used to transmit data over transmission media.

5. **B.** Advanced Encryption Standard (AES) uses 128-, 192-, or 256-bit keys. Data Encryption Standard (DES) uses 56-bit keys. 3DES uses 56-, 112-, or 168-bit keys. MD5 is a hashing algorithm used to enforce integrity.

6. **B.** Data Encryption Standard (DES) uses 56-bit keys and is a weak encryption protocol. Advanced Encryption Standard (AES) uses 128-, 192-, or 256-bit keys. MD5 and SHA are hashing algorithms, but the question is asking about encryption.

7. **C.** Triple Data Encryption Standard (3DES) is an improvement over DES and encrypts data using multiple keys and multiple passes of the DES algorithm. Data Encryption Standard (DES) uses a single 56-bit key and encrypts the data one time. Advanced Encryption Standard (AES) use a single 128-bit, 192-bit, or 256-bit key, and is preferable over 3DES, but if hardware doesn't support AES, 3DES may be used. MD5 is a hashing algorithm used to enforce integrity.

8. **A.** Data encrypted with a public key can only be decrypted with the matching private key, and data encrypted with the private key can only be encrypted with the matching public key. The same asymmetric key used to encrypt data cannot decrypt the same data. Depending on the usage, either the public key or the private key can encrypt or decrypt.

9. **A.** RSA uses prime numbers to generate public and private keys. Secure Hash Algorithm (SHA) is a hashing algorithm that can ensure the integrity of data, and it doesn't use a key. S/MIME and PGP digitally sign and encrypt e-mail, and both use RSA, but they don't generate keys with prime numbers.

10. **D.** Elliptic curve cryptography is an encryption technology commonly used with small mobile devices, and it provides strong confidentiality using the least amount of computing resources. Steganography is the practice of hiding data within a file. Triple Data Encryption Standard (3DES) is an improvement over DES and is used when AES is not supported. Pretty Good Privacy (PGP) uses RSA and public key cryptography to secure e-mail.

11. **B.** Steganography is the practice of hiding data within a file and comparing hashes between two apparently identical files can verify if data is hidden within a file. A certificate revocation list (CRL) is a list of revoked certificates. A key is used for encryption, but a hash can't discover a key. A digital signature is an encrypted hash of a message, but it wouldn't be in a graphic file.

12. **B.** Protected Extensible Authentication Protocol Transport Layer Security (PEAP-TLS) uses TLS for the authentication process, and TLS requires a certificate provided by a certification authority (CA). File Transfer Protocol (FTP) is transferred in clear text and does not use certificates. Advanced Encryption Standard (AES) is a symmetric algorithm and doesn't use a CA. A Public Key Infrastructure (PKI) issues and manages certificates used in asymmetric encryption and verifies a certificate's authenticity.

13. **D.** Digital signatures provide authentication (verified identification) of the sender, integrity of the message, and non-repudiation. Advanced Encryption Standard (AES) is a symmetric encryption algorithm that uses 128-, 192-, or 256-bit keys, but encryption doesn't verify identities or integrity. A certificate revocation list (CRL) is a list of revoked certificates.

14. **C.** A digital signature provides non-repudiation (in addition to authentication and integrity) and is encrypted with the sender's private key. Encryption provides confidentiality, but if the e-mail is encrypted with the sender's private key, anyone with the publically available public key can decrypt it. A certification authority (CA) validates a certificate with a certificate revocation list (CRL), but the digital signature doesn't validate the certificate. A one-time pad is a hardcopy printout of encryption keys on different pages of a pad of paper.

15. **C.** Sally uses Joe's public key (the recipient's public key) to encrypt the data, and because Joe is the only person with Joe's private key, Joe is the only person that can decrypt the data. Sally would use her private key to create a digital signature, but would not use her keys for encryption. Sally would not have access to Joe's private key.

16. **C.** The website provides its public key in a certificate, and the user's system uses this to encrypt a symmetric key. The symmetric key encrypts data in the session. Private keys are kept

private so the website will not provide its private key to the user. Message Digest 5 (MD5) is a hashing algorithm that can ensure the integrity of data, but it doesn't use a key.

17. **D.** Secure/Multipurpose Internet Mail Extensions (S/MIME) can encrypt e-mail at rest (stored on a drive) and in transit (sent over the network). Hash-based Message Authentication Code (HMAC) and RACE Integrity Primitives Evaluation Message Digest (RIPEMD) are both hashing algorithms used to provide integrity. Pretty Good Privacy (PGP, not PII) can also encrypt e-mail.

18. **B.** Pretty Good Privacy (PGP) uses RSA and public key cryptography, and e-mail is encrypted with the recipient's public key (Sally's public key). Users will never give out their private key. A recovery key is used to recover encrypted data if the user's private key is inaccessible. Steganography doesn't use a key.

19. **B.** A Public Key Infrastructure (PKI) is a group of technologies used to request, create, manage, store, distribute, and revoke digital certificates used with asymmetric encryption. Asymmetric (not symmetric) encryption allows two entities to privately share symmetric keys without any prior communication. Advanced Encryption Standard (AES) is a symmetric encryption algorithm that uses 128-, 192-, or 256-bit keys. Message Digest 5 (MD5) is a hashing algorithm that can ensure the integrity of data.

20. **C.** A certificate authority (CA) within a public key infrastructure (PKI) verifies authenticity of certificates. The certificate revocation list (CRL, not CRILL) includes a list of revoked certificates and is published by the CA. Digital signatures provide authentication (verified identification) of the sender, integrity, and non-repudiation for e-mail. A recovery agent can recover an encryption key or encrypted data if the original key is lost.

21. **C.** If the certificate authority (CA) isn't trusted, web browsers will display a message indicating that the site's certificate is not trusted. If the CA's root certificate is in the trusted root certification store, the certificate will be trusted. If a certificate is in the certification revocation list (CRL), the browser will indicate the certificate is revoked, but it won't indicate a lack of trust. If it's not in the CRL, it indicates it is not revoked.

22. **A, B.** Valid reasons to revoke a certificate include key compromise and CA compromise. A certificate is not revoked in response to loss of data or a database breach unless this actually compromised the key or the CA.

23. **C.** A certificate revocation list (CRL) is a list of revoked certificates, and regularly retrieving a copy of the CRL to validate certificates reduces the risk of using compromised certificates. The trusted root certification authorities store identifies trusted certificate authorities (CAs). A key escrow stores a copy of private keys used within a public key infrastructure (PKI) for recovery purposes. RSA is a public key encryption method based on prime numbers.

24. **A.** A key escrow stores a copy of private keys used within a public key infrastructure (PKI) that can be used if the original private key is lost or inaccessible. Public keys are publically available and do not need to be stored in escrow. Revoked certificates are identified in a certificate revocation list (CRL) and there's no need to keep a copy of revoked certificates. Digital signatures provide authentication (verified identification) of the sender, integrity of the message, and non-repudiation for e-mail.

25. **C.** Public Key Infrastructure (PKI) recovery agents can recover private keys or, in some cases, recover encrypted data using a different key. Public keys are public and do not need to be recovered. A certification revocation list (CRL) is a publically available list of revoked certificates. Message Digest 5 (MD5) is a hashing algorithm that can ensure the integrity of data, but it does not use a key.

26. D. If an organization uses a recovery agent, the recovery agent can decrypt the file, in some cases by recovering a copy of the private key and in other cases by using a special recovery agent key. Data encrypted with a public key cannot be decrypted with the same public key. A private key is stored in escrow, but a public key would not be stored in escrow.

Chapter 11

Exploring Operational Security

CompTIA Security+ objectives covered in this chapter:

2.1 Explain risk related concepts
- Importance of policies in reducing risk
  - Privacy policy
  - Acceptable use
  - Security policy
  - Mandatory vacations
  - Job rotation
  - Separation of duties
  - Least privilege

2.2 Carry out appropriate risk mitigation strategies
- Incident management
- User rights and permissions reviews
- Implement policies and procedures to prevent data loss or theft

2.3 Execute appropriate incident response procedures
- Basic forensic procedures
  - Order of volatility
  - Capture system image
  - Network traffic and logs
  - Capture video
  - Record time offset
  - Take hashes
  - Screenshots
  - Witnesses
  - Track man hours and expense

- Damage and loss control
- Chain of custody
- Incident response: first responder

2.4 Explain the importance of security related awareness and training

- Security policy training and procedures
- Personally identifiable information
- Information classification: sensitivity of data (hard or soft)
- Data labeling, handling, and disposal
- Compliance with laws, best practices, and standards
- User habits
  - Data handling
  - Clean desk policies
  - Personally owned devices
- Use of social networking and P2P

2.8 Exemplify the concepts of confidentiality, integrity, and availability (CIA)

5.2 Explain the fundamental concepts and best practices related to authentication, authorization, and access control

- Least privilege
- Separation of duties
- Mandatory vacations
- Job rotation

5.3 Implement appropriate security controls when performing account management

- Mitigates issues associated with users with multiple account/roles

Organizations often develop security policies. These provide guiding principles to the professionals who implement security throughout the organization. One of the goals is to reduce security incidents. However, security incidents still occur, and incident response policies provide the direction on how to handle them.

Exploring Security Policies

Security policies lay out a security plan within a company. They are written documents created as an early step to mitigate risks. When created early enough, they help ensure that personnel consider and implement security throughout the life cycle of various systems in the company.

Policies include brief, high-level statements that identify goals based on an organization's overall beliefs and principles. After creating the policy, the organization creates guidelines and procedures to support the policies. While the policies are often high-level statements, the guidelines and procedures provide details on policy implementation.

Security controls enforce the requirements of a security policy. For example, a security policy may state that internal users must not use peer-to-peer (P2P) applications. A firewall with appropriate rules to block these applications provides a technical implementation of this policy. Similarly, administrators can use port scanning tools to detect the applications running on internal systems contrary to the policy.

Remember this

Security policies are written documents that identify a security plan. Security controls (including technical, management, and operational controls) enforce security policies.

A security policy can be a single large document or divided into several smaller documents, depending on the needs of the company. The following sections identify many of the common elements of a security policy.

Clean Desk Policy

A clean desk policy directs users to keep their areas organized and free of papers. The primary security goal is to reduce threats of security incidents by ensuring the protection of sensitive data. More specifically, it helps prevent the possibility of data theft or inadvertent disclosure of information.

Imagine an attacker going into a bank for a bank loan and meeting a loan officer. The loan officer has stacks of paper on his or her desk, including loan applications from various customers. If the loan officer steps out, the attacker can easily grab some of the documents, or simply take pictures of the documents with a mobile phone.

Beyond security, organizations want to present a positive image to customers and clients. Employees with cluttered desks with piles of paper can easily turn off customers.

However, a clean desk policy doesn't just apply to employees who meet and greet customers. It also applies to employees that don't interact with customers. Just as dumpster divers can sort through trash to gain valuable information, anyone can sort through papers on a desk to learn information. It's best to secure all papers to keep them away from prying eyes.

Remember this

A clean desk policy requires users to organize their areas to reduce the risk of possible data theft. It reminds users to secure sensitive data and may include a statement about not writing down passwords.

Some items left on a desk that can present risks include:

- Keys
- Cell phones
- Access cards
- Sensitive papers
- Logged-in computer
- Printouts left in printer
- Passwords on sticky notes
- File cabinets left open or unlocked
- Personal items such as mail with PII

Some people want to take a clean desk policy a step further by scrubbing and sanitizing desks with antibacterial cleaners and disinfectants on a daily basis. They are free to do so, but that isn't part of a security-related clean desk policy.

Account Management Policies

Chapter 2 introduced account management as a logical access control. Accounts provide access to systems and networks, and account management involves the creation, deletion, and disabling of accounts.

When accounts aren't managed, they can pose significant vulnerabilities to the organization. Account management policies provide direction for administrators to address and prevent these vulnerabilities. This section describes common elements included in an account management policy.

User Privilege Policy

Privileges are the rights and permissions assigned to users. Rights identify what a user can do, such as changing the system time or rebooting a system, and permissions define access to resources, such as being able to read or modify a file.

A user privilege policy ensures that users have only the rights and permissions needed to perform their job and no more. In other words, it dictates the use of the principle of least privilege (described in chapter 2). For example, if Joe needs to print to a printer, you should grant him print permission for that printer but nothing else.

Many operating systems automatically enforce this. For example, in the discretionary access control (DAC) model used by Microsoft operating systems, users own files. When a user creates a new file, the user is granted full access to the file, but no one else is given direct access to the file. Files will *inherit* permissions assigned to folders, so other users may have access based on inheritance, but the operating system doesn't assign these additional permissions directly to newly created files. Only the creator has access by default.

Administrators often use group-based privileges (described in chapter 2 as part of role-based access control) to enforce a user privilege policy. In other words, instead of administrators assigning privileges directly to a user, they add the user account to a group, and assign privileges to the group. This simplifies user administration and helps enforce least privilege. If an employee is reassigned or promoted, the administrator simply adds the employee to groups related to the new job and removes the account from groups related to the previous job.

Chapter 8 introduced a user rights and permission review as a security audit. This review ensures that the policy is being followed, users don't have more privileges than they need, and inactive accounts are either disabled or deleted.

> ### Remember this
>
> The principle of least privilege ensures that users are granted rights and permissions needed to perform assigned tasks and nothing else. Operating systems enforce this by giving only the file creator full access to newly created files. Administrators enforce it with group-based privileges. Rights and permissions reviews discover violations.

Require Administrators to Use Two Accounts

It's common to require administrators to have two accounts. They use one account for regular day-to-day work. It has the same limited privileges as a regular user. The other account has elevated privileges required to perform administrative work, and they use this only when performing administrative work. The benefit of this practice is that it reduces the exposure of the administrative account to an attack.

For example, when malware infects a system, it often attempts to gain additional rights and permissions using privilege escalation techniques. It may exploit a bug or flaw in an application or operating system. Or, it may simply assume the rights and permissions of the logged in user.

If an administrator logs on with an administrative account, the malware can assume these elevated privileges. In contrast, if the administrator is logged on with a regular user account, the malware isn't able to escalate its privileges through this account.

> ### Remember this
>
> Requiring administrators to use two accounts, one with administrator privileges and another with regular user privileges, helps prevent privilege escalation attacks.

This also reduces the risk to the administrative account for day-to-day work. Imagine Joe is an administrator and he's called away to a crisis. It is very possible for him to walk away without locking his computer. If he was logged on with his administrator account, an attacker walking by can access the system and have administrative privileges. While systems often have password-protected screen savers, these usually don't start until about ten minutes or longer after a user walks away.

Account Disablement Policy

An account disablement policy (sometimes called an account expiration policy) specifies when to disable accounts. This policy directs disabling accounts for ex-employees or employees taking a leave of absence. If the account is not disabled, the employee or someone else can use it for attacks.

> ### Remember this
> An account disablement or expiration policy ensures that inactive accounts are disabled. Some companies also disable accounts when users take a leave of absence.

For example, chapter 6 mentioned the case at Fannie Mae, where a UNIX engineer was terminated but retained account access. He installed a logic bomb set to go off on January 31 that would have deleted data and backups for about four thousand servers. While another administrator discovered the logic bomb before it went off, a more stringent account disablement policy would have avoided the risk completely.

Organizations often identify a specific exit process when terminating an employee. For example, HR personnel may describe rights and benefits to the employee. However, from a security perspective, the process often includes disabling accounts during the exit interview. When an exit process isn't used, accounts may be left enabled. The organization will typically delete the account after a period of time, such as after three months. This gives managers an opportunity to retrieve any files used by the account.

It's also possible to set accounts to expire after a certain time period. For example, if an organization hired a contractor for a ninety-day period, an administrator can set the account to expire in ninety days. When the account expires, it's automatically disabled.

Change Management Policy

Chapter 5 introduced the change management process. As a reminder, change management ensures changes to IT systems do not result in unintended outages and provides an accounting structure or method to document all the changes. A change management policy provides overall direction for change management processes.

Patch management (also covered in chapter 5) is usually included in a change-management process. Patch management ensures that systems are kept up to date and reduces risks associated with known vulnerabilities. The patch management process includes testing, deploying, and verifying changes from patches. When included with change management, change management provides documentation of the process.

Most change-management procedures start with a change request. Designated personnel review the change, and, once it's approved, a technician implements the change. Each step of the process is documented. The entire process is documented at each stage. The documentation ensures everyone is aware of the change, it can be easily reversed if necessary, and can be reproduced if a system needs to be rebuilt after an outage.

> ### Remember this
>
> Security policies are written documents that identify a security plan. Security controls (including technical, management, and operational controls) enforce security policies.

Hey! Who Moved My Changes?

In one environment where I worked, several technicians spent the weekend troubleshooting a problem that was negatively affecting services. They ultimately identified two grossly misconfigured servers. Through a slow, painful process, they identified all the incorrect configurations and returned the services to 100 percent by the end of the weekend.

On Monday, another group of technicians came in and realized that the changes they made on Friday to two servers were all undone. The changes made on Friday were not communicated to the technicians working on the weekend, and the changes were not adequately tested, resulting in unintended service loss.

The Monday technicians were upset that the work they did on Friday was undone. The weekend technicians were upset that they wasted their time troubleshooting an undocumented change. The end users suffered through reduced services.

Effective change management ensures that changes have the least effect on services, are well documented, and all personnel are adequately informed of the changes. Without an accounting structure to document changes, it's difficult to ensure personnel are informed of changes.

Portable Device Policies

As mentioned several times throughout this book, USB drives represent significant risks to an organization. They can transport malware without the user's knowledge and can be a source of data leakage. Malicious users can copy and steal a significant amount of information using an easily concealable thumb drive. Users can misplace these drives, and the data can easily fall into the wrong hands.

Because of the risks, it's common for an organization to include security policy statements to prohibit the use of USB flash drives and other mobile storage devices. Notice that the restriction isn't only on the flash drives though.

Many personal music devices, such as MP3 players, use the same type of flash drive memory as a USB flash drive. Users can plug them into a system and easily copy data to and from a system. Additionally, many of today's phones include storage capabilities using the same type of memory.

> **Remember this**
> USB thumb drives are a source of data leakage and malware distribution. Personal music devices can also store data and are often included in policies designed to prevent data leakage.

Mobile phones present other risks. For example, most cell phones include camera capabilities and have the capability of transmitting audio without the user's knowledge. Some organizations prohibit the possession of mobile phones within some areas, and they strictly enforce the policy. For example, I know of one organization where security personnel randomly scan employees for mobile phones using an electronic device. If security personnel find a mobile phone, they confiscate it and the employee is immediately fired.

Personnel Policies

Companies frequently develop polices to specifically define and clarify issues related to personnel. This includes personnel behavior, expectations, and possible consequences. Personnel learn these policies when they are hired and as changes occur.

Some of the policies directly related to personnel are:

- Acceptable use
- Mandatory vacations
- Separation of duties
- Job rotation

Acceptable Use

An acceptable use policy defines proper system usage. It will often describe the purpose of computer systems and networks, how users can access them, and the responsibilities of users when accessing the systems.

> **Remember this**
> An acceptable use policy defines proper system usage. Users are often required to read and sign an acceptable use policy when hired, as well as periodically, such as with annual security training.

This policy will often include definitions and examples of unacceptable use. For example, users may be prohibited from using company resources for personal business, such as shopping on the Internet or visiting websites that are unrelated to their work.

Many organizations require users to read and sign a document indicating they understand the acceptable use policy when they're hired and in conjunction with annual security training. In many cases, organizations post the policy on an intranet site and sign it electronically. Other methods, such as logon banners or e-mails, help reinforce an acceptable use policy.

Mandatory Vacations

Mandatory vacation policies help detect when employees are involved in malicious activity, such as fraud or embezzlement. As an example, employees in positions of fiscal trust, such as stock traders or bank employees, are often required to take an annual vacation of at least five consecutive workdays.

For embezzlement actions of any substantial size to succeed, an employee would need to be constantly present in order to manipulate records and respond to different inquiries. On the other hand, if an employee is forced to be absent for at least five consecutive workdays, the likelihood of any illegal actions succeeding is reduced, since someone else would be required to answer the queries during the employee's absence.

Mandatory vacations aren't limited to only financial institutions, though. Many organizations require similar policies for administrators. For example, an administrator may be the only person required to perform sensitive activities such as reviewing logs. A malicious administrator can overlook or cover up certain activities revealed in the logs. However, a mandatory vacation would require someone else to perform these activities and increase the chance of discovery.

Of course, mandatory vacations by themselves won't prevent fraud. Most companies will implement the principle of defense in depth by using multiple layers of protection. Additional policies may include separation of duties and job rotation to provide as much protection as possible.

> ### *Remember this*
> Mandatory vacation policies require employees to take time away from their job. These policies help to reduce fraud and discover malicious activities.

Separation of Duties

Separation of duties is a principle that prevents any single person or entity from being able to complete all the functions of a critical or sensitive process. It's designed to prevent fraud, theft, and errors.

Accounting provides the classic example. It's common to divide accounting departments into two divisions: Accounts Receivable and Accounts Payable. Personnel in the Accounts Receivable division review and validate bills. They then send the validated bills to the personnel in the Accounts Payable division, who pay the bills.

If Joe was the only person doing both functions, it would be possible for him to create and approve a bill from Joe's Most Excellent Retirement Account. After approving the bill, Joe would then pay it. If Joe doesn't go to jail, he may indeed retire early at the expense of the financial health of the company.

Separation of duties policies also apply to IT personnel. Consider network defense. A firewall is a preventative control that attempts to prevent attacks and a network-based intrusion detection system (NIDS) is a detective control that attempts to detect attacks. If a single administrator managed both systems, it's possible that issues could be overlooked resulting in errors. However, by separating the tasks between two people, it reduces the possibility of errors.

As another example, a group of IT administrators may be assigned responsibility for maintaining a group of database servers, but do not have access to security logs on these servers. Instead, security administrators regularly review these logs, but these security administrators will not have access to data within the databases.

Consider what should happen if one of the IT administrators is promoted and is now working as a security administrator? Based on separation of duties, this administrator should now have access to security logs, but access to the data within the databases should be revoked. However, if the administrator's permissions to the data are not revoked, the administrator will have more permissions than needed violating the principle of least privilege. A user rights and permissions review will often discover these types of issues.

> ### *Remember this*
>
> Separation of duties prevents any single person or entity from being able to complete all the functions of a critical or sensitive process by dividing the tasks between employees. Job rotation policies require employees to change roles on a regular basis. This helps ensure that employees cannot continue with fraudulent activity indefinitely.

Job Rotation

Job rotation is a concept that has employees rotate through different jobs to learn the procedures and processes in each. From a security perspective, job rotation helps to prevent or expose dangerous shortcuts or even fraudulent activity. Knowledge is shared with multiple people, and no one person can retain explicit control of any process or data.

For example, your company could have an accounting department. As mentioned in the separation of duties section, you would separate accounting into two divisions—Accounts Receivable and Accounts Payable. Additionally, you could rotate personnel in and out of jobs in the two divisions. This would ensure more oversight over past transactions and help ensure that employees are following rules and policies.

In contrast, if a single person always performs the same function without any expectation of oversight, the temptation to go outside the bounds of established policy increases.

Job rotation policies work well together with separation of duties policies. A separation of duties policy helps prevent a single person from controlling too much. However, if an organization only used a separation of duties policy, it is possible for two people to join together in a scheme to defraud the company. If a job rotation policy is also used, these two people will not be able to continue the fraudulent activity indefinitely.

Job rotation policies also apply to IT personnel. For example, the policy can require administrators to swap roles on a regular basis, such as annually or quarterly. This prevents any single administrator from having too much control over a network.

I'll Go to Jail Before I Give You the Passwords!

The city of San Francisco had an extreme example of the dangers of a single person with too much explicit knowledge or power. A network administrator with Cisco's highest certification of Cisco Certified Internetwork Expert (CCIE) made changes to the city's network, changing passwords so that only he knew them and ensuring that he was the only person with administrative access.

It could be that he was taking these actions to protect the network that he considered his "baby." He was the only CCIE, and it's possible he looked on others as simply not having the knowledge necessary to adequately maintain the network. Over the years, fewer and fewer people had access to what he was doing, and his knowledge became more and more proprietary. Instead of being malicious in nature, he may have simply been protective, even if overly protective.

At some point, his boss recognized that all the information eggs were in the basket of this lone CCIE. It was just too risky. What if the CCIE was hit by one of the San Francisco trolleys? What would they do? The boss asked him for some passwords and he refused, even when faced with arrest. Later, he gave law enforcement personnel passwords that didn't work.

He was charged with four counts of tampering with a computer network and kept in custody with a $5 million bail. In April 2010, he was convicted of one felony count and sentenced to four years in prison. This is a far fall from his reported annual salary of $127,735.

The city of San Francisco had to bring in experts from Cisco, and the city reported costs of $900,000 to regain control of their network. Following his conviction, the CCIE was ordered to pay $1.5 million in restitution.

What's the lesson here? Internal security controls, such as creating and enforcing policies related to rotation of duties, separation of duties, and cross training, may have been able to avoid this situation completely. If this CCIE truly did have good intentions toward what he perceived as his network, these internal controls might have prevented him from going over the line into overprotection and looking at the world through the bars of a jail cell.

Security Awareness and Training

Many organizations create a security education and awareness plan to identify methods of raising the security awareness of employees. The primary goal is to minimize the risk posed by users and help to reinforce user compliance with security policies.

Training often helps users understand the risks. By understanding the risks, they are more likely to comply with the security policies.

For example, many users are unaware of the risks associated with USB flash drives. They know that USB flash drives are very convenient and restricting their use sometimes makes it more difficult to do their job. However, they don't always know that an infected USB drive may infect a system as soon as it's plugged in, and an infected system will infect any other USB drives plugged into the system. With a little bit of training, users understand the risks and are more likely to comply with a restrictive USB flash drive policy.

The success of any security awareness and training plan is directly related to the support from senior management. If senior management supports the plan, middle management and employees will also support it. On the other hand, if senior management does not show support for the plan, it's very likely that it won't be supported throughout the organization.

Security awareness training isn't a one-time event. Personnel are trained when they are hired and periodically afterwards. For example, it's common to have annual refresher training. This informs users of current and updated threats and helps reinforce the importance of user compliance.

> ### *Remember this*
>
> A primary goal of security awareness and training is to reinforce user compliance with security policies and help reduce risks posed by users. The success of any security awareness and training plan is dependent on the support of senior management. Because security issues change over time, it's common to provide periodic refresher training.

Training can include a wide variety of topics depending on the organization. Some of the topics include:

- Security policy contents
- Acceptable use and user responsibilities
- Classification of both hard and soft information
- Protection of personally identifiable information
- Importance of data labeling, handling, and disposal
- Compliance with relevant laws, best practices, and standards
- Threat awareness including current malware and phishing attacks
- User habits that represent risks such as with passwords and tailgating
- Use of social networking sites and peer-to-peer applications and how they result in data leakage

The following section on data policies covers many of these topics, while other topics were covered in previous chapters.

Data Policies

Every company has secrets. Keeping these secrets can often make the difference between success and failure. A company can have valuable research and development data, customer databases, proprietary information on products, and much more. If the company cannot keep private and proprietary data secret, it can directly affect its bottom line.

Data policies assist in the protection of data and help prevent data leakage. This section covers many of the different elements that may be contained in a data policy.

Information Classification

As a best practice, organizations take the time to identify, classify, and label data they use. Data classifications ensure that users understand the value of data, and the classifications help protect sensitive data. Classifications can apply to hard data (printouts) and soft data (files).

As an example, the U.S. government uses classifications such as "Top Secret," "Secret," "Confidential," and "Unclassified" to identify the sensitivity of data. Private companies often use terms such as "Proprietary," "Private," "Classified," or "Public."

Remember this

Organizations classify data to ensure that users understand the value of the data and to help protect sensitive data. Data labeling ensures that users know what data they are handling and processing.

Data Labeling and Handling

Data labeling ensures that users know what data they are handling and processing. For example, if an organization classified data as confidential, private, sensitive, and public, they would also use labeling to identify the data. These labels can be printed labels for media such as backup tapes. It's also possible to label files using file properties, headers, footers, and watermarks.

The labels and classifications an organization uses are not as important as the fact that they use labels and classifications. Organizations take time to analyze their data, classify it, and provide training to users to ensure the users recognize the value of the data.

Consider a company that spends millions of dollars on research and development (R&D) trying to develop or improve products. The company values this data much more than data publically available on its website, and it needs to protect it. However, if employees have access to the R&D data and it's not classified or labeled, they may not realize its value and may not protect it.

For example, a web content author may write an article for the company's website touting its achievements. If the R&D data isn't classified and labeled, the author may include some of this R&D data in the article, inadvertently giving the company's competitors free access to valuable data. While the R&D employees will easily recognize the data's value, it's not safe to assume that everyone does. On the other hand, if the data included confidential or proprietary labels, anyone would recognize its value and take appropriate steps to protect it.

Chapter 9 presented information on backups. As a reminder, it's important to protect backups with the same level of protection as the original data. Labels on backup media help administrators easily identify the value of the data on the backups.

Storage and Retention Policies

A storage and retention policy identifies where data is stored and how long it is retained. For example, a storage policy often dictates that users must store all data on servers instead of local workstations. One of the benefits is that administrators can back up data on the server to ensure they have copies of user data. If users store data on their individual systems, it makes it much more difficult and expensive to back up data.

Retention policies help reduce legal liabilities, and this is another reason they're used. For example, imagine if a retention policy states that the company will only keep e-mail for one year. A court order requiring all e-mail from the company can only expect to receive e-mail from the last year.

On the other hand, if the organization doesn't have a retention policy, they may need to provide e-mail from the past ten years or longer in response to a court order. This can require an extensive amount of work by administrators to recover archives or search for specific e-mails. Additionally, investigations can uncover other embarrassing evidence from previous years. The retention policy helps avoid these problems.

Some laws mandate the retention of data for specific time frames, such as three years or longer. For example, laws mandate the retention of all White House e-mails indefinitely. If a law applies to an organization, the retention policy reflects the same requirements.

Remember this

Storage and retention policies identify where data is stored and how long it is retained. In some cases, the retention policies can limit a company's exposure to legal proceedings and reduce the amount of labor required to respond to court orders.

Personally Identifiable Information

Personally identifiable information (PII) is personal information that can be used to personally identify an individual. Some examples of PII are:

- Full name
- Birthday and birth place
- Medical and health information
- Street or e-mail address information
- Personal characteristics, such as biometric data
- Any type of identification number, such as a Social Security number or driver's license number

In general, you need two or more pieces of information to make it PII. For example, "John Smith" is not PII by itself, since it can't be traced back to a specific person. However, when you connect the name with a birthdate, an address, medical information, or other data, it is PII.

When attackers gain PII, they often use it for financial gain at the expense of the individual. For example, attackers steal identities, access credit cards, and empty bank accounts. Whenever possible, organizations should minimize the use, collection, and retention of PII. If it's not kept, it can't be compromised. On the other hand, if they collect PII and attackers compromise the data, the company is liable.

The number of security breach incidents resulting in the loss of PII continues to rise. For example, a Veteran's Administration employee copied a database onto his laptop that contained PII on over twenty-six million U.S. veterans. He took the laptop home and a burglar stole it. The VA then went through the painful and expensive process of notifying all of the people who were vulnerable to identity theft, and the affected individuals spent countless hours scouring their records for identity theft incidents. Even though police later recovered the laptop, the VA paid $20 million to settle a lawsuit in the case.

Chapter 5 mentioned several other instances, such as the attack on Sony's PlayStation Network that compromised more than seventy-seven million customer records resulting in direct expense of over $171 million.

Each of these instances resulted in potential identity theft and the loss of goodwill and public trust of the company. Both customers and employees were negatively impacted, and the companies were forced to spend time and energy discussing the incident, and spend money trying to repair their reputations.

> ### *Remember this*
>
> Personally identifiable information (PII) includes information such as a full name, birthdate, biometric data, and identifying numbers such as an SSN. Organizations have an obligation to protect PII and often identify procedures for handling and retaining PII in data policies.

Protecting PII

Organizations have an obligation to protect PII. There are many laws that mandate the protection of PII including international laws, federal laws, and local regulations. Organizations often develop policies to identify how they handle, retain, and distribute PII, and these policies help ensure they are complying with relevant regulations. When a company doesn't use a specific PII policy, it will usually identify methods used to protect PII in related data policies.

Additionally, many laws require a company to report data losses due to security breaches. If an attack results in the loss of customer PII data, the company is required to report it and notify affected individuals. As an example, Arizona enacted a security breach notifica

tion law that requires any company doing business in Arizona to notify customers of security breaches. Most states in the United States have similar laws, and similar international laws

exist.

One of the common reasons data seems to fall into the wrong hands is that employees don't understand the risks involved. They may not realize the value of the data on a laptop, or they may casually copy PII data onto a USB flash drive. As mentioned previously, data classification and labeling procedures help employees recognize the data's value and help protect sensitive data.

Training is also important. One of the goals of security professionals is to reinforce the risks of not protecting PII. When employees understand the risks, they are less likely to risk customer and employee data to identity theft.

> ## Remember this
>
> PII requires special handing and policies for data retention. Employees should be trained not to give out any type of personal information. Many laws mandate the reporting of attacks resulting in PII data losses.

Privacy Policy

It's almost a business requirement today for a company to have a website. Customers expect a website and often look for it to get additional information about a company. When it doesn't exist, customers often go elsewhere. However, websites have additional requirements such as a privacy policy.

A privacy policy identifies how a website collects, uses, and discloses information about visitors. For example, web forms collect e-mail addresses and other information from users. The privacy policy indicates whether the company uses this information internally only or if it sells or shares it with other entities.

Many states, such as California, Nebraska, and Pennsylvania, have specific laws requiring privacy policies. For example, a California law requires websites to conspicuously post a privacy policy on the site. This law applies to any website that collects information about California residents, regardless of where the website is located.

You can usually find a link to a privacy policy on the site's main page. For example, if you go to Google.com, you'll find a link labeled "Privacy," and by clicking on it, you'll see its privacy policy.

Social Networking Sites

Millions of people interact with each other using social networking sites like Facebook and Twitter. Facebook allows people to share their lives with friends, family, and others. Twitter allows people to tweet about events as they are happening. From a social perspective, these technologies allow people to easily share information about themselves with others.

However, from a security perspective, they present some significant risks, especially related to inadvertent information disclosure. Attackers can use these sites to gain information about individuals and then use that information in an attack.

Users often post personal information such as birthdates, their favorite colors or books, the high school they graduated from, graduation dates, and much more. Some sites use this personal information to validate users when they forget or need to change their password. For example, imagine Sally needs to reset her password for a bank account. The website may challenge her to enter her birthdate, favorite book, and graduation date for validation. If Sally posts all this information on Facebook, an attacker can use it to change the password on the bank account.

In some cases, attackers have used personal information from social networking sites to launch scams. For example, an attacker first identifies the name of a friend or relative using the social networking site. The attacker then impersonates the friend or relative in an e-mail, claiming they were robbed and are stuck in a foreign country. The attacker ends with a plea for help asking the victim to send money via wire transfer.

It's also worth noting that social networking sites have become one of the methods that employers use to collect information on prospective employees. In 2010, Microsoft surveyed U.S. human resources professionals and learned that 70 percent of them had rejected a job application based on information they found online.

Remember this

Improper use of social networking sites can result in inadvertent information disclosure. Information available on these sites can also be used to launch attacks against users.

P2P

Peer-to-peer (P2P or file sharing) applications allow users to share files such as music, video, and data over the Internet. Instead of a single server providing the data to end users, all computers in the P2P network are peers, and any computer can act as a server to other clients.

The first widely used P2P network was Napster, an online music-sharing service that operated between 1999 and 2001. Users copied and distributed MP3 music files between each other, and these were often pirated music files. The files were stored on each user's system, and as long as the system was accessible on the Internet, other users could access and download the files. A court order shut down Napster due to copyright issues, but it later reopened as an online music store. Other P2P software and P2P networks continue to appear and evolve.

Organizations usually restrict the use of P2P applications in networks, but this isn't because of piracy issues. Instead, a significant risk with P2P applications is data leakage. Users are often unaware of what data they are sharing. Another risk is that users are often unaware of what data the application downloads and stores onto their systems, causing them to host inappropriate data. Two examples help illustrate these data leakage risks.

Information concentrators search P2P networks for information of interest and collect it. In March 2009, investigators discovered an information concentrator in Iran with over two hundred documents containing classified and secret U.S. government data. This included classified information about Marine One, the helicopter used by the president. While the information about Marine One made the headlines, the attackers had much more information. For example, this concentrator included Iraq status reports and lists of soldiers with privacy data.

How did this happen? Investigations revealed that a defense contractor installed a P2P application on a computer. The computer had access to this data, and the P2P application shared it.

The media latched onto the news about Marine One, so this story was widely published. However, it's widely believed that much more data is being mined via P2P networks. Most end users don't have classified data on their systems, but they do have PII, such as banking information or tax data. When an attacker retrieves data on a user's system and empties a bank account, it may be a catastrophe to the user, but it isn't news.

A second example affected a school-age child. It's popular to use these P2P sharing programs to share music files, but they are often used to share other data. One school-age girl was browsing data she found on her computer and discovered a significant number of pornographic pictures. She did not seek these or deliberately download them. Instead, as a member of the P2P network, the P2P application used her system to store files shared by others.

Organizations can restrict access to P2P networks by blocking access in firewalls. Additionally, port scanners can scan open ports of remote systems to identify P2P software. Organizations often include these checks when running a port scanner as part of a vulnerability scan.

> **Remember this**
> Data leakage occurs when users install P2P software and unintentionally share files. Organizations often block P2P software at the firewall and detect running software with port scans.

Decommissioning Systems

When computers reach the end of their life cycles, organizations donate them, recycle them, or sometimes just throw them away. From a security perspective, you need to ensure that the computers don't include any data that may be useful to people outside your organization or damaging to your organization if it's released.

It's common for organizations to have a checklist to ensure that a system is sanitized prior to being released. The goal is to ensure that all usable data is removed from the system.

Hard drives represent the greatest risk since they hold the most information, so it's important to take additional steps when decommissioning old hard drives. Simply deleting a file on a drive doesn't actually delete it. Instead, it marks the file for deletion and makes the space available for use. Similarly, formatting a disk drive won't erase the data. There are many recovery applications available to recover deleted data, file remnants, and data from formatted drives.

Different methods of sanitizing a disk drive and removing all useable data include:

- **Bit level overwrite**. Different programs are available that will write patterns of ones and zeroes multiple times to ensure that data originally on the disk is unreadable. This process ensures that the disk doesn't contain any data.
- **Degauss the disks**. A degausser is a very powerful electronic magnet. Passing a disk through a degaussing field will render the data on the disk unreadable, and it will often destroy the motors of the disk. Degaussing of backup tapes will sanitize a tape without destroying it.
- **Physical destruction**. If the disk includes classified or proprietary data, simply overwriting it may not be enough. Instead, the computer disposal policy may require the destruction of the drive. For example, technicians can remove disk platters and sand them down to the bare metal.

> **Remember this**
>
> Old hard drives are sanitized as part of the decommissioning process. A common method uses bit level erasure and overwrites the drive by writing a series of ones and zeroes multiple times on the drive.

It's also worth mentioning that hard drives can be in other devices besides computers. For example, many copy machines include disk drives. If these disk drives aren't sanitized, it can also result in a loss of confidentiality.

Incident Response Policies

Many organizations create incident response policies to help personnel identify and respond to incidents. A security incident is an adverse event or series of events that can negatively affect the confidentiality, integrity, or availability of data or systems within the organization, or that has the potential to do so. Some examples include:

- Attacks
- Release of malware
- Security policy violations
- Unauthorized access of data
- Inappropriate usage of systems

For example, an attack resulting in a data breach is an incident. Once the organization identifies a security incident, it will respond based on the incident response policy.

One of the first responses is to contain the incident. This can be as simple as unplugging the system's network interface card to ensure it can't communicate on the network. However, the system shouldn't be powered down or manipulated at all until forensics experts have an opportunity to collect evidence.

After identifying the incident and isolating the system, forensic experts may begin a forensic evaluation depending on the incident. A forensic evaluation helps the organization collect and analyze data as evidence it can use in the prosecution of a crime. In general, forensic evaluations proceed with the assumption that the data collected will be used as evidence in court. Because of this, forensic practices protect evidence to prevent modification and control evidence after collecting it.

> ### Remember this
>
> An incident response policy defines an incident and incident response procedures. The first step to take after identifying an incident is to contain or isolate the problem. This is often as simple as disconnecting a computer from a network. A forensic evaluation collects, controls, and evaluates evidence from incidents.

After the forensic evidence collection process, administrators will recover or restore the system to bring it back into service. This assumes, of course, that the system itself isn't collected as evidence. Recovery of a system may require a simple reboot or it may require a complete rebuild of the system, depending on the incident.

Organizations also review security controls to identify vulnerabilities after an incident. It's very possible the incident provides some valuable lessons. The organization may modify procedures or add additional controls to prevent a reoccurrence of the incident.

The following sections cover some of the important elements of an incident response policy relevant to the Security+ exam.

Containment

The first response after identifying the incident is to contain or isolate the problem. Often administrators do this by simply disconnecting the cable from the network interface card to disconnect a computer from the network.

For example, you can isolate an attacked server by disconnecting it from the network. You can isolate a network from the Internet by modifying access control lists on a router or a network firewall.

This is similar to how you'd respond to water spilling from an overflowing sink. You wouldn't start cleaning up the water until you first turn off the faucet. The goal of containment is to prevent the problem from spreading to other areas or other computers in your network, or to simply stop the attack.

Incident Response Team

An incident response team is composed of employees with expertise in different areas. Organizations refer to the team as a computer incident response team (CIRT), security incident response team (SIRT), or simply IRT. Combined, they have the knowledge and skills to respond to an incident. Team members may include:

- **Senior management**. Someone needs to be in charge with enough authority to get things done.
- **Network administrator/engineer**. A technical person needs to be included who can adequately understand technical problems and relay the issue to other team personnel.
- **Security expert**. Security experts know how to collect and analyze evidence using different forensic procedures.
- **Communications expert**. If an incident needs to be relayed to the public, a public relations person should be the one to do so.

Due to the complex nature of incidents, the team often has extensive training. Training includes concepts such as how to identify and validate an incident, how to collect evidence, and how to protect the collected evidence.

First responders are the first security-trained people who arrive on the scene. The term comes from the medical community, where the first medically trained person to arrive on the scene of an emergency or accident is a first responder. A first responder could be someone from the incident response team or someone with adequate training to know what the first response steps should be. The incident response policy documents initial steps or at least the goals of first responders.

Basic Forensic Procedures

Once the incident has been contained or isolated, the next step is a forensics evaluation. What do you think of when you hear "forensics"? A lot of people think about the TV program *CSI* (short for "crime scene investigation") and all of its spin-offs. These shows demonstrate the phenomenal capabilities of science in crime investigations.

Computer forensics analyzes evidence from computers to determine details on computer incidents, similar to how CSI personnel analyze evidence from crime scenes. It uses a variety of different tools to gather and analyze computer evidence. Computer forensics is a growing field, and many educational institutions offer specialized degrees around the science.

While you may not be the computer forensic expert analyzing the evidence, you should know about some of the basic concepts related to gathering and preserving the evidence.

Forensic experts use a variety of forensic procedures to collect and protect data after an attack. A key part of this process is preserving the evidence. In other words, they ensure that they don't modify the data as they collect it, and they protect it after collection. Just as a rookie cop wouldn't walk through the blood at a crime scene (at least not more than once), employees shouldn't access systems that have been attacked or power them down.

For example, files have properties that show when they were last accessed. However, in many situations, accessing the file modifies this property. This can prevent an investigation from identifying when an attacker accessed the file. Additionally, data in a system's memory includes valuable evidence, but turning a system off deletes this data. In general, first responders do not attempt to analyze evidence until they have taken the time to collect and protect it.

Forensic experts have specialized tools they can use to capture data. For example, many experts use EnCase by Guidance Software or Forensics Toolkit by Access Data. These tools can capture data from memory or disks. This includes documents, images, e-mail, webmail, Internet artifacts, web history, chat sessions, compressed files, backup files, and encrypted files. They can also capture data from smartphones and tablets.

Order of Volatility

Order of volatility refers to the order in which you should collect evidence. "Volatile" doesn't mean it's explosive, but rather that it is not permanent. In general, you should collect evidence starting with the most volatile and moving to the least volatile.

For example, random access memory (RAM) is lost after powering down a computer. Because of this, it is important to realize you shouldn't power a computer down if it's suspected to be involved in a security incident.

A processor can only work on data in RAM, so all the data in RAM indicates what the system was doing. This includes data a user has been working on, system processes, network processes, application remnants, and much more. All of this can be valuable evidence in an investigation, but the evidence is lost when the computer is turned off.

Many forensic tools include the ability to capture volatile data. Once it's captured, experts can analyze it and gain insight into what the computer and user were doing.

> ### Remember this
> RAM is volatile and is lost when a computer is powered down. Data in RAM includes processes and applications, and data recently accessed by a user. Memory forensics analyzes data in RAM.

In contrast, data on disks remains on the drive even after powering a system down. This includes any files and even low-level data such as the master boot record on a disk. However, it's important to protect the data on the disk before analyzing it, and a common method is by capturing an image of the disk.

The order of volatility from most volatile to least volatile is:

- Data in RAM, including cache and recently used data and applications
- Data in RAM, including system and network processes
- Data stored on local disk drives
- Logs stored on remote systems
- Archive media

Capture Images

An image is a snapshot of data in memory or a snapshot of a drive. Chapter 5 introduced disk images as a common method used to deploy systems. These system disk images include mandatory security configurations and help ensure a system starts in a secure state. Forensic analysts use similar processes to capture images for analysis.

A forensic image of a disk captures the entire contents of the drive. Some tools use bit-by-bit copy methods that can read the data without modifying it. Other methods include hardware devices connected to the drive to write-protect it during the copy process. A distinct difference between standard system images and forensic images is that a forensic image is an exact copy and does not modify the original. This isn't always true with system imaging tools.

An important element in creating forensic copies is to ensure that the data on the hard drive is not modified. Said another way, forensic copies ensure the integrity of the disk evidence is not compromised during the copy process.

Remember this

A forensic image is a bit-by-bit copy of the data and does not modify the data during the capture. Experts capture an image of the data before analysis. Analysis can modify the data so forensic experts analyze the image (or copies of the image) and keep the original data in an unmodified state.

All of these methods capture the entire contents of the disk, including system and user files, and files marked for deletion but not overwritten. Similarly, many tools include the ability to capture data within volatile memory and save it as an image.

After capturing an image, experts create a copy and analyze the copy. They do not analyze the original disk and often don't even analyze the original image. They understand that by analyzing the contents of a disk directly, they can modify the contents. By creating and analyzing forensic copies, they never modify the original evidence.

Take Hashes

Hashes provide integrity and prove that data has not been modified. Hashing is an important element of forensic analysis to provide proof that collected data has retained integrity.

Chapter 10 covered hashes and hashing. As a reminder, a hash is simply a number. You can execute a hashing algorithm against data as many times as you like, and as long as the data is the same, the hash will be the same. The focus in chapter 10 was on using hashes with files and messages. An image (from RAM or a disk) is just a file, and you can use hashing with forensic images to ensure image integrity.

For example, after capturing an image of volatile RAM, an expert can create a hash of the image. Hashing algorithms include MD5 and SHA variations such as SHA-1 or SHA-256.

Some tools allow you to create a hash of an entire drive. These verify that the imaging process has not modified data. For example, you can create a hash of a drive before capturing the image and after capturing the image. If the hashes are the same, it verifies that the imaging process did not modify the drive.

Additionally, you can run the same hashing algorithm against the drive later to prove the original drive did not lose integrity. As long as the hashes are the same, it proves the evidence has not been modified. On the other hand, if the hashes are different, it indicates the original drive has lost integrity. This may have occurred accidentally or through deliberate evidence tampering.

> ### Remember this
>
> Forensic analysts sometimes make a copy of the image to analyze, instead of analyzing the first image they capture. If they ever need to verify the integrity of the copy, they run the same hashing algorithm against it. Again, as long as the hash is the same, they known the analyzed data is the same as the captured data.

Network Traffic and Logs

A forensic investigation will often include an analysis of network traffic and available logs. This information helps the investigators recreate events leading up to, and during an incident.

As an example, an organization may want to prove that a specific computer was involved in an attack. One way is to match the media access control (MAC) address used by the attacking computer with an existing computer. The MAC address is permanently assigned to a network interface card, and even though the operating system can be manipulated to use a different MAC, the actual MAC isn't changed. In contrast, the IP address and name of the computer are not permanently assigned, and it is relatively easy to change them.

Chapter 8 covered protocol analyzers, and Figure 8.1 showed a capture with an expanded packet. Data within packets identify computers involved in a conversation based on their IP address and their MAC address. If a data capture shows a MAC address matches the actual MAC address of a suspected computer, it provides a strong indication the computer was involved in the attack.

> ### *Remember this*
> Network traffic and logs can identify computers and some of their activity. One way to identify computers involved in attacks is with a MAC address. The MAC address is more definitive than an IP address or a computer name.

Similarly, if the attack came from the Internet, the IP address can be traced back to the Internet Service Provider (ISP). ISPs issue IP addresses to users and the ISP logs identify exactly who was issued an IP address at any given time. For example, when David Kernell hacked into Sarah Palin's Yahoo e-mail account in 2008, the attack was quickly traced back to him based on his IP address.

Chapter 8 presented information on logs. Logs record what happened during an event, when it happened, and what account was used during the event. You may remember that a Security log records logon and logoff events. Similarly, many applications require users to authenticate, and applications also log authentication events. All of these logs can be invaluable in recreating the details of an event after a security incident, including the identity of the account used in the attack.

Chain of Custody

A key part of incident response is collecting and protecting evidence. A chain of custody is a process that provides assurances that evidence has been controlled and handled properly after collection. Forensic experts establish a chain of custody when they first collect evidence.

Security professionals use a chain-of-custody form to document this control. The chain-of-custody form identifies who had custody of the evidence and where it was stored the entire time since collection. A proper chain of custody ensures that evidence presented in a court of law is the same evidence that security professionals collected.

As an example, imagine that Bob collected a USB thumb drive as part of an investigation. However, instead of establishing a chain of custody, he simply stores the drive on his desk with the intention of analyzing it the next day. Is it possible that someone could modify the contents of the thumb drive overnight? Absolutely. Instead, he should immediately establish a chain of custody and lock the drive in a secure storage location.

> ### *Remember this*
> A chain of custody provides assurances that evidence has been controlled and handled properly after collection. It documents who handled the evidence and when.

If evidence is not controlled, it can be modified, tampered with, or otherwise corrupted. Courts will rule the evidence inadmissible if there is a lack of adequate control, or even a lack of documentation showing that adequate control was maintained. However, the chain of custody proves that the evidence has been handled properly.

Capture Video

Chapter 2 introduced video surveillance methods such as closed circuit television (CCTV) systems. These can be used as a detective control during an investigation. They provide reliable proof of a person's location and activity. For example, if a person is stealing equipment or data, video may provide proof.

I remember a high school student was working nights at a local grocery store. The store had a delivery of beer in a tractor-trailer they hadn't unloaded yet but kept backed up to the store loading dock overnight. The student stole several cases of beer thinking the crime was undetectable. However, the entire scene was recorded on video, and when he showed up for work the next evening, the store promptly called the police and provided a copy of the video. The video provided reliable proof that simply couldn't be disputed.

Record Time Offset

In some cases, times are expressed clearly, making it easy to identify the time of an event. However, in other cases the displayed time is based on an offset. Consider Figure 11.1.

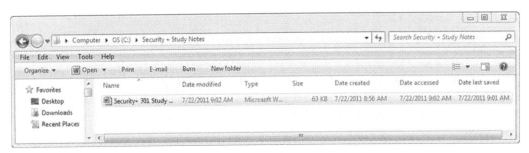

Figure 11.1: Windows Explorer showing file times

In the figure, you can easily identify the exact times when the file was created, last accessed, and saved. In this case, the date is easy to identify as July 22, 2011. However, in other cases, the file is coded.

For example, Greenwich Mean Time (GMT) identifies time based on the location. I live in the Eastern Standard Time (EST) zone, so you can express the last accessed time as 9:02 a.m. EST. However, GMT uses an offset, so the same time is also 1:02 p.m. GMT.

Similarly, many recorders use time offsets to identify times on tape recordings rather than the actual time. For example, a recording may use a displayed counter to identify the time that has passed since the recording started. Imagine that the counter advances 1000 ticks or counts per hour. If the counter indicates an event occurred at an offset time of 1500 and the recording started at midnight, then the time of the event was 1:30 a.m.

When analyzing time stamps of any evidence, it's important to understand that these times are often based on an offset. If you can't identify the offset, you may not be able to identify the actual time.

Screenshots

Screenshots are simply pictures of what is displayed on the screen of a computer. If you want to capture exactly what a user was doing, or specific displays, a screenshot is the perfect solution.

For example, Figure 11.1, shown previously, is a screenshot of Windows Explorer. You can save screenshots as graphics files and embed these graphics into documents. Many operating systems include the ability to capture the screen and save it to the clipboard. For example, you can capture the screen of almost any system by pressing the PrtScn key found on most keyboards. Many applications such as Snagit allow you to capture screenshots from specific windows or applications, any region of the screen, and even scrolling windows such as a long web page.

Witnesses

Another element of an investigation is interviewing witnesses. Witnesses provide firsthand reports of what happened and when it happened. However, witnesses won't necessarily come forward with relevant information unless they're asked. Often witnesses don't recognize what information is valuable.

For example, imagine an attacker that tailgated behind an employee without showing credentials. The employee may notice, but not give it much thought, especially if tailgating is common in the organization. If the attack resulted in loss of equipment or data, an investigator may get a good description of the attacker just by interviewing witnesses.

Track Man Hours and Expense

Investigations can take an extraordinary amount of time and for any business, time is money. When budget time rolls around, the departments that can accurately identify how much time and money they spent are more likely to get their requested budget approved.

Additionally, quantitative risk assessments base decisions using specific monetary amounts, such as cost and asset values. If an incident required involvement by security professionals on an incident response team, the man hours and expenses incurred by the incident response team needs to be included in the assessment. Including this data improves the accuracy of the cost values used in the quantitative risk assessment.

Chapter 11 Exam Topic Review

When preparing for the exam, make sure you understand these key concepts covered in this chapter.

Security Policies

- A security policy is a written document that identifies a security plan for an organization. Security controls enforce security policies.
- Clean desk policies require users to organize their desks and surrounding areas to reduce the risk of possible data theft and password compromise.
- User privilege policies enforce the principle of least privilege and ensure users have only the rights and permissions needed to perform their job and no more. Rights and permissions reviews identify when user privilege policies are not enforced.
- Account policies often require administrators to have two accounts. This helps prevent privilege escalation and other attacks.
- Account disablement or expiration policies ensure that inactive accounts are disabled.
- USB thumb drives are a source of data leakage and malware distribution. Security policies often restrict the use of USB thumb drives and other portable devices such as music players.
- An acceptable use policy defines proper system usage for users. Users are often required to read and sign an acceptable use policy when hired, and in conjunction with refresher training.
- Mandatory vacation policies require employees to take time away from their job. These policies help to reduce fraud and discover malicious activities by employees.
- Job rotation policies require employees to change roles on a regular basis. These policies help to prevent employees from continuing with fraudulent activities.
- Separation of duties policies separate individual tasks of an overall function between different entities or different people.
- Security awareness and training practices reinforce user compliance with security policies and help reduce risks posed by users.
- Information classification practices help protect sensitive data by ensuring users understand the value of data. Data labeling ensures that users know what data they are handling and processing.
- Storage and retention policies identify how long data is retained. They can limit a company's exposure to legal proceedings and reduce the amount of labor required to respond to court orders.
- Personally identifiable information (PII) is used to personally identify an individual. Examples include full name, birthdate, addresses, medical information, and more.
- PII requires special handling and policies for data retention. Many laws mandate the protection of PII, and require informing individuals when an attack results in the compromise of PII.

- A privacy policy identifies what data is collected from users on a web site. Many laws require a privacy policy.
- Improper use of social networking sites can result in inadvertent information disclosure. Attackers gather information from these sites to launch attacks against users.
- P2P software is a source of data leakage. Organizations often block P2P software at the firewall and run port scans to detect P2P on end user systems.
- Sanitization procedures ensure data is removed from decommissioned systems. Specialized applications erase disk drives by writing a series of ones and zeroes multiple times on the drive.

Incident Response Policies

- An incident response policy defines an incident and response procedures.
- The first step to take after identifying an incident is to contain or isolate the problem. Disconnecting a computer from a network will isolate it.
- Some data is more volatile than other data, and the order of volatility refers to the order experts collect evidence.
- A memory forensics analysis retrieves information from RAM, such as data a user has been working on, system processes, network processes, application remnants, and more. RAM is volatile and must be captured before a system is powered down.
- Hard drive imaging creates a forensic copy and prevents the forensic capture and analysis from modifying the original evidence. A forensic image is a bit-by-bit copy of the data and does not modify the data during the capture.
- Hashing, using algorithms such as MD5 or SHA-256, provides integrity for image captures. Taking a hash before and after capturing a disk image verifies that the capturing process did not modify data.
- Hashes can reveal evidence tampering or, at the very least, that evidence has lost integrity.
- Network traffic and logs identify computers and network activity. A MAC address (captured by a protocol analyzer) can identify a computer.
- A chain of custody documents how evidence has been controlled and who has handled it after the initial collection. It provides assurances that evidence has been controlled and handled properly.

Chapter 11 Practice Questions

1. An organization recently created a security policy. Of the following choices, what is a technical implementation of security policy?
    A. Training
    B. Acceptable use acknowledgment
    C. Implicit deny rule in a firewall
    D. Job rotation

2. An organization wants to reduce the possibility of data theft. Of the following choices, what can assist with this goal?
    A. Requiring the use of USB thumb drives to store data
    B. Removing DLP devices
    C. Store copies of the data in the cloud
    D. Clean desk policy

3. An organization requires administrators to have two accounts. One account has administrator access and the other account is a regular user account. What can this help prevent?
    A. Whaling
    B. Vishing
    C. Escalation of privileges
    D. Command injection

4. An attacker is using an account from an employee that left the company three years ago. What could prevent this?
    A. Password expiration policy
    B. Job rotation policy
    C. Account expiration policy
    D. Separation of duties policy

5. A company prohibits the use of USB flash drives to prevent data leakage. Of the following choices, what could the company also do to reduce data leakage?
    A. Prohibit personal music devices
    B. Remove labels from backup media
    C. Prohibit the storage of backups off-site
    D. Prohibit DLP devices

6. What policy informs users of proper system usage?
    A. Acceptable use policy
    B. Clean desk policy
    C. Data labeling policy
    D. Data classification policy

7. Employees in the accounting department are forced to take time off from their duties on a regular basis. What would direct this?
   A. Account disablement policy
   B. Mandatory vacation policy
   C. Job rotation policy
   D. Dual accounts for administrators

8. Two administrators within an organization perform different functions and have different privileges. They are required to swap roles annually. What policy would direct this?
   A. Mandatory vacation policy
   B. Separation of duties policy
   C. Least privilege policy
   D. Job rotation policy

9. A group of server administrators maintains several database servers, but they cannot access security logs on these servers. Security administrators can access the security logs, but they cannot access data within the databases. What policy is the company using?
   A. Separation of duties policy
   B. Policy requiring dual accounts for administrators
   C. Job rotation policy
   D. Mandatory vacations policy

10. A company provides employees with annual security awareness training. Of the following choices, what is the most likely reason the company is doing this?
    A. To increase the number of security incidents
    B. To educate users about changes in the IT network
    C. To eliminate malware attacks
    D. To reinforce user compliance with security policies

11. A company is creating a security awareness and training plan for employees. Of the following choices, what will affect its success the most?
    A. Support from senior management
    B. Acceptance by employees
    C. Technical controls used
    D. Method of training

12. Why would an organization use information classification practices?
    A. To enhance phishing
    B. To enhance whaling
    C. To protect sensitive data
    D. To ensure PII is publically available

13. Of the following choices, what is a primary benefit of data labeling?
    A. To identify data collected from a public web site
    B. To prevent the handling of PII
    C. To identify PII
    D. Ensure that employees understand data they are handling

14. A company was recently involved in a legal issue that resulted in administrators spending a significant amount of time retrieving data from archives in response to a court order. The company wants to limit the time spent on similar events in the future. What can it do?
    A. Implement separation of duties policies
    B. Implement privacy policies
    C. Create storage and retention policies
    D. Perform user rights reviews

15. Which of the following is PII when it is associated with a person's full name?
    A. Pet's name
    B. Birthdate
    C. Favorite book
    D. Favorite color

16. Your company has a public website. Where could you identify what data is collected from users on this website?
    A. PII policy
    B. Privacy policy
    C. Clean desk policy
    D. Data retention policy

17. Organizations often restrict employee access to social networking sites from work locations. What are they trying to prevent?
    A. Information disclosure
    B. Employee morale
    C. Risks from DoS attacks
    D. Risks from DDoS attacks

18. An organization is disposing of old hard drives. What should security personnel do to prevent data leakage?
    A. Sanitize the drive using bit level overwrites
    B. Delete all data files
    C. Format the drive
    D. Remove operating system files

19. An administrator recently discovered an active attack on a database server. The server hosts customer PII and other data. What should the administrator do first?
    A. Create a chain of custody
    B. Create an image of the memory
    C. Disconnect the server from the network
    D. Create an image of the disks

20. Of the following choices, what is a likely response to a security breach?
    A. Backup data
    B. Begin a forensic evaluation
    C. Enable a NIDS
    D. Encrypt data with AES-128

21. Investigators suspect that an internal computer was involved in an attack, but the computer has been turned off. What information is unavailable for an investigation? (Choose all that apply.)
    A. Memory
    B. Network processes
    C. Files
    D. System processes
    E. Master boot record

22. What should a forensics expert do before analyzing a hard drive for evidence?
    A. Create a listing of files
    B. Identify the last file opened on the system
    C. Create an image of the system memory
    D. Image the drive

23. How can a forensic analysis ensure the integrity of an image of a computer's memory?
    A. Use AES-128
    B. Use SHA-256
    C. Encrypt the image
    D. Power the system down before capturing the image

24. A forensic expert collected a laptop as evidence. What provides assurances that the system was properly handled while it was transported?
    A. System log
    B. Security log
    C. Chain of custody
    D. Forensic hash

25. A forensic expert created an image copy of a hard drive and created a chain of custody. What does the chain of custody provide?

    A. Confidentiality of the original data

    B. Documentation on who handled the evidence

    C. Verification of integrity with a hash

    D. Proof that the image wasn't modified

Chapter 11 Practice Question Answers

1. **C.** Firewall rules (including the implicit deny rule) provide technical implementation of security policies. The other choices are not technical controls. Organizations provide security awareness training to reinforce user compliance with security policies and to minimize the risk posed by users. It's common to have users sign an acceptable use statement when hired and periodically afterwards, such as during annual security refresher training. Job rotation policies require employees to change roles on a regular basis.

2. **D.** A clean desk policy requires users to organize their areas to reduce the risk of possible data theft and password compromise. USB thumb drives increase the risk of data theft and data leakage. Data Loss Prevention (DLP) devices such as network-based DLPs can detect data leakage. Because cloud computing stores data in unknown locations accessible via the Internet, you lose physical control of the data.

3. **C.** Requiring administrators to use two accounts in this way helps prevent privilege escalation attacks. Whaling is a phishing attack that targets high-level executives. Vishing is a form of phishing that uses recorded voice over the telephone. A command injection attack is any attempt to inject commands into an application such as a web-based form.

4. **C.** An account disablement or account expiration policy ensures that inactive accounts are disabled. A password expiration policy requires changing the password, but wouldn't disable the account unless the user or attacker didn't change the password. Job rotation policies require employees to change roles on a regular basis but don't affect accounts. A separation of duties policy separates individual tasks of an overall function between different people.

5. **A.** Personal music devices use the same type of memory as USB flash drives, so by prohibiting them, it can reduce data leakage. Backup media should be labeled to ensure employees recognize the value of the data. As a disaster recovery best practice, a copy of backups should be stored off-site. Network-based Data Loss Prevention (DLP) systems can examine and analyze network traffic and detect if confidential company data is included to reduce data leakage.

6. **A.** An acceptable use policy defines proper system usage for users. A clean desk policy requires users to organize their areas to reduce the risk of possible data theft and password compromise. Data labeling and classification policies help users understand the value of data and data labeling ensures that users know what data they are handling and processing.

7. **B.** Mandatory vacation policies require employees to take time away from their job and help to detect fraud or malicious activities. An account disablement policy specifies when to disable accounts. Job rotation policies require employees to change roles on a regular basis. Dual accounts for administrators help prevent privilege escalation attacks.

8. **D.** Job rotation policies require employees to change roles on a regular basis. Mandatory vacation policies require employees to take time away from their job and help detect malicious activities. A separation of duties policy separates individual tasks of an overall function between different people. Least privilege ensures that users are granted only the rights and permissions needed to perform assigned tasks but doesn't require swapping roles.

9. **A.** A separation of duties policy separates individual tasks of an overall function between different people, and in this case it is separating maintenance of the database servers with security oversight of the servers. Dual accounts for administrators (one for administrative use and one for regular use) help prevent privilege escalation attacks. Job rotation policies require employees to change roles on a regular basis. Mandatory vacation policies require employees to take time away from their job and help detect malicious activities.

10. **D.** Organizations provide security awareness training to reinforce user compliance with security policies and to minimize the risk posed by users. The goal is to reduce, not increase, the number of incidents. End users don't need to be educated about the IT network, but an acceptable use policy does educate them about proper system usage. Training may educate users about malware, but it's not possible to eliminate all malware attacks.

11. **A.** The success of a security education and awareness plan is directly related to the amount of support from senior management. If senior management supports the plan, employees will accept it. Technical controls (such as a firewall) enforce security but are not typically included in a security awareness and training plan. Multiple methods of training and different environments require different methods.

12. **C.** Information classification practices help protect sensitive data by ensuring that users understand the value of data. Phishing and whaling are attacks via e-mail. Personally identifiable information (PII) requires special handling and should not be publically available.

13. **D.** Data classifications ensure that users understand the value of data and data labeling ensures that users know what data they are handling and processing. A privacy policy identifies data collected from a public website. Personally identifiable information (PII) requires special handling, but it is not possible to prevent handling PII. Data labeling identifies all types of data and classifications, not just PII.

14. **C.** Storage and retention policies identify how long data is retained. They can limit a company's exposure to legal proceedings and reduce the amount of labor required to respond to court orders. A separation of duties policy separates individual tasks of an overall function between different people but doesn't affect data retention. A privacy policy identifies what data is collected from users on a website. User rights reviews can identify violations in a user privilege policy.

15. **B.** A birthdate is personally identifiable information (PII) when it is combined with a full name. Other answers are not PII.

16. **B.** A privacy policy identifies what data is collected from users on a website. A PII policy identifies procedures for handling and retaining PII but wouldn't necessarily identify data collected from a website. A clean desk policy requires users to organize their areas to reduce the risk of possible data theft and password compromise. A data retention policy identifies how long to keep data.

17. **A.** A risk resulting from the improper use of social networking sites is information disclosure. Some organizations allow access to various Internet sites to increase morale (not prevent it), but they provide training to users on the risks. Denial-of-service (DoS) and distributed DoS (DDoS) attacks are launched against systems, not users, so accessing the social networking sites doesn't present risks of DoS or DDoS attacks.

18. **A.** A bit level overwrite process writes a series of ones and zeroes on a drive and ensures that the disk is sanitized before disposing of it. File deletion and drive formatting can be undone in many situations and doesn't ensure the data is removed. All files and data should be removed, not just operating system files.

19. **C.** Containment is an important first step after verifying an incident, and disconnecting the server will contain this incident. A chain of custody provides assurances that evidence (such as memory or disk images) has been controlled and handled properly after collection, but this isn't done before containing the problem.

20. **B.** Once an organization identifies an incident and contains it, it will begin a forensic evaluation. It's too late to back up data *after* a breach. A network intrusion detection system (NIDS) can detect attacks, but a NIDS should be running at all times, not just after a breach. Encryption of data with AES-128 will protect confidentiality, but it won't help after the breach.

21. **A, B, D.** Data in memory is volatile and not available after turning a system off. Additionally, any processes or applications are not running when the system is powered off, since this information is stored in volatile memory. Files are stored on disks, and disk data (including the master boot record) remains available even after turning off power to the system.

22. **D.** Hard drive imaging creates a forensic copy and prevents the forensic analysis from modifying the original evidence. Listing or identifying files is part of analysis and should not be done before an image is created. It's valuable to create an image of system memory before powering down a system, but this is unrelated to analyzing a hard drive.

23. **B.** You can ensure integrity with hashing algorithms such as SHA-256, and this includes images of memory and images of disks. Advanced Encryption Standard 128 (AES-128) is an

encryption algorithm that uses 128 bits, but encryption helps ensure confidentiality, not integrity. Information in memory is lost if the system is powered down.

24. **C.** A chain of custody provides assurances that evidence has been controlled and handled properly after collection. The System log records system events such as when a service stops and starts, and the Security log records auditable events such as user logons and logoffs, but neither documents transportation. A forensic hash provides assurances that an image or file has not been modified.

25. **B.** A chain of custody provides assurances that evidence has been controlled and documents who handled the evidence. The expert may create a hash before and after capturing the image to prove the image wasn't modified, but this provides integrity and is not related to a chain of custody. Confidentiality is provided with encryption, not a chain of custody.

CompTIA Security+ Practice Exam

Use this practice exam as an additional study aid before taking the live exam. An answer key with explanation is available at the end of the practice exam.

1. An organization hosts online gaming and wants to ensure that customer data hosted within the datacenter is protected. It implements several access controls, including a mantrap. What is the organization trying to protect?
    A. Social engineering
    B. Availability
    C. Confidentiality
    D. Integrity

2. What can you use to ensure that stored data has retained integrity?
    A. BIA
    B. Hashing
    C. Digital signatures
    D. SaaS

3. Your organization is considering virtualizing some servers in your network. Of the following choices, what can virtualization provide?
    A. Confidentiality
    B. Integrity
    C. Availability
    D. Encryption

4. What can you do to increase the key space of a password?
    A. Use only uppercase or lowercase letters
    B. Use uppercase, lowercase, numbers, and special characters
    C. Use password history with a minimum password age
    D. Ensure that passwords expire

5. Users in your organization can use a self-service password reset system. What does this provide?
    A. Password policy enforcement
    B. Password deletion
    C. Account expiration reset
    D. Password recovery

6. A user must use a thumbprint scanner to gain access to his laptop. What type of authentication is being used?

    A. Something the user knows

    B. Something the user has

    C. Something the user is

    D. CAC

7. Of the following choices, what method is the most difficult for an attacker to falsify?

    A. Passwords

    B. XSRF

    C. Biometrics

    D. Usernames

8. What makes up a two-factor authentication system?

    A. Two distinct items, one from two of the authentication factors

    B. Two distinct items from any single authentication factor

    C. Two distinct items from each of the authentication factors

    D. One distinct item from each of the authentication factors

9. Which one of the following accurately identifies a three-factor authentication system?

    A. A username, password, and PIN

    B. A token, password, and a retina scan

    C. A token, a password, and a PIN

    D. A fingerprint, retina scan, and password

10. Which of the following authentication protocols uses a key distribution center to generate tokens?

    A. LDAP

    B. AES

    C. 3DES

    D. Kerberos

11. Users in your network are able to log onto their local system, and after logging on they are able to access encrypted files on a server without reentering their password. What is being used?

    A. Discretionary access control (DAC)

    B. Single sign-on

    C. Multifactor authentication

    D. Least privilege

12. An organization suspects that equipment and confidential data is being removed from the organization. What could it use to provide verification that this is or isn't occurring?
    A. Video surveillance
    B. Spyware
    C. Regular user access review
    D. Change management

13. An organization wants to simplify user administration. What strategy would it use?
    A. Implement a password policy
    B. Require users to provide their passwords to the administrator
    C. Assign permissions to users individually
    D. Implement access based on groups

14. Which of the following best describes RBAC?
    A. Single-factor authentication
    B. Job function specific
    C. Two-factor authentication
    D. A method of increasing user administration

15. Users in your organization are issued proximity cards. What factor of authentication is being used?
    A. Something a user knows
    B. Something a user has
    C. Something a user is
    D. Something a user wants

16. A datacenter includes servers with highly sensitive data, and management wants reliable proof to determine if specific individuals access the datacenter. What should be used?
    A. Security log
    B. Access list
    C. Mantrap
    D. Video surveillance

17. An attacker followed an authorized user into a secure area after the authorized user opened the door with an access card. What type of attack is this?
    A. Mantrap
    B. Fuzzing
    C. Tailgating
    D. ARP poisoning

18. You want to ensure that users must use passwords with at least eight characters and a mix of at least three of the following four character types: uppercase, lowercase, numbers, and symbols. What would you use?

    A. An account lockout policy

    B. A password policy

    C. A training program

    D. IPsec encryption

19. An administrator needs to record any access to a file server. The record should include the date and time when the user accessed the system, and the user's identity. What supports this?

    A. Time of day restrictions

    B. Kerberos log

    C. Account login log

    D. User rights log

20. Of the following choices, what provides the most secure method of transferring files between two computers on a network?

    A. FTP

    B. TFTP

    C. SFTP

    D. AES

21. Of the following choices, what is most often used to remotely administer a UNIX or Linux system?

    A. Terminal Services

    B. Remote Desktop Services

    C. SCP

    D. SSH

22. Of the following choices, what identifies computers on the Internet and some internal networks using a long string of numbers and characters?

    A. NAT

    B. IPv4

    C. IPv6

    D. ICMP

23. What port does Telnet use?

    A. 22

    B. 23

    C. 443

    D. 500

24. Your organization hosts a Microsoft SQL Server database in the internal network. You want to ensure that the firewall blocks access to this database from the Internet. What port should you block?
    A. 22
    B. 23
    C. 443
    D. 1433

25. Of the following choices, what would be the easiest to use to help you determine what services are running on a remote server?
    A. Port scanner
    B. Sniffer
    C. CRL
    D. Load balancer

26. An audit of the firewall logs shows that attackers are attempting to remotely login to systems using remote desktop protocols. The security administrator decides to block the port to prevent this activity. What port should the administrator close?
    A. 20
    B. 22
    C. 389
    D. 3389

27. A file server failed and a user was unable to access it. After repairing the problem, you attempt to ping the server to verify it was working. The ping fails, but the user is able to access the server. What is the most likely reason why the ping fails?
    A. A router between you and the file server is blocking ICMP
    B. TCP and UDP is blocked at a router between you and the file server
    C. A flood guard blocked the ping
    D. A host enumeration sweep is running

28. Of the following choices, what are you most likely to see as the last rule in a firewall's ACL?
    A. Implicit deny
    B. Block ICMP
    C. Allow FTP traffic
    D. Filter spam

29. Your organization wants to prevent attackers from performing host enumeration sweeps. What can be done to prevent these sweeps?
    A. Block ICMP at the network perimeter
    B. Allow ICMP at the network perimeter
    C. Block FTPS at the network perimeter
    D. Block SMTP at the network perimeter

30. What services does a proxy server provide?
    A. Forwards requests for services from a client
    B. Reduces usage of cache
    C. Ensures that all URLs are allowed
    D. Filters traffic into a network

31. Which of the following controls can detect smurf attacks?
    A. Firewall
    B. NIDS
    C. Honeypot
    D. NAC

32. A security company wants to identify and learn about the latest unknown attacks. What can it use?
    A. Nothing, the attacks are unknown
    B. Honeypot
    C. MAC filtering
    D. Evil twin

33. An IPS is monitoring data streams looking for malicious behavior. When it detects malicious behavior, it blocks the traffic. What is this IPS using?
    A. Smurf detection
    B. Honeypot
    C. Content inspection
    D. Port scanner

34. An administrator wants to detect and mitigate malicious activity on the network. What should the administrator use?
    A. NIDS
    B. NIPS
    C. HIDS
    D. HIPS

35. An organization wants to implement a wireless network using the strongest encryption and authorization methods possible. Of the following choices, what provides the best solution?
    A. WEP with RADIUS
    B. WPA2 Personal
    C. WPA Enterprise
    D. WPA2 with CCMP

36. An attacker is trying to break into your wireless network. Of the following choices, what security controls can the attacker easily bypass with a protocol analyzer? (Choose all that apply.)
    A. WPA2-PSK
    B. MAC filtering
    C. WPA2 with CCMP
    D. Disabled SSID broadcast

37. You regularly perform wireless audits around your organization's campus. While war driving, you discover many unauthorized devices connected to the network. What can explain this?
    A. Rogue access point
    B. Low power level on the WAP
    C. Incorrectly placed antenna on the WAP
    D. Bluesnarfing

38. What would you use to protect against loss of confidentiality of data stored on a mobile phone?
    A. Hashing
    B. Evil twin
    C. Encryption
    D. IPsec

39. Of the following choices, what can you use in tunnel mode for a VPN?
    A. SSL
    B. ICMP
    C. HTTPS
    D. IPsec

40. What does NAC provide for an organization?
    A. Strong security for a large number of VPN clients
    B. A method of observing attackers using zero day exploits
    C. Access to a network based on predetermined characteristics
    D. An encrypted tunnel over the Internet

41. What can an organization use to deploy systems in compliance with its strict security guidelines?
    A. Network access control
    B. Honeypots
    C. Change management
    D. Security templates

42. Users have been complaining that their systems are running slow when interacting with a Windows e-mail server. What can an administrator use to check the performance of the mail server?
    A. Security templates
    B. Performance Monitor
    C. Imaging software
    D. Data Loss Prevention system

43. An organization is planning to implement virtualization technology within its datacenter. Of the following choices, what benefit will this provide?
    A. Eliminate VM escape attacks
    B. Reduce the datacenter footprint
    C. Ensure systems include mandated security configurations
    D. Provide the accounting structure for system modifications

44. A security professional routinely researches security threats by releasing new versions of malware on a system and observing the activity. Of the following choices, what will provide the best protection to reduce risks to the production environment?
    A. HIDS
    B. NIDS
    C. NIPS
    D. Virtual system

45. Your organization regularly tests and deploys patches. What types of attacks will this prevent?
    A. Zero day attacks
    B. Unknown attacks
    C. Known attacks
    D. Hotfix attacks

46. A vendor released a firmware update that applies to several routers used in your organization, and you have updated each of the routers. Where should you document the completion of this work?
    A. Security log
    B. Change management system
    C. CCTV
    D. ACL

47. What is a TPM?
    A. A method used to erase data on lost mobile devices such as mobile phones
    B. A hardware chip that stores encryption keys
    C. A system that can examine and analyze e-mail to detect if confidential data is included
    D. A removable device that stores encryption keys

48. Your organization needs to improve the performance of SSL sessions on an e-commerce server. What can they use to improve performance while also providing a secure method of storing the digital certificates used by the SSL sessions?

   A. HSM

   B. CA

   C. A private CRL

   D. A database

49. Your organization has a significant amount of research and development data it wants to protect against data leakage. Of the following choices what presents the greatest risk?

   A. Users copying the data to a USB flash drive

   B. Users sending encrypted backup tapes to an offsite location

   C. Users sending data over the network with IPsec

   D. Users transmitting data to an FTP server with FTPS

50. A company needs to deploy a large database for a new venture. It does not want to purchase servers or hire additional personnel until it has proven the venture can succeed. What can it use?

   A. IaaS

   B. PaaS

   C. SaaS

   D. HSM

51. Sally is helping a user whose system is running slow and randomly rebooting. While troubleshooting it, she realizes she no longer has administrative rights on the system. What is a likely cause of these symptoms?

   A. Adware

   B. Rootkit

   C. DDoS

   D. Spam

52. Your organization issues laptops to employees used while on the road. Of the following choices, what software does not enhance their security? (Choose two.)

   A. Spam filter

   B. Host-based firewall

   C. Antivirus software

   D. NIDS

   E. NIPS

53. Of the following choices, what can antivirus software detect? (Choose all that apply.)

   A. Pharming

   B. Virus

   C. Worm

   D. Trojan horse

54. Of the following choices, what provides the best protection against malware for computers with Internet access?
    A. Antivirus software
    B. Anti-spam software
    C. Updated antivirus software
    D. Updated anti-spyware software

55. Of the following choices, what best represents an attack designed to obtain information from a specific person?
    A. Spear phishing
    B. Tailgating
    C. Trojan
    D. Phishing

56. What type of attack is launched from multiple systems from different geographic locations?
    A. DoS
    B. DDoS
    C. SYN flood
    D. Kiting

57. Of the following choices, what provides the best testing for in-house developed application?
    A. Internal black box testing
    B. Internal white box testing
    C. Third party black box testing
    D. Third party white box testing

58. A web application developer uses code to check data entered into a web form. The code prevents the web application from sending certain characters or commands to other servers. What is the developer using?
    A. Cross-site scripting
    B. SQL injection
    C. Input validation
    D. NOOP sleds

59. Which of the following is related to a buffer overflow attack?
    A. NOOP instructions
    B. Small initialization vector
    C. Spear phishing
    D. Pharming

60. An attacker recently used a SQL injection attack against a company's website. How can the company prevent future SQL injection attacks?
    A. Add SSL encryption
    B. Add input validation
    C. Add antivirus software
    D. Add cross-site scripting capabilities

61. A web application is blocking users from including HTML tags in data inputs. What is it trying to prevent?
    A. Cross-site scripting
    B. Trojans
    C. Rootkits
    D. SQL injection

62. Which of the following choices are valid risk management methods? (Choose all that apply).
    A. Risk acceptance
    B. Risk avoidance
    C. Risk deterrence
    D. Risk elimination
    E. E. Risk transference

63. A company briefly considered providing an additional service to its customers. However, it decided not to provide the service due to the risks involved. What method of risk management is the company using?
    A. Risk acceptance
    B. Risk avoidance
    C. Risk deterrence
    D. Risk mitigation
    E. Risk transference

64. An organization wants to identify how threats may affect it without actually exploiting the findings. What can it do?
    A. Perform a risk assessment
    B. Hire external black box testers
    C. Perform a penetration test
    D. Perform a fuzz test

65. A security administrator is using a tool in a passive attempt to identify weaknesses. What type of tool is this?
    A. Penetration test
    B. Fuzz tester
    C. Vulnerability scanner
    D. IDS

66. An organization wants to assess security on its network during normal business hours without affecting users. What type of assessment should it use?
    A. Penetration test
    B. Protocol analysis
    C. Vulnerability scan
    D. Black box

67. Of the following choices, what represents the most important information a penetration test can provide when compared with a vulnerability scan?
    A. Information on the impact of a threat
    B. Information on security controls
    C. Information on vulnerabilities
    D. Information on system configuration

68. A black box tester is attempting data exfiltration. What will the tester most likely attempt after gaining access to a system?
    A. Vulnerability scan
    B. Privilege escalation
    C. Erase rules of engagement logs
    D. Create chain of custody

69. What can an attacker use to identify vulnerabilities in an application?
    A. Protocol analyzer
    B. Port scanner
    C. Fuzzing
    D. IPS

70. Why is it important to gain consent from a system owner prior to starting a penetration test?
    A. This is not a requirement
    B. A penetration test can cause increased performance
    C. A penetration test can cause system instability
    D. A penetration test can reduce system resource usage

71. What tool allows an administrator to view unencrypted network traffic?
    A. Vulnerability scanner
    B. PKI
    C. Protocol analyzer
    D. HSM

72. You want to check a log to determine when a service was stopped. What log would you check?
    A. System
    B. Application
    C. Firewall
    D. Security

73. What does RAID-1 provide for a system?
    A. Authentication
    B. Availability
    C. Confidentiality
    D. Integrity

74. Commercial power provided to a remote location has problems with power fluctuations, resulting in occasional server crashes. What can the organization implement to protect against power fluctuations?
    A. UPS
    B. Generators
    C. HVAC system
    D. Hot and cold aisles

75. An organization stores backups on tapes. Of the following choices, what is an important step related to these tapes?
    A. Ensure tapes are not labeled
    B. Store the tapes with the servers
    C. Throw tapes away after usable service lifetime expires
    D. Store a copy of the backup off-site

76. Which of the following continuity of operations solutions is the least expensive?
    A. Hot site
    B. Cold site
    C. Warm site
    D. BIA site

77. An organization maintains an off-site location as a contingency for a disaster at the main site. The location includes all the necessary servers to support the critical functions, but it does not have up-to-date data. What type of site is this?
    A. Hot site
    B. Cold site
    C. Warm site
    D. HSM site

78. Of the following choices, what is included in a DRP?
    A. Report or testing results
    B. CRL
    C. List of vulnerabilities
    D. Hierarchical list of critical systems

79. What can an HVAC system control to reduce potential damage from electrostatic discharges?
    A. Humidity
    B. Hot and cold aisles
    C. Temperature
    D. Air flow

80. What can you use to prevent data loss in a CAT 6 cable?
    A. Fiber optics
    B. Unshielded cable
    C. RAID
    D. EMI shielding

81. A system administrator wants to create a unique identifier for an executable file. Of the following choices, what can be used?
    A. RC4
    B. Public key
    C. Private key
    D. SHA

82. Two entities share the same secret key. What type of encryption are they using?
    A. Asymmetric
    B. Symmetric
    C. Public key
    D. HMAC

83. A new security policy has mandated that executives within a company must encrypt all e-mail they send and receive between each other. Of the following choices, what can support this?
    A. MD5
    B. TPM
    C. SHA-1
    D. RSA

84. A user discovered text in a document that is so small it looks like a dash. What best describes this?
    A. Steganography
    B. Elliptic curve cryptography
    C. CRL
    D. RIPEMD

85. Sally sent an encrypted e-mail with a digital signature to Joe. Joe wants to verify the e-mail came from Sally. How can this be achieved?
    A. Use Sally's private key to verify the digital signature
    B. Use Sally's private key to decrypt the e-mail
    C. Use Sally's public key to verify the digital signature
    D. Use Sally's public key to decrypt the e-mail

86. What type of key is used to sign an e-mail message?
    A. Sender's public key
    B. Sender's private key
    C. Recipient's public key
    D. Recipient's private key

87. Sally sent an encrypted e-mail with a digital signature to Joe. What would Joe's public key provide in this situation?
    A. Integrity
    B. Non-repudiation
    C. Confidentiality
    D. Availability

88. A web browser indicates that the issuer of a certificate is not recognized. What is a likely reason?
    A. The certificate is a self-signed certificate
    B. The certificate does not include the private key
    C. The certificate does not include the public key
    D. The certificate is using weak encryption

89. What includes a list of compromised or invalid certificates?
    A. CA
    B. Digital signature
    C. S/MIME
    D. CRL

90. Where can a key be stored so that someone can recover data even if the original key is destroyed?
    A. Recovery agent
    B. CRL
    C. Digital signature
    D. Key escrow

91. An organization wants users to organize their areas to reduce data theft. What would it most likely use to identify this requirement?
    A. Clean desk policy
    B. Requirement for administrators to have two accounts
    C. Whaling education
    D. Privacy screens

92. An operating system automatically ensures that if a user creates a file, the user is the only person granted access to the file. What principle is this operating system using?
    A. Least privilege
    B. Multifactor authentication
    C. Separation of duties
    D. Due care

93. An organization wants to ensure that if employees do engage in any fraudulent activities, they won't be able to continue them indefinitely. What policy would provide this protection?
    A. Separation of duties policy
    B. Job rotation policy
    C. Acceptable use policy
    D. Data labeling policy

94. An IT manager has assigned daily responsibility of managing the network-based firewall to one administrator, and daily responsibility of monitoring the network-based intrusion detection system (IDS) to another administrator. What policy is the manager trying to follow?
    A. Mandatory vacations policy
    B. Policy requiring administrators to use two accounts
    C. Job rotation policy
    D. Separation of duties policy

95. An organization is planning annual security awareness training. Of the following choices, what is likely to be combined with this training?
    A. Creation of a BIA
    B. Signing an acceptable use statement
    C. ALE analysis
    D. Publishing the CRL

96. Of the following choices, what requires special handling related to retention and distribution of data?
    A. Virtual servers
    B. PII
    C. VLAN
    D. CRL

97. Employees share personal information, such as pictures and family updates, online. Of the following choices, what can an attacker use to gain this information?
    A. Company websites
    B. E-mail
    C. Mandatory vacation policy
    D. Social networking sites

98. Anonymous reports indicate a user is processing inappropriate data on a computer. However, a search of files on the system doesn't indicate anything inappropriate. What else can a security administrator do to investigate this?
    A. Capture an image of the hard drive
    B. Examine the firewall logs
    C. Perform memory forensics
    D. Implement password masking

99. Of the following choices, what can help a forensic expert identify evidence tampering with a disk drive?
    A. Chain of custody
    B. Imaging
    C. AES-128
    D. Hashing

100. The computer incident response team (CIRT) is trained on documenting the location of data they collect in an investigation. What does this documentation provide?
    A. Integrity
    B. Basis for imaging
    C. Chain of custody
    D. Least privilege

Security+ Practice Exam Answers

When checking your answers, take the time to read the explanation. Understanding the explanations will help ensure you're prepared for the live exam. The explanation also shows the chapter or chapters where you can get more detailed information on the topic.

1. **C.** Confidentiality ensures that data is only viewable by authorized users and can be ensured with access controls such as a mantrap (or encryption). A mantrap protects against the social engineering tactic of tailgating. Availability can be ensured with sound power and cooling systems and various fault tolerance and redundancy techniques. Integrity is enforced with hashing. See chapters 1 and 2.

2. **B.** Hashing is used to ensure that data has retained integrity. If hashes captured on different days are different, it indicates that the data has lost integrity. Software as a Service (SaaS) is an application (such as web mail) provided through cloud-based technologies. See chapter 1.

3. **C.** Virtualization technologies can increase availability be reducing unplanned downtime. Confidentiality is enforced with encryption, and integrity is enforced with hashing, but virtualization technologies do not directly affect confidentiality, integrity, or encryption. See chapters 1 and 5.

4. **B.** The combination of different characters in a password makes up the key space, and using all character types (uppercase, lowercase, numbers, and special characters) increases the key space. Using only uppercase or lowercase letters limits the key space. Password history and minimum password age prevent users from reusing passwords. Password expiration requires users to change their password regularly. See chapter 1.

5. **D.** A self-service password reset system provides password recovery. Users are able to prove their identity through some piece of information (such as their first dog's name) and they can either retrieve their original password or the system can create a new password for them and require them to change it immediately. A password policy ensures passwords are sufficiently strong and changed periodically. While a password reset system can delete a password, this is not the best answer, since the purpose of the password reset system is to recover the password. Accounts can be disabled, but a password reset system doesn't expire accounts. See chapter 1.

6. **C.** A thumbprint scanner is using biometrics in the *something you are* (or something the user is) factor of authentication. A password or PIN is an example of something the user knows. A token or smart card is an example of something the user has. A common access card (CAC) is a form of photo identification and can also function as a smart card. See chapter 1.

7. **C.** Biometrics are the most difficult for an attacker to falsify or forge since it represents a user based on personal characteristics such as a fingerprint. Passwords can be cracked with password crackers. Cross-site request forgery (XSRF) is an attack where users are redirected to different sites

than they intended to visit. Usernames can often be discovered simply by learning a user's name and understanding how the username is derived (such as first name dot last name—for example, darril.gibson). See chapter 1.

8. **A.** The three factors of authentication are *something you know, something you have*, and *something you are*, and two-factor authentication uses two distinct items, with one from two of the three factors. Using two items from a single authentication factor (such as a PIN and a password in the *something you know* factor) does not provide two-factor authentication. Two-factor authentication doesn't require an element in each of the three factors. See chapter 1.

9. **B.** A token is in the *something you have* factor, a password is in the *something you know* factor, and a retina scan is in the *something you are* factor. None of the other answers includes methods in each of the three factors. A password and PIN are both in the *something you know* factor. A fingerprint and retina scan are both in the *something you are* factor. See chapter 1.

10. **D.** Kerberos uses a key distribution center (KDC) to generate tokens (also called tickets). The Lightweight Directory Access Protocol (LDAP) specifies formats and methods to query directories and is used to manage objects (such as users and computers) in an Active Directory domain. AES and 3DES are symmetric encryption protocols, not authentication protocols. See chapter 1.

11. **B.** Single sign-on (SSO) refers to the ability of a user to log on or access multiple systems by providing credentials only once. DAC is an access control method used by Microsoft operating systems, where every object has an owner and the owner has full control over the object. Multifactor authentication combines more than one factor (*something you know, something you have*, and *something you are*). The principle of least privilege ensures that users are granted the rights and permissions needed to perform assigned tasks, and nothing else. See chapter 1.

12. **A.** Video surveillance is a detective security control that can be used to verify that equipment and confidential data is not being removed. Spyware is a form of malware and wouldn't provide verification that equipment is being stolen. A regular user access review is an audit that verifies users have appropriate permissions and accounts are disabled for terminated employees. A change management system helps ensure that changes don't result in unintended outages through a change, and includes the ability to document changes. See chapter 2.

13. **D.** Access based on groups, or roles, simplifies user administration. A password policy ensures users create strong passwords, but doesn't necessarily simplify user administration. Passwords should be known by only one person and never shared. Assigning permissions to users individually greatly increases user administration. See chapter 2.

14. **B.** The role-based access control (RBAC) model is job function specific. RBAC is not an authentication model. Access is based on roles, or groups, and it simplifies user administration. See chapter 2.

15. **B.** A proximity card is in the *something you have* (or something a user has) factor of authentication. Something a user knows is something like a password or PIN. Biometrics is used for something a user is. Something a user wants is not used as a factor of authentication. See chapters 1 and 2.

16. **D.** Video surveillance provides reliable proof that someone has entered a room. Logs are useful, but users can be impersonated or claim they were impersonated (but an impersonation claim isn't possible with video). An access list identifies who is authorized into a space, but not who actually entered. A mantrap prevents tailgating. See chapter 2.

17. **C.** Tailgating (also called piggybacking) occurs when one user follows closely behind another user without using credentials. A mantrap prevents tailgating. Fuzzing, or fuzz testing, sends invalid, unexpected, or random data to a system to detect buffer overflow vulnerabilities. An ARP poisoning attack sends false hardware address updates to a switch. See chapters 2 and 6.

18. B. A password policy can be implemented to ensure that users create complex passwords based on a password complexity definition. An account lockout policy can lockout users if they enter the incorrect password a predetermined number of times (such as three). Training is useful, but it wouldn't ensure that users used complex passwords. IPsec can be used to encrypt data in motion, but it doesn't affect password policies. See chapter 2.

19. **C.** An account login log will record the date and time when a user logs into a local system, and when a user accesses a system over the network. Time of day restrictions can be used to prevent users from logging in at certain times or from making connections to network resources at certain times. Kerberos does not support accounting and does not have a log that records access. A user rights log (rarely maintained) documents rights granted to users. See chapter 2.

20. **C.** Secure File Transfer Protocol (SFTP) is a secure implementation of FTP, an extension of Secure Shell (SSH), and it transmits data using port 22. FTP transmits data in clear text and is not secure. Trivial FTP is a form of FTP using UDP to transmit smaller amounts of data than FTP. AES provides secure encryption of data, but it doesn't include a method of transferring files. See chapter 3.

21. **D.** Secure Shell (SSH) is commonly used to remotely administer UNIX and Linux systems (informally called *nix systems) since it provides a secure channel. Microsoft systems use Terminal Services and Remote Desktop Services to remotely administer systems. SCP copies encrypted files over a network using SSH. See chapter 3.

22. **C.** IPv6 uses 128-bit IP addresses and is expressed with eight groups of four hexadecimal characters (0 to 9 and A to F). NAT translates private IP addresses to public and public IP addresses back to private. IPv4 addresses use dotted decimal format with decimal numbers, but not characters. Diagnostic tools such as ping use ICMP to discover computers. See chapter 3.

23. **B.** Telnet uses port 23. SSH, SFTP, and SCP use port 22. HTTPS uses port 443. IKE (used with an IPsec VPN connection) uses port 500. See chapter 3.

24. **D.** Microsoft SQL server uses ports 1433 by default. SCP, SFTP, and SSH use port 22. Telnet uses port 23. HTTPS uses port 443. See chapter 3.

25. **A.** A port scanner scans a system for open ports and helps identify what services are running on the remote server. A sniffer (also called a protocol analyzer) captures traffic that you can analyze, but this isn't as easy as using a port scanner. A CRL is a list of revoked certificates. A load balancer can optimize and distribute data workloads across multiple computers. See chapter 3.

26. **D.** Port 3389 is the default port for remote administration (Terminal Services and Remote Desktop Services) and closing this port blocks remote administration. Port 20 is the FTP data port. SCP, TFTP, and SSH all use port 22. LDAP uses port 389. See chapter 3.

27. **A.** Blocking Internet Control Message Protocol (ICMP) at a router will block pings, but it will not block other traffic (such as the traffic used to connect to the server). If TCP and UDP were blocked, it blocks almost all traffic. A flood guard detects and corrects against SYN flood attacks. A host enumeration sweep uses ICMP to discover hosts, but it would not block pings and is also blocked if ICMP is blocked. See chapter 3.

28. **A.** Most firewalls have an implicit deny statement (such as **drop all** or **deny any any**) at the end of an access control list (ACL) to block all traffic not previously allowed. While many firewalls block ICMP traffic to block ICMP attacks, and block pings, this is not likely to be the last rule. Only firewalls that want to allow FTP traffic would have a rule to allow it. Firewalls can't filter spam. See chapter 3.

29. **A.** Host enumeration sweeps use Internet Control Message Protocol (ICMP) to identify active hosts similar to how a ping verifies a single client is operational, and they can be blocked by blocking ICMP. If ICMP is allowed, the sweeps would work. FTPS uses SSL to secure FTP, and SMTP is related to e-mail, but neither is related to host enumeration sweeps. See chapter 3.

30. **A.** A proxy server forwards requests for services from a client. It caches requests to reduce Internet bandwidth usage. Proxy servers can filter URLs to block access to specific URLs from clients. It filters traffic out of a network when filtering URLs, but does not filter traffic into a network. See chapter 3.

31. **B.** A network-based intrusion detection system (NIDS) can detect many types of attacks, including smurf attacks. Firewalls can't detect attacks but can block them. A honeypot is a server designed to look valuable to an attacker and can help administrators learn about zero day exploits. A NAC system can restrict access to a network, but not detect attacks. See chapters 4 and 5.

32. **B.** A honeypot is a server designed to look valuable to an attacker and can help administrators learn about zero day exploits, or previously unknown attacks. MAC filtering is a form of network access control, but can't be used to detect or learn about attacks. An evil twin is a rogue access point with the same SSID as an authorized access point. See chapter 4.

33. **C.** Many intrusion prevention systems (IPSs) use content inspection techniques to monitor data streams in search of malicious code or behaviors. Smurf is a type of attack, not a method of detection. A honeypot is a server designed to look valuable to an attacker, can divert attacks, and helps organizations identify the latest unknown attacks. A port scanner looks for open ports on a system to determine running services and protocols. See chapters 3 and 4.

34. **B.** A network-based intrusion prevention system (NIPS) can detect and mitigate malicious activity by blocking it. In contrast, a NIDS would only detect the activity. Host-based IDSs and IPSs only detect malicious activity on the host. See chapter 4.

35. **C.** Wi-Fi Protected Access (WPA) Enterprise is the strongest since it combines a strong wireless protocol (WPA) with authentication in Enterprise mode using an 802.1X server (implemented as RADIUS). WEP is not strong and should not be used. WPA2 Personal uses a PSK. WPA2 with CCMP is strong, but it doesn't specify Enterprise mode, so it implies WPA2-PSK and isn't the best choice. See chapter 4.

36. **B, D.** An attacker using a protocol analyzer (sniffer) can easily defeat both MAC filtering and disabled SSID broadcasts. WPA2-PSK and WPA2 with CCMP (based on AES) are both strong. See chapter 4.

37. **A.** A rogue access point is an unauthorized wireless station, and when connected to a network, unauthorized users may be able to use it to connect to the network. While the power level and antenna affect the footprint, they would not directly result in unauthorized users. Bluesnarfing allows an attack to access data on a Bluetooth-enabled phone. See chapter 4.

38. **C.** Encryption protects against loss of confidentiality for data, including data stored on a mobile phone. Hashing helps ensure integrity. An evil twin is a rogue access point with the same SSID as an authorized access point. IPsec can encrypt traffic over the wire (such as in a VPN tunnel) but doesn't protect data at rest, such as on a mobile phone. See chapters 4 and 5.

39. **D.** IPsec operates in tunnel mode when used for a VPN, and in transport mode when used internally. SSTP (using SSL) secures VPN traffic but it does not include a tunnel mode. ICMP is a diagnostic protocol that includes tools such as ping. HTTPS secures HTTP traffic with SSL or TLS. See chapter 4.

40. **C.** Network access control (NAC) provides access to a network based on predetermined characteristics, such as up-to-date antivirus software, operating systems with current patches and fixes, and enabled firewalls. A VPN concentrator provides strong security for a large number

of VPN clients. A honeypot is a server designed to look valuable to an attacker, can divert attacks, and helps organizations identify attackers using zero day exploits. IPsec is one method created encrypted tunnels over the Internet, but NAC does not encrypt traffic or create tunnels. See chapter 4.

41. **D.** You can use security templates to deploy security settings to multiple systems. Network access control inspects clients for specific health conditions and can redirect access to a remediation network for unhealthy clients. A honeypot can divert malicious attacks to a harmless area of your network, away from production servers. A change management system helps ensure that changes don't result in unintended outages and includes the ability to document changes. See chapter 5.

42. **B.** Performance Monitor is a tool used within Windows systems to create performance baselines and view system performance. You can use security templates to deploy the same security setting to multiple systems. Imaging software can capture images of systems for deployment to multiple systems. A network-based Data Loss Prevention system can examine and analyze network traffic and detect if confidential company data is included. See chapter 5.

43. **B.** Virtualization can reduce the datacenter's footprint by reducing the number of physical servers and eliminate wasted resources. VM escape is an attack run on virtual machines allowing the attacker to access and control the physical host, and adding more virtual servers will not eliminate VM escape attacks. Imaging and baselines ensure systems include mandated security configurations and are applied the same to both physical and virtual systems. A change management system defines the process and accounting structure for system modifications. See chapter 5.

44. **D.** Malware can be released in an isolated virtual system and it will not affect other systems. Intrusion detection and prevention systems such as HIDS, NIDS, and NIPS provide a level of protection for a production environment. However, there is no guarantee that they will detect and isolate new versions of malware as effectively as an isolated virtual system, and it's certainly not a good idea to release malware in a production environment to observe it. See chapter 5.

45. **C.** Patches protect against known attacks by fixing known vulnerabilities. A zero day attack is an attack on an undisclosed or unknown vulnerability and patches only protect against known or disclosed vulnerabilities. There is no such thing as a hotfix attack. See chapter 5.

46. **B.** A change management system helps ensure that changes don't result in unintended outages through a change, and includes the ability to document changes. A security log is an automated log for systems used to record security events as they occur. A CCTV is a detective control that can record video. An ACL is a list of rules identifying what traffic is allowed and what traffic is denied. See chapter 5.

47. B. A Trusted Platform Module (TPM) is a hardware chip that is included on the motherboard of many laptops, and it stores encryption keys used for full drive encryption. Remote wipe is a method used to erase data on lost mobile devices such as mobile phones. A network-based DLP can examine e-mail and detect if confidential company data is included. An HSM is a removable hardware device that stores RSA keys and provides encryption services. See chapter 5.

48. A. You can use a hardware security module (HSM) with Secure Sockets Layer (SSL) accelerators to store keys, or digital certificates used in SSL sessions. A CA issues, manages, and verifies the authenticity of certificates which are used in SSL sessions, but a CA does not improve the performance of SSL sessions. A CRL is a list of revoked certificates and it is always public, not private. A database is not a secure method of storing digital certificates and cannot improve the performance of SSL sessions. See chapters 5 and 9.

49. A. The greatest risk is users copying data to a USB flash drive. Every other answer includes some type of encryption, and encryption protects against loss of confidentiality resulting from data leakage. A copy of backup tapes should be stored offsite, and if they're encrypted it provides additional protection. IPsec and FTPS are both encryption protocols used when transferring data over a network. See chapter 5.

50. A. It can use Infrastructure as a Service (IaaS) to rent access to hardware, such as servers, limiting its hardware, personnel costs, and server room footprint. PaaS provides cloud customers with an easy-to-configure operating system and on-demand computing capabilities. SaaS is a cloud-based technology that provides access to software or applications such as web-based e-mail over the Internet. An HSM is a removable device that can generate and store RSA keys used for asymmetric encryption and decryption. See chapter 5.

51. B. A slow-running system that randomly reboots indicates a malware infection, and modification of administrative rights indicates a process with system level or kernel access, which can only be a rootkit. Adware may open and close windows with advertisements but wouldn't modify administrative access. A DDoS is an attack launched from multiple computers and results in loss of services. Spam is unwanted e-mail and isn't necessarily malicious. See chapter 6.

52. D, E. A network-based intrusion detection system (NIDS) and network-based intrusion prevention system (NIPS) are network devices and would not be installed on a mobile computer. However, a spam filter will filter unsolicited e-mail, a host-based firewall can prevent intrusions into the system, and antivirus software detects and blocks malware. See chapters 3 and 6.

53. B, C, D. Antivirus software can detect viruses, worms, and Trojan horses. However, pharming is an attack that redirects website traffic to another bogus website, and antivirus software does not detect pharming. See chapter 6.

54. **C.** Updated antivirus software has current definitions and provides the best protection against malware for computers accessing the Internet. Antivirus software without updated signatures is vulnerable to newly released viruses. Anti-spam software can filter out unwanted or unsolicited e-mail (also called spam). Anti-spyware software detects spyware but doesn't provide the best protection against all malware, such as viruses, worms, Trojans, logic bombs, rootkits, and spyware. See chapter 6.

55. **A.** A spear phishing attack targets a specific person or specific groups of people, such as employees of a company. Tailgating occurs when one user follows closely behind another user without using credentials, and mantraps help prevent tailgating. A Trojan appears to be something useful but instead includes something malicious. Phishing sends e-mail to users with the purpose of tricking them into revealing personal information (such as bank account information), but it doesn't target a specific person. See chapter 6.

56. **B.** A distributed denial-of-service (DDoS) attack includes attacks from multiple systems and often comes from computers joined to a botnet. A DoS attack comes from a single system, and a SYN flood is an example of a DoS attack. Kiting registers domain names for short periods to avoid paying for the domain name. See chapter 7.

57. **C.** Third party black box testing is done by an external entity with no prior knowledge of the application and is an effective method for testing applications. White box testers have full knowledge of the application, which can influence their testing. Internal politics can affect the effectiveness of internal testers. See chapter 7.

58. **C.** Input validation checks the validity of data before using it and can help prevent SQL injection, buffer overflow, and cross-site scripting attacks. Cross-site scripting is an attack that allows attackers to embed malicious code into a website. SQL injection is an attack using SQL statements, which are entered into a web form that doesn't use input validation. Many buffer overflow attacks use a string of no-operation commands as NOOP sleds, which are preventable with input validation. See chapter 7.

59. **A.** Many buffer overflow attacks use a string of no-operation commands as a NOOP sled. WEP implemented RC4 with small initialization vectors (IVs) allowing an IV attack (not a buffer overflow attack) to discover the key. Spear phishing is an e-mail attack targeting employees of a specific organization. Pharming is an attack that redirects a website's traffic to another website. See chapter 7.

60. **B.** Input validation checks the validity of data before using it and can help prevent SQL injection, buffer overflow, and cross-site scripting attacks. SSL can protect confidentiality of data by encrypting it, and antivirus software protects against malware such as viruses and Trojans, but neither protect against SQL injection attacks. Cross-site scripting is an attack that allows attackers to embed malicious code into a website, and you wouldn't want to enable cross-site scripting capabilities. See chapter 7.

61. **A.** Web applications reduce cross-site scripting attacks by filtering out hypertext and JavaScript tags using input validation. A Trojan is malware that appears to be something useful to a user, and a rootkit provides attackers with system level access, but filtering HTML tags does not block them. SQL injection attacks use SQL statements and input validation helps prevent SQL injection attacks. See chapter 7.

62. **A, B, C, E.** Valid methods of risk management include acceptance, avoidance, deterrence, transference, and mitigation (not included in the answers). It is not possible to eliminate risk. See chapter 8.

63. **B.** An organization can avoid a risk by not providing a service, using an application, or participating in a risky activity. Organizations often accept a risk when the cost of the control exceeds the cost of the risk. Risks deterrence attempts to discourage attacks with preventative controls, such as a security guard. Risk mitigation reduces risks through internal controls. Organizations can transfer a risk by purchasing insurance. See chapter 8.

64. **A.** A risk assessment (or risk analysis) identifies threats and vulnerabilities. Black box testers start with zero knowledge of a tested system and attempt a penetration test. A fuzz test sends random data to an application to detect potential problems, but it can exploit a vulnerability. See chapter 8.

65. **C.** A vulnerability scanner performs passive scans to identify weaknesses and does not attempt to exploit them. A penetration test is active (not passive) since it attempts to exploit weaknesses and can cause instability in systems. A fuzz tester is an active tool that sends random data to a system and can potentially result in an outage. An intrusion detection system (IDS) can detect attacks, but not weaknesses. See chapter 8.

66. **C.** A vulnerability scan can be conducted during normal business hours without affecting users. A penetration test is active and can potentially affect users. You can use a protocol analyzer (sniffer) to view headers and contents in IP packets. Black box testing is a form of penetration testing where the testers do not have any prior knowledge of the system. See chapter 8.

67. **A.** A penetration test can help determine the impact of a threat by demonstrating the magnitude of damage that is possible. Vulnerability scans can passively test security controls, identify vulnerabilities, and identify common misconfiguration, but they don't demonstrate the impact of a threat. See chapter 8.

68. **B.** A black box tester performs penetration tests without any prior knowledge and would need to use privilege escalation to extract data after gaining access to a system. The vulnerability scan is done at the beginning of a penetration test. The rules-of-engagement document identifies boundaries of a test and expectations of the testers, but there are no rules-of-engagement logs. The chain of custody is a document used with forensic evidence to document who handled evidence. See chapter 8.

69. **C.** Fuzzing sends random data to an application, and attackers can use fuzz testers to identify vulnerabilities within applications. A protocol analyzer can capture and analyze IP packets and a port scanner can detect open ports, but they aren't the best choice to check vulnerabilities in an application. An organization uses an intrusion prevention system (IPS) to detect and block attacks. See chapter 8.

70. **C.** It's important to gain consent from a system owner prior to penetration testing since testing can cause system instability. If consent isn't obtained, the tester can be viewed as a black hat (malicious) attacker. Penetration tests can reduce (not increase) performance due to increased (not reduced) system resource usage. See chapter 8.

71. **C.** A protocol analyzer can capture packets to view unencrypted network traffic, including the data and IP header. A vulnerability scanner can scan systems for vulnerabilities and determine which ones are most susceptible to an attack. A public key infrastructure (PKI) includes elements used for asymmetric encryption. A hardware security module (HSM) is a removable or external device that provides encryption services. See chapter 8.

72. **A.** The System log records system such as when a service stops and starts. The Security log records auditable events, such as user logons and logoffs. The Application log records events from individual applications. A firewall log can record what traffic is passed and what traffic is blocked. See chapter 8.

73. **B.** RAID-1 (mirroring) increases availability with fault tolerance. Authentication provides verification of a user's identity. Confidentiality ensures that data is viewable by authorized users only and can be ensured with access controls or encryption. Integrity provides assurances that data has not been modified, tampered with, or corrupted. See chapter 9.

74. **A.** An uninterruptible power supply (UPS) uses a battery to provide temporary power and provides fault tolerance for power fluctuations. Generators provide long-term power if commercial power fails. Heating, ventilation, and air-conditioning (HVAC) systems increase availability by ensuring that equipment doesn't fail due to overheating. Hot and cold aisles regulate cooling to reduce cooling costs while also increasing availability. See chapter 9.

75. **D.** A copy of backups should be kept in an off-site location for retention purposes. It is a best practice to label tapes for easy identification. The tapes should be stored with the servers. Tapes should be sanitized or destroyed when they are no longer usable, and not just thrown away. See chapter 9.

76. **B.** Cold sites are the least expensive. Hot sites are the most expensive. There is no such thing as a BIA site. See chapter 9.

77. **C.** A warm site is a cross between a hot site (which has everything needed for operations) and a cold site (which only has power and connectivity). A hardware security module (HSM) is a

removable or external device that provides encryption services, but there is no such thing as an HSM site. See chapter 9.

78. **D.** A disaster recovery plan (DRP) includes a hierarchical list of critical systems. A DRP includes a testing element to validate the plan, but not the results of the test. A certificate revocation list (CRL) is a public list of revoked certificates. Vulnerability assessments (not DRPs) identify vulnerabilities. See chapter 9.

79. **A.** Humidity controls reduce the potential for static discharges, and damage from condensation. HVAC systems often use hot and cold aisles to control temperature and air flow and can increase availability by ensuring that equipment doesn't fail due to overheating. However, these controls do not prevent damage from electrostatic discharge. See chapter 9.

80. **D.** EMI shielding can prevent data loss in twisted pair cables (such as CAT 5, 5E, and 6). CAT 6 cable is twisted pair and can't include fiber optics. Shielded (not unshielded) helps prevent data loss. RAID disk drives provide fault tolerance for systems and improve availability. See chapter 9.

81. **D.** Secure Hash Algorithm (SHA) is a hashing algorithm that can ensure the integrity of data including executable files. RC4 is an encryption algorithm, not a hashing algorithm. Public and private keys are used in asymmetric encryption. See chapter 10.

82. **B.** Symmetric encryption uses a single key for encryption of data and decryption of data. Asymmetric encryption (sometimes called public key encryption) uses a matched key pair (public and private keys) for encryption and decryption. Hash-based Message Authentication Code (HMAC) is a hashing algorithm, not encryption. See chapter 10.

83. **D.** RSA is a public key encryption method, and e-mail applications such as S/MIME and PGP use RSA to secure e-mail. MD5 and SHA-1 are hashing algorithms used to ensure integrity. A Trusted Platform Module (TPM) is a hardware mechanism that supports full disk encryption. See chapter 10.

84. **A.** Steganography is the practice of hiding data within a file, and reducing the font size to reduce readability is one possible method. Elliptic curve is an encryption technology commonly used with small wireless devices. A certificate revocation list (CRL) is a list of revoked certificates published by a certification authority (CA). RACE Integrity Primitives Evaluation Message Digest (RIPEMD) is a hashing algorithm. See chapter 10.

85. **C.** Digital signatures provide authentication (verified identification) of the sender and are decrypted with the sender's public key (Sally's public key). Sally's private key encrypts the digital signature, but it is kept private and would not be available to Joe's system. Sally's keys are not involved in encryption. Instead, Joe's public key would be used for encryption. Joe's private key is used for decryption, but the question asks about verification of the sender, not encryption. See chapter 10.

86. **B.** A digital signature is an encrypted hash of a message, encrypted with the sender's private key. The recipient decrypts the hash using the sender's public key. Recipient keys are used with encryption, but not with a digital signature. See chapter 10.

87. **C.** E-mail is encrypted using the recipient's public key (Joe's public key in this case), and encryption provides confidentiality. A digital signature is an encrypted hash of a message, encrypted with the sender's private key, and it provides integrity and non-repudiation. Availability ensures that systems are up and operational when needed and often addresses single points of failure, but does not use public keys. See chapter 10.

88. **A.** A self-signed certificate is not issued from a certificate authority (CA) in the trusted root certification authority store, so the CA is not recognized. The certificate would include the public key but never the private key, since the private key is private. Weak encryption would not indicate a certificate is not recognized. See chapter 10.

89. **D.** A certificate revocation list (CRL) is a list of revoked certificates, and certificates are revoked if they are compromised or invalid. A certificate authority (CA) publishes the CRL, making it publically available. Digital signatures provide authentication (verified identification) of the sender, integrity of the message, and non-repudiation. Secure/Multipurpose Internet Mail Extensions (S/MIME) secures e-mail with encryption and digital signatures. See chapter 10.

90. **D.** A key escrow stores copies of user's private keys to ensure that the loss of the original key does not result in data loss. A recovery agent can recover a key, or data, if the original key is destroyed. However, copies of the original key aren't stored with the recovery agent, and the question is specifically asking where the key is stored. A certificate revocation list (CRL) identifies revoked certificates. Digital signatures provide authentication (verified identification) of the sender, integrity of the message, and non-repudiation but do not store copies of keys. See chapter 10.

91. **A.** A clean desk policy directs users to keep their areas organized and free of sensitive data. Requiring administrators to use two accounts helps prevent privilege escalation attacks. Whaling is a phishing attack that targets high-level executives, and whaling education trains employees about phishing. Privacy screens can reduce the threat of shoulder surfing. See chapter 11.

92. **A.** The principle of least privilege ensures that users are granted the rights and permissions needed to perform assigned tasks, and nothing else. Multifactor authentication uses more than one factor to authenticate users. Separation of duties prevents any single entity from being able to complete all the functions of a critical or sensitive process. Due care refers to the steps a company must take to protect against risks. See chapter 11.

93. **B.** A job rotation policy requires employees to change roles on a regular basis. This policy would help prevent employees from continuing with fraudulent activities. A separation of duties policy separates individual tasks of an overall function between different people and helps

prevent an employee even starting fraudulent activities. An acceptable use policy defines proper system usage for users but doesn't detect fraudulent activities. Data labeling ensures that users know what data they are handling and processing. See chapter 11.

94. **D.** A separation of duties policy separates individual tasks of an overall function between different people. In this case, the overall function is network defense; one technician is managing prevention (the firewall) and the other technician is managing detection (the NIDS). Mandatory vacation policies require employees to take time away from their job and help detect malicious activities. Dual accounts for administrators (one for administrative use and one for regular use) help prevent privilege escalation attacks. Job rotation policies require employees to change roles on a regular basis. See chapter 11.

95. **B.** It's common to have users sign an acceptable use statement when hired and periodically afterwards, such as during annual security refresher training. A business impact analysis (BIA) identifies critical functions and services but is not associated with training. Annual loss expectancy (ALE) identifies losses with hard numbers in a quantitative risk assessment. The certificate revocation list (CRL) is a public list of revoked certificates. See chapter 11.

96. **B.** Personally identifiable information (PII) requires special handling due to many laws and regulations. Virtualization does not change the requirements for handing or retaining data. Virtual local area networks do not affect the retention of data. A certificate revocation list (CRL) is a public list of revoked certificates. See chapter 11.

97. **D.** A common way users share personal information is through social networking sites, and when they do so, attackers can use these sites to gain information and launch attacks. Users would not share personal data on a company website, and attacks do not have easy access to user's e-mail. Mandatory vacation policies require employees to take time away from their job and help to detect fraud or malicious activities, but they do not help attackers gain information. See chapter 11.

98. **C.** Memory forensics captures an image of volatile RAM and examines the contents. The memory includes recently accessed data, such as files. Hard drive imaging creates a forensic copy and prevents a forensic analysis from modifying the original data, but the administrator already searched the drive. Firewall logs include data on network traffic, but not about data processed on the system. Password masking displays a character, such as an asterisk, when a user types in a password. See chapter 11.

99. **D.** Hashing provides integrity for disk drives and can identify evidence tampering. If the current hash of a disk drive is different from the hash created when the drive was collected, it proves the drive has been modified. A chain of custody provides assurances that evidence has been controlled and handled properly after collection, and imaging is used to create forensic copies, but neither provide integrity. Advanced Encryption Standard 128 (AES-128) is an

encryption algorithm that uses 128 bits, but encryption helps ensure confidentiality, not integrity. See chapter 11.

100. **C.** A chain of custody provides assurances that evidence has been controlled and handled properly after collection. Hashing provides integrity. Imaging is used to protect the original evidence, but doesn't affect the chain of custody. The principle of least privilege ensures that users are granted the rights and permissions needed to perform assigned tasks, and nothing else. See chapter 11.

Appendix A—Acronym List

This acronym list provides you with a quick reminder of many of the different security-related terms along with a short explanation. Where appropriate, the concepts are explained in greater depth within the book. You can use the index to identify the specific pages on which the topics are covered.

802.1x—A port-based authentication protocol. Wireless can use 802.1X. For example, WPA2-Enterprise mode uses an 802.1X server (implemented as a RADIUS server) to add authentication.

3DES—Triple Digital Encryption Standard. A symmetric algorithm used to encrypt data and provide confidentiality. It was originally designed as a replacement for DES. It uses multiple keys and multiple passes and is not as efficient as AES, but is still used in some applications, such as when hardware doesn't support AES.

AAA—Authentication, Authorization, and Accounting. AAA protocols are used in remote access systems. For example, TACACS+ is an AAA protocol that uses multiple challenges and responses during a session. Authentication verifies a user's identification. Authorization determines if a user should have access. Accounting tracks a user's access with logs.

ACE—Access Control Entry. Identifies a user or group that is granted permission to a resource. ACEs are contained within a DACL in NTFS.

ACL—Access control list. A list of rules used to grant access to a resource. In NTFS, a list of ACEs makes up the ACL for a resource. In a firewall, an ACL identifies traffic that is allowed or blocked based on IP addresses, networks, ports, and some protocols (using the protocol ID).

AES—Advanced Encryption Standard. A symmetric algorithm used to encrypt data and provide confidentiality. AES is quick, highly secure, and used in a wide assortment of cryptography schemes. It includes key sizes of 128 bits, 192 bits, or 256 bits.

AES256—Advanced Encryption Standard 256 bit. AES sometimes includes the number of bits used in the encryption keys and AES256 uses 256-bit encryption keys.

AH—Authentication Header. IPsec includes both AH and ESP. AH provides authentication and integrity, and ESP provides confidentiality, integrity, and authentication. AH is identified with protocol ID number 51.

ALE—Annualized loss expectancy. Used to measure risk with annualized rate of occurrence (ARO) and single loss expectancy (SLE). The ALE identifies the total amount of loss expected for a given risk. The calculation is SLE x ARO = ALE.

AP—Access point, short for wireless access point (WAP). APs provide access to a wired network to wireless clients. Many APs support isolation mode to segment wireless uses from other wireless users.

ARO—Annualized rate of occurrence. Used to measure risk with annualized loss expectancy (ALE) and single loss expectancy (SLE). The ARO identifies how many times a loss is expected to occur in a year. The calculation is SLE x ARO = ALE.

ARP—Address Resolution Protocol. Resolves IP addresses to MAC addresses. ARP poisoning attacks can redirect traffic through an attacker's system by sending false MAC address updates. VLAN segregation helps prevent the scope of ARP poisoning attacks within a network.

AUP—Acceptableuse policy. An AUP defines proper system usage. It will often describe the purpose of computer systems and networks, how users can access them, and the responsibilities of users when accessing the systems.

BCP—Business continuity plan. A plan that helps an organization predict and plan for potential outages of critical services or functions. It includes disaster recovery elements that provide the steps used to return critical functions to operation after an outage. A BIA is a part of a BCP and the BIA drives decisions to create redundancies such as failover clusters or alternate sites.

BIA—Business impact analysis. The BIA identifies critical business or mission requirements and includes elements such as Recovery Time Objectives (RTOs) and Recovery Point Objectives (RPOs), but it doesn't identify solutions.

BIOS—Basic Input/Output System. A computer's firmware used to manipulate different settings such as the date and time, boot drive, and access password.

BOTS—Network Robots. An automated program or system used to perform one or more tasks. A malicious botnet is group of computers called zombies and controlled through a command-and-control server. Attackers use malware to join computers to botnets. Zombies regularly check in with the command-and-control server and can launch DDoS attacks against other victims. Botnet activity often includes hundreds of outbound connections, and some botnets use Internet Relay Chat (IRC) channels.

CA—Certificate Authority. An organization that manages, issues, and signs certificates and is part of a PKI. Certificates are an important part of asymmetric encryption. Certificates include public keys along with details on the owner of the certificate and on the CA that issued the certificate. Certificate owners share their public key by sharing a copy of their certificate.

CAC—Common Access Card. A specialized type of smart card used by United States Department of Defense. It includes photo identification and provides confidentiality, integrity, authentication, and non-repudiation for the users. It is similar to a PIV.

CAN—Controller Area Network. A standard that allows microcontrollers and devices to communicate with each other without a host computer.

CCMP—Counter Mode with Cipher Block Chaining Message Authentication Code Protocol. An encryption protocol based on AES used with WPA2 for wireless security. It is more secure then TKIP, used with the original release of WPA.

CCTV—Closed-circuit television. This is a detective control that provides video surveillance. Video surveillance provides reliable proof of a person's location and activity. It can be used by an organization to verify if any equipment or data is being removed.

CERT—Computer Emergency Response Team. A group of experts that respond to security incidents. Also known as CIRT, SIRT, or IRT.

CHAP—Challenge Handshake Authentication Protocol. Authentication mechanism where a server challenges a client. MS-CHAPv2 is an improvement over CHAP and uses mutual authentication.

CIA—Confidentiality, integrity, and availability. These three form the security triad. Confidentiality helps prevent the unauthorized disclosure of data. Integrity provides assurances that data has not been modified, tampered with, or corrupted. Availability indicates that data and services are available when needed.

CIRT—Computer Incident Response Team. A group of experts that respond to security incidents. Also known as CERT, SIRT, or IRT.

COOP—Continuity of Operations Plan. A COOP site provides an alternate location for operations after a critical outage. A hot site includes personnel, equipment, software, and communications capabilities of the primary site with all the data up to date. A hot site can take over for a failed primary site within an hour. A cold site will have power and connectivity needed for COOP activation, but little else. A warm site is a compromise between a hot site and a cold site.

CRC—Cyclical Redundancy Check. An error detection code used to detect accidental changes that can affect the integrity of data.

CRL—Certification Revocation List. A list of certificates that have been revoked. Certificates are commonly revoked if they are compromised. The certificate authority (CA) that issued the certificate publishes a CRL, and a CRL is public.

DAC—Discretionary Access Control. An access control model where all objects have owners and owners can modify permissions for the objects (files and folders). Microsoft's NTFS uses the DAC model. Other access control models are MAC and RBAC.

DACL—Discretionary Access Control List. List of Access Control Entries (ACEs) in Microsoft's NTFS. Each ACE includes a security identifier (SID) and a permission.

DDoS—Distributed denial-of-service. An attack on a system launched from multiple sources intended to make a computer's resources or services unavailable to users. DDoS attacks are often launched from zombies in botnets. DDoS attacks typically include sustained, abnormally high network traffic. A performance baseline helps administrators detect a DDoS. Compare to DoS.

DEP—Data Execution Prevention. A security feature in some operating systems. It helps prevent an application or service from executing code from a nonexecutable memory region

DES—Digital Encryption Standard. An older symmetric encryption standard used to provide confidentiality. DES uses 56 bits and is considered cracked.

DHCP—Dynamic Host Configuration Protocol. A service used to dynamically assign TCP/IP configuration information to clients. DHCP is often used to assign IP addresses, subnet masks, default gateways, DNS server addresses, and much more.

DLL—Dynamic Link Library. A compiled set of code that can be called from other programs.

DLP—Data Loss Protection. A network-based DLP system can examine and analyze network traffic. It can detect if confidential company data or any PII data is included in e-mail and reduce the risk of internal users e-mailing sensitive data outside the organization.

DMZ—Demilitarized zone. Area between two firewalls separating the Internet and an internal network. A DMZ provides a layer of protection for Internet-facing servers. It allows access to a server or service for Internet users while segmenting and protecting access to the internal network.

DNS—Domain Name System. Used to resolve host names to IP addresses. DNS is the primary name resolution service used on the Internet and is also used on internal networks. DNS uses port 53. DNS poisoning attempts to modify or corrupt cached DNS results. A pharming attack is a specific type of DNS poisoning attack that redirects a website's traffic to another website.

DoS—Denial-of-service. An attack from a single source that attempts to disrupt the services provided by another system. Examples include SYN flood, smurf, and some buffer overflow attacks. Compare to DDoS.

DRP—Disaster recovery plan. A document designed to help a company respond to disasters, such as hurricanes, floods, and fires. It includes a hierarchical list of critical systems and often prioritizes services to restore after an outage. Testing validates the plan. Recovered systems are tested before returning them to operation, and this can include a comparison to baselines. The final phase of disaster recovery includes a review to identify any lessons learned and may include an update of the plan.

DSA—Digital Signature Algorithm. A digital signature is an encrypted hash of a message. The sender's private key encrypts the hash of the message to create the digital signature. The recipient decrypts the hash with the sender's public key, and, if successful, it provides authentication, non-repudiation, and integrity. Authentication identifies the sender. Integrity verifies the message has not been modified. Non-repudiation is used with online transactions and prevents the sender from later denying they sent the e-mail.

EAP—Extensible Authentication Protocol. An authentication framework that provides general guidance for authentication methods. Variations include LEAP and PEAP

ECC—Elliptic curve cryptography. An asymmetric encryption algorithm commonly used with smaller wireless devices. It uses smaller key sizes and requires less processing power than many other encryption methods

EFS—Encrypting File System. A feature within NTFS on Windows systems that supports encrypting individual files or folders for confidentiality.

EMI—Electromagnetic interference. Interference caused by motors, power lines, and fluorescent lights. Cables can be shielded to protect signals from EMI. Additionally, EMI shielding prevents signal emanation, so it can prevent someone from capturing network traffic.

ESP—Encapsulating Security Protocol. IPsec includes both AH and ESP. AH provides authentication and integrity, and ESP provides confidentiality, integrity, and authentication. ESP is identified with protocol ID number 50.

FTP—File Transfer Protocol. Used to upload and download files to an FTP server. FTP uses ports 20 and 21. Secure FTP (SFTP) uses SSH for encryption on port 22. FTP Secure (FTPS) uses SSL or TLS for encryption.

FTPS—File Transfer Protocol Secure. An extension of FTP that uses SSL or TLS to encrypt FTP traffic. Some implementations of FTPS use ports 989 and 990.

GPG—GNU Privacy Guard (GPG). Free software that is based on the OpenPGP standard. It is similar to PGP but avoids any conflict with existing licensing by using open standards.

GPO—Group Policy object. Group Policy is used within Microsoft Windows to manage users and computers. It is implemented on a domain controller within a domain. Administrators use it to create password policies, lock down the GUI, configure host-based firewalls, and much more.

GPS—Global Positioning System. GPS tracking can help locate lost mobile devices. Remote wipe, or remote sanitize, erases all data on lost devices. Full disk encryption protects the data on the device if it is lost.

GRE—Generic Routing Encapsulation. A tunneling protocol developed by Cisco Systems.

GUI—Graphical user interface. Users interact with the graphical elements instead of typing in commands from a text interface. Windows is an example of a GUI.

HDD—Hard disk drive. A disk drive that has one or more platters and a spindle. In contrast, USB flash drives use flash memory.

HIDS—Host-based intrusion detection system. An IDS used to monitor an individual server or workstation. It protects local resources on the host such as the operating system files.

HIPS—Host-based intrusion prevention system. An extension of a host-based IDS. Designed to react in real time to catch an attack in action.

HMAC—Hash-based Message Authentication Code. An HMAC is a fixed length string of bits similar to other hashing algorithms such as MD5 and SHA-1, but it also uses a secret key to add some randomness to the result.

HSM—Hardware security module. A removable or external device that can generate, store, and manage RSA keys used in asymmetric encryption. High-volume ecommerce sites use HSMs to increase the performance of SSL sessions. High-availability clusters needing encryption services can use clustered HSMs.

HTML—Hypertext Markup Language. Language used to create web pages served on the Internet. HTML documents are displayed by web browsers and delivered over the Internet using HTTP or HTTPS. It uses less than and greater than characters (< and >) to create tags. Many sites use input validation to block these tags and prevent cross-site scripting attacks.

HTTP—Hypertext Transfer Protocol. Used for web traffic on the Internet and in intranets. HTTP uses port 80.

HTTPS—Hypertext Transfer Protocol Secure. Encrypts HTTP traffic with SSL or TLS using port 443.

HVAC—Heating, ventilation, and air conditioning. HVAC systems increase availability by regulating airflow within datacenters and server rooms. They use hot and cold to regulate the cooling, thermostats to ensure a relatively constant temperature, and humidity controls to reduce the potential for static discharges, and damage from condensation. They are often integrated with fire alarm systems and either have dampers or the ability to be turned off in the event of a fire.

IaaS—Infrastructure as a Service. A cloud computing technology useful for heavily utilized systems and networks. Organizations can limit their hardware footprint and personnel costs by renting access to hardware such as servers. Compare to PaaS and SaaS.

ICMP—Internet Control Message Protocol. Used for diagnostics such as ping. Many DoS attacks use ICMP. It is common to block ICMP at firewalls and routers. If ping fails, but other connectivity to a server succeeds, it indicates that ICMP is blocked.

ID—Identification. For example, a protocol ID identifies a protocol based on a number. AH is identified with protocol ID number 51 and ESP is identified with protocol ID number 50.

IDS—Intrusion detection system. A detective control used to detect attacks after they occur. A signature-based IDS (also called definition-based) uses a database of predefined traffic patterns. An anomaly-based IDS (also called behavior-based) starts with a performance baseline of normal behavior and compares network traffic against this baseline. An IDS can be either host-based (HIDS) or network-based (NIDS). In contrast, a firewall is a preventative control that attempts to prevent the attacks before they occur. An IPS is a preventative control that will stop an attack in progress.

IEEE—Institute of Electrical and Electronic Engineers. International organization with a focus on electrical, electronics, and information technology topics. IEEE standards are well respected and followed by vendors around the world.

IGMP—Internet Group Management Protocol. Used for multicasting. Computers belonging to a multicasting group have a multicasting IP address in addition to a standard unicast IP address.

IIS—Internet Information Services. A Microsoft Windows web server. IIS comes free with Microsoft Windows Server products.

IKE—Internet Key Exchange. Used with IPsec to create a secure channel over port 500 in a VPN tunnel.

IM—Instant Messaging. Real-time direct text-based communication between two or more people, often referred to as chat.

IMAP4—Internet Message Access Protocol v4. Used to store e-mail on servers and allow clients to manage their e-mail on the server. IMAP4 uses port 143.

IPS—Intrusion prevention system. A preventative control that will stop an attack in progress. It is similar to an active IDS except that it's placed in line with traffic. An IPS can actively monitor data streams, detect malicious content, and stop attacks in progress.

IPsec—Internet Protocol Security. Used to encrypt traffic on the wire and can operate in both tunnel mode and transport mode. It uses tunnel mode for VPN traffic. IPsec is built into IPv6, but can also work with IPv4 and it includes both AH and ESP. AH provides authentication and integrity, and ESP provides confidentiality, integrity, and authentication. IPsec uses port 500 for IKE with VPN connections.

IPv4—Internet Protocol version 4. Identifies hosts using a 32-bit IP address. IPv4 is expressed in dotted decimal format with decimal numbers separated by dots or periods like this: 192.168.1.1.

IPv6—Internet Protocol version 6. Identifies hosts using a 128-bit address. IPv6 is expressed as eight groups of four hexadecimal characters (numbers and letters), such as this: FE80: 0000:0000:0000: 20D4:3FF7:003F:DE62.

IRC—Internet Relay Chat. A form of real-time Internet text messaging often used with chat sessions. Some botnets have used IRC channels to control zombie computers through a command and control server.

IRT—Incident Response Team. A group of experts that respond to security incidents. Also known as CERT, CIRT, or SIRT.

ISP—Internet Service Provider. Company that provides Internet access to customers.

IV—Initialization vector. An provides randomization of encryption keys to help ensure that keys are not reused. WEP was susceptible to IV attacks because it used relatively small IVs. In an IV attack, the attacker uses packet injection, increasing the number of packets to analyze, and discovers the encryption key.

KDC—Key Distribution Center. Part of the Kerberos protocol used for network authentication. The KDC issues time-stamped tickets that expire.

L2TP—Layer 2 Tunneling Protocol. Tunneling protocol used with VPNs. L2TP is commonly used with IPsec (L2TP/IPsec). L2TP uses port 1701.

LAN—Local area network. Group of hosts connected within a network.

LANMAN—Local area network manager. Older authentication protocol used to provide backward compatibility to Windows 9x clients. LANMAN passwords are easily cracked due to how they are stored.

LDAP—Lightweight Directory Access Protocol. Language used to communicate with directories such as Microsoft's Active Directory. It provides a central location to manage user accounts and other directory objects. LDAP uses port 389 when unencrypted and port 636 when encrypted.

LEAP—Lightweight Extensible Authentication Protocol. A modified version of the Challenge Handshake Authentication Protocol (CHAP) created by Cisco.

MAC—Mandatory Access Control. Access control model that uses sensitivity labels assigned to objects (files and folders) and subjects (users). SELinux (deployed in both Linux and UNIX platforms) is a trusted operating system platform using the MAC model. Other access control models are DAC and RBAC.

MAC—Media access control. A 48-bit address used to uniquely identify network interface cards. It also called a hardware address or a physical address, and is commonly displayed as six pairs of hexadecimal characters. Port security on a switch can limit access using MAC filtering. Wireless access points can use MAC filtering to restrict access to only certain clients, though an attacker can easily beat this.

MAC—Message authentication code. Method used to provide integrity for messages. A MAC uses a secret key to encrypt the hash. Some versions called HMAC.

MAN—Metropolitan area network. A computer network that spans a metropolitan area such as a city or a large campus

MBR—Master Boot Record. An area on a hard disk in its first sector. When the BIOS boots a system, it looks at the MBR for instructions and information on how to boot the disk and load the operating system. Some malware tries to hide here.

MD5—Message Digest 5. A hashing function used to provide integrity. MD5 uses 128 bits. A hash is simply a number created by applying the algorithm to a file or message at different times. The hashes are compared to each other to verify that integrity has been maintained.

MITM—Man in the middle. A MITM attack is a form of active interception allowing an attacker to intercept traffic and insert malicious code sent to other clients. Kerberos provides mutual authentication and helps prevent MITM attacks.

MS-CHAP—Microsoft Challenge Handshake Authentication Protocol. Microsoft's implementation of CHAP. MS-CHAPv2 provides mutual authentication.

MTU—Maximum Transmission Unit. The MTU identifies the size of data that can be transferred.

NAC—Network access control. Inspects clients for health and can restrict network access to unhealthy clients to a remediation network. Clients run agents and these agents report status to a NAC server. NAC is used for VPN and internal clients. MAC filtering is a form of NAC.

NAT—Network Address Translation. A service that translates public IP addresses to private and private IP addresses to public. It hides addresses on an internal network.

NIDS—Network-based intrusion detection system. IDS used to monitor a network. It can detect network-based attacks, such as smurf attacks. A NIDS cannot monitor encrypted traffic, and cannot monitor traffic on individual hosts.

NIPS—Network-based intrusion prevention system. An IPS that monitors the network. An IPS can actively monitor data streams, detect malicious content, and stop attacks in progress.

NIST—National Institute of Standards and Technology. NIST is a part of the U.S. Department of Commerce, and it includes an Information Technology Laboratory (ITL). The ITL publishes special publications related to security that are freely available for download here: http://csrc.nist.gov/publications/PubsSPs.html.

NOOP—No operation, sometimes listed as NOP. NOOP instructions are often used in a buffer overflow attack. An attacker often writes a large number of NOOP instructions as a NOOP sled into memory, followed with malicious code.

NOS—Network Operating System. Software that runs on a server and enables the server to manage resources on a network.

NTFS—New Technology File System. A file system used in Microsoft operating systems that provides security. NTFS uses the DAC model.

NTLM—New Technology LANMAN. Authentication protocol intended to improve LANMAN. The LANMAN protocol stores passwords using a hash of the password by first dividing the password into two seven-character blocks, and then converting all lowercase letters to uppercase. This makes LANMAN easy to crack. NTLM stores passwords in LANMAN format for backward compatibility, unless the passwords are greater than fifteen characters. NTLMv1 is older and has known vulnerabilities. NTLMv2 is newer and secure.

NTP—Network Time Protocol. Protocol used to synchronize computer times.

OS—Operating system. For example, SELinux is a trusted OS that can help prevent malicious code from executing.

OVAL—Open Vulnerability Assessment Language. International standard proposed for vulnerability assessment scanners to follow.

P2P—Peer-to-peer. P2P applications allow users to share files such as music, video, and data over the Internet. Data leakage occurs when users install P2P software and unintentionally share files. Organizations often block P2P software at the firewall and detect running software with port scans.

PaaS—Platform as a Service. Provides cloud customers with an easy-to-configure operating system and on-demand computing capabilities. Compare to IaaS and SaaS.

PAP—Password Authentication Protocol. An older authentication protocol where passwords are sent across the network in clear text. Rarely used today.

PAT—Port Address Translation. A form of network address translation.

PBX—Private Branch Exchange. A telephone switch used to telephone calls.

PEAP—Protected Extensible Authentication Protocol. PEAP provides an extra layer of protection for EAP. PEAP-TLS uses TLS to encrypt the authentication process by encapsulating and encrypting the EAP conversation in a Transport Layer Security (TLS) tunnel. Since TLS requires a certificate, PEAP-TLS requires a certification authority (CA) to issue certificates.

PED—Personal Electronic Device. Small devices such as cell telephones, radios, CD players, DVD players, video cameras, and MP3 players.

PGP—Pretty Good Privacy. Commonly used to secure e-mail communications between two private individuals but is also used in companies. It provides confidentiality, integrity, authentication, and non-repudiation. It can digitally sign and encrypt e-mail. It uses both asymmetric and symmetric encryption.

PII—Personally Identifiable Information. Information about individuals that can be used to trace a person's identity, such as a full name, birthdate, biometric data, and identifying numbers such as a Social Security number (SSN). Organizations have an obligation to protect PII and often identify procedures for handling and retaining PII in data policies.

PIN—Personal identification number. A number known by a user and entered for authentication. PINs are often combined with smart cards to provide two-factor authentication.

PIV—Personal identity verification card. A specialized type of smart card used by United States federal agencies. It includes photo identification and provides confidentiality, integrity, authentication, and non-repudiation for the users. It is similar to a CAC.

PKI—Public Key Infrastructure. Group of technologies used to request, create, manage, store, distribute, and revoke digital certificates. Certificates are an important part of asymmetric encryption. Certificates include public keys along with details on the owner of the certificate and on the CA that issued the certificate. Certificate owners share their public key by sharing a copy of their certificate.

POP3—Post Office Protocol v3. Used to transfer e-mail from mail servers to clients. POP3 uses port 110.

POTS—Plain old telephone service. Voice grade telephone service available.

PPP—Point-to-Point Protocol. Used to create remote access connections.

PPTP—Point-to-Point Tunneling Protocol. Tunneling protocol used with VPNs. PPTP uses TCP port 1723.

PSK—Pre-shared key. A secret shared among different systems. Wireless networks support Personal Mode, where each device uses the same PSK. In contrast, Enterprise Mode uses an 802.1x or RADIUS server for authentication.

PTZ—Pan tilt zoom. Refers to cameras that can pan (move left and right), tilt (move up and down), and zoom to get a closer or a wider view.

RA—Recovery agent. A designated individual who can recover or restore cryptographic keys. In the context of a PKI, a recovery agent can recover private keys to access encrypted data.

RADIUS—Remote Authentication Dial-In User Service. Provides central authentication for remote access clients. RADIUS encrypts the password packets and uses UDP. In contrast, TACACS+ encrypts the entire authentication process and uses TCP.

RAID—Redundant Array of Inexpensive (or Independent) Disks. Multiple disks added together to increase performance or provide protection against faults.

RAID-0—Disk striping. RAID-0 improves performance but does not provide fault tolerance.

RAID-1—Disk mirroring. RAID-1 uses two disks and provides fault tolerance.

RAID-5—Disk striping with parity. RAID-5 uses three or more disks and provides fault tolerance.

RAM—Random Access Memory. Volatile memory within a computer that holds active processes, data, and applications. Data in RAM is lost when the computer is turned off. Inspection of RAM can discover hooked processes from rootkits. Memory forensics analyzes data in RAM.

RAS—Remote Access Service. A server used to provide access to an internal network from an outside location. RAS is also known as Remote Access Server and sometimes referred to as Network Access Service (NAS).

RBAC—Role-based access control. An access control model that uses roles to define access and it is often implemented with groups. A user account is placed into a role, inheriting the rights and permissions of the role. Other access control models are MAC and DAC.

RBAC—Rule-based access control. An access control model that uses rules to define access. Rule-based access control is based on a set of approved instructions, such as an access control list. Other access control models are MAC and DAC.

RC—Ron's Code or Rivest's Cipher. Symmetric encryption algorithm that includes versions RC2, RC4, RC5, and RC6. RC4 is a secure stream cipher, and RC5 and RC6 are block ciphers.

RFI—Radio frequency interference. Interference from RF sources such as AM or FM transmitters. RFI can be filtered to prevent data interference, and cables can be shielded to protect signals from RFI.

RIPEMD—RACE Integrity Primitives Evaluation Message Digest. A hash function used for integrity. It creates fixed length hashes of 128, 160, 256, or 320 bits.

RPO—Recovery Point Objective. A Recovery Point Objective identifies a point in time where data loss is acceptable. It is related to the RTO and the BIA often includes both RTOs and RPOs.

RSA—An asymmetric algorithm used to encrypt data and digitally sign transmissions. It is named after its creators, Rivest, Shamir, and Adleman, and RSA is also the name of the company they founded together. RSA relies on the mathematical properties of prime numbers when creating public and private keys.

RSTP—Rapid Spanning Tree Protocol. An improvement over STP. STP and RSTP protocols are enabled on most switches and protect against switching loops, such as those caused when two ports of a switch are connected together.

RTO—Recovery Time Objective. An RTO identifies the maximum amount of time it can take to restore a system after an outage. It is related to the RPO and the BIA often includes both RTOs and RPOs.

RTP—Real-time Transport Protocol. A standard used for delivering audio and video over an IP network.

S/MIME—Secure/Multipurpose Internet Mail Extensions. Used to secure e-mail. S/MIME provides confidentiality, integrity, authentication, and non-repudiation. It can digitally sign and encrypt e-mail, including the encryption of e-mail at rest (stored on a drive) and in transit (data sent over the network). It uses RSA, with public and private keys for encryption and decryption, and depends on a PKI for certificates.

SaaS—Software as a Service. Applications provided over the Internet. Webmail is an example of a cloud-based technology. Compare to IaaS and PaaS.

SCAP—Security Content Automation Protocol. A method with automated vulnerability management, measurement, and policy compliance evaluation tools

SCP—Secure copy. Based on SSH, SCP allows users to copy encrypted files over a network. SCP uses port 22.

SCSI—Small Computer System Interface. Set of standards used to connect peripherals to computers. Commonly used for SCSI hard disks and/or tape drives.

SDLC—Software Development Life Cycle. A software development process. Many different models are available.

SDLM—Software Development Life Cycle Methodology. The practice of using a SDLC when developing applications.

SELinux—Security-Enhanced Linux. A trusted operating system platform that prevents malicious or suspicious code from executing on both Linux and UNIX systems. It is one of the few operating systems that use the MAC model.

SFTP—Secure FTP. An extension of Secure Shell (SSH) using SSH to transmit the files in an encrypted format. SFTP transmits data using port 22.

SHA—Secure Hash Algorithm. A hashing function used to provide integrity. SHA1 uses 160 bits, and SHA-256 uses 256 bits. Hashing algorithms always provide a fixed-size bit-string regardless of the size of the hashed data. By comparing the hashes at two different times, you can verify integrity of the data.

SHTTP—Secure Hypertext Transfer Protocol. An alternative to HTTPS. Infrequently used.

SID—Security identifier. Unique set of numbers and letters used to identify each user and each group in Microsoft environments.

SIM—Subscriber Identity Module. A small smart card that contains programming and information for small devices such as cell phones.

SIRT—Security Incident Response Team. A group of experts that respond to security incidents. Also known as CERT, CERT, or IRT.

SLA—Service level agreement. An agreement between a company and a vendor that stipulates performance expectations, such as minimum uptime and maximum downtime levels.

SLE—Single loss expectancy. Used to measure risk with annualized loss expectancy (ALE) and annualized rate of occurrence (ARO). The SLE identifies the expected dollar amount for a single event resulting in a loss. The calculation is SLE x ARO = ALE.

SMTP—Simple Mail Transfer Protocol. Used to transfer e-mail between clients and servers and between e-mail servers and other e-mail servers. SMTP uses port 25.

SNMP—Simple Network Management Protocol. Used to manage network devices such as routers or switches. SNMP agents report information via notifications known as SNMP traps, or SNMP device traps.

SONET—Synchronous Optical Network Technologies. A multiplexing protocol used to transfer data over optical fiber.

SPIM—Spam over Internet Messaging. A form of spam using instant messaging that targets instant messaging users

SPOF—Single point of failure. An SPOF is any component whose failure results in the failure of an entire system. Elements such as RAID, failover clustering, UPS, and generators remove many single points of failure.

SQL—Structured query language. Used by SQL-based databases, such as Microsoft's SQL Server. Websites integrated with a SQL database are subject to SQL injection attacks. Input validation with forms and stored procedures help prevent SQL injection attacks. Microsoft's SQL Server uses port 1433 by default.

SSH—Secure Shell. SSH encrypts a wide variety of traffic such as Secure File Transfer Protocol (SFTP), Telnet, and Secure Copy (SCP). SSH uses port 22.

SSID—Service Set Identifier. Identifies the name of a wireless network. Disabling SSID broadcast can hide the network from casual users but an attacker can easily discover it with a wireless sniffer. It's recommended to change the SSID from the default name.

SSL—Secure Sockets Layer. Used to encrypt traffic on the wire. SSL is used with HTTPS to encrypt HTTP traffic on the Internet using both symmetric and asymmetric encryption algorithms. SSL uses port 443 when encrypting HTTPS traffic.

SSO—Single sign-on. Authentication method where users can access multiple resources on a network using a single account. SSO can provide central authentication against a federated database for different operating systems.

SSTP—Secure Socket Tunneling Protocol. A tunneling protocol that encrypts VPN traffic using SSL over port 443.

STP—Spanning Tree Protocol. Protocol enabled on most switches that protects against switching loops. A switching loop can be caused if two ports of a switch are connected together, such as those caused when two ports of a switch are connected together.

STP—Shielded twisted pair. Cable type used in networks that includes shielding to prevent interference from EMI and RFI. It can also prevent data from emanating outside the cable.

SYN—Synchronize. The first packet in a TCP handshake. In a SYN flood attack, attackers send this packet, but don't complete the handshake after receiving the SYN/ACK packet. A flood guard is a logical control that protects against SYN flood attacks.

TACACS—Terminal Access Controller Access-Control System. An older remote authentication protocol that was commonly used in UNIX networks. TACACS+ is more commonly used.

TACACS+—Terminal Access Controller Access-Control System+. Provides central authentication for remote access clients and used as an alternative to RADIUS. TACACS+ uses TCP port 49, compared with TACACS, which uses UDP port 49. It encrypts the entire authentication process, compared with RADIUS, which only encrypts the password. It uses multiple challenges and responses.

TCO—Total cost of ownership. A factor considered when purchasing new products and services. TCO attempts to identify the cost of a product or service over its lifetime.

TCP—Transmission Control Protocol. Provides guaranteed delivery of IP traffic using a three-way handshake.

TCP/IP—Transmission Control Protocol/Internet Protocol. Represents the full suite of protocols.

TFTP—Trivial File Transfer Protocol. Used to transfer small amounts of data with UDP port 69. In contrast, FTP is used to transfer larger files using TCP ports 20 and 21.

TKIP—Temporal Key Integrity Protocol. Wireless security protocol introduced to address the problems with WEP. TKIP was used with WPA but many implementations of WPA now support CCMP.

TLS—Transport Layer Security. Used to encrypt traffic on the wire. TLS is the replacement for SSL and like SSL, it uses certificates issued by CAs. PEAP-TLS uses TLS to encrypt the authentication process and PEAP-TLS requires a CA to issue certificates.

TPM—Trusted Platform Module. This is a hardware chip on the motherboard included on many newer laptops. A TPM includes a unique RSA asymmetric key, and it can generate and store other keys used for encryption, decryption, and authentication. TPM provides full disk encryption.

UAT—User Acceptance Testing. One of the last phases of testing an application before its release.

UDP—User Datagram Protocol. Used instead of TCP when guaranteed delivery of each packet is not necessary. UDP uses a best-effort delivery mechanism.

UPS—Uninterruptible power supply. A battery backup system that provides fault tolerance for power and can protect against power fluctuations. UPS provide short-term power giving the system enough time to shut down smoothly, or to transfer to generator power. Generators provide long-term power in extended outages.

URL—Universal Resource Locator. Address used to access web resources, such as http://GetCertifiedGetAhead.com. Pop-up blockers can include URLs of sites where pop-ups are allowed.

USB—Universal Serial Bus. A serial connection used to connect peripherals such as printers, flash drives, and external hard disk drives. Data on USB drives can be protected against loss of confidentiality with encryption. They combine high volume and transfer speeds with ease of concealment and often result in data leakage.

UTP—Unshielded twisted pair. Cable type used in networks that do not have any concerns over EMI, RFI, or cross talk. If these are a concern, STP is used.

VLAN—Virtual local area network. A VLAN can logically group several different computers together, or logically separate computers, without regard to their physical location. It is possible to create multiple VLANs with a single switch.

VM—Virtual machine. A virtual system hosted on a physical system. A physical server can host multiple VMs as servers. Virtualization can reduce the footprint of an organization's server room or datacenter, and helps eliminate wasted resources. It also helps reduce the amount of physical equipment, reducing overall physical security requirements. A VM escape is an attack that allows an attacker to access the host system from within the virtual system.

VoIP—Voice over IP. A group of technologies used to transmit voice over IP networks. Vishing is a form of phishing that sometimes uses VoIP.

VPN—Virtual private network. Provides access to a private network over a public network such as the Internet. VPN concentrators provide VPN access to large groups of users.

VTC—Video teleconferencing. A group of interactive telecommunication technologies that allow people in two or more locations to interact with two-way video and audio transmissions.

WAF—Web application firewall. A firewall specifically designed to protect a web application, such as a web server. A WAF inspects the contents of traffic to a web server, can detect malicious content, and block it.

WAP—Wireless access point, sometimes just called an access point (AP). Increasing the power level of a WAP increases the wireless coverage of the WAP. Decreasing the power levels, decreases the coverage. Coverage can also be manipulated by moving or positioning the wireless antenna.

WEP—Wired Equivalent Privacy. Original wireless security protocol. Had significant security flaws and was replaced with WPA, and ultimately WPA2. WEP used RC4 incorrectly making it susceptible to IV attacks.

WIDS—Wireless intrusion detection system. An IDS used for wireless networks.

WIPS—Wireless intrusion prevention system. An IPS used for wireless networks.

WLAN—Wireless local area network. Network connected wirelessly.

WPA—Wi-Fi Protected Access. Replaced WEP as a wireless security protocol without replacing hardware. Superseded by WPA2.

WPA2—Wi-Fi Protected Access version 2. Newer security protocol used to protect wireless transmissions. It supports CCMP for encryption, which is based on AES and stronger than TKIP which was originally released with WPA. In Enterprise Mode, it can use RADIUS to support 802.1x authentication. In personal mode, it uses a preshared key (PSK).

WTLS—Wireless Transport Layer Security. Used to encrypt traffic for smaller wireless devices.

XML—Extensible markup language. Used by many databases for inputting or exporting data. XML uses formatting rules to describe the data.

XTACACS—Extended Terminal Access Controller Access-Control System. An improvement over TACACS developed by Cisco Systems and proprietary to Cisco systems. TACACS+ is more commonly used.

XSRF—Cross-site request forgery. An attack that causes users to perform actions on websites without their knowledge. In some cases, attackers use header manipulation to steal cookies and harvest passwords.

XSS—Cross-site scripting. It scripting allows an attacker to redirect users to malicious websites and steal cookies. E-mail can include an embedded HTML image object or a JavaScript image tag as part of a malicious cross-site scripting attack. Websites prevent cross-site scripting attacks with input validation to detect and block input that include HTML and JavaScript tags. Many sites prevent the use of < and > characters to block cross-site scripting.

Index

Numbers and Symbols

3DES, **420**, 421, 445
802.1X, **76**, 155, 193
802.11, **188–189**, 76, 192, 196, 349

A

Acceptable use, **464–465**, 468
Access control lists (ACL), 113
    DAC, 101–103
    Firewall rules, 161
    Implicit deny, 60
    RBAC, 97
    Routers and ACLs, 158
    VPNs, 203–204
Access control models, 97–104
    Discretionary access control (DAC),
      101–103
    Mandatory access control (MAC), 103–104
    Role– and rule-based access control
      (RBAC), 97–100
Access controls, 97–112
Account disablement policy, 462
    And routine audits, 347
    Disabling and deleting accounts, 118
    Preventative control, 95
Account lockout policies, 67
    Account access review, 119
    Use with passwords, 64
Account management, **117–120**, 269
    Account access review, 119
    Account disablement policy, 462
    Account expiration, 119
    Account management policies, 460–462
    Account policy enforcement, 118–120

Centralized and decentralized account
    management, 117
Disabling and deleting accounts,118
Group based privileges, **98–100**, 460
Issues associated with users with
    multiple account/roles
Time-of-day restrictions, 118–119
User assigned privileges, **97**, 98, 460
Account policy enforcement, 118–120
    Disablement, **119**, 462
    Expiration, 119
    Lockout, 67
    Password complexity, 114–115
    Password length, 115
    Recovery, 63
Active IDS, 184–187
    Corrective control, 96
    IDS vs IPS 186–187
Ad-hoc changes and change management 95,
    96, 239
Ad-hoc wireless, 200
Advanced persistent threat (APT), 339
Adware, 272–273
AES (Advanced Encryption Standard), **420**, 418
    Compared to Blowfish and TwoFish, 422
    Compared to DES and 3DES, 420–421
    Symmetric encryption, 418
    Use in email, 434–435
ALE (annualized loss expectancy), 333
All-in-one security appliances, 162
Anomaly based IDS, 182–183
Antenna placement, wireless, 189
    And war driving, 198
Anti-malware, 273–275
    Anti-spam, 271

Anti-spyware, 275
Antivirus, 273–274
Heuristic-based detection, 274
Host-based firewalls, 159
Pop-up blockers, 272–273, 300
Signature-based detection, 274
Application attacks, 307–317
Buffer overflow, 308–309
Cookies and attachments, 300
Cross-site scripting, 312
Directory traversal/command injection, 314
Header manipulation, 301
LDAP injection, 314
Malicious add-ons, 300
Session hijacking, 300
SQL injection, 309–311
XML injection, 311–312
Zero day, 185, 223–224
Application security, 304–307
Application configuration baseline (proper settings), 224–226
Application hardening, 304
Application patch management, 304, 235–238
Changing defaults, 305
Cross-site request forgery (XSRF), 313
Cross-site scripting prevention, 312
Disabling unnecessary accounts, 305
Eliminate backdoors, 305
Fuzzing, 314
Input validation, 306–307
Secure coding, 306
Vendor guidelines, 304
Architecture review, 340
ARO (annualized rate of occurrence), 333
ARP, 137
ARP poisoning, **301–302**, 299
Asymmetric encryption, 422–427, 409
Certificates, 424–426
Diffie–Hellman, 427
Digital signatures, 431–433
RSA, 426
Attack surface, 337
Attacks, 294–303
Application attacks, 307–317
ARP poisoning, 301–302
Botnet, 297–298
Buffer overflow attacks, 308–309
Client–side attacks, 316

Cross-site request forgery (XSRF), 313
Cross-site scripting, 312
Denial-of-service (DoS), 294–296
Directory traversal/command injection, 314
Distributed denial-of-service (DDoS), 297
DNS poisoning, 318
Fuzzing, 314
Header manipulation, 301
IV attack, 191
Kiting, 302
LDAP injection, 314
Malicious add-ons, 300
Malicious insider threat, 330
Man-in-the-middle, 299, 302
Pharming, 317
Phishing, 278–281
Privilege escalation, 275, 338
Replay, 299–300
Session hijacking, 300
Smurf, 296
Spam, 271
Spear phishing, 279–280
Spim, 271
Spoofing, 298
SQL injection , 309–311
SYN flood, 295–296
Transitive access and client–side attacks, 316
Vishing, 281
XMAS attack, 298–299
XML injection, 311–312
Zero day, 185, 223–224
Audit, 346–347
Account access review, 119–120
Detective control, 96
Firewall logs, 163
Non–repudiation, 59–60, 409
Operating system logs, 350–351
User rights and permissions reviews, 347
Wireless audit via war driving, 198
Authentication, 61–80
CACs and PIVs, 69–70
Comparing identification, authentication, and authorization, 61–62
Identity proofing, 62–63
Multifactor authentication, 72–73
Mutual authentication, **74–75**
Remote access authentication, 76–80

Self-service password reset systems, 53
Single factor, 63, 72–73
Single sign-on, 75
Smart cards, 68–69
Three factors of authentication, 63–73
Tokens or key fobs, 70
Authentication services, 73–80
Kerberos, 73–74
LDAP, 74
RADIUS, 78–79
TACACS, 79, 142
TACACS+, 79–80, 142
XTACACS, 79, 142
Authorization, 61–62
Availability, 57–58
Balancing CIA, 58–59
Concepts of confidentiality, integrity and
availability (CIA), 54–58
COOP sites, 385–388
Environmental controls, 391–394
Failsafe/secure vs Failopen, 394
High availability, 370–376, 244–245
Subnetting and availability, 143–146
Virtualization and availability, 232–233, 234

B

Backdoors, 273, 305
Backup policies, 381
Backups, 376–382
Backup policies, 381
Differential backups, 378–379
Full backups, 378
Incremental backups, 379
Protecting backups, 381
Restoring a full backup, 378
Restoring a full/differential backup set,
379
Restoring a full/incremental backup set,
379
Testing backups, 380
Baselines, **224–228**, 94
Baseline reporting, 227, 340
Configuration baseline, 226
Group Policy, 224–225
Performance baselines and baseline
reporting, 227
Security baselines, 224–225
Security templates, 225–226
Behavior based IDS, 182–183
Biometrics, 70–72

Black box testing, 344, 306
Blogs.GetCertifiedGetAhead.com
Blowfish, 422
Bluetooth wireless, 200–202
Bluejacking, 201
Bluesnarfing, 201
Discovery mode, 201
Botnet, **297–298**, 265
Buffer overflow, 308–309
Buffer overflow attacks, 308–309
Input validation, 306–307
Business continuity, 363–396
Backups, 376–382
Business continuity plan (BCP), 383–391
Business impact analysis, 383–384
Contingency planning, 389–390
Continuity of operations (COOP site),
385–388
Disaster recovery, 388–389
Mean time between failure, 385
Mean time to restore, 386
Planning and testing, 388
Recovery point objective (RPO), 385
Recovery time objective (RTO), 384
Redundancies, 370–376
Single point of failure, 370–371
Succession planning, 390
Business impact analysis, 383–384

C

Cable locks, 111–112
Camera vs. guard (detection vs prevention),
95–96, 109–111
CCMP, 192
CCTV (closed circuit television), 109–111
Certificate authority (CA), 438–439
And digital certificates, 424–426
CRLs, 441–442
Certificates, 424–426
Asymmetric encryption, 422
Certificate authority (CA), 438–439
Certificate revocation list (CRL), 441–442
Certificate trust paths, 439–440
Public key, 425
Revoking certificates, 441–442
Self-signed certificates, 440–441
Validating certificates, 442–443
Chain of custody, 481
Change management, 238–239
Change management policy, 462–463

CHAP, 77–78
Cipher locks , 106
Clean desk policy, 459–460
Client–side attacks, 316
Cloud computing, 248–251
    Drawbacks, risks, 251
    Infrastructure as a Service (IaaS), 250
    Platform as a Service (PaaS), 250
    Software as a Service (SaaS), 249
Clustering, 373–374
Code review, 306, 340
Cold site, 387
Command injection/directory traversal, 314
Common access card (CAC), 69–70
Confidentiality, **54–55**, 409, 234
    Concepts of confidentiality, integrity and
      availability (CIA), 54–58
    Cryptography, 409
    Encryption, 417–424
    Protecting confidentiality with
      encryption, 241–244, 417–424
Configuration Baseline, 226, 230
Containment, 476–477
Content inspection, 162
Contingency planning, 389–390
Continuity of operations (COOP site), 385–388
    Cold site, 387
    Hot site, 386
    Warm site, 387
Controls, 92–97, 104–119
    Corrective controls, 96
    Detective controls, 96
    Logical access controls, 111–119
    Management controls, 94
    Operational controls, 94–95
    Physical security controls,105–112
    Preventative controls, 95–96
    Technical controls, 93–94
Cookies and attachments, 300
Core security principles, 54–60
    Availability, 57–58
    Balancing CIA, 58
    Confidentiality, 54–55
    Integrity, 55–56
Corrective controls, 96
Cross-site request forgery (XSRF), 313
Cross-site scripting, 312
Cryptography, 407–444
    Asymmetric encryption, 422–427
    Confidentiality, 54–55,

Digital signatures, 431–433
Elliptic curve cryptography, 194, 427
Hashing, 409–417
Integrity, 55–56
Key escrow, 443–444
Non–repudiation, 59–60, 409
Quantum cryptography, 428–429
Steganography, 427–428
Symmetric encryption, 418–422
Symmetric vs. asymmetric, 417, 418–422,
    422–427

D

Data encryption, 417–424
    Database, 242
    Individual files, 241
    Mobile devices, 246–248
    Removable media, 246–247
    Whole disk, 244, 246–247
Data security , 239–248
    Categories, 240
    Cloud computing, 251
    Data Loss Prevention (DLP), 245–246
    Data security, 468–475
    Hardware based encryption devices,
      242–245
    Information classification: sensitivity of
      data (hard or soft), 469
    Labeling, handling and disposal, 469–
      470
    Leakage, 245–248
    Protecting confidentiality with
      encryption, 241–244, 417–424
    Software-based encryption, 241–242
    Training, 468
Data Loss Prevention (DLP), 245–246
Data policies, 469–472
    Data labeling and handling, 469–470
    Information classification, 469
    Personally identifiable information (PII),
      471–472
    Privacy policy, 472–473
    Storage and retention policies, 470
Database servers, 140
    SQL injection attacks, 311
DDoS (Distributed denial-of-service) attack,
    297
Decommissioning systems, 475
Defense in depth, 59–60
DES (Data Encryption Standard), 420

Design reviews, 340

Detection controls vs. prevention controls, 95–96

   Camera vs. guard, 95–96, 109–111

   IDS vs. IPS, 186–187

Device encryption, 202

Device policy, 116

Differential backups, 378–379

Digital signatures, 431–433

Directory traversal/command injection, 314

Disabling and deleting accounts, 118

Disaster recovery, 388–389

   Backup / backout contingency plans or policies, 389–390

   Backups, execution and frequency, 382

   Disaster recovery plan (DRP), 388–389

   IT contingency planning, 389–390

   Redundancy and fault tolerance, 370–376

   Succession planning, 390

   Testing, 390–391

Discretionary access control (DAC), 101–103

   SIDs and DACLs, 101

Distributed denial-of-service (DDoS) attack, 297

DLP (Data Loss Prevention), 245–246

   Protecting data in motion, 240

   Vulnerability scanning, 240

DMZ (demilitarized zone), 164–165

DNS (Domain Name System), 317–318, 140

   DNS poisoning, 318

Domain name kiting, 302

Door access systems, 105–107

   Cipher locks, 106

   Proximity cards, 106–107

DoS (Denial-of-service) attack, 294–296, 303

Dumpster diving, 282

E

E-mail

   E-mail protocols, 141

   E-mail servers, 316

   Encrypting e-mail, 433

   Malware, 264, 266, 273

   PGP/GPG, 435

   Phishing, 278–280

   Protecting e-mail, 431

   S/MIME, 435

   Signing e-mail with digital signatures, 431–433

   Social engineering, 276

   Spam and spam filters, 163

   Web-based SaaS, 248–249, 271

EAP, LEAP, PEAP, 194

Education and awareness training, 68, 277, 468

Elliptic curve cryptography (ECC), 194, 427

EMI shielding, 394–395

Encryption, **417–424**, 409

   AES, 420

   Asymmetric encryption, 422–427

   Block vs stream cipher, 419

   Confidentiality, 54–55, 234

   Encrypting data on the wire, 138

   Encrypting HTTPS Traffic with SSL and TLS, 436–438

   Hardware security module (HSM), 243–245

   Hardware-based encryption, 242–245

   IPsec, 205–206

   Mobile devices, 202, 247–248

   One-time pads, 421–422

   Portable storage devices, 246–247

   Protecting confidentiality with encryption, 241–244, 417–424

   RC4, 421

   RSA, 427

   Software-based encryption, 241–242

   Steganography, 427–428

   Symmetric encryption, 418–422

   Transport encryption protocols, 138, 139, 429–430

   Trusted Platform Module (TPM), 243–244

   TwoFish, 422

   Whole disk encryption, 244, 246–247

Environmental controls, 391–396

   EMI shielding, 394–395

   Environmental monitoring, 392–393

   Fire suppression, 391–392, 394

   Hot and cold aisles, 393

   HVAC (heating, ventilation, and air conditioning), 392–394

   Temperature and humidity controls, 393

Errata,

   GetCertifiedGetAhead.com/errata

Error and exception handling, 306–307

Evil twin, 199–200

F

Failover cluster, **373–374**, 57, 234, 371, 384, 391

Failsafe/secure vs. failopen, 394

False positives, 183
Faraday cage, 395
Fault tolerance, 370–376
  Clustering, 373–374
  Load balancing, 374–375
  RAID, 371–373
Fingerprinting, 337
Fire suppression, 391–392
Firewall, 159–164
  Firewall logs and log analysis, 163
  Firewall rules, 161
  Host-based firewalls, 159–160
  Implicit deny, 161
  Network-based firewalls, 160–161
  Routers and firewalls, 159
  Web application firewall (WAF), 161–162
  Web security gateways and appliances, 162
First responder, incident response, 477
Flood guards, 296
Footprint, 189–190, 231–232
  Environmental/physical, 231–232
  Reducing with virtualization, 231–232
  Wireless, 189–190
Forensic procedures, 477–484
  Capture images, 479
  Capture video, 482
  Chain of custody, 481
  Containment, 476–477
  Damage and loss control, 476–477
  Network traffic and logs, 480
  Order of volatility, 478
  Record time offset, 482
  Screenshots, 483
  Take hashes, 480
  Track man hours and expense, 483
  Witnesses, 483
FTP (File Transfer Protocol), 139
  FTPS (File Transfer Protocol Secure), 139
  SFTP (Secure File Transfer Protocol), 139
  TFTP (Trivial File Transfer Protocol), 139
Full backups, 378
Fuzzing, 314

G

Generator, 376
GetCertifiedGetAhead.com
GPS tracking, 202
Gray box testing, 344
Group based privileges, 98–100

Group policy, 113–116, 224–225
  Baselines, 225
  Device policy, 116
  Domain password policy, 116
  Password policy, 114–115

H

Hardening, 223–224, 304–305
  Application hardening, 304–305
  Baselines, 224–228
  Changing defaults, 305
  Disabling unnecessary accounts, 305
  Disabling unnecessary services, 223–224
  Eliminating unneeded applications, 224
  Imaging, 228–230
  Security templates, 225–226
  Server hardening, 223–224
Hardware based encryption devices, 242–245
  Hard drive, 244, 246–247
  HSM, 243–245
  TPM, 243–244
  USB encryption, 241–242
Hardware security , 111–112
  Cable locks, 111–112
  Locking cabinets, 111–112
  Safe, 111–112
Hardware security module (HSM), 243–245
Hashing, 409–417
  Forensics, 480
  Hashing files, 411–13
  Hashing messages, 413–414
  HMAC, 411
  Integrity, 409–417
  MD5, 410
  RIPEMD, 415
  SHA, 410–411
  Steganography, 427–428
Header manipulation, 301
Help,
  Blogs.GetCertifiedGetAhead.com
  GetCertifiedGetAhead.com
Heuristic based IDS, 182–183
HIDS (host-based intrusion prevention system), 180
High availability , 370–376, 244–245
HMAC, 411
Hoaxes , 266–267
Honeynet, 186
Honeypot, 185
Host security, 223–230

Host software baselining, 224–230
Host-based firewalls, 159–160
Hot and cold aisles, 393
Hot site, 386
HSM (Hardware security module) 243–245
HTTP (Hypertext Transfer Protocol) 139
    With proxy server, 166–167
HTTPS (Hypertext Transfer Protocol Secure)
        139, 430
    With SSL or TLS, 138, 429
    With proxy server, 166–167
    With RC4, 421
    Encrypting HTTPS Traffic with SSL and
        TLS, 436–438
Hub, 153
HVAC (heating, ventilation, and air
conditioning), 392–394
    Fire suppression, 391–392
    Hot and cold aisles, 393

I

ICMP (Internet Control Message Protocol), 137
Identification, 61–63
    Identification vs. authentication, 61–62
Identity proofing, 62–63
IDS (intrusion detection system) 179–187
    Active IDS, 184
    Alarms, Alerts, and Trends, 183
    Anomaly based, 182–183
    Behavior based, 182–183
    False positives, 183
    Heuristic based, 182–183
    HIDS, 180
    IDS vs. IPS, 186–187
    NIDS, 180–181
    Passive IDS, 185
    Signature based, 182
IEEE 802.1X, **76**, 155, 193
IEEE 802.11, **188 – 189**, 76, 192, 196, 349
Imaging, 228–230
    Baseline configuration, 228–230
    Forensics, 479
IMAP4, 140
Impersonation, 282
Implicit deny, 60, 113, 159, 161
Incident response
    Containment, 476–477
    First responder, 477
    Forensic procedures, 477–484
    Incident response policies, 476–477

Incident response team, 477
Incremental backups, 379
Information classification: sensitivity of data
(hard or soft), 469
Infrastructure as a Service (IaaS), 250
Injection attacks, 306–314
    Directory traversal/command injection,
        314
    Fuzzing, 314
    Input validation, 306–307
    LDAP injection, 314
    SQL injection attack, 311
    XML Injection, 311–312
Input validation, 306–307
  Protect against:
    Buffer overflow attacks, 309
    Cross-site scripting attacks, 313
    Directory traversal/command injection
        attacks, 314
    SQL injection attacks, 311
    Transitive access and client–side attacks,
        316
Integrity, 55–56
    Concepts of confidentiality, integrity and
        availability (CIA), 54–58
    Digital signatures, 431–433
    Forensic images, 479–480
    Hashing, 409–417
    Rootkits and file integrity checkers,
        270
Interference, 198, 394–395
Intrusion detection system (IDS) 179–187
IP, 137
IPS (intrusion prevention system),179, 180
    IDS vs. IPS, 186–187
IPsec, 138, 141–142, 430
    Encrypting data in motion, 240
    IPsec as a Tunneling Protocol, 205
    L2TP and IPsec, 205–206
    NAT and IPsec, 206
    VPN, 204–205
IPv4, 137, 142–143
    Network Address Translation (NAT), 166
    Public and private IP addresses, 165–166
IPv6, 137, 142–143
Isolation mode, wireless, 200
IV attack, 191

J

Job rotation, 466–467

K

Kerberos, **73–74**
Key escrow, 443–444
Kiting, 302

L

L2TP, **205–206**, 141–142, 147, 166, 430
LANMAN, 416
LDAP, 74, 140
    LDAP injection, 314
LEAP, 194
Least privilege, 112–113, 94
    And RBAC, 100
    User privilege policy, 460
Load balancers, 374–375
Logic bomb, 269
Logical access controls, 111–119
Logs, 350–352
    Access logs, 108
    Audit logs, 59
    Event logs, 350–351
    Firewall logs and log analysis, 163
    Forensic analysis, 480
    Monitoring, 350
    Operating system logs, 350–351
    Reviewing logs, 352
    Security logs, 351
Loop protection, 156

M

MAC filter, MAC filtering, 195–196, 209
Malicious add-ons, 300
Malicious insider threat, 330
Malware, 264–275
    Adware, 272–273
    Anti-spyware software, 275
    Antivirus software, 273–274
    Backdoors, 305
    Botnet, 297–298
    Delivery, 265
    Hoaxes, 266–267
    Logic bomb, 269
    Privilege escalation, 275
    Rogueware, 277–278
    Rootkits, 270–271
    Scareware, 277–278
    Spyware, 271–272
    Trojan horse, 267–268
    Trusted operating system, 275
    Virus, 265–266
    Worms, 267
Malware inspection, 162
Man-in-the-middle attack, 299, 302
    and Kerberos, 73
Management controls, 94
Mandatory access control (MAC), 103–104
Mandatory vacations, 465
Mantraps, 109
MD5, 410
Mean time between failure, 385
Mean time to restore, 386
Mitigation and deterrent techniques, 60–61,
    92–120
    Detective controls, 96
    Hardening, 223–224, 304–305
    Monitoring system logs, 350–351
    Physical security, 105–112
    Port security, 155
    Prevention controls, 95
Mobile devices, 202, 247–248
    Device encryption, 202
    GPS tracking, 202
    Remote wipe/sanitation, 202, 247–248
    Screen lock, 247
    Strong password, 202
    Voice encryption, 202
MS–CHAP and MS-CHAPv2, 77–78
Multifactor authentication, **72–73**, 63, 69, 70
Mutual authentication, **74–75**
    Kerberos, 61
    Man-in-the-middle, 299, 302
    MS–CHAPv2, 77–78

N

NAC (network access control), 207–209
NAT (Network Address Translation), 166
    NAT and IPsec, 206
NetBIOS, 140, 148
Network bridging, 157
Network-based firewalls, 160–161
NIDS (network-based intrusion prevention
    system), 180–181
    Anomaly based, 182–183
    Behavior based, 182–183
    Heuristic based, 182–183
    Signature based, 182
Non–repudiation, 59–60, 409
    Digital signature, 431–433
NTLM/NTLMv2, 416–417

O

Objectives (Security+ objectives to chapter map) 8–20
One-time pad, 421–422
Operational controls, 94–95
Order of volatility, 478
OVAL (Open Vulnerability and Assessment Language), 352

P

P2P, 473
Packet sniffing, 345–346
PAP, 77
Passive IDS, 185
Passwords, 63 – 68
  Changing passwords, 66
  Domain password policy, 116
  Password history, 66 – 67
  Password policy, 116
  Password-cracking, 348, 65
  Resetting passwords, 66, 63
  Sharing passwords, 66
  Something you know factor, 63 – 68
  Storing passwords, 65–66
  Strong passwords, 64–65
  Training, 68
Patch management, 235–238
  Change management, 238–239
  Deploying patches, 236
  Scheduling patches, 238
  Testing patches, 237
PEAP, 194
Penetration testing, 342–345
  Obtaining consent, 345
  Passive vs Active, 342
  White box, gray box, black box testing, 344
Performance baselines and baseline reporting, 227
Personal identification verification card (PIV), 69–70
Personally identifiable information (PII), 471
  Protecting PII, 472
Personnel policies, 464–467
PGP/GPG, 435
Pharming, 317
Phishing, 278–281
  Spear phishing, 279–280
  To install malware, 279

To validate e-mail addresses, 279
To get money, 279–280
Vishing, 281
Whaling, 280–281
Physical security, 105–112
  Controls, 105–112
  Door access systems, 105–107
  Fencing, 105
  Hardware locks, 111–112
  Mantraps, 109
  Physical access control—ID badges, 107–108
  Physical access lists and logs, 108
  Proximity readers
  Security guards, 109
  Video surveillance (CCTV), 109–111
Platform as a Service (PaaS), 250
Policies, see Security Policies
Pop-up blockers, 272–273, 300
POP3, 140
Port scanners, 152–153
Port security, 155
  802.1x, **76**, 155, 193
  Disabling unused ports, 155
  MAC limiting and filtering, 209, 194
Portable device policies, 463
Ports, 147–153
  Combining the IP Address and the port, 148–149
  Importance of ports in security, 151
  Port scanners, 152–153
  Ports table, 148
  Well-known ports, 147–151
Power level controls, wireless, 189
Power redundancies (UPS, generator), 375–376
PPP, 141
PPTP, 141
Preventative controls, 95–96
Privacy policy, 472–473
Private key **422–425**, 409, 417, 426, 430–437
Private IP addresses, 165–166
Privilege escalation, 275, 338, 461
  Penetration testing, 343
Protocol analyzer, 345–346
Protocols, 136–148
  Application protocols, 139–140
  Connectivity protocols, 136–137
  E-mail protocols, 141
  Encryption protocols, 138
  Remote access protocols, 141–142

Proxies, 166–168
Proximity cards, 106–107
Proxy server, 166–168
    Caching, 167
    Content filters, 167–168
Public IP addresses, 165–166
Public key, **422–425**, 409, 417, 426, 430–437
Public key infrastructure (PKI), 438–444
    Certificate authorities, 438–439
    Digital certificates, 424–426
    Key escrow, 443–444
    Private key, 422–425
    Public key, 422–425
    Recovery agent, 444
    Registration, 441
    Trust models, 440

Q

Qualitative risk assessment, 334–335
Quantitative risk assessment, 333–334
Quantum cryptography, 428–429

R

RADIUS, **78–79**, 77, 142, 207
    With WPA2 and 802.1X, 190, 193
RAID (Redundant array of inexpensive disks),
    371–373
RC4, 421
Reconnaissance, 336
Recovery agent, 444
Recovery Point Objective (RPO), 385
Recovery Time Objective (RTO), 384
Redundancy, 370–376
    Disk redundancy (RAID), 371–373
    Fault tolerance, 370–376
    Load balancing, 374–375
    Power redundancy (UPS, generator),
    375–376
    Server redundancy (failover clusters),
    373–374
    Single point of failure, 370–371
    Site redundancy (hot, cold, warm),
    385–388
Remote access, 202–209
    Authentication, 76–80
        CHAP, 77–78
        IEEE 802.1X, 76
        MS–CHAP and MS–CHAPv2, 78
        PAP, 77
        RADIUS, 78–79

        TACACS/XTACACS, 79, 142
        TACACS+, 79–80, 142
    MAC filtering, 209
    Network access control (NAC), 207–209
    Remote access protocols, 204–205
    Tunneling, 203–206
    VPN, 203
Remote administration, Remote Desktop
    Services, 141
Remote wipe/sanitation, 202, 247–248
Replay attack, 299–300
    And Kerberos, 73
Reporting, alarms, alerts, trends, 183
RIPEMD, 415
Risk, 60–61, 329–335
    Calculation (SLE, ARO, ALE), 333
    Cloud computing risks, 251
    Impact, 334
    Likelihood, 334
    Penetration testing, 342–345
    Quantitative vs. qualitative, 332–334
    Risk acceptance, 332
    Risk assessment, 332–335
    Risk avoidance, 332
    Risk deterrence, 332
    Risk management, 331
    Risk mitigation, 332
    Risk transference, 332
    Threat vs. likelihood, 329–330
    Threats, 329–330
    Virtualization risks, 233–234
    Vulnerabilities, 330–331
    Vulnerability assessment, 339–340
Risk assessment, 332–335
    Documenting, 335
    Qualitative risk assessment, 334–335
    Quantitative risk assessment, 333–334
    Vulnerability assessment, 339–340
Risk calculation, 333–335
    Impact, 334
    Likelihood, 334
    SLE, ARO, ALE, 333
Risk management, 331–332
Rogue access point, 198–199
Rogueware, 277–278
    As a Trojan horse, 268
Role/rule-based access control (RBAC), 97–100
    Establishing access with groups as roles, 98
Rootkits, 270–271
    Detecting with antivirus software, 273
    Detecting with SHA hashing, 410–411

Router
  Implicit deny, 159
  Routers and ACLs, 158
  Routers and firewalls, 159
RSA, 426
  Asymmetric encryption, 422–423
  With PGP/GPG, 435–436
  With S/MIME, 435

S

S/MIME (Secure/Multipurpose Internet Mail
  Extensions), 435–436
Scareware, 277–278
  As a Trojan horse, 268
SCP (Secure Copy), 138
Screen lock, 247
Screenshots, forensics, 483
Secure coding, 306–307
  Error and exception handling, 306–307
  Input validation, 306–307
Security awareness and training, 68
Security baselines, **224–225**, 340
Security guards, 109
Security policies, 458–475
  Acceptable use, 464–465
  Account disablement policy, 462
  Account management policies, 460–462
  Backup policies, 381
  Change management policy, 462–463
    Change management, 238–239
    Preventative control, 95
  Clean desk policy, 459–460
  Data policies, 469–472
  Job rotation, 466–467
  Least privilege, 112–113
  Mandatory vacations, 465
  Personnel policies, 464–467
  Portable device policies, 463
  Privacy policy, 472–473
  Security awareness and training, 68
  Separation of duties, 465
  Storage and retention policies, 470
  User privilege policy, 460
Security templates, 225–226
Self-service password reset systems, 53
Separation of duties, 465
Server attacks, 307–317
  Database servers, 315
  DNS servers, 316
  E-mail servers, 316
  Web servers, 308–314

Session hijacking, 300
SFTP (Secure File Transfer Protocol), 139
SHA, 410–411
Shielding, 394–396
  Faraday cage, 395
  Shielding cables, 395
  TEMPEST, 396
Shoulder surfing, 282–283
SIDs and DACLs, 101
Signature based IDS, 182
Single point of failure, **370–371**, 234
Single sign-on (SSO), 75
SLE (single loss expectancy), 333
Smart cards, 68–69
  CACs and PIVs, 69–70
  Multifactor authentication, 72–73
Smartphone security, 202
SMTP, 140
Smurf attack, 296
Sniffer, 345–346
SNMP (Simple Network Management Protocol),
  140
Social engineering, 276–283
  Dumpster diving, 282
  Education and awareness training,
    277
  Hoaxes, 266–267
  Impersonation, 282
  Phishing, 278–281
  Rogueware and scareware, 277–278
  Shoulder surfing, 282–283
  Tailgating, 108–109, 281
  Vishing, 281
  Whaling , 280–281
Social networking, 473, 468
Software as a Service (SaaS), 249
Software Development Life Cycle (SDLC),
  305–306
Spam and spam filters, **271**, 162–163
Spear phishing, 279–280
Spim, 271
Spoofing, 298
Spyware, 271–272
SQL injection attack, 311
  Input validation, 306–307
SSID, changing and broadcasting, 196–197
SSL (Secure Sockets Layer), 138, 429, 436–438
  Encrypting FTPS, 139
  Encrypting HTTPS, 139, 436–438
  Encrypting LDAP, 74, 140
  With asymmetric encryption, 423–424

With HSM, 244–245
With SSTP, 205
SSH (Secure Shell), 138, 430
    Encrypting data in motion, 240
    Encrypting SCP, 138
    Encrypting SFTP, 139
    Encrypting Telnet, 140
Steganography, 427–428
Storage and retention policies, 470
Subnetting, 143–146
    Calculating subnet IP addresses with a
        calculator, 144–146
    Subnetting and availability, 143–146
Succession planning, 390
Switch, 153–156
    Loop protection, 156
    Network bridging, 157
    Physical security of a switch, 156
    Port security, 155
    Security benefit, 155
    VLAN, 156–157
Symmetric encryption, 418–422
    3DES, 420–421
    AES, 420
    Block vs stream cipher, 419
    Blowfish, 422
    DES, 420
    One-time pad, 421–422
    RC4, 421
    TwoFish, 422
SYN flood attack, 295–296, 137

T

TACACS/XTACACS, 79, 142
TACACS+, **79–80**, 77, 142, 207
Tailgating, **108–109**, **281**, 276, 468
TCP, 136
TCP/IP protocols, 136–143
Technical controls, 93–94
Telephony, 203
TELNET, 140
TEMPEST, 396
TFTP (Trivial File Transfer Protocol), 139
Threats, 329–330
    Malicious insider threat, 330
    Threat modeling, 330
Three factors of authentication, 63–73
Time-of-day restrictions, 118–119
TKIP, 192
TLS (Transport Layer Security), 138, 429, 436–438

Encrypting FTPS, 139
Encrypting HTTPS, 139, 436–438
Encrypting LDAP, 74, 140
    With asymmetric encryption, 423–424
Tokens or key fobs, **70**, 68
TPM (Trusted Platform Module), 243–244
Training, 277, 468
    Acceptable use, 464–465
    Data labeling, handling and disposal,
        469–470
    P2P, 473
    Passwords, 68
    Personally identifiable information,
        471–472
    Policies, 95, 468–475
    Security policy
    Social engineering, 277
    Social networking, 473, 468
    Tailgating, 108
Transitive access and client–side attacks, 316
Transport encryption, 138, 139, 429–430
    HTTPS, 139, 430, 436–438
    IPsec, 138, 141
    SSH, 138, 430
    SSL, 138, 429
    TLS, 138, 429
Trojan horse, 267–268
Trust models, 440
Trusted OS (operating system), 275
Trusted Platform Module (TPM), 243–244
Tunneling, 203–206
    IPsec, 205–206
    L2TP, 205–206
    VPN, 203
TwoFish, 422

U

UDP, 137
Uninterrupted power supply (UPS), 375–376
URL filtering, 162
User assigned privileges, **97**, 98, 460
User habits
    Clean desk policies, 459–460
    Data handling, 469–470
    Password behaviors, 63 – 68
    Personally owned devices, 202, 246–248
    Tailgating, 108–109, 281
    Training, 68, 277, 468
User privilege policy, 460
User rights and permissions review, 347

V

Video monitoring and surveillance, 109–111
Virtualization, 230–234
    Benefits, 231–233
    Drawbacks, Risks, 233–234
    VM Escape, 233–234
Viruses, 265–267
Vishing, 281
VLAN (virtual local area network), 156–157
    VLAN segregation, 303
    Network bridging, 157
VM Escape, 233–234
Voice encryption, 202
VPN (Virtual private network), 203–206
    Concentrators, 80
    DMZ, 164–165
    IPsec, 138
    L2TP, 205–206
    NAC, 207–209
    NAT and IPsec, 166, 206
    Remote access authentication, 76–80
    Remote access protocols, 141–142
    Site-to-site VPNs, 206
    Tunneling, 203–206
Vulnerabilities, 330–331
Vulnerability assessment, 339–340
Vulnerability scanning, 341–342
    Honeypots and honeynets, 185–186
    Passively vs active, 342
    Port scanner, 152–153
    Protocol analyzer, 345–346
    Sniffer, 345–346
    White box, gray box, black box testing, 344

W

War chalking, 198
War driving, 198
    To discover rogue access points, 198–199
Warm site, 387
Web application firewall (WAF), 161–162
Web browser concerns, 300
    Cookies, 300
    Malicious add-ons, 300
    Session hijacking, 300

Web security gateways and appliances, 162
Web servers, 308–314
Well-known ports, 148–149
    Ports table,148
WEP, 190–191
    IV attack, 191
    vs. WPA/WPA2 and preshared key, 192–193
Whaling, 280–281
White box testing, 344
Wireless, 188–202
    Antenna placement and power level controls, 189
    Attacks, 190–191
    Bluejacking, 201
    Bluesnarfing, 201
    CCMP, 192
    EAP, LEAP, and PEAP, 194
    Evil twin, 199–200
    Footprint, 189–190
    Interference, 198
    Isolation mode, 200
    IV attack,191
    MAC filtering, 195–196
    Packet sniffing, 345–346
    Rogue access points, 198–199
    SSID, changing and broadcasting, 196–197
    TKIP,192
    War driving and war chalking, 198
    WEP, 190–191
    WPA/WPA2, 192–193
    WTLS and ECC, 194
Worms, 267, 265
WPA/WPA2, 192
    Personal and Enterprise modes, 193
WTLS (Wireless Transport Layer Security), 194

X

XTACACS, **79**, 77, 142
XMAS attack, 298–299
XML injection, 311–312

Z

Zero day, 185, 223–224

21501572R00309

Made in the USA
Lexington, KY
17 March 2013